A
CHRISTIAN ROSENKREUTZ
ANTHOLOGY

"Christian Rosenkreutz felt it to be his mission to make it possible for every human being, no matter where he stands in modern life, to rise to spiritual heights."

— Rudolf Steiner

A CHRISTIAN ROSENKREUTZ ANTHOLOGY

Compiled and Edited by

Paul M. Allen

in collaboration with
Carlo Pietzner

Rudolf Steiner Publications
Blauvelt, New York

For
Joan, Morven and Temora

PUBLISHERS' NOTE

The appearance of the limited, first edition of this book was welcomed by appreciative readers in many countries, and we are grateful for the letters and expressions of interest we continue to receive concerning it.

Meanwhile we have had repeated requests from college and university circles for an edition of this work, designed for classroom and student reference use, particularly in connection with adult education courses. Therefore in order to meet this need we are issuing this second, revised edition.

We are happy to announce that in recognition of his scholarship in the research and compilation of *A Christian Rosenkreutz Anthology* and his outstanding work during fourteen years as Senior Editor for Rudolf Steiner Publications, Paul M. Allen has recently been awarded an Honorary Doctorate. His new book, *Vladimir Soloviev, Russian Mystic*, will shortly appear in our Steinerbooks series. — *The Publishers*

Second Edition, 1974

Library of Congress Catalog Card Number 68-13130

Manufactured in the United States of America

TABLE OF CONTENTS

A LETTER FROM THE BROTHERHOOD TO T.V. .. , NOT BY T.V. NEC'LY

PREFACE

Through the writings and lectures of the Austrian philosopher and educator, Rudolf Steiner (1861-1925), our
present-day comprehension of the significance of Christian
Rosenkreutz has entered an entirely new phase. Already at
the turn of the century in his *Mysticism at the Dawn of the
Modern Age,* Rudolf Steiner discussed the lives and work of
certain outstanding men whose spiritual aspirations were
motivated by the Rosicrucian impulse. In a number of lectures during the following years, he returned again and
again to this theme, indicating the profound importance of
Christian Rosenkreutz and his teaching. Finally, with the appearance of his essay on *The Chymical Wedding of Christian Rosenkretuz* in 1917, Rudolf Steiner gave the key to
an appreciation of the work itself as well as a means of distinguishing between the genuine and spurious which have appeared under the name of Rosicrucianism over the past
three centuries.

By means of his writings and lectures on Rosicrucian
themes, Rudolf Steiner has removed the elements of secrecy
and exclusiveness which long have surrounded this subject.
Appealing solely to what he termed "good will and healthy
common sense" in his readers, he opened the way to a clear
understanding of true Rosicrucianism as it has manifested
itself in the course of history. He traced the Rosicrucian path
of spiritual striving up to our present time, and showed that

See Reference Notes, beginning p. 635

today new requirements call upon men to discover correspondingly new methods of spiritual development. — In Rudolf Steiner's Science of Spirit, or Anthroposophy, these new methods are to be found in "a path of knowledge leading from the spiritual in the human being to the spiritual in the universe."

In the present volume will be found what long have been regarded as "the true Rosicrucian writings" — *The Chymical Wedding of Christian Rosenkreutz,* in the complete English translation by Ezechiel Foxcroft, 1690, and *The Fame and Confession of the Fraternity of the Rosy Cross,* as translated by Thomas Vaughan, 1652. These are supplemented by other writings related to the Rosicrucian theme by Robert Fludd, Hinricus Madathanus, etc.

The Secret Symbols of the Rosicrucians, published in the late 18th century — though it includes many items of far earlier origin — long regarded as one of the most important and exceedingly rare Rosicrucian works, is reproduced here in its entirety, with the German original and an English translation on facing pages. This is supplemented by a broad selection of other rare illustrations and facsimiles of Rosicrucian interest.

Particular attention is drawn to the *Editorial and Reference Notes* at the end of the volume. These are designed to aid in a fuller appreciation of the themes touched upon in the main text of the book, and to assist the reader in finding his way to other sources dealing with the life and mission of Christian Rosenkreutz. The annotated Bibliography and Chronological List of Rudolf Steiner's works on Rosicrucian subjects are also included for the same purpose.

We wish to thank the following institutions which have made many valuable source materials available for study: The British Museum and Dr. Williams' Library, London; The Bodleian Library and Ashmolean Museum, Oxford; The Congressional Library, Washington; the Libraries of Harvard and Columbia Universities and of the Metropolitan Museum of Art, New York, and The New York Public Library.

Lastly, our warm thanks go to the many friends, both in this country and in Europe, who have aided the preparation of this volume by helpful suggestions, and particularly by the generous loan of books and illustrative materials — many of them very rare.

Paul M. Allen

Alvastra,
South Egremont,
Massachusetts.

A MAN IN ARMOR, by Rembrandt. Reproduced by permission of the Glasgow Art Gallery and Museum, Scotland. - Rudolf Steiner once identified this as a portrait of Christian Rosenkreutz as he appeared in the Netherlands in the 17th century.

INTRODUCTION

by
CARLO PIETZNER

The Chymical Wedding of Christian Rosenkreutz, Anno 1459 is generally considered to have been written by Johann Valentin Andreae (1586-1654) in the beginning of the 17th century, though it appeared in print only in 1616 in Strassburg. It was the third and perhaps the most influential publication through which the *Fraternitas Rosae Crucis* became a historical controversy. Its existence had been made known widely through an earlier publication, the *Fama Fraternitatis Rosae Crucis* which was first printed in Cassel in 1614 (together with part of a satirical-allegorical work by the Italian writer, Boccalini, *The General Reformation of the World*). The *Fama* was followed by the *Confessio* of the Fraternity, published at Frankfurt a.M. in 1615. Both these works are included in this present volume.

Andreae, who became a Protestant Theologian and Pastor of considerable repute, was a very young man of about seventeen or eighteen years and a student at Tuebingen when he wrote *The Chymical Wedding*. A prolific writer, he later denounced this work as a hoax, distancing himself from his first inspiration, for which his soul and his pen had been willing and subtle tools. He altogether denied authorship of the *Fama* and *Confessio,* but in riper years showed some feeling for them when he exchanged letters with the celebrated educator, Johann Amos Comenius.

In 1620 Andreae sketched for his learned Protestant friends the plan for a *Societas Cristiana (Societas literaria et christiana* or *Fraternitas christiana).* The Thirty Years

See Reference Notes, beginning p. 635

11

War destroyed all hope of fulfilling this plan, and most of its collaborators as well. Eight years later Andreae along with four friends founded a Christian Union. But eventually in his age he passed the torch to Comenius and wrote in one of his letters to him in 1629: "We were some men of note who came together for this purpose about eight years after the jest with the silly *Fama*."

The fact remains, however, that *The Chymical Wedding* was and is regarded as a work which could not have been composed by a young man who — however studious — would have had to work within his limited horizon, and still less would this have been the case had he intended it to be a deliberate hoax, which he wished his readers to believe in 1619, only three years after publication of *The Chymical Wedding*, in his book, *Turris Babel, The Tower of Babel*.

Rudolf Steiner, at the end of his essay which follows, provides the explanation of this enigma of the earliest-known Rosicrucian writings. His suggestion is even more significant when coupled with his observation made in another place concerning Gotthold Ephraim Lessing: "There is a difference between the good Swabian pastor, Johann Valentin Andreae, who wrote those conventional theological treatises, and Lessing. Had Lessing been Andreae, merely transported into the 18th century, he might perhaps have written in his youth a beautiful treatise on *The Education of the Human Race*, bringing in the idea of repeated earth-lives. But he was not Andreae; he was Lessing, Lessing who had no visions, who even — so it is said — had no dreams. He banished the inspirer — unconsciously of course. If the inspirer had wanted to take possession of him in his youth, Lessing would have said, Go away, I have nothing to do with you. He followed the path that was normal for an educated man in the 18th century. And so it was only in old age that he was mature enough to understand what had been with him throughout his life. It was with him as it would have been with Andreae if the latter had also banished the inspirer, had written no trivial, edifying sermons and theological treatises, but had waited until he reached a grey old age and had then written *The Chymical Wedding of Christian Rosenkreutz*."

Manuscripts of the Rosicrucian writings mentioned above had been in circulation much earlier than the printed texts, and in interested circles had prepared a climate of anticipation, the eruptive power of which can hardly be overestimated, when the documents at last appeared in print. For example, as early as 1603 *The Chymical Wedding* had been read by some people, and the *Fama* was circulated in manuscript in 1610 in the Austrian Tyrol, as Rudolf Steiner stated. His remark is substantiated by a printed reply appended to the first edition of the *Fama* (August 1614, Cassel), but which had been independently printed in 1612 by the author, a certain Adam Haselmeyer, a notary public to Archduke Maximilian, fourth son of Emperor Maximilian II, who became Governor of Tirol and Oberoesterreich in 1595. After studying the manuscript of the *Fama* in 1610 and waiting for two years to contact the Rosicrucian Brotherhood, Haselmayer published his own *Reply to the Laudible Fraternity of the Rosy Cross,* signing himself, *"Archiducalis Alumnus Notarius seu Judex Ordinarius Caesareus,* at present dwelling at the village of Heiligencreutz near Hall in Tirol: a Response in all good faith to the *Fama Fraternitatis."* It is said that this publication had an unhappy sequel, for Haselmeyer was seized by the Jesuits and put into irons on the galleys.

The confusion as to the authenticity of the first Rosicrucian writings, the enmity they aroused, and the pronouncements of the apologists who espoused the cause of the Fraternity have not ceased to this day. However, what had been attempted in Middle Europe with these first writings was overwhelmed and swept away in the holocaust of the Thirty Years War. Individual expressions of varying sincerity and insight can be traced over all the civilized world for the next century and a half. These took the form of a spiritual pursuit of knowledge of Nature, gradually giving way to purely materialistic concepts of natural science as we know it today, or found expression in a variety of attempts to pursue ideas designed to safeguard spiritually-developed social organisms. In *The Chymical Wedding* both are shown to have the same origin. To trace this spiritual impulse into the past, with decreasing spiritual perception, became an obsession with occult societies; to follow trends into later manifestations proved to be increasingly uncertain, surrounded as they soon were by charlatanry and fraud.

There is one even earlier manifestation of the incipient impulse of *The Chymical Wedding,* to which attention should be drawn. Like the castle to which Christian Rosenkreutz is led in *The Chymical Wedding,* — the "Temple," which is always the expression of the *ordo,* the order of all perfect being, be it natural or of the nature of true social forms — today one can still visit a remarkable building. This is the Bohemian castle known as Karlstejn, some twelve miles from Prague, situated on a wooded hill near the River Beroun.

Karlstejn was built between 1348 and 1365 with great spiritual purpose by the Bohemian and German King and Emperor, Charles IV, "the last Initiate on the throne of the Emperors," as Rudolf Steiner described him. The ingenious and beautiful building was constructed in a special manner according to the plans of the king himself. The lofty tower was the most conspicuous feature among the separate buildings, surrounded by mighty walls and battlements. These buildings were connected by carefully planned corridors and series of steps, chief among them being a spiral stairway which led into the very center and crown of the whole edifice — the Chapel of the Holy Cross.

This stairway is reached from the Chapter Church, which is painted with apocalyptic murals and representations of certain reliquary-presentations to the Emperor through the French Dauphin, later King Charles V, and also through Peter of Lusignan, King of Cyprus and Jerusalem. Separated from this church by a gate is a small *Privatorium,* the Emperor's private chapel of St. Catherine, into which he used to retreat on Maundy Thursday, remaining there until the Resurrection-Mass was celebrated on Easter Sunday morning. From this floor the stairway already mentioned leads into the gilded vault of the Chapel of the Holy Cross, a marvel of spatial harmony and color. However, the badly restored and partially destroyed paintings accompanying the ascending stairs, though representing scenes from the lives of Saints Wenzel and Ludmilla, require special attention. Rudolf Steiner once remarked about them: "I was recently in a castle in Middle Europe in which there is a chapel and where one can find, symbolized, thoughts from the turning-point of this new era. In the whole stairway are rather primitive paintings, but what can be found painted throughout this whole stairway — even if the paintings are primitive? — *The Chymical Wedding of Christian Rosenkreutz!* — One walks through this *Chymical Wedding,* finally reaching a Chapel of the Grail." (From a lecture given in Berlin, July 16, 1918.)

In addition to photographs of the castle and details of some of the paintings mentioned by Rudolf Steiner, in this present volume will be found a detailed description of the castle and its spiritual importance written by the late Dr. Ita Wegman.

Among the paintings on the walls of the stairway in castle Karlstejn certain forms can indeed be recognized as belonging to the cycle of images which are those of *The Chymical Wedding,* but also — strangely — of other pictures and figures, of which we must now speak.

One other work which is also included in this volume, appeared in 1785/88 in Altona: *Die geheimen Figuren der Rosenkreutzer, The Secret Symbols of the Rosicrucians,* concerning which Rudolf Steiner made the following observations:

"In the year 1785 the collected esoteric representations of the Rosicrucians came to expression in the work, *Die geheimen Figuren der Rosenkreuzer,* by Hinricus Madathanus Theosophus. In a certain limited way this publication contains indications of everything which had been at work in the preceding century, and which only then came to expression in certain works which were compiled and collected by Hinricus Madathanus Theosophus. Again a hundred years later we can see the effects of the stream of the Rosicrucians come to expression in the work of H. P. Blavatsky, especially in the book, *Isis Unveiled.* Much of the content of these figures has been written down there. A store of occult wisdom of the Occident is contained there, which is far from being exhausted, even if the composition of the book is sometimes rather confused. It is interesting to compare

Die geheimen Figuren der Rosenkreuzer by Hinricus Madathanus Theosophus with the work of H. P. Blavatsky. We must chiefly take into consideration the *first* part of this publication (*Isis Unveiled*), which has been written in the sense of the *Figuren*." (From a lecture given in Neuchâtel, September 27, 1911.)

In this work of figures and symbols, the result of the earliest teaching of the founder of the Rosicrucian Brotherhood is noted down. As will be seen upon examination, *Die geheimen Figuren* consists of two parts. A third part is known to have been published, but only one copy (in Hamburg) has been known to exist in recent times. It appears, however, that of several handwritten copies at least one or two found their way into the United States with the wave of early settlers in Pennsylvania who had to flee religious persecution in Middle Europe and some of whom had knowledge of or contacts with those from whose testimony Hinricus Madathanus Theosophus may have compiled his book. Specimen pages from one of these handwritten copies brought to Pennsylvania in Colonial times are included among the illustrations in the present volume, and should be compared with similar pages of *Die geheimen Figuren*.

As in the imagery of *The Chymical Wedding*, ordinary language and concepts of the intellect were not sufficient to approximate the imaginations which had been conveyed at the beginning of an era of new spiritual development. This new epoch with its increasing longing for a new spiritual ideal of the whole human being, even though it was first to be overshadowed by the triumph of the intellect alone, — this new era had begun with the return in 1413 of the founder of the Fraternity, Christian Rosenkreutz, from the Orient, and his final elevation to *Eques aurei Lapidis*, Knight of the Golden Stone, in 1459 on the seventh day of *The Chymical Wedding*.

It required further and greater powers of mind before new spiritual insight was to be translated into that vehicle of thought and being which today becomes available to modern humanity. Many were the often despairing attempts; here and there their traces can be followed with awe by the student, and of the whole tapestry only a small part of the pattern is recorded in the literature remaining to us.

However, the metamorphosis of *The Chymical Wedding* into modern times is clearly indicated in the Introduction to the English translation in the present book, and its substance can be tangibly encountered in the essay by Rudolf Steiner. Since the publication of this essay in 1917 Rosicrucianism requires no apologia. While many may continue to hesitate before accepting the historic validity of the vast, often contradictory literature on the subject, while others — for reasons of their own — may deny themselves the enlightenment to be derived from spiritual research, even though it is accessible to vertification through application of their thinking capacity, and while yet others may be deterred from probing deeper because of a variety of distressing activities pretending to serve Rosicrucian impulses, Rudolf Steiner's essay, here published in English for the first time, constitutes the essence of such human experiences as can rightfully be called Rosicrucian.

Like some other written works by Rudolf Steiner, this essay does not lend itself to easy reading. On the contrary, it requires careful participation. As it follows the form of its subject, of which it is an interpretation, it thereby reveals to the attentive reader *its own* structure, leading to an awareness of progress in his experience, comparable perhaps to a guided entrance into some previously unknown and dimly-lit edifice whose rooms, by their own harmonious sequence, begin to shed increasing light over the plan of the entire structure. Moreover, the one so guided may feel his own involvement in the ordered building, and begin to divine the dependence of its completion upon himself.

Rudolf Steiner's essay prepares one for the acknowledgment of a certain attitude which, independent of learning or upbringing, circumstances or environment, can be recognized as forming the basis of the most prevalent longing of modern man, be it conscious or unconscious. In every epoch such an ideal, appropriate to human evolution, tries to fulfill itself in countless individual attempts. The essay indicates the extent to which — in each moment of time — man can hope to become himself to the fullest extent. This attitude here represented as achieved by Christian Rosenkreutz and his companions in the course of the seven days' development of *The Chymical Wedding*, will permit actions of such harmonizing force as will be akin to those forces in Nature which can overcome its disparate and inharmonious tendencies. The presence of such men in social life can then be a continuing source of health-giving influence.

In five sentences Rudolf Steiner expresses what can thus live in souls who wish to work into human life in the sense of Christian Rosenkreutz:

"It was to be far from them to think out of any spirit other than the one revealing itself in the creations of nature; and they were to see man's work as a continuation of nature's works.

"They were not to place their work in the service of human impulses, but were to make these impulses into mediators for the works of the spirit.

"They were to serve men lovingly, so that in the relation between man and man the creative spirit could be manifested.

"By anything of worth the world could give they were not to let themselves be led, aside from their striving for the worth the spirit can confer upon all human labor.

"They were not, like bad Alchemists, to fall into the error of confusing the physical with the spiritual. Bad Alchemists think that the physical means of prolonging life or similar objectives are the highest good, forgetting that the physical is of value only so long as its existence is a rightful manifestation of the underlying spirit."

These sentences contain the social laws to be achieved by inner effort, and which for our present time continue to be the prerequisites for building social forms patterned upon that threefold organism of which man himself is the measure. They may be said to be the result of inner processes represented in pictorial form in *The Chymical Wedding*. These processes — based upon due preparation — are alternations between enhancements of consciousness and resulting chemical (alchymical) changes in the finest structures of the human being, involving salt, sulphur and mercurial-liquid processes within man. They are the chemical wedding of spiritual forces of perception with their evolving organs, the interaction of function and instrument, of "Faith and Love, of the King and Queen," in the castle of the body of Hope.

THE CHYMICAL WEDDING OF CHRISTIAN ROSENKREUTZ

by
RUDOLF STEINER

Translated by Carlo Pietzner

Anyone who knows what the human soul experiences when it has opened the gates into the spiritual world, need only read a few pages of the *Chymical Wedding of Christian Rosenkreuz of the Year 1459* to recognize that the descriptions given in this book are based upon genuine spiritual experience. Subjectively created pictures soon betray themselves to a reader with such experience because neither in their own form nor in their sequence do they entirely correspond with reality. — It is from this point of view that the *Chymical Wedding* can be considered first of all. One can follow the experiences with the soul, as it were, and can investigate what can be said of them through insight into spiritual realities. Untroubled by all that has been written about this book we shall consider it only from the above-mentioned point of view. We shall take everything from what the book itself would say. Only then can one speak about questions raised by many before a sufficient basis has been created for their queries.

See Reference Notes, beginning p. 635

The First Day

The experiences of the pilgrim to the Chymical Wedding are arranged in seven days' labor of the soul. The first day begins with an Imagination appearing before the soul of the seeker which causes him to decide upon undertaking the journey. The description is given in such a way that it shows the special care taken to differentiate between what the seeker is able to understand at the time of the Vision and what is still hidden from him. Likewise, what approaches the seer from the spiritual world without the participation of his will is distinguished from what is brought about through his will. The first experience is not brought about arbitrarily, neither is it fully understood by the seer. It gives him the possibility of entering the spiritual world, but it does not meet him unprepared. Seven years previously it was intimated to him through "a bodily vision" that he would be called to participate in the Chymical Wedding. The expression, *"bodily vision,"* cannot be misunderstood by anyone who grasps the whole spirit of the book. It is no vision of a diseased or half-dreaming soul-life but a perception attainable by the spiritual seer, the content of which stands before his soul with the same reality as a percept stands before the physical eye. That the one having these experiences could have such a vision presupposes a mood of soul which is not that of ordinary human consciousness. This latter knows only the alternating conditions of sleeping and waking and, between these, that of dreaming, the experience of which, however, is not related to reality. In this ordinary consciousness the soul knows itself to be related to reality through the senses, but when this relation ceases in sleep it is not knowingly connected with reality nor with itself and its inner experiences. And what connection with reality the soul has while dreaming it cannot, at first, comprehend. At the time of the "bodily vision" the pilgrim to the Chymical Wedding had already remembered a different consciousness from the ordinary one. He had realized that the soul can perceive even when, as regards the senses, it is in a condition similar to that of sleep. The concept of the soul living apart from the body and experiencing reality in such a state has become valid for him. He knows that the soul can so strengthen itself that in its separateness from the body it can unite with the spiritual world just as through bodily sense organs it is able to be united with nature. That such a union was possible and that it awaited him, he had experienced through the "bodily vision." The actual experience of this union could not come to him through the vision. It was this for which he had waited. It represented itself to him as the participation in the "Chymical Wedding;" thus he was prepared for a renewed life in the spiritual world.

This experience of renewal comes to him on the eve of the Easter Festival, at a time of an exalted mood of soul. He feels as if a storm is raging around him. Thus it is made clear to him that he experiences a reality not dependent on perception by means of the physical body. He is lifted out of the condition of balance as regards world forces, into which man is placed through his physical body. His soul does not share in the life of the physical body, but feels united only with the (etheric) body of formative forces which interpenetrates the physical. This formative-forces body, however, is not inserted within the balance of the world forces but within the mobility of that supersensible world which stands next to the physical and is first perceived by man when the gates of spirit vision open. It is only in the physical world that the forces rigidify into the state of balance demanded by definite form; in the spiritual world perpetual mobility rules. That he is caught up into this movement comes to the seeker's consciousness through the perception of a violent storm. — Out of the indeterminate character of this perception is revealed *the manifestation of a spiritual being.* This revelation occurs through a definitely formed Imagination. The spirit-being appears in a blue mantle covered with stars, but this description must be kept free from all that the dilettante esotericist would so gladly "explain" symbolically. We have to do with a non-physical experience which the one experiencing it expresses in a picture for himself and others. The blue, star-spangled mantle is indeed no more a symbol for the blue night-sky, or anything of the sort, than is the idea of a rose tree in ordinary consciousness a symbol for the sunset-glow. In supersensible perception a much more animated and conscious activity of the soul is present than in that of the senses.

— In the case of the wanderer to the "Chymical Wedding" this activity is exercised by the formative forces body, just as in physical sight the eyes are the mediators for the physical body. This activity of the formative forces body may be compared with the stimulation of outstreaming light. Such light falls upon the spirit being, who is revealed. It is rayed back by the latter. The seer thus perceives his own out-raying light, and beyond and by virtue of its limits he beholds the being who limits and reflects his own light. Through this connection of the spirit being with the spirit light of the formative forces body, "blue" appears, the stars being that part of the spirit light which is not rayed back but absorbed by the being. The spirit being has objective reality; the picture by which this being is revealed is a modification brought about by it in the raying-out of the formative forces body. This Imagination must not be confused with a vision. The subjective experience of one having such an Imagination is something completely different from that of the visionary. The visionary lives in his vision through an inner compulsion; the one experiencing Imagination unites this to the spiritual being described, or to a spiritual event, with the same conscious inner freedom with which a word or a sentence is used to express an object of the senses. Anyone with no knowledge of the nature of the spiritual world might suppose that it is wholly unnecessary to clothe the pictureless experiences of this spiritual world in Imaginations that evoke the semblance of the visionary. To this it must be objected that in reality it is not the Imagination that is the essential thing in what is spiritually perceived, but that this is the means through which what is essential must reveal itself in the soul. A sense colour can be perceived without the definite activity of an eye just as little as one can experience something spiritual without meeting it from within by a definite Imagination. But this does not hinder the use of pure concepts, such as are customary in natural science or philosophy, for representing spiritual experiences attained through Imagination. The present article uses such concepts in describing the content of the *Chymical Wedding*. However, in the seventeenth century when J. V. Andreae wrote the book it was not yet customary to use such concepts to any great extent; the direct Imagination, through which the supersensible beings and events had been experienced, was represented.

In the spiritual form which revealed itself to the pilgrim to the Chymical Wedding, he recognized the being able to give him the right impulse for the journey. Through his meeting with this figure he feels himself to be standing consciously in the spiritual world. The manner in which he stands there points to the special direction of his path of knowledge. He does not follow the way of the *mystic* in the narrower sense, but travels the path of the *alchemist*. In order to understand the following description we must eliminate from the idea of "alchemy" all that has been associated with it through superstition, fraud, thirst for adventure, and so on. We must think of what was striven for by the honest, unprejudiced seekers of truth who formed this concept. They wished to recognize the legitimate relations between the objects of nature which are not conditioned by natural activity itself but by a spirit-being who manifests through nature. They sought for supersensible forces active in the sense world which cannot, however, be recognized by means of the senses. The pilgrim to the "Chymical Wedding" takes the path of such investigators. In this sense he is a representative of the alchemistic quest. As such he is convinced that the supersensible forces of nature are hidden from ordinary consciousness. In his inner being he has brought about the experiences which enable the soul, through their effects, to use the formative forces body as organ of perception. Through this organ of perception he attains a vision of the supersensible forces of nature. In a spiritual form of existence which can be experienced outside the realm of sense-perception and the ordinary intellectual activity, he wishes above all to recognize the supersensible forces of nature outside man, and then, equipped with the knowledge of these forces, to penetrate the real nature of the human body itself. He believes that through a knowledge which will be attained by the soul in union with the formative forces body, now being operated apart from the physical organism, it will be possible to penetrate to the nature of man's bodily being, and thereby come nearer to the mystery which is accomplished by the cosmos through this being. For the ordinary consciousness this mystery is veiled; man lives in it, but he does not see through the experience. By starting from the supersensible knowledge of nature, the pilgrim to the Chymical Wedding wishes finally to reach a vision of the supersensible nature of man. By this method of invetigation he is an alchemist in contrast to the mystic in the narrower sense of the term. The mystic also strives for a different experience of the human being than is possible with the ordinary consciousness. However, he does not choose the way leading to a use of the formative forces body independently of the physical body. He starts from a vague feeling that a penetration of the physical body by the formative forces body, deeper than is customary in waking life, leads one from a connection with what is of a physical nature to a union with man's spiritual nature. With his conscious being the alchemist strives to draw himself out of the ordinary connection with the bodily, and to enter the world which, as "the spiritual in nature," lies behind the realm of the sense-perceptible world. The mystic seeks to lead the conscious soul deeper into its connection with the bodily in order to dip down consciously into that realm of the corporeal which hides itself from self-consciousness when the latter is filled with the perceptions of the senses. The mystic does not always seek to give himself a full account of this striving. All too often he is inclined to describe his path quite differently. But in most instances the mystic is a poor exponent of his own being. This is connected with the fact that certain feelings are linked up with the spiritual quest. Because the soul of the mystic, through a kind of self-illusion, wishes to overcome the connection with the body, as experienced in ordinary consciousness, not only a certain contempt for this connection takes possession of him, but a contempt for the body itself. Therefore the soul will not admit that its mystical experience is based upon an even closer connection with the body than is usual. — Through this more inner connection with himself the mystic perceives an alteration in his thinking, feeling and willing. He devotes himself to this perception without developing the inclination to become clear as to the basis of the alteration. Although the change is due to a dipping down deeper into his body, it appears to him as a spiritualization of his inner life. And he is fully justified in so regarding it. For the perceptive faculty is nothing other than that form of existence which the soul experiences when standing in the relation with the body which is the basis of ordinary waking consciousness. If the soul connects itself more deeply with the body than is the case in this latter form of existence, then it experiences a relation of the human being to the world which is more spiritual than that produced by the senses. The ideas which then arise are condensed to Imaginations. These Imaginations are revelations of the powers which the body of formative forces exercises on the physical body. They remain hidden for the ordinary consciousness. Feeling is strengthened to such a degree that the etheric-spiritual forces, streaming from the cosmos and acting upon the human being, are experienced as through an inner touch. In willing, the soul knows itself to be given over to a spiritual activity which incorporates man in a supersensible connection with the world from which he separates himself through the subjective will of the ordinary consciousness. Real mysticism arises only when man brings his fully conscious soul into closer connection with the body as described above, and through the compulsion of the bodily organization, is not driven to pathological visions or dimmed consciousness. True mysticism is a striving to experience that inner human spirituality which for the ordinary consciousness is submerged by sense-perception. True alchemy makes itself independent of sense-perception in order to behold the spiritual nature of the world that is external to man, but is concealed by sense-perception. Before entering into the inner being of the soul, the mystic must bring himself into such a condition that the soul is not exposed to an extinguished or dimmed consciousness resulting from the enhanced counter-thrust which it experiences through a more intimate connection with the body. Before he enters the spiritual world lying behind the physical, the alchemist needs a strengthening of his soul so that the latter will not lose itself in the beings and events of that world. The mystical and the alchemical ways of investigation lie in opposite directions. The mystic enters directly into man's own spiritual being. His aim, which may be called the "Mystical Marriage," is the union of the conscious soul with his own spiritual being. The alchemist wishes to wander through the spirit realm of nature, in order that by means of the forces of knowledge won in this region, he may afterward behold the spirit-nature of man. His aim is the "Chymical Marriage," the union with the spirit region of nature. Not until after this union does he wish to experience the vision of man's being.

Both alchemist and mystic experience in the very beginning of their way a mystery which according to its nature cannot be penetrated by the ordinary consciousness. It is connected with the relationship between the human body and human soul. As soul-being man lives truly in the spiritual world; but at his present stage of evolution in world-becoming he has no proper capacity of orientation in the realm of spirit. Through the forces of his ordinary consciousness he can only establish a relation to himself and to the world outside him because the body provides the direction for the soul activity. The body is so placed within the world that it corresponds with the cosmic harmony. While the soul lives within sense-perception and ordinary intellectual activity, it is given up to the body with just that force by which the body is able to transmit to it its own harmony with the cosmos. If the soul raises itself out of this experience, in the mystical or alchemical direction, it is then necessary to take care that it does not lose this harmony with the universe attained by the body. Without such precaution it is threatened on the mystical path with the loss of its spiritual connection with the cosmos, and on the alchemical path with the loss of capacity for distinguishing between truth and error. Without such care, the mystic, through this closer connection with the body would so densify the force of self-consciousness that, overpowered in his own life by this force, he would no longer be able to co-experience the world-life. Thereby with his consciousness he would enter into the realm of a different spiritual world from the one which corresponds with that of man. (In my writings on the science of spirit I have called it the Luciferic world.) The alchemist, without due care, would lose the power of distinguishing between truth and illusion. In the great relationships of the cosmos illusion is a necessity. However, at his present stage of evolution man cannot fall a victim to it because the realm of sense-perception is his safeguard. Were this illusion not in the background of human world-experience, man could not develop the different stages of his consciousness. For illusion is the driving force for this development of consciousness. At the present stage of this development of human consciousness illusion must indeed work for the arising of consciousness, but illusion itself must remain in the unconscious. If it appeared in the consciousness it would overpower the truth. As soon as the soul takes the alchemistical path, it enters the region of spirit behind sense-perception, and it falls into the vortex of illusion where it can rightly preserve its being only if out of its experience in the sense-world it brings with it a sufficient capacity for distinguishing between error and truth. If it has not taken the precaution to acquire such a capacity, then the whirl of illusion will drive it into a world where it must lose itself. (In my writings on the science of spirit I have called this the Ahrimanic world.) — The mystic, before entering on his path, needs to bring his soul into such a condition that his own life does not become overpowering; the alchemist must reinforce the sense for truth so that it will not be lost to him, even when he is not supported by sense-perception and the understanding connected with it.

The bearer of the experiences described in the *Chymical Wedding* is aware that on his path as alchemist he needs a strengthened capacity for distinguishing between truth and illusion. According to the life-connections out of which he enters upon his alchemical path, he seeks to gain his support out of Christian truth. He knows what unites him with Christ has already brought to unfoldment within his life in the sense world a force in his soul leading to truth, which does not need the support of the senses and can therefore hold good when this support is no longer present. In this attitude his soul stands before the being in blue garments who shows him the way to the Chymical Wedding. To begin with, this being could just as well belong to the world of error and illusion as to that of truth. The pilgrim to the Chymical Wedding must distinguish. But his capacity for distinction would be lost, and error would overpower him if he could not, within the supersensible experience, remember what unites him with an inner force to truth in the sense-world. Out of his own soul there arises what has happened within it through Christ. And over and above his light the Christ-light also radiates from his body of formative forces, toward this being who is revealed. The right Imagination is formed. *The letter* which shows him the way to the Chymical Wedding contains the sign of Christ and the words: *In hoc signo vinces.* — The pilgrim knows he is connected with the being who appears by a force which points to the truth. If the force which led him into the supersensible world were to incline toward illusion, he would stand before a being who would injure his power of memory for the Christ-Impulse living within him. He would then be attended only by the misleading powers which attract man when the supersensible world brings forces to meet him which are injurious for his being and his will.

The content of the letter conveyed to the pilgrim by that being concerning the Chymical Wedding, in a form of expression belonging to the fifteenth century, is a description of his relationship with the spiritual world insofar as he can be conscious of it at the beginning of the first day of his spiritual experience. The sign by which the words are accompanied, brings to expression how the mutual relationship between the physical body, the body of formative forces, and the soul-spirit has taken shape in him. It is fully significant for him that he can perceive how this condition of his human nature stands in harmony with cosmic relationships. "By diligent reckoning and calculation" of his "annotated planets" he has found that this condition in him might possibly arise at the moment when it now occurs. The "astrology" intended here will be understood neither by proponents or opponents of modern astrology. With good reason has the exponent of the *Chymical Wedding* added to the title of his book *the Year 1459.* He was aware that the mood of soul of the one having this experience must correspond with the mood which is reached at a definite point of time in world-becoming, if the inner soul-mood and the outer world-content are not to come into disharmony. The soul which has become independent of ordinary sense-perception must meet the external supersensible world-content harmoniously, if through the concord of both that condition of consciousness is to arise which forms the *Chymical Wedding.* Whoever believes that the constellation of "the annotated planets" contains a mysterious force which determines the condition of human experience, is like someone who might suppose that the position of the hands of his watch have the power to cause him to take the walk which the circumstances of his life require of him at a certain hour.

In the letter *three temples* are indicated. At the time he receives the letter, the one who has the experience does not understand what is meant by them. He who perceives in the spiritual world must know that at times Imaginations are assigned him which at first he must forgo understanding. He must receive them as Imaginations and let them ripen within his soul as such. During the ripening they bring forth in man's inner being the power necessary for understanding them. If the observer were to try to explain them at the moment of their revelation, he would do this with an insufficient power of understanding and with distorted thinking. In spiritual experience much depends on a man having the patience to make observations, at first simply to accept them, and to wait with understanding them until the right moment arrives. What the pilgrim to the Chymical Wedding learns on the first day of his spiritual experiences, he describes as having been announced to him "seven years" before. He dared not then form an intellectual opinion as to the meaning of the "vision" but had to wait until the "vision" had worked long enough in his soul for him henceforth to experience with understanding.

The appearance of the spirit-being in the blue, starry mantle and the conveyance of the letter to him are experiences which the pilgrim to the Chymical Wedding has without the free decision of his own soul leading him to them. He then proceeds to further experiences through such a free decision. He enters into a sleep-like condition, bringing him dream-experiences, the contents of which have reality. This is possible because after the experiences he has already had, he can, through sleep, enter into a relationship with the spiritual world different from the usual one. The ordinary experience during sleep does not link man's soul to the spiritual world by such bonds as would be capable of giving him valid concepts of reality. The soul of the pilgrim, however, is transformed. It is so strengthened inwardly that in the dream experience it can perceive what of this experience is connected with the spiritual world in which it dwells. And through such an experience the soul first experiences its own newly-won relationship through *the Imagination of the Tower* in which the dreamer is enclosed, and from which he wishes to be freed. The soul experiences consciously what is experienced unconsciously in ordinary existence when in sleep the soul passes over from the realm of sense experience to that of the supersensible form of existence. The cramping and distress in the tower are the expression of the sense experiences within the soul from the sphere of which the soul is extricating itself. What binds the soul to the body in such a way that the result is ordinary sense experience, are the life-forces that engender growth. Under these forces alone, consciousness could never arise. What is merely living, remains unconscious. For the arising of consciousness, together with illusion, serves those forces which destroy life. If in himself man did not bear all that leads him to physical death, he certainly could live in a physical body, but he could not develop consciousness within it. For the ordinary consciousness, the connection between the death-bringing forces and this consciousness remains hidden. As with the one experiencing the Chymical Wedding, this connection must appear before the "spiritual eye" of anyone wishing to develop a consciousness for the spiritual world. He must realize that the *"ice-grey man"* is bound up with his existence — that being which, according to its nature, bears within it the forces of old age. Only that soul can participate in the vision within the realm of spirit which, while in this domain, sees working upon it the force hidden in ordinary life behind the ageing process. This force has power to tear the soul away from the realm of sense-experience. — The reality of the dream lies in that the pilgrim to the Chymical Wedding becomes conscious through it that henceforth he can encounter nature and the human world with a mood of soul enabling him to perceive in both what is hidden from ordinary consciousness. Thereby he becomes ready for the experiences of the next day.

The Second Day

The beginning of the description of the second day immediately indicates how nature appears to the pilgrim in a new
way. But he is meant not only to see what is behind nature;
he is to gain a deeper insight than with ordinary consciousness
into the motives of human will and action. The writer of the
Chymical Wedding wishes to say that this ordinary consciousness learns to know the external aspect of will and of action
alone, and that therefore with this consciousness men become
aware only of this external aspect of their will and action.
The deeper lying, spiritual impulses which pour out of the
spiritual world into this willing and acting, and form the human social life, remain unknown to this consciousness. Man
can live in the belief that a definite motive leads him to his
action, while in truth this motive is only the conscious mask
for something that remains unconscious. Insofar as men regulate their *social life* with their ordinary consciousness, forces
lay hold of this common life that do not belong to the real
aims of human evolution which are wholesome for men. Other forces must be placed in opposition to these, forces derived
from supersensible consciousness, which must then be incorporated into the social activity. It is to the knowledge of such
forces that the pilgrim to the Chymical Wedding has to be
led. He is to look through men and to penetrate to their inner
being, for the latter is something quite different from what
they believe they are or what they assume their position to
be according to the social order determined by ordinary consciousness. — The picture of nature which reveals itself to ordinary consciousness is very different from the picture of a human social order. But the supersensible forces of nature which
spiritual consciousness learns to know are related to the supersensible forces which work in the human social order.
The alchemist strives for a knowledge of nature that for
him is to be the foundation of a true knowledge of man. This
path to this knowledge must the pilgrim to the Chymical
Wedding seek. Not only *one* such path, however, but several
are shown to him. *The first* leads to a region where the intellectual ideas of ordinary consciousness that are won through
sense perception influence the process of supersensible expe-

rience, so that, through the working together of both spheres of experience, insight into reality is killed. *The second* shows that the soul may lose patience if compelled to wait long for spiritual revelations in order to allow what at first can only be received as incomprehensible revelation, continually to ripen. *The third* demands men who, through their already attained, but unconscious readiness are allowed to see in a brief time what others have to attain only through long struggle. *The fourth* brings man to meet all the forces which, out of the supersensible world, becloud and alarm his consciousness when this latter wishes to tear itself free from sense-experience. — Which path is taken by this or the other soul depends upon the state it has attained through the experiences of ordinary consciousness before entering on the spiritual pilgraimage. It cannot "choose" in the ordinary sense, for the choice would come from physical consciousness which is not adapted for making decisions about supersensible things. The pilgrim to the Chymical Wedding recognizes the impossibility of such a choice. But he also knows that his soul has been sufficiently strengthened to conduct itself in a supersensible world so as to be directed rightly when such direction comes from the spiritual world itself. The Imagination of being set free "from the tower" gives him this knowledge. *The Imagination of the "Black Raven"* which snatches the offered food from the *"white dove,"* calls up in the soul of the pilgrim a certain feeling; and this feeling, produced out of supersensible, imaginative perceptions leads along the way which the ordinary consciousness would not have been permitted to choose. — On this path he comes to perceive man and human relationships in the light which is not accessible to experience in a sense body. He passes through a *portal* into a dwelling where men behave in accordance with the supersensible forces which pour themselves into their souls. Through the experiences he has within this dwelling he should awaken to the new life he will be obliged to lead, when enough of this experience is grasped by his supersensible consciousness. — Many of those who have pronounced judgment on *The Chymical Wedding of Christian Rosencreutz* have expressed the opinion that it is nothing more than a satirical romance concerning the activity of certain sects, or adventurous alchemists, or something of the kind. Perhaps, however, a true insight into the experiences the author of this book assigns to the pilgrim "at the portal" shows that the satirical mood of later parts of the work is really to be traced to soul experiences of such seriousnesss that they assume a form of mere satire only to those who wish to remain in the sphere of the senses. It would be well to bear this in mind in the perusal of the further experiences of the pilgrim to the Chymical Wedding.

The second day's labor brings to the soul experiences which decide whether the spiritual seeker whom Johann Valentin Andreae is describing, will attain the faculties for true spiritual perception or whether his soul will be surrounded by a world of spiritual error. For his capacity of perception these experiences are clothed in *the Imagination of entering a castle* where the world of spiritual experience is administered. Such Imaginations are possible not only to the genuine but also to the spurious spirit-seeker. The soul may come to them when following certain trends of thought and feeling which enable it to imagine surroundings not derived from impressions of the senses. — From the way Andreae describes *the company of false seekers of the spirit* within which the "Brother of the Red Rose Cross" finds himself on "the second day" we realize that the secret of the difference between the true and the untrue seeker is well known to him. Anyone in a position to estimate rightly such inner proof of the spiritual insight of the author of the *Chymical Wedding* can no longer be in doubt concerning the true character of this book nor the intentions of Andreae, its author. It is obviously written to show men of earnest striving the connection between the sense world and the spiritual, and to explain to them the forces which, out of knowledge of the spiritual world, can be awakened in the human soul for the social and moral life. The unsentimental, humorously satirical mode of Andreae's presentation does not contradict but confirms the deep earnestness of his aim. Not only can one feel this earnestness in the apparently unimportant scenes, but we also realize that Andreae presents his pictures like one who does not wish to becloud the mind of his reader through sentimentality concerning the mysteries of the spiritual world, but would rather create in him the mood of a soul-free, self conscious and reasonable attitude toward this world. Although the control of thought and feeling can enable anyone to form Imaginations of the spiritual world, this faculty by no means guarantees that by these Imaginations he will be brought into a genuine relation to the spiritual world. In this field of imaginative experience the Rosicrucian brother finds himself surrounded by numerous souls who indeed live in Imaginations of the spiritual world but who, through their inner condition, are not able to come into genuine contact with it. The possibility of such genuine contact depends upon how the seeker for the spirit relates his soul to the sense world before he approaches the threshold of the spiritual world. This relationship creates a mood of soul which is carried across the threshold and which reveals itself in the spirit world by the acceptance or rejection of the seeker. *The right disposition of soul* can be attained only by the seeker's readiness to lay aside at the threshold all that conditioned his relation to the world of sense-reality. All impulses of heart and mind that through his outer position in life and destiny gave him the sense of the character and the worth — the weight — of his personality must cease to be active during the time he is in the spiritual world. If this necessity of becoming again as a little child is felt to be difficult, still more repugnant is it to the ordinary feelings to suppress the kind of judgment by which one finds one's way about in the sense-world. One must acquire insight into the fact that this latter kind of judgment applies and has value only in this world, and within the spiritual world itself must men be ready to learn how to judge in the spirtual world. From the moment of his entrance into the castle, the Rosicrucian brother develops the mood of soul that springs from a feeling for these necessities. He does not allow himself to be lead into a room where the others would spend the first night within the castle, but remains in the hall which he has reached through all that is possible as a result of his participation in the events of the second day. Thus he guards himself from bringing his soul into a region of the spiritual world with which he is not yet able to connect himself worthily in his innermost forces. This mood of soul which prevents him from penetrating further into spiritual places than the experiences of the second day warrant, works in his soul throughout the night and equips him with a power of perception and will which he will need on the following day. Those seekers who accompanied him and have not the faculty of this soul-mood must be rejected by the spiritual world on the following day because they cannot develop the fruits of this mood. Without these fruits it is impossible for them through actual inner forces to unite the soul with that world by which it is, so to speak, only outwardly surrounded.

The events at the portals, the encounter with the lion, the reading of the inscriptions on the two pillars at the entrance, and various events of the second day are experienced by the Rosicrucian brother so that one sees that his soul is weaving in the mood described above. He experiences things in such a way that everything related only to the ordinary intellect bound up with the sense world remains unknown to him, and he perceives only that part which appears to his deeper soul forces in a spiritually visible connection. — *The encounter with "the terrible lion"* at the second portal forms part of the spirit-seeker's self-knowledge. The Rosicrucian brother experiences it so that it works as an Imagination on his deeper soul forces, but he does not know what it signifies for his position in the spiritual world. This judgment, of which he is ignorant, is pronounced by the "Guardian" who stands near the lion whom he calms, and who addresses these words to the pilgrim which are in accord with the contents of a letter which, again, are unknown to the pilgrim: "Now welcome in God's Name to the man whom I would have liked to see long ago." The supersensible picture of the "terrible lion" is the result of the Rosicrucian brother's state of soul. This condition of soul is reflected in the formative forces region of the spiritual world and produces the Imagination of the lion. In this reflection a picture of the seer's own self is presented. In the sphere of spiritual reality he is a different being from what he is during his existence in the sense world. The active forces of the sense world mould him into a physical human image. However, in the domain of the spirit he is not yet "man," but is a being that can be imaginatively expressed by the animal form. All that displays itself within physical existence as instincts, emotions, impulses of feelings and will is held in fetters within this existence through the life of ideas and perception bound to the sense-body, itself the outcome of the sense-world. If a man desires to leave this sense-world he must beome aware of all that, outside this world, is no longer attached to him through the gifts of the sense world, and he must be led into the right path through new gifts emanating from the world of spirit. He must behold himself as he was *before* becoming man in the sense-world. This perception is given to the Rosicrucian brother through his meeting with the lion, which is the picture of his own being *before* becoming man. — To avoid misunderstanding it may here be noted that the form in which man existed before becoming man, at which the fundamental being of man looks in a spiritual way, has nothing to do with the animal state that Darwinism considers to be connected with the descent of the human race. For the animal form that appears to spiritual vision is such as can, through its very nature, belong only to the world of formative forces. Within the sense world it can exist only as a subconscious part of man's nature. — That he encounters this part of his being which is usually fettered to the sense-body, is expressed in the mood of soul in which the Rosicrucian brother enters the castle. He is unprejudiced as regards what he is to experience, and does not allow the latter to be obscured by judgments originating from the intellect bound to the sense world. Later he has to observe just such obscurity in those who have come without the right mood of soul. These also have seen and passed the "terrible lion," for this depends only upon their having taken into their soul the appropriate thoughts and feelings. But in their case the effect of this spiritual vision was not strong enough to induce the laying aside of that faculty of judgment which belongs to the sense world. Their way of judging appears as vain boasting to the spiritual eye of the Rosicrucian brother within the spiritual realm. They presume to see Plato's ideas, to count the atoms of Democritus, pretend to see the invisible, whereas in truth they see nothing. By this it is shown that they cannot unite their inner soul forces with the world which now surrounds them. They lack consciousness of the real demands made by the spiritual world upon those who strive to see. The Rosicrucian brother is able to form the connection between his soul powers and the realm of the spirit during the following days, because during the second day he admits to himself that he is unable to see and do the things the intruders claim to see and do. His feeling of helplessness later becomes the power to experience spiritually. He must allow himself to be fettered at the end of the second day because he is to feel the fetters of soul-impotence in face of the spiritual world until this helplessness has been exposed sufficiently long to the light of consciousness to be transmuted into power.

The Third Day

Andreae wishes to show how the *seven liberal arts* into which men organized the knowledge attainable in the sense-world in the Middle Ages, should work as preparation for knowledge of the spirit. These seven branches of knowledge were reckoned as Grammar, Dialectic, Rhetoric, Arithmetic, Geometry, Music and Astronomy. From the description in the *Chymical Wedding* it is evident that Andreae considers that the Rosicrucian brother and his legitimate companions, as well as the intruders, are equipped with the knowledge attainable through these "liberal arts." But the possession of it differs in all who have arrived. The legitimate seekers, and above all the Rosicrucian brother whose experiences are being described, have made this knowledge their own in such a way that through its possession their souls have developed the power to receive from the spiritual world what has still had to remain unknown for these seven "liberal arts." Their souls have been so prepared through these arts that they not only know what is to be known by and through them, but this knowledge can give them the necessary weight for having experiences in the spiritual world. For intruders, however, the weight of these arts has not become weight of soul. Their souls have not acquired the true world content which these arts contain. On the third day the Brother of the Rose Cross takes part in *the weighing of the souls*. This is described by the Imagination of the scales upon which the souls are weighed to ascertain whether to their own weight as man they have added what corresponds to the seven other weights. These seven weights are the imaginative representatives of the "seven liberal arts."

Within his own soul the Rosicrucian brother has not only the content which has grown out of the seven weights but also a surplus. This benefits another personality who in himself is not considered sufficiently mature, but is guarded against expulsion from the spiritual world by the true seeker of the spirit. In mentioning this episode Andreae shows how well acquainted he is with the secrets of the spiritual world. Of all the soul-forces already developed in the sense world, love is the only one that can remain unchanged by the passage of the soul into the spiritual world. To help weaker men attain the forces one possesses oneself can be done in the world of sense, and it can likewise be accomplished through what is bestowed upon one in the realm of the spirit.

The manner of Andreae's description of *the illegitimate intruders' expulsion* from the spirit world shows that through his writing he desires to make his contemporaries conscious of how far removed a man can be from the spiritual world and therefore from true reality who, although familiar with various descriptions of the way to this world, has remained a stranger to the consciousness of a real inner change of soul. An unbiased perusal of the *Chymical Wedding* discloses that one of the author's aims is to show his contemporaries how destructive for true human evolution are those who interfere with life by means of impulses that place themselves into illegitimate relationship to the world of the spirit. Particularly for his own time Andreae envisions right social, moral, and other human community aims of mankind through proper knowledge of the spiritual foundations of existence. Because of this, in his description he throws a clear light upon all that becomes injurious to human progress because its aims are derived from an unsound relationship with the spirit-world.

On the third day, after having experienced the expulsion of the unlawful intruders, the Brother of the Rose Cross feels the possibility arising of so using his faculties of understanding that the latter is suited to the spiritual world. His possession of this capacity appears before his soul in *the Imagination of the unicorn* bowing before a lion. Thereupon, by his roaring the lion calls forth a dove who brings him an olive branch. This he swallows. Were we to consider this as a symbol rather than a real Imagination, we might say that it pictured an event within the soul of the spiritual seeker through which he feels himself capable of thinking what is spiritual. But such an abstract idea would not express the full essence of that soul-event which, in fact, we are considering. For the event is experienced in such a manner that the sphere of personal sense-perception is extended beyond the boundary of the physical body. In the spirit realm the seer experiences beings and events external to his own essential being just as man experiences processes going on within his own body during his usual waking consciousness. When such extended consciousness arises, mere abstract conceptions cease, and the Imagination appears as the necessary form of expression for what is experienced. When, nevertheless, we try to express these experiences in terms of abstract ideas, as is necessary at present for the wider communication of knowledge derived from the science of spirit, then these Imaginations must be brought into the appropriate form of ideas. Andreae omits this in the *Chymical Wedding* for he aims at describing, without alteration, the experiences of the spirit-seeker in the middle of the fifteenth century, at which time it was not customary to translate experienced Imaginations into ideas and concepts.

When the imaginative perception reaches the stage of maturity, as with the Rosicrucian Brother on the third day, the soul is enabled, with its inner life, to enter that realm of reality in which Imaginations originate. With the attainment of this faculty man can observe in a new way the beings and events of the sense world from a viewpoint in the spirit-world. He sees to what extent these beings and events flow from their true supersensible source. Andreae explains that the Rosicrucian Brother succeeds in acquiring this power to a greater degree than his companions. He arrives at the stage when he sees the *library of the castle* and the *burial of the kings* from a spiritual point of view. This is made possible by the fact that he can use his own will to a high degree in the imaginative world. His comrades can perceive only what comes to them from external powers, without such strong activity of their own will. The Rosicrucian Brother learns more from "the funeral of the kings" than is "found written in all books." The view of these burials is brought into direct connection with seeing the glorious "*Phoenix*." In the beholding of these, the secret of death and of birth is revealed. These two threshold-events of our life hold sway only in the sense world. In the spirit, birth and death do not correspond to a becoming and passing away, but represent a transmutation of one form of life into another. The nature of birth and death can be understood only when viewed from a standpoint removed to the sense world, from a realm in which they themselves do not exist.

In recording how the Rosicrucian Brother makes his way to the "burial of the kings" and perceives in the picture of the phoenix the rise of a new kingly power out of the death of the old kings, Andreae wishes to describe the particular path of a spirit-seeker in the middle of the fifteenth century. The latter was *a turning point in time* for the spiritual experience of humanity. Then it was that the mode of approach to the spiritual world, valid for many previous centuries, was changed. In the sphere of man's external life this change arose through the growing mode of modern thought in natural science and other transformations in the life of the people on earth during this period. In the realm of that world in which the scientist of the spirit searches for the secrets of existence, is revealed in connection with such turning points of time, the passing away of one particular tendency of human soul-forces and the beginning of another. Despite all the other revolutionary events in the historical progress of humanity, the character of spiritual vision remained practically the same from Graeco-Roman times until the fifteenth century. The spiritual instinctive understanding, rooted in man's heart and mind, which at this period was the essential characteristic of his soul powers, had to be transferred to the realms of spiritual reality, and there transmuted into the power of spiritual perception. From the middle of the fifteenth century, in place of this soul power, there arose that understanding which, liberated from the instinctive forces, worked in the light of full consciousness of self. To raise this understanding to the power of perceptive consciousness becomes the task of the spirit-seeker.

In Christian Rosenkreuz, as the leading Brother of the Rose Cross, Andreae describes a personality who has entered the spiritual world by the method which ended in the fifteenth century. The experiences of the *Chymical Wedding* bring before the eye of his soul this ending of the one and the arising of a new method of approach. He must therefore penetrate certain secrets which the rulers of the castle, who would prefer to continue the administration of the spiritual life along the old lines, would fain hide from him. For his contemporaries Andreae wishes to portray the foremost spiritual investigator of a declining epoch, one who perceives in the spiritual field the death of that epoch and the birth of a new one. He found that his contemporaries were still satisfied with the traditions of the old epoch, that they wished to continue to open the way to the spiritual world by their own traditional methods. He wished to say to them: Your path is fruitless; the greatest who has most recently followed it, has seen how useless it is; realize what he has perceived and you will develop a feeling for a new path. In his own time he wanted to set up *Christian Rosenkreuz's spiritual path* as the legacy of the spiritual investigation of the fifteenth century, so as to show that initiative for a new way of spiritual investigation must be taken. The present-day scientist of the spirit, if he understands the signs of his time, still finds himself continuing the efforts that originated with Johann Valentin Andrae. He meets with the strongest opposition from those spirit-seekers who by means of a renewal or rejuvenation of old spiritual-scientific traditions seek to open the way into the supersensible world.

Andreae speaks with gentle indications of the prospects of knowledge which must result through the perceptive consciousness of mankind in the period following the middle of the fifteenth century. Christian Rosenkreuz makes his way to a great *globe,* through which the dependence of earthly events upon extra-earthly, cosmic impulses is placed before his soul. This indicates the first glimpse into a "knowledge of the heavens," starting with the Copernican view of the universe, which, however, Christian Rosenkreuz considers only a beginning, able to give only what has meaning for the physical world. To this day modern natural science carries out its researches in the sense of this beginning. In its picture of the world it sees the earth surrounded by "events in the heavens," which it endeavors to grasp through intellectual concepts alone. Within the earth-sphere itself it seeks for the forces behind the essential processes of earthly events. When investigating the conditions under which the seed of a new being arises within the maternal being, it notes only the forces which are related to the earthly ancestors in the stream of heredity. It is quite unconscious of the fact that during the forming of the seed "the heavenly periphery of the earth" is working into the earthly happenings, and the maternal being is merely the place within which the extra-terrestrial cosmos is shaping the seed. By this mode of thought the causes of historical events are sought exclusively in facts preceding these events in earthly life. It ignores the super-earthly impulses which fertilize earthly facts so that from the events of one epoch those of the next may proceed. This way of thinking admits extra-earthly influence as working merely upon the lifeless earth processes. The prospect of an organic, a spiritual "knowledge of the heavens" is disclosing itself to Christian Rosenkreuz; this can have nothing in common with the ways of ancient astrology, but rests upon the same foundations for the supersensible as does Copernicanism for the sense world.

We may note how competently Andreae treats the imaginative life in the *Chymical Wedding*. All the wisdom that comes to Christian Rosenkreuz as revelation and without the exercise of his own will, Andreae shows as appearing through forces finding their representation in *images of a feminine nature*; and where the personal will of the spiritual investigator makes its way, this is pictured through the male element — by *images of boys leading the way*. In the human being, whether physically man or woman, the male and female hold sway as polar opposites. Andreae gives his characterizations with this in view. What has to do with concepts and thoughts will be put in the right relation to what is of the nature of will when this relation is represented in pictures that are reminiscent of male and female in the world of the senses. — Once more it should be remarked as a precaution against misunderstanding, that the Imagination of the male and the female, is not to be confused with the relation between man and woman in the sense-world, any more than has the Imagination of the animal form appearing to perceptive consciousness to do with the animal nature related by current Darwinism to mankind. At the present time many think that they can penetrate to hidden secrets of existence through the physiology of sex. Even a superficial knowledge of the real science of the spirit could convince them that such efforts, instead of leading toward the mysteries of existence, lead far away from them. In any case, it is nonsense to bring the teaching of such a personality as Andreae into any kind of connection with the physiology of sex.

In a very clear manner Andreae points to something of importance when he includes in a secret way in the *Chymical Wedding* a description of the *"virgin"* whom he brings into particularly close relationship with the seeker of the spirit. This "virgin" is the imaginative representation of supersensible knowledge, which instead of being gained upon the physical plane like the "seven liberal arts," has to be drawn from the realm of the spirit. In a somewhat enigmatic way the virgin gives her name — it is "Alchemy." By this Andreae wishes to show that true alchemy is a science different from those evolved from ordinary consciousness. According to his view the alchemist accomplishes his work with perceptible substances and forces, not because he wishes to investigate the effects in the sense world, but because he would let the supersensible manifest through the physical process. Through the physical process he wishes to penetrate to a supersensible one. It is in the way he regards the process that what he performs differs from the research of the ordinary scientist.

The "third day's" experiences include the complete overcoming of the belief that the kind of judgment to which man is accustomed in the sense world can be, in unchanged form, a guiding power in the supersensible world. Among the company in which Christian Rosenkreuz finds himself *questions* are propounded, all of which lead to the end that decisive answers are withheld. Reality is richer than the faculty of judgment based upon the intellect nurtured by the sense world. — After the description of these experiences Andreae also introduces a *"Duchess;"* in this way he brings Christian Rosenkreuz into relationship with that supersensible kind of knowledge which is characterized through her: Theology. In what manner this is to affect the human heart and soul, is pictured. Of special significance is the fact that after all these experiences, in the following night nevertheless the spirit seeker is again visited by a *dream* in which he is shown a door that he desires to open, that offers him, however, considerable and prolonged resistance. This picture is produced within his soul through the idea that all previous experiences should not be considered as possessing any intrinsic value through their immediate content, but that they are only generators of a force which will have to be subjected to still further efforts.

The Fourth Day

The "fourth day" is decisive for the spiritual pilgrim insofar as his position in the supersensible world is concerned. Once more he meets the lion. *The ancient inscription,* brought toward him by the lion, contains essentially the demand that he should approach the source from which Inspirations flow from the spiritual world. The soul satisfied with mere imaginative experience could only allow itself to be addressed, as it were, from the spiritual world and to use the power of its own will to make these revelations comprehensible. If the full power of the "I" is to enter the supersensible world this "I" has to carry its own consciousness into that world. In the spiritual world the soul must rediscover the "I" with its sense-experiences. In a certain way the memory of the kind of experiences one has in the sense-world must emerge in the supersensible world. Andreae makes this clear by introducing a *"comedy"* on the "fourth day", that is, a phantom-picture of events in the physical world. In the beholding of this phantom-picture obtained in the supersensible realm, the "I" of the spirit-seeker is strengthened so that he feels the firm connection between that part of his soul which experiences in the supersensible world and that part which is active through the body in the world of the senses.

Out of insight into Andreae's competent method of description the conviction will arise that he desired to speak to his contemporaries in a most serious manner concerning a path into the world of spirit, adapted to the epoch of human development in the sixteenth century, at the beginning of which the author of the *Chymical Wedding* feels himself placed. The fact that at first a realization of the idealistic claims he set up before his contemporaries was hindered by serious obstacles, was due to the devastating confusion of the Thirty Years War, with all it brought over into the more modern era. But progress in human evolution is possible only when personalities of an attitude similar to that of Johann Valentin Andreae oppose the retarding forces of certain world-currents by others of a truly constructive nature. Whether Andreae succeeded in describing Christian Rosenkreuz as a spirit-seeker able to point effectively from his spiritual experiences of a past epoch to the new path appropriate for the new era, can only be decided if we can show that the last "days" of the *Chymical Wedding* relate experiences which open out a perspective into this period, — if Christian Rosenenkreuz is able to carry his "I" over into the new period.

The most significant experience for Christian Rosenkreuz on the fourth day is his introduction to the kings, and their subsequent beheading. The author of the *Chymical Wedding* indicates the nature of this experience by means of *symbolic figures standing upon a small altar.* In these symbols the human soul can behold its relationship to the universe and its becoming. By such symbols spiritual investigators have always tried to bring intimately before the soul how their own being lives within the cosmic being. The *book* points to the throught-content of man which, in conformity with the human organization, is an influx of objective world-creative thought into the soul. Through the *"little light"* it is indicated that these world-creative thoughts are active as light-ether in the universe, and in man become productive of knowledge and illumination. The playing into it of *Cupid* and his blowing upon the light refers to the spirit-seeker's perception that light and love are the two forces which, as polar opposites, are etherically at the basis of all existence and becoming. We only judge this perception correctly, however, when we see in the physical light and the love active on the physical plane, the materially effective revelations of original spiritual forces. In the primal spiritual force of light the creative thought element of the world lives freely, and within love lives the creative will element. A *"sphere"* is shown among the symbols to indicate how human experience in encountering cosmic life is a member of this cosmic life. The *clock* speaks of how the soul is interwoven with the progress of cosmic time, just as the sphere is interwoven with its spatial existence. The *little well* from which blood-red water flows, and *the skull with the serpent* show how birth and death appear to the seer as founded in the world-all. These symbols are among the very oldest. Valentin Andreae uses these symbolic representations in a manner similar to that which was used in the meeting-places of very ancient times, and which served such societies where men were admitted for initiation into the mysteries of life. Since Andreae uses them in the same manner, he shows that in his opinion they are imaginations truly based on the evolution of the human soul, which can stimulate it to perceive the mysteries of existence.

It must be asked: What is signified by the *"Hall of the Kings"* into which Christian Rosenkreuz is led, and what did he experience through *the presence of the Kings and their beheading?* The symbols point to the answer. The spiritual seeker is to behold how with his own being he is grounded in the Cosmic Being. What is in him he should perceive in the world; what is within the world he should perceive within himself. He can only do this when he sees in the objects and events, world pictures of what works and weaves in himself; no longer seeing these inner experiences merely as ideas proceeding out of his own soul, but perceiving them in pictures that represent the growth and becoming of the whole cosmos. *The kings* stand before Christian Rosenkreuz to indicate: thus do your soul-powers live within your own inner being; and the kings' experiences reflect events that under certain conditions must take place in the soul. Christian Rosenkreuz faces what happens in the "Hall of the Kings" in such manner that in it all his soul beholds itself. The beheading of the kings is an event in the evolution of his own soul. He has arrived in the "Hall of the Kings" with those forces of knowledge which are still of the same nature as they were before gaining entrance into the spiritual world. Through living into this world, however, these *forces of knowledge* have experiences that are also related to the material world. Not only does the spiritual world light up in face of the soul, but the material world also reveals itself before the latter in forms that cannot be seen in their full significance by anyone remaining with his powers of observation within the realm of matter. To these experiences belong the revealing of the divided nature of man's being. The forces forming the basis of physical growth are shown to be active also in phenomena generally considered as of a soul nature. The power of memory, the impulses for forming representations, prove to be dependent upon the same kind of physical condition as does growth. But the forces of growth work in such a way that during man's childhood and youth they are in progressive development, after which they decrease, finally becoming the cause of death, whereas memory and the forces for forming ideas, from a certain very early period of life, take on the possiblity of decline. In each waking period these forces pass through the same process of decline which the whole organism experiences in the second half of life until death. In every period of sleep this decline is compensated for, and memory and the forces of forming ideas undergo a resurrection. Man's soul organism is grafted like a parasite upon the whole human organism, and thus can supply the condition for memory and representations, because in the course of the day it follows along the path to death which in the course of earthly life the whole organism traverses. In this way, for the spiritual investigator, the soul-organism becomes a metamorphosis of the whole organism. The soul organism appears as that part of the complete organism that in a more intensive manner develops the forces responsible for the manifestation of life between birth and death, so that in the soul these forces may become the basis for the conceptual life. Into the daily decline of the forces of the soul-organism flows the creative cosmic being of thought, thus becoming the conceptual life of man. It is essential for the spirit-seeker to perceive the material foundation of soul-processes as the transmuted general processes of matter of the whole organism. It is a paradoxical fact that first of all one sees the material conditions of the soul life when on one's way to the spirit. This fact can be the starting-point of a temptation. One can remain at the point of discovery that soul events manifest themselves in their material form, and so while seeking the spirit one can be driven into a materialistic world conception. But if one really penetrates what is in question, the opposite takes place. In the material basis of the life of soul one observes the creative spiritual powers which reveal themselves through formations of substances, and thereby one prepares for oneself the possibility of recognizing the spirit at the basis of the whole organism and its life-course.

Christian Rosenkreuz is thus confronted with the important experience which reveals to him an alchemy accomplishing its work within the processes of nature. The material processes of the whole organism are transformed before his spiritual eye. They become something out of which the soul events flash forth like the light in the external process of combustion. But thereby these soul-events reveal themselves also where they reach their limits. They correspond to the processes in the organism which lead to death. Christian Rosenkreuz is brought before the "kings" of his own soul-being — before his powers of knowledge. They appear to him as a metamorphosis of the whole organism. But the forces of growth are changed into cognitional powers only by accepting death into themselves. For this reason they can carry in them only the knowledge of what is dead. — In all processes of nature death is included in such a way that the non-living exists in everything. It is upon what is non-living that our ordinary process of knowledge is directed. Because it is dead it grasps the inorganic, understanding the plant and all that is living only insofar as they are touched by the non-living. Every plant contains inorganic processes, over and above what it is as a living entity. Ordinarily these inorganic processes are grasped by our forces of knowledge; but they do not grasp what is living. What is living becomes visible only insofar as it manifests itself in the non-living. Christian Rosenkreuz witnesses the death of his "soul kings," his forces of knowledge, as these arise from the metamorphosis of the material forces of the whole organism without man passing over from the *alchemy of nature* to the *alchemy of art*. This has to take place in such a way that within his soul man gives his forces of knowledge a character they do not possess through their merely organic evolutionary processes. What essentially dwells within the ascending powers of growth, upon which death has not yet encroached, has to be awakened in the forces of cognition. Nature-alchemy must be carried further.

The Fifth Day

This further development of nature-alchemy forms the work of the fifth day of the *Chymical Wedding*. The vision of the spirit-seeker must penetrate into the processes nature effects when she brings forth growing life. And he must lead this creative activity of nature over into the forces of knowledge without allowing death to prevail in the transition from processes of growth to those of soul. The forces of knowledge he receives from nature as dead entities which he has to animate by restoring everything of which nature deprived them when it brought about their alchemical transmutation into powers of cognition. As he moves toward this goal, a temptation approaches him. He must descend into the region where through the force of love, nature charms life from what, inherently, is striving toward death. Here he is in danger of his vision being seized upon by those instincts that prevail in the lower regions of substances. He has to learn to recognize how in matter, which bears the stamp of death, lives an element related to the love underlying every renewal of life. This exposure of the soul to temptation is very significantly described by Andreae when he makes Christian Rosenkreuz appear before the *Venus* while Cupid is playing his role. And clearly indicated is how the spirit-seeker here referred to, is not restrained by the temptation from pursuing his way further by his own soul forces alone, but also by the working of other powers. If Christian Rosenkreuz had to tread only his own path of knowledge the latter could have ended with the temptation. The fact that this is not the case indicates what Andreae wishes to portray. On his spiritual path Christian Rosenkreuz is meant to show the way from a past epoch to the dawn of another. The active powers of the courses of time help him to permeate his "I" with the powers of knowledge suitable for the new period. Therefore he can proceed on his journey to the "tower" by participating in the alchemical process through which the dead cognitional powers experience their resurrection. Through this also on this journey he now possesses the power of listening to the *Siren's Song* of love without falling victim to its seductions. The spiritual primeval force of love must work upon him, but he may not allow its manner of manifestation in the sense world to mislead him on his way. In the *Tower of Olympus* occurs the permeation of the dead cognitional forces with those impulses which in the ordinary human organism hold sway only in the process of growth. How Christian Rosenkreuz is allowed to take part in this event because his soul development is to proceed in accordance with the changing forces of the times, is indicated. Instead of going to sleep he goes into the garden, looks up at the starry heavens and observes to himself: "Because I thus have a good opportunity to ponder over astronomy I found that on this night a conjunction of planets takes place such as is not often to be seen."

The Sixth Day

In the experiences of the sixth day are given detailed descriptions of the various Imaginations that make clear in Christian Rosenkreuz's soul how the dead forces of cognition evolved by the organism in the ordinary journey through life are transmuted into supersensible powers of perception. Each of these Imaginations corresponds to an experience of the soul in relation to its own powers when it realizes how what until now could be permeated only by death, becomes capable of knowingly allowing the living to stir within it. The single pictures would be differently described by any other spirit-seeker than Andreae. But it is not a question of the content of single pictures, but of the transformation of man's soul forces through his having before him in a succession of Imaginations such pictures as the reflection of this transformation.

Christian Rosenkreuz is portrayed in the *Chymical Wedding* as the spirit-seeker who feels the approach of that period when humanity will view nature's phenomena differently from the epoch passing away with the fifteenth century. In this coming period, as he observes nature man will no longer be able to perceive the spiritual content of the objects and events of nature through this observation alone. This can lead to a denial of the spiritual world if man does not admit the existence of a path of knowledge by which the material basis of the soul-life can be penetrated, and yet the being of the spirit be received into this knowledge. To be able to effect this, one must be able to shed spiritual light upon this material basis. One must be able to perceive how nature proceeds as it shapes its active forces into a soul organism through which death is revealed, in order then to hear from the being of nature itself the mystery of how spirit can confront spirit when the creative activity of nature is guided to awaking the dead cognitional forces to a higher life. Thereby a knowledge is developed which, as spirit-knowledge, finds its place within reality. For knowledge of this kind is a further shoot on the living being of the world; through it is continued the evolution of reality which prevails from the first primeval beginnings of existence up to the life of man. Thus alone is developed into higher forces of knowledge, what as a germ is preconditioned in nature, but which is held back from the working of nature itself at the point where, in the metamorphosis of existence, the cognition for what is dead should be developed. — The objection that such a continuation of nature's activity beyond what is attained by it in the human organism would lead beyond reality and into the unreal, will not be made by anyone who penetrates into the evolution of nature itself. For everywhere evolution consists in the progress of the forces of growth being arrested at certain points in order to bring about revelations of the endless possibilities of new forms at certain stages of human existence. Thus in the human organization also is a possibility of formation stayed. But just as in the green leaf of the plant such a possibility is arrested, and yet the formative forces of the plant's growth advance beyond this form, making the colored leaf of the blossom appear at a higher stage, so can man progress from the formation of his forces of knowledge which are directed toward what is dead, to a higher stage of these forces. He experiences the character of reality in this progress by becoming aware that through it he receives the soul-organ into himself for the comprehension of the spirit in its supersensible revelation, just as the transformation of the green leaf into the colored flower-organ of the plant prepares the capacity that expands itself into the formation of the fruit.

The Seventh Day

After the art-alchemical process is completed, Christian Rosenkreuz is named *"Knight of the Golden Stone."* One would have to enter deeply into a purely historical description if one wished to expatiate on the name "Golden Stone" from literature — some trustworthy but, for the greater part, fraudulent — and to indicate its use. But to enter into this literature is not the purpose of this article. However, we may simply indicate the conclusions concerning the use of the name as derived from a perusal of this literature. The individuals who are to be taken seriously who have used this name, "The Golden Stone," desired to indicate by it that it is possible to regard the dead stone-nature so as to grasp its relation to what is living and what is coming to life. The serious alchemist believed it would be possible for artificial processes of nature to be produced in which what is dead and of a stony character could be employed, but in which, when rightly observed, something of what goes on when nature itself weaves the dead into the living and becoming can be recognized. Through the perception of quite distinct processes in what is dead, one would grasp traces of the creative activity of nature and with it the being of the spirit ruling in the phenomena. The symbol for the dead that is recognized as the revelation of the spirit, is "The Golden Stone." Whoever examines a corpse in its essential, actual nature, recognizes how what is dead is gathered up within the general process of nature. It is the form of the corpse, however, which protests against this general nature-process. This form can only be a result of spirit-permeated life. The general processes of nature must destroy what has been formed by spirit-permeated life. The alchemist is of the opinion that what ordinary human knowledge can grasp of the whole of nature is only as much as man can be identified by his corpse. A higher knowledge should find in natural phenomena what is related to it, as the spirit-permeated life is related to the corpse. Such is the striving for "The Golden Stone." Andreae so speaks of this symbol that he clearly means only those can understand what to do with "The Golden Stone" who have experienced what he describes as the six days' work. He wishes to show that anyone who has spoken of this without knowing the nature of the transformation of the cognitional forces, can have only an illusion in mind. In Christian Rosenkreuz he strives to describe a personality who can speak in an authoritative way about something often spoken of without authority. He wishes to defend the truth against what is wrongly spoken about the search for the spiritual world.

Christian Rosenkreuz and his companions, after they have become actual workers on "The Golden Stone," receive *a memento with the two sayings*: "Art is the servant of nature," and "Nature is the daughter of time." Out of their spirit-knowledge they are to work in harmony with these guiding tenets. In the latter the six days' experiences are comprised and characterized. Nature reveals its mysteries to him who through his art enables himself to continue its creative work. But in this continuation he cannot succeed unless in his art he has first listened to the meaning of nature's will, and unless he has recognized how nature's revelations arise through its infinite faculty of evolution, coming forth from the womb of time in finite forms of existence.

In his connection with the king on the seventh day, we are shown how Christian Rosenkreuz as spirit-seeker now stands in relation to his transformed faculties of knowledge. It is shown how as "Father," he himself gave them birth. And his relation to the *"First Gatekeeper"* is a relation to a part of his own being, i.e., to what as "Astrologus," before the transformation of his cognitional forces, searched for the laws determining human life but was not then equal to facing the temptation resulting when the spirit-seeker comes to a situation like that in which Christian Rosenkreuz was placed at the beginning of the fifth day upon confronting Venus. One succumbing to this temptation finds no entrance to the spiritual world. He knows too much to be entirely shut away from it, but he cannot enter. He has to stand guard before the door until another appears and falls victim to the same temptation. Christian Rosenkreuz supposes himself to have succumbed and thus to have been condemned to take over *The Office of Watchman*. But this watchman is part of himself, and because he can survey it with the other part that is transformed, he is able to overcome it. He becomes watchman of his own soul life, but this guardianship does not hinder him from establishing free connection with the spiritual world. By reason of his seven days' experience Christian Rosenkreuz has become a knower of the spirit who, with the power conferred on him by this experience, can work in the world. What Christian Rosenkreuz and his associates accomplish in external life will flow from that spirit out of which the works of nature itself flow. Through their work they will bring into human life harmony which will be an image of the harmony working in nature, capable of conquering opposing inharmonies. The presence of such people in the *social order* is to be a continuously working impulse toward a health-sustaining way of life. When people ask what are the best laws for living together, for the social life of men on earth, Andreae points to Christian Rosenkreuz and his companions. He answers: The social order cannot be regulated by ideas expressed in thoughts as to how this or that shall be done, but by what may be said by those who strive to live in the spirit manifesting itself through existence. What guides those souls who, in the sense of Christian Rosenkreuz, wish to work in the life of man, is expressed in *five sentences:*

> It was to be far from them to think out of any spirit other than the one revealing itself in the creations of nature; and they were to see man's work as a continuation of nature's works.

> They were not to place their work in the service of human impulses, but were to make these impulses into mediators for the works of the spirit.

They were to serve men lovingly, so that in the relation between man and man the creative spirit could be manifested.

By anything of worth the world could give they were not to let themselves be led, aside from their striving for the worth the spirit can confer upon all human labor.

They were not, like bad Alchemists, to fall into the error of confusing the physical with the spiritual. Bad Alchemists think that the physical means of prolonging life or similar objectives are the highest good, forgetting that the physical is of value only so long as its existence is a rightful manifestation of the underlying spirit.

At the end of the narrative of *The Chymical Wedding* Andreae describes Christian Rosenkreuz' "homecoming." In all externals he is the same as he was before his experiences. His new condition of life is different from the old only in that henceforth he will carry his "higher man" within himself, as the ruler of his consciousness, and what he accomplishes will be what the "higher man" can effect through him. The transition from the last experiences of the seventh day to the finding-himself-at-home in his ordinary surroundings is not described. "Here two or three pages are missing." One could imagine there might be people who would be especially curious about what these *missing pages* contain. This latter is what only he can know who himself has undergone an individual experience of the transformation of his soul-nature. Such a one knows that everything leading to this experience has a universally human significance which is communicated as one communicates the experience of a journey. The reception of what has been experienced by the ordinary man is, on the contrary, something quite personal; it is different for each one and cannot be understood by another in the same way as by the one who has experienced it. That Valentin Andreae has not described this transition into the customary conditions of life can serve as further proof that through *The Chymical Wedding* is expressed true knowledge of what had to be described.

* * *

The foregoing exposition is an attempt to describe what is expressed in *The Chymical Wedding* entirely through consideration of the content of this work as revealed to the author. It should confirm the judgment that in this writing published by Andreae, the direction is shown that must be followed when anything concerning the true character of higher knowledge is to be known. And this exposition seeks to make clear that in *The Chymical Wedding* we have a picture of the special kind of spiritual knowledge demanded since the fifteenth century. For those who understand this document as does the author of this exposition, it is *a historical account of a European spiritual stream going back to the fifteenth century,* a stream seeking to acquire knowledge about that relationship of everything which lies behind the phenomena of the external world.

There exists, however, a fairly extensive literature concerning the effect of the work of Johann Valentin Andreae, in which is discussed whether his published writings can be regarded as actual proof of the existence of a spiritual stream of this nature. In these writings this stream is indicated to be that of Rosicrucianism. Certain investigators consider that the whole affair of Andreae and his Rosicrucian writings is simply a literary joke intended to ridicule the sentimentality to be found wherever the mysteries of higher knowledge are discussed. From this point of view, this Rosicrucianism would be a fantasy-picture created by Andreae for the express purpose of making fun of the wild talk of sentimentalists or of fraudulent mystics. The author of this exposition considers it unnecessary to trouble his readers with much of what is put forward in this way against the seriousness of Andreae's intentions, because he is of the opinion that a correct study of what *The Chymical Wedding* contains affords sufficient basis for understanding what it means to convey. Evidence based on material other than these contents can have no effect upon this opinion. One who recognizes the full weight of inner reasons, is of the conviction that external documentary evidence is to be valued according to these inner reasons, and not that the inner should receive its value from the outer. Therefore if what is said here takes its position outside the purely historical literature concerning Rosicrucianism, no adverse criticism of historical research is intended. All that is meant here is that the point of view taken in this exposition makes a full discussion of Rosicrucian literature unnecessary. Let us therefore add only a few remarks.

It is a known fact that the manuscript of *The Chymical Wedding* was completed by 1603. It first made its public appearance in 1616 after Andreae, in 1614, had published his other Rosicrucian document, *Fama Fraternitatis R.C.* It was this publication above all that gave rise to the belief that Andreae spoke only in jest of the existence of a Rosicrucian Society. This belief was later supported by Andreae's own statement that Rosicrucianism was not a thing he would have cared to defend. There is much in his later writings and in his letters to support the interpretation that his sole purpose was to invent stories concerning this spiritual stream for the mystification of fanatics and the curious. As a rule, in making use of such evidence no heed is paid to what misunderstandings works like those of Andreae are exposed. What he himself later said about this can be estimated rightly only when one realizes that he was obliged to speak in that manner after enemies had appeared who severely condemned this spiritual movement as heresy; that adherents had come forward who were fanatical or were alchemical swindlers, distorting everything for which Rosicrucianism stood. But even when all this is taken into consideration, when one is willing to accept the thought that Andreae, who appears later as a pietistic writer, soon after the publication of the Rosicrucian writings showed himself averse to owning as his what was expressed in those writings, through such considerations one does not reach a sufficiently well-grounded opinion on the relation of this personality to Rosicrucianism. Indeed, even if one is willing to go so far as to deny Andreae the authorship of the *Fama,* on historical grounds one is not willing to do so with regard to *The Chymical Wedding.*

There is also another point of view from which the matter must be considered historically. The *Fama Fraternitatis* appeared in 1614. We may first of all leave undecided whether with this work Andreae wished to approach serious readers in order to tell them about the spiritual path known as Rosicrucianism. But two years after the appearance of the *Fama*, *The Chymical Wedding,* which had already been completed thirteen years before, was published. In 1603 Andreae was still a very young man (seventeen years of age). Are we to suppose that he was sufficiently mature to have started a ghost among the sentimentalists of his day by presenting them with Rosicrucianism, an image of his power of fantasy, as a sop for their mockery? Besides, if in the *Fama,* which in manuscript was already being read in the Tyrol by the year 1610, he was wishing to speak of Rosicrucianism in a serious way, how was it that as a quite young man, in *The Chymical Wedding* he composed a document that he published as information concerning true Rosicrucianism two years after the *Fama*? In fact, the questions about Andreae seem to become so entangled that this complicates any merely historical solution. We should not be able to protest against any merely historical investigator trying to make it credible that Andreae may have lighted upon the manuscripts — perhaps in the possession of his family — of *The Chymical Wedding* and the *Fama,* that he published them for some reason in his youth, but later repudiated the spiritual bent expressed in them. Were this a fact, however, why did not Andreae simply announce that this was the case?

With the help of the science of spirit one can reach a totally different conclusion. There is no need to connect the content of *The Chymical Wedding* with Andreae's age at the time he wrote it, nor with his powers of judgment. As far as the content is concerned, this document shows itself to be written out of *Intuition.* It is possible for things of this kind to be written down by people with a certain aptitude for them, even if their own powers of judgment and experience in life take no part in what is thus written. And what is written down nevertheless can be the conveying of full reality. On the basis of its content one is compelled to accept *The Chymical Wedding* as a communication about an actually existing spiritual current. The assumption that Valentin Andreae wrote it out of Intuition sheds a light upon the attitude toward Rosicrucianism he adopted later. As a young man he had the capacity to give a picture of this spiritual current without calling upon his own means of knowledge. Andreae's own path of knowledge found its development later when he became the pietistic theologan, whereas his spiritual receptivity that could reflect Intuition receded in his soul. Later he himself philosophized about what he had written in his youth. He did this as early as 1619 in his *Turris Babel* (Tower of Babel). The connection between the later Andreae and the Andreae who wrote out of Intuition in his youth, did not become clear to him. If in this way we consider Andreae's attitude toward what was contained in *The Chymical Wedding,* we are obliged to keep in mind what the document contains without relation to anything expressed by him at any time concerning his connections with Rosicrucianism. What it was possible to reveal about this spiritual stream in Andreae's day was set forth by a personality fitted to do so. Whoever believes from the outset that it is impossible for the spiritual life as it takes effect in world phenomena to be revealed in such a way as this, will certainly be constrained to reject what is said here. There may be people, however, who, without superstitious prejudices, will quietly consider the "case of Andreae," and by it gain the conviction of the possibility of this kind of revelation.

King's College, Cambridge University, from an early 19th century engraving. Here Ezechiel Foxcroft made the first English translation of *The Chymical Wedding of Christian Rosenkreutz* between 1656 and his death in 1674, while he was Mathematics Lecturer at the College.

THE ENGLISH TRANSLATION OF THE CHYMICAL WEDDING

by

PAUL M. ALLEN

Ever since its initial publication in 1616 *The Chymical Wedding,* sometimes called *The Hermetic Romance of Christian Rosenkreutz,* has intrigued a wide circle of readers. The artistry and charm of its word-pictures, the occasional touches of ironic humor, the element of suspense, along with the tale of its somewhat mysterious origin at the hands of the young student, Johann Valentin Andreae, have sustained an interest in this unusual book. More than this, however, from its first appearance to our own day, spiritually perceptive readers have discovered in *The Chymical Wedding,* a profound picture-book, a "spiritual diary" of utmost importance, its "revealed secrets" conveying truths indispensable to the well-being of the individual, and to the establishment of a healthy community life among the family of mankind. To many it has become a trustworthy interpreter of the phenomenology of those events inevitably accompanying each individual who strives to follow the path leading to a real knowledge and experience of the spiritual world. Today's physical, psychological and spiritual distress should suffice to recommend serious consideration of *The Chymical Wedding* to anyone attempting to comprehend the nature and activity of those forces at work behind external happenings, creating the signature of our modern life.

*

The first English translation of *The Chymical Wedding* was made by Ezechiel Foxcroft and was published in 1690, just

See Reference Notes, beginning p. 635

seventy-five years after its appearance in German. Those in a position to compare Andreae's text with Foxcroft's translation will observe how well the latter renders the meaning while preserving the particular flavor and spirit of the original. This unusual example of the translator's art is due to Foxcroft's own intuitive grasp of *The Chymical Wedding,* for although biographical details concerning him are somewhat limited, sufficient is known to indicate that he was a man of unusual spiritual interests and attainments.

Born in London in 1633, the son of a merchant, Ezechiel Foxcroft attended Eaton and at 16 entered King's College, Cambridge, from which he graduated B.A. in 1652 and M.A. in 1656. He was a Fellow of King's College 1652-74 and Senior Proctor of the University, 1673-74.

Foxcroft is remembered in connection with the so-called "touch" healings of various types of diseases by the famous Valentine Greatrakes of Affane in County Waterford, Ireland. When Greatrakes came to England in 1666 his fame had preceded him and thousands of sick people thronged to him from all parts of the country. Among the many famous men who witnessed the "touching" of the sick by Greatrakes were the eminent scientist, Robert Boyle and the philosopher, Ralph Cudworth, a leading member of the Cambridge Platonists, pupil of Henry More and author of the well-known *True Intellectual System of the Universe.* Foxcroft's name appeared prominently among those endorsing Greatrakes' successful treatment of the sick, particularly in a tract published at Oxford titled *The Miraculous Conformist; or, an Account of several marvelous Cures, performed by the stroking of the hands of Mr. Valentine Greatrakes; with a physical Discourse thereupon, in a letter to the Hon. Robert Boyle; with a letter relating to some other of his miraculous Cures, attested by E. Foxcroft, A.M., and Fellow of King's College, Cambridge.*

At first glance it might appear that Greatrakes was merely another of those charlatans common in the history of the healing arts, and that Foxcroft's endorsement might well be considered evidence of poor judgment and even questionable integrity. That this was by no means the case, however, is borne out by a letter published in *The Gentleman's Magazine* for

January 1779 describing Greatrakes' life and work. The letter concludes: "On the strictest inquiry no sort of blemish was ever thrown upon his character, nor did any of those curious and learned persons who espoused his cause draw any implications upon themselves."

Foxcroft was doubtless one of that circle of men who found at Ragley, the estate of Lady Conway in Warwickshire a congenial atmosphere for their philosophical, religious and scientific discussions. For among the guests who met regularly at this beautiful country place were Henry More, Ralph Cudworth, Greatrakes and many another "curious and learned person" including such famous visitors from the Continent as Franz Mercurius van Helmont and Baron von Rosenroth, the co-authors of the great caballistic work, the *Caballa Denudata,* and many others. In such a company it is highly probable that *The Chymical Wedding* was discussed with considerable interest, and it well may have been here that Foxcroft's attention was drawn to the work in the first place.

One fact of interest concerning the English translation of *The Chymical Wedding* is that it was not published until fourteen years after Foxcroft's death at the age of forty-one in 1674, just twenty years after the decease of Andreae.

*

In 1652, the same year that Foxcroft was made Fellow of King's College, the well-known Thomas Vaughan, by many regarded as the spiritual successor of the great Oxford scientist and Rosicrucian apologist, Robert Fludd, published a small volume of some sixty-four pages titled *The Fame and Confession of the Fraternity of R:C:, commonly, of the Rosie Cross.* This work created a sensation among the literati of England as it had upon its publication thirty-eight years before in Cassel after several years' circulation in manuscript form.

Thomas Vaughan was well known to the circle at Ragley, not only for this translation of the *Fame and Confession* which evoked lively interest there, but also for his own work which had appeared two years earlier. This was his *Anthroposophia Theomagica; A Discourse of the Nature of Man and his State after Death, grounded on his Creator's proto-Chemistry and verified by a Practical Examination of Principles in the Great World,* London, 1650. Dedicated "To the

Most Illustrious and Truly Bretheren R.C. (Rosy Cross, i.e., Rosicrucians) Elders of Election and Peaceable Apostles of the Church in this Storm-Driven Age. Salutation from the Center of Peace."

Incidentally, the title of Vaughan's important work was doubtless drawn from Robert Fludd's famous treatise, the *Summum Bonum,* (1629) a defense of the claims of the Brotherhood of the Rosy Cross, with the title-page bearing the emblematic rose springing from a cross stem. A long disquisition on the significance of the Rose and the Cross is followed by an explanation of what Fludd calls "Theomagica," which he terms "the wisdom of God . . the hidden wisdom," "the divine life in and by the Word of God — God's government of the angelic Hierarchies, the natural science of a moral and politic philosophy" — and which he sums up in the one word *Anthroposophia.*

A notation on its title page that Vaughan's *Anthroposophia Theomagica* was "printed for H. Blunden" is of unusual significance, for it connects this work with yet another stream of spiritual life with which it is unquestionably related. No doubt the "H. Blunden" referred to Humphrey Blunden who, along with the Advocate of the Inner Temple, John Sparrow and the latter's cousin, John Ellistone, formed the circle of the first English translators of the writings of the great Silesian mystic, Jacob Boehme. Thus the Rosicrucian impulses at work in the teaching of Robert Fludd flower out into that of Thomas Vaughan, link up with the translators of Jacob Boehme in 17th century England, and at length include the Cambridge Senior Proctor, Ezechiel Foxcroft . .

*

Vaughan's *Anthroposophia Theomagica* was translated and published in Germany in 1704 and again at Berlin in 1782 It seems highly significant that only two years later, in August 1784 Johann Wolfgang von Goethe began writing his "Rosicrucian fragment," as he later called it. This was his remarkable poem, *Die Geheimnisse, The Mysteries,* with its impressive pictures of the circle of the Rosicrucian Brotherhood like "a Salutation from the Center of Peace" in a "Storm-Driven Age," to use Vaughan's words of dedication, mentioned above.

Goethe's relationship with the Rosicrucian writing by no

means ceased at this point, however. In a letter addressed to Frau von Stein on June 28, 1786, just two years after his work on *The Mysteries,* he wrote: "I have just read *The Wedding of Christian Rosenkreutz;* from this there will be a good fairy tale to be told at the right time, but it will have to be reborn, for it cannot be enjoyed in its old skin." — And nine years later this "good fairy tale" of Goethe actually did appear in the well-known periodical, *Die Horen,* under the title, "The *Green Snake and the Beautiful Lily.* Indeed, in Goethe's word, the latter is *The Chymical Wedding of Christian Rosenkreutz,* no longer "in its old skin," but artistically metamorphosed through the spiritually creative faculties of Goethe and "reborn" in a totally new artistic guise.

*

For the 150th anniversary of Goethe's birth which occurred in 1899, Rudolf Steiner wrote an essay on Goethe's Fairy Tale, which in the meanwhile had been translated into English by Thomas Carlyle and published in Fraser's Magazine in 1832, the year of Goethe's death. In his essay, titled *The Character of Goethe's Spirit,* Rudolf Steiner shows how the motifs of the Goethe Fairy Tale present "in delicate imaginative pictures. . . the development of the human soul from the state in which it feels itself a stranger to the supersensory, to that enhanced consciousness in which the life spent in the world of the senses permeates itself with the supersensory world of the spirit in such a way that the two become *one.*" (Both the Carlyle translation of the Goethe Fairy Tale and Rudolf Steiner's essay are included in the volume titled *The Portal of Initiation,* by Rudolf Steiner, Rudolf Steiner Publications, New Jersey, 1961. It will be found very helpful to compare Carlyle's translation of Goethe's Fairy Tale with the Foxcroft translation of *The Chymical Wedding of Christian Rosenkreutz.*)

Finally in 1910 Rudolf Steiner took up the threads descending from *The Chymical Wedding,* artistically "reborn" in Goethe's Fairy Tale, and wove them into a modern drama. This work bears the significant title, *The Portal of Initiation, A Rosicrucian Mystery,* thus indicating its relationship to that spiritual stream out of which it had come and to which it belongs. Through this drama Rudolf Steiner said he sought "to show how the influx of spiritual ideas, of spiritual life into our civilization is to be regarded."

Seven years later, amidst the tragic events of World War One, recognizing their fateful impact upon the present and future of all mankind, Rudolf Steiner forged yet another link in the spiritual chain extending from earlier centuries into our own time. This took the form of an essay on *The Chymical Wedding* which he wrote for a magazine with a broad public circulation in Germany.

In this essay Rudolf Steiner shows how humanity's age-old quest for the spirit, evidenced in the "spiritual diary", *The Chymical Wedding of Christian Rosenkreutz,* finds new orientation in modern terms through the Science of Spirit, or Anthroposophy. Rising out of true Rosicrucian foundations, this knowledge is a prerequisite if mankind is rightly to experience "the streaming down of spiritual life into man on earth" in our time.

A SUGGESTION

It is recommended that the reading of the following Rosicrucian texts be accompanied by reference to the notes beginning on page 635.

THE
HERMETICK
ROMANCE:
OR THE
CHYMICAL
VVEDDING

Written in high Dutch By
Chriſtian Roſencreutz.

Tranſlated by *E. Foxcroft*, late Fellow of
Kings Colledge in *Cambridge*.

Licenſed, & Entred according to **Order.**

Ne Aſino ſubſterne Roſas.

Printed, by *A. Sowle*, at the *Crooked-Billet* in *Hol-*
loway-Lane Shoreditch: And ſold at the *Three-Kyes*
in *Nags-Head-Court Grace-Church-ſtreet*, 1690.

The First Day

On an Evening before *Easter*-Day, I sate at a Table, and having (as my Custom was) in my humble Prayer sufficiently conversed with my Creator, and considered many great Mysteries (whereof the Father of Lights his Majesty had shewn me not a few) and being now ready to prepare in my Heart, together with my dear *Paschal Lamb,* a small unleavened, undefiled Cake; All on a sudden ariseth so horrible a Tempest, that I imagined no other but that through its mighty force, the Hill whereon my little House was founded, would flye in pieces. But in as much as this, and the like from the Devil (who had done me many a spight) was no new thing to me; I took courage, and persisted in my Meditation, till some body after an unusual manner, touched me on the Back; whereupon I was so hugely terrified, that I durst hardly look about me; yet I shewed my self as cheerful as (in the like Occurrences) humane frailty would permit; Now the same thing still twiching me several times by the Coat, I looked back, and behold it was a fair and glorious *Lady,* whose Garments were all *Skye-colour,* and curiously (like Heaven) bespangled with golden *Stars,* in her right Hand she bare a *Trumpet* of beaten Gold, whereon a Name was ingraven (which I could well read in) but am as yet forbidden to reveal it. In her left Hand she had a great bundle of *Letters of all Languages,* which she (as I afterwards understood) was to carry into all *Countries.* She had also large and beautiful *Wings,* full of *Eyes* throughout, wherewith she could mount aloft, and flye swifter than any *Eagle.* I might perhaps been able to take further notice of her, but because she staid so small time with me, and terror and amazement still possessed me, I was fain to be content. For as soon as I turned about, she turned her *Letters* over and over, and at length drew out a small one, which with *great Reverence* she laid down upon the Table, and without giving one word, departed from me. But in her mounting upward, she gave so mighty a *blast* on her gallant Trumpet, that the *whole Hill* echoed thereof, and for a full *quarter* of an hour after, I could hardly hear my own Words.

See Reference Notes, beginning p. 635

68

In so unlooked for an adventure I was at a loss, how either to advise, or assist my poor self, and therefore fell upon my Knees, and *besought* my Creator to permit nothing contrary to my *Eternal* Happiness to befall me; whereupon with fear and trembling, I went to the Letter, which was now *so heavy,* as had it been meer Gold, it could hardly have been so weighty. Now as I was diligently viewing it, I found a little *Seal,* whereupon a curious Cross with this Inscription, IN HOC SIGNO VINCES, was ingraven.

Now as soon as I espied this Sign I was the more comforted, as not being ignorant that such a Seal was little acceptable, and much less useful to the *Devil*. Whereupon I tenderly opened the Letter, and within it, in an *Azure* Field, in *Golden* Letters, found the following Verses written.

> *This day, this day, this, this*
> *The Royal Wedding is.*
> *Art thou thereto by Birth inclin'd,*
> *And unto joy of God design'd,*
> *Then may'st thou to the Mountain trend,*
> *Whereon three stately* Temples *stand,*
> *And there see all from end to end.*
>   *Keep watch, and ward,*
>   *Thy self regard;*
> *Unless with diligence thou* bathe,
> *The Wedding can't thee harmless save:*
> *He'l dammage have that here delays;*
> *Let him beware, too light that weighs.*

Underneath stood *Sponsus* and *Sponsa*.

As soon as I had read this Letter, I was presently like to have fainted away, all my Hair stood on end, and a cold Sweat trickled down my whole Body. For although I well perceived that this was the appointed *Wedding*, whereof seven Years before I was acquainted in a *bodily Vision,* and which now so long time I had with great earnestness attended,* and which lastly, by the account and calculation ot the *Plannets,* I had most diligently observed, I found so to be, yet could I

---

*awaited

69

never fore-see that it must happen under so grievous and perilous conditions. For whereas I before imagined that to be a well-come, and acceptable Guest, I needed only be ready to appear at the Wedding; I was now directed to Divine *Providence,* of which until this time I was never certain. I also found by my self, the more I *examined* my self, that in my Head there was nothing but gross mis-understanding, and blindness in mysterious things, so that I was not able to comprehend even those things which lay *under* my Feet, and which I daily conversed with, much less that I should be born to the searching out, and understanding of the Secrets of Nature; since in my opinion Nature might every where find a more *vertuous* Disciple, to whom to intrust her precious, though temporary, and changeable Treasures. I found also that my bodily behaviour, and outward good Conversation, *and Brotherly Love* toward my Neighbour, was not duly purged and cleansed; Moreover the tickling of the Flesh manifested it self, whose affection was bent only to Pomp and Bravery, and Worldly Pride, and not to the good of mankind: And I was always contriving how by this art I might in a short time abundantly increase my profit and advantage, rear up stately Palaces, make my self an everlasting Name in the World, and other like *Carnal* designs. But the obscure Words concerning the *Three Temples* did particularly afflict me, which I was not able to make out by any after-Speculation, and perhaps should not yet, had they not been wonderfully revealed to me. Thus sticking betwixt Hope and Fear, examining my self again and again, and finding only my own Frailty and *Impotency,* not being in any wise able to succour my self, and exceedingly amazed at the fore-mentioned threatning; at length I betook my self to my usual and most secure course; after I had finished my earnest and most fervent *Prayer,* I laid me down in my Bed, that so perchance my good *Angel* by the Divine permission might appear, and (as it had sometimes *formerly* happened) instruct me in this doubtful affair, which to the praise of God, my own good, and my Neighbours faithful and hearty warning and amendment did now likewise fall out. For I was yet scarce fallen asleep, when me-thought, I, together with a *numberless multitude* of men lay fettered with great Chains in a *dark Dungeon,*

70

wherein without the least glimps of Light, we swarmed like Bees one over another, and thus rendred each others affliction more grievous. But although neither I, nor any of the rest could *see* one jot; yet I continually heard one heaving himself *above* the other, when his Chains or Fetters were become ever so little lighter, though none of us had much reason to shove up the other, since we were all *Captive Wretches*. Now as I with the rest had continued a good while in this affliction, and each was still reproaching the other with his *blindness* and *captivity*, at length we heard many *Trumpets* sounding together, and Kettle Drums beating so artifically thereto, that it even revived and rejoyced us in our Calamity. During this Noise the *cover* of the Dungeon was from above lifted up, and a little *light* let down unto us. Then first might truly have been discerned the bustle we kept, for all went pesle-mesle, and he who perchance had too much *heaved* up himself, was forced down again under the others Feet. In brief, each one strove to be *uppermost,* neither did I my self linger, but with my weighty Fetters slipt up from under the rest, and then heaved my self upon a *Stone,* which I laid hold of; howbeit, I was several times caught at by others, from whom yet as well as I might, with Hands and Feet I still guarded my self. For we imagined no other but that we should all be set at *Liberty,* which yet fell out quite otherwise. For after the Nobles who looked upon us from above through the Hole, had a while recreated themselves with this our strugling and lamenting, a certain *hoary-headed Ancient* Man called to us to be quiet, and having scarce obtained it, began (as I still remember) thus to say on.

> *If wretched Mankind would forbear*
> *Themselves so to uphold,*
> *Then sure on them much good confer,*
> *My righteous Mother would:*
> *But since the same will not insue,*
> *They must in Care and Sorrow rue,*
> *And still in Prison lie.*
> *Howbeit, my dear Mother will*
> *Their Follies over-see,*
> *Her choicest Goods permitting still*

Too much in th' Light to be.
Though very rarely it may seem
That they may still keep some esteem,
Which else would pass for Forgery.
Wherefore in honour of the Feast
  We this day solemnize,
That so her Grace may be increast,
  A good deed she'l devise.
For now a Cord shall be let down,
And whosoe'er can hang thereon,
  Shall freely be releast.

He had scarce done speaking, when an Antient *Matron* commanded her Servants to let down the Cord *seven times* into the Dungeon, and draw up whosoever could hang upon it. Good God! that I could sufficiently describe the hurry and disquiet that then arose amongst us; For every one strove to get to the Cord, and yet only hindred each other. But after seven Minutes a sign was given by a little Bell, whereupon at the *first Pull* the Servants drew up *four.* At that time I could not come near the Cord by much, having (as is before-mentioned) to my huge misfourtune, betaken my self to a *Stone* at the Wall of the *Dungeon,* and thereby was disabled to get to the Cord which descended in the middle. The Cord was let down the second time, but divers, because their Chains were too *heavy,* and their Hands too *tender,* could not keep their hold on the Cord, but with themselves beat down *many another,* who else perhaps might have held fast enough; Nay, many an one was forcably *pulled* off by another, who yet could not himself get at it; so mutually *envious* were we even in this our great misery. But they of all others most moved my Compassion, whose weight was so heavy, that they tore their very hands from their Bodies, and yet could not get up. Thus it came to pass that at these five times very few were drawn up. For as soon as the sign was given, the Servants were so nimble at the draught, that the most part tumbled one upon another, and the Cord, this time especially, was drawn up very *empty.* Whereupon the greatest part, and even I my self, despaired of Redemption, and called upon *God* that he would have pitty on us, and (if possible) deliver us out of this obscurity, who also then heard some of us: For when the Cord came down the sixth time, some of them hung themselves fast upon it; and whilst in the drawing up, the Cord swung from one side to the other, it (perhaps by the will of God) came to me, which I suddainly catching, uppermost above all the rest, and so at length beyond hope came out; whereat I exceedingly rejoyced, so that I perceived not the *Wound,* which in the drawing up I received on my *Head* by a sharp Stone, till I with the rest who were released (as was always before done) was fain to help at the seventh and last pull, at which time through straining, the *Blood* ran down all over my *Cloathes,* which I nevertheless for joy regarded not. Now when the last draught whereon the most of all hung, was finished; The Matron caused the Cord to be laid away, and willed her aged Son (at which I much wondred) to declare her Resolution to the rest of the Prisoners; who after he had a little bethought himself spoke, thus unto them.

> *Ye Children dear*
> *All present here,*
> *What is but now compleat and done,*
> *Was long before resolved on:*
> *What er'r my Mother of great Grace*
> *To each on both sides here hath shown,*
> *May never Discontent mis-place;*
> *The joyful time is drawing on,*
> *When every one shall equal be,*
> *None Wealthy, none in Penury.*
> *Who er'e receiveth great Commands*
> *Hath work enough to fill his Hands.*
> *Who er'e with much hath trusted been,*
> *'Tis well if he may save his Skin.*
> *Wherefore your Lamentations cease,*
> *What is't to waite for some few days;*

As soon as he had finished these Words, the Cover was again put to and locked down, and the Trumpets and Kettle-Drums began afresh, yet could not the noise thereof be so loud, but that the bitter Lamentation of the Prisoners which arose in the Dungeon was heard above all, which soon also caused my

Eyes to *run-over*. Presently after the Antient Matron, together with her Son sate down upon seats before prepared, and commanded the Redeemed should be told. Now as soon as she understood the number, and had written it down in a Gold-yellow Tablet, she demanded every ones Name, which were also written down by a little page; having viewed us all, one after another, she sighed, and spoke to her Son, so as I could well hear her, "Ah how hartily am I grieved for the poor Men in the Dungeon! I would to God I durst release them all," whereunto her Son replyed; "It is Mother thus ordained of God, against whom we may not contend. In case we all of us were Lords, and possessed all the Goods upon Earth, and were seated at Table, who would there then be to be bring up the Service?" whereupon his Mother held her peace, but soon after she said; "Well, however, let these be freed from their Fetters; which was likewise presently done, and I, except a few was the last; yet could I not refrain, but (though I still looked upon the rest, bowed my self before the Antient Matron, and thanked God that through her, had graciously and fatherly vouch-safed to bring me out of such Darkness into the Light: After me the rest did likewise, to the satisfaction of the Matron. Lastly, to every one was given a piece of Gold for a Remembrance, and to spend by the way, on the one side whereof was stamped the rising Sun, on the other (as I remember) these three letters, D L. S, And therewith every one had License to depart, and was sent to his own Business with this annexed Intimation, *That We to the Glory of God should benefit our Neighbours, and reserve in silence what we had been intrusted with,* which we also promised to do, and so departed one from another; But in regard of the Wounds which the Fetters had caused me, I could not well go forward, but halted on both Feet, which the Matron presently espying, laughing at it, and calling me again to her said thus to me, My Son, let not this defect afflict thee, but call to mind thy *Infirmities,* and therewith thank God who hath permitted thee even in this World, and in the state of thy imperfection to come into so *high* a light, and keep these wounds for my sake. Whereupon the Trumpets began again to sound, which so affrighted me that I *awoke,* and then first perceived that it was only a *Dream,* which was so strongly impressed upon my imagination, that I was still perpetually troubled about it, and me thought I was yet sensible of the wounds on my feet. Howbeit, by all these things I well understood that God had vouchsafed that I should be present at this *mysterous and bidden Wedding;* wherefore with *Child-like* confidence I returned thanks to his *Divine* Majesty, & besought him, that he would further preserve me in his fear, that he would daily fill my Heart with Wisdom and Understanding, and at length graciously (without my desert) conduct me to the desired end. Hereupon I prepared my self for the *way,* put on my *white* linnen Coat, girded my Loyns, with a *Blood-red* Ribbon bound-cross-ways over my Shoulder: In my Hat I stuck *four red* Roses, that I might the sooner by this Token be taken notice of amongst the throng. For food I took *Bread,* Salt, and Water, which by the counsel of an understanding person I had at certain times used, not without profit, in the like occurrences. But before I parted from my *Cottage,* I first in this my dress, and wedding Garment, fell down upon my *Knees,* and besought *God,* that in case such a thing were, he would vouchsafe me a good issue. And thereupon in the presence of God I made a vow, that if any thing through his grace should be revealed unto me, I would employ it neither to my *own* honour nor authority in the World, but to the spreading of his *Name,* and the service of my *Neighbour.* And with this vow, and good hope I departed out of my Cell with joy.

The Second Day

I was hardly got out of my Cell into a *Forrest*, when me thought that the whole *Heaven* and all the Elements had already trimmed themselves against* this *Wedding*. For even the Birds in my opinion chanted more pleasantly then before, and the young Fawns skipped so merrily, that they rejoyced my *old Heart*, and moved me to sing: wherefore with a loud Voice I thus began:

> *With mirth thou pretty* Bird *rejoice,*
> *Thy Maker's praise in-hanced.*
> *Lift up thy shrill and pleasant Voice,*
> *Thy God is high advanced.*
> *Thy food before he did provide,*
> *And gives it in a fitting side,*
> *Therewith be thou sufficed.*
> *Why should'st thou now unpleasant be,*
> *Thy wrath against God venting?*
> *That he a little* Bird *made thee,*
> *Thy silly head tormenting?*
> *Because he made thee not a Man,*
> *O peace, he hath well* thought *thereon.*
> *Therewith be thou sufficed.*
> *What is't I'd have poor earthly worm,*
> *By God (as'twere) inditing,*
> *That I should thus 'gainst Heaven storm*
> *To force great arts by fighting?*
> *God will out-braved be by none,*
> *Who's good for naught, may hence be gone,*
> *O man b' herewith sufficed.*
> *That he no* Caesar *hath thee fram'd,*
> *To pine therefore 'tis needless*
> *His Name perhaps thou hadst defam'd*
> *Whereof he was not heedless.*
> *Most clear and bright Gods eyes do shine,*
> *He pierces to thy heart within,*
> *And cannot be deceived.*

---

*against—in preparation for (-Ed.)

This sang I now from the bottom of my Heart throughout the whole Forrest, so that it resounded from all parts, and the Hills repeated my last words, until at length I espyed a curious *green* Heath, whither I betook my self out of the *Forrest*. Upon this Heath stood three lovely tall *Cedars,* which by reason of their *breadth* afforded an excellent and desired *shade,* whereat I greatly rejoyced; for although I had not hitherto gone far, yet my earnest longing made me very faint, whereupon I hasted to the Trees to rest a little under them, but as soon as I came somewhat nigher, I espyed a *Tablet* fastned to one of them, on which (as afterwards I read) in curious Letters the following words were written:

Hospes salve: si quid tibi forsitan de nuptijs *Regis* auditum, Berba haec perpende. *Quatuor viarum* optionem per nos tibi *Sponsus* offert, per quas omnes, modo non in devias delabaris, ad Regiam ejus aulam pervenire possis. Prima brevis est, sed periculosa, et quae te in varios *scopulous* deducet ex quibus vix te expedire licebit. Altera *longior,* quae circumducet te, non abducet, *plana* est et *facilis,* si te *Magnetis* auxilio neque ad dextrum, neque finistrum abduci patiaris. Tertia vere *Regia* est, quae per varias Regis nostri delicias et spectacula viam tibi reddet jucundam. Sed quod vix millisimo hactenus obtigit. Per quartam *nemini hominum* licebit ad Regiam pervenire, utpote quae consumens et non nisi corporibus *incorruptibilibus* conveniens est. Elige nunc extribus quam velis, et in ea *constans* permane. Scito autem quamcumque ingressus fueris, ab immutabili *fato* tibi ita *destinatum,* nec nisi cum maximo vitae periculo regredi fas esse. Haec sunt quae te scivisse voluimus; sed heus cave ignores, quanto cum *periculo* te huic viae commiseris, nam si te vel minimi *delicit* contra Regis nostri leges nosti obnoxium, quaeso dum adhuc licet per eandem viam qua accessisti domum to confer quam citissime.*

---

*God save you, Stranger; if you have heard anything concerning the wedding of the *King,* consider these words. By us the *Bridegroom* offers you a choice between *four ways,* all of which, if you do not collapse on the path, can bring you to his royal court. The first is short but dangerous, and one which will lead you into *rocky places,* through which it will hardly be possible to pass. The second is

Now as soon as I had read this Writing, all my joy was near vanished again, and I who before Sang merrily, began now inwardly to Lament. For although I saw all the *three ways* before me, and understood that hence forward it was vouchsafed me, to make choice of one of them; yet it troubled me that in case I went the stony and *rocky* way, I might get a miserable and deadly fall, or taking the *long* one, I might wander *out* of it through *by-ways,* or be otherway's detained in the great Journey. Neither durst I hope, that I amongst thousands should be the very He, who should choose the *Royal* way. I saw likewise the *Fourth* before me, but it was so invironed with *Fire* and *Exhalations,* that I durst not (by *much*) draw near it, and therefore again and again considered, whether I should return back, or take any of the ways before me. I well weighted my own *unworthiness,* but the Dream still comforted me, that I was delivered out of the Tower, and yet I durst not confidently rely upon a Dream; whereupon I was so variously perplexed, that for very great weariness, hunger and thirst seized me, whereupon I presently drew out my *Bread,* cut a slice of it, which a snow-white *Dove* of whom I was not aware, sitting upon the Tree, espyed and therewith (perhaps according to her wonted manner) came down, and betook her self very familiarly to me, to whom I willingly imparted my food, which she received, and so with her prettiness did again a little refresh me. But as soon as her enemy a most *black Raven* perceived it, he streight darted himself down upon the Dove, and taking no notice of me,

---

longer and takes you roundabout; it is *plain* and *easy* if by the help of the *Magnet* you turn neither to the left nor the right. The third is that truly *Royal* road, which through various pleasures and pageants of our King affords you a happy journey. But so far this latter has hardly been granted to one in a thousand. By the fourth *no man* will reach the place, because it is a consuming path, possible only for *incorruptible* bodies. Now choose which you will of the three and *persevere* in it. For know that whichever you enter, that is the one immutable *Destiny* has chosen for you, nor can you turn back except at great *danger* to life. These are the things we wish you to know; but Beware, for you know not with how much peril you commit yourself to this path, for if you know yourself to be obnoxious to the laws of our King by the smallest *fault,* I implore you to return quickly to your house by the way you came, while it is still possible. (—Ed. transl.)

would needs force away the Dove's meat, who could no otherwise guard her self but by *flight*; whereupon they both *together* flew toward the *South,* at which I was so hugely incensed and grieved, that without thinking what I did, I made hast after the filthy Raven, and so against my will ran into *one* of the forementioned ways a whole Fields length; and thus the Raven being chased *away,* and the Dove delivered, I then first observed what I had inconsiderately done, and that I was already entred into a way, from which under peril of great punishment I durst not retire. And though I had still herewith in some measure to comfort my self, yet that which was worst of all to me, was, that I had *left my Bag* and *Bread* at the *Tree,* and could never retrieve them: For as soon as I turned my self about, a *contrary* wind was so strong against me, that it was ready to fell me. But if I went forward on my way, I perceived no hinderance at all: From whence I could easily conclude, that it would cost me my life, in case I should set my self against the *Wind)* wherefore I patiently took up my cross, got up on my feet, and resolved, since so it must be, I would use my utmost endeavour to get to my Journeys end before night. Now although many apparent *byways* shewed themselves, yet I still proceeded with my *Compass,* and would not budge one step from the Meridian Line; howbeit the way was oftentimes so *rugged* and unpassable, that I was in no little doubt of it. On this way I constantly thought upon the *Dove* and *Raven,* and yet could not search out the meaning, until at length upon a high Hill afar off I espyed a stately Portal, to which not regarding how far it was distant both from me and the way I was in, I hasted, because the Sun had already *hid* himself under the *Hills,* and I (by far) could elsewhere espy no abiding place, and this verily I ascribe only to God, who might well have permitted me to go forward in this way, and withheld my Eyes that so I might have gazed beside this Gate. To which (as was said) I now made mighty haste, and reached it by so much *Daylight,* as to take a very competent view of it. Now it was an exceeding *Royal beautiful Portal,* whereon were carved a multitude of most *noble Figures* and Devices, every one of which (as I afterwards learned) had its peculiar Signification; Above was fixed a pretty large Tablet, with these Words, *Procul hinc, procul ite profani*, and other things more, that I was earnestly forbidden to relate. Now as soon as I was come under the Portal, there streight stepped forth one in a *Sky-coloured* habit, whom I in friendly manner saluted, which though he thankfully returned, yet he instantly demanded of me my Letter of Invitation. O how glad was I that I had then brought it with me! For how easily might I have forgotten it (as it also chanced to others) as he himself told me! I quickly presented it, wherewith he was not only Satisfied, but (at which I much wondred) shewed me abundance of respect, saying, Come in my *Brother*, an acceptable Guest you are to me; and withal intreated me not to with-hold my Name from him. Now having replyed, that I was a Brother of the *Red-Rosie Cross*, he both wondred, and seemed to rejoyce at it, and then proceeded thus, My Brother have you nothing about you wherewith to purchase a Token? I answered my ability was small, but if he saw any thing about me he had a mind to, it was at his service. Now he having requested of me my *Bottle* of Water, and I granted it, he gives me a *golden Token* whereon stood no more but these two Letters, S. C. intreating me that when it stood me in good stead, I would remember him. After which I asked him, how many were got in before me, which he also told me, and lastly out of meer Friendship gave me a *sealed Letter* to the second Porter. Now having lingered some time with him, the Night grew on: Whereupon a great *Beacon* upon the Gates was immediately fired, that so if any were still upon the way, he might make haste thither. But the way where it finished at the Castle, was on both sides inclosed with *Walls,* and planted with all sorts of excellent Fruit-Trees, and still on every third Tree on each side Lanthorns were hung up, wherein all the Candles were already lighted with a glorious Torch by a *beautiful Virgin,* habited in *Skye-colour,* which was so noble and Majestick a Spectacle, that I yet delayed somewhat *longer* than was requisite. But at length after sufficient Information, and an advantageous Instruction, I friendly departed from the first Porter. On the way, though I would gladly have known what was written in my Letter, yet since I had no reason to mistrust the Porter, I forbare my purpose, and so went on the way, until I came likewise to the *second Gate,* which although it was very like

1st gate

the other, yet was it adorned with Images & *mystick significations*. In the affixed *Tablet* stood *Date & dabitur vobis*. Under this Gate lay a terrible grim *Lion* chain'd, who as soon as he espi'd me arose & made at me with great roaring; whereupon the second Porter who lay upon a *Stone* of Marble, awaked, and wished me not to be troubled or affrighted, and then drove back the *Lion,* and having received the Letter which I with trembling reached him, he read it, and with very great respect spake thus to me; Now well-come in Gods Name unto me the man whom of long time I would gladly have seen. Mean while he also drew out a *token,* and asked me whether I could purchase it? But I having nothing else left but my *Salt,* presented it to him, which he thankfully accepted. Upon this token again stood only two Letters, namely, S. M. Being now just about to enter discourse with him, it began to ring in the Castle, whereupon the Porter counselled me to run apace, or else all the paines and labour I had hitherto taken would serve to no purpose, for the *Lights* above began already to be *extinguished;* whereupon I dispatched with such haste that I heeded not the Porter, in such anguish was I, and truly it was but necessary, for I could not run so fast but that the Virgin, after whom all the *lights* were *put* out, was at my heels, and I should never have found the way, had not she with her Torch afforded me some light; I was more-over constrained to enter the very next to her, and the Gate was so suddenly clap't to, that a part of my *coate* was locked out, which I verily was forced to leave behind me; for neither I, nor they who stood ready without and called at the Gate could prevail with the Porter to *open* it again, but he delivered the Keys to the Virgin, who took them with her into the Court. Mean time I again surveyed the Gate, which now appeared so *rich,* as the whole World could not equal it; just by the Door were two Columns, on one of them stood a pleasant Figure with this Inscription *Congratulor.* The other having its Countenance vailed was sad, and beneath was written, *Condoleo*. In brief, the Inscriptions and Figures thereon, were so dark and mysterious, that the most dextrous man upon Earth could not have expounded them. But all these (if God permit) I shall e'er long publish and explain. Under this Gate I was again to give my Name, which was this last time written down in a little Vellum-Book, and immediately with the rest dispatched to the Lord *Bridegroom*. Here it was where I first received the *true* Guest token, which was somewhat less than the former, but yet much heavier, upon this stood these Letters S. P. N. Besides this, a new pair of Shoes were given me, for the Floor of the Castle was laid with pure shing Marble; my *old Shoes* I was to give away to one of the Poor (whom I would) who sate in throngs, howbeit in very good order, under the Gate. I then bestowed them on an old man; after which two Pages with as many Torches, conducted me into a little Room; there they willed me to sit down on a Form, which I did, but they sticking their Torches in two holes, made in the Pavement, departed and left me thus sitting alone. Soon after I heard a noise, but saw nothing, and it proved to be certain men who stumbled in upon me; but since I could see nothing, I was fain to suffer, and attend what they would do with me; but presently perceiving them to be *Barbers,* I intreated them not to justle me so, for I was content to do whatever they desired, whereupon they quickly let me go, and so one of them (whom I could not yet see) fine and gently cut away the *Hair* round about from the *Crown of my Head,* but on my Forehead, Ears and Eyes he permitted my *Ice-grey* Locks to hang. In his first incounter (I must confess) I was ready to dispair, for inasmuch as some of them shoved me so forceably, and I could yet see nothing, I could think no other but that God for my *Curiosity* had suffered me to miscarry. Now these invisible Barbers carefully gathered up the *Hair* which was cut off, and carried it away with them. After which the *two* Pages entred again, and heartily laughed at me for being so terrified. But they had scarce spoken a few Words with me, when again a little Bell began to ring; which (as the Pages informed me) was to give notice for assembling; whereupon they willed me to rise, and through many Walks, Doors and winding Stairs lighted me into a spacious *Hall.* In this Room was a great multitude of guests, Emperors, Kings, Princes, and Lords, Noble and Ignoble, Rich, and Poor, and all sorts of People, at which I hugely marviled, and thought to my self, ah, how gross a fool hast thou been to ingage upon this Journey with so much bitterness and toil, when (behold) here are even those fellows whom thou well know'st, and yet hadst never any reason to *esteem*. They are now all *here,* and thou with all thy Prayers and Supplications art hardly got in at last. This and more the Devil at that time injected, whom I notwithstanding (as well as I could) directed to the issue. Mean time one or other of my acquaintance here and there spake to me: Oh Brother *Rosencreutz!* art thou here too; yea, (my Brethren) replied I, the *Grace* of God hath helped me in also; at which they raised a mighty laughter, looking upon it as ridiculous that there should be need of *God* in so slight an occasion. Now having demanded each of them concerning his way, and found that most were forced to clamber over the *Rocks,* certain Trumpets (none of which we yet saw) began to sound to the Table, whereupon they all seated themselves, every one as he judged himself above the rest; so that for me and some *other sorry* Fellows there was hardly a *little Nook* left at the lower-most Table. Presently the two Pages entred, and one of them said Grace in so handsom and excellent a manner, as rejoyced the very Heart in my Body. Howbeit, certain great Sr *John's* made but little reckoning of them, but fleired and winked one at another, biting their Lips within their Hats, and using more the like unseemly Gestures. After this Meat was brought in, and albeit none could *be seen,* yet every thing was so orderly managed, that it seemed to me as if every Guest had had his proper Attendant. Now my Artists having somewhat recruted themselves, and the Wine having a little removed shame from their Hearts, they presently began to vaunt and brag of their *Abilities:* One would prove this, another that, and commonly the most sorry *Idiots* made the loudest noise. Ah, when I call to mind what *preternatural* and impossible enterprises I then heard, I am still ready to vomit at it. In fine, they never kept in their order, but when ever one Rascal here, another there, could insinuate himself in between the *Nobles;* Then pretended they the finishing of such *Adventures* as neither *Sampson,* nor yet *Hercules* with all their strength could ever have atchieved: This would discharge *Atlas* of his burden; The other would again draw forth the three-headed *Cerberus* out of Hell. In brief, every man had his own Prate, and yet the great *Lords* were so simple that they believed their pretences, and the Rogues so audacious, that although one or other of them was here and there rapped over the Fingers with a Knife, yet they flinched not at it, but when any one perchance had filched a Gold-Chain, then would all hazard for the like. I saw one who heard the rustling of the Heavens: The second could see *Plato's* Ideas: A third could number *Democritus's* Atoms. There were also not a few pretenders to the *perpetual motion*. Many an one (in my opinion) had good *understanding*, but assumed too to much to himself, to his own destruction. Lastly, there was one also who would needs out of hand perswade us that he saw the *Servitors* who attended, and would still have pursued his Contention, had not one of those invisible waiters reached him so handsom a cuff upon his lying Muzzle, that not only he, but many more who were by him, became as mute as Mice. But it best of all pleased me, that all those, of whom I had any *esteem*, were very quiet in their business, and made no loud cry of it, but acknowledged themselves to be *mis-understanding* men, to whom the mysteries of Nature were too high, and they themselves much too small. In this Tumult I had almost cursed the day wherein I came hither; For I could not but with anguish behold that those lewd vain People were above at the Board, but I in so *sorry* a place could not, however rest in quiet, one of these Rascals scornfully reproaching me for a motly Fool. Now I thought not that there was yet one Gate *behind*, through which we must pass, but imagined I was during the whole Wedding, to continue in this scorn, contempt and indignity, which yet I had at no time deserved, either of the Lord Bridegroom or the Bride; And therefore (in my opinion) he should have done well to have sought out some other Fool to his Wedding than me. Behold, to such *impatience* doth the Iniquity of this World reduce simple hearts. But this really was one part of my *Lameness*, whereof (as is before mentioned) I dreamed. And truly this clamour the longer it lasted, the more it increased. For there were already those who boasted of false and imaginary *Visions*, and would perswade us of palpably lying Dreams. Now there sate by me a very fine *quiet Man*, who oftentimes discoursed of excellent matters, at length he said, *Behold my Brother, if any one should now come who were willing to instruct these blockish People in the right way, would he be heard?* No, verily, replyed I. *The world*, said he, *is now re-solved (whatever comes on it) to be cheated, and cannot abide to give Ear to those who intend its good. Seest thou also that same Cocks-Comb, with what whimsical Figures and foolish conceits he allures others to him. There one makes Mouthes at the people with the unheard-of Mysterious Words. Yet be-lieve me in this, the time is now coming when those shame-ful Vizards shall be plucked off, and all the World shall know what Vagabond Imposters were concealed behind them. Then perhaps that will be valued which at present is not esteemed.* Whilst he was thus speaking, and the clamour the longer it lasted, the worse it was, all on a suddain there began in the Hall such excellent and stately *Musick,* as all the days of my Life I never heard the like; whereupon every one held his peace, and attended what would become of it: Now there were in this Musick all sorts of *stringed* Instruments imagi-nable, which sounded together in such harmony, that I for-got my self, and sate so unmovable, that those who sate by me were amazed at me, and this lasted near half an hour, where-in none of us spake one word, For as soon as ever any one was about to open his Mouth, he got an unexpected blow, neither knew he from whence it came: Me thought since we were not permitted to see the Musicians, I should have been glad to view only all the Instruments they made use of. After half an hour this Musick *ceased* unexpectly, and we could neither see *nor* hear any thing further. Presently after, be-fore the Door of the Hall began a great *noise* sounding and beating of *Trumpets,* Shalms and Kettle-Drums, also Master-like, as if the Emperor of *Rome* had been entring; where-upon the Door opened of it self, and then the noise of the Trumpets was so loud, that we were hardly able to indure it. Mean while (to my thinking) many thousand *small Tapers* came into the Hall, all which of themselves marched in so very exact an order as altoghether amazed us, till at last the two forementioned Pages with bright Torches, lighting in a most beautiful *Virgin,* all drawn on a gloriously gilded Tri-umphant Self-moving Throne, entred the Hall. It seemed to me she was the very same who before on the way kindled, and put out the Lights, and that these her Attendants were the very same whom she formerly placed at the Trees. She was not now as before in Skye-colour, but arrayed in a *snow-white* glittering Robe, which sparkled of pure Gold, and cast such a lustre that we durst not steadily behold it. Both the Pages were after the same manner habited (albeit somewhat more slightly); as soon as they were come into the middle of the Hall, & were descended from the Throne, all the small Taers made obeisance before her: Whereupon we all stood up from our Benches, yet every one staid in his own place. Now she having to us, and we again to her, shewed all Respect and Reverence; in a most pleasant Tone she began thus to speak;

> *The King my Lord most gracious,*
> *Who now's not very far from us.*
> *As also his most lovely Bride,*
> *To him in troth and honour ti'd;*
> *Already, with great joy indu'd,*
> *Have your arrival hither view'd;*
> *And do to every one, and all*
> *Promise their Grace in special;*
> *And from their very Hearts desire,*
> *You may it at the time acquire;*
> *That so their future Nuptial joy*
> *May mixed be with none's annoy.*

Hereupon with all her small Tapers she again courteously bowed, and presently after began thus:

> *In the Invitation writ, you know.*
> *That no man called was hereto*
> *Who of God's rarest gifts good store*
> *Had not received long before,*
> *Adorned with all requisit's,*
> *As in such cases it befit's.*
> *How though they cannot well conceit*
> *That any man's so desperate,*
> *Under conditions so hard,*
> *Here to intrude without regard;*
> *Unless he have been first of all,*
> *Prepared for this Nuptial;*
> *And therefore in good hopes do dwell*

That with all you it will be well:
Yet men are grown so bold, and rude,
Not weighing their inepitude,
As still to thrust themselves in place
Whereto none of them called was:
No Cocke-comb here himself may sell,
No Rascal in with others steal;
For they resolve without all let
A Wedding pure to celebrate.
So then the Artists for to weigh,
Scales shall be fix'd the ensuing day;
Whereby each one may lightly find
What he hath left at home behind.
If here be any of that Rout
Who have good cause themselves to doubt,
Let him pack quickly hence aside;
For that in case he longer bide,
Of grace forelor'n, and quite undone
Betimes he must the Gantlet run:
If any now his Conscience gall,
He shall tonight be left in th' Hall
And be again releas't by morn,
Yet so he hither ne'er return.
If any man have confidence,
He with his waiter may go hence,
Who shall him to his Chamber light
Where he may rest in peace tonight;
And there with praise await the Scale
Or else his Sleep may chance to faile.
The others here may take it well,
For who aim's 'bove what's possible,
'Twere better much he hence had pas't,
But of you all wee'l hope the best.

As soon as she had done speaking this, she again made reverence, and sprung cheerfully into her Throne, after which the Trumpets began again to sound, which yet was not of force to take from many their grievous Sighs. So they again conducted her invisibly away, but the most part of the small

Tapers remained in the Room, and still one of them accompanied each of us. In such perturbation 'tis not well possible to express what pensive Thoughts and Gestures were amongst us. Yet the most part resolved to await the Scale, and in case things sorted not well, to depart (as they hoped) in peace. I had soon cast up my *reckoning,* and being my Conscience convinced me of all ignorance, and *unworthiness,* I purposed to stay with the rest in the Hall, and chose much rather to content my self with the Meal I had already taken, than to run the Risco of a *future repulse.* Now after that every one by his small Taper had serverally been conducted into a Chamber (each as I since understood into a peculiar one) There staid *nine* of us, and amongst the rest he also, who *discoursed* with me before at the Table. But although our small Tapers left us not, yet soon after within an hours time one of the fore-mentioned Pages came in, and bringing a great bundle of *Cords* with him, first demanded of us whether we had concluded to stay there, which when we had with Sighs affirmed, he *bound* each of us in a several place, and so went away with our small Tapers, and left us poor Wretches *in Darkness.* Then first began some to perceive the imminent danger, and I my self could not refrain Tears. For although we were not forbidden to speak, yet *anguish* and *affliction* suffered none of us to utter one word. For the Cords were so wonderfully made, yet none could cut them, much less get them off his Feet: yet this comforted me, that still the future gain, of many an one, who had now betaken himself to rest, would prove very little to his satisfaction. But we by only one Nights Pennance might expiate all our presumption: till at length in my sorrowful thoughts I fell asleep; during which I had a *Dream;* Now although there be no great matter in it, yet I esteem it not impertinent to recount it: Me thought I was upon an *high Mountain,* and saw before me a great & large Valley, in this Valley were gathered together an unspeakable *multitude* of People, each of which had at his Head a *Thread,* by which he was hanged up towards Heaven, now one hung high, another low, some stood even quite upon the Earth. But in the Air there flew up and down an *ancient* Man, who had in his hand a pair of Sheers, wherewith here he *cut* one's, and there another's thread. Now he that was nigh the Earth was so much the readier, & fell without noise, but when it happened to one of the *high* ones, he fell, so that the Earth quaked. To some it came to pass that their Thread was so stretched, that they came to the Earth before the Thread was cut. I took pleasure in this tumbling, and it joyed me at the Heart, when he who had *over-exalted* himself in the Air, of his Wedding, got so shameful a fall, that it carried even some of his Neighbours along with him. In like manner it also rejoiced me, that he who had all this while kept himself *near the Earth*, could come down so fine and gently, that even his next men perceived it not. But being now in my highest fit of Jolity, I was unawares jogged by one of my fellow Captives, upon which I was awaked, and was very much discontented with him; Howbeit, I considered my Dream, and recounted it to my Brother, who lay by me on the other side; who was not dissatisfied with it, but hoped some Comfort might thereby be pretended. In such discourse we spent the remaining part of the Night, and with longing exspected the Day.

dream 2 w/in a dream

89

The Third Day

Now as soon as the lovely day was broken, and the *bright Sun,* having raised himself above the Hills, had again betaken himself, in the high Heaven, to his appointed office; My good Champions began to rise out of their Beds, and leisurely to make themselves ready unto the Inquisition. Whereupon, one after another, they came again into the Hall, and giving us a good morrow, demanded how we had Slept to Night; and having espied our Bonds, there were some that reproved us for being so cowardly, and that we had not (much rather) as they, *hazarded upon* all adventures. Howbeit, some of them whose Hearts still smote them made no loud cry of the business. We excused our selves with our *ignorance,* hoping we should now soon be set at Liberty, and learn wit by this disgrace, that they on the contrary had not yet altogether escaped, & perhaps their greatest *danger* was still to be expected: At length each one being again assembled, the *Trumpets* began now again to sound & the Kettle Drums to beat as formerly, and we then imagined no other but that the Bridegroom was ready to present himself; which nevertheless was a huge mistake. For it was again the *yesterday's Virgin* who had arrayed her self all in *red Velvet,* and girded her self with a *white Scarfe.* Upon her Head she had a *green Wreath* of Laurel, which hugely became her. Her train was now no more of *small Tapers,* but consisted of two hundred Men in *Harnis,* who were all (like her) cloathed in *red* and *white.* Now as soon as they were alighted from the Throne, she comes streight to us Prisoners, and after she had Saluted us, she said in few words; That some of you have been sensible of your wretched condition is hugely pleasing to my most mighty Lord, and he is also resolved you shall fare the better for it; And having espied me in my Habit, she laughed and spake, good lack! hast thou also submitted thy self to the Yoke, I imagined thou wouldst have made thy self very smug; with which Words she caused my Eyes to run over. After which she commanded we should be unbound, and cuppled together and placed in a station where we might well behold the Scales. For, said she, it may yet fare better with them, than with the Presumptious, who yet stands here at

Liberty. Mean time the Scales which were intirely of *Gold* were hung up in the midst of the Hall; There was also a little Table covered with red *Velvet,* and *seven weights* placed thereon. First of all stood a pretty great one, next four little ones; lastly, two great ones severally; And these Weights in proportion to their bulk were so *heavy,* that no man can believe or comprehend it: But each of the *Harnised men* had together with a naked Sword a *strong rope;* These she distributed according to the number of Weights into seven bands, and out of every band chose one for their proper weight; and then again sprung up into her high Throne. Now as soon as she had made her reverence, with a very *Shrill* Tone she began thus to speak:

> *Who int' a Painters room does go*
> *And nothing does of painting know,*
> *Yet does in prating thereof, pride it;*
> *Shall be of all the World derided.*
>   *Who into th' Artists order goes,*
> *And thereunto was never chose;*
> *Yet with pretence of skill does pride it;*
> *Shall be of all the World derided.*
>   *Who at a Wedding does appear,*
> *And yet was ner'e intended there;*
> *Yet does in coming highly pride it;*
> *Shall be of all the World derided.*
>   *Who now into this Scale ascends,*
> *The weights not proving his fast Friends,*
> *And that it bounces so does ride it;*
> *Shall be of all the World derided.*

As soon as the Virgin had done speaking, one of the Pages commanded each one to place himself according to his order, and one after another to step in: which one of the *Emperors* made no scruple of, but first of all bowed himself a little towards the Virgin, and afterwards in all his stately Attire went up: where upon *each* Captain laid in his weight; which (to the wonder of all) he stood out. But the *last* was too heavy for him, so that forth he must; and that with much anguish that (as it seemed to me) the Virgin her self had pitty on him, who also beckned to her people to hold their peace, yet was the good Emperor bound and delivered over to the Sixth band. Next him again came forth *another Emperor,* who stept hautily into the Sacle, and having a great *thick Book* under his Gown, he imagined not to fail; But being scarce able to abide the third weight, and being unmercifully flung down, and his Book in that affrightment flipping from him, all the Soldiers began to laugh, and he was delivered up bound to the third band. Thus it went also with some others of the Emperors, who were all shamefully laughed at and captived. After these comes forth a little *short Man* with a curled brown Beard *an Emperor* too, who after the usual reverence got up also, and held out so steadfastly, that me thought, and there been more weights ready, he would have outstood them; To whom the Virgin immediately arose, and bowed before him, causing him to put on a Gown of *red Velvet,* and at last reached him a branch of Laurel, having good store of them upon her Throne, upon the steps whereof she willed him to sit down. Now how, after him it fared with the rest of the Emperors, Kings and Lords, would be too long to recount; but I cannot leave unmentioned that few of those great *personages* held out. Howbeit sundry *eminent vertues* (beyond my hopes) were found in many. One could stand out this, the second another, some two, some three, four or five, but few could attain to the just perfection; but every one who failed, was miserably laughed at by the bands. After the Inquisition had also passed over the Gentry, the learned, and unlearned, and the rest, and in each condition perhaps *one,* it may be, *two,* but for the most part none, was found perfect, it came at length to those honest Gentlemen the vagabond *Cheaters,* and rascally *Lapidem Spitalanficum* makers, who were set upon the Scale with such scorn, that I my self for all my grief was ready to burst my Belly with laughing, neither could the very Prisoners themselves refrain. For the most part could not abide that severe trial, but with *Whips* and Scourges were jerked out of the Scale, and led to the other Prisoners, yet to a suiteable band. Thus of so great a throng so few remained, that I am ashamed to discover their number. Howbeit there were Persons of quality *also* amongst them, who notwithstanding were

INQUISITION: all are measured vs. scale: 7 weights correspond to virtues...only a couple out of 100's make it (like the rest) honoured with Velvet *Robes* and wreaths of Laurel.

The Inquisition being compleatly finished, and none but we poor coupled hounds standing aside; At length one of the Captains stepped forth, and said, Gratious Madam, if it please your Ladyship let these poor men, who *acknowledged* their mis-understanding, be set upon the Scale also without their incurring any danger of penalty, and only for recreation's sake, if perchance any thing that is right may be found amongst them. In the first place I was in great perplexity, for in my anguish this was my only comfort, that I was not to stand in such ignominy, or to be lashed out of the Scale. For I nothing doubted but that many of the Prisoners wished that they had stay'd ten Nights with us in the Hall. Yet since the Virgin consented, so it must be, and we being untied were one after another set up: Now although the most part miscarried, yet they were neither laughed at, nor scourged, but peaceably placed on one side. My *Companion* was the fifth, who held out *bravely,* whereupon all, but especially the Captain who made the request for us, applauded him, and the Virgin shewed him the usual respect. After him again two more were dispatched in an instant. But I was the *eighth*; Now as soon as (with trembling) I stepped up, my Companion who already sat by in his *Velvet,* looked friendly upon me, and the Virgin her self smiled a little. But for as much as I out-stayed *all the* Weights, the Virgin commanded them to draw me up by force, wherefore three *men* moreover *hung* on the otherside of the Beam, and yet could nothing prevail. Whereupon one of the Pages immediately stood up, and cryed out exceeding loud, T H A T ' S H E: Upon which the other replyed, *Then let him gain his Liberty,* which the Virgin accorded; and being received with due Ceremonies, The choice was given me to release *one of* the Captives, whosoever I pleased; Whereupon I made no long deliberation, but elected the *first* Emperor whom I had long pittied, who was immediately set free, and with all respect seated amongst us. Now the last being set up, and the Weights proving too heavy for him, in the mean while the Virgin espied my *Roses,* which I had taken out of my Hat into my Hands, and thereupon presently by her Page graciously requested them of me, which I readily sent her. And so this first *Act* was finished about *ten* in the fore-noon. Whereupon the Trumpets began to sound again, which nevertheless we could not as yet see. Mean time the Bands were to step aside with their Prisoners, and expect the judgment. After which a Council of the seven Captains and us was set, and the business was propounded by the Virgin as President, who desired each one to give his opinion, how the Prisoners were to be dealt with. The first opinion was. That they should all be put to *Death,* yet one more severely than another: namely those who had presumptuously intruded themselves contrary to the Express conditions; others would have them kept close prisoners. Both which pleased neither the *President,* nor me. At length by one of the Emperors (the same whom I had freed) my Companion, and my self the affair was brought to this point; That first of all the principal *Lords* should with a befitting respect be led out of the Castle; others might be carried out somewhat more scornfully. These would be stripped, and caused to run out naked; The fourth with Rods, Whips, or Dogs, should be hunted out. Those who the day before willingly surrendred themselves, might be suffered to depart without any blame. And last of all those Presumptuous ones, and they who behaved themselves so unseemly at Dinner the day before, should be punished in *Body and Life* according to each Mans demerit. This opinion pleased the Virgin well, and obtained the upper hand. There was moreover another Dinner vouchsafed them, which they were soon acquainted with. But the Execution was deferred till twelve at noon, Herewith the *Senate arose,* and the *Virgin* also, together with her Attendants returned to her usual quarter; But the uppermost Table in the Room was allotted to us, they requesting us to take it in good part till the Business were fully dispatched. And then we should be conducted to the *Lord Bridegroom* and the *Bride,* with which we were at present well content. Mean time the Prisoners were again brought into the Hall, and each Man seated according to his Quality; they were likewise enjoyned to behave themselves somewhat more civilly than they had done the day before, which yet they needed not to be have been admonished, for without this, they had already put up their pipes. And this I can boldly say, not with flattery, but in the love of truth, that commonly those persons who were of the *highest Rank,* best understood how to behave themselves in so unexpected a misfourtune. Their Treatment was but indifferent, yet with respect, neither could they yet see their *Attendants,* but to us they were visible, whereat I was exceeding joyful. Now although Fourtune had exalted us, yet we took not upon us more than the rest, advising them to be of good Cheer, the event would not be so ill. Now although they would gladly have understood the Sentence of us, yet we were so deeply obliged that none durst open his Mouth about it. Nevertheless we comforted them as well as we could, drinking with them to try if the Wine might make them any thing cheerfuller. Our Table was covered with *red Velvet,* beset with drinking-Cups of pure *Silver* and *Gold;* which the rest could not behold without amazement and very great anguish. But e'er we had seated our selves, in came the two Pages, presenting every one in the *Bride-groom's* behalf, the *Golden Fleece* with a *flying Lyon,* requesting us to wear them at the Table, and as became us, to observe the Reputation and Dignity of the Order, which his Majesty had now vouchsafed us, and should suddenly be ratified with sutable Ceremonies. This we received with profoundest submission, promising obediently to perform whatsoever his Majesty should please. Besides these, the noble Page had a Schedule, wherein we were set down in order. And for my part I should not otherwise be desirous to conceal my place, if perchance it might not be interpreted to Pride in me, which yet is expresly against the *fourth* Weight. Now because our entertainment was exceeding stately, we demanded one of the Pages, whether we might not have leave to send some choice bit to our Friends and Acquaintance, who making no difficulty of it, every one sent plentifully to his acquaintance by the waiters, howbeit they saw none of them; and forasmuch as they knew not whence it came, I was my *self* desirous to carry somewhat to one of them, but as soon as I was risen, one of the Waiters was presently at my Elbow, saying *He desired me to take friendly warning, for in case one of the Pages had seen it, it would have come to the King's Ear, who would certainly have taken it amiss of me; but since none had observed it but him-*

self, he purposed not to betray me, but that I ought for the time to come to have better regard to the dignity of the order: With which words the Servant did really so astonish me, that for a long time after I scarce moved upon my Seat, yet I returned him Thanks for his faithful warning, as well as in haste and affrightment I was able. Soon after the Drums began to beat again, to which we were already accustomed: For we well knew it was the *Virgin,* wherefore we prepared our selves to receive her, who was now coming in with her usual Train, upon her high Seat, one of the Pages bearing before her a very tall Goblet of Gold. And the other, a Patent in Parchment: Being now after a marvellous *artificial* manner alighted from the Seat, she takes the Goblet from the Page, and presents the same in the King's behalf, saying, *That it was brought from his Majesty, and that in honour of him we should cause it to go round.* Upon the cover of this Goblet stood *Fortune* curiously cast in Gold, who had in her Hand a *red flying* Ensign, for which cause I drunk somewhat the more sadly, as having been but too well acquainted with Fortune's way-wardness. But the Virgin as well as we, was adorned with the Golden *Fleece* and Lyon, whence I observed, that perhaps she was the president of the Order. Wherefore we demanded of her how the Order might be named? she answered, That it was not yet seasonable to discover it, till the affair with the Prisoners were dispatched. And therefore their Eyes were still held; and what had hitherto happened to us, was to them only for an Offence and Scandal, although it were to be accounted as nothing, in regard of the honour that attended us. Hereupon she began to distinguish the *Patent* which the other Page held into two different parts, out of which about thus much was read before the first company.

That they should confess that they had too lightly given Credit to false fictitious Books, had assumed too much to themselves, and so came into this Castle, albeit they were never invited into it, and perhaps the most part had presented themselves with design to make their Market here, and afterwards to live in the greater Pride and Lordliness; And thus one had seduced another, and plunged him into this disgrace and ignominy, wherefore they were deservedly to be soundly punished.

Which they with great humility readily acknowledged, and gave their Hands upon it. After which a severe check was given to the rest, much to this purpose.

That they very well knew, and were in their Consciences convinced, that they had forged false fictitious Books, had befooled others, and cheated them, and thereby had diminished Regal dignity amongst all. They knew in like manner what ungodly deceitful Figures *they had made use of, in so much as they spared not even the* Divine Trinity, *but accustomed themselves to cheat People all the Country over. It was also now as clear as Day with what Practices they had indeavoured to ensnare the true Guests, and introduce the Ignorant: in like manner, that it was manifest to all the World, they they* wallowed *in open Whoredom, Adultery, Gluttony, and other Uncleannesses: All which was against the express Orders of our Kingdom. In brief, they knew they had disparaged Kingly Majesty, even amongst the common sort, and therefore they should confess themselves to be* manifest convicted Vagabond-Cheaters, Knaves *and* Rascals, *whereby they deserved to be cashiered from the company of civil People, and severely to be punished.* The good *Artists* were loath to come to this Confession, but inasmuch as not only the Virgin her self threatned, and sware their death, but the other party also vehemently raged at them, and unanimously cryed out, that they had most wickedly seduced them out of the Light: They at length, to prevent a huge misfortune, confessed the same with dolour, and yet withal alledged that what had herein happened was not to be animadverted upon them in the worst sense. For in as much as the *Lords* were absolutely resolved to get into the Castle, and had *promised* great sums of Money to that effect, each one had used all Craft to seize upon something, and so things were brought to that pass, as was now manifest before their Eyes. But that it succeeded not, "*They in their opinion had dis-deserved no more than the Lords themselves*; As who should have had so much understanding as to consider that in case any one had been sure of getting in, he would not, in so great Peril, for the sake of a slight gain, have clambered over the Wall with them." Their Books also *sold so mightily,* that whoever had no other mean to maintain himself, was fain to ingage in such a Cousenage. They hoped moreover, that if a right Judgment were made, they should be found no way to have miscarried, as having behaved themselves towards the Lords, as became Servants, upon their *earnest entreaty*. But answer was made them, that his Royal Majesty had determined to punish all, and every man, albeit one more severely than another. For although what had been alledged by them was partly true, and *therefore the Lords should not wholly be indulged*, yet they had good reason to prepare themselves for Death, who had so presumptuously obtruded themselves, and perhaps seduced the more ignorant against their will; As likewise they who with *false Books* had violated Royal Majesty, as the same might be evinced out of their *very Writings* and Books.

Hereupon many began most pitteously to lament, cry, weep, intreat, and prostrate themselves, all which notwithstanding could avail them nothing, and I much marvelled how the Virgin could be so resolute, when yet their misery caused *our Eyes* to run over, and moved our Compassion (although the most part of them had procured us much trouble, and vexation) For she presently dispatched her Page, who brought with him all the *Curiassiers* which had this day been appointed at the Scales, who were commanded each of them to take his own to him, and in an orderly Procession, so as still each Curiassier should go with one of the *Prisoners*, to conduct them into her great Garden. At which time each one so exactly recognised his own Man, that I marvelled at it. Leave also was likewise given to my yesterday *Companions* to go out into the Garden unbound, and to be present at the Execution of the Sentence. Now as soon as every Man was come forth, the Virgin mounted up into her *High Throne,* requesting us to sit down upon the Steps, and to appear at the Judgment, which we refused not, but left all standing upon the Table (except the Goblet, which the Virgin committed to the Pages keeping) and went forth in our Robes upon the Throne, which of it self *moved* so gently as if we had passed in the Air, till in this manner we came into the *Garden,* where we arose altogether. This Garden was not extraordinary curious, only it pleased me that the Trees were planted in so good order. Besides there ran in it a most costly *Fountain,* adorned with wonderful Figures and Inscriptions, and strange Characters, (which God willing I shall mention in a future *Book*) In this Garden was raised a wooden Scaffold, hung about with curiously painted figured Coverlets. Now there were four *Galleries* made one over another, the first was more glorious than any of the rest, and therefore covered with a *white Taffata Curtain,* so that at that time we could not perceive who was behind it. The second was empty and uncovered. Again the two last were covered with *red* and *blew Taffata.* Now as soon as we were come to the Scaffold, the Virgin bowed her self *down* to the ground, at which we were mightily terrified: For we might easily guess that the *King* and *Queen* must not be far off; Now we also having duely performed our Reverence, The Virgin lead us up by the winding Stairs into the second Gallery, where she placed her self uppermost, and us in our former order. But how the *Emperor* whom I had released, behaved himself towards me, both at this time, as also before at the Table, I cannot, without slander of wicked Tongues, well relate. For he might well imagine in what Anguish and Sollicitude he now should have been, in case he were at present to attend the Judgment with such ignominy, and that only through *me* he had not attained such Dignity and Worthiness. Mean time the Virgin who first of all brought me the Invitation, and whom hitherto I had never since seen, stepped in; First she gave one blast upon her Trumpet, and then with a very loud Voice declared the Sentence in this manner.

The Kings Majesty my most gratious Lord could from his heart wish, that all and every one here Assembled, had upon his Majesties Invitation presented themselves so qualified, as that they might (to his honour) with greatest frequency have adorned this his appointed Nuptial and joyful Feast. But since it hath otherwise pleased Almighty God, his Majesty hath not whereat to murmur, but must be forced, contrary to his own Inclination, to abide by the antient and laudable Constitutions of this Kingdom. But now, that his Majesty's innate Clemency may be celebrated over all the World, he hath thus far absolutely dealt with his Council and Estates, that the usual Sentence shall be considerably lenified. So that in the first place he is willing to vouchsafe to the Lords *and* Potentates, *not only their lives intirely, but also freely and frankly to dismiss them; friendly and courteously intreating your Lordships not at all to take it in evil part that you cannot be present at his Majesties Feast of Honour; But to remember that there is notwithstanding more imposed upon your Lordships by God Almighty (who in the distribution of his Gifts hath an incomprehensible* Consideration) *than you can duely and easily sustain. Neither is your Reputation hereby prejudiced, although you be rejected by this our Order, since we cannot at once all of us, do all things. But for as much as your Lordships have been* seduced *by base Rascals, it shall not on their part, pass unrevenged. And furthermore his Majesty resolveth shortly to communicate with your Lordships a Catalogue of* Hereticks *or* index Expurgatorius, *that you may henceforward be able with better judgment to discern between the Good and the Evil. And because his Majesty e're long also purposeth to rummage his Library, and offer up the seductive Writings to* Vulcan, *he friendly, humbly, and courteously intreats every one of your Lordships to put the same in Execution with your own, whereby it is to be hoped that all evil and Mischief may for the time to come be remedied. And you are withal to be admonished, never henceforth so inconsiderately to covet an entrance hither, least the former excuse of Seducers be taken from you, and you fall into Disgrace and Contempt with all Men. In fine, for as much as the Estates of the Land have still somewhat to demand of your Lordships, his Majesty hopes that no Man will think much to redeem himself with a* Chain *or what else he hath about him, and so in friendly manner to depart from us, and through our safe conduct to betake himself home again.*

The others who stood not at the first, third, *and* fourth weight, *his Majesty will not so lightly dismiss. But that they also may now experience his Majesty's gentleness, it is his* Command, *to strip them* stark naked, *and so send them forth.*

Those who in the second and fifth *weight were found too light, shall besides Stripping, be noted with one, two or more Brand-marks, according as each one was lighter, or heavier.*

They who were drawn up by the sixth *or* seventh, *and not by the rest, shall be somewhat more* gratiously *dealt withal, and so forward. For unto every combination there was a certain punishment ordained, which were here too long to recount.*

They who yesterday separated themselves freely of their own accord, shall go out at Liberty without any blame.

Finally, the convicted vagabond-Cheaters who could move up none of the weights, shall as occasion serves, be punished in Body and Life, with the Sword, Halter, Water and Rods. And such Execution of Judgment shall be inviolably observed for an Example unto others.

Herewith our Virgin *broke* her Wand, and the other who read the Sentence, blowed her Trumpet, and stepped with most profound Reverence towards those who stood behind the Curtain. But here I cannot omit to discover somewhat to the Reader concerning the number of our Prisoners; of whom those who weighed *one,* were *seven;* those who weighed *two,* were *twenty one;* they who *three, thirty five;* they who *four, thirty five;* those who *five, twenty one;* those who *six, seven;* but he that came to the *seventh,* and yet could not *well* raise it, He, was only one, and indeed the same whom I released. Besides, of them who wholly failed there were many: But of those who drew all the weights from the ground, but few. And these as they stood severally before us, so I diligently numbred, and noted them down in my Table-Book; And it is very admirable that amongst all those who weighed any thing, none was equal to another. For although amongst those who weighed three, there were thirty five, yet one of them weighed the first, *second,* and third, another the third, fourth, and *fifth,* a third, the fifth, sixth, and seventh and so on. It is likewise very wonderful that amongst one hundred twenty six who weighed any thing, none was equal to another; And I would very willingly name them all, with each Mans weight, were it not as yet forbidden me. But I hope it may hereafter be published with the *Interpretation.*

Now this Judgment being read over, the Lords in the first place were well satisfied, because in such severity they durst not look for a mild sentence. For which cause they gave more than they were desired, and each one redeemed himself with

101

Chains, Jewels, Gold, Monies and other things, as much as they had about them; and with reverence took leave. Now although the King's Servants were forbidden to jear any at his going away, yet some unlucky Birds could not hold laughing, and certainly it was sufficiently ridiculous to see them pack away with such speed, without once looking behind them. Some desired that the promised *Catalogue* might with the first be dispatched after them, and then they would take such order with their Books as should be pleasing to his Majesty; which was again assured. At the Door was given to each of them out of a Cup *a Draught of* FORGETFULNESS, that so he might have no further memory of misfortune.

After these the *Voluntiers* departed, who because of their ingenuity were suffered to pass, but yet so as never to return again in the same fashion, But if to them (as likewise to the others) any thing *further* were revealed, then they should be well-come Guests.

Mean while others were stripping, in which also an inequality (according to each mans demerit) was observ'd. Some were sent away naked, without other hurt. Others were driven out with small Bells. Some were scourged forth. In brief the punishments were so various, that I am not able to recount them all. In the end it came to the last also with whom somewhat a longer time was spent, for whilst some were hanging, some beheading, some forced to leap into the Water, and the rest otherwise dispatching, much time was consumed. Verily at this execution my Eyes ran over, not indeed in regard of the punishment, which they otherwise for their impudency well deserved, but in contemplation of *humane blindness*, in that we are continually busiing our selves in that which ever since the first Fall hath been hitherto *Sealed* up to us. Thus the Garden which so lately was quite full, was soon emptied; so that besides the Souldiers there was not a man left. Now as soon as this was done, and silence had been kept for the space of five minut's; There came forward a beautiful snow-*white Unicorn* with a golden coller (having it in certain Letters) about his neck: In the same place he bowed himself down upon both his fore-feet, as if hereby he had shown honour to the Lyon, who stood so immoveably upon the fountain, that I took him to be of stone or brass, who immediately took the naked *Sword* which he bare in his Paw, and brake it in the middle in two, the pieces whereof to my thinking sunk into the *Fountain*: after which he so long roared, until a *white-Dove* brought a branch of *Olive* in her bill, which the Lyon devoured in an instant, and so was quieted. And so the Unicorn returned to his place with joy. Hereupon our Virgin lead us down again by the winding staires from the Scaffold, and so we again made our reverence toward the Curtain. We were to wash our hands and heads in the Fountain, and there a little while to wait in our order. till the King through a certain secret Gallery were again returned into his Hall, and then we also with choice Musick, Pomp, State and pleasant discourse were conducted into our former lodging: And this was done about four in the afternoon. But that in the meanwhile the time might not seem too long to us, the Virgin bestowed on each of us a noble *Page,* who were not only richly habited, but also exceeding learned, so that they could so aptly discourse upon all subjects, that we had good reason to be ashamed of our selves. These were commanded to lead us up and down the Castle yet but into certain places and if possible, to *shorten* the time according to our desire. Mean time the Virgin took leave with this consolation, that at Supper she would be with us again, and after that celebrate the Ceremonies of the hanging up of the *Weights,* requesting that we would in patience waite till the next day, for on the morrow we must be presented to the King. She being thus departed from us, each of us did what best pleased him. One part viewed the excellent paintings, which they copied out for themselves, and considered also what the wonderful Characters might signifie. Others were fain to recruit themselves again with *meat* and drink. I indeed caused my Page to conduct me (together with my Companion) up and *down* the Castle, of which walk it will never repent me as long as I have a day to live. For besides many other glorious Antiquities, the Royal *Sepulcher* was also shewed me, by which I learned more than is extant in *all Books.* There in the same place stands also the glorious *Phoenix* (of which two years since I published a particular small discourse) And am resolved (in case this my narration shall prove useful) to set forth several and peculiar Treatises, concerning the *Lyon, Eagle, Griffon, Falcon* and other like, together with their Draughts and Inscriptions. It grieves me also for my other Conforts, that they neglected such pretious Treasures. And yet I cannot but think it was the special will of God it should be so. I indeed reaped the most benefit by my Page, for according as each ones *genius* lay, so he led his intrusted into the quarters and places which were pleasing to him. Now the *Kyes* hereunto belonging were committed to my Page, and therefore this good Fortune happened to me before the rest; For although he invited others to come in, yet they imagining such *Tombs* to be only in the Church-yard, thought they should well enough get thither, when ever any thing was to be seen there. Neither shall these *Monuments* (as both of us copied and transcribed them) be *withheld* from my thankful Schollars. The other thing that was shewed us two was the Noble *Library* as it was altogether before the *Reformation*. Of which (albeit it rejoyces my Heart as often as I call it to mind) I have so much the less to say, because the *Catalogue* thereof is very shortly to be published. At the entry of this Room stands a *great* Book, the like whereof I never saw, in which all the Figures, Rooms, Portals, also all the Writings, Riddles and the like, to be seen in the whole Castle, are delineated. Now although we made some promise concerning *this* also, yet at present I must contain my self, and first learn to know the World better. In every Book stands its *Author* painted; whereof (as I understood) many were to be *burnt,* that so even their memory may be blotted out from amongst the Righteous. Now having taken a full view hereof, and being scarce gotten forth, another *Page* came running to us, and having whispered somewhat in our Pages ear, he delivered up the *Kyes* to him, who immediately carried them up the winding Stairs; But our Page was very much out of *Countenance,* and we setting hard upon him with Intreaties, He declared to us that the *King's Majesty* would by no means permit that either of the two, namely the *Library* and *Sepulchers,* should be seen by any Man and therefore he besought us as we tendered his Life, to discover it to no Man, he having already utterly denied it: Whereupon both of us stood hovering between Joy and Fear, yet it continued in silence, and no Man

secrets of
the Order's learning

made further inquiry about it. Thus in both places we consumed three hours, which does not at all repent me. Now although it had already strucken *Seven,* yet nothing was hitherto given us to *eat,* howbeit our hunger was easie to be abated by constant *Revivings,* and I could be well content to fast all my Life long with such Entertainment. About this time the Curious *Fountains,* Mines, and all kind of Art-Shops, were also shown us, of which there was none but surpassed all our Arts, though they should all be melted into one Mass. All their Chambers were built in *semi-circle,* that so they might have before their Eyes the costly Clock-work which was erected upon a fair Turret in the Center, and regulate themselves according to the course of the *Planets,* which were to be seen on it in a glorious manner. And hence I could easily conjecture wherein our *Artists* failed, howbeit its none of my duty to inform them. At length I came into a spacious Room (shown indeed to the rest a great while before) in the middle whereof stood a terestrial Globe, whose Diameter contained thirty Foot, albeit near half of it, except a little which was covered with the steps, was let into the Earth. Two Men might readily turn this Globe about with all its Furniture, so that more of it was never to be seen, but so much as was above the Horizon. Now although I could easily conceive that this was of some special use, yet could I not understand whereto those *Ringlets* of Gold (which were upon it in several places) served; At which my Page laughed, and advised me to view them more narrowly. In brief, I found there *my native Country noted with Gold also*: Whereupon my Companion sought his, and found that so too. Now for as much as the same hapened in like manner to the rest who stood by, The Page told us of a certain that it was yesterday declared to the Kings Majest'y by their old *Atlas* (so is the Astronomer named) that all the gilded points did exactly answer to their native Countries, according as had been shown of each of them. And therefore He also, as soon as he perceived that I *undervalued my self and that nevertheless there stood a point upon my native Country,* moved one of the Captains to intreat for us, that we should be set upon the Scale (without our Peril) at all Adventures; Especially seeing *one of our Native Coun-*

tries had a notable good Mark: And truly it was not without cause that He, the Page who had the greatest power of all the rest, was bestowed on me. For this I then returned him thanks, and immediately looked more diligently upon my native Country, and found more over that besides the *Ringlet,* there were also certain delicate *streaks* upon it, which nevertheless I would not be thought to speak to my own praise or glory. I saw much more too upon this Globe than I am willing to discover. Let each Man take into consideration why every City produceth not a Philosopher. After this he lead us quite into the Globe, which was thus made; On the Sea (there being a large square besides it) was a Tablet, whereon stood three Dedications, and the Author's name, which a Man might gently lift up and by a little joyned Board, go into the *Center,* which was capable of four Persons, being nothing but a round Board whereon we could sit and at ease by broad-daylight (it was now already dark) contemplate the Stars, to my thinking they were mere *Carbuncles* which glittered in an agreeable order, and moved so gallantly, that I had scarce any mind ever to go out again, as the Page afterwards told the Virgin, with which she often twitted me: For it was already Supper time, and I had so much amused my self in the Globe, that I was almost the last at Table; wherefore I made no longer delay, but having again put on my *Gown* (which I had before layd aside) and stepping to the Table, the waiters treated me with so much reverence and honour, that for shame I durst not look up, and so unawares permitted the Virgin, who attended me on one side, to stand, which she soon perceiving twitched me by the Gown, and so led me to the table. To speak any further concerning the Musick, or the rest of that magnificent entertainment, I hold it needless both because it is not possible sufficiently to express it, and I have above reported it according to my power. In brief, there was nothing there but Art and Amaenity. Now after we had each to other related our employment since noon (howbeit, not a word was spoken of the Library and Monuments) being already merry with the Wine, the Virgin began thus: My Lords, I have a great contention with one of my Sisters: In our Chamber we have an *Eagle,* Now we cherish him with such diligence, that each of us in disirous to be the best beloved, and upon that score have many a Squabble. On a day we concluded to go both together to him, and toward whom he should shew himself most friendly, hers should be properly be; this we did, and I (as commonly) bare in my hand a branch of Lawrel, but my Sister had none. Now as soon as he espyed us both, he immediately gave my Sister another branch which he had in his Beak, and offered at mine, which I gave him. Now each of us hereupon imagined her self to be best beloved of him; which way am I to resolve my self? This modest proposal of the Virgin pleased us all mighty well, and each one would gladly have heard the Solution, but in as much as they all looked upon me, and desired to have the beginning from me, my mind was so extreamly confounded that I knew not what else to do with it but propound another in its stead, and therefore said Gracious Lady, your Ladyships question were easily to be resolved if one thing did not perplex me. I had two Companions, both which loved me exceedingly; now they being doubtful which of them was most dear to me, concluded to run to me unaware, and that he whom I should then embrace should be the right; this they did, yet one of them could not keep pace with the other, so he staid behind and wept, the other I embraced with amazement. Now when they had afterwards discovered the business to me, I knew not how to resolve my self, and have hitherto let it rest in this manner, until I may find some good advice herein. The Virgin wondered at it, and well observed where about I was, whereupon she replied, well then let us both be quit; and then desired the solution from the rest. But I had already made them wise. Wherefore the next began thus. In the City where I live, a Virgin was lately condemned to death, but the Judge being something pittiful towards her, caused it to be proclaimed that if any man desired to become the Virgins Champion, he should have free leave to do it. Now she had two Lovers, the one presently made himself ready, and came into the lists to expect his adversary, afterwards the other also presented himself, but coming somewhat too late, he resolved nevertheless to fight, and willingly suffer himself to be vanquished, that so the Virgin's life might be preserved, which also succeeded according. *Whereupon each challenged her: Now my Lords instruct me, to which of them of right belongeth she?* The Virgin could hold no longer, but said, I thought to have gained much information, and am my self gotten into the Net, but yet would gladly hear whether there be any more behind; yes, that there is, answered the third, a Stranger adventure hath not been yet recounted than that which happened to my self. In my Youth I loved a worthy Maid: Now that this my love might attain its wished end, I was fain to make use of an ancient Matron, who easily brought me to her. Now it happened that the Maid's Brethren came in upon us just as we three were together, who were in such a rage that they would have taken my Life, but upon my vehement Supplication, they at length forced me to swear to take *each of them for a Year,* to my wedded Wife. *Now tell me my Lords, should I take the old, or the young one first?"* We all laughed sufficiently at this riddle, and though some of them muttered one to another thereupon, yet none would undertake to unfold it. Hereupon the fourth began. In a certain City there dwelt an honourable Lady, who was beloved of all, but especially by a young noble Man, who would needs be too importunate with her; at length she gave him this determination, that in case he would, in a cold Winter, lead her into a fair green Garden of Roses, then he should obtain, but if not, he must resolve never to see her more. The noble Man travelled into all Countries to find such a Man as might perform this, till at length he lite upon a little old Man that promised to do it for him, in case he would assure him of half his Estate; which he having consented to the other was as good as his word. Whereupon he invited the foresaid Lady home to his Garden, where contrary to her expectation she found all things green, pleasant and warm, and withal remembring her promise, she only requested that she might once more return to her Lord, to whom with Sighs and Tears she bewailed her lamentable condition: But for as much as he sufficiently perceived her faithfulness, he dis-dispatched her back to her Lover, who had so dearly purchased her, that she might give him Satisfaction. This Husband's integrity did so mightily affect the noble man, that he thought it a sin to touch so honest a Wife; so he sent her home again with honour to her Lord. Now the little Man perceiving such Faith in both these, would not, how poor soever he were, be the least, but restored the noble Man all his Goods again, and went his way. Now (my Lords) I know not which of these persons may have shown the greatest ingenuity? Here our Tongues were quite cut off. Neither would the Virgin make any other reply, but only that another should go on. Wherefore the fifth, without delay, began. My Lords, I desire not to make long work; who hath the greater joy, he that beholdeth what he loveth, or he that only thinketh on it? He that beholdeth it, said the Virgin; nay answered I; hereupon arose a contest, wherefore the sixth called out, My Lords I am to take a Wife; now I have before me a maid, a married Wife, and a Widdow; ease me of this doubt, and I will afterwards help to order the rest. It goes well there, replyed the seventh, where a man hath his choice, but with me the case is otherwise; in my youth I loved a fair and vertuous Virgin from the bottom of my Heart, and she me in like manner: howbeit because of her Friends denyal we could not come together in wedlock: Whereupon she was married to another, yet an honest and discreet Person, who maintained her honourably and with affection, until she came into the paines of Child-birth, which went so hard with her that all thought she had been dead, so with much state, and great mourning she was interred. Now I thought with my self, during her Life thou couldst have no part in this Woman, but yet now dead as she is thou mayst embrace and Kiss her sufficiently; whereupon I took my Servant with me, who dug her up by Night; Now having opened the Coffin and locked her in my Arms, and feeling about her Heart, I found still some little motion in it, which increased more and more from my warmth, till at last I perceived that she was indeed still alive; wherefore I quietly bare her home, and after I had warmed her chilled Body with a costly Bath of Herbs, I committed her to my Mother until she brought forth a fair Son, whom (as the Mother) I caused faithfully to be nursed. After two days (she being then in a mighty amazement) I discovered to her all the forepassed affair, requesting her that for the time to come she would live with me as a Wife, against which she thus excepted, in case it should be grievous to her Husband who had well and honourably maintained her. But if it could otherwise be, she was the present obliged in love to one as well as the other. Now after two Months (being then to make a Journey elsewhere) I invited her Husband as a Guest, and amongst other things demanded of him, whether if his deceased Wife should come home again, he could be content to receive her, and he affirming it with Tears and Lamentations, at length I brought him his Wife together with his Son, and an account of all the fore-passed business, intreating him to ratifie with his consent my fore-purposed espousals. After a long dispute he could not beat me from my right, but was fain to leave me the Wife. But still the contest was about the Son. Here the Virgin interrupted him, and said, It makes me wonder how you could double the afflicted Mans grief. How, answered he, was I not then concerned? Upon this there arose a dispute amongst us, yet the most part affirmed that he had done but right. Nay, said he, I freely returned him both his Wife and Son. Now tell me (my Lords) was my honesty, or this Man's joy the greater? These words had so mightily cheared the Virgin that (as if it had been for the sake of these two) she caused a health to go round. After which the rest of the proposals went on somewhat perplexedly, so that I could not retain them all, yet this comes to my mind, that one said, that a few years before he had seen a Physitian, who bought a parcel of Wood against Winter, with which he warmed himself all Winter long; but as soon as the Spring returned he sold the very same Wood again, and so had the use of it for nothing: Here must needs be skill, said the Virgin, but the time is now past. Yea, replyed my Companion, who ever understands not how to resolve all the Riddles, may give each Man notice of it by a proper Messenger, I conceive he will not be denied. At this time they began to say Grace, and we arose altogether from the Table, rather satisfied and merry than glutted; and it were to be wished that all *Invitations* and Feastings were thus to be kept. Having now taken some few turns up and down the Hall again, the Virgin asked us whether we desired to begin the Wedding. Yes, said one, noble and vertuous Lady; whereupon she privately dispatched a Page, and yet in the mean time proceeded in discourse with us. In brief she was already become so familiar with us, that I adventured and requested her Name. The Virgin smiled at my Curiosity, but yet was not moved, but replyed, *My Name contains five and fifty, and yet hath only eight Letters, the third is the third part of the fifth, which added to the sixth will produce a Number, whose root shall exceed the third it self by just the first, and it is the half of the fourth. Now the fifth and the seventh are equal, the last and the first are also equal, and make with the second as much as the sixth hath, which contains just four more than the third tripl'd. Now tell me, my Lord, how am I called?* The answer was intricate enough to me, yet I left not off so, but said, noble and vertuous Lady, may I not obtain one only Letter? *Yea* (said she) *that may well be done.* What then (replyed I again) may the seventh contain? *It contains* (said she) *as many as there are Lords here.* With this I was content, and easily found her Name, at which she was well pleased, with assurance that much *more* should yet be revealed to us. Mean time certain Virgins had made themselves ready, and came in with great Ceremony. First of all two Youths carried Lights before them, one of them was of a jocond Countenance, sprightly Eyes and gentile Proportion. The other lookt something angerly, whatever he would have, must be, as I afterwards perceived. After them first followed four Virgins; one looked shame-facedly towards the Earth, very humble in Behavior; The second also was a modest, bashful Virgin; The third, as she entered the Room seemed amazed at somewhat, and as I understood, she cannot well abide where there is too *much Mirth.* The fourth brought with her certain small *wreaths,* thereby to manifest her Kindness and Liberality. After these four came two which were somewhat more gloriously Apparelled; they saluted us courteously; One of them had a Gown of *Skye* coulour spangled with golden Stars; The others was *green,* beautified with red and white stripes. On their Heads they had thin flying *Tissaties,* which did most becomingly adorn them. At last came one alone, who had on her head a *Coronet,* but rather looked up towards Heaven, than towards Earth. We all thought it had been the Bride, but were much mistaken, although otherwise in Honour, Riches and State she much surpassed the *Bride;* and she afterwards ruled the whole Wedding. Now on this occasion we all followed our Virgin, and fell down on our Knees, howbeit she shewed her self extream humble, offering every one her hand, and admonishing us not to be too much surprized at this, for this was one of her smallest Bounties, but to lift up our Eyes to our Creator, and learn hereby to acknowledge his Omnipotency, and so proceed in our enterprised course, employing this Grace to the praise of God, and the good of Man. In sum, her words were quite different from those of our *Virgin*, who was somewhat *more worldly*. They pierced even through my Bones and Marrow. *And thou*, said she further to me, *hast received more than others, see that thou also make a larger return*. This to me was a very strange Sermon; for as soon as we saw the Virgins with the Musick, we imagined we must presently fall to Dancing, but that time was not as yet come. Now the Weights, whereof mention hath been before made, stood still in the same place, wherefore the Queen (I yet knew not who she was) commanded each Virgin to take *up* one, but to our Virgin she gave her own, which was the last and *greatest*, and commanded us to follow behind; our Majesty was then somewhat abated, for I well observed that our Virgin was but too good for us, & that we were not so highly reputed as we our selves were almost in part willing to phantasie. So we went behind in our order, and were brought into the first Chamber, where our Virgin in the first place hang up the *Queen's* weight, during which an excellent spiritual Hymn was Sung; there was nothing costly in this Room save only certain curious little *Prayer Books* which should never be missing. In the midst was erected a Pulpit, very convenient for Prayer, where in the *Queen* kneeled down, about her we were all fain to kneel and pray after the Virgin, who read out of a Book, That this Wedding might tend to the Honour of God, and our own benefit. Afterwards we came into the second Chamber, where the *first Virgin* hung up her weight also, and so forward till all the Ceremonies were finished. Hereupon the *Queen* again presented her Hand to every one, and departed thence with her Virgin. Our President staied yet a while with us. But because it had been already two hours night, she would no longer detain us; me thought she was glad of our Company, yet she bid us

good night, and wished us quiet rest, and so departed friendly, although *unwillingly* from us. Our Pages were well instructed in their business, and therefore shewed every Man
his Chamber, and stayed also with us in another Pallet, that
in case we wanted any thing we might make use of them. My
Chamber (of the rest I am not able to speak) was royally furnished with rare *Tapistries,* and hung about with Paintings.
But above all things I delighted in my Page, who was so excellently spoken, and experienced in the *Arts,* that he yet
spent me another hour, and it was half an hour after three
when first I fell asleep. And this indeed was the first night
that I slept in quiet, and yet a scurvy Dream would not suffer
me to rest; For I was all the night troubled with a *Door*
which I could not get open, but at last I did it. With these
phantasies I passed the time, till at length towards day I
awaked.

The Fourth Day

I Still lay in my Bed, and leisurely survieghed all the noble Images and Figures up and down about my Chamber, during which on a sudden I heard the *Musick* of Coronets, as if they had been already in Procession. My Page skipped out of the Bed as if he had been at his wits end, and looked more like one dead than living; In what case I then was, is easily immaginable, for, said he, *"The rest are already presented to the King;* I knew not what else to do, but weep out-right, and Curss my own sloathfulness; yet I dressed my self, but my Page was ready long before me, and ran out of the Chamber to see how affairs might yet stand. But he soon returned, and brought with him this joyful news, that the time indeed was not yet but only I had over-*slept* my Breakfast, they being unwilling to waken me because of my Age; But that now it was time for me to go with him to the *Fountain* where the most part were assembled; With this Consolation my Spirit returned again, wherefore I was soon ready with my Habit, and went after the Page to the *Fountain* in the aforementioned Garden, where I found that the *Lyon* instead of his Sword had a pretty large Tablet by him. Now having well viewed it, I found that it was taken out of the ancient Monuments, and placed here for some especial Honour. The Inscription was somewhat worn out with age, and therefore I am minded to set it down here, as it is, and give every one leave to consider it.

HERMES PRINCEPS.
POST TOT ILLATA
GENERI HUMANO DAMNA,
DEI CONSILIO:

ARTISQUE ADMINICULO,
MEDICINA SALUERIS FACTUR
HEIC FLUO.

Bibat ex me qui potest: lavet, qui vult:
turbet qui audet:
BIBITE FRATRES, ET VIVITE.

⚕ ꙅ):XXꙆICϓ ⱳⱳⰶꙶ

This Writing might well be read and understood, and may therefore fitly be here placed, because easier than any of the rest: Now after we had first washed our selves out of the Fountain, and every Man had taken a draught out of an intirely Golden Cup, we were once more again to follow the Virgin into the Hall, and there put on new Apparel, which was all of Cloth of *Gold* gloriously set out with Flowers. There was also given to every one another Golden *Fleece*, which was set about with pretious Stones, and various Workmanship according to the utmost skill of each Artificer. On it hung a weighty Medal of Gold, whereon were figured the *Sun* and *Moon* in opposition; but on the other side stood this Poesie, *The light of the Moon shall be as the light of the Sun, and the light of the Sun shall be seven times lighter than at present.* But our former Jewels were layed in a little Casket, and committed to one of the Waiters. After this the Virgin lead us out in our order, where the Musitians waited ready at the door, all apparalled in *red Velvet* with white Guards. After which a *Door* (which I never saw open before) to the Royal winding-Stairs was unlocked; There the Virgin led us together with the Musick, up *three hundred sixty five* Stairs, there we saw nothing but what was of extream costly and artificial Workmanship; and still the further we went, the more glorious still was the Furniture, until at length at the top we came under a *painted.* Arch, where the *sixty* Virgins attended us, all Richly Apparelled; Now as soon as they had bowed to us, and we as well as we could, had returned our reverence, our Musitians were dispatched away, who fain to go down the winding-Stairs again, the Door being shut after them. After this a little Bell was tolled; then came in a beautiful Virgin who brought every one a wreath of Laurel; But our Virgins had Branches given them: Mean while a Curtain was drawn up; Where I saw the *King* and *Queen* as they sate there in their Majesty, and had not the yesterday Queen so faithfully warned me, I should have forgotten my self, and have equalled this unspeakable glory to Heaven. For be-

Virgin
led procession up
365 stairs to meet
K & Q

115

sides that the Room glistered of meer Gold and pretious Stones; the *Queen's Robes* were moreover so made that I was not able to behold them. And whereas I before esteemed any thing for handsom, here all things so much surpassed the rest, as the Stars in Heaven are elevated. In the mean time the Virgin stept in, and so each of the Virgins taking one of us by the hand, with most profound Reverence presented us to the *King:* Whereupon the Virgin began thus to speak. *That to honour your Royal Majesties, (most gratious King and Queen) these Lords here present have adventured hither with peril of Body and Life; your Majesties have reason to rejoyce, especially since the greatest part are qualified for the inlarging of your Majesties Estates and Empire, as you will find the same by a most gratious and particular examination of each of them. Herewith I was desirous thus to have them in Humility presented to your Majesties, with most humble suit to discharge me of this my Commission, and most gratiously to take sufficient information from each of them, concerning both my Actions and Omissions.* Hereupon she laid down her Branch upon the ground. Now it would have been very fitting for one of us to have put in and spoken somewhat on this occasion, but seeing we were all troubled with the *falling* of the *Uvula,* at length the old *Atlas* stept forward and spoke on the *King's* behalf; *Their Royal Majesties do most gratiously rejoyce at your arrival, and will that their Royal Grace be assured to all, and every Man: And with thy Administration, gentle Virgin, they are most gratiously satisfied, & accordingly a Royal Reward shall therefore be provided for thee; yet it is still their intention, that thou shalt this day also continue with them, in as much as they have no reason to mistrust thee.* Hereupon the Virgin humbly took up the Branch again. And so we for this first time were to step aside with our Virgin. This room was square on the front, five times broader than it was long; but towards the West it had a great Arch like a Porch, wherein stood in circle three glorious Royal *Thrones,* yet the middle-most was somewhat higher than the rest. Now in each Throne sate two persons, in the first sate a very antient *King* with a gray Beard, yet his Consort was extraordinary fair and young. In the third Throne sate a black *King* of middle Age, and by him a dainty old Matron, not Crowned, but covered with a Vail. But in the middle sate the two *young Persons,* who tho' they had likewise Wreaths of Laurel upon their Heads, yet over them hung a large and costly *Crown.* Now albeit they were not at this time so fair as I had before imagined to my self, yet so it was to be. Behind them on a round Form sat for the most part antient Men, yet none of them (at which I wondered) had any Sword, or other Weapon about him, Neither saw I any other Life-guard, but certain Virgins which were with us the day before, who sate on the sides of the Arch: Here can I not pass in silence how the little *Cupid* flew to and again there, but for the most part he hovered and played the wanton about the great *Crown;* sometimes he seated himself in between the two Lovers, somewhat smiling upon them with his Bow. Nay, sometimes he made as if he would shoot one of us; In brief, this *Knave* was so full of his waggery, that he would not spair even the *little Birds,* which in multitudes flew up and down the Room, but tormented them all he could. The Virgins also had their pastimes with him, but whensoever they could catch him, it was not so easie a matter for him to *get from* them again. Thus this little *Knave* made all the sport and mirth. Before the *Queen* stood a small, but unpressibly curious *Altar:* wherein lay a *Book* covered with black *Velvet,* only a little over-layed with *Gold;* by this stood a small Taper in an *Ivory Candlestick,* now although it were very *small,* yet it burnt *continually,* and stood in that manner, that had not *Cupid,* in sport, now and then puffed upon it, we could not have conceived it to be Fire. By this stood a Sphere or Celestial Globe, which of its self turned clearly about. Next this, a small striking-Watch, by that a little *Christal* Pipe or *Syphon-Fountain,* out of which perpetually ran a clear *blood-red Liquor;* and last of all a Scull, or *Death's Head;* in this was a *white Serpent,* which was of such a length, that though she crept circle-wise about the rest of it, yet her Taile still remained in one of the Eye-holes, until her Head again entered at the other, so she never stirred from her Scull, unless it happened that *Cupid* twitched a little at her, for then she slipt in so suddenly, that we all could not choose but marvel at it: Together with this *Altar,* there were up and down the Room wonderful

Images, which moved themselves, as if they had been alive, and had so strange a contrivance, that it would be impossible for me to relate it all: likewise as we were passing out, there began such a marvellous kind of vocal Musick, that I could not certainly tell, whether it were performed by the Virgins who yet stayed behind, or by the Images themselves. Now we being for this time satisfied, went thence with our Virgins, who, the Musitians being already present, led us down the winding Stairs again, but the Door was diligently locked and bolted. As soon as we were come again into the Hall; one of the Virgins began: *I wonder, Sister, that you durst adventure your self amongst so many Persons: My Sister,* replyed our President, *I am fearful of none so much as of this Man,* pointing at me; This speech went to the Heart of me: For I well understood that she mocked at my *Age,* and indeed I was the oldest of them all. Yet she comforted me again with promise. That in case I behaved my self well towards her, she would easily rid me of this burden. Mean time a Collation was again brought in, and every one's Virgin seated by him, who well knew how to shorten the time with handsome discourses: But what their discourses and sports were I dare not blab out of School. But most of the questions were about the Arts, whereby I could lightly gather that both young and old were conversant in the Sciences. But still it run in my thoughts how I might become young again, whereupon I was somewhat the sadder; This the Virgin perceived, and therefore began, *I dare lay anything, if I lye with him to night, he shall be pleasanter in the morning.* Hereupon they began to laugh, and albeit I blushed all over, yet I was fain to laugh too at my own ill-luck. Now there was one there that had a mind to return my disgrace again upon the Virgin; whereupon he said, *I hope not only we, but the Virgins too themselves will bear witness in behalf of our Brother, that our Lady President hath promised her self to be his Bedfellow to Night: I should be well content with it,* replyed the Virgin, *if I had no reason to be afraid of these my Sisters, there would be no hold with them should I chuse the best and handsomest for my self, against their will.* My Sister presently began another, *We find hereby that thy high Office makes thee not proud; wherefore if by thy permission we might by lot part the Lords here present, amongst us, for Bed-fellows, thou shouldst with our good-will have such a Prerogative.* We let this pass for a · Jeast, and began again to discourse together. But our Virgin could not leave tormenting us, and therefore began again, *My Lords, how if we should permit Fourtune to decide which of us must lie together to Night?* Well, said I, if it may be no otherwise, we cannot refuse such a proffer. Now because it was concluded to make this tryal after Meat, we resolved to sit no longer at Table, so we arose, and each one walked up and down with his Virgin. *Nay,* said the Virgin, *It shall not be so yet, but let us see how Fortune will couple us;* upon which we were separated asunder: But now first arose a dispute how the business should be carried, but this was only a premediated device, for the Virgin instantly made the proposal that we should mix our selves together in a Ring, and that she beginning to count from her self, the *seventh,* was to be content with the folling *seventh,* whether it were a Virgin, or man; for our parts we were not aware of any craft, and therefore permitted it so to be; but when we thought we had very well mingled our selves, the Virgins nevertheless were so subtil, that each one knew her station before-hand: The Virgin began to reckon, the seventh next her was again a Virgin, the third seventh a Virgin likewise, and this happened so long till (to our amazement) all the *Virgins* came forth, and *none of* us was hit; Thus we poor pittiful Wretches remained standing alone, and were moreover forced to suffer our selves to be *jeared* too, and confess we were very handsomely couzened. In short, who ever had seen us in our order, might sooner have expected the Skye to fall, then that it should never have come to our turn. Herewith our sport was at an end, and we were fain to satisfie our selves with the Virgins Waggery. In the interm, the little wanton *Cupid* came also in unto us; But because he presented himself on behalf of their Royal Majesties, and delivered us a Health (as from them) out of a golden Cup, and was to call our Virgins to the King, withal declaring he could at this time tarry no longer with them, we could not sufficiently sport our selves with him: So with a due return of our most humble thanks we let him flye forth again. Now because (in the interm) the mirth began to fall into my Consort's

Feet, and the Virgins were nothing sorry to see it, they quickly lead up a civil Dance, whom I rather beheld with pleasure, then assisted. For my Mercurialists were so ready with their Postures, as if they had been long of the Trade. After some few Dances our president came in again, and told us how the Artists and Students had offered themselves to their Royal Majesties, for their Honour and Pleasure, before their departure to act a Merry Comedy; and if we thought good to be present at it, and to waite upon their Royal Majesties to the House of the *Sun,* it would be acceptable to them, and they would most gratiously acknowledge it: Hereupon in the first place we returned our most humble thanks for the Honour vouchsafed us, not only so, but moreover most submissively tendered our small service, which the Virgin related again, and presently brought word to attend their Royal Majesties (in our order) in the Gallery, whither we were soon led, and staid not long there; for the Royal Procession was just ready, yet without any Musick at all. The unknown Queen who was Yesterday with us, went foremost, with a small and costly Coronet, apparrelled in *white* Sattin, she carried nothing but a small Crucifix which was made of a Pearl, and this very day wrought between the young King and his Bride. After her went the six fore-mentioned Virgins in two ranks, who carried the King's Jewels belonging to the little Altar: next to these came the three Kings. The Bridegroom was in the midst of them in a plain dress, only in *black Sattin,* after the Italian Mode. He had on a small round black Hat, with a little black pointed Feather, which he courteously put off to us, thereby to signifie his favour towards us. To him we bowed our selves, as also to the first, as we had been before instructed. After the Kings came the three Queens, two whereof were richly habited, only she in the middle went likewise all in *black,* and Cupid held up her Train; after this intimation was given to us to follow, and after us the Virgins, till at last old *Atlas* brought up the rear. In such Procession, through many stately Walks, we at length came to the House of the *Sun,* there next to the King and Queen, upon a richly furnished Scaffold, to behold the fore-ordained Comedy: We indeed, though Separated, stood on the right Hand of the Kings, but the Virgins on the left, except those, to whom the

Royal Ensignes were committed. To them was allotted a peculiar standing at top of all. But the rest of the attendants were fain to stand below between the columns, and therewith to be content. Now because there are many remarkable Passages in this Comedy, I will not omit in brief to run it over.

First of all came forth a very *ancient King,* with some Servants; before whose *Throne* was brought a little *Chest,* with mention that it was found upon the Water, Now it being opened, there appeared in it a lovely *Babe,* together with certain Jewels, and a small Letter of Parchment sealed, and superscribed to the King. Which the King therefore presently opened, and having read it, wept; and then declared to his Servants how injuriously the King of the *Moores* had deprived his Aunt of her Country, and had exstinguished all the Royal Seed even to his Infant, with the Daughter of which Country he had now purposed to have matched his Son. Hereupon he Swore to maintain perpetual enmity with the *Moore,* and his Allies, and to revenge this upon him; and therewith commanded that the Child should be tenderly nursed, and to make preparation against the *Moore.* Now this provision and the discipline of the young Lady (who after she was a little grown up was committed to an ancient Tutor) continued all the first *Act*; with many very fine and laudable sports besides.

In the interlude a *Lyon and* Griffon were set at one another, to fight, and the *Lyon got* the victory; which was also a pretty sight.

In the second *Act,* the *Moore,* a very black treacherous Fellow, came forth also; who having with vexation understood that his Murder was discovered, and that too a little Lady was craftily stollen from him; began thereupon to consult how by stratagem he might be able to encounter so powerful an adversary, whereof he was at length advised by certain *Fugitives* who by reason of Famine fled to him: So the young Lady contrary to all mens expectation, fell again into his Hands: Whom, had he not been wonderfully deceived by his own Servants, he had like to have caused to be slain. Thus this *Act* too was concluded with a marvelous triumph of the *Moore.*

In the third *Act* a great *Army* on the *King's* party was raised against the *Moore,* and put under the conduct of an antient valiant Knight, who fell into the *Moores* Country, till at length he forceably rescued the young *Lady* out of the Tower, and Apparrelled her a new. After this in a *trice* they erected a glorious Scaffold, and placed their young Lady upon it: presently came *twelve Royal* Embassadors, amongst whom the fore-mentioned Knight made a Speech, alledging that the King his most gracious Lord had not only heretofore delivered her from death, and even hitherto caused her to be royally brought up (though she had not behaved her self altogether as became her) But moreover his Royal Majesty had, before others, elected her, to be a Spouse for the young *Lord* his Son; and most gratiously desired that the said espousals might be really executed in case they would be sworn to his Majesty upon the following Articles. Hereupon out of a Patent he caused certain glorious conditions to be read, which if it were not too long, were well worthy to be here recounted. In brief, the young Lady took an Oath inviolably to observe the same; returning thanks withal in most seemly sort for this so high a Grace. Whereupon they began to sing to the Praise of God, of the King, and the young Lady; and so for this time departed.

For sport, in the mean while, the four Beasts of *Daniel,* as he saw them in the Vision, and hath at large described them, were brought in, all which had its certain *signification*.

In the fourth *Act* the young Lady was again *restored* to her lost Kingdom, and *Crowned,* and for a space, in this array, conducted about the place with extraordinary joy: after this many and various Embassadors presented themselves, not only to wish her prosperity, but also to behold her Glory. Yet it was not long that she preserved her Integrity, but soon began again to look wantonly about her, and to wink at the Embassadors and Lords; wherein she truly acted her part to the Life.

These her manners were soon known to the *Moore,* who would by no means neglect such an opportunity, and because her Steward had not sufficient regard to her, she was easily blinded with great promises, so that she had no good confidence in her King, but privily submitted her self to the intire disposal of the *Moore*. Hereupon the *Moore* made haste, and having (by her consent) gotten her into his Hands, he gave her good words so long till all her Kingdom had subjected it self to him: After which in the third Scene of this *Act,* he caused her to be led forth, and first to be stript stark naked, and then upon a scurvy wooden Scaffold to be bound to a Post, and well scourged, and at last sentenced to *Death*. This was so woful a Spectacle, that it made the Eyes of many to run over. Hereupon thus *naked* as she was, she was cast into Prison, there to expect her Death, which was to be procured by *Poyson,* which yet killed her not, but made her Leprous all over: Thus this *Act* was for the·most part lamentable.

Between, they brought forth *Nebuchadnezzar's* Image, which was adorn'd with all manner of Arms, on the Head, Breast, Belly, Legs and Feet, and the like; of which too more shall be spoken in the future explication.

In the fifth *Act* the young King was acquainted with all that had passed between the *Moore* and his future Spouse, who first interceeded with his Father for her, intreating that she might not be left in that condition; which his Father having agreed to, Embassadors were dispatched to comfort her in her Sickness and Captivity, but yet withal to give her notice of her inconsideratedness. But she would not yet receive them, but consented to be the *Moore's Concubine,* which was also done, and the young King was acquainted with it.

After this comes a band of Fools, each of which brought with him a Cudgel, where with in a trice they made a great Globe of the World, and soon undid it again. It was fine sportive Phantasie.

In the sixth *Act* the young King resolved to bid battle to the *Moore,* which also was done. And albeit the *Moore* was discomfitted, yet all held the young King too for dead. At length he came to himself again, released his Spouse, and committed her to his Steward and Chaplain.

The first whereof tormented her mightily; at last the leaf turned over, and the Priest was so insolently wicked, that he would needs be above all, until the same was reported to the young King, who hastily dispatched one who broke the Neck of the Priest's mightiness, and adorned the Bride in some measure for the Nuptials.

After the *Act* a vast artificial *Elephant* was brought forth. He carried a great Tower with Musitians: which was also well-pleasing to all.

In the last *Act* the Bride-groom appeared in such pomp as is not well to be believed, and I was amazed how it was brought to pass: The Bride met him in the like Solemnity. Whereupon all the People cried out *VIVAT SPONSUS, VIVAT SPONSA*. So that by this Comedy they did with all congratulate our King and Queen in the most stately manner: Which (as I well observed) pleased them most extraordinary well.

At length they made some pasces about the stage in such Procession, till at last they altogether began thus to Sing.

I

This time full of love
Does our joy much improve
Because of the King's Nuptial;
And therefore let's Sing
That from all parts't may ring,
Blest be he that granted us all.

II

The Bride most exquisitely faire:
Whom we attended with long care
To him in troth's now plighted:
We fully have at length obtain'd,
The same for which we did contend:
He's happy, that's fore-sighted.

III

Now the Parents Kind and good
By intreaties are subdu'd:
Long enough in hold was she mew'd;
In honour increase,
Till Thousands arise.
And spring from your own proper Blood.

After this thanks were returned, and the Comedy was finished with joy, and the particular good liking of the Royal Persons wherefore, (the Evening also being already hard by) they departed together in their fore-mentioned order: But we were to attend the Royal Persons up the winding Stairs into the forementioned Hall, where the Tables were already richly furnished, and this was the first time that we were invited to the Kings table. The little Altar was placed in the midst of the Hall, and the six fore-named Royal Ensignes were laid on it. At this time the young King behaved himself very gratiously towards us, but yet he could not be heartily Merry; But howbeit he now and then discoursed a little with us, yet he often sighed, at which the little Cupid only mocked, and playd his waggish tricks. The old King and Queen were very serious, only the *Wife* of one of the ancient Kings was gay enough, the cause whereof I yet understood not. During this, the Royal Persons took up the first Table, at the second we only Sate. At the third, some of the principal Virgins placed themselves: The rest of the Virgins, and Men, were all fain to wait. This was performed with such state and solemn stilness, that I am affraid to make many words of it. Here I cannot leave untouched how that all the Royal Persons, before Meat, attired themselves in *Snow*-white glittering Garments, and so sate down to Table. Over the Table hang the fore-mentioned great Golden Crown, the pretious Stones whereof, without any other Light, would have sufficiently illuminated the Hall. However all the Lights were kindled at the *small Taper* upon the Altar; what the reason was I did not certainly know. But this I took very good notice of, that the young King frequently sent Meat to the white *Serpent* upon the little Altar, which caused me to muse. Almost all the Prattle at this Banquet was made by little Cupid, who could not leave us (and me indeed especially) untormented. He was perpetually producing some *Strange* matter. However, there was no considerable Mirth, all went silently on: from whence I, by my self, could imagin some great imminent Peril. For there was no Musick at all heard; but if we were demanded any thing, we were fain to give short round answers, and so let it rest. In short, all things had so strange a face, that the *sweat began* to trickle down all over my Body;

and I am apt to believe that the stout-heartedst Man alive
would then have lost his courage. Supper being now almost
ended, the young King commanded the Book to be reached
him from the little Altar. This he opened, and caused it once
again by an old Man to be propounded to us, whether we resolved to abide with him in *Prosperity* and Adversity;
which we having with trembling consented to, he further
cause us sadly to be demanded, whether we would give him
our Hands on it, which, when we could find no evasion, was
fain so to be. Hereupon one after another arose, and with his
own Hand writ himself down in this Book, When this also was
performed, the little *Christal Fountain,* together with a
very small Christal Glass was brought near, out of which all
the Royal Persons one after *another Drank,* afterwards it was
reached to us too, and so forward to all Persons, and this was
called, *the Draught of Silence.* Hereupon all the Royal Persons presented us their Hands, declaring that in case we did
not now stick to them, we should now and *never more hereafter* see them; which verily made our Eyes run over. But
our president engaged her self and promised very largely on
our behalf, which gave them Satisfaction. Mean time a little
Bell was tolled, at which all the Royal Persons waxed so
mighty bleak, that we were ready utterly to despair. They
quickly put off their *white* Garments again, and put on intirely *black* ones; The whole Hall likewise was hung about
with black Velvet, the Floor was covered with black Velvet,
with which also the Ceiling above (all this being before Prepared) was over-spread. After that the Tables were also removed away, and all had seated themselves round about
upon the Form, and we also had put on *black* habits, in comes
our President again, who was before gone out, and brought
with her six black Taffeta Scarffs, with which she bound the
six Royal Persons Eyes. Now when they could no longer see,
there were immediately brought in by the Servants six covered *Coffins,* and set down in the Hall, also a low black Seat
placed in the midst. Finally, there steps in a very *cole-black*
tall Man, who bare in his hand a sharp Ax. Now after that
the old King had been first brought to the Seat, his *Head* was
instantly whipt off, and wrapped up in a black Cloth, but the
Blood was received into a great *golden Goblet,* and placed

with him in this Coffin that stood by, which being covered, was set aside. Thus it went with the rest also, so that I thought it would at length have come to me too, but it did not; For as soon as the six *Royal Persons* were Beheaded, the black Man went out again; after whom another followed, who Beheaded *him* too just before the Door, and brought back his Head together with the Ax, which were laid in a little Chest. This indeed to me seemed a bloody Wedding, but because I could not tell what would yet be the event, I was fain for that time to captivate my understanding until I were further resolved. For the Virgin too, seeing that some of us were faint-*hearted* and wept, bid us be content. For, said she to us, *The Life of these standeth now in your hands, and in case you follow me, this Death shall make many alive.* Herewith she intimated we should go sleep, & trouble our selves no further on our part, for they should be sure to have their due right; And so she bad us all good night, saying, *That she must watch the dead Corps this night:* We did so, and were each of us conducted by our Pages into our Lodgings. My Page talked with me of sundry and various matters (which I still very well remember) and gave me cause enough to admire at his understanding: But his intention was to lull me asleep, which at last I well observed, whereupon I made as though I was fast asleep, but no sleep came into my Eyes, and I could not put the Beheaded out of my mind. Now my Lodging was directly over against the great *Lake,* so that I could well look upon it, the Windows being nigh the Bed. About midnight, as soon as it had struck twelve, on a sudden I espied on the *Lake* a great *Fire,* wherefore out of fear I quickly opened the Window to see what would become of it; Then from far I saw seven *Ships* making forward, which were all stuck full of Lights. Above on the top of each of them hovered a *Flame,* that passed to and fro, and sometimes descended quite down, so that I could lightly judge that it must needs be the *Spirits* of the Beheaded. Now these Ships gently approched to Land, and each of them had no more than one Mariner. As soon as they were now gotten to Shore, I presently espied our Virgin with a *Torch* going towards the Ships, after whom the six covered Coffins, together with the little Chest, were carried; and each of them privily laid in a

127

Ship. Wherefore I awaked my Page too, who hugely thanked me, for having run much up and down all the day, he might quite have overslept this, tho' he well knew it. Now as soon as the Coffins were laid in the Ships, all the Lights *were* extinguished, and the six *Flames* passed back together over the *Lake,* so that there was no more but one Light in each Ship for a Watch. There were also some hundreds of Watchmen who had encamped themselves on the Shore, and sent the Virgin back again into the Castle, who carefully bolted all up again; so that I could well judge that there was nothing more to be done this night, but that we must expect the day; so we again betook our selves to rest. And I only of all my Company had a Chamber towards the Lake, and saw this, so that now I was also extream weary, and so fell asleep in my manifold Speculations.

The night was over, and the dear wished for day broken, when hastily I got me out of the Bed, more desirous to learn what might yet insue, than that I had sufficiently slept; Now after that I had put on my Cloaths, and according to my custom was gone down the Stairs, it was still too early, and I found no body else in the Hall, wherefore I intreated my Page to lead me a little about in the Castle, and shew me somewhat that was rare, who was now (as always) willing, and presently lead me down certain steps under ground, to a great iron Door, on which the following Words in great Copper Letters, were fixed.

VENVS

This I thus copied, and set down in my Table-Book. NOW after this Door was opened, the Page led me by the hand though a very dark Passage, till we came again to a very little Door, that was now only put too, For (as the Page informed me) it was first opened but yesterday when the Coffins were taken out, and had not been since shut. Now as soon as we stepped in, I espied the most pretious thing that Nature ever created: For this Vault had no other light but from certain huge great *Carbuncles;* And this (as I was informed) was the *King's Treasury.* But the most glorious and principal thing, that I here saw, was a *Sepulcher* (which stood in the middle) so rich that I wondred it was no better guarded: whereunto the Page answered me, *That I had good reason to be thankful to my Planet, by whose influence it was, that I had now seen certain pieces which no humane Eye else (except the King's Family) had ever had a view of.* This Sepulcher was *triangular,* and had in the middle of it a Kettle of polished Copper, the rest was of pure Gold and pretious Stones; In the Kettle stood an Angel, who held in his Arms an unknown Tree, from which it continually dropped Fruit into the Kettle; and as oft as the Fruit fell into the Kettle, it turned into *Water* too, and ran out from thence into three small Golden Kettles standing by. This little Altar was supported by these three Animals, an *Eagle,* and *Ox* and a *Lyon,* which stood on an exceeding costly Base. I asked my Page what this might signifie; *Here,* said he, *lies Buried* Lady Venus, *that Beauty which hath undone many a great Man, both in Fourtune, Honour, Blessing and Prosperit*y. After which he shewed me a Copper Door on the Pavement. *Here* (said he) *if you please, we may go further down;* I still follow you (replyed I) so I went down the steps, where it was exceeding dark, but the Page immediately opened a little Chest, wherein stood a small *ever-burning Taper,* at which he Kindled one of the many Torches which lay by. I was mightily terrified, and seriously asked how he durst do this? He gave me for answer. *As long as the Royal Persons are still at rest, I have nothing to fear.* Herewith I espied a rich Bed ready made, hung about with curious Curtains, one of which he drew, where I saw the Lady *Venus stark-naked* for he heaved up the Coverlets too) lying there in such Beauty, and a fashion so surprizing, that I was almost besides my self, neither do I yet know whether it was a piece thus Carved, or an humane Corps that lay dead there; For she was altogether immoveable, and yet I durst not touch her. So she was agin covered, and the Curtain drawn before her, yet she was still (as it were) in my Eye. But I soon espyed behind the Bed a Tablet, on which it was thus written.

7 and the page!

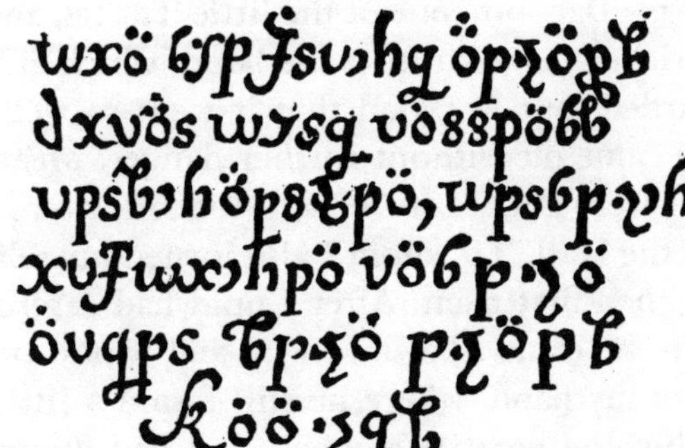

[decorative text in an unknown / cipher script]

VENUS WILL AWAKE
→ BIRTH TO A KING

I asked my Page concerning this Writing, but he laughed, with promise that I should know it too. So he putting out the Torch, we again ascended: Then I better viewed all the little Doors, and first found, that on every corner there burned a small Taper of *Pyrites,* of which I had before taken no notice; for the Fire was so clear, that it looked much liker a Stone than a Taper. From this heat the Tree was forced continually to *melt,* yet it still produced new Fruit. *Now behold* (said the Page) *what I heard revealed to the King by* Atlas, *When the Tree* (said he) *shall be quite melted down, Then shall* Lady Venus *awake, and be the Mother of a* King. Whilst he was thus speaking, in flew the little Cupid, who at first was somewhat abashed at our presence, but seeing us both look more like the Dead then the Living, he could not at length refrain from Laughing, *Demanded what Spirit had brought me thither,* whom I with trembling answered, that I had lost my way in the Castle, and was by chance come hither, and that the Page likewise had been looking up and down for me, and at last lited upon me here, I hoped he would not take it amiss. *Nay then 'tis well enough yet,* said Cupid, *my old busie Gransir, but you might lightly have served me a scurvy trick, had you been aware of this* Door. *Now I must look better to it,* and so he put a strong Lock on the Copper Door, where we before descended. I thanked God that he lited upon us no sooner, my Page too was the more jocond, because I had so well helped him at this pinch. *Yet can I not* (said Cupid) *let it pass unrevenged, that you were so near stumbling upon my dear Mother;* with that he put the point of his Dart into one of the little Tapers, and heating it a little, pricked me with it on the hand, which at that time I little regarded, but was glad that it went so well with us, and that we came off without further danger. Meantime my Companions were gotten out of Bed too, and were again returned into the Hall. To whom I also joyned my self, making as if I were then first risen. After Cupid had carefully made all fast again, he came likewise to us, and would needs have me shew him my hand, where he still found a little drop of blood, at which he heartily laughed, and bad the rest have a care of me, I would shortly end my days. We all wondred how Cupid could be so merry, and have no sence at all of the yesterday's sad passages. But he was no what troubled. Now our President had in the mean time made her self ready for the Journey, coming in all in *black Velvet*, yet she still bare her branch of Laurel, her Virgins too had their Branches. Now all things being in readiness, the Virgin bid us first drink somewhat, and then presently prepare for the procession: wherefore we made no long tarrying, but followed her out of the Hall into the Court. In the Court stood six Coffins, and my Companions thought no other but that the six Royal Persons lay in them, but I well observed the device. Yet I knew not what was to be done with these other. By each Coffin were eight *muffled* Men. Now as soon as the Musick went (it was so mournful and dolesome a tune, that I was astonished at it) they took up the Coffins, and we (as we were ordered) were fain to go after them into the formentioned Garden, in the midst of which was erected a wooden Edifice, having round about the Roof a glorious Crown, and standing *upon seven* Columns; within it were formed six Sepulchers, and by each of them a stone, but in the middle it had a round hollow rising stone: In these Graves the Coffins were quietly and with many Cerimonies layed: The stones were shoved over them, and they shut fast. But the little Chest was to lie in the middle. Herewith were my Companions deceived, for they imagined no other but that the Dead Corps were there. Upon the top of all there was a great Flag, having a *Phoenix painted* on it, perhaps

C. R. IS PRICKED BY
CUPID, FOR "ALMOST"
FINDING HIS MOTHER

132

therewith the more to delude us. Here I had great occasion to thank God that I had seen more than the rest. Now after the Funerals were done, the Virgin, having placed her self upon the middle-most Stone, made a short Oration, *That we should be constant to our ingagements, and not repine at the pains we were hereafter to undergo, but be helpful in* restoring *the present buried* Royal Persons to Life *again, and therefore without delay to rise up with her, to make a Journey to the Tower of* Olympus, *to fetch from thence Medicines useful and necessary for this purpose.* This we soon agreed to, and followed her through another little door quite to the Shore. There the seven fore-mentioned *Ships* stood all empty; on which all the Virgins stuck up their *Laurel Branches,* and after they had distributed us in the six Ships, they caused us in Gods name thus to begin our Voyage, and looked upon us as long as they could have us in sight, after which they with all the Watch-men returned into the Castle. Our Ships had each of them a peculiar device. Five of them indeed had the five *regular Bodies,* each a several one, but mine in which the Virgin too sate, carried a Globe. Thus we sailed on in a singular order, and each had only two Mariners. Foremost went the Ship *a,* in which, as I conceive the *Moor* lay, in this were *twelve Musitians,* who played excellent well, its device was a Pyramid. Next followed three a breast, *b, c,* and *d,* in which we were disposed, I sate in *c.* In the midst behind these came the two fairest and stateliest Ships, *e* and *f,* stuck about with many Branches of Laurel, having no Passengers in them; their Flags were the *Sun* and *Moon.* But in the rear only one Ship *g,* in this were *Forty Virgins.* Now being thus passed over this Lake, we first came through a narrow Arm, into the right Sea,

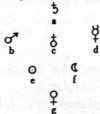

where all the Syrens, Nymphs, and Sea-Goddesses had attended us; wherefore they immediately dispatched a Sea-Nymph to us to deliver their Present and Offering of Honour to the

Wedding. It was a costly, great, set, round, and Orient Pearl; the like to which hath not at any time been seen, either in ours, or yet in the new World. Now the Virgin having friendly received it, the Nymph further intreated that audience might be given to their Divertisements, and to make a little stand, which the Virgin was content to do, and commanded the two great Ships to stand into the middle, and with the rest to incompass them in *Pentagon*. After which the Nymphs fell into a ring about them, and with a most delicate sweet voice began thus to sing.

I

There's nothing better here below,
Than beauteous, noble, Love;
Whereby we like to God do grow,
And none to grief do move.
Wherefore let's chant it to the King,
That all the Sea thereof may ring.
   We question; Answer you.

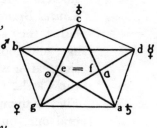

II

What was it that at first us made?
   'Twas Love.
And what hath Grace a fresh conveigh'd?
   'Tis Love.
Whence was't (pray tell us) we were born?
   Of Love
How came we then again forlorn?
   Sans Love.

III

Who was it (say) that us conceived?
   'Twas Love.
Who Suckled, Nursed, and Reliev'd?
   'Twas Love.
What is it we to our Parents owe?
   'Tis Love.

What do they us such kindness show?
          Of Love.

IV

Who get's herein the Victory?
          'Tis Love.
Can Love by search obtained be?
          By Love.
How may a Man good works perform?
          Through Love.
Who into one can two transform?
          'Tis Love.

V

Then let our Song sound,
Till it's Eccho rebound.
To Loves honour and praise,
Which may ever encrease
With our noble Princes, the King,
          and the Queen,
The Soul is departed, their Body's within.

VI

And as long as we live,
God gratiously give;
That as great Love and Amity,
They bear each other mightily;
So we likewise, by Loves own Flame,
May reconjoyn them once again.

VII

Then this annoy
Into great Joy
(If many thousand younglings deign)
Shall change, and ever so remain.

They having with most admirable concent and melody finished this Song, I no more Wondred at *Ulisses* for stopping the Ears of his Companions; for I seemed to my self the most unhappy man alive, that Nature had not made me too so trim a creature. But the *Virgin* soon dispatched them, and commanded to set Sail from thence; wherefore the Nymphs too after they had been presented with a long *red Scarff* for a gratuity; went off, and dispersed themselves in the Sea. I was at this time sensible, that *Cupid* began to work with me too, which yet tended but very little to my Credit, and for as much as my giddiness is likely to be nothing beneficial to the Reader, I am resolved to let it rest as it is. But this was the very wound that in the first Book I received on the head in a Dream: and let every one take warning by me of loitering about *Venus's* Bed, for *Cupid* can by no means brook it. After some Hours, having in friendly discourses made a good way, we came within Ken of the Tower of *Olympus,* wherefore the Virgin commanded by the discharge of some Pieces to give the signal of our approach, which was also done; And immediately we espyed a great *white* Flag thrust out, and a small gilded Pinnace sent forth to meet us. Now as soon as this was come to us, we perceived in it a very ancient man, the Warden of the Tower, with certain Guards cloathed in *white*, of whom we were Friendly received, and so conducted to the Tower. This Tower was Situated upon an *Islan*d exactly *square,* which was invironed with a *Wall* so firm and thick, that I my self counted two hundred and *sixty* passes over. On the other side of the wall was a fine Meadow with certain little Gardens, in which grew strange, and to me unknown, Fruits; and then again an inner Wall round about the Tower. The Tower of it self was just as if *seven round Towers* had been built one by another, yet the middlemost was somewhat the higher, and within they all entred one into another, and had seven Storys one above another. Being thus come to the Gates of the Tower, we were led a little aside on the Wall, that so, as I well observed, the Coffins might be brought into the Tower without our taking notice; of this the rest knew nothing. This being done, we were conducted into the Tower at the very bottom, which albeit it were excellently painted, yet we had here littil recreation, for this was nothing but a *Laboratory,* where we were fain to beat and wash Plants, and pretious Stones, and all Sorts of Things, and extract their Juice and Essence, and put up the same in Glasses, and deliver them to be laid up. And truly our Virgin was so busie with us, and so full of her directions, that she knew how to give each of us employment enough, so that in this Island we were fain to be meer *drudges,* till we had atcheived all that was necessary for the restoring of the Beheaded Bodies. Meantime (as I afterwards understood) three Virgins were in the first Apartment washing the Corps with all diligence. Now having at *length almost* done with this our preparation, nothing more was brought us, but some broath with a little draught of Wine, whereby I well observed, that we were not here for our pleasure; for when we had finished our days work too, every one had only a Mattress laid on the Ground for him, wherewith we were to content our selves. For my part I was not very much troubled with sleep, and therefore walked out into the Garden, and at length came as far as the Wall; and because the Heaven was at that time very clear, I could well drive away the time in contemplating the *Stars;* By chance I came to a great pair of Stone-Stairs, which led up to the top of the Wall. And because the Moon shone very bright, I was so much the more confident, and went up, and looked too a little upon the Sea, which was now exceeding calm; and thus having good opportunity to consider better of Astronomy, I found that this present Night there would happen such a conjunction of the Planets, the like to which was not otherwise suddenly to be observed. Now having looked a good little into the Sea, and it being just about Midnight, as soon as it had struck Twelve, I beheld from far the *Seven Flames* passing over Sea hitherward, and betaking themselves to the top of the Spire of the Tower. This made me somewhat affraid; for as soon as the Flames had setled themselves, the Winds arose, and began to make the Sea very Tempestuous. The Moon also was Covered with clouds, and my joy ended with such fear, that I had scarce time enough to hit upon the Stairs again, and begake my self again to the Tower. Now whether the Flames tarried any longer, or passed away again,

I cannot say: For in this obscurity I durst no more venture abroad: So I laid me down upon my Mattress, and there being besides in the *Laboratory* a pleasant and gently purling Fountain, I fell a Sleep so much the sooner. And thus this fifth day too was concluded with Wonders.

a - х	b - ծ	c - ɔꙅ	d - б	e - ρρg
f - Ⅎ	g - ꞡ	h - bh	i - ꙅꙅ [-y?]	k - ҟ ꞧ
l - Ꝺ	m - ȯ	n - ӧ	o - ó	r - ꙅ
s - ꞵꙅ	t - ꞡ	u - ʊ	w - ꞷ	z - ꝫ

The Sixth Day.

Next morning, after we had awakend one another, we sate together a while to discourse what might yet be the event of things. For some were of opinion that they should all be inlivened again together. Others contradicted it, because the decease of the ancients was not only to *restore* life, but increase too to the young ones. Some imagined that they were not put to death, but that others were beheaded in their stead. We having now talked together a pretty long while in comes the Old Man to us, and first saluting us, looks about him to see if all things were ready, and the processes enough done. We had herein so behaved our selves, that he had no fault to find with our diligence, whereupon he placed all the Glasses together, and put them into a case. Presently come certain youths bringing with them some Ladders, Roapes, and large Wings, which they laid down before us, and departed. Then the old Man began thus: My Dear Sons, one of these three things must each of you this day constantly bear about with him. Now it is free for you either to make a choice of one of them, or to cast lots about it. We replied, we would choose. Nay; said he, let it rather go by lot. Hereupon he made three little Schedules, in one he writ *Ladder,* on the second *Rope,* on the third *Wings;* These he laid in an Hat, and each man must draw, and whatever he happened upon, that was to be his. Those who got the *Ropes,* imagined themselves to be in the best case, but I chanced on a *Ladder,* which hugely afflicted me, for it was twelve-foot long, and pretty weighty, and I must be forced to carry it, whereas the others could handsomly coyle their Ropes about them: and as for the *Wings,* the old Man joyned them so nearly on to the third sort, as if they had grown upon them. Hereupon he turned the Cock, and then the Fountain ran no longer, and we were fain to remove it, from the middle out of the way. After all things were carried off, he taking with him the Casket with the Glasses, took leave, and locked the Door fast after him, so that we imagined no other but that we had been imprisoned in this Tower. But it was hardly a quarter of an Hour before a round Hole at the very *top* was uncovered, where we saw our Virgin, who called to us, and bad us good Morrow, desiring us to *come* up. They with the Wings were instantly above through the hole. Only they with the Ropes were in evil plight. For as soon as ever one of us was up, he was commanded to draw up the Ladder to him. At last each mans Rope was hanged on an Iron Hook, so every one was fain to climb up by his Rope as well as he could, which indeed was not compassed without Blisters. Now as soon as we were all well up, the hole was again covered, and we were friendly received by the Virgin. This Room was the whole breadth of the Tower it self, having *Six* very stately *Vestries* a little raised above the Room, and to be entred by the ascent of three Steps. In these *Vestries* we were distributed, there to pray for the Life of the King and Queen, mean while the Virgin went in and out at the little Door *a,* till we had done. For as soon as our process was absolved, there was brought in, and placed in the middle through the little Door, by twelve persons (which were formerly our Musitians) a wonderful thing of a *longish* shape, which my Companions took only to be a Fountain. But I well observed that the *Corps's* lay in it, for the inner Chest was of an oval Figure, so large that Six Persons might well lie in it one by another. After which they again went forth, fetched their Instruments, and conducted in our Virgin, together with her she-attendants, with a most delicate noise of Musick. The Virgin carried a little Casket, but the rest only Branches, and small Lamps, and some too lighted Torches. The Torches were immediately given into our Hands, and we were to stand about the Fountain in this order.

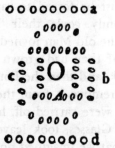

First stood the *Virgin* A with her attendants in a Ring round about with the Lamps & branches *c,* next stood we with our Torches *b,* then the *Musitians a* in a long rank, last of all the rest of the Virgins *d* in another long rank too. Now whence the Virgins came, or whether they dwelt in the Castle, or whether they were brought in by night, I know not, for all their Faces were covered with delicate white Linnen, so that I could not know any of them. Hereupon the Virgin opened the Casket, in which there was a round thing wrapped up in a piece of green double Taffata. This she laid in the uppermost Kettle, and then covered it with the lid, which was full of holes, and had besides a Rim, on which she poured in some of the Water which we had the day before prepared, whence the Fountain began immediately to run, and through four small Pipes to drive into the little Kettle; beneath the undermost Kettle there were many sharp points, on which the Virgins stuck their Lamps, that so the heat might come to the Kettle, and make the Water Seeth. Now the Water beginning to Simper, by many little holes at *a*, it fell in upon the Bodies, and was so hot, that it *dissolved* them all, and turned them *into* Liquor. But what the above said round wrapt up thing was, my Companions knew not, but I understood that it was the Moor's Head, from which the Water conceived so great heat. At *b* round about the great Kettle, there were again many holes, in which they stuck their Branches; now whether this was done of necessity, or only for Ceremony, I know not; However these Branches were continually besprinkled by the Fountain, whence it afterwards dropt somewhat of a deeper *Yellow* into the Kettle. This lasted for near two Hours, that the Fountain still constantly ran of it self; but yet the longer, the fainter it was. Mean time the Musitians went their way, and we walked up and down in the Room; and truly the Room was so made, that we had opportunity enough to pass away our time: There was, for Images, Paintings, Clock-works, Organs, Springing Fountains, and the like, nothing forgotten. Now it was near the time that the Fountain ceased, and would run no longer: upon which the Virgin commanded a round Golden Globe to be brought. But at the bottom of the Fountain there was a Tap, by which she let out all the matter that was dissolved by those hot Drops (whereof certain quarts were then *very Red*) into the Globe. The rest of the Water which remained above in the Kettle, was poured out. And so this Fountain (which was now become much lighter) was again carried forth. Now whether it was opened abroad, or whether any thing of the Bodies that was further useful, yet remained, I dare not cer-

141

tainly say: But this I know, that the Water that was emptied into the Globe was much *heavier* then *six,* or yet more of us were well able to bear, albeit for its bulk it should have seemed not too heavy for one man. Now this Globe being with much ado gotten out of Doors, we again sate alone. But I perceiving a trampling over head, had an Eye to my Ladder. Hear one might take notice of the strange opinions my Companions had concerning this Fountain: For they not imagining but that the Bodies lay in the Garden of the Castle, knew not what to make of this kind of working, but I thanked God that I awaked in so opportune a time, and saw that which helped me the better in all the Virgins business. After one quarter of an hour the cover above was again lifted of, and we commanded to come up, which was done as before with Wings, Ladders, and Ropes. And it did not a little vex me, that whereas the Virgins could go up another way, we were fain to take so much toil; yet I could well judge there must be some *special* reason in it, and we must leave somewhat for the *Old Man* to do too. For even those with the Wings had no advantage by them but when they were to mount through the Hole. Now being gotten up thither also, and the Hole shut again, I saw the Globe hanging by a strong Chain in the middle of the Room. In this Room was nothing else but meer Windows, and still between two *Windows* there was a Door, which was covered with nothing but a great polished Looking-Glass; and these Windows and Looking-Glasses were so optically opposed one to another, that although the Sun (which now shined exceeding bright) beat only upon one Door, yet (after the Windows towards the Sun were opened, and the Doors before the Looking-Glasses drawn aside) in all quarters of the Room there was nothing but *Suns,* which by artificial *Refractions* beat upon the whole golden Globe hanging in the midst; and for as much as the same (besides that brightness) was polished, it gave such a Lustre, that none of us could open our Eyes, but were therefore forced to look out at Windows till the Globe was well heated, and brought to the desired effect. Here I may well avow that in these Mirrours I have seen the most wonderful Spectacle that ever Nature brought to light; for there were Suns in all places, and the Globe in the middle shined yet

HANGING GOLDEN GLOBE:

ILLUMINATED BY MIRRORS TO REFLECT SUN

brighter, so that, but for one twinkling of an Eye, we could no more indure it than the Sun it self. At length the Virgin commanded to shut up the Looking-Glasses again, and to make fast the Windows, and so let the Globe cool again a little; and this was done about seven of the Clock. Wherefore we thought good, since we might now have leisure a little to refresh our selves with a Breakfast: This Treatment again was right Philosophical, and we had no need to be affraid of Intemperance, yet we had no want. And the hope of the future joy (with which the Virgin continually comforted us) made us so jocond that we regarded not any pains, or inconvenience. And this I can truly say too concerning my Companions of high quality, that their minds never ran after their *Kitchin or Table,* but their pleasure was only to attend upon this adventurous Phisick, and hence to contemplate the Creator's Wisdom and Omnipotency. After we had taken our Refection, we again settled our selves to work, for the Globe was sufficiently cooled; which with toil and labour we were to lift off the Chain and set upon the Floor. Now the dispute was how to get the Globe in sunder, for we were commanded to divide the same in the midst. The conclusion was that a sharp pointed Diamond would best do it. Now when we had thus opened the Globe, there was nothing of *redness* more to be seen, but a lovely great snow-white Egg: It most mightily rejoyced us, that this was so well brought to pass. For the Virgin was in perpetuall care, least the Shell might still be too tender. We stood round about this Egg as jocond as if we our selves had laid it. But the Virgin made it presently be carried forth, and departed her self too from us again, and (as all ways) locked the Door to. But what she did abroad with the Egg, or whether it were some way privately handled, I know not, neither do I believe it. Yet we were again to pause together for one quarter of an hour, till the third hole were opened, and we by means of our instruments were come upon the fourth Stone or Floor. In this Room we found a great Copper Kettle filled with *yellow Sand,* which was warmed with a gentle Fire, afterwards the Egg was raked up in it, that it might therein come to perfect maturity. This Kettle was exactly square, upon one side stood these two verses, Writ in great Leters.

GOLDEN GLOBE →

SNOW-WHITE EGG

O. BLI. TO. BIT. MI. LI.
KANT. I. VOLT. BIT. TO. GOLT.

On the second side were these three Words.

SANITAS. NIX. HASTA.

The third had no more but this one Word.
F. I. A. T.

But on the hindermost past stood an enitre Inscription running thus.

QUOD.

Ignis: Aer: Aqua: Terra:

SANCTIS REGUM ET REGI-

NARUM NOSTR:

Cineribus

Eripere non potuerunt.

Fidelis Chumicorum Turba

IN HANC URNAM

Contulit.

A .

144

Now whether the Sand or Egg were hereby meant, I leave
to the learned to dispute, yet do I my part, and omit nothing
undeclared. Our Egg being now ready was taken out; But
it needed no cracking, for the *Bird* that was in it soon freed
himself, and shewed himself very jocond, yet he looked very
Bloody and unshapen: We first set him upon the warm Sand,
so the Virgin commanded that before we gave him any thing
to eat, we should be sure to make him fast, otherwise he
would give us all work enough. This being done too, food
was brought him, which surely was nothing else than the
Blood of the Beheaded, deluted again with prepared water,
by which the Bird grew so fast under our eyes, that we well
saw why the Virgin gave us such warning of him. He bit
and scratcht so devillishly about him, that could he have had
his will upon any of us, he would soon have dispatched him.
Now he was wholly *black,* and wild, wherefore other meat
was brought him, perhaps the blood of another of the *Royal
Persons,* whereupon all his black Feathers moulted again,
and instead of them there grew out Snow-*white-Feathers.*
He was somewhat tamer too, and suffered himself to be more
tractable, nevertheless we did not yet trust him. At the third
feeding his Feathers began to be so curiously *coloured,* that
in all my Life I never saw the like colours for Beauty. He
was also exceeding tame, and behaved himself so friendly
with us, that (the Virgin consenting) we released him from
his Captivity. *'Tis now reason* (began our Virgin) *since
by your diligence, and our old man's consent, the Bird has
attained both his Life, and the highest Perfection, that he be
also joyfully Consecrated by us.* Herewith she commanded
to bring in Dinner, and that we should again refresh our
selves, since the most troublesome part of our Work was now
over, and it was fit we should begin to enjoy our passed Labours. We began to make our selves merry together. Howbeit
we had still all our Mourning Cloaths on, which seemed
somewhat reproachful to our Mirth. Now the Virgin was perpetually inquisitive, perhaps to find to which of us her future
purpose might prove serviceable. But her discourse was for
the most part about *melting;* and it pleased her well when
one seemed expert in such compendious Manuals, as do pe-
culiarly commend an Artist. This Dinner lasted not

145

above three quarters of an hour; which we yet for the most part spent with our Bird, whom we were fain constantly to feed with his meat: But he still continued much at the same growth. After Dinner we were not long suffered to digest our Meat; but after that the Virgin together with the Bird was departed from us. The fifth Room was set open to us, whither we got too after the former manner, and tendred our Service. In this Room a Bath was prepared for our Bird, which was so coloured with a fine white Powder, that it had the appearance of meer Milk. Now it was at first cool when the Bird was set into it: He was mighty well pleased with it, drinking of it, and pleasantly sporting in it. But after it began to heat by reason of the Lamps that were placed under it, we had enough to do to keep him in the Bath. We therefore clapt a cover on the Kettle, and suffered him to thrust his head out through a hole, till he had in this sort lost all his Feathers in this Bath, and was as smooth as a new-born Child, yet the heat did him no further harm, at which I much marvelled; for in this Bath the Feathers were quite consumed, and the Bath was thereby tinged into *blew;* at length we gave the Bird air, who of himself sprung out of the Kettle, and was so glitteringly smooth, that it was a pleasure to behold it. But because he was still somewhat wild, we were fain to put a collar, with a Chain, about his Neck, and so led him up and down the Room. Mean time a strong Fire was made under the Kettle, and the Bath sodden away till it all came to a *blew* Stone, which we took out, and having first pounded it, we were afterwards fain to grind it on a Stone, and finally with this colour to paint the Bird's whole Skin over: Now he lookt much more strangely, for he was all *blew*, except the head, which remained *white*. Herewith our work on this Story too was performed; And we (after the Virgin with her *blew Bird* was departed from us) were called up through the hole to the sixth Story; which was done too, there we were mightily troubled, for in the midst a little Altar, every way like that in the King's Hall above described, was placed. Upon which stood the six fore-mentioned *particulars,* and he him self (the Bird) made the *seventh.* First of all the little *Fountain* was set before him, out of which he drunk a good draught, afterwards he pecked upon the *white Serpent* until she bled mightily. This Blood we were to receive into a Golden Cup, and pour it down the *Birds* Throat, who was mighty averse from it, then we dipt the *Serpents* head in the *Fountain,* upon which she again revived, and crept into her *Deaths-head,* so that I saw her no more for a long time after. Mean time the Sphere turned constantly on, until it made the desired conjunction. Immediately the watch Struck one, upon which there was a going another *conjunction.* Then the Watch struck two. Finally, whilst we were observing the third conjunction, and the same was indicated by the Watch, the poor Bird of himself submissively laid down his Neck upon the Book, and willingly suffered his Head (by one of us thereto chosen by lot) to be *smitten off.* Howbeit he yielded not one drop of *Blood,* till he was opened on the Breast, and then the *Blood* spun out so fresh and clear as if it had been a Fountain of Rubies. His Death went to the heart of us, and yet we might well judge, that a naked Bird would stand us in little stead. So we let it rest, and removed the little Altar away and assisted the Virgin to burn the Body (together with the little Tablet hanging by) to Ashes, with Fire kindled at the little *Taper;* afterwards to cleanse the same several times, and to lay them in a Box of Cypress-Wood. Here I cannot conceal what a trick I and three more were served; After we had thus diligently taken up the Ashes, The Virgin began to speak thus. *My Lords, we are here in the sixth Room, and have only one more before us, in which our trouble will be at an end, and then we shall return home again to our Castle, to awaken our most gratious Lords and Ladies. Now albeit I could heartily wish, that all of you, as you are here together, had behaved your selves in such sort, that I might have given you Commendations to our most renowned King and Queen, and you have obtained a suitable Reward; yet because, contrary to my desire, I have found amongst you these four* (herewith she pointed at me and three more) *lazy and sluggish Labourators, and yet according to my good-will to all and every one, am not willing to deliver them up to condign punishment; However, that such Negligence may not remain wholly unpunished, I am purposed thus concerning them, that they shall only be excluded from the* future seventh *and most Glo-*

147

rious action of all the rest, and so too they shall incur no further blame from their Royal Majesties. In what a case we now were at this Speech, I leave others to consider: For the Virgin so well knew how to keep her countenance, that the Water soon ran over our Baskets, and we esteemed our selves the most unhappy of all men. After this the Virgin by one of her Maids (whereof there were many always at hand) caused the Musitians to be fetcht, who were with Cornets to blow us out of Doors with such scorn and derision that they themselves could hardly sound for *laughing.* But it did *particularly* mightily afflict us that the *Virgin* so vehemently laughed at our *weeping, anger & impatience,* and that there might well perhaps be some amongst our Companions who were glad of this our misfortune. But it proved otherwise. For as soon as we were come out at the Door, the Musitians bid us be of good cheere and follow them up the winding Staires; They led us up to the seventh Floor under the Roof, where we found the *old Man,* whom we had not hitherto seen, standing upon a *little round* Furnace. He received us friendly, and heartily congratulated us, that we were hereto chosen by the Virgin; but after he understood the affright we had conceived, his belly was ready to burst with Laughing, that we had taken such good Fortune so hainously. Hence said he, My Dear Sons learn, *That Man never knoweth how well God intendeth him.* During this discourse the Virgin also with her little *Box* came running in, who (after she had sufficiently laughed at us) emptied her Ashes out into another Vessel, and filled hers again with other matter, saying, she must now go cast a Mist before the other Artists Eyes, that we in the mean time should obey the old Lord in whatsoever he commanded us, and not remit our former diligence. Herewith she departed from us into the seventh Room whither she called our Companions. Now what she first did with them there, I cannot tell, for they were not only most earnestly forbidden to speak of it, but we too by reason of our business, durst not peep on them through the Ceiling. But this was our work, we were to *moisten the* Ashes with our fore-prepared *Water till* they became altogether like a very thin Dough. After which we set the matter over the Fire, till it was well *heated,* then we cast it thus hot as it was into two *little* forms or moulds, and so let it cool a little (here we had leisure to look a while upon our Companions through certain crevises made in the Floor) they were now very busie at a Furnace, & each was himself fain to blow up the Fire with a pipe, and they stood thus blowing about it, as if they were herein wondrously preferred before us. And this blowing lasted so long till our old Man rouzed us to our work again; So that I cannot say what was done afterwards. We having opened our little forms, there appeared two beautiful bright and almost *Transparent little* Images, the like to which Mans Eye never saw, a Male and a Female, each of them only *four* inches long; and that which most mightily surprised me, was, that they were not hard, but limber and fleshy, as other human Bodies, yet had they no Life: So that I do most assuredly believe that the Lady *Venus's* Image was also made after some such way. These Angelically fair Babes we first laid upon two little Sattin Cushonets, and beheld them a good while, till we were almost besotted upon so exquisite an object. The old Lord warned us to forbear, and continually to instill the *Blood* of the Bird (which had been received into a little Golden Cup) drop after drop into the Mouths of the little Images, from whence they apparently to the Eye *encreased;* and whereas they were before very small, they were now (according to proportion) much more beautiful; so that worthily all Limners ought to have been here, and have been ashamed of their Art in respect of these productions of Nature. Now they began to grow so *big,* that we lifted from the little Cushonets, and were fain to lay them upon a long Table, which was covered with white Velvet. The old man also commanded us to cover them over up to the Breast with a piece of the fine *white double* Taffata, which because of their unspeakable beauty, almost went against us; but that I may be brief, before we had in this manner quite spent the *Blood,* they were already in their perfect *full* growth, they had Gold-yellow curled Hair, and the above-mentioned figure of *Venus* was nothing to them. But there was not yet any natural warmth, or sensibility in them, they were dead Figures, yet of a lively and natural colour: and since care was to be taken that they grew not too great, the old Man would not permit any thing more to be given them,

149

but quite covered their Faces too with the Silk, and caused the Table to be *stuck* round about with Torches. Here I must warn the Reader that he imagine not these Lights to have been of *necessity,* for the old Man's intent hereby, was only that we should not observe when the *Soul* entred into them, as indeed we should not have taken notice of it, in case I had not twice before seen the *Flames;* However, I permitted the other three to remain in their belief, neither did the old Man know that I had seen any thing more. Hereupon he bid us sit down on a Bench over against the Table: presently the Virgin came in too with the Musick and all furniture, and carried two curious white Garments, the like to which I had never seen in the Castle, neither can I describe them, for I thought no other but that they were meer *Christal,* but they were gentle, and not transparent, so that I cannot speak of them. These she laid down upon a Table, and after she had disposed her Virgins upon a Bench round about, she and the old Man began many *Leger-demain* tricks about the Table, which was done only to *Blind* us. This (as I told you) was managed under the roof, which was wonderfully formed, for on the inside it was arched into seven Hemispheres, of which the middlemost was somewhat the highest, and had at top a little round hole, which was nevertheless shut, and was observed by none else. After many Ceremonies, stept in *six* Virgins, each of which bare a large Trumpet, which were rouled about with a green glittering and burning material like a wreath, one of which the old Man took, and after he had removed some of the lights at top, and uncovered their Faces, he placed one of the Trumpets upon the *Mouth* of one of the Bodies in such manner, that the upper and wider part of it was directed just against the forementioned hole. Here my Companions always looked upon the Images, but I had other thoughts; for as soon as the foliage or wreath about the shank of the Trumpet was kindled, I saw the hole *at top* open, and a bright *stream* of Fire shooting down *the* Tube, and passing into the Body: whereupon the hole was again covered, and the Trumpet removed. With this device my Cmmpanions were deluded, so that they imagined that life came into the Image by means of the *Fire* of the foliage, for as soon as he received the *Soul* he twinckled

SOULS (FLAMES OF FIRE) INSTILLED INTO THE 2 FIGURES → ALIVE

with his Eyes, howbeit he scarce stirred. The second time he placed another Tube upon its Mouth, and kindled it again, and the Soul was let *down* through the Tube. This was repeated upon each of them *three times,* after which all the Lights were exstinguished and carried away. The Velvet Carpets of the Table were cast together over them, and immediately a travilling Bed was unlocked and made ready, into which thus wrapped up they were born, and so after the Carpets were taken off them, they were neatly laid by each other, where with the Curtains drawn before them, they slept a good while. (Now was it also time for the Virgin to see how our other Artists behaved themselves, they were well pleased, because (as the Virgin afterwards informed me) they were to *work in Gold,* which is indeed a piece also of this art, but not the most *Principal,* most necessary, and best: They had indeed too a part of these *Ashes,* so that they imagined no other, but that the whole Bird was provided for the sake of *Gold,* and that life must thereby be restored to the deceased) during which we sate very still, attending when our married couple would awake, thus about half an hour was spent. For then the wanton *Cupid* presented himself again, and, after he had saluted us all, flew to them behind the Curtain, tormenting them so long till they awaked. This happened to them with very great amazement, for they imagined no other but that they had hitherto slept from the very hour in which they were beheaded. *Cupid,* after he had awaked them, and renewed their acquaintance one with another, stepped a side a little, and permitted them both somewhat better to *recruit* themselves, mean time playing his tricks with us; and at length he would needs have the *Musick* fetcht to be somewhat the merrier. Not long after the Virgin her self comes: And after she had most humbly saluted the young King and Queen (who found themselves somewhat faint) and kissed their hands, she brought them the two forementioned curious *Garments,* which they put on, and so stepped forth. Now there were already prepared two very curious *Chaires,* wherein they placed themselves: and so were by us with most profound Reverence congratulated; for which the King in his own Person most gratiously returned his thanks, and again *re-assured* us of all Grace. It was already about

151

five of Clock, wherefore they could make no longer stay, but as soon as ever the chiefest of their furniture could be laden, we were to attend the young Royal Persons down the winding Stairs, through all Doors and watches unto the Ship, in which they inbarqued themselves, together with certain Virgins, and Cupid, and sailed so mighty swift that we soon lost sight of them, yet they were met (as I was informed) by certain stately Ships: Thus in four Hours time they had made many *Leagues* out at Sea. After five of Clock the Musitians were charged to carry all things back again to the Ships, and to make themselves ready for the Voyage. But because this was somewhat long a doing, the old *Lord* commanded forth a party of his concealed Soldiers, who had hitherto been planted in the Wall, so that we had taken no notice of any of them, whereby I observed that this Tower was well provided against opposition. Now these Soldiers made quick work with our stuff, so that no more remained further to be done, but to go to Supper. Now the Table being compleatly furnished, the Virgin brings us again to our Companions where we were to carry our selves as if we had truly been in a Lamentable condition, and forbear laughing. But they were always smiling one upon another, howbeit some of them too simpathized with us. At this Supper the old *Lord* was with us too, who was a most sharp Inspector over us: For none could propound any thing so discreetly, but that he knew how either to confute it, or amend it, or at least to give some good document upon it. I learned most by this *Lord,* and it were very good that each one would apply himself to him, and take notice of his procedure, for then things would not so often, and so untowardly Miscarry. After we had taken our nocturnal refection, the old Lord led us into his Closets of Rarities, which were here and there dispersed amongst the Bulworks, where we saw such wonderful productions of Nature, and other things too which man's wit in imitation of Nature had invented, that we needed a Year more sufficiently to surveigh them: Thus we spent a good part of the Night by Candle-light. At last, because we were more inclined to Sleep than see many Rarities, we were lodged in Rooms in the Wall, where we had not only costly good Beds, but also besides extra-ordinary handsom Chambers, which made us the more wonder why we were the day before forced to undergo so many hardships. In this Chamber I had good rest; and being for the most part without care, and weary with continual Labour, the gentle rushing of the Sea helped me to a sound and sweet Sleep, for I continued in one Dream from eleven of Clock till eight in the morning.

The Seventh Day

After eight of clock I awaked, and quickly made my self ready, being desirous to return again into the Tower, but the dark passages in the Wall were so many, and various, that I wandred a good while before I could find the way out. The same happened to the rest too, till at last we all met again in the neather most Vault, and habits intirely *yellow* were given us, together with our golden Fleeces. At that time the Virgin declared to us that we were Knights of the *GOLDEN STONE,* of which we were before ignorant. After we had now thus made our selves ready, and taken our Breakfast, the old Man presented each of us with a medal of Gold; on the one side stood these Words,

AR. NAT. MI.

On the other these,

TEM. NA. F.

Exhorting us moreover we should entreprize nothing beyond and against this token of remembrance. Herewith we went forth to the Sea, where our Ships lay so richly equipped, that it was not well possible but that such brave things must first have been brought thither. The Ships were *twelve in number,* six of ours, and six of the old Lord's, who caused his Ships to be freighted with well appointed Soldiers. But he betook himself, to us, into our Ship, where we all were together; In the first the Musitians Seated themselves, of which the old Lord had also a great number, they sailed before us to shorten the time. Our Flags were the *twelve Celestial* Signs, and we sate in *Libra;* besids other things, our Ship had also a noble and curious Clock, which shewed us all the *Minutes.* The Sea too was so calm, that it was a singular pleasure to Sail. But that which surpassed all the rest, was the old Man's discourse, who so well knew how to pass away our time with wonderful Histories, that I could have been content to Sail with him all my Life long. Mean time the Ships passed on amain, for before we had sailed two hours the Mariner told us that he already saw the whole Lake almost covered with Ships, by which we could conjecture they were come out to meet us, which also proved true: For as soon, as we were gotten out of the Sea into the Lake by the forementioned River, there presently stood in to us five hundred Ships, one of which sparkled with mere Gold and pretious Stones, in which sate the King and Queen, together with other Lords, Ladies, and Virgins of high Birth. As soon as they were well in Ken of us the pieces were discharged on both sides, and there was such a din of Trumpets, Shalms, and Kettle Drums that all the Ships upon the Sea capered again. Finally, as soon as we came near they brought about our Ships together, and so made a stand, Immediately the old *Atlas* stepped forth on the King's behalf, making a short, but handsom oration, wherein he wellcomed us, and demanded whether the Royal Presents were in readiness. The rest of my Companions were in an huge amazement, whence this King should arise, for they imagined no other but that they must again *awaken* him. We suffered them to continue in their wonderment, and carried our selves as if it seemed strange to us too. After *Atlas's* oration out steps our old Man, making somewhat a larger reply, wherein he wished the King and Queen all happiness and increase, after which he delivered up a curious small Casket, but what was in it, I know not; only it was committed to Cupid, who hovered between them both, to keep. After the oration was finished, they again let off a joyful Volle of Shot, and so we sailed on a good time together, till at length we arrived at another Shore. This was near the first Gate at which I first entred: At this place again there attended a great Multitude of the King's Family together with some hundreds of Horses. Now as soon as we were come to shore, and disembarqued, the King and Queen presented their Hands to all of us one with another with singular kindness; and so we were to get up on Horseback. Here I desire to have the Reader friendly intreated not to interpret the following Narration to any vain glory or pride of mine, but to credit me thus far, that if there had not been a special necessity in it, I could very well have utterly concealed this honour which was shewed me. We were all one after another distributed amongst the Lords. But our *old* Lord, and I most unworthy,

155

were to ride even with *the* King, each of us bearing a snow *white* Ensign, with a Red Cross: I indeed was made use of because of my Age, for we both had long *grey* Beards, and Hair. I had besides fastened my token round about my Hat, of which the young King soon took notice, and *demanded if I were he, who could at the Gate* redeem *these tokens?* I answered in most humble manner, Yea. But he laughed on me, saying, *There henceforth needed no Ceremony; I was HIS Father.* Then he asked me, *Wherewith I had redeemed them?* I replied, with *Water* and Salt: whereupon he wondred who had made me so wise; upon which I grew somewhat more confident, and recounted unto to him how it had happened to me with my *Bread,* the Dove, and the Raven, and he was pleased with it, and said expresly, *That it must needs be, that* God *had herein vouch safed me a singular happiness.* Herewith we came to the first gate where the Porter with the blew Cloaths waited, who bare in his Hand a supplication. Now as soon as he spied me even with the King, he delivered me the *supplication,* most humbly beseeching me to mention his ingenuity towards me before the King: Now in the first place I demanded of the King, what the condition of this *Porter* was? who friendly answered me, *That he was a very famous and rare* Astrologer, *and always in high regard with the Lord his Father. But having on a time committed a fault against* Venus, *and beheld her in her Bed of rest, This punishment was therefore imposed upon him, that he should so long wait at the first Gate, till some one should release him from thence.* I replied, may he then be released? *Yes,* said the King, *if any one can be found that hath as highly* transgressed *as himself, he must stand in his stead, and the other shall be free.* This word went to my Heart, for my Conscience convinced me that I was the offender, yet I held my peace, & herewith delivered the supplication. As soon as he had read it, he was mightily ᵗerrified, so that the Queen, who (with our Virgins, and that other Queen besides, of whom I made mention at the hanging of the Weights) rid just behind us observed it, & therefore asked him, what this Letter might signifie. But he had no mind that he should take notice of it, but putting up the Paper, began to discourse of other matters, till thus in about three hours time we came

WHITE ENSIGN,
RED CROSS

quite to the Castle, where we alighted, and waited upon the King into his forementioned Hall. Immediately the King called for the old *Atlas* to come to him in a little Closet, and shewed him the writing, who made no long tarrying, but rid out again to the Porter to take better Cognizance of the matter. After which the young King with his Spouse, and other Lords, Ladies and Virgins sate down. Then began our Virgin highly to commend the diligence we had used, and the pains and labour we had undergone, requesting we might be royally rewarded, and that she henceforward might be permitted to enjoy the benefit of her commission. Then the old Lord stood up too, and attested that all that the Virgin had spoken was true, and that it was but equity that we should both on both parts be contented. Hereupon we were to step out a little; and it was concluded that each man should make some possible wish, and accordingly obtain it; for it was not to be doubted, but that those of *understanding* would also make the *best* wish: So we were to consider of it till after Supper. Mean time the King and Queen for recreations sake, began to fall to play together. It looked not unlike Chesse, only it had other Laws; for it was the *Vertues* and Vices one against another, where it might ingeniously be observed with what Plots the Vices lay in *wait* for the Vertues, and how to re-encounter them again. This was so properly and artifically performed, that it were to be wished, that we had the like game too. During the game, in comes *Atlas* again, and makes his report in private, yet I blushed all over. For my Conscience gave me no rest; after which the King presented me the supplication to read, and Contents whereof were much to this purpose: First he wished the King prosperity, and increase; that his seed might be spread abroad far and wide: Afterwards he remonstrated that the time was now accomplished, wherein according to the Royal promise he ought to be *released*. Because *Venus* was already uncovered by one of his Guests, for his observations could not lie to him. And that if his Majesty would please to make a strict and diligent enquiry, he would find that she had been uncovered, and in case this should not prove to be so, he would be content to remain before the Gate all days of his life. Then he sued in the most humble manner, that upon peril of Body and Life

[handwritten marginal note: PORTER AT THE GATE : DOOMED TO STAND THERE TILL SOMEONE ELSE CAME WHO HAD COMMITTED THE SAME CRIME (i.e. LOOKED UPON Venus) — LIKE C.R., WHO SAYS NOTHING...]

he might be permitted to be present at this Nights supper, he was in good hopes to spye out the very Offendor, and obtain his wished freedom. This was expresly and handsomly indicted, by which I could well perceive his ingenuity, but it was too sharp for me, and I could well have endured never to have seen it. Now I was casting in my mind whether he might perchance be helped through my wish, so I asked the King, whether he might not be released some other way: No, replyed the King, because there is a special consideration in the business. However, for this Night, we may well gratifie him in his desire; so he sent one forth to fetch him in. Mean time the Tables were prepared in a spatious Room, in which we had never been before, which was so compleat, and in such manner contrived, that it is not possible for me only to begin to describe it. Into this we were conducted with singular Pomp, and Ceremony. Cupid was not at this time present. For (as I was informed) the disgrace which had happened to his Mother, had somewhat angred him. In brief, my offence, and the Supplication which was delivered were an occasion of much sadness, for the King was in perplexity how to make inquisition amongst his Guests, and the more because thus even they too, who were yet ignorant of the matter, would come to the knowledge of it. So he caused the Porter himself, who was already come, to make his strict surveigh, and shewed himself as pleasnat as he was able. Howbeit at length they began again to be merry, and to bespeak one another with all sorts of recreative and profitable discourses. Now how the treatment and other Ceremonies were then performed, it is not necessary to declare, since it is neither the Reader's concern, nor serviceable to my design. But all exceeded more in art, and human invention, than that we were overcharged with drinking. And this was the last, and noblest Meal at which I was present. After the Bancket the Tables were suddainly taken away, and certain curious Chairs placed round about in circle, in which we together with the King, and Queen, both their old Men, the Ladies and Virgins, were to sit. After which a very handsom Page opened the abovementioned glorious little Book, when *Atlas* immediately placing himself in the midst, began to bespeak us to the ensuing purpose. That his Royal Majesty had not yet committed to oblivion the service we had done him, and how carefully we had attended our duty, and therefore by way of retribution had elected all and each of the Knights of the Golden Stone. That it was therefore further necessary not only once again to oblige our selves towards his Royal Majesty, but to vow too upon the following Articles, and then his Royal Majesty would likewise know how to behave himself towards his liege People. Upon which he caused the Page to read over the Articles: which were these.

I. You my Lords the Knights, shall swear, that you shall at no time ascribe your order either unto any *Devil* or Spirit, but only to God your *Creator,* and his hand-maid *Nature.*

II. That you will Abominate all Whoredom, Incontinency and Uncleaness, and not defile your order with such Vices.

III. That you through your Talents will be ready to assist all that are worthy, and have need of them.

IV. That you desire not to employ this honour to worldly Pride and high Authority.

V. That you shall not be willing to live longer than God will have you.

At this last Article we could not choose but laugh sufficiently, and it may well have been placed after the rest, only for a conceit. Now being to vow to them all by the King's Scepter, we were afterwards with the usual Ceremonies installed Knights, and amongst other Priviledges set over *Ignorance, Poverty, and Sickness*; to handle them at our pleasure. And this was afterwards ratified in a little Chappel (whither we were conducted in all Procession) and thanks returned to God for it. Where I also at that time to the honour of God hung up my Golden Fleece and Hat, and left them there for an eternal memorial. And because every one was there to write his Name, I writ thus;

ARTICLES

159

Summa Scientia nihil Scire.

Fr. CHRISTIANUS ROSENCREUTS.

Eques aurei Lapidis.

Anno. 1459.

Others writ otherwise, and truly each as seemed him good. After which we were again brought into the Hall, where being sate down, we were admonished quickly to bethink our selves what every one would wish. But the King and his party retired into a little Closet, there to give audience to our wishes. Now each man was called in severally, so .hat I cannot speak of any man's proper wish, I thought nothing could be more praise-worthy than in honour of my order to demonstrate some laudable vertue. And found too that none at present could be more famous, and cost me more Trouble than *Gratitude*. Wherefore not regarding that I might well have wished somewhat more dear and agreeable to my self, I vanquished my self, and concluded, even with my own peril, to free the *Porter* my Benefactor. Wherefore being now called in, I was first of all demanded, whether, having read the supplication, I had observed, or suspected nothing concerning the offendor? upon which I began undauntedly to relate how all the business had passed. How through Ignorance I fell into that mistake, and so offered my self to undergo all that I had thereby demerited. The King, and the rest of the Lords wondered mightily at so un-hoped for confession, and so wished me to step aside a little. Now as soon as I was called for in again, *Atlas* declared to me, that although it were grievous to the King's Majesty, that I whom he loved above others, was fallen into such a mischance, yet because it was not possible for him to Transgress his ancient usages, he knew not how else to absolve me, but that the other must be at Liberty, and I placed in his stead, yet he would hope that some other would soon be apprehended, that so I might be able to go home again. However, no release was to be hoped for, till the Marriage Feast of his future Son. This Sentence had near cost me my life, and I first hated my self

CR CONFESSES TO
HAVING SEEN VENUS;
THE PORTER, HIS BENE-
FACTOR, GOES FREE —
CR IS DOOMED TO
THE PORTER'S SPOT, HE
THINKS ...

and my twatling Tongue, in that I could not hold my peace, yet at last I took courage, and because I considered there was no remedy, I related how this Porter had bestowed a token on me, and commended me to the other, by whose assistance I stood upon the Scale, and so was made partaker of all the honour and joy already received. And therefore now it was but equal that I should shew my self grateful to my Benefactor: and because the same could no way else be done, I returned thanks for the sentence, and was willing gladly to sustain some inconvenience for his sake, who had been helpful to me in coming to so high place. But if by my wish any thing might be effected, I wished my self at home again, and that so he by me, and I by my wish might be at Liberty. Answer was made me, that the wishing stretched not so far. However I might well wish him free. Yet it was very pleasing to his Royal Majesty, that I had behaved my self so generously herein, but he was affraid I might still be ignorant, into what a miserable condition I had plunged my self through this my curiosity. Hereupon the good man was pronounced free, and I with a sad heart was fain to step aside. After me the rest were called for too, who came jocundly out again, which was still more to my smart; for I imagined no other, but that I must finish my life under the Gate. I had also many pensive thoughts running up and down in my Head, what I should yet undertake, and wherewith to spend the time, at length I considered that I was now old, and according to the course of nature, had few years more to live: And that this anguish and melancholy Life would easily dispatch me, and then my doorkeeping would be at an end: And that by a most happy Sleep I might quickly bring my self into the Grave. I had sundry of these thoughts, Sometimes it vexed me that I had seen such galant things, and must be *robbed* of them. Sometimes it rejoyced me that yet before my end I had been accepted to all joy, and should not be forced so shamefully to depart. This was the last and worst shock that I sustained; During these my Cogitations the rest were ready. Wherefore after they had received a good night from the King and Lords, each one was conducted into his Lodging. But I most wretched Man had no body to shew me the way, and yet must moreover suffer my self to be tormented, and that I might be certain of my future function, I was fain to put on the Ring, which the other had before worn. Finally, the King exhorted me, that since this was now the last time I was like to see him in this manner: I should however behave my self according to my place, and not against the order: Upon which he took me also in his Arms, and *kissed* me, all which I so understood, as if in the morning I must sit at my Gate. Now after they had all a while spoken friendly to me, and at last presented their Hands, committing me to the divine protection: I was by both the old Men, the Lord of the Tower, and *Atlas* conducted into a glorious Lodging, in which stood three Beds, and each of us lay in one of them, where we yet spent almost two, & c.

Here are wanting about two Leaves in quarto, and he (the Author hereof) whereas he imagined he must in the morning be Door-Keeper, returned home.

FINIS.

THE
FAME
AND
CONFESSION
OF THE
FRATERNITY
OF
R: C:

Commonly, of the

Rosie Cross.

WITH
A Præface annexed thereto, and a short
Declaration of their Physicall
Work.

By EUGENIUS PHILALETHES.

Jarch: apud Philostrat:

Καὶ γὰρ κέρδ⊙ οἶη, μήτε πιστύιν,
μήτε ἀπιστῶν πᾶσιν.

Veritas in Profundo.

London, Printed by *J. M.* for *Giles Calvert*, at the
black spread Eagle at the West end of Pauls. 1652

WE, the Bretheren of the *Fraternity* of the R.C. bestow our Greeting, Love and Prayers upon each and everyone who reads this our *Fama* of Christian intent.

Seeing the only Wise and Merciful God in these latter days hath poured out so richly his mercy and goodness to Mankind, wherby we do attain more and more to the perfect knowledge of his Son Jesus Christ and *Nature,* that justly we may boast of the happy time, wherein there is not only discovered unto us the half part of the World, which was heretofore unknown & hidden, that he hath also made manifest unto us many wonderful, and never-heretofore seen, Works and Creatures of *Nature,* and more over hath raised men, indued with great Wisdom, which might partly renew and reduce all Arts (in this our Age spotted and imperfect) to perfection; so that finally Man might thereby understand his own Nobleness and Worth, and why he is called *Microcosmus,* and how far his knowledg extendeth in Nature.

Although the rude World herewith will be but little pleased, but rather smile and scoff thereat; also the Pride and Covetousness of the Learned is so great, it will not suffer them to agree together; but were they united, they might out of all those things which in this our Age God doth so richly bestow upon us, collect *Librum Naturae,* or a perfect Method of all Arts: but such is their opposition, that they still keep, and are loth to leave the old course, esteeming *Porphiry, Aristotle,* and *Galen,* yea and that which hath put a meer shew of learning, more than the clear and manifested Light and Truth; who if they were now living, with much joy would leave their erroneous Doctrines. But here is too great weakness for such a great Work: And although in *Theologie, Physic,* and the *Mathematic,* the Truth doth manifest it self; nevertheless the old Enemy by his subtilty and craft doth shew himself in hindering every good purpose by his Instruments and contentious wavering people. To such an intent of a general Reformation, the most godly and highly illuminated Father, our Brother, *C. R.* a German, the chief and original of our Fraternity, hath much and long time laboured, who by reason of his poverty (although descended of Noble Parents) in the fifth year of his age was placed in a

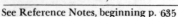

See Reference Notes, beginning p. 635

Cloyster, where he had learned indifferently the *Greek* and *Latin* Tongues, who (upon his earnest desire and request) being yet in his growing years, was associated to a Brother, *P. A. L.* who had determined to go to the Holy Land.

Although this Brother dyed in *Ciprus,* and so never came to *Jerusalem,* yet our Brother C. R. did not return, but shipped himself over, and went to *Damasco,* minding from thence to go to *Jerusalem*; but by reason of the feebleness of his body he remained still there, and by his skill in Physick he obtained much favour with the *Turks:* In the mean time he became by chance acquainted with the Wise men of *Damasco* in *Arabia,* and beheld what great Wonders they wrought, and how *Nature* was discovered unto them; hereby was that high and noble Spirit of Brother C. R. so stired up, that *Jerusalem* was not so much now in his mind as *Damasco;* also he could not bridle his desires any longer, but made a bargain with the *Arabians,* that they should carry him for a certain sum of money to *Damasco;* he was but of the age of sixteen years when he came thither, yet of a strong Dutch constitution; there the Wise received him (as he himself witnesseth) not as a stranger, but as one whom they had long expected, they called him by his name, and shewed him other secrets out of his Cloyster, whereat he could not but mightily wonder: He learned there better the *Arabian* Tongue; so that the year following he translated the Book *M.* into good *Latin,* which he afterwards brought with him. This is the place where he did learn his Physick, and his Mathematicks, whereof the World hath just cause to rejoyce, if there were more Love, and less Envy. After three years he returned again with good consent, shipped himself over *Sinus Arabicus* into *Egypt,* where he remained not long, but only took better notice there of the Plants and Creatures; he sailed over the whole *Mediterranean* Sea for to come unto *Fez,* where the *Arabians* had directed him. And it is a great shame unto us, that wise men, so far remote th'one from th' other, should not only be of one opinion, hating all contentious Writings, but also be so willing and ready under the seal of secrecy to impart their secrets to others.

Every year the *Arabians* and *Affricans* do send one to another, inquiring one of another out of their Arts, if happily

165

they had found out some better things, or if Experience had weakened their Reasons. Yearly there came something to light, whereby the *Mathematica, Physic* and *Magic* (for in those are they of *Fez* most skilful) were amended; as there is now adays in *Germany* no want of learned Men, *Magicians, Cabalists, Physicians,* and *Philosophers,* were there but more love and kindness among them, or that the most part of them would not keep their secrets close only to themselves. At *Fez* he did get acquaintance with those which are commonly called the Elementary Inhabitants, who revealed unto him many of their secrets: As we *Germans* likewise might gather together many things, if there were the like unity, and desire of searching out of secrets amongst us.

Of these of *Fez* he often did confess, that their *Magia* was not altogether pure, and also that their *Cabala* was defiled with their Religion; but notwithstanding he knew how to make good use of the same, and found still more better grounds of his Faith, altogether agreeable with the Harmony of the whole World, and wonderfully impressed in all Periods of times, and thence proceedeth that fair Concord, that as in every several kernel is contained a whole good tree or fruit, so likewise is included in the little body of Man the whole great World, whose Religion, policy, health, members, nature, language, words and works, are agreeing, sympathizing, and in equal tune and melody with God, Heaven and Earth; and that which is dis-agreeing with them, is error, falsehood, and of the Devil, who alone is the first, middle, and last cause of strife, blindness, and darkness in the World: Also, might one examine all and several persons upon the Earth, he should find that which is good and right, is always agreeing with it self; but all the rest is spotted with a thousand erroneous conceits.

After two years Brother C. R. departed the City *Fez,* and sailed with many costly things into *Spain,* hoping well, he himself had so well and so profitably spent his time in his travel, that the learned in *Europe* would highly rejoyce with him, and begin to rule, and order all their Studies, according to those sound and sure Foundations. He therefore conferred with the Learned in *Spain,* shewing unto them the Errors of our Arts, and how they might be corrected, and from whence they should gather the true *Inditia* of the Times to come, and wherein they ought to agree with those things that are past; also how the faults of the Church and the whole *Philosopia Moralis* was to be amended: He shewed them new Growths, new Fruits, and Beasts, which did concord with old *Philosophy*, and prescribed them new *Axiomata*, whereby all things might fully be restored: But it was to them a laughing matter; and being a new thing unto them, they feared that their great Name should be lessened, if they should now again begin to learn and acknowledg their many years Errors, to which they were accustomed, and wherewith they had gained them enough: Who-so loveth unquietness, let him be reformed.

The same Song was also sang to him by other Nations, the which moved him the more (because it happened to him contrary to his expectation,) being then ready bountifully to impart all his Arts and Secrets to the Learned, if they would have but undertaken to write the true and infallible *Axiomata*, out of all Faculties, Sciences and Arts, and whole *Nature*, as that which he knew would direct them, like a Globe, or Circle, to the onely middle Point, and *Centrum*, and (as it is usual among the *Arabians*) it should onely serve to the wise and learned for a Rule, that also there might be a Society in *Europe*, which might have Gold, Silver, and precious Stones, sufficient for to bestow them on Kings, for their necessary uses, and lawful purposes: with which such as be Governors might be brought up, for to learn all that which God hath suffered Man to know, and thereby to be enabled in all times of need to give their counsel unto those that seek it, like the Heathen Oracles: verily we must confess that the world in those days was already big with those great Commotions, laboring to be delivered of them; and did bring forth painful, worthy men, who brake with all force through Darkness and Barbarism, and left us who succeeded to follow them: and assuredly they have been the uppermost point in *Trygono igneo,* whose flame now should be more and more brighter, and shall undoubtedly give to the World the last Light.

Such a one likewise hath *Theophrastus** been in Vocation

*Theophrastus, Paracelsus of Hohenheim

167

nevertheless hath he diligently read over the Book *M.*: whereby his sharp *ingenium* was exalted; but this man was also hindered in his course by the multitude of the learned and wise-seeming men, that he was never able peaceably to confer with others of his Knowledg and Understanding he had of *Nature.* And therefore in his writing he rather mocked these busie bodies, and doth now shew them altogether what he was; yet nevertheless there is found with him well grounded the aforenamed *Harmonia,* which without doubt he had imparted to the Learned, if he had not found them rather worthy of subtil vexation, than to be instructed in greater Arts and Sciences; he then with a free and careless life lost his time, and left unto the World their foolish pleasures.

But that we do not forget our loving Father, Brother *C. R.* he after many painful Travels, and his fruitless true Instructions, returned again into *Germany,* the which he (by reason of the alterations* which were shortly to come, and of the strange and dangerous contentions) heartily loved: There, although he could have bragged with his Art, but specially of the transmutations of Metals; yet did he esteem more Heaven, and the Citizens thereof, Man, then all vain glory and pomp.

Nevertheless he built a fitting and neat habitation, in the which he ruminated his Voyage, and Philosophy, and reduced them together in a true Memorial. In this house he spent a great time in the *Mathematicks,* and made many fine Instruments, *ex omnibus hujus artis partibus,* whereof there is but little remaining to us, as hereafter you shall understand. After five years came again into his mind the wished for Reformation; and in regard he doubted of the ayd and help of others, although he himself was painful, lusty, and unwearisom, he undertook, with some few adjoyned with him, to attempt the same: wherefore he desired to that end, to have out of his first Cloyster (to the which he bare a great affection) three of his Brethren, Brother *G. V.* Brother *J. A.* and Brother *J. O.* who besides that, they had some more knowledg in the Arts, than at that time many others had, he did binde those three unto himself, to be faith-

---

*i.e., the Reformation

ful, diligent, and secret; as also to commit carefully to writing, all that which he should direct and instruct them in, to the end that those which were to come, and through especial Revelation should be received into this Fraternity, might not be deceived of the least sillable and word.

After this manner began the Fraternity of the *Rosie Cross;* first, by four persons onely, and by them was made the Magical Language and writing, with a large Dictionary, which we yet dayly use to Gods praise and glory, and do finde great wisdom therein; they made also the first part of the Book *M:* but in respect that that labor was too heavy, and the unspeakable concourse of the sick hindred them, and also whilst his new building (called *Sancti spiritus*) was now finished, they concluded to draw and receive yet others more into their Fraternity; to this end was chosen brother *R. C.* his deceased fathers brothers son, brother *B.* a skilful Painter, *G.* and *P. D.* their Secretary, all *Germains* except *J. A.* so in all they were eight in number, all batchelors and of vowed virginity, by those was collected a book or volumn of all that which man can desire, wish, or hope for.

Although we do now freely confess, that the World is much amended within an hundred years, yet we are assured, that our *Axiomata* shall unmovably remain unto the Worlds End, and also the world in her highest & last Age shall not attain to see any thing else; for our *Rota* takes her beginning from that day when God spake *Fiat,* and shall end when he shall speak *Pereat;* yet Gods Clock striketh every minute, where ours scarce striketh perfect hours. We also stedfastly beleeve, that if our Brethren and Fathers had lived in this our present and clear light, they would more roughly have handled the Pope, *Mahomet,* Scribes, Artists, and Sophisters, and had shewed themselves more helpful, not simply with sighs, and wishing of their end and consummation.

When now these eight Brethren had disposed and ordered all things in such manner, as there was not now need of any great labour, and also that every one was sufficiently instructed, and able perfectly to discourse of secret and manifest Philosophy, they would not remain any longer together, but as in the beginning they had agreed, they separated themselves into several Countries, because that not only their *Axi-*

omata might in secret be more profoundly examined by the learned, but that they themselves, if in some Country or other they observed any thing, or perceived some Error, they might inform one another of it.

Their Agreement was this; First, That none of them should profess any other thing, than to cure the sick, and that *gratis*. 2. None of the Posterity should be constrained to wear one certain kind of habit, but therein to follow the custom of the Country. 3. That every year upon the day *C.** they should meet together at the house *S. Spiritus,* or write the cause of his absence. 4. Every Brother should look about for a worthy person, who after his discease might succeed him. 5. The word *C. R.* should be their Seal, Mark, and Character. 6. The Fraternity should remain secret one hundred years. These six Articles they bound themselves one to another to keep; and five of the Brethren departed, only the Brethren *B.* and *D.* remained with the Father *Fra: R. C.* a whole year; when these likewise departed, then remained by him his Cousen and Brother *J. O.* so that he hath all the days of his life with him two of his Brethren. And although that as yet the Church was not cleansed, nevertheless we knew that they did think of her, and what with longing desire they looked for: Every year they assembled together with joy, and made a full resolution of that which they had done; there must certainly have been great pleasure, to hear truly and without invention related and rehearsed all the Wonders which God hath poured out here and there through the World. Every one may hold it out for certain, that such persons as were sent, and joyned together by God, and the Heavens; and chosen out of the wisest of men, as have lived in many Ages, did live together above all others in highest Unity, greatest Secrecy, and most kindness one towards another.

After such a most laudable sort they did spend their lives; and although they were free from all diseases and pain, yet notwithstanding they could not live and pass their time appointed of God. The first of this Fraternity which dyed, and that in *England,* was *J. O.* as Brother *C.* long before had foretold him; he was very expert, and well learned in *Cabala,* as

---

*i.e. Christmas Day

his Book called *H*. witnesseth: In *England* he is much spoken of, and chiefly because he cured a young Earl of *Norfolk* of the Leprosie. They had concluded, that as much as possibly could be their burial place should be kept secret, as at this day it is not known unto us what is become of some of them, yet every ones place was supplyed with a fit successor; but this we will confesse publickly by these presents to the honour of God, That what secret soever we have learned out of the book *M*. (although before our eyes we behold the image and *pattern* of all the world) yet are there not shewn unto us our misfortunes, nor hour of death, the which only is known to God himself, who thereby would have us keep in a continual readiness; but hereof more in our Confession, where do we set down 37 Reasons wherefore we now do make known our Fraternity, and proffer such high Mysteries freely, and without constraint and reward: also do we promise more gold than both the Indies bring to the King of *Spain*; for *Europe* is with child and wil bring forth a strong child, who shall stand in need of a great godfathers gift.

After the death of *J. O.* Brother *R. C.* rested not, but as soon as he could, called the rest together, (and as we suppose) then his grave was made; although hitherto we (who were the latest) did not know when our loving father *R. C.* died, and had no more but the bare names of the beginners, and all their successors to us; yet there came into our memory, a secret, which through dark and hidden words, and speeches of the 100 years, brother *A.* the successor of *D.* (who was of the last and second row and succession, and had lived amongst many of us,) did impart unto us of the third row and succession; otherwise we must confess, that after the death of the said *A.* none of us had in any manner known any thing of Brother *R. C.* and of his first fellow-brethren, than that which was extant of them in our Philosophical *Bibliotheca,* amongst which our *Axiomata* was held for the chiefest, *Rota Mundi,** for the most artificial, and *Protheus*

Rotae Mundi—A kind of cosmic "clock" or "wheel," described by Raimundus Lullus (1235-1315) in his *Ars Magna* and later by G.W.V. Leibnitz (1646-1716) in his *De Arte Combinatoria*. See also Rudolf Steiner, Lecture 10 in his Nuremberg cycle on *The Apocalypse.—Ed.*

[margin, handwritten:]

1st brother's death: J.O.

we know all things, except:

mentions the Confession

promise of gold ref. to Europe, macrocosm

A.

author tells of his acquisition of knowledge, after 100 years

Protheus; Meaning? "the most profitable."

the most profitable. Likewise we do not certainly know if these of the second row have been of the like wisdom as the first, and if they were admitted to all things. It shall be declared hereafter to the gentle Reader, not onely what we have heard of the burial of *R. C.* but also made manifest publickly by the foresight, sufferance and commandment of God, whom we most faithfully obey, that if we shall be answered discreetly and Christian-like, we will not be afraid to set forth publickly in Print, our names, and sirnames, our meetings, or any thing else that may be required at our hands.

public statement promised, if …

Now the true and fundamental relation of the finding out of the high illuminated man of God, *Fra: C. R. C.* is this: After that *A.* in *Gallia Narbonensi* was deceased, then succeeded in his place, our loving Brother *N. N.* this man after he had repaired unto us to take the solemn oath of fidelity and secrecy, he informed us *bona fide,* That *A.* had comforted him in telling him, that this Fraternity should ere long not remain so hidden, but should be to all the whole *German* Nation helpful, needful, and commendable; of the which he was not in any wise in his estate ashamed of. The year following after he had performed his School right, and was minded now to travel, being for that purpose sufficiently provided with *Fortunatus* purse, he thought (he being a good *Architect*) to alter something of his building, and to make it more fit: in such renewing he lighted upon the memorial Table which was cast of brasse, and containeth all the names of the brethren, with some few other things; this he would transfer in another more fitting vault: for where or when *Fra: R. C.* died, or in what country he was buried, was by our predecessors concealed and unknown unto us. In this Table stuck a great naile somewhat strong, so that when he was with force drawn out, he took with him an indifferent big stone out of the thin wall, or plaistering of the hidden door, and so unlooked for uncovered the door; wherefore we did with joy and longing throw down the rest of the wall, and cleared the door, upon which that was written in great letters, *Post 120 annos patebo,** with the year of the Lord o[o] under it; there-

prediction

finding CR's tomb

---

*"After 120 years I will open."
[o]1484.

fore we gave God thanks and let it rest that same night, because first we would overlook our *Rotam*: but we refer our selves again to the Confession, for what we here publish is done for the help of those that are worthy, but to the unworthy (God willing) it will be small profit: For like as our door was after so many years wonderfully discovered, also there shall be opened a door to *Europe* (when the wall is removed) which already doth begin to appear, and with great desire is expected of many.

In the morning following we opened the door, and there appeared to our sight a Vault of seven sides and corners, every side five foot broad, and the height of eight foot; Although the Sun never shined in this Vault, nevertheless it was enlightned with another sun, which had learned this from the Sun, and was scituated in the upper part in the Center of the sieling; in the midst, in stead of a Tomb-stone, was a round Altar covered over with a plate of brass, and thereon this engraven:

A. C. R.C. Hoc universi compendium
unius mili sepulchrum feci. *

Round about the first Circle or Brim stood,

Jesus mihi omnia. °

In the middle were four figures, inclosed in circles, whose circumscription was,

    1. *Nequaquam vacuum.*
    2. *Legis Jugum.*
    3. *Libertas Evangelij.*
    4. *Dei gloria intacta.* #

---

*For *unius* read *vivus.* "This compendium of the Universe I made in my lifetime to be my tomb."

°"Jesus is my all."

#"A vacuum exists nowhere.
The yoke of the Law
The Liberty of the Gospel
The Entire Glory of God."

This is all clear and bright, as also the seven sides and the two *Heptagoni*: so we kneeled altogether down, and gave thanks to the sole wise, sole mighty and sole eternal God, who hath taught us more than all mens wit could have found out, praised be his holy name. This Vault we parted in three parts, the upper part or sieling, the wall or side, the ground or floor.

Of the upper part you shall understand no more of it at this time, but that it was divided according to the seven sides in the triangle, which was in the bright center; but what therein is contained, you shall God willing (that are desirous of our society) behold the same with your own eys; but every side or wall is parted into ten squares, every one with their several figures and sentences, as they are truly shewed, and set forth *Concentratum* here in our book.

The bottom again is parted in the triangle, but because therein is discribed the power and rule of the inferior Governors, we leave to manifest the same, for fear of the abuse by the evil and ungodly world. But those that are provided and stored with the heavenly Antidote, they do without fear or hurt, tread on, and bruise the head of the old and evil serpent, which this our age is well fitted for: every side or wall had a door for a chest, wherein there lay divers things, especially all our books, which otherwise we had, besides the *Vocabular* of *Theoph: Par. Ho.** and these which daily unfalsifieth we do participate.⁰ Herein also we found our Father's *Itinerarium,* and *vitam,* whence this relation for the most part is taken. In another chest were looking-glasses of divers virtues, as also in other places were little bells, burning lamps, & chiefly wonderful artificial Songs; generally al done to that end, that if it should happen after many hundred years, the Order or Fraternity should come to nothing, they might by this onely Vault be restored again.

Now as yet we had not seen the dead body of our careful and wise Father, we therefore removed the Altar aside, there we lifted up a strong plate of brass, and found a fair and worthy body, whole and unconsumed, as the same is here

---

*"Theophrastus Paracelsus of Hohenheim"

⁰or, "and which we daily communicate unfalsified"

lively counterfeited, with all the Ornaments and Attires; in his hand he held a parchment book, called T,[+] the which next unto the Bible, is our greatest treasure, which ought not lightly to be delivered to the censure of the world. At the end of this book standeth this following *Elogium**

Granum pectori Jesu insitum.

C. Ros. C. ex nobili atque splendida Germaniae R.C. familia oriundus, vir sui seculi divinis revelationibus subtilissimis imaginationibus, indefessis laboribus ad coelestia, atque humana mysteria; arcanave admissus postquam suam (quam Arabico, & Africano itineribus Collegerat) plusquam regiam, atque imperatoriam Gazam suo seculo nondum convenientem, posteritati eruendam custo divisset & jam suarum Artium, ut & nominis, fides acconjunctissimos herides instituisset, mundum minutum omnibus motibus magno illi respondentem fabricasset hocque tandem preteritarum, praesentium, & futurarum, rerum compendio extracto, centenario major non morbo (quem ipse nunquam corpors expertus erat, nunquam alios infestare sinebat) ullo pellente sed spiritu Dei evocante, illuminatam animam (inter Fratrum amplexus & ultima oscula) fidelissimo creatori Deo reddidisset, Pater dilectissimus, Fra: suavissimus, praeceptor fidelissimus amicus integerimus, a suis ad 120 annos hic absconditus est.

[+]Testament or Thesaurus.

*A Grain Buried in the Breast of Jesus. C. Ros. C., sprung from the noble and renowned German family of R.C.; a man admitted into the Mysteries and secrets of heaven and earth through the divine revelations, subtle cogitations and unwearied toil of his life. In his journeys through Arabia and Africa he collected a treasure surpassing that of Kings and Emperors; but finding it not suitable for his times, he kept it guarded for posterity to uncover, and appointed loyal and faithful heirs of his arts and also of his name. He constructed a microcosm corresponding in all motions to the Macrocosm and finally drew up this compendium of things past, present and to come. Then, having now passed the century of years, though oppressed by no disease, which he had neither felt in his own body nor allowed to attack others, but summoned by the Spirit of God, amid the last embraces of his bretheren he rendered up his illuminated soul to God his Creator. A beloved Father, an affectionate Brother, a faithful Teacher, a loyal Friend, he was hidden here by his disciples for 120 years.

175

Underneath they had subscribed themselves,

1 *Fra: I. A. Fr. C. H. electione Fraternitatis caput.*[o]
2 *Fr: G. V. M. P. C.*
3 *Fra: R. C. Iunior haeres S. Spiritus.*
4 *Fra: B.M.P.A. Pictor & Architectus.*
5 *Fr: G. G. M. P. I. Cabalista.*

Secundi Circuli.

1 *Fra: P. A. Successor, Fr: I. O. Mathematicus.*
2 *Fra: A. Successor Fra. P. D.*
3 *Fra: R. Successor patris C. R. C. cum Christo triumphantis.*

At the end was written,
Ex Deo nascimur, in Jesu morimur, per Spiritum Sanctum reviviscimus. [*]

At that time was already dead Brother *I. O.* and *Fra: D* but their burial place where is it to be found? we doubt not but our *Fra: Senior* hath the same, and some especial thing layd in Earth, and perhaps likewise hidden: we also hope that this our Example will stir up others more deligently to enquire after their names (whom we have therefore published) and to search for the place of their burial; for the most part of them, by reason of their practice and physick, are yet known, and praised among very old folks; so might perhaps our *Gaza* be enlarged, or at least be better cleared.

Concerning *Minutum Mundum,* we found it kept in another little Altar, truly more finer than can be imagined by any understanding man; but we will leave him undescribed, untill we shal truly be answered upon this our true hearted *Famam;* and so we have covered it again with the plates, and set the altar thereon, shut the door, and made it sure, with all our seals; besides by instruction and command of

---

[o] By the choice of Fr. C. H., head of the Fraternity.

[*] Out of God we are born, in Jesus we die, through the Holy Spirit we are reborn.

176

our *Rota*, there are come to sight some books, among which is contained *M.* (which were made in stead of household care by the praise-worthy *M. P.*) Finally we departed the one from the other, and left the natural heirs in possession of our Jewels. And so we do expect the answer and judgment of the learned, or unlearned.

Howbeit we know after a time there will now be a general reformation, both of divine and humane things, according to our desire, and the expectation of others: for it's fitting, that before the rising of the Sun, there should appear and break forth *Aurora*, or some clearness, or divine light in the sky; and so in the mean time some few, which shall give their names, may joyn together, thereby to increase the number and respect of our *Fraternity*, and make a happy and wished for beginning of our *Philosophical Canons*, prescribed to us by our brother *R. C.* and be partakers with us of our treasures (which never can fail or be wasted) in all humility, and love to be eased of this worlds labor, and not walk so blindly in the knowledge of the wonderful works of God.

But that also every Christian may know of what Religion and belief we are, we confess to have the knowledge of Jesus Christ (as the same now in these last days, and chiefly in *Germany*, most clear and pure is professed, and is now adays cleansed and voyd of all swerving people, Hereticks, and false Prophets,) in certain and noted Countries maintained, defended and propagated: Also we use two Sacraments, as they are instituted with all *Formes* and *Ceremonies* of the first renewed Church. In *Politia* we acknowledge the *Roman* Empire and *Quartam Monarchiam** for our Christian head; albeit we know what alterations be at hand, and would fain impart the same with all our hearts, to other godly learned men; notwithstanding our hand-writing which is in our hands, no man (except God alone) can make it common, nor any unworthy person is able to bereave us of it. But we shall help with secret aid this so good a cause, as God shal permit or hinder us: For our God is not blinde, as the Heathens *Fortuna*, but is the Churches Ornament, and the honor of

---

*The Fourth Kingdom, *see* Daniel 7: 16-28.

the Temple. Our *Philosophy* also is not a new Invention, but as *Adam* after his *fall* hath received it, and as *Moses* and *Solomon* used it; also she ought not much to be doubted of, or contradicted by other opinions, or meanings; but seeing the truth is peaceable, brief, and always like her self in all things, and especially accorded by with *Jesus in omni parte* and all members. And as he is the true Image of the Father, so is she his Image; It shal not be said, this is true according to *Philosophy*, but true according to *Theologie;* And wherein *Plato, Aristotle, Pythagoras* and others did hit the mark, and wherein *Enoch, Abraham, Moses, Solomon* did excel; but especially wherewith that wonderful book the *Bible* agreeth. All that same concurreth together, and make a Sphere or Globe, whose total parts are equidistant from the Center, as hereof more at large and more plain shal be spoken of in Christianly Conference.

But now concerning (and chiefly in this our age) the ungodly and accursed *Gold-making,* which hath gotten so much the upper hand, whereby under colour of it, many runagates and roguish people do use great villanies, and cozen and abuse the credit which is given them: yea now adays men of discretion do hold the transmutation of Mettals to be the highest point, and *fastigium* in *Philosophy,* this is all their intent, and desire, and that God would be most esteemed by them, and honored, which could make great store of Gold, and in abundance, the which with unpremeditate prayers, they hope to attain of the alknowing God, and searchers of all hearts: we therefore do by these presents publickly testifie, That the true *Philosophers* are far of another minde, esteeming little the making of Gold, which is but a *parergon;* for besides that they have a thousand better things.

And we say with our loving Father *R. C. C. Phy: aurum nisi quantum aurum,* for unto them the whole nature is detected: he doth not rejoyce, that he can make Gold, and that, as saith Christ, the devils are obedient unto him; but is glad that he seeth the Heavens open, and the Angels of God ascending and descending, and his name written in the book of life. Also we do testifie that under the name of *Chymia* many books and pictures are set forth in *Contumeliam gloria Dei,* as we wil name them in their due season, and

178

wil give to the pure-hearted a Catalogue, or Register of them: And we pray all learned men to take heed of these kinde of Books; for the enemy never resteth, but soweth his weeds, til a stronger one doth root it out. So according to the wil and meaning of *Fra: C. R. C.* we his brethren request again all the learned in *Europe,* who shal read (sent forth in five Languages) this our *Famam* and *Confessionem,* that it would please them with good deliberation to ponder this our offer, and to examine most nearly and most sharply their Arts, and behold the present time with all diligence, and to declare their minde, either *Communicato consilio,* or *singulatim* by Print.

And although at this time we make no mention either of our names, or meetings, yet nevertheless every ones opinion shal assuredly come to our hands, in what language so ever it be; nor any body shal fail, who so gives but his name to speak with some of us, either by word of mouth, or else if there be some lett in writing. And this we say for a truth, That whosoever shal earnestly, and from his heart, bear affection unto us, it shal be beneficial to him in goods, body and soul; but he that is false-hearted, or onely greedy of riches, the same first of all shal not be able in any manner of wise to hurt us, but bring himself to utter ruine and destruction. Also our building (although one hundred thousand people had very near seen and beheld the same) shal for ever remain untouched, undestroyed, and hidden to the wicked world, *sub umbra alarum tuarum Jehova.**

A Preface of the Confession to the
Reader who is desirous of
Wisdom.

Here Gentle Reader, you shal finde incorporated in our Confession thirty seven Reasons of our purpose, and intention, the which according to thy pleasure thou mayst seek out and compare them together: thou mayst also consider with thy self, if they be weighty, and sufficient enough to bring and perswade thee for to take our parts.

---

*"Under the shadow of thy wings, Jehovah"

Verily it requires no smal pains to confirm that which men have not yet seen, but when it shal once com to light we doubt not, but they will then justly be ashamed of such doubts, and conjectures. And as we do now altogether securely, free ly, and without any hurt call the *Pope* of *Rome* Antichrist, the which heretofore was held for a deadly sin, and such in all Countries were put to death for it. So we know certainly, that the time shal likewise come, that that which we yet keep in secret, we shal openly, freely, and with a loud voice publish and confess it before al the world; the which *Gentle Reader* wish with us with all thy heart, that it may happen with speed.

[margin: claims]
[margin: RC's, tov?]
[margin: anti-Pope]

Confessio Fraternitatis,
Or,
The Confession *of the laudable Fraternity of the most honorable Order of
the* Rosie Cross, *written to
the Learned of* Europe.

[margin: "... to the learned".]

Whatsoever there is published, and made known to every one, concerning our *Fraternity,* by the foresaid *Fama,* let no man esteem lightly of it, nor hold it as an idle or invented thing, and much less receive the same, as though it were onely a meer conceit of ours. It is the Lord *Jehovah* (who seeing the Lords Sabbath is almost at hand, and hastened again, his period or course being finished, to his first beginning) doth turn about the course of Nature; and what heretofore hath been sought with great pains, and dayly labor, is now manifested unto those who make small account, or scarcely once think upon it; but these which desire it, it is in a manner forced and thrusted upon them, that thereby the life of the godly may be eased of all their toyl and labor, and be no more subject to the storms of unconstant Fortune; but the wickedness of the ungodly thereby, with their due and deserved punishment, be augmented and multiplied.

[margin: a NEW CYCLE...]

Although we cannot be by any suspected of the least Heresie, or of any wicked beginning, or purpose against the worldly Government; we do condemn the East and the West, (meaning the *Pope* and *Mahomet*) blasphemers against our

[margin: condemnation of Pope & Mahomet cf 184]

Lord Jesus Christ, and offer and present with a good will to the chief head of the Romish Empire, our prayers, secrets, and great treasures of Gold.

Yet we have thought good, and fit for the Learned sakes, to add somewhat more to this, and make a better explanation, if there be any thing too deep, hidden, and set down over dark in the *Fama*, or for certain reasons were altogether omitted, and left out; hoping herewith the Learned will be more addicted unto us, and be made far more fitter and willing for our purpose.

Concerning the alteration and amendment of *Philosophy*, we have (as much as at this present is needful) sufficiently declared, to wit, that the same is altogether weak and faulty; yet we doubt not, although the most part falsly to alledge that she (I know not how) is sound and strong, yet notwithstanding she fetches her last breath and is departing.

But as commonly, even in the same place or Country where there breaketh forth a new unaccustomed disease, Nature also there discovereth a medicine against the same; so there doth appear for so manifold infirmities of *Philosophy*, the right means, and unto our *Patria* sufficiently offered, whereby she may become sound again, which is now to be renewed and altogether new.

No other *Philosophy* we have, than that which is the head & sum, the foundation and contents of all faculties, sciences and arts, the which (if we will behold our age) containeth much of *Theology* and medicine, but little of the wisdom of Lawyers, and doth diligently search both heaven and earth: or, to speak briefly thereof, which doth manifest and declare sufficiently Man; whereof then all Learned who will make themselves known unto us, and come into our brotherhood, shall finde more wonderful secrets by us then heretofore they did attain unto, and did know, or are able to believe or utter.

Wherefore, to declare briefly our meaning hereof, we ought to labor carefully that there be not onely a wondering at our meeting and adhortation, but that likewise every one may know, that although we do highly esteem and regard such mysteries and secrets, we nevertheless hold it fit, that the knowledge thereof be manifested and revealed to many.

For it is to be taught and believed, that this our unhoped willing offer wil raise many and divers thoughts in men, unto whom (as yet) be unknown *Miranda sexta aetatis*, or those which by reason of the course of the world, esteem the things to come like unto the present, and are hindred through all manner of importunities of this their time, so that they live no otherwise in the world, then blinde fools, who can, in the clear Sun-shine day, discern and know nothing, then onely by feeling.

Now concerning the first part, we hold this, that the Meditations, knowledge and inventions of our loving Christian Father (of all that, which from the beginning of the world, *Mans Wisdom,* either through Gods Revelation, or through the service of the Angels and spirits, or through the sharpness and deepness of understanding, or through long observation, use and experience, hath found out, invented brought forth, corrected, and till now hath been propagated & transplanted) are so excellent worthy and great, that if all books should perish, and by Gods almighty suffrance, all writings, & all lerning should be lost, yet the posterity will be able onely thereby to lay a new foundation, and bring truth to light again; the which perhaps would not be so hard to do if one should begin to pull down and destroy the old ruinous building, and then begin to enlarge the fore Court, afterwards bring the lights in the Lodgings, and then change the doors, staples and other things according to our intention.

But to whom would not this be acceptable, for to be manifested to every one rather than to have it kept and spared, as an especial ornament for the appointed 'time to come?

Wherefore should we not with all our hearts rest and remain in the onely truth (which men through so many erroneous and crooked ways do seek) if it had onely pleased God to lighten unto us the sixth *Candelabrum?* were it not good that we needed not to care, not to fear hunger, poverty, sickness and age?

Were it not a precious thing, that you could always live so, as if you had liv'd from the beginning of the world, and moreover, as you should stil live to the end thereof? Were it not excellent, you dwel in one place, that neither the people which dwel beyond the River *Ganges* in the *Indies* could

182

hide any thing, nor those who live in *Peru* might be able to keep secret their counsels from thee?

Were it not a precious thing, that you could so read in one onely book, and withal by reading understand, and remember all that, which in all other books (which heretofore have been, and are now, and hereafter shal come out) hath been, is, and shal be learned, and found out of them?

How pleasant were it, that you could so sing, that in stead of stony rocks you could draw to* the pearls and precious stones, in stead of wilde beasts, spirits, and in stead of hellish *Pluto,* move the mighty Princes of the world?

O ye people, Gods counsel is far otherwise, who hath concluded now to encrease and enlarge the number of our *Fraternity,* the which we with such joy have undertaken, as we have heretofore obtained this great treasure without our merits, yea without any our hopes, and thoughts; and purpose with the like fidelity to put the same in practice, that neither the compassion nor pity of our own children (which some of us in the *Fraternity* have) shal draw us from it, because we know that these unhoped for goods cannot be inherited, nor by chance be obtained.

If there be some body now, which on the other side wil complain of our discretion, that we offer our Treasures so freely, and without any difference to all men, and do not rather regard and respect more the godly, learned, wise, or princely persons, then the common people; those we do not contradict, seeing it is not a slight and easie matter; but withall we signifie so much, that our *Arcana* or Secrets will no ways be common, and generally made known: Although the *Fama* be set forth in five languages, and is manifested to every one, yet we do partly very well know, that the unlearned and gross wits will not receive, nor regard the same; as also the worthiness of those who shall be accepted into our Fraternity are not esteemed and known of us by Mans Carefulness, but by the Rule of our Revelation and Manifestation. Wherefore if the unworthy cry and call a thousand times, or if they shall offer and present themselves to us a thousand times, yet God hath commanded our ears, that they should

---

*"to yourself pearls..."

hear none of them: yea, God hath so compassed us about with his Clouds, that unto us his servants no violence or force can be done or committed; wherefore we neither can be seen or known by any body, except he had the eyes of an Eagle. It hath been necessary that the *Fama* should be set forth in every ones Mother Tongue, because those should not be defrauded of the knowledg thereof, whom (although they be unlearned) God hath not excluded from the happiness of this Fraternity; the which shall be divided and parted into certain degrees; as those which dwell in the City *Damcar* in *Arabia,* who have a far different politick order from the other *Arabians.* For there do govern only wise and understanding men, who by the Kings permission make particular Laws; according unto which example also the Government shall be instituted in *Europe* (whereof we have a description set down by our Christianly Father) when first is done and come to pass that which is to precede. And thenceforth our Trumpet shall publiquely sound with a loud sound, and great noise, when namely the same (which at this present is shewed by few, and is secretly, as a thing to come, declared in Figures and Pictures) shall be free, and publiquely proclaimed, and the whole World be filled withall. Even in such manner as heretofore, many godly people have secretly and altogether desperately pusht at the Popes Tyranny, which afterwards, with great earnest, and especial zeal in *Germany,* was thrown from his seat, and trodden under-foot, whose final fall is delayed, and kept for our times, when he also shall be scratched in pieces with nails, and an end be made of his Asses cry, by a new voyce: The which we know is already reasonably manifest and known to many learned men in *Germany,* as their Writings and secret Congratulations do sufficiently witness the same.

We could here relate and declare what all the time, from the year of our Lord 1378. (in which year our Christian Father was born) till now, hath happened, where we might rehearse what alterations he hath seen in the World these one hundred six years of his life, which he hath left to our Brethren and us after his decease to peruse: But brevity, which we do observe, will not permit at this present to make rehearsal of it, till a more fit time: At this time it is enough for

184

these which do not despise our Declaration, having therefore briefly touched it, thereby to prepare the way for their acquaintance and friendship with us.

secret — 186 law. [handwritten margin note]

To the Good: for Reform, join the Fast [handwritten margin note]

Yea, to whom it is permitted, that he may see, and for his instruction use those great Letters and Characters which the Lord God hath written and imprinted in Heaven and Earths Edifice, through the alteration of Government, which hath been from time to time altered and renewed; the same is already (although as yet unknown to himself) ours: And as we know he will not despise our inviting and calling, so none shall fear any deceit; for we promise, and openly say, That no mans uprightness and hopes shall deceive him, whosoever shall make himself known unto us under the Seal of Secrecy, and desire our Fraternity.

To the evil... [handwritten margin note]

But to the false Hypocrites, and to those that seek other things then Wisdom, we say and witness by these presents publickely, we cannot be made known, and be betrayed unto them; and much less they shall be able to hurt us any manner of way without the Will of God; but they shall certainly be partakers of all the punishment spoken of in our *Fama;* so their wicked Counsels shall light upon themselves, and our Treasures shall remain untouched and unstirred, until the Lion doth come, who will ask them for his use, and imploy them for the confirmation and establishment of his Kingdom. We ought therefore here to observe well, and make it known unto every one, that God hath certainly and most assuredly concluded to send and grant to the World before her end, which presently there upon shall ensue, such a Truth, Light, Life and Glory, as the first man *Adam* had, which he lost in Paradise, after the which his successors were put, and driven with him to misery: Wherefore there shall cease all servitude, falshood, lyes, and darkness, which by little and little, with the great Worlds Revolution, was crept into all Arts, Works and Governments of Men, and have darkened the most part of them. For from thence are proceeded an innumerable sort of all manner of false Opinions and Heresies, that scarce the wisest of all was able to know whose Doctrine and Opinion he should follow and embrace, and could not well and easily be discerned; seeing on the one part they were detained, hindered, and brought into Errors through the respect of the

Philosophers and learned men, and on the other part through true experience. All the which, when it shall once be abolished and removed, and in stead threof a right and true Rule instituted, then there will remain thanks unto them which have taken pains therein; but the Work it self shall be attributed to the Blessedness of our Age.

As we now willingly confess, that many principal men by their Writings will be a great furtherance unto this Reformation which is to come; so we desire not to have this honour ascribed to us, as if such Work were only commanded and imposed upon us; but we confess, and witness openly with the Lord Jesus Christ, that it shall first happen that the stones shall arise, and offer their service, before there shall be any want of Executors and Accomplishers of Gods Counsel: yea the Lord God hath already sent before certain Messengers, which should testifie his Will, to wit, some new Stars, which do appear and are seen in the Firmament in *Serpentario* and *Cygno*, which signifie and give themselves known to every one, that they are powerful *Signacula* of great weighty matters. So then, the secret hid Writings and Characters are most necessary for all such things which are found out by Men: Although that great Book of Nature stand open to all Men, yet there are but few that can read and understand the same. For as there is given to Man two instruments to hear, likewise two to see, and two to smell, but only one to speak, and it were but vain to expect speech from the ears, of hearing from the eyes: So there hath been Ages or Times which have seen, there have also been Ages that have heard, smelt, and tasted: now there remains yet that which in short time, honour shall be likewise given to the Tongue, and by the same; what before times hath been seen, heard, and smelt, now finally shall be spoken and uttered forth, *viz.* when the World shall awake out of her heavy and drowsie sleep, and with an open heart, bare-head and barefoot, shall merrily and joyfully meet the now arising Sun.

These Characters and Letters, as God hath here and there incorporated them in the holy Scripture the *Bible,* so hath he imprinted them most apparently into the Wonderful Creation of Heaven and Earth, yea in all Beasts. So that like as the *Mathematician* or *Astronomer* can long before see and know the Eclipses which are to come, so we may verily fore-know and fore-see the darkness of Obscurations of the Church, and how long they shall last: From the which Characters or Letters we have borrowed our *Magick* writing, and have found out, and made a new Language for our selves, in the which withall is expressed and declared the Nature of all Things: So that it is no wonder that we are not so eloquent in other Languages, the which we know that they are altogether disagreeing to the Languages of our forefathers, *Adam* and *Enoch,* and were through the Babylonical Confusion wholly hidden.

But we must also let you understand, that there are yet some *Eagles Feathers* in our way, the which do hinder our purpose. Wherefore we do admonish every one for to read diligently and continually the holy *Bible;* for he that taketh all his pleasures therein, he shall know that he prepared for himself an excellent way to come in to our *Fraternity:* For as this is the whole sum and content of our Rule, That every Letter or Character which is in the World ought to be learned and regarded well; so those are like unto us, and are very near allyed unto us, who do make the holy *Bible* a Rule of their life, and an aim and end of all their studies; yea to let it be a *Compendium* and Content of the whole World: And not only to have it continually in the mouth, but to know how to apply and direct the true understanding of it to all times and Ages of the World. Also, it is not our Custom to prostitute and make so common the holy *Scriptures;* for there are innumerable Expounders of the same; some alledging and wresting it to serve for their Opinion, some to scandal it, and most wickedly do liken it to a Nose of Wax, which alike should serve the *Divines, Philosophers, Physicians* and *Mathematicians,* against all the which we do openly witness and acknowledg, That from the beginning of the World there hath not been given unto Men a more worthy, a more excellent, and more admirable and wholesom Book then the holy *Bible*; Blessed is he that hath the same, yea more blessed is he who reads it diligently, but most blessed of all is he that truly understandeth the same, for he is most like to God, and doth come most near to him. But whatsoever hath been said in the *Fama* concerning the Deceivers against the Transmu-

secret
lang.
184–186

Read Bible =
Compendium of whole
world

tation of *Mettals,* and the highest *Medicine* in the World, the same is thus to be understood, that this is so great gift of God we do in no manner set at naught, or despise it. But because she bringeth not with her always the knowledg of *Nature,* but this bringeth forth not only *Medicine,* but also maketh manifest and open unto us innumerable *Secrets* and *Wonders;* Therefore it is requisite, that we be earnest to attain to the understanding and knowledg of *Philosophy.* And moreover, excellent Wits ought not to be drawn to the Tincture of *Mettals,* before they be exercised well in the knowledg of *Nature.* He must needs be an unsatiable Creature, who is come so far, that neither Poverty nor Sickness can hurt him; yea, who is exalted above all other men, and hath Rule over that, the which doth anguish, trouble and pain others, yet will give himself again to idle things, as to build houses, make Wars, and use all manner of Pride, because he hath of Gold and Silver infinite store.

God is far otherwise pleased, for he exalteth the *lowly,* and pulleth down the *proud* with disdain; to those which are of *few words* he sendeth his holy Angel to speak with them, but the *unclean Bablers* he driveth in the Wilderness and solitary places: The which is the right Reward of the *Romish Seducers,* who have vomitted forth their *Blasphemies* against *Christ,* and as yet do not abstain from their Lyes in this clear shining Light: In *Germany* all their Abominations and detestable Tricks have been disclosed, that thereby he may fully fulfill the measure of sin, and draw near to the end of his punishment. Therefore one day it will come to pass, that the Mouth of those Vipers will be stopped, and the three double Horn will be brought to nought, as thereof at our Meeting shall more plain and at large be discoursed.

For Conclusion of our *Confession,* we must earnestly admonish you, that you put away, if not all, yet the most Books written by false *Alchimists,* who do think it but a Jest, or a Pastime, when they either misuse the holy *Trinity,* when they do apply it to vain things, or deceive the people with most strange Figures, and dark Sentences and Speeches, and cozen the simple of their money; as there are now adays too many such Books set forth, which the Enemy of Mans Welfare doth dayly, and will to the end, mingle among the good

Seed, thereby to make the Truth more difficult to be beleeved, which in her self is simple, easie, and naked; but contrarily Falshood is proud, haughty, and coloured with a kind of Lustre of seeming godly and of humane Wisdom. Ye that are wise eschew such Books, and turn unto us, who seek not your moneys, but offer unto you most willingly our great *Treasures:* We hunt not after your Goods with invented lying *Tinctures,* but desire to make you Partakers of our Goods: We speak unto you not by *Parables,* but would willingly bring you to the right, simple, easie, and ingenuous Exposition, Understanding, Declaration and Knowledg of all *Secrets.* We desire not to be received of you, but invite you unto our more than Kingly Houses and Palaces, and that verily not by our own proper motion, but (that you likewise may know it) as forced unto it, by the Instigation of the Spirit of God, by his Admonition, and by the Occasion of this present time.

What think you, loving people, and how seem you affected, seeing that you now understand and know, That we acknowledg our selves truly and sincerely to profess *Christ,* condemn the *Pope,* addict our selves to the true *Philosophy,* lead a *Christian life,* and dayly call, intreat and invite many more unto our *Fraternity,* unto whom the same Light of God likewise appeareth? Consider you not at length how you might begin with us, not only by pondering the Gifts which are in you, and by experience which you have in the Word of God, beside the careful Consideration of the Imperfection of all *Arts,* and many other unfitting things, to seek for an amendment therein; to appease God, and to accommodate you for the time wherein you live. Certainly if you will perform the same, this profit will follow, That all those Goods which *Nature* hath in all parts of the World wonderfully dispersed, shall at one time altogether be given unto you, and shall easily disburden you of all that which obscureth the Understanding of Man, and hindereth the working thereof, like unto the vain *Epicides,* and Excentrick *Astronomical Circles.*

But those Pragmatical and busie-headed men, who either are blinded with the glistering of Gold, or (to say more truly) who are now honest, but by thinking such great Riches should never fail, might easily be corrupted, and brought to Idleness, and to riotous proud living: Those we do desire that they would not trouble us with their idle and vain crying. But let them think, that although there be a *Medicine* to be had which might fully cure all Diseases, nevertheless those whom God hath destinated to plague with Diseases, and to keep them under the Rod of Correction, such shall never obtain any such *Medicine*.

Even in such manner, although we might inrich the whole World, and endue them with Learning, and might release it from Innumerable Miseries, yet shall we never be manifested and made known unto any man, without the especial pleasure of God; yea, it shall be so far from him whosoever thinks to get the benefit, and be Partaker of our Riches and Knowledg, without and against the Will of God, that he shall sooner lose his life in seeking and searching for us, then to find us, and attain to come to the wished Happiness of the *Fraternity* of the *Rosie Cross*.

the evil cannot
find us, and
will not, even

Chymische Hoch-
zeit:
Christiani Rosencreutz.
ANNO 1459.

Arcana publicata vilescunt; & gra-
tiam prophanata amittunt.

Ergo: ne Margaritas obijce porcis, seu
Asino substerne rosas.

Straßburg,
In Verlägung / Lazari Zetzners.
Anno M. DC. XVI.

Title Page of First Edition of *The Chymical Wedding of Christian Rosenkreutz*, 1616. The book was published four times that year in Strassburg, with
this title page.

Straßburg/

SIMPLEX SPES   PRUDENTIA FIRMA.

Gedruckt bey Conrad Scher/

Im Jahr/ M. DC. XVI.

Printer's Device and Colophon from the First Edition of *The Chymical Wedding*, Strassburg, 1616. This device appears at the end of the book and was *not* included in any of the other three editions printed that same year.

Johann Valentin Andreae in 1616, the year of the appearance of *The Chymical Wedding of Christian Rosenkreutz*. Published in his *Turbo sive moleste et frustra per Cuncta Divagans ingenium, in theatrum productum. Helicone juxta Parnassum*, 1616.

Johann Valentin Andreae (1586-1654), a portrait supposedly painted from life. His signature and family coat of arms are reproduced below.

Johann Valentin Andreae, from an engraving made late in life. The words of *The Chymical Wedding* are those of Andreae; the deeds were those of Christian Rosenkreutz.

The Sign of Invitation to the Chymical Wedding. Facsimile of the title page of *The Monad, Hieroglyphically, Mathematically, Magically, Cabalistically and Anagogically Explained,* by Dr. John Dee, advisor to Queen Elizabeth I, published at Antwerp, 1564. Dedicated to Maximilian, King of Bohemia, this work is important for an understanding of the esoteric significance of the sign on the letter of invitation to *The Chymical Wedding* sent to Christian Rosenkreutz.

Cutting the Egg of the Philosophers. Reminiscent of the same scene in *The Chymical Wedding*, this engraving is by Johannes Theodorus de Bry (1561-1623), famous copper engraver at Frankfort a.M., illustrator of works by Fludd, Maier, and many others. This plate is from Michael Maier's *Atalanta Fugiens*, 1618.

The Seven Maidens. An engraving by deBry from the *Musaeum Hermeticum*,
1625. A choir of seven maidens sings to the accompaniment of a lyre within
a grotto, while above three figures display alchemical symbols of fire, water,
and of "universal matter." These maidens are comparable to the seven virgins
in *The Chymical Wedding*, who in turn have been compared to the seven
Liberal Arts.

The Rebirth of the King. From *Splendor Solis* by Solomon Trismosin, "teacher of Paracelsus," 1582. The details of the plate invite comparison with motifs in *The Chymical Wedding* and *The Parabola*.

Elias Ashmole, F.R.S., 1617-1692. An engraving published in London, 1707. Founder of the Ashmolean Museum, Oxford, compiler of the *Theatrum Chemicum Britannicum*, 1652, Ashmole was a famous patron of the hermetic arts, associated with astrologers, scholars, alchemists, cabbalists and Rosicrucians alike. A manuscript draft of *The Fame and Confession of the Brothers of the Rosy Cross* in his own handwriting is preserved at Oxford, attesting his personal interest in Risocrucian matters.

Unicorn, Deer, Lion and Fountain. Motifs associated with *The Chymical Wedding* are clearly visible in this reproduction of one of the Unicorn Tapestries at the Cloisters of the Metropolitan Museum of Art in New York. In the *Book of Lambspring*, 1625, is said, "In the Body (the Forest) is the Soul (the Deer) and the Spirit (the Unicorn). One who knows how to tame and control them by Art, to yoke them together and lead them in and out of the Forest, may with right be called a Master, for he has gained the Golden Flesh."

Three Philosophers, a painting by Giorgione (c.1478-1511), Vienna, Staats-galerie. Clad in green and white the neophyte sits upon the ground, indica-tive of his beginning rank, face hopefully lifted toward the future. The central figure, dressed in red and wearing a turban, his posture radiating alertness and energy, contrasts strongly with the patriarch on the right, clad in a robe of violet and gold, holding in his hand a page of manuscript covered with hermetic writing and cabalistic signs. It has been observed that this painting is based upon profound Rosicrucian wisdom.

Robert Fludd, (1574-1637) the English Rosicrucian Apologist. From an engraving, frontispiece to his *Philosophia Sacra*, 1626.

Rosicrucian Design from the Title Page of Robert Fludd's *Summum Bonum,
The Highest Good,* subtitled "True Magic, Cabala, Alchemy, of the True
Brothers of the Rose Cross," Frankfort, 1629. Part IV of this work, titled *The
Rosicrucian Brotherhood,* is included in the present volume. A rose of 49 petals
rises from a stem in cross-form, from which 11 leaves grow. At the right are
four bee-hives, at the left two spider webs within a wooden frame. Wisdom
and industry are clearly indicated, and the motto, *The Rose gives the Bees
Honey,* arches over the whole vignette.

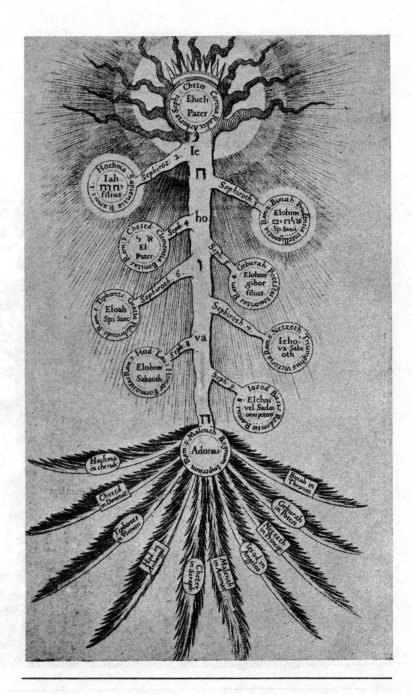

The Tree of the Sephiroth, an engraving by deBry from the *Works* of Robert Fludd, 1624. As Fludd explains in his *Rosicrucian Brotherhood*, Cabala is one of the pillars of the House of Wisdom of the Rosicrucians. The divine power émanates downward from *Kether*, the Crown, in the world of the *Ain Soph*, finally manifesting itself in ten ranks of Spiritual Hierarchies, each of which has a profound relationship with the world of Nature and Man.

The Tree of the Philosophers, from *Philosophia Reformata*, 1622, by Johann Daniel Mylius, physician from the Wetterau. Designs reminiscent of *The Chymical Wedding* and *The Secret Symbols* surround the tree, beneath which stand the adept and the student, comparable to the figures in Plate VIII of the Khunrath series in the present book.

MICHAELIS MAJERI
VIATORIUM,
hoc eft,
DE MONTIBVS PLANETARVM
septem seu Metallorum;
TRACTATUS tam utilis, quàm perspicuus,
quo, ut Indice Mercuriali in triviis, vel
Ariadnêo filo in Labyrintho, seu Cyno-
surâ in Oceano Chymicorum errorum
immenso, quilibet rationalis, veritatis a-
mans, ad illum, qui in montibus sese ab-
didit DE Rubea-petra Alexicacum, o-
mnibus Medicis desideratum, investi-
gandum, uti poterit.
OPPENHEIMII
Ex typographia HIERONYMI GALLERI,
Sumptibus JOH. THEODORI de BRY.
M DC XVIII.

Michael Maier (c.1568-1622) and his *Viatorium, De Montibus Planetarium septem seu Metallorum,* title page engraved by deBry, 1618. This outstanding German defender of the Rosicrucians, author of many works, including *Silentium post Clamores,* "the most learned scientist of his time," was responsible for making the *Fama* and *Confessio* known widely on the Continent. He is thought to have been the emissary of the Rosicrucian Brotherhood in Germany, who, on his visit to England about 1615, initiated Robert Fludd. The portrait of Maier at the top of the page is flanked by allegroical studies of Planets, Metals, and Signs of the Zodiac.

A Mystical Drawing in the Works of Jacob Boehme. Included in the 1682
edition, edited by Johann Georg Gichtel (1638-1710), whom H. P. Blavatsky
described as "an Initiate and Rosicrucian," who perhaps used these plates
to disseminate Rosicrucian teachings. The drawing above is clearly identical
with one in *The Secret Symbols of the Rosicrucians*, 1785. It has been suggested that this drawing—and others in the series—may have been the work
of Dionysius Andreas Freher (1649-1728).

Jacob Boehme (1575-1624), *Teutonicus Philosophus*, "the shoemaker of Goerlitz," from a contemporary woodcut. Though it was long thought that Boehme's
profound writings on mystical theology were the fruit of personal inspiration
alone, modern scholars are inclined to believe that though he lacked formal
schooling, he was widely read and owed much to his circle of learned friends,
among them Dr. Balthazar Walther, whom the late Albert Steffen identified
as a Rosicrucian, in his essay on Boehme. Dr. Walther gave the title *Aurora*
to Boehme's first work. Goethe touches upon the significance of this title in
Faust: "The world of spirits is not shut away. . . . Up Student! bathe, without
dismay, Thy earthly breast in morning red!" The *Fama, Confessio* and *Chymical Wedding* all appeared in Boehme's lifetime, and he must have known
about them and perhaps studied them.

The Temple of Pansophia, from the anonymous work, *Compass of the Wise*, Berlin, 1779. The two columns which also form a leading motif in Khunrath's *Amphitheater* are shown wreathed with roses, with Sun, Moon and planets above, their "fatherly" and "motherly" influences streaming downward upon the seven-pillared structure, reminiscent of the House of Wisdom described by Solomon.

Secret
Symbols of the Rosicrucians

of the 16th and 17th Centuries

Secret Symbols
of the
Rosicrucians

of the 16th & 17th Centuries

FIRST BOOK

Brought to light for the first time from an old manuscript

ALTONA, 1785

Edited and printed by J. D. A. Eckhardt,
Commissioned by the Bookstore of Mr. Herold in Hamburg

Geheime
Figuren der Rosenkreuzer,

aus dem 16ten und 17ten Jahrhundert.

Erstes Heft.

Aus einem alten Mscpt. zum erstenmal ans Licht gestellt.

Altona, 1785.

Gedruckt und verlegt von J. D. A. Eckhardt; in Commission in der Heroldschen Buchhandlung in Hamburg.

The Teachings of the Rosicrucians
of the 16th and 17th Centuries

— O R —

A Simple ABC Booklet

For Young Students

Practising Daily in the School of the Holy Ghost

MADE CLEAR TO THE EYES BY PICTORIAL FIGURES

For the Exercises of the New Year

— IN THE —

Natural and Theological Light

by a Brother of the Fraternity { **C H R I S T I** / of the Rosy-Cross } P. F.

FOR THE FIRST TIME MADE PUBLIC

and

WITH SEVERAL FIGURES OF SIMILAR CONTENT ADDED BY P. S.

IMMA NUEL

I AM A FLOWER
OF SHARON,
AND A ROSE IN
THE VALLEY

CANT. 2 . V. 1.

ALTONA
Printed and Published by Joh. Dav. Ad. Eckhardt, Book-Printer to H. M. the King of Denmark.

Die Lehren der Rosenkreuzer
aus dem 16ten und 17ten Jahrhundert.

Oder

Einfältig ABC Büchlein

für junge Schüler

so sich täglich fleissig üben in der Schule des H. Geistes;

Bildnißweise vor die Augen gemahlet

zum neuen Jahrs-Exercitio

in dem

Natürlichen und Theologischen Lichte

von einem Bruder der Fraternitaet $\left\{ \begin{array}{c} \text{CHRISTI} \\ \text{des Rosenkreuzes} \end{array} \right\}$ P. F.

zum erstenmal öffentlich bekannt gemacht,

und

mit einigen Figuren von gleichem Inhalt vermehret durch P. S.

IMMA NUEL

Ich bin eine Blume
zu Saron, und eine
Rose im Thal.
Cant 2. v. I.

Altona,
gedruckt und verlegt von Joh. Dav. Ad. Eckhardt, Königl. Dän. privil. Buchdrucker.

215

The Almighty, Alone-Wise, and Omniscient GOD and LORD hath given understanding to Man, above all other creatures, so that he may know his works and not leave them unexplored. Now since this Man, whom the All-wise GOD hath inspired thereto, hath this high and profound secret Work and the great secret of the ancient *Water-Stone of the Wise,* he must needs prove himself aright. If ever there is a natural thing on earth, it is the Preparation and the *Magysterium* of the Philosopher's Stone, natural and not of man's making, but wholly the work of Nature, for the *Artist* addeth nothing thereto. Nature alone directeth the growing, as doth every tiller of the soil with his fruits and plants; only he must be subtle in mind and have the grace of GOD, so that he may direct the same as the work becomes evident in the boiling and through *successive* time: namely, in the beginning there is the *Subjectum,* which one doth receive from Nature directly into the hand. Therein lieth hidden the Universal Tincture of all metals, animals, and plants. It is a rough *Corpus,* having neither the figure nor form of an animal or plant, but is in the beginning a rough, earthy, heavy, viscous, tough and nebulous substance on which Nature hath stopped; but when the enlightened man openeth these matters, investigateth them in *Digestion,* and with its thick foggy shadows with which it is surrounded, he purifieth and permitteth the hidden to emerge, and through further *Sublimation* its innermost soul, which is hidden therein, is also separated from it and brought into a bodily form. Then one will find what Nature hath hidden in such a once shapeless substance and what power and *Magnalia* the Supreme Creator hath given to and implanted in this *Creato.* For GOD hath this *Creato* for all other creatures, as in the beginning of creation this power was implanted, and He still giveth it daily, so that it would otherwise not only be impossible for a man to bring such natural work to the desired end, much less to create herein anything useful. But the good and gracious GOD doth not begrudge man the treasures and goods which He hath implanted in Nature, else He would not have granted such things to His creatures; nay, He hath created everything good for man, and hath made him to be Lord over His creation. Therefore it is fitting for man to understand and to undertake such a natural philosophical work, for otherwise such a highly-gifted and wonderful creation would have been in vain, and we would view Nature like the dumb animals which run about, and we would go vainly after God's counsel and we would not fit into the ends of Nature. *Deus autem et Natura, nihil faciunt frustra.* (But God and Nature do nothing in vain). But GOD Almighty ruleth in all such things, He ordereth and provideth that oats and fodder be placed before the ass and the horse, but that the rational human being be served with more costly and more delicious food. Therefore those who try to investigate and who long for such a deeply hidden *Arcanum* and great treasure, in the proper way, do not have to depend upon the harvest of the ignorant, who have no understanding under the Light of our Sun.

The *Philosophers* and wise men, as well as *Neoterici* and *Veteres,* have had many disputations about this secret art, and have tried to point out, with many different names, allegories, and wondrously strange sophistical words what that *Subjectum* and its *Essentia* are, and what kind of a *Materia,* what kind of a *Corpus,* what kind of a *Subjectum,* and what a wonderful thing and secret a *Creatura* it is, which hath embodied such mighty, strange, and heavenly powers, and with which, after

Es hat der allmächtige, allein weise und allwissende Gott und Herr, dem Menschen vor allen andern Thieren mit Vernunst begabet, daß er sein Werk erkennen und unersucht nicht lassen soll. Als hat dieser Mensch, welchen der allwissende Gott dazu erwecket, dieses hohen und tiefen verborgenen Werks und der grossen Heimlichkeit des uralten Wasser-Steins der Weisen sich billig anzunehmen, dann so irgend ein natürlich Ding auf der Welt ist, so ist die Bereitung und das *Magisterium* des philosophischen Steins natürlich und nicht eines Menschen, sondern ganz und gar der Natur ihr Werk, denn der *Artist* thut nichts dazu, ohn allein daß er die Natur ins Wachsen richtet, wie ein jeder Ackersmann mit seinen Früchten und Pflanzungen auch thut; allein daß er spitzfindig an Verstand, und die Gnade von Gott habe, daß er derselben Gang regiere, wie das Werk sich in der Kochung und durch die Zeit *successive* erzeiget: nemlich Anfangs das *Subjektum*, welches man von der Natur in die Hand empfähet, darinnen die Universal-Tinctur aller Metallen, Thieren und Gewächsen verborgen liegt, ist ein ungeschlachtes *Corpus*, hat weder Gestalt noch Form einiges Thieres oder Gewächses, sondern ist anfangs ein rauhes, irdisches, schweres, schleimiges, zähes und nebelwässeriges Wesen, an welchem die Natur hat aufgehäret; wenn aber der erleuchtete Mensch diese Materien aufthut, dieselbe in der *Digestion* ersuchet, und seinen dicknblichten Schatten, mit welchen es umgeben, *purificiret*, und löst das Verborgene hervor triechen, und durch fernere *Sublimation* ihm seine innerliche Seele, so darin verborgen, auch aus ihm diviret, und in ein corporalisch Wesen gebracht wird, alsdenn findet man was die Natur in solcher zuvor ungeschlachten Gestalt verstecket, und was für Kraft und *Magnalia* der höchste Schöpfer in diesem *Creato* eingepflanzet und verliehen hat, denn Gott hat diesem *Creato* für allen andern Creaturen, gleich Anfangs der Erschaffung, solche Kraft eingepflanzet, und beggbet sie noch täglich, wo das nicht alse, wäre keinem Menschen auf Erden möglich solch natürlich Werk zu gewünschtem Ende zu bringen, geschweig hierinnen einen einigen Nutz zu schaffen. Aber der leutselige gute Gott, der mißgönnet dem Menschen die Schätze und die Güter, so er der Natur eingepflanzet, mit nichten nicht; er hätte sonsten den Creaturen solches nicht verliehen, sondern hat alles dem Menschen zu gut erschaffen, und über sein Geschöpf den Menschen zum Herren gemacht. Darum solch natürlich philosophisch Werk dem Menschen zu erkennen und auch zu erlangen wohl zustehet, denn solch hoch begabt und wunderlich Geschöpf wäre sonst vergebens ins Mittel gelegt, und liesen wir vorüber wie die Kühe unbetrachtend die Natur, und ginge Gottes Rath leer abe, und bekäme die Natur ihre Endschaft nicht. *Deus autem & Natura, nihil faciunt frustra.* (Gott aber und die Natur thun nichts vergebens.) Es hält aber Gott der Allmächtige in solchen allen das Regiment, ordnets und machts, daß einem Esel und Pferd der Haber und das Futter wird vorgeschüttet, dem vernünstigen Menschen aber köstlichere und lieblichere Speise vorgetragen wird. Derowegen diejenigen, so solchen tief versteckten *Arcano* und hohen Schatz gebührlicher Weise begehren nachzusetzen und zu ergründen, haben sich an der Ignoranten carpiren nicht zu kehren, denn sie haben keinen Verstand im Licht der Natur.

Es haben aber die *Philosophi* und weise Männer, sowohl die Neoterici als die Veteres von dieser geheimen Kunst mancherlen disputiret, und mit vielen unterschiedlichen Namen, Parabolen und wunderbarlichen fremden sophistischen Worten das Subjektum und dessen Essentia angedeutet, was für eine *Materia*, für ein *Corpus*, für ein *Subjektum*, ja für ein Wunderding und geheime Creatur es sey, welchem so mächtige, wunderliche und himmlische Kraft einverleibet sey, nach welcher *Digestion* und Reinigung dem Menschen, Thieren, Gewächsen und Metallen man helfen, und auf deren Gesundheit und Perfection höchsten Grad bringen, und viel anders mit demselben ausrichten könne. So haben sie doch alle, was wahre *Philosophi* gewesen, und noch seyn, einhellig mit verwechselten Reden und Schriften nur auf einen einigen *Scopum* und einzige *Materiam* die Filii Sapientiae weisen und zeigen wollen. Hier ist aber bey dem Wesentlichen ein grosses Still-

Digestion and purification, one can help human beings, animals, plants, and metals, and one can bring their health and perfection up to the highest degree, and one can also do many other marvellous things with it. Nevertheless all those who were and still are true *Philosophi*, have unanimously pointed out one single *Scopum* and one only *Materiam*, the *Filii Sapientiat*, writing various and manifold speeches and scripts about it. Concerning the essential thing, however, there is only silence, and that silence hath fast-locked their mouths, and placed a solid *Sigill* upon them, for if it should become as common knowledge as brewing and baking, the world would soon perish.

There are many who have searched for that only *Res*, which *solvit se ipsum, coagulat se ipsum, se ipsum impraegnat, mortificat et vivicat* (dissolveth itself, coagulateth itself impregnateth itself, killeth and bringeth to life again), but most of these searchers, who have lost themselves while searching, failed. Then it is such a thing as is nearest gold; and it is such a thing as the poor as well as the rich can gain, be it whatever it may. But it threaten≥th the *Philosophi execrationem divinam*, and invoketh the curse of God upon him who with his own mouth might *expressly* speak on this *Subjectum*.

When the Philosophers pronounced an *Execration*, Almighty God did respect and grant their appeal, and gave unto them what He had until then kept in His own hands for several thousand years. Now the aforesaid *Subjectum* is of such a nature that it, our *Magnesia*, doth not only contain a small proportioned *quantity* of the universal *Spiritus Vitalis* in itself, but also hath some of the heavenly power condensed and compressed within it. Many who found it were so intoxicated by its fumes that they remained in their place and could no longer raise themselves. Only a wise man and one who knoweth these things can take a measure of this same fluid and carry it home from whatever place he may have found it, be it from the depths of the mountains or any other place where it may be met. The poor and the rich are quite free, by the singular and abounding grace of God, to take this, so that he goeth homeward with it in to his house, and placeth it behind the furnace or in any other room where it pleaseth him, and where it is convenient for him, and he may begin to work and to experiment with it, for he can leave off so quickly that even his own servants do not notice it. For it doth not go so slovenly with this natural work as it doth with the common alchemists with their bungling work, with their charcoal-burning, smelting and refining, and whatever more they may do. But it is a work which one can keep in a closed casket in whatever room he wisheth, alone that not even a cat come upon it, and, should it be necessary, he can well carry on his craft, only taking care that the furnace have a threefold testing, and that he keep it at the right heat, and let Nature takes its own course. When finally the *Solution* is taken out of the *Terrestriaet*, and is strengthened by long *Digestion*, it is set free from the *Crudae Materiae*, and is prepared and reborn in the most subtle form. Subsequently, of course, this sharp and potent *Spiritus* is at certain times given a well-measured *quantity*, after the fashion of drinking and nourishing, *per modum inibitionis et nutritionis*. And its potency is thus condensed and daily becometh as new supports for its brethren, and active therein. Dost thou indeed think that one canst bring forth such work and such potency in unmeasured hidden intensity, a *Spiritus Vitalis*? The *crudae materiae* or *Subjectum* cometh from the *Astris* and *Constellation* of the heavens into its earthly kingdom, from which is then drawn the *spiritus universi secretur* of the Philosophers, which is the *Mercurius* of the Wise, and it is the beginning, the means, and the end, in which the *Aurum Physicum* is determined and hidden, which the common alchemist thinks to extract out of common gold, but in vain. Meanwhile, the *Philosophi* deal much in their writings with *Sol* and *Luna*, which of all metals are the most durable in the △. But this is not to be understood literally, for their *Sol* and *Luna*, when they are brought to their inner *puritaet*, through true, natural, seemly, and philosophical *praeparation* may well be compared with the celestial bodies, such as the Sun and the Moon, which with their brightness illuminate day and night, the upper and the lower *Firmament*. Therefore these two noble metals, like the *Sol* and *Luna* of the Philosophers, resemble by nature the human body, and to him who knoweth how to prepare them

rightly and use them wisely they give much health, and except and above this nothing else is to be prepared, but the one threefold point of the *Universalis*, for the *Spiritus* to be found in these two said things produceth consistency, strength and virtue, amongst other things.

Now the man pardoned by God can prepare and make ready an object or substance of the above mentioned red or white, of *Sol* and *Luna*, which is called the *Lapidem Philosophorum*, or the very ancient *Water-Stone of the Wise*, from the substance in which God placed such potency at the creation or genesis of the world, or the oft-mentioned materials or *Subjectum* which God, out of love and grace, implanted in the highly-endowed divine man. But I believe, therefore, that the divine substance which was left to him in the first *Creation* of the world, of the *Spiritu Vitali*, of the *Inspiration*, hath survived in all kinds of creatures. All received the same *Spiritum* in the aforesaid *Massam*, and firmly secluded in the lowest depths of the earth, and it was indicated and left to the Wise Men to disinter it, to extract it, to use it, and to perform the same *Miracula* with it, through the holy wisdom which is still implanted in it and with which it is supplied daily.

Both substances mentioned above as Sun and Moon or red and white, or rather the *Praeparation* ♀ is and *Mercurii*, are the ingredients in the *Composition* of our *Lapidis Philosophorum*. Now then the *Materia* are in the beginning through sufficient and oft-repeated *Sublimentiones* purified and cleansed, and then weighed carefully, and then soon composed; also thou must not be ignorant of what is the potency and occasion of both of the said ingredients, but thou must know how to arrange both *Pondera, secundum proportionem Physicam* (according to the analogy of Physics), for a good portion of the ☿ *ii* is encumbered with a small portion of *animae Solis vel Sulphuris*, and then unite both with a delicate hand, so that finally the *Praeparation* and the most difficult work is completed.

But thou wilt have to know that thou must first tinge thy ☿ um with the red *Tinctur*, yet it will not become red *in continenti*, but remaineth white, for the *Mercurius* hath the privilege of wanting to be tinged first before all others. The *Philosophi* also tell what to do in addition with the *Anima solis* of this *Tinctur* of the *Mercurii*, and from whence it shall be taken. The *Ferment* of gold is gold, just as the *Ferment* of dough is dough. Moreover, it is the *Ferment* of gold out of its own nature, and then its potency is perfect when it is transformed back into earth. And then this is first the beginning of the Philosophers, the right and true *Prima Materia Philosophorum metallorum* (the first *Materia* of the metals of the Philosophers). From then on the true Masters, experienced in the Art, begin to stimulate their *Ingeniam* and attain to the Great Work. And then the *Artifex* continues further with such work and, through God's blessing, bringeth it to the end, to which it tendeth and where it is embodied by God, namely, to the highly-blessed Philosopher's Stone. So that from nothing else than *per Spiritum universali Secretum* the true *materia prima Philosophorum* is prepared and made ready. Who now understandeth well this *Spiritum Secretum* understandeth also, without doubt, the secrets and wonders of Nature and hath the perception of the light of Nature. For he is *motus harmonicus Sympaticus* and *magneticus*, from which originates the *Harmonia and Concordantia*, the magnetic and sympathetic power or effect of the uppermost and of the lowermost. But note that the natures of both ingredients are unlike each other in the beginning because of their opposed qualities. For one is warm and dry, the other is cold and moist, and they must of course be united. But when this is about to occur, then their opposed qualities must slowly be changed and equalised, so that neither nature through intense fire divest the other of its potency. For thou canst never collect them, because both natures must rise simultaneously in the fire's power. Then the *Discrasia* will be taken from the *Corpori*, and an *Aequalitas* and good *Temperatur* is established, which occureth through a moderate and constant boiling.

For when both of the natures *Sulphur* and *Mercurius* are enclosed in a very narrow space and are maintained with moderate heat, they begin to abate from their opposed charac-

schweigen, welche ihnen selbsten ein Maul-Schloß an den Mund geleget, und ein festes Sigill aufgedrücket, denn wenn es so gemein würde, als Brauen und Backen, müste die Welt zu Grunde gehen.

Diese einzige *Res* aber, welche *solvit se ipsum, coagulat se ipsum, se ipsum impraegnat, mortificat & vivicat,* (sich selber auflöset, von selbst gerinnet, sich selber befeuchtet und schwängert, tödtet und wieder lebendig machet,) hat viele Nachsucher gehabt, aber denen meisten aller gefehlet, welche sich in dem Nachforschen verstiegen haben. Dann es so ein Ding ist, welches dem Golde am nächsten ist: und ist ein solch Ding, daß es der Arme sowol als der Reiche zu Händen bringen kann, es sey jetzo auch wo es wolle. Es dräuen aber die *Philosophi execrationem divinam,* und rufen den Fluch Gottes über solchen, welcher das *Subjectum* mit seinem Munde *expresse* aussage.

Ob welcher Philosophen *Execration* der allmächtige Gott auch halten thut, und ihr Anrufen erstattet, und nunmehr in etlichen tausend Jahren unter Händen gehabt hat. Also ist es aber mit gedachtem *Subjecto* beschaffen, dann dieselbe unsere *Magnesia* hat nicht nur des allgemeinen *Spiritus Vitalis* eine geringe proportionirte *Quantität* in sich, sondern ist von der himmlischen Kraft also wohl *condensiret* und compreß gemacht, daß von des Dunstes viele trunken worden, daß es da an seinem Orte lieget, und kann ihm selber nicht mehr aufhelfen, so dann im Verständigen, so solcher Materien kundig, dazu kommt, es sey in der Tiefe eines Berges, oder sonsten wo er sie möge antreffen, nimt desjenigen Saftes ein Lägel voll, denn es aus sonderer und überreicher Gnaden Gottes darnach zu greifen Armen und Reichen frey stehet, der gehe damit heimwerts in sein Haus hinter den Ofen oder anderm Gemach, wohin ihm bequem zu seyn gefallen thut, und sahe damit zu bauen und zu laboriren an, denn er kann es also behende einhalten, daß auch sein eigen Hausgesind solches nicht gewahr werde. Denn es gehet mit diesem natürlichen Werk also suderisch zu, wie es mit dem gemeinen Laboranten ihrem Sudelwerk, als Kohlenbrennen, Schmelzen, Abtreiben, und was deren mehr sey, sondern ist ein Werk, welches einer in einem verschlossenen Kasten halten kann, in was für ein Gemach er will, allein daß keine Katze ihm drüber komme, und wenn es die Noth erfodern sollte, kann er sein Handwerk dabey gar wohl treiben, nur daß er den Ofen, welcher dreyfacher Bewährung gemacht sey, wisse mit der rechten Wärme ihn zu stellen, und der Natur ihren Gang lasse. Wenn ihm nun durch die *Solution* die *Terrestritaet* entnommen, und durch lange *Digestion* acuirt, der *Crudae materiae* entledigt, zum subtilesten zugerichtet und wiedergebohren, auch nachmals erst wiederum den hochgebohrnen *scilicet* diesen scharfen und kräftigen *Spiritus,* nach Art einer Eintrinkung und Ernährung, *per modum imbibitionis* und *nutritionis* zu gewissen Zeiten eine gebührliche *Quantitaet* vielmahlen zugesetzt, und seine Kraft über besagtes auf solche Weise *condensiret,* und denn täglich also neue Pfeiler von seinen Brüdern zukommen, und darein getrieben worden, wie meinest du wohl, daß man solches Werk bringen könne, denn solche Kraft und unermeßlich verborgene Stärke *Spiritus Vitalis,* kömt der *crudae materiae* oder *Subjecti* von den *Astris* und *Constellation* des Himmels her in seinem Erdreich, daraus denn die Philosophen *Spiritus universi secretus* gezogen wird, welches ist der Weisen ihr *Mercurius,* und ist ihr Anfang, das Mittel und das Ende, und ist verborgen ist das *Aurum Physicum,* welches die gemeinen Laboranten vermeinen aus dem gemeinen Golde zu erbähren, aber vergeblich. Dieweil die *Philosophi* viel von *Sol* und *Luna* in ihren Schriften handeln, welche unter den Metallen die beständigsten im △ sind, es ist aber solches nicht nach dem Buchstaben zu verstehen, denn ihr *Sol* & *Luna,* wo sie zu ihrer innerlichen *puritaet* gebracht werden, und durch die rechte natürliche gebührliche und philosophische *praeparation* sich wohl vergleichen, dem himmlischen Gestirn als *Sol* und *Luna,* oder in ihrer Klarheit erleuchten Tag und Nacht, das obere und untere Firmament. Derowegen diese zwey edeln Metallen, als der Philosophen ihr *Sol* & *Luna,* so von Natur dem menschlichen Leibe gleich seyn, solche hohe Gesundheit, wer sie recht brauchet, und auch zu präpariren weiß, eingiessen können, und daß ausser den darüber nichts anders denn allein der Einige dreyfaltige Punct des *Universalis* zu präpariren ist, es ist aber der *Spiritus,* so in diesen gedachten beyden beschlossen, schaftlich, und würket solche Beständigkeit, Kraft und Tugend, wie in andern Dingen mehr.

Da nun der von Gott begnadigte Mensch eine Sache oder Ding von obgedachten Roth oder Weis, oder *Sol* & *Luna,* welches man *Lapidem Philosophorum* oder den uralten Wasserstein der Weisen nennet, zurichten und bereiten kann aus einer Creatur, in welche Gott in der Schöpfung oder Erschaffung der Welt solche Kraft geleget, oder obgedachter Materien oder *Subjecto* den hochbegabten Männern Gottes zu Lieb und Wohlgefallen eingepflanzet. Ich halte es aber davor, daß das göttliche Wesen, was ihm in der ersten *Creation* der Welt von dem *Spiritu Vitali* von der *Inspiration*

derselben in allerley Creaturen überblieben, allen denselben *Spiritum* in diese erste genannte *Massam* eingesteckt, und zu unterst in die tiefe Erden also fest verschlossen und den weisen Männern denselben zu erheben, auszufertigen, zu gebrauchen, und gleiche *Miracula* damit zu begehen durch seine heilige Weisheit angedeutet und hinterlassen habe, und noch täglich solches *armiret* und einpflanzet.

Obgedachte beyde Stück als Sonn und Mond oder Roth und Weiß, oder vielmehr die *Praeparation* ♁ïs und *Mercurii,* welche beyde Stücke denn die *Ingredientien* sind in der *Composition* unsers *Lapidis Philosophorum,* dann wann die *Materialia* anfangs durch gnugsame und öfft wiederholte *Sublimationes* purificiret und gereiniget, nachmahlen fleissig abgewogen und alsbald darinne componiret; aber was die Kraft und Gelegenheit der gedachten beyden Ingredienten sey, muß dir nicht unwissend seyn, sondern der beyden *Pondera* wissen anzustellen, *secundum proportionem Physicam,* (nach physicalischer Eintheilung,) dann des ♄ïi ein gutes Theil läst sich mit einer geringen Theil *animae Solis vel Sulphuris* seejigen, alsdenn mit einem zierlichen Handgriff solches vereinigen, so ist alsdann die *Praeparation* und das schwereste Werk verrichtet.

Aber das ist zu wissen, daß du must deinen ♄um mit der rothen *Tinctur* zuforderst tingiren, er wird aber nicht *in continenti* roth, sondern bleibet weiß, er der *Mercurius* hat den Vorzug, daß er für allen andern der erste will tingiret seyn, dazu mit der *Anima solis* von dieser *Tinctur* des *Mercurii,* auch woher dieselbe soll genommen werden, melden die *Philosophi.* Das *Ferment* des Goldes (ist Gold,) wie der *Ferment* des Teiges, Teig ist. *Item* es ist das *Ferment* des Goldes aus seiner Natur, und alsdenn ist seine Kraft vollkommen, wann es in eine Erde verkehrt ist worden, dann das ist erst der Philosophen Anfang, die rechte wahre *Prima materia Philosophorum metallorum,* (die erste *Materia* der Metallen der Philosophen,) von dannen an die rechten und in der Kunst erfahrnen Meister erst ihr *Ingenium* zu spannen anfahen, und zum hohen Werke kommen, und fähret dann der *Artifex* mit solchen Werk weiter fort, und bringt es durch Gottes Segen zu dem Ende, dahin es *inclinirt* und von Gott einverleibet, nemlich zu dem hochgebenedeyten Stein der Weisen, daß also aus nichts anders denn allein *per Spiritum universi Secretum* die wahrhafte *materia prima Philosophorum* zugerichtet und bereitet wird. Welcher nun diesen *Spiritum Secretum* recht erkennen thut, der versiehet auch zweifelsohne, die Geheimnisse und Wunder der Natur, und hat das Erkenntniß des Lichts der Natur, dann ist *motus harmonicus Sympaticus* und *magneticus,* dahero die *Harmonia* und *Concordantia* die magnetische und sympatetische Kraft oder Würkung der Obern und Untern entstehen. Werk aber, daß beyder Ingredientien Naturen anfangs einander ungleich seind, wegen ihrer widerwärtigen Qualitäten, denn eins ist warm und trocken, das andere ist kalt und feucht, die müssen nun allerdings vereiniget werden, wenn aber nun dis geschehen soll, müssen deren widerwärtigen Qualitäten allgemach verändert und verglichen werden, und daß sich ja keines Natur durch allzustark Feuer eine für die andere über sich begebe, denn du sie nimmer zusammen zu bringen vermöchtest, denn beyde Naturen müssen zugleich in des Feuers Regierung auffsteigen, alsdann wird die *Discrasia* dem *Corpori* benommen, und eine *Aequalitas* und gute *Temperatur* eingeführet, welches geschieht durch eine mässige und anhaltende Kochung.

Denn wenn also die beyden Naturen *Sulphur & Mercurius* in dem engen viel eingeschlossen und mit der mässigen Wärme continuiret, so fangen sie an von ihrem widerwärtigen Wesen nachzulassen, und vereinbaren sich, bis sie endlich qualificiret, daß eine *Conspiration* und zugleich Auffsteigen werde, und stehet denn am Glase allerdings eines, sind bereit sich zu verheyrathen, alsdann steckt der Bräutigam seiner Braut einen güldnen Ring an, sagen die *Philosophi.* Und wenn also der *Mercurius* mit seinem *Sulphur* als Wasser und Erden mit einander nach der Gebühr gekocht werden, so werfen sie alle ihre Ueberflüssigkeiten hinweg, und fügen sich die reinen Theile je länger je mehr zusammen, und daß es keines *corlicibi* entlediget, sonsten verhindern die unreinen Theile die Vereinigung und den *Ingress.*

Denn der *Mercurius,* als das erste *Corpus,* ist ganz grob, und kann *per minima* nicht vermischt noch perpetuiret werden, denn kein *Corpus* in das andere eingehet, noch mit ihm *vere* und *in radice* vereiniget wird. Soll aber den Sachen geholfen werden, daß eine wahre *Tinctur* zugerüst werde, so muß aus diesem ein neu *spiritulisch Corpus* bereitet werden, welches aus beyden entsprungen; denn nach der *Purification* nimmet eins des andern Tugend an sich, und wird aus vielen eines, *numero & virtute* (an Zahl und Vermögen) wenn aber das Feuer allzu stark, und nicht nach Erfoderung der Natur sollte regieret werden, so würden diese obgedachte zwey entweder ersticket oder zertrennet, nachdem sie ihren lieblichen Gang nicht hätten, und würde entweder nichts oder ein verderbtes Werk

ter and to unite, until finally they have all the qualities. They become one *Conspiration* and rise at the same time, and certainly at the top of the glass standeth *numero* one. They are ready to wed, and then the bridegroom placeth a golden ring on his bride, say the *Philosophi*. And when thus the *Mercurius* with its *Sulphur*, like water and earth with each other, become duly boiled (and the longer the more) they cast away all their superfluities and the pure parts join each other and dispose of their *corlicibi;* otherwise the impure parts prevent unification and the *Ingress*.

For the *Mercurius*, as the first *Corpus*, is entirely crude and can *per anima* be neither mixed nor perpetuated, for neither *Corpus* entereth the other nor will be united with it either *vere* or *in radice*. But should these things be so helped that a true *Tinctur* will be formed, there must be prepared out of this a new spiritual *Corpus* which cometh forth out of both, for after the purification one taketh the virtues of the other, and out of several become one, *numero et virtute* (in number and power). But if the fire should be much too intense and should not be controlled according to the requirements of Nature, these two above-mentioned would be either suffocated or separated. If they did not have their right mode of preparation, they would become either nothing or a spoiled work and a *Monstrum*. But when one proceedeth prudently and with a duly tempered heat, then both substances will rise in the *Sublimation* uppermost in the glass or cupola. Then when thou pluckest these lovely flowers, thou canst enjoy them already *particularia*.

But thou canst observe the *motum occultum naturae* as little as thou canst either hear or see the grass growing, for one can neither observe nor notice the increase and development of these two ingredients, *Mercurii* and *Sulphuris*, because of their subtle, hidden, and slow *Progressus* from hour to hour. Only by marks set from week to week can it be observed and a conclusion drawn, for the inner fire is very delicate and subtle. But however slow it may be, it doth not stand still until it cometh to the end where its *intent* is to be seen, as in all plants, unless it then be that such subtle and expert boiling is hindered through the all too-strong heat of the sun and is burnt out, or is hindered through suddenly appearing cold; *ergo qui scit occultum motum naturae, scit perfectum decoctionem* (therefore he who knoweth the hidden movement of Nature, knoweth also the perfect boiling or preparation). This *motum* should now take its natural and self-determined course, although one can neither hear nor see it, as also one cannot comprehend the *Centra et ignem invisibilem seminum invisibilium* (the Centre and invisible fire of the invisible seed). Therefore thou must commit such a matter to Nature alone, and observe it and not once try to oppose Nature, but have all confidence in it until it bringeth forth its fruit.

When one treateth Nature with a gentle and agreeable heat, it doeth and effecteth everything out of itself, which for the furnishing of a *Creati* or the introduction of a new form is a matter of necessity; for the Divine Word *Fiat* still abideth in all creatures and in all plants, and hath its mighty power in these times as well is in the beginning.

There are, however, four chief *Virtutes* and *potentias* of which noble Nature maketh use in every boiling; thereby it doth complete its work and bringeth it to an end.

The First Virtus

Is and is called *appellativa et attractiva*, for it is possible for it to attract to itself from far or near, food of which it is desirous out of results and places agreeable to its nature, and it can grow and increase. And here it hath a magnetic power, like that of a man for a woman, the *Mercurius* or the *Sulphur*, the dry for the moist, the *Materia* for the form. Therefore the axiom of the Philosophers is: *natura naturam amat, amplectitur prosequitur*. *Omnia namquam crescentia, dum radices agunt et vivant, succum ex Terra attrahunt, atque avide arripiunt illud, quo vivere et augmentari sentiunt — i.e.*, Nature loveth nature, surroundeth it, and followeth it. For all plants, when they strike root and begin to live, suck sap out of the earth, and draw to themselves avidly that whereby they sense they can live and multiply themselves. For where there is hunger

and thirst, food and drink will be received with avidity and this *Virtus* and *potentia* will be aroused, and it cometh from the heat and average dryness.

The Second Virtus and Potentia

Is and is called *natura retentiva et coagulativa*. For Nature not only alone is useful to it and serveth it for its continuation and is advantageous when it lacketh that which it eagerly produceth from itself, but hath also with it the bond with which it draweth and bringeth and holdeth it to itself. Yea, Nature even changeth it into itself, for as it hath chosen of these two the purest parts, it separateth the rest and bringeth to the mouth and maketh it grow, and is in no need of any other *calcination* or *fixation; natura naturam continet* (Nature retaineth nature), and such skill cometh from its dryness, for the cold constricteth the gained and evenly-formed parts and drieth them in the *Terrae*.

The Third Virtus and Potentia

naturae in rebus generandis et augmentandis.

Est Virtus digestiva, quae fit per putrefactionem seu in putrefactione (is the digestive power, which occurs through the putrefaction or in the putrefaction), in moderate and temperate heat and moisture. For Nature directeth, changeth, and introduceth one kind and quality, the crudeness is done away with, the bitter is made sweet, the harsh is made mild, the rough is made smooth, the immature and wild is made tame, that which was formerly incapable is now made skillful and efficient; and leadeth to the final intended execution and perfection of the Work, and representeth the *Ingredientia* to the *Composition*.

The Fourth Potentia naturae

Est virtus expulsiva mundificativa, segregativa (the expelling, purifiying, separating power) which separateth and divideth, which purifieth and cleanseth, which washeth during the *Sublimation* or *Decoction*. It setteth from *Sordibus* and darkness and bringeth forth a pure, transparent, powerful or illuminated *Corpus* or substance; it collecteth the *Partes homogeneis*, and is gradually set free from the *heterogeneis*, repulseth the *Vitia* and everything alien, inspecteth the crude, and giveth every part a special place. This is caused by and cometh from the agreeable constant heat in appropriate moisture, and that is the *Sublimation* and mature fruit, which will now fall out of the husk. Therefore it is in the beginning designed by Nature and artisans, namely the *Patiens* is set free from the *Agente*, and will be perfected. *Nam liberatio illa a partibus heterogeneis est vita et perfectio omnis Rei. — i.e.*, for the liberation of these unequal and opposed parts is the life and perfection of all things. For the *Agens* and *Patiens* which until now have been contending with each other, so that each affecteth and rendereth resistance according to its opponent's resistance — *i.e.*, as much as possible it would like to break its opponent's resistance and they must not unite during the time of their *Decoction*, but the best part must gain the victory and expel the impure, and subjugate it.

Now when all *Naturalis potentia* have done their *officium*, then cometh forth the new birth and as the mature fruit presenteth itself in all other plants, so also now in our *Subjecto* and natural work which, when perfected, quite surprisingly doth not at all resemble any more its first beginning and hath no more quality, and is neither cold nor dry, neither moist nor warm, and is neither *masculus* nor *foemina*. For cold is there itself turned into heat, and the dry into the moist, the heavy into the light, for it is a new *Quinta Essentia*, a *Corpus Spirituale*, and hath become a *Spiritus corporalis*, such a *Corpus* as is clear and pure, transparent and crystallike; one which Nature itself, could never have produced as long as the world hath stood. The *Artifex* and the enlightened man, however, *auxiliante Deo et natura* (by the aid of God and Nature), produceth through his intellect and art, and he placeth it there by itself. So that subsequently he encountereth a *Miracula* and that is called: *Unguentum anima, aurum Philosophorum, flos auri* (the unguent, the soul, the philosophers' gold, the flower of gold). *Theophrastus* and others call it *Gluten aquilae*.

Now what is shown about the four *potentiis naturae*.

und *Monstrum* daraus. Wann aber bescheidentlich mit gebührender temperirter Wärme verfahren wird, so steigen in der *Sublimation* beyde Stücke zu
oberst im Glase oder Helme auf; dieser lieblichen Blumen, wenn du sie ab-
brichst, kanst du schon genießen *particularia*.

Aber den *motum occultum naturae* kanst du so wenig vernehmen,
als wie du das Gras weder sehen noch hören kanst wachsen, denn das Zunehmen und Aufwachsen dieser beyden Ingredientien, *Mercurii* und *Sulphuris*,
kann man nicht wegen ihres subtilen verborgenen und langsamen *Progreßus*
alle Stund observiren und merken, sondern von Woche zu Woche allein bey
einem dazu gesteckten Zeichen abnehmen, spühren und die Rechnung machen.
Denn das inwendige Feuer ist ganz zart und subtil, ja wie langsam. es
auch ist, so stehet es doch nicht still, bis daß es zu dem Ende kommet,
dahin sein *intent* ist, wie in allen Gewächsen auch zu sehen, es wäre denn
daß solche subtile und meisterliche Kochung durch auswendig allzu starke Hitze
der Sonnen verstöhret und ausgebrannt oder einfallende Kälte also gehindert
würde; *ergo qui scit occultum motum naturae, scit perfectum decoctionem;* (derohalben welcher die verborgene Bewegung der Natur weiß, der
weiß auch die völlige Koch- oder Bereitung) soll nun diesem *motui* sein natürlicher und eigenwilliger Gang gelassen werden, ob man ihn schon weder sehen
noch hören kann, wie man denn auch die *Centra & ignem invisibilem
seminum invisibilium* (die Mittelpuncte und das unsichtbare Feuer derer
unsichtbaren Saamen) nicht begreiffen kann, darum must du solches allein
der Natur befehlen, und ihr zusehen und nicht einreden, denn nur einmal,
sondern ihr alles vertrauen, bis sie ihre Geburt hervor bringet.

Die Natur, wenn man ihr eine sanfte und angenehme Wärme wider-
fahren läst, so thut und vollführet sie für sich selbst alles dasjenige, was zu
Ausrüstung eines *Creati* und Einführung einer neuen Form vonnöthen ist:
denn das Wort Gottes *Fiat* steckt noch in allen Creaturen und in allen Gewächsen, und hat seine mächtige Kraft, sowohl nach dieser Zeit als vom Anfang.

Es sind aber fürnemlich vier *Virtutes & potentias* deren sich die edle
Natur in einer jedweden Kochung gebraucht, dadurch sie ihre Werke verserti-
get und zu Ende bringet.

Die erste Virtus

Ist und heisset *appellativa & attractiva*, da sie aus Enden oder Orten so
ihr der Natur zu haben annehmlich, und zu haben möglich, es sey fern oder
nahe, dadurch sie sich erhalten, wachsen und zunehmen kann, Nahrung an
sich ziehet, derselben begierig ist, und hierinnen die magnetische Kraft hat,
als der Mann das Weib, der *Mercurius* den *Sulphur*, Trocken das Feuchte,
die *Materia* die Form, daher der Philosophen ihr Sentenz, *natura naturam amat, amplectitur prosequitur. Omnia namque crescentia, dum
radices agunt & vivunt, succum ex Terra attrahunt, atque avide arripiunt illud, quo vivere se & augmentari sentiunt.* d. i. Die Natur liebt
die Natur, umfasset sie, und folgt ihr nach: Denn alle Gewächse, indem sie
Wurzel fassen und zu leben anfangen, ziehen den Saft aus der Erde an sich,
und reissen dasjenige begierlich zu sich, wodurch sie leben und sich vermehren
können. Denn wo Hunger und Durst ist, da wird Speise und Trank mit
Begierde angenommen, und wird diese *Virtus* und *potentia* erwecket, und
kommt her von der Wärme und mittelmäßigen Trockniß.

Die andere Virtus und Potentia

Ist und heisset *natura retentiva & coagulativa*, denn die Natur nicht
allein was ihr nützlich und zu ihrer Fortsetzung dienet und fördelich, wenn sie
entweder aus Mangel desjenigen, dessen sie begierlich von sich selbst an sich
bringet, sondern sie hat auch bey sich selbst das Band, mit welchem sie dasjenige so sie ziehet und herzu bringet auch an sich hält, ja dasselbe in sich verändert, so sie doch unter diesen beyden die reinesten Theile auserwählet, die
übrigen abscheidet und zum Ausgang bringet und ihn wachsend machet, und
bedarf sie die keiner andern *calcination* oder *fixation; natura naturam
retinet,* (die Natur hält die Natur zurück) und solche Geschicklichkeit kommet
her von der Trockniß, da die Kälte die erworbene und gleichförmige Theile
constringiret und der *Terrae* eintrocknet.

Die dritte Virtus & potentia
naturae in rebus generandis & augmentandis.

Est Virtus digestiva,,quae sit per putrefactionem seu in putrefactione,
(ist die verdauende Kraft, welche geschieht durch die Fäulung oder in der
Fäulung) in mäßiger und temperirter Wärme und Feuchtigkeit, da die Natur
digeriret, verändert, eine Art und Qualität einführet, das Rohe zeitiget,
das Bittere süß, das Herbe mild, das Rauhe gelind, und das Unzeitige und
Wilde heimisch, was anfangs untüchtig, jetzo geschickt und tüchtig macht,
und zur endlichen vorhabenden Werks Ausführung und Vollkommenheit führet, und die *Ingredientia* zur *Composition* darstellet.

Die vierte Potentia naturæ.

Est virtus expulsiva mundificativa. segregativa. (die austreibende,
reinigende und absondernde Kraft) die absondert, scheidet, welche in währender *Sublimation* oder *Decoction* reiniget und mundiret, wäschet, von den
Sordibus und Finsterniß entlediget, und rein, lauter, kräftig oder illuminirt
Corpus oder Wesen hervor bringet, indem sie die *Partes homogeneis* samm-
let, und von den *heterogeneis* allgemählig entlediget, die *vitia* und alles
fremde abstosset, das grobe mustert, jeden Theil seine besondere Stelle giebet,
solches wird verursacht und kommt her von der lieblichen anhaltenden Wärme
in gebührlicher Feuchtigkeit, und das ist, daß der *Sublimation* die rein-
zeitige Frucht, so nun aus den Hülsen fallen will, darum es anfangs von
der Natur und Artisten vorgenommen worden, nemlich das *Patiens* von
dem *Agente* entlediget, und derowegen perficiret werde. *Nam liberatio
illa a partibus heterogeneis est vita & perfectio omnis Rei,* d. i. dann
diese Befreyung von denen ungleichen und widrigen Theilen, ist das Leben
und die Vollkommenheit jeder Sache. Denn das *Agens* und *Patiens*, welches bishero mit einander streitig, daß ein jegliches gewürket und Widerstand
gethan hat, nach seines Gegenparts Widerstand, (das ist) um so viel
ihm möglich und er seine Widerwärtigen hat brechen mögen, müssen sich
in währender Zeit ihrer *Decoction* nicht einigen, sondern der beste Theil
muß den Sieg behalten, und das Unreine ausstossen und unter sich bringen.

Wenn nun alle *Naturales potentiae* ihr *officium* gethan haben, alsdenn kömmt eine neue Geburt hervor, und erzeiget sich die zeitige Frucht, wie
in allen andern Gewächsen also auch in unserm *Subjecto* und natürlichen
Werk, welches, wann es ausgearbeitet, ganz wunderlich, und seinem ersten
Anfang ganz und gar nicht mehr gleich siehet, und gar keine Qualität mehr
hat, welche weder kalt noch trocken, und weder feucht noch warm, auch
weder *masculus* noch *foemina*. Denn das Kalte ist daselbst verkehret in das
Warme, und das Trockene in das Feuchte, das Schwere ist leicht, und das
Leichte schwer worden; denn es ist eine neue *Quinta Essentia, ein Corpus
Spirituale,* und *Spiritus corporalis* worden, ein solch *Corpus*, welches
lauter und rein, durchsichtig und crystallinisch ist; welches die Natur für sich
selber niemahlen, so lange die Welt gestanden hat, ausarbeiten mögen; der
Artifex und erleuchte Mensch aber *auxiliante Deo & natura* bringts herfür
durch seinen Verstand und Kunst, und stellet es ihm selber dar, damit er
nachmahlen *miracula* begegnet, und das heisset: *Unguentum, anima, aurum Philosophorum, flos auri.* (Die Seele, die Salbe, das Gold der
Philosophen, die Blume des Goldes.) *Theophrastus* und andere nennen
es *Gluten aquilae.*

Was nun von den vier *potentiis naturae* ist angezeigt, dieselben
werden vollbracht vermittelst des Feuers, welches muß heimlich, fein sitt-
sam, natürlich und unverbrennlich seyn, der Natur angenehm, und derselben
gemäß, stetig anhaltend, und also dem Werke fürderlich seyn, es sind aber
fürnemlich zweyerley Feuer in diesem Werk wohl in acht zu haben, nemlich
das äußerliche elementische Feuer, welches der *Artifex* erstruiret, und dem
Werk beybringt, darnach das innerliche, angebohrne und natürliche Feuer der
Materien. Wiewohl auch in allen dreyen ansahenden Dingen oder Geschlechten als in den *Animalibus, Vegetabilibus* und *Mineralibus* ein natürlich
Feuer sich findet, dadurch es angetrieben und beweget, sein Leben erhalten,
gestärkt, gegrössert, und also ihre angebohrne Kraft der Gebährung und ein-
gepflanzte Tugend nach jedes Eigenschaft fortsetzen kann.

Aber das Feuer, so in unserm *Subjecto*, ist unter den Creaturen und
Mineralien das geringste in ihm selber, so hat in ihm verborgen die aller-
wunderlichste, kräftigste Feure, gegen welchen das äußerliche Feuer als Wasser
zu achten ist, denn kein gemein elementisch Feuer kann das feine Gold, so die
allerbeständigste Substanz unter allen Metallen ist, verzehren und zunichte machen, es sey das Feuer auch so stark es immer wolle, aber der Philosophen ihr
essentialisch △ und ▽ das thuts allein.

Wann wir nun dasjenige Feuer hätten, womit Moses das güldene
Kalb verbrannt, und es auf das Wasser stäubete, und dem Volk Israel zu
trinken gab, *Exod.* 33 Cap., laß mir solches ein alchymisch Stücklein seyn
von Mose dem Mann Gottes! er war aber in der egyptischen Kunst gelehret
und darinn erzogen. Oder welches Feuer der Prophet *Jeremias* versteckt
unten an dem Berge, auf welchen Berg Moses das gelobte Land gesehen und
allda gestorben, welches Feuer nach 70 Jahren von den Wissenden der alten
Priester Nachkömmlinge nach Wiederkehr des Gefängnisses von Babel erhoben
ward, und aber mittler weile dieser Zeit im Berge sich resolviret, und zu einem dick-
lichen Wasser worden war. 2 Maccab. 1. u. 2. Cap. Was meinest du, ob
wir uns nicht dabey wärmen, und im Winter uns des Frostes erwehren
wollten.

Solches Feuer aber schläfet in unserm *Subjecto* ganz ruhig und still,
und hat von ihm selbst keine Bewegung. Soll nun dieses heimliche und ver-

the same had been effected by means of the fire, which must be incombustible, pleasing to Nature, and according to Nature it must continue steadily and must also be advantageous to the Work: but in this Work two kinds of fires are to be particularly well attended to, namely: the outer elementary fire which the *Artifex* constructeth and which he applieth to the Work, and after that the inner, innate, and natural fire of the substances. Though in all three primary things or genera there is to be found a natural fire as in the *Animalibus*, *Vegetabilibus*, and *Mineralibus*, through which it started and moved, maintained life, was strengthened and increased; and can continue its innate power of bringing forth and of implanted virtue according to the character of each.

But the fire which is in our *Subjecto* is in itself not least amongst creatures and minerals. It hath hidden within itself the most wonderful, the most potent fire against which the outer fire seemeth like water, for no common elementary fire can consume and destroy the pure gold which is the most durable substance amongst all metals, however intense the fire may be, but the essential $\triangle$ and ∇ of the Philosophers alone doeth it.

If we had to-day that fire with which Moses burned the golden calf and ground it to powder and strewed it upon the water and which he gave to and made the Children of Israel drink of it (*Exodus*, ch. 32) — let such be a piece of alchemical work of Moses, the man of God! For he was instructed in the Egyptian art and skilled therein. Or the fire which the prophet *Jeremias* hid beneath the foot of the mountain, from which Moses saw the Promised Land and whereon he died, the fire which was recovered seventy years later by the Wise Men, the descendants of the old priests after the return from the Babylonian Captivity. But in the meantime the fire was changed in the mountain and became dense water (II *Maccab.*, ch. 1 and 2). What thinkest thou? should we not warm ourselves at it and keep from us the frost in winter?

Such fire slumbereth in our *Subjecto* quietly and peacefully and hath no movement of itself. Should now this secret and hidden fire help its own *Corpori*, so that is may rise and have its effect, and manifest its might and power, so that the Artist may reach the desired and predestined end, it must be aroused through the outer elementary fire, be kindled and be brought into its course. This fire may be in lamps, or of whatever kind thou dost like, or contrive, for it alone is sufficiently capable of executing the activity with ease, and such fire and outer heat must be tended and maintained all the time until the end of the *Sublimation*, so that the inner and essential fire be kept alive, in order that the two indicated fires may help each other and the outer fire let the inner fire be worthy, until in its appointed time it becometh so strong and intense a fire that it will soon burn to ashes, pulverise, turn into itself, and make equal to itself all that is put into it but which is nevertheless of its own kind and nature.

Nevertheless it is necessary for every *Artifex*, at the cost of his desired end, to know that between these two abovementioned fires, he maintaineth certain proportions between the outermost and the innermost, and that he kindle his fire rightly, for if he maketh it too weak, then the Work cometh to a standstill, and the outermost fire is not able to raise the inner one, and in so far as he stirreth it up moderately several times, it yieldeth a slow effect and a very long process, and when he hath waited with such patience and hath his data, he then finally reacheth his intended goal. But if one maketh a stronger fire than befitteth this process, and it be speeded up, then the inner fire suffereth, it is entirely incapable, the Work will surely be destroyed, and the hasty one will never attain his end.

If after lasting *Decoction* and *Sublimation* the noble and pure parts of the *Subjecti* are gradually, with the advantage of a calculated time, separated and set free from the crude earthly and useless substance, the impulse in such activity must be according to Nature and must be adjusted with such moderation that it will be agreeable, pleasing, and advantageous to the inner fire, in order that the inner essential fire be not destroyed through all too-intense heat, or even extin-

guished and made useless. Nay, rather it will be maintained in its natural degree, be strengthened, whilst the pure and subtle parts come together and convene, the crude being separated, so that they combine and the best will achieve the aforesaid end in view. Therefore thou must learn from Nature that degree of fire which Nature useth in its operations until it bringeth its fruit to maturity, and from this learn *Reason* and make calculation. For the inner essential fire is really that which bringeth the *Mercurium Philosophorum* to *aequalitaet;* but the outer fire stretcheth forth to it a hand so that the inner fire will not be hindered in its operation, therefore the outer must have concordance with the inner and must adjust itself according to the same, *vice versa.* Then in such use of the universal elementary fire it must be led toward the inner natural heat, and the outer heat hath to be adjusted to it, so that such doth not surpass in the *Creato* the power of the moist and warm *Spiritus*, which is wholly *subtil;* if otherwise, the warm nature of the said *Spiritus* would soon be dissolved, and it could not hold itself together any more, and would have no potency; it followeth therefrom that a fire more intense than is necessary for reviving and maintaining the inner natural fire implanted in our *Materiae* can only be for hindrance and deterioration. *In natura et illius Creatis et generationibus sit tua Imaginatio,* — *i.e.*, upon Nature and what hath been created or brought forth by her, mediate thou. Therefore bring the moist *Spiritum* into the earth, make it dry, *agglutinirs* and *figurs*, with an agreeable fire. Thus shalt thou also bring the *Animam* into the dead *Corpus* and restore what thou hast taken away, and thou restorest the soulless and dead to life and to rise again and be equipped, but whatever hath driven it will not stand the heat, for it will not become constant as if it were to be received spontaneously from itself with good will, with joy and with desire, and be deeply impressed.

And that is *sicci cum humido naturalis unio et ligamentum optimum* (the natural unification of the dry with the moist and also the best tie). Yea, if one really desireth to discuss this matter: the Wise Men mention three kinds of fire, each of which taketh charge of the *operis magni*, so that each best form in particular must in wisdom and good readiness have governed this also. And so he will not work as one blind, but in an understanding and prudent manner, as befitteth an intelligent *Philosophus.*

The first is the outer fire, which the *Artist* or watchman maketh, which the Wise Men call *ignem frontem*, upon which *Regimen* dependeth the safety or the ruin of the entire Work, and this in two ways: *nemium sumiget cave* (take heed that it doth not smoke too much), but it is also said: *combure igne fortissimo* (burn it with the strongest fire).

The second fire is the nest wherein the *Phoenix* of the Philosophers hath its abode, and hatcheth itself therein *ad regenerationem.* This is nothing else than the *Vas Philosophorum.* The Wise Men call it *ignem corticum*, for it is written that the *Phoenix* bird collected all fragrant wood whereon it cremateth itself. If this were not so, the *Phoenix* would freeze to death and it could not attain to its *Perfection. Sulphura Sulphuribus continentur* (Sulphurs are maintained by sulphurs). For the nest should protect, assist, cherish and keep the brood of the bird unto the final end.

The third however is the true innate fire of the noble *Sulphuris*, itself to be found *in radice subjecti*, and is an *Ingredient*, and it *quieteth* the *Mercurium* and fashioneth it: that is the real Master, yea, the true *Sigillum Hermetis.* Concerning this fire *Crebrerus* writeth: *In profundo mercurii est Sulphur, quod tandem vincit frigiditatem et humiditatem in Mercurio. Hoc nihil aliud est, quam parvus ignis occultus in mercurio, quod in mineris nostris exitatur et longo temporis successe digerit frigiditatem et humiditatem in mercurio.* — *i.e.,* In the essence of the *Mercurii* is a sulphur which finally conquereth the coldness and the moisture in the *Mercurio.* This is nothing else than a small fire hidden in the *Mercurio*, which is aroused in our *Mineris*, and in the fulness of time it absorbeth the coldness and moisture in the *Mercurio* or removeth them, and that is also said about the fire.

FINIS

bergene Feuer seinem eigenem *Corpori* helfen, daß es sich möge erheben und seine Wirkung haben, und seine Macht und Kraft erzeigen, daß der Artist zum gewünschten und prädestinirten Ende komme, so muß es durch das äusserliche elementische Feuer erweckt, angezündet, und in seinen Lauf gebracht werden, es sey das Feuer in *Lampen*, oder was Gattung dir gefällt, angestellt, denn es allein gnugsam den Handel auszuführen bequem und tüchtig ist, und muß solch Feuer und äusserliche Wärme die ganze Zeit bis zum Ende der *Sublimation* serviren und erhalten, damit das innerliche essentialische Feuer im Leben gericht werde, daß also die zwey angezeigte Feuer einander helfen, und das Aeussere das Innere ihm lassen empfohlen seyn, bis auf seinen bestimmten Termin, daß es ein solch kräftig und inbrünstig Feuer wird, daß es alsobald alles dasjenige, so ihm zugesetzt, doch seiner Art und Natur ist, zur Aschen bringet, pulverisiret, in sich verkehrt, und seines Gleichen macht.

Indessen aber ist einem jeden *Artifici* bey Verlust seines gewünschten Endes zu wissen vonnöthen, daß er zwischen beyden diesen obgedachten Feuern, als dem äussersten und innersten die gewisse Proportion halte, und sein Feuer recht entzünde, denn macht ers zu schwach, so stehet das Werk stille, und mag das äusserste Feuer das innere nicht erheben, und sofern er solches je etlichen maassen rege macht, gibt es eine langsame Würkung und sehr langen Proceß, mag doch endlich sein vorgesetztes Ziel bey dem, so mit Geduld auswarten thut, und seine Nachrichtigung hat, erreichen; gibt man dann ein stärker Feuer, denn ihm gebühret und das innere Feuer erleiden mag, und will damit eilen, so ist es ganz untüchtig und wird das Werk allerdings zerstöhret, und erreichet der Eilende nimmer sein Ende.

Denn nachdem in währender *Decoction* und *Sublimation* die edeln und reinen Theile des *Subjecti* allgemach mit Vortheil der angelegten Zeit von dem groben irdischen und untüchtigem Wesen abgeschieden und erlediget sollen werden, so muß der Treiber in solcher Wirkung der Natur nach, und daß es mit solcher *Moderation* angestellet werde, daß es dem innerlichen Feuer annehmlich, lieblich und förderlich sey, damit das innerliche essentialische Feuer durch allzustarker Hitze nicht zerstöhret oder gar ausgelöscht werde und untüchtig gemacht, sondern vielmehr in seinem natürlichen Grad erhalten, gestärkt, inmittelst sich die reinen und subtilen Theile sammlen und zusammen sich thun, das Grobe aber sich absondert, damit sich zusammen thut, das Beste den vorgesetzten Zweck erreichen möge. Darum must du solchen Grad des Feuers von der Natur lernen, wie die in ihrer Würkung handelt, bis sie ihre Frucht zur Zeitigung bringe, und hieraus ein *Raison* schöpfen und Rechnung machen. Denn das innerliche essentialische Feuer ist eigentlich dasjenige Ding, so den *Mercurium Philosophorum* zur *aequalitaet* bringet; das äussere Feuer aber beut ihm die Hand, damit es an seiner *Operation* nicht verhindert werde, darum muß das Aeussere mit dem Innern eine Concordanz haben, und nach demselben zurichten *vice versa*. Denn es muß in solcher Anstellung des gemeinen elementischen Feuers die innerliche natürliche Wärme geführet, und die äusserliche Wärme darnach sich reguliren, damit solche der Gewalt des feuchten und warmen *Spiritus*, welche ganz *subtil* sind, in dem *Creato* nicht übertreffe: wo anders, so würde gemeldtem *Spiritus* warme Natur alsobald resolviret, und könnte sich nicht mehr zusammen halten, noch einige Macht haben, derohalben was mehr und stärker denn zu Erweckung und Erhaltung des innerlich natürlichen unseter *Materien* eingepflanztes Feuer, ist alles zur

Verhinderniß und zur Verderbniß. *In natura & illius Creatis & generationibus sit tua Imaginatio.* d. i. In der Natur, und was von ihr gezeuget oder hervorgebracht wird, sey deine Betrachtung. Darum bringe den feuchten *Spiritum* ein in die Erde, machts trocken, *agglutinirs* und *figirs* mit lieblichen Feuer, denn so wirst du so wohl einführen die *Animam* in das todte *Corpus*, und welchem du es genommen restituiren, dem entseelten und erstorbenen zum Leben, und wieder auferstehen und armiten, was aber mit Gewalt eingetrieben wird, hält sich nicht wohl in der Probe, denn es wird nicht beständig, als wenn es von ihm selbst gutwillig mit Lust und Begierd angenommen imprimiret wird.

Und das ist *ficci cum humido naturalis unio & ligamen tum optimum*, (die natürliche Vereinigung des Trockenen mit dem Feuchten, und das beste Band.) Ja wenn man eigentlich von der Sache reden will, so melden die weisen Männer von dreyerley Feuer, deren ein jedweder, so des *operis magni* sich annimt, eines jedweden insonderheit bester Forma im Wissen und guter Bereitschaft auch diese zu regieren haben muß, so er anders nicht blinder, sondern wissender und vorsichtiger Weise arbeiten will, als einem verständigen *Philosopho* zustehet.

Das erste ist das äussere Feuer, so der *Artist* oder Hüter anstellt, welches die Weisen *ignem frontem* nennen, auf welches *Regimen* gleichwohl des ganzen Werks Heil und Verderben stehet, und solches auf zweyerley Weise, denn es heisset: *nimium fumiget cave*, (nimm dich in acht daß es nicht zu viel rauche) und heist auch wiederum: *combure igne fortissimo*, (verbrenne es mit dem stärksten Feuer.)

Das andere Feuer ist das Nest, darinnen sich der Philosophen *Phoenix* einlogiret, und darinnen *ad regenerationem* sich ausbrütet, ist anders nichts denn das *Vas Philosophorum*. Die Weisen nennen es *ignem corticum*, denn man schreibet, daß der Vogel *Phoenix* all wohlriechendes Holz zusammen trage, darinnen er sich selber verbrenne, wo daß nicht wäre, müste *Phoenix* ersterben, und könnte zu seiner *Perfection* nicht kommen. *Sulphura Sulphuribus continentur*, (Schwefel wird durch Schwefel unterhalten.) Denn das Nest soll den Vogel seine Jungen bewahren, helfen, foviren, und bis ans letzte End erhalten.

Das dritte aber ist das recht innerlich angebohrne Feuer des edlen *Sulphuris*, so in radice *subjecti* sich findet, und ein *Ingredienz* ist, und den *Mercurium* stillet und ihn *figiret*: das ist der rechte Meister, ja das wahre *Sigillum Hermetis*. Von diesem Feuer schreibet *Crebrerus*: In *profundo mercurii est Sulphur, quod tandem vincit frigiditatem & humiditatem in Mercurio. Hoc nihil aliud est, quam parvus ignis occultus in mercurio, quod in mineris nostris excitatur & longo temporis successe digerit frigiditatem & humiditatem in mercurio.* d. i. Im Grunde des *Mercurii* ist ein Schwefel, welcher endlich die Kälte und Feuchte im *Mercurio* überwindet. Dieses ist nichts anders denn ein reines Feuer, so im *Mercurio* verborgen steckt, welches in unsern *Mineris* erwecket wird, und durch Länge der Zeit die Kälte und Feuchte im *Mercurio* digeriret oder hinweg nimmt, und das sey auch also von dem Feuer gesagt.

FINIS.

IF A PHILOSOPHER YOU WISH TO BE,
Where on this globe lives a man so wise,
Who'll ever learn what four ones do comprise,
And even if he'd know all this,
He'd still always be an apprentice.
Therefore, O human, with all thy might,
Recognise God and thyself in God's and nature's light,
Both these lights God pours into thee,
That a likeness of him thou mayest be,
He is one fourfold God, let thou be told,
As thou art a piece of clay fourfold.
This maketh nature to thee well known,
With wisdom, light and understanding to thee is it shown.

LET ONLY PATIENCE DWELL IN THEE.
To nothing can thine eye be blind,
Be it of body or of mind.
Therefore be thankful to thy God,
Who in time this before thee hast brought.
Be thou not jealous of the scoffer's fame,
Do not begrudge every mocker's great name.
With sophisticated vanity they strut,
Unbeknownst to them is what thou'st got.
Be happy with what God to thee gave,
Defy, that four in one they have.
Fiat and Amen, be my treasure,
A fourfold sphere always together.

O DOMINE QUAM MIRABILIA SUNT OPERA TUA.

Lord, thine eternal Spirit is in all Things.
Salvator ☿ Mundi

Four fires are floating in this world,
Wherein God holdeth a Center,

That is locked up in four,
Out of which Heaven and Earth were poured.

SPECULUM DIVINUM OCCULTUM ATOUE

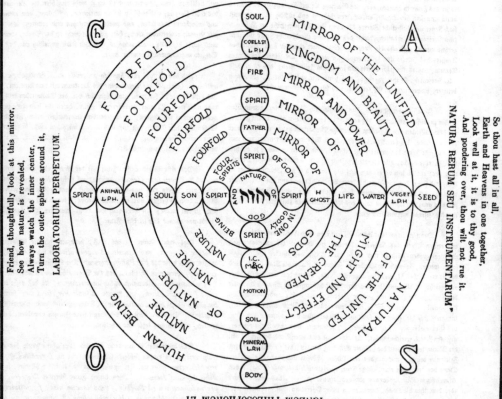

Friend, thoughtfully look at this mirror,
See how nature is revealed,
Always watch the inner center,
Turn the outer spheres around it,
LABORATORIUM PERPETUUM.

NATURA RERUM SEU INSTRUMENTARUM"
So thou hast all in all,
Earth and Heavens in one together,
Look well at it, it is to thy good,
And pondering over, thou wilt not rue it.

Notice Nature in its strength,
Look at its great life-power.

From God it, and all things spring,
And return to their centers again.

Coel. & ☿ Terra.

There is never a Philosopher who Nature's ultimate Principle doth not know.

Look well for the golden Magnet. If thou findest it thou wouldest get rid of thy sorrows.
Study well the law KNOW THYSELF, that thou may not be deceived any more.
Unum sunt omnia, per quod omnia.
Make known to thee the Terra Sancta, so that thou mayest not go astray.

Wilt du ein Philoſophus ſeyn,   So laß Geduld bey dir ziehen ein.

Welcher Menſch lebt in dieſer Welt,
der auſſern was vier eins in ſich hält,
und ob er ſchon deſſen kundig iſt,
bleibt dennoch Lehrjung zu aller Friſt.
Darum o Menſch erkenne Gott und dich,
nach dem göttlichen und natürlichen Licht,
welche Gott beyde in dich geleit,
auf daß du ſeyſt ein Bild ihm gleich,
wie er iſt ein viereiniger Gott,
und du ein vierfach Erdenklott.
Das giebt Weisheit, Licht und Verſtand,
macht dir Natur und alles bekannt.

Und mag nichts Geiſt- noch Leibliches
vor deinen Augen verbergen ſich.
Dafür dank Gott aus Herzensgrund,
der dir ſolchs in der Zeit thut kund.
Der Spötter Ruhm und groſſen Namen
laß dich nicht irren, noch darum grämen.
Was du haſt bleibt ihnen unbekannt,
ſie prangen mit ihren Sophiſten Tand.
Freu du dich deiner Gottes Gaben,
trutz, daß ſie vier in eins haben,
Mein Schatz bleibt Fiat und Amen,
ein vierfach Sphær immer beyſammen.

O Domine quam mirabilia ſunt Opera tua.

Herr dein unvergänglicher Geiſt iſt in allen Dingen.

Salvator ☿ Mundi

Vier Feuer ſchweben in der Welt   Das in Vieren iſt verſchloſſen,
Darinnen Gott ein Centrum hält,   Daraus Himmel und Erden gefloſſen.

SPECULUM DIVINUM OCCULTUM ATQUE

Schau die Natur in ihrer Kraft,   Von Gott ſie und alle Dinge entſpringen
Merk auf ihr groſſe Lebensmacht,   Und wieder in ihr Centrum dringen.

Coel. & ☿ Terra.

Das iſt nimmer ein Philoſophus, dem der Natur Grund nicht bewußt.

Such den güldnen Magnet. Findeſt du den, kömmſt aus allem Leid.
Studier wohl das γνωθισ αυτον, ſo wirſt du kommen aus falſchen Wahn.
Unum ſunt omnia, per quod omnia.
Die Terra Sancta mache dir bekannt, kömmſt leichtlich aus dem Irregang.

225

The outer and the inner Mind
Without God's light you cannot find.

God is free everywhere
Within and without all creatures
GOD
Time measure of Nature
The Angel with six wings
I.

God is the Alpha and Omega
The Beginning and the End
FATHER
Time-Measure of the Law
Lion with six wings
II.

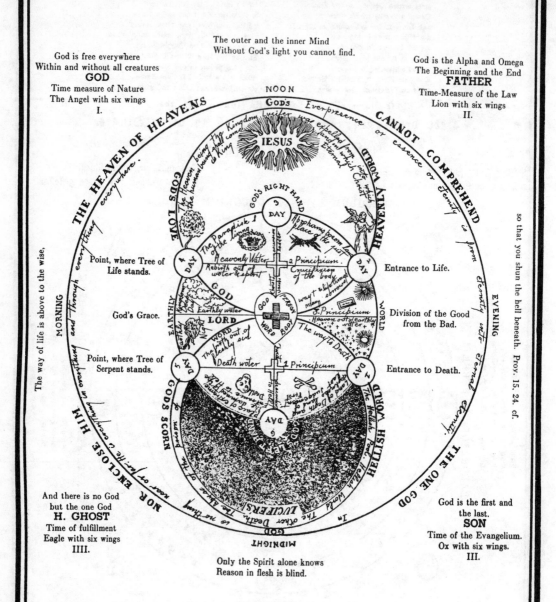

Point, where Tree of
Life stands.

God's Grace.

Point, where Tree of
Serpent stands.

Entrance to Life.

Division of the Good
from the Bad.

Entrance to Death.

And there is no God
but the one God
H. GHOST
Time of fulfillment
Eagle with six wings
IIII.

God is the first and
the last.
SON
Time of the Evangelium.
Ox with six wings.
III.

Only the Spirit alone knows
Reason in flesh is blind.

the hellish world have their effects. And the darkness cannot conquer the light. It also shows that the land of the dead, the entrance to hell or superficial darkness, where there is wailing and gnashing of teeth, as well as the land of the living, the heavenly paradise or third heaven are from this world. And that the human being has all these things in his heart; heaven and hell, light and darkness, life and death.

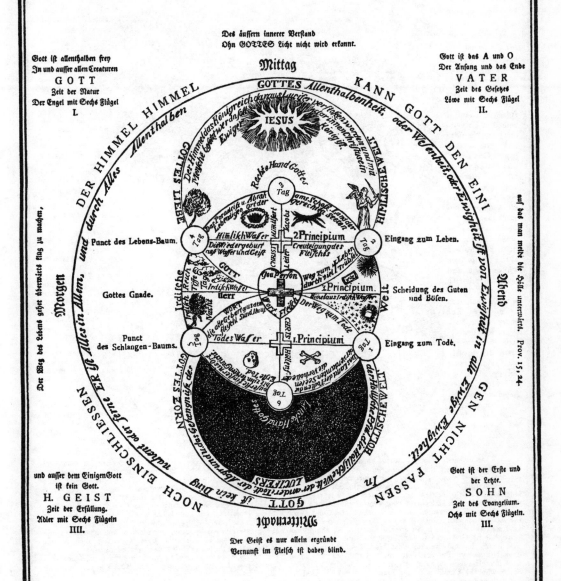

höllische Welt ihre Würkungen haben.   Und vermag die Finsterniß das Licht nicht.   Auch wie das Land der Todten,
die Vorhölle oder die äusserste Finsterniß, da Heulen und Zähnklappen ist, sowol als das Land der Lebendigen,
das himmlische Paradeiß oder der dritte Himmel, nicht ausser dieser Welt sey.   Und daß der Mensch alle Dinge,
Himmel und Hölle, Licht und Finsterniß, Leben und Tod, in seinem Herzen habe.

The Tree of Good and Evil Knowledge

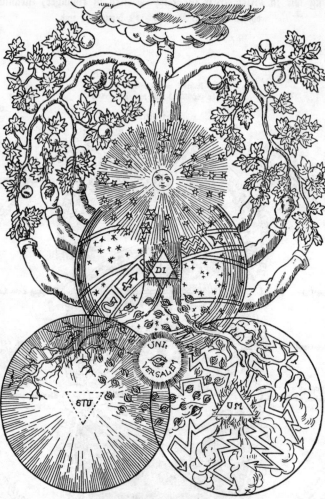

THERE IS ONE TREE

bearing two kinds of fruits. Its name is the tree of the knowledge of good and evil. Like its name, are its fruits; namely, good and bad fruits of life and death, of love and hate, of light and darkness. This tree was put before Adam, and even if he had in his innocence the liberty to look upon it as a tree of God's wonders. God's prohibition did not allow him to place his desire in it and eat of it, but threatened that (if he would do so) he would die from its fruit. For this was a tree of division where good and evil battled with each other; but in a battle there can be no life: For battle brings forth destruction, and destruction brings forth death, life lives in the sweet unity of love. Therefore, when Adam ate from this tree, a battle started within him, and in this battle he lost his life.

Nevertheless wretched men will not learn through such fall and damage. His desire is still for that tree and its fruits. Man is always desirous to have the division of manifold things, and man is always battling, when he could return to the unity of simplicity, if he only would come in peace. Life's light stands in the middle to point out to men the way to this first rest, and the Father in the heaven lets his Sun rise over good and evil: But everything grows after its own fashion, and man is only too apt to look upon the stars of the many-foldness, and in his own discretion, to choose them for his ladders, though they make him stray many times from the true light, and detain him in the whirlpool of uncertainty. This whirlpool of uncertainty leads more and more out of the innermost face of the Sun into the outer (world) and can find neither end nor place of rest, unless it leads from the outer (world) back again and seeks the beginning, from which all the smaller star-lights originated.

There is also among 7 stars, hardly one turning its rays inward to direct the searching mind to Bethlehem, and amongst 7 eyes winding around the whirlpool of searching desire is hardly one which stands towards the Sabbath in the innermost; but the restless movement of the working days move them through all spheres, and even if they take a look at God's wonders, they only look upon the surface and every eye looks upon that which is shown through its own desire. God made man to live in an eternal Sabbath, he should not work, but let God work in him, he should not take with his own hands, but only receive what God bestowed plentifully upon His mercy. But man left the Sabbath, and wanted to work himself, raised his hand against the law to take in his own desire what he should not have taken. Therefore, God let him fall, and since he had despised the quiet, he had to feel painfully the restlessness. In such restlessness of life all children of man still extend their hands, trying to grasp their pleasures. And as is their understanding and will, so is their grasping. Some grasp for the good, some grasp for the evil. Some grasp for the fruit, some only for the leaves, some for a branch with fruits and leaves on it. And they derive pleasure from the things they have grasped, these poor fools do not know that all their pain and labor had only been a *Studium particulare*. They grasp for pieces, where they could obtain the whole. They seek for quiet and cannot find it; for they look from the outside into the restlessness of movement, which dwells in the inner solitude of the inner *Centri*, and though one may grasp more than the other, it is still piece-work. At times there may be one amongst 7 hands coming near the secret and it grasps the whole stem of the tree at that point where all the divided branches return to unity. But even this hand is still far from the roots of the tree, only grasping and holding the secret from the outside and cannot yet see it from the inside. For the root of this tree is understood only by the eye of wisdom, standing in the *Centro* of all spheres. These roots go from the visible world of mingled good and evil, into the sphere of the invisible world. This eye looks with the greatest peace upon the wonders of all movements and also looks through all the other eyes, wandering about outside of the rest in the unrest, all those eyes which want to see for themselves without the right eye of wisdom, from which they have received all their seeing-power. This eye can prove all spirits, how intelligent, pure and acute they be. It understands the sources of good and evil. Plain before it is light and darkness. It understands time and eternity, visible and invisible, present and future things, earthly and heavenly things, things of the body and things of the spirit, high and deep, outwardliness and inwardliness. And nevertheless, none of these things are disturbed by it, for the eye lives in the *Centro* of peace, where everything stands in equality outside of any strife, and whatever it sees it possesses. For in the *Centro* of its peace is its kingly throne, everything being subject to it. Therefore, dear man! If thou wouldst return to right understanding and right peace, cease from thy works and let God alone work in thee, so that the eye of wisdom will open in thine own self and thou wilt attain a *studio particulari ad universale* and One find All.

Der Baum der Erkenntniß Gutes und Böses.

Es ist ein einziger Baum, der träget zweyerley Früchte. Sein Name ist, der Baum der Erkenntniß Gutes und Böses. Wie sein Name ist, so sind auch seine Früchte, nemlich, gute und böse, Früchte des Lebens und des Todes, der Liebe und des Zorns, des Lichts und der Finsterniß. Dieser Baum ward Adam in seiner Unschuld vorgestellet, und wiewohl er Freyheit hatte, denselben als einen Baum der Wunder Gottes anzuschauen; so wollte doch das göttliche Verbot ihm nicht verstatten, daß er seine Begierde darein setzen und davon essen sollte; sondern drohete ihm, daß er von seiner Frucht des Todes sterben würde. Denn es war der Baum der Scheidlichkeit, da Gutes und Böses in der Zertheilung mit einander stritte; im Streite aber mag das Leben nicht bestehen: denn der Streit gebieret Zerbrechung, und Zerbrechung gebieret den Tod; das Leben aber wohnet in der süßen Einigkeit der Liebe. Darum als Adam von diesem Baume gegessen hatte, so ward der Streit in ihm rege, und in diesem Streit muste er sein Leben verliehren.

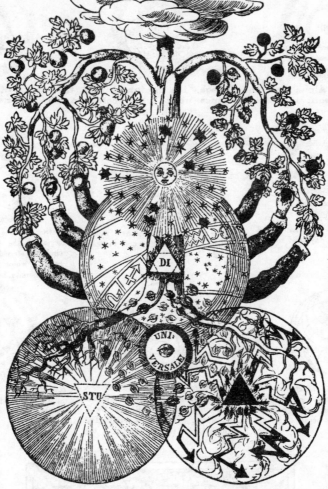

Dennoch will der elende Mensch durch solchen Fall und Schaden noch nicht klüger werden. Seine Begierde stehet immer nach diesem Baum und seinen Früchten. Er lüstert nach der Scheidlichkeit der Vielfalt, und ist immer im Streite, da er doch in die Ruhe kommen könte, wann er nur wieder in die Einheit der Einfalt kehren wollte. Das Licht des Lebens stehet in der Mitten daß es dem Menschen den Weg zur ersten Ruhe zeige, und der Vater im Himmel läßt seine Sonne aufgehen über Böses und Gutes: aber ein jedes wächset nach seiner Art, und der Mensch ist mehr geneigt auf die Sterne der Vielheit zu sehen, die er sich in seinem Gutdünken zu seinen Leitern erwählet, da sie ihm doch oft von dem wahrhaftigen Lichte vielmahl abführen und in dem Wirbel der Ungewißheit aufhalten, der sich immer mehr und mehr von dem inwendigen Angesichte der Sonnen in das Aeußere herauswindet und sein Ende noch Stätte der Ruhe finden mag, wo er sich nicht wieder von Außen hinein windet, und den Anfang suchet, davon alle kleinere Sternen-Lichter ausgegangen sind.

So ist auch unter 7 Sternen kaum einer der seine Strahlen einwärts kehret, daß sie das forschende Gemüthe nach Bethlehem weisen könnten; und unter 7 Augen, welche sich in dem Wirbel der forschenden Begierde herum winden, ist kaum ein einiges, das nach dem Sabbat in das Innere gerichtet stehet; sondern die unruhige Beweglichkeit der Werkel-Tage treibet sie durch alle Sphären, und ob sie wol einen Blick in die Wunder Gottes thun, so sehen sie doch, weil sie in das Aeussere gekehret sind, dieselben nur von aussen an, und schauet ein jegliches Auge nur dasjenige, worein es von seiner Begierde geführet wird. Der Mensch war von Gott zu einem beständigen Sabbat erschaffen, er sollte selbst nicht wirken, sondern Gott in sich wirken lassen; er sollte nicht mit seinen Händen sich selber etwas nehmen, sondern nur empfahen, was ihnen von Gottes Güte reichlich dargeboten ward. Allein er verließ den Sabbat und wollte selbst wirken, er streckte wider das Gebot seine Hand aus, in eigener Begierde zu nehmen, was ihm nicht zu nehmen vergönnet war; darum ließ ihn Gott dahin fallen, und weil er die Ruhe verachtet hatte, so muste er hernach die Unruhe mit Schmerzen fühlen. In solcher Unruhe des selbstwirkenden Lebens strecken alle Menschenkinder noch immer ihre Hand aus, und wollen dasjenige ergreifen, wodurch sie ihre Vergnügung zu erlangen suchen; und wie der Verstand und Wille bey ihnen ist, so ist auch ihre Ergreifen. Einige Hände greifen nach dem Guten; Einige Hände greifen nach dem Bösen. Etliche greifen nach der Frucht; Etliche nur nach den Blättern; Etliche ergreifen einen Zweig mit Frucht und Blättern. Was nun ein jeder ergriffen hat, daran ergötzet er sich, und wissen die armen Leute nicht, daß alle ihre Mühe und Wirken nur ein Studium particulare sey. Sie greifen alle nach dem Stückwerk, und können das Ganze erlangen. Sie suchen die Ruhe und finden sie nicht: denn sie suchen sie von Aussen in der Unruhe der Bewegung, da sie doch in der innern Stille des innern Centri wohnet; und ob einer gleich mehr ergreifet als der andere, so ist es dennoch Stückwerk. Zuweilen ist unter 7 Händen eine, welche dem Geheimniß nahe kömmt, und den ganzen Stamm des Baums an demjenigen Orte fasset, wo die zertheilten widerwärtigen Reiche seiner Aeste wieder in die Einheit gehen. Allein sie ist noch ferne von der Wurzel des Baums; sie greifet und tastet das Geheimniß nur von Aussen, und siehet es noch nicht recht von Innen. Denn die Wurzel dieses Baums, welche durch die Sphæram der aus gut und böse gemischten sichtbaren Welt in die Sphären der unsichtbaren Welt gehet, da Licht und Finsterniß in sich selber wohnen, wird nur von dem Auge der Weisheit verstanden, welches in dem Centro aller Sphären stehet. Dieses Auge schauet in der höchsten Ruhe die Wunder aller Bewegungen, und siehet durch alle andere Augen, welche ausser der Ruhe in der Unruhe herumschweifen, und ohne das rechte Auge der Weisheit vor sich selber sehen wollen, da sie doch alle ihr Sehen von demselben empfangen haben. Dieses Auge kann alle Geister prüfen, wie verständig, lauter und scharf sie sind. Es versteht, woher Gutes und Böses entspringet. Licht und Finsterniß ist vor ihm offenbar. Zeit und Ewigkeit, Sichtbares und Unsichtbares, Gegenwärtiges und Zukünftiges, Irdisches und Himmlisches, Leibliches und Geistliches, Hohes und Tiefes, Aeusserliches und Innerliches wird von ihm verstanden. Und doch wird es von deren keines beunruhiget, denn es wohnet im Centro der Ruhe, da alles ausser dem Streite in der Gleichheit stehet, was es siehet das besitzet es auch. Denn im Centro seiner Ruhe ist der königliche Thron, dem alles unterworfen ist. Darum, o lieber Mensch! willst du wieder zum rechten Bestande und zu der rechten Ruhe kommen, so höre auf von deinen Werken, und laß Gott allein in dir wirken, so wird das Auge der Weisheit sich in dir aufthun, und du wirst a studio particulari ad universale gelangen, und in Einem, Alles finden.

I am the Alpha and the Omega, the beginning and the end, saith the Lord,
God liveth in a Light, since no one can come to Him, or near Him.

This is the Omega, which has caused so many many evil days and restless nights.

This is the trifling matter over which so many hundreds of people moaned in vain.

Notice here the eternal end without beginning, the eternal revelation and circle, in eternal love, willpower and centro ☉ whose principle reveals itself since eternity began.

You will see in this the eternal nature in its seven apparitions, revealing itself in the centro○ of the eternal bottomless depth since eternity began.

The Centrum of the eternal bottomless depth of light and darkness is in the infinite inexpressable width and depth everywhere. Therefore is said: The light inhabits the darkness and the darkness cannot grasp it.

An eternal holy fire
An infinite God sent flame
A heavenly secret

} The great indescribable spirit of fire, inexplorable in eternity.

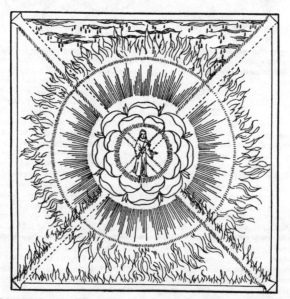

Harmonious Conception of the Light of Nature.
FROM WHICH YOU CAN DEDUCE THE RESTORATION & RENOVATION OF ALL THINGS EMBLEMATIC.

Ich bin das A und O, der Anfang und das Ende, spricht der HErr.
Gott wohnet in einem Lichte, da niemand hin oder zu ihm kommen kann.

Dieses O ist es, daß vielen so viele böse Tage und unruhige Nächte verursachet hat.

Dieses geringschätzige Wesen ist es, darüber so viel hundert Menschen so viele vergebliche Seufzer gethan haben.

Merk allhier den ewigen Ausgang ohne Anfang, den ewigen Aufschluß und Einschluß, so sich auf der ewigen Liebe, Willen und Centro ☉, und dessen Grund sich von Ewigkeit eröfnet und offenbaret.

Man verstehet allhier die ewige Natur mit ihren sieben Gestalten, so auf dem Centro ☉ des ewigen Ungrundes von Ewigkeit sich eröffnet und offenbahret.

Das Centrum des ewigen Ungrundes des Lichts und der Finsterniß ist in der unendlichen und unmeldlichen Weite und Tiefe überall. Darum heißet es, das Licht wohnet in der Finsterniß, und die Finsterniß begreift es nicht.

Ein ewiges heiliges Feuer } Der grosse unbe-
Eine unendlich göttl. Flamme } schreibliche Feuer-
Ein himmlisches Geheimniß } geist, in Ewigkeit
unerforschlich.

Harmonische Vorstellung aus dem Lichte der Natur.
Daraus die Wiederherstellung und Neumachung aller Dinge emblematice abzunehmen ist.

231

The art makes him a lord, not a servant.
Do not make haste, stay on the right track,
So thou wilt have much profit and much joy.

The art is just, true and certain to the
Man who fears God and is assiduous,
And behaves rightly towards all natures.

If God grants many things in thy life,
Give plentifully to the poor,
Be faithful and silent about the art,

For this surely is God's will,
Keep truth and faith, think of me,
So thou wilt be free from all evil.

1604

MONS PHILOSOPHORUM.

The soul of men everywhere was lost through a fall, and the health of the body suffered through a fall, Salvation came to the human soul through IEHOVA, Jesus Christ. The bodily health is brought back through a thing not good to look at. It is hidden in this painting, the highest treasure in this world, in which is the highest medicine and the greatest parts of the riches of nature, given to us by the Lord IEHOVA. It is called *Pator Metallorum*, well known to the philosopher sitting in front of the mountain-cave, easy to obtain for anybody. But the sophists in their sophistic garb, tapping on the walls, recognise him not. At the right is to be seen *Lepus*, representing the art of chemistry, marvellously white, the secrets of which with fire's heat are being explored. To the left one can see freely what the right *Clavis artis* is; one cannot be too subtle with it, like a hen hatching a chicken. In the midst of the mountain, before the door stands a courageous Lion in all its pride, whose noble blood the monster-dragon is going to shed; throwing him into a deep grave, out of it comes forth a black raven, then called *Ianua artis*, out of that comes *Aquila alba*. Even the crystal refined in the furnace will quickly show you on inspection *Servum fugitivum*, a wonder-child to many artists. The one effecting this all is *Principium laboris*. On the right hand in the barrel are *Sol* and *Luna*, the intelligence of the firmament. The Senior plants in it *Rad. Rubeam and albam*. Now you proceed with constancy and *Arbor artis* appears to you, with its blossoms it announces now *Lapidem Philosophorum*. Over all, the crown of the glory, ruling over all treasures.

Be diligent, peaceful, constant and pious, pray that God may help thee. And if thou attain, never forget the poor. Then thou wilt praise God with the legion of the angels, now and forever.

MONS PHILOSOPHORUM.

Die Kunst ist gerecht, wahr und gewiß,
Dem, der gottesfürchtig, fleißig ist,
Und braucht sich der Naturen recht.

Macht ihn zum Herrn, nicht zum Knecht,
Eil nicht, bleib auf der rechten Bahn,
So wirst du Nutz und Freud viel han.

Und gönn't es Gott dir in dein'm Leben,
So thu reichlich den Armen geben,
Sey treu, und halt die Kunst im Still.

Denn das ist gewißlich Gottes Will,
Halt Treu und Glaub, denk mein dabey,
So bleibst du aller Nachred frey.

Die Seel des Menschen überall
Verlohren ist durch einen Fall,
Durch einen Fall des Leibs Gesundheit
Verlohren und zerrüttet leid't.
Der Seel ein Heil wiederbracht ist,
Welches ist IEHOVA Jesus Christ.
Des Leibes Gesundheit wiederbringt
Von Angesicht ein schlechtes Ding,
Welches ist verborgen in diesem Gemähld,
Der höchste Schatz in dieser Welt,
In ihm ist die höchste Medicin
Auch der größte Theil der Reichthum,
Welchen uns der HERRE IEHOVA
In der Natur fürstellet da,
Pater Metallorum genannt,
Den Philosophis wohl bekannt,
Sitzend wol für des Berges Höht,
Jedermann er sich darbeut feil,
Aber von Sophisten, so verblendt,
Am wenigsten er wird erkennt,

So an den Wänden herummer tappen,
Behängt mit sophistischen Lappen.
Zur Rechten wird gesehen da
Lepus, deut der Kunst Chymia,
Wunderbar'rweiß, und derselben Art
Erforscht wird durch des Feuers Grab,
Zur Linken denn find man auch frey;
Was der rechte Clavis artis sey;
Gleich wie ausbrüht die Henn das Huhn,
Zu subtil kann man ihm nicht thun.
Im Mittel des Berges vor der Thür
Steht der tapfre Löw mit großer Zier,
Welchen denn Drache Ungeheuer,
Vergeußt sein edles Blut so theuer;
Wirfst ihn wol in ein tiefes Grab,
Davon entspringt der schwarze Rab;
Welches denn Ianua artis heist,
Aquila alba davon entspreust;
Selbst der Crystall im Ofen stän,
Wird dir zeigen mit Augenschein,

Servum fugitivum geschwind,
Vielen Artisten ein Wunder-Kind.
Principium laboris ist
Der Mittler genannt zu aller Frist,
Dann auch im Faß zur rechten Hand
SOL LUNA des Firmaments Verstand.
Der Senior so pflanzen thut,
Rad. Rubeam & albam gut.
Nun fährst du fort mit Beständigkeit,
Arbor artis sich dir erzeigt.
Mit seiner Blüt verkündet er nun,
Lapidem Philosophorum.
Darob die Kron der Herrlichkeit,
Herrschend über alle Schätzeweit.
Sey fleißig, friedsam, beständig fromm,
Bitt daß dir GOtt zu Hülfe komm.
Erlangst du das, so laß dir sein
Die Armen stets befohlen seyn,
So wirst du mit der Engel Schaar
GOtt loben jetzt und immerbar.

Mercy - Choice.

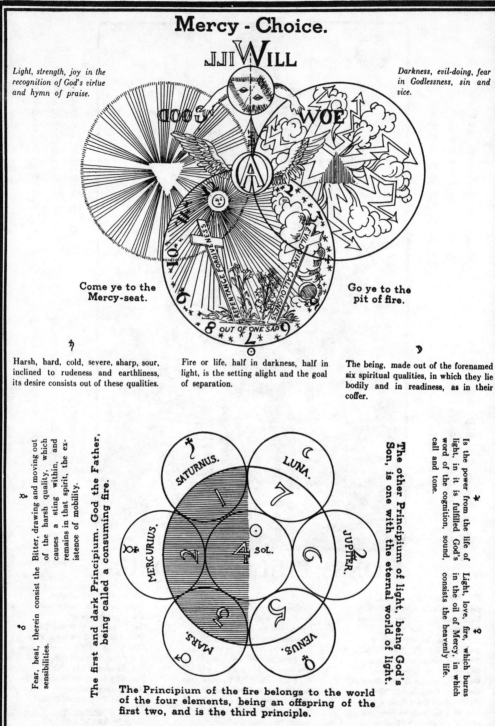

Will

Light, strength, joy in the recognition of God's virtue and hymn of praise.

Darkness, evil-doing, fear in Godlessness, sin and vice.

GOOD

WOE

Come ye to the Mercy-seat.

Go ye to the pit of fire.

OUT OF ONE SAP

♄ Harsh, hard, cold, severe, sharp, sour, inclined to rudeness and earthliness, its desire consists out of these qualities.

☉ Fire or life, half in darkness, half in light, is the setting alight and the goal of separation.

☽ The being, made out of the forenamed six spiritual qualities, in which they lie bodily and in readiness, as in their coffer.

☿ Fear, heat, therein consist the Bitter, drawing and moving out of the harsh quality, which causes a sting within, and remains in that spirit, the existence of mobility.

☿ The first and dark Principium. God the Father, being called a consuming fire.

SATURNUS. LUNA. MERCURIUS. SOL. JUPITER. MARS. VENUS.

♃ The other Principium of light, being God's Son, is one with the eternal world of light.

♂ Is the power from the life of Light, love, fire, which burns light, in it is fulfilled God's word of the cognition, sound, call and tone.

♀ in the oil of Mercy, in which consists the heavenly life.

The Principium of the fire belongs to the world of the four elements, being an offspring of the first two, and is the third principle.

Whenever the first three qualities of the first dark Principii gain the upper hand, then the others are tied up around their Centro and all seven are evil. Then Saturnus stands for avarice, Mercurius for envy, Mars for wrath, Sol for vanity, Venus for lewdness, Jupiter for cunning and Luna for bodily desire, which are the seven evil spirits ruling within the old human being.

But when the three in the Principio of light have the upperhand and are born out of the dark Centro, so that they are in accordance with their innermost depths of light, which is the new birth in man, all seven are good, and then Saturnus stands for compassion, Mercurius for doing good, Mars for gentleness, Sol for humility, Venus for chastity, Jupiter for wisdom, and Luna for Christ's flesh or body.

WILLE

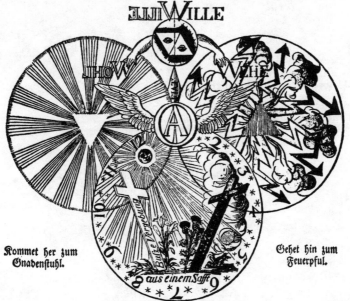

Licht, Kraft, Freude in Erkenntniß Gottes, Tugend u. Lobgesang.

Finsterniß, Bosheit, Angst in Gottlosigkeit, Sünde und Laster.

Kommet her zum Gnadenstuhl.

Gehet hin zum Feuerpful.

♄ Herbe, hart, kalt, strenge, scharf, sauer, zur Grobheit und Irdischheit geneigt, als in welchen Eigenschaften dessen Begierlichkeit besteht.

☉ Feuer oder Leben, halb in der Finsterniß, halb im Licht, ist die Anzündung und das Scheideziel.

☽ Der vorigen sechs geistlichen Eigenschaften gemachtes Wesen, in welchen sie so die Leiblichkeit und Bereitlichkeit, als in ihren Kasten ruhen.

☿ Bitter, Ziehen und Bewegen aus der herben Qualität, welchen ein Stechen darinnen verursacht, und stehet in diesen Geist — Wesen der Beweglichkeit.

♂ Angst, Hitze, darinnen steht die Empfindlichkeit.

Das erstere finstere Principium, so Gott der Vater, so fern Er ein verzehrend Feuer genennet wird.

Das andere, als des Lichts Principium, so Gott der Sohn, und der ewigen Lichtwelt eigen.

♃ Ist die Kraft aus dem Lichtleben, daraus gehet auf das göttliche Wort oder die Erkenntniß, Hall, Schall und Ton.

♀ Licht, Liebe, Feuer, welches in Oel der Gnaden brennet, und darinnen bestehet das himmlische Leben.

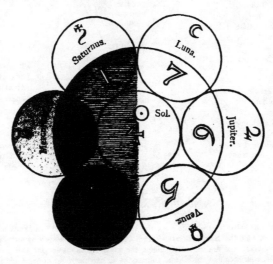

Des Feuers Principium gehöret zur Vier-Elementischen Welt, als eine Ausgeburt aus den zwey Ersten, und ist das dritte Principium.

Wann die drey ersten Eigenschaften des Ersten finstern Principii die Oberhand haben, so sind die übrigen in ihrem Centro verschlungen, und alle sieben böse, als Saturnus der Geiz, Mercurius der Neid, Mars der Zorn, Sol die Hoffarth, Venus die Unzucht, Jupiter die List, und Luna das Fleisch, welches die sieben bösen Geister sind, so in dem alten Menschen herrschen.

Wann aber die drey im Lichts-Principio die Oberhand haben, und aus dem finstern Centro ausgebohren sind, so sind sie nach ihrem innersten Grunde des Lichts, welches die neue Geburt im Menschen ist, alle Sieben gut, und heißt Saturnus sodann die Barmherzigkeit, Mercurius das Wohlthun, Mars die Sanftmuth, Sol die Demuth, Venus die Keuschheit, Jupiter die Weisheit, und Luna Christi Fleisch oder Leib.

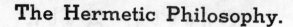

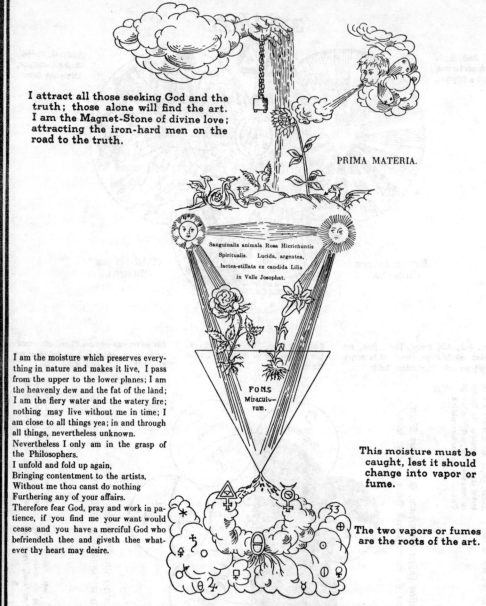

I attract all those seeking God and the truth; those alone will find the art. I am the Magnet-Stone of divine love; attracting the iron-hard men on the road to the truth.

PRIMA MATERIA.

Sanguinalis animala Rosa Hierichuntis Spiritualis. Lucida, argentea, lactea-stillata ex candida Lilia in Valle Josophat.

FONS Miraculv-rum.

I am the moisture which preserves everything in nature and makes it live, I pass from the upper to the lower planes; I am the heavenly dew and the fat of the land; I am the fiery water and the watery fire; nothing may live without me in time; I am close to all things yea; in and through all things, nevertheless unknown.
Nevertheless I only am in the grasp of the Philosophers.
I unfold and fold up again,
Bringing contentment to the artists,
Without me thou canst do nothing
Furthering any of your affairs.
Therefore fear God, pray and work in patience, if you find me your want would cease and you have a merciful God who befriendeth thee and giveth thee whatever thy heart may desire.

This moisture must be caught, lest it should change into vapor or fume.

The two vapors or fumes are the roots of the art.

The Prima Materia derives its existence from the Fiat, the Word of creation. And this Word comes from the Father who is the creator of all things, and the Spirit radiates from both: This is God's life giving air. Then, too, air brings to life everything within the elements. The fire warms all things, the water refreshes, delights and saturates all things: And the nitrous earth, Mother-like, nourishes and sustains all things; the air was born out of fire, and in turn makes the fire burn, that it may live, but air in the form of water is food for the fire, and the fire burns into this element: Water and dew of the ground, the greasy fat dew of the ground, the earth as keeper of nitrous salt nourishes it. For the womb of the earth is the sulphuric nitrous-salt of nature, the one good thing God has created in this visible world.

The same Salt-Mother of the elements is the nitrous, aluminous and spiritual gumosic water, ⊖ earth or crystal, which has Nature in its womb, a Son of the Sun, and a Daughter of the Moon. It is a Hermaphrodite, born out of the wind, a phoenix living in fire, a pelican, reviving his dear young ones with its blood; the young Icarus, drowned in the water, whose nurse is the earth, whose Mother is the wind, whose Father is the fire, the water her caretaker and drink, one stone and no stone, one water and no water, nevertheless a stone of living power and a water of living might; a sulphur, a mercury, a salt, hidden deep in nature, and which no fool has ever known nor seen.

Deus vendit sua dona pro labore.

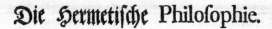

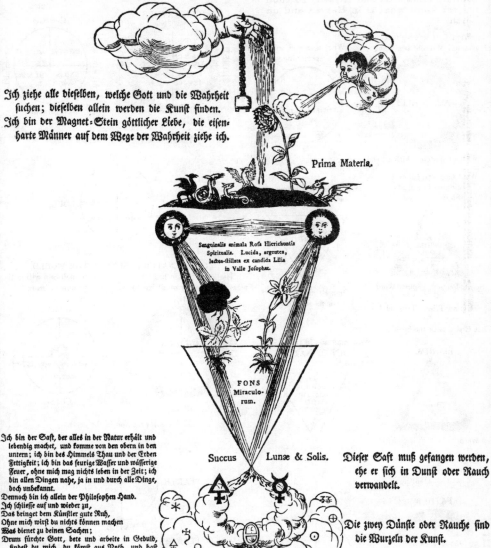

Ich ziehe alle dieselben, welche Gott und die Wahrheit
suchen; dieselben allein werden die Kunst finden.
Ich bin der Magnet=Stein göttlicher Liebe, die eisen=
harte Männer auf dem Wege der Wahrheit ziehe ich.

Prima Materia.

Sanguinalis animata Rosa Hierichuntis
Spiritualis. Lucida, argentea,
lactea-stillata ex candida Lilia
in Valle Josophat.

FONS
Miraculo-
rum.

Succus   Lunæ & Solis.

Ich bin der Saft, der alles in der Natur erhält und
lebendig machet, und komme von den obern in den
untern; ich bin des Himmels Thau und der Erden
Fettigkeit; ich bin das feurige Wasser und wässerige
Feuer, ohne mich mag nichts leben in der Zeit; ich
bin allen Dingen nahe, ja in und durch alle Dinge,
doch unbekannt.
Dennoch bin ich allein der Philosophen Hand.
Ich schliesse auf und wieder zu,
Das bringet dem Künstler gute Ruh,
Ohne mich wirst du nichts können machen
Was dienet zu deinen Sachen;
Drum fürchte Gott, bete und arbeite in Geduld,
findest du mich, du kömst aus Noth, und hast
einen gnädigen Gott, der dir ist hold, und giebet
was dein Herz begehret.

Dieser Saft muß gefangen werden,
ehe er sich in Dunst oder Rauch
verwandelt.

Die zwey Dünste oder Rauche sind
die Wurzeln der Kunst.

Die Prima Materia hat ihren Unterhalt aus dem Fiat und Wort der Schöpfung. Und das Wort ist aus dem Vater, wodurch alle Dinge gemacht sind, und der
Geist gehet von beyden aus, und ist die göttliche lebendigmachende Luft. Also macht die Luft in den Elementen alle Dinge lebendig. Das Feuer erwärmet alle
Dinge, das Wasser erquicket, labet und tränket alle Dinge; und die nitrossche Erde, als eine Mutter, ernähret und unterhält alle Dinge; also hat das Feuer die
Luft gebohren, und die Luft bläst das Feuer wiederum auf, daß es lebet; aber die Luft verändert ins Wasser ist des Feuers Speise, und in dies Element, Wasser und
Grundfeuchte, als in die schmierige fette Grundfeuchtigkeit, brennt das Feuer, und die Erde als ein Mitersalzhalter, reicht die Nahrung dafür, und in ihrem Bauch
wohnen alle diese Elemente, denn in diesem Bauch ist das sulphurische Mitersalz der Natur, das einige gute Ding, das Gott geschaffen hat in dieser sichtbaren Welt.
Dieselbe Salz: Mutter der Elemente ist das nitrossche, aluminossche, geistige, gumossche Wasser, ☉ Erde oder Crystal, welche die Natur in ihrem
Bauch hat, ein Sohn der Sonnen, und eine Tochter des Mondes. Es ist ein Hermaphrodit, welchen der Wind in seinem Bauch getragen hat; ein Phönix, im
Feuer lebend; ein Pelican, der seine todte Jungen mit seinem Blut wieder lebendig macht; der im Wasser ertrunkne junge Ikarus, dessen Säugmutter die Erde ist,
der Wind seine Mutter, das Feuer sein Vater, das Wasser seine Säuberinn und Trank, ein Stein und kein Stein, ein Wasser und kein Wasser, und dennoch ein
Stein lebendiger Kraft, und ein Wasser lebendiger Macht; ein Sulphur, ein Mercurius, ein Salz, welche die Natur verborgen in ihr trägt, und kein Unweiser
nimmer gekannt noch gesehen hat.

Deus vendit sua dona pro labore.

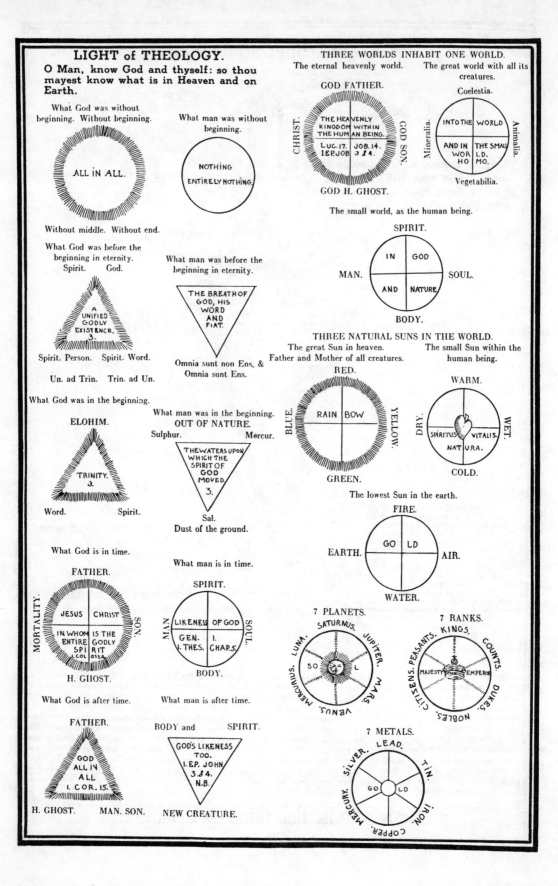

Theologisch Licht.

O Mensch erkenne Gott und dich: so weist du
was im Himmel und auf Erden ist.

Was war Gott ohn Anfang.   Was war der Mensch ohn Anfang.

Ohn Anfang.

Alles in Allem.   Nichts ganz Nichts.

Ohn Mittel.   Ohn Ende.

Was war Gott vor dem Anfang   Was war der Mensch vor dem
in der Ewigkeit.   Anfang in der Ewigkeit.

Geist.   Gott,

Ein einiges
göttliches
Wesen.

Das Hauchen Gottes,
sein
WORT
und
Fiat.

Geist. Person.   Geist. Wort.

Un. ad Trin.   Trin. ad Un.

Omnia sunt non Ens, &
Omnia sunt Ens.

Was war Gott am Anfang.   Was war der Mensch am Anfang.

ELOHIM.   Aus der Natur.

Sulphur.   Mercur.

H.
Dreyfaltigkeit.

Das Wasser
darauf der Geist
des Herrn
schwebet.

Wort.   Geist.

Sal.
Erdenklos.

Was ist Gott in der Zeit.   Was ist der Mensch in der Zeit.

Vater.   Geist.

Jesus   Christus

in welchem   die ganze
Fülle der   Gottheiten
2. Co   loß. a.

Ebenbild.   Gottes.

Gen.   L.
1. Thes   Sal. s.

Menschheit.   Sohn.   Mensch.   Seel.

H. Geist.   Leib.

Was ist Gott nach der Zeit.   Was ist der Mensch nach der Zeit.

Vater.   Leib und   Geist.

Gott
Alles
in Allem.
1. Cor. 15.

H. Geist.   Mensch. Sohn.   Neue Creatur.

Drey Welten wohnen in Einer Welt.

Die ewige himmlische Welt.   Die grosse Welt mit allen Geschöpfen.

Gott Vater.   Coelestia.

Christus.   Gott Sohn.   Mineralia.

Das Him
im Men
reich
schen.

Luc. 17.
1 Ep. Joh.

Joh. 14.
3 & 4.

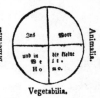

Ins   Wort

und in   die kleine
Ge   Welt
Ho   mo.

Animalia.

Gott H. Geist.   Vegetabilia.

Die kleine Welt, als der Mensch.

Geist.

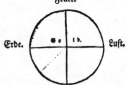

Mensch.   In   Gott   Seel.

und der   Natur.

Leib.

Drey natürliche Sonnen in der Welt.

Die grosse Sonne am Himmel.   Die kleine Sonne in dem Menschen
Vater und Mutter aller Creaturen.   das

Roth.   Warm.

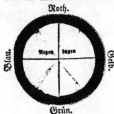

Blau.   Regen bogen   Gelb.

Grün.

Trocken.   Feucht.

Spiritus   Vitalis
Natu   ra.

Kalt.

Die unterste Sonne in der Erden.

Feuer.

Erde.   So ld.   Luft.

Wasser.

7 Planeten.   7 Stände.

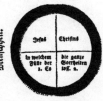

Saturnus.

Luna.   Jupiter.

L

Mercurius.   Mars.

Venus.

Könige.

Bauer.   Gelehrte.

Handwer.   Majest.

Soldat.

7 Metallen.

Bley.

Silber.   Zinn.

Kupfer   Eisen.

Queck-silber.

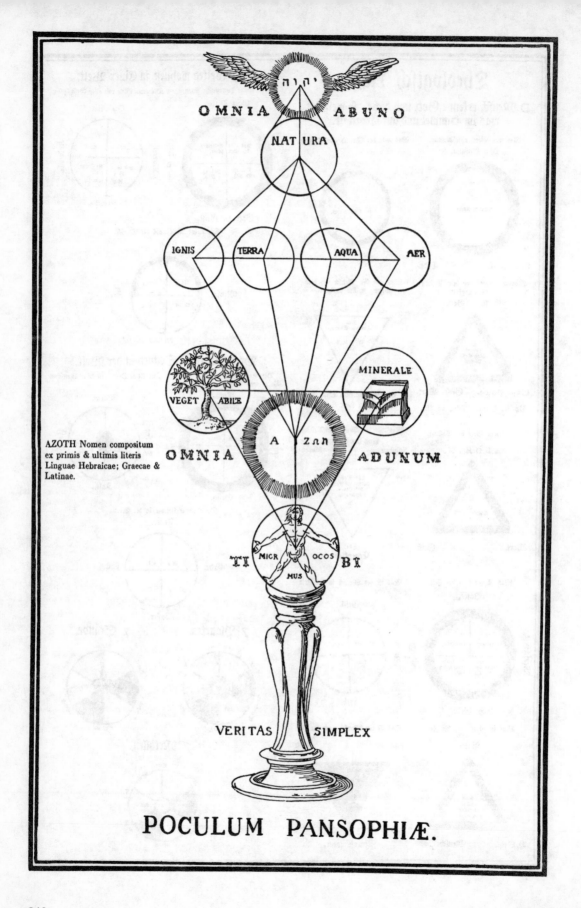

POCULUM PANSOPHIÆ.

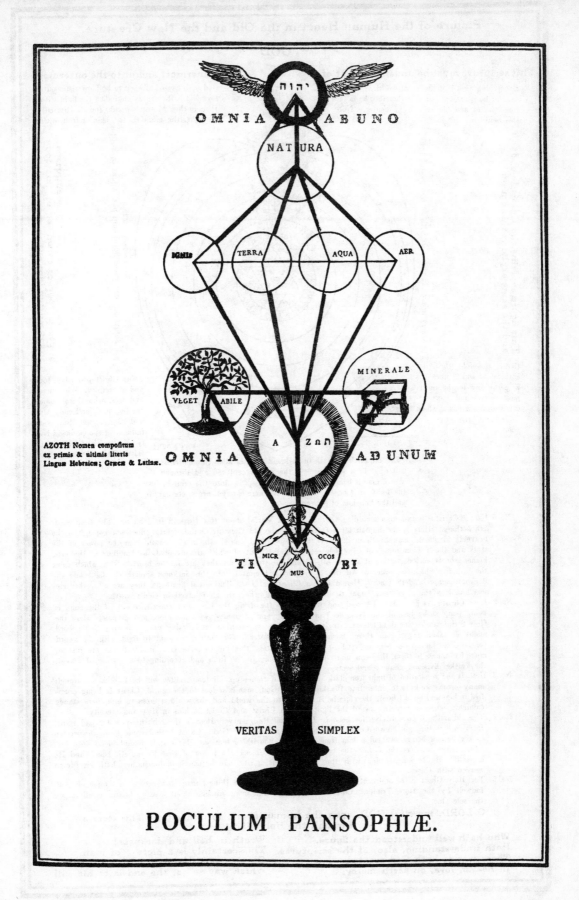

POCULUM PANSOPHIÆ.

241

Picture of the Human Heart in the Old and the New Creature.

GOD

This scripture must be understood out of the innermost and unto the outermost.

Everything that is in the great world, is in man too, for he is created out of it therefore he is the small world and his heart is his center. Note this well!

God hath caused all men to be born again out of love and hath already enkindled the light within them in their Mother's womb, and He Himself, is the light, the morning star, shining from within them.

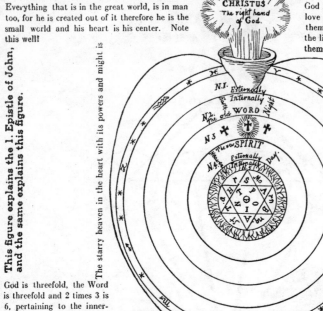

This figure explains the 1. Epistle of John, and the same explains this figure.

The starry heaven in the heart with its powers and might is

subject to vanity, and time being past, then everything will be again in eternity.

A heart is wide at the top, narrow at the bottom, to be opened to God, closed to earthliness.

God is threefold, the Word is threefold and 2 times 3 is 6, pertaining to the innermost person and morningstar within our heart, which is Jesus Christ, the one point.

Jesus Christ yesterday, today and in eternity. Who there is and was, who there cometh, the beginning and end, Alpha and Omega, in Him is the fullness of the Godhead bodily. Hallelujah, Gloria in Excelsus Deo. Amen.

The old birth of death in darkness must be slain through cross and suffering, in a wide circle is the reason captured and through the Word, man is being led back into the spirit, into the rebirth, into the light, in Christo, where alone there is quiet, peace, eternal life and the kingdom of heaven.

No. 1 Here is Christus born a man according to the flesh of Maria, about this He said in John 6. The flesh pacifieth nothing. Here is the human birth from Adam, the old Creature, sinful, mortal, does not come into the heavenly kingdom, man liveth in darkness, blindness, night and death, in his reason from the power of the stars and the 4 Elements, out of which come sickness, out of which are invented the handling of the arts, higher schools, ecclesiastical and secular offices and position, so far they are in the heart. Over which rules the authority which God ordered. All this is in vain and mortal, into this darkness shineth the light and the darkness comprehendeth it not. Herein belong Christians, Jews, Turks and heathens, they are altogether sinners and lack the glory they ought to have before God; they are all resolved in God's wrath.

No. 2. Here Christus is grieved in his soul and tempted by the devil, the innermost conscience out of the stars is being tempted by lust of the eyes, deed of the flesh and of vanity, with assurance and despair. Here the Holy Scriptures become dead letters, bringing forth sects, superstitious and fleshly priests, fearing God's word might be taken away from them, meaning the dead letter. The authorities want to fight with the sword for religion, killing the believers, Christ and His apostles, thinking to serve God, divine things are just so much foolishness to them, they can understand Christ only in the flesh and according to the tribe of David, they make divisions, cliques, and sects.

No. 3. Here is the separation of light from darkness, the dawn comes up, all temporalites will be foresaken, through many sorrows we have to enter into the kingdom of God, man is a fool to the world, Christ is being crucified in him and he in Christ, therefore he is a cross to the world and the world a cross to him, here stands calmness, whoever turneth toward the light lives in Christ and Christ in him in time and eternity.

No. 4. The old hath to go entirely: for behold: I make all things new. Here is the rebirth by water and spirit, from on high through the word of truth, a new creature born of God. Christ hath become flesh, ressurected in the human being, awakening him from the dead, nourishing him with his real flesh and blood unto life. Christ is the word of the father, the book of life, the Gospel, the power of God He causeth belief, and He blesseth. He is king, ruling with the sword of the spirit, man becometh divine nature, hath his life in heaven with Christ.

No. 5. The Holy Ghost is the ointment, teacheth men innermost Divine things; man hath become a temple of God, indwelt by the Holy Trinity. Christ in man, God and man, cringing about love. Christus is all in all, the sole One.

O LORD, merciful GOD, open the human heart, to understand Thy secrets through the Holy Ghost.

Who hath well understood the figure,
Hath understanding, also, of the scriptures.
Three worlds hath God created,
In heaven love, on earth mercy,

Wrath in hell and darkness;
This certainly is a picture of man.
On this earth he only hath to choose
Which way to go, the end is to his will.

Abbildung des menschlichen Herzens von der Alten und Neuen Creatur.

GOTT

CHRISTUS zur Rechten Gottes

Diese Schrift muß von Innen heraus und   **von Außen hinein verstanden werden.**

Alles was in der großen Welt ist, das ist auch im Menschen, denn er ist daraus geschaffen, darum ist er die kleine Welt, und hat alles in dem Mittelpunct seines Herzens. Das merke wohl.

Gott hat alle Menschen aus Liebe wiedergebohren, und ihnen das Licht schon in Mutterleibe wiederum angezündet, und er ist selber das Licht, der Morgenstern, scheinet von Innen heraus.

Diese Figur erkläret die I. Epist. Johannes, und dieselbe erkläret diese Figur.

Der gestirnte Himmel mit seiner Wirkung und Kräften ist der Eitelkeit

Ein Herz ist unten eng, und obenher sehr weit, Daß es Gott offen sey, verschert der Irdigkeit.

unterworfen, und ist die Zeit vergangen, dann kömt alles wieder in die Ewigkeit.

N1.
N2. das WORT
N3. das GEIST Neue
N4. Euserlich

GOTT WORT GEIST

VATER SOHN GEIST

Gott ist dreyfaltig, das Wort ist dreyfaltig, und 2 mal 3 ist 6, belangend die innerliche Person, und den Morgenstern in unsern Herzen, der ist JESUS CHRISTUS der einige Punct.

Jesus Christus gestern, heut und in Ewigkeit, der da ist, der da war, der da kömt, der Anfang und Ende, A und O, in ihm ist die Fülle der Gottheit leiblich worden. Hallelujah, Gloria in Excelsus Deo. Amen.

Die alte Geburt des Todes in der Finsterniß, die muß durch Kreuz und Leiden getödtet werden, die Vernunft im weiten Zirkel wird gefangen, und der Mensch wird durchs Wort wieder zurück in den Geist geführet, in die Wiedergeburt, ins Licht, in Christo, da ist allein Ruhe, Friede, ewiges Leben und Himmelreich.

No. 1. Allhier ist CHRISTUS nach dem Fleisch aus Maria Mensch gebohren, tödlich, davon sagt er Joh. 6. das Fleisch ist kein nutze. Allhier ist des Menschen Geburt aus Adam, die alte Creatur, sündlich, tödlich, kömt nicht ins Himmelreich, der Mensch lebet in der Finsterniß, Blindheit, Nacht und Tod, in seiner Vernunft aus der Sternen Kraft, und den 4 Elementen, daraus entstehen Krankheiten, und werden erfunden die Handthierung, Künste, hohe Schulen, geistliche und weltliche Aemter und Stände, solche seind im Herzen. Darüber herrschet die Obrigkeit von Gott verordnet. Diß alles ist eitel und des Todes, in diese Finsterniß scheinet das Licht, und die Finsterniß kann es nicht begreifen. Hierein gehören Christen, Juden, Türken, Heiden, sie sind allzumal Sünder, und mangeln des Ruhms den sie an Gott haben sollen; sie sind alle unter dem Zorn Gottes beschlossen.

No. 2. Allhier wird CHRISTUS im Geiste betrübet, vom Teufel versucht, das innerliche Gewissen aus den Sternen wird angefochten, mit Augenlust, Fleischeslust und hoffärtigen Leben, mit Sicherheit und Verzweifelung. Allhier ist die heilige Schrift der todte Buchstab, macht Secten, Aberglauben, fleischliche Priester, fürchten sich man werde ihnen Gottes Wort nehmen, und meynen den todten Buchstaben. Die Obrigkeit will die Religion mit dem Schwerdt verfechten, tödtet die Rechtgläubigen, Christum und seine Apostel, meynen sie thun Gott einen Dienst daran, die göttlichen Dinge sind ihnen lauter Thorheit, können Christum nicht anders als nur nach dem Fleisch und nach dem Geschlecht David verstehen, machen Spaltungen, Rotten und Secten.

No. 3. Allhier ist die Scheidung des Lichts von der Finsterniß, die Morgenröthe geht auf, alles Zeitliche wird verlassen, durch viel Trübsal müssen wir ins Reich Gottes eingehen, der Mensch wird der Welt zum Narren, Christus wird in ihm gekreuziget, und er in Christo, darum ist er der Welt ein Kreuz, und sie ist ihm ein Kreuz, allhier steht die Gelassenheit, wer sich gegen das Licht kehret, der lebet in Christo, und Christus in ihm, in Zeit und Ewigkeit.

No. 4. Das Alte muß ganz weg, siehe ich mache alles neu. Allhier ist die Wiedergeburt aus Wasser und Geist, von oben herab, durch das Wort der Wahrheit, eine neue Creatur aus Gott gebohren. Christus wird darin Fleisch, stehet im Menschen auf, weckt ihn von den Todten, speiset ihn mit seinem wahren Fleisch und Blut zum Leben, Christus ist das Wort des Vaters, das Buch des Lebens, das Evangelium, die Kraft Gottes, wirket den Glauben, machet selig. Er ist König, regieret mit dem Schwerdt des Geistes, der Mensch wird göttlicher Natur, hat seinen Wandel im Himmel bey Christo.

No. 5. Der heilige Geist ist die Salbung, lehret den Menschen inwendig GÖTTliche Dinge; der Mensch ist ein Tempel Gottes, darinn wohnet die heilige Dreyfaltigkeit. Christus im Menschen, Gott und Mensch, wirkend die Liebe. CHRISTUS alles in allen, das einige EINS.

O HERR, barmherziger GOTT, schleuß auf der Menschen Herzen, durch deinen H. GEIST, deine Geheimniß zu verstehen.

Wer die Figur recht hat erkannt,
Der hat auch wol der Schrift Verstand;
Drey Welten Gott geschaffen hat,
Im Himmel Lieb, auf Erden Gnad,

Zorn in der Höll und Finsterniß,
Ein Bild der Mensch, des ist gewiß;
Auf Erd steht er im Scheide-Ziel,
Das End schleust sich wohin er will.

TABULA SMARAGDINA HERMETIS.

VERBA SECRETORUM HERMETIS.

It is true, certain, and without falsehood, that whatever is below is like that which is above; and that which is above is like that which is below: to accomplish the one wonderful work. As all things are derived from the One Only Thing, by the will and by the word of the One Only One who created it in His Mind, so all things owe their existence to this Unity by the order of Nature, and can be improved by Adaptation to that Mind.

Its Father is the Sun; its Mother is the Moon; the Wind carries it in its womb; and its nurse is the Earth. This Thing is the Father of all perfect things in the world. Its power is most perfect when it has again been changed into Earth. Separate the Earth from the Fire, the subtle from the gross, but carefully and with great judgment and skill.

It ascends from earth to heaven, and descends again, new born, to the earth, taking unto itself thereby the power of the Above and the Below. Thus the splendor of the whole world will be thine, and all darkness shall flee from thee.

This is the strongest of all powers, the Force of all forces, for it overcometh all subtle things and can penetrate all that is solid. For thus was the world created, and rare combinations, and wonders of many kinds are wrought.

Hence I am called HERMES TRISMEGISTUS, having mastered the three parts of the wisdom of the whole world. What I have to say about the masterpiece of the alchemical art, the Solar Work, is now ended.

TABULA SMARAGDINA HERMETIS.

VERBA SECRETORUM HERMETIS.

Wahrhaftig ohne Lügen gewiß, und auf das allerwahrhaftigste, dies, so Unten, ist gleich dem Obern, und dies, so Oben, ist gleich dem Untern, damit man kann erlangen und verrichten Wunderdinge eines einigen Dinges. Und gleich wie alle Dinge von einem Dinge alleine geschaffen, durch den Willen und Gebot eines Einigen, der es bedacht: also entstehen auch alle Dinge nunmehro aus diesem einigen Dinge, durch Ordnung der Natur. Sein Vater ist die Sonne, und seine Mutter der Mond; Die Luft trägt es gleich als in ihrer Gebährmutter; Seine Ernährerin oder Säugamme ist die Erde. Dies Ding ist der Ursprung aller Vollkommenheiten so in der Welt sind. Seine Kraft ist am vollkommensten wann es wieder in Erde verwandelt ist. Scheide alsdann die Erde vom Feuer, und das Subtile oder Dünne vom Dicken oder Groben, sein lieblich mit grossen Verstand und Bescheidenheit. Es steigt von der Erde gen Himmel, und von dannen wiederum zur Erde, und nimmt an sich die Kraft des Obern und Untern. Also wirst du haben die Herrlichkeit der ganzen Welt. Derohalben weiche von dir aller Unverstand und Unvermögenheit. Dies ist von aller Stärke die stärkste Stärke: denn es kann überwinden alle subtile Dinge, und kann durchdringen ein jedes hart oder vest Ding. Also ist die Welt geschaffen, dahero entstehen seltsame Vereinigungen, und werden mancherley Wunder gewürket, welcher Weg dieselbige zu würken dieser ist. Derhalben bin ich genannt worden: Hermes Trismegistus, habe drey Theile der Weisheit der ganzen Welt. Dies sey gesagt von dem Meisterstück der chymischen Kunst.

INTERPRETATION and EXPLANATION of the
TABULA SMARAGDINA HERMEDIS

This picture, plain and insignificant in appearance,
  Concealeth a great and important thing.
Yea, it containeth a secret of the kind
  That is the greatest treasure in the world.
For what on this earth is deemed more excellent
  Than to be a Lord who ever reeketh with gold,
And hath also a healthy body,
  Fresh and hale all his life long,
Until the predestined time
  That cannot be overstepped by any creature.
All this, as I have stated, clearly
  Is contained within this figure.
Three separate shields are to be seen,
  And on them are eagle, lion, and free star.
And painted in their very midst
  Artfully stands an imperial globe.
Heaven and Earth in like manner
  Are also placed herein intentionally,
And between the hands outstretched towards each other
  Are to be seen the symbols of metals.
And in the circle surrounding the picture
  Seven words are to be found inscribed.
Therefore I shall now tell
  What each meaneth particularly
And then indicate without hesitation
  How it is called by name.
Therein is a secret thing of the Wise
  In which is to be found great power.
And how to prepare it will also
  Be described in the following:
The three shields together indicate
  Sal, Sulphur, and *Mercurium.*
The *Sal* hath been one *Corpus* that
  Is the very last one in the Art.
The *Sulphur* henceforth is the soul
  Without which the body can do nothing.
Mercurius is the spirit of power,
  Holding together both body and soul,
Therefore it is called a medium
  Since whatever is made without it hath no stability.
For soul and body could not die
  Should spirit also be with them.
And soul and spirit could not be
  Unless they had a body to dwell in,
And no power had body or spirit
  If the soul did not accompany them.
This is the meaning of the Art:
  The body giveth form and constancy,
The soul doth dye and tinge it,
  The spirit maketh it fluid and penetrateth it.
And therefore the Art cannot be
  In one of these three things alone.
Nor can the greatest secret exist alone:
  It must have body, soul, and spirit.
And now what is the fourth,
  From which the three originate,
The same names teach thee
  And the sevenfold star in the lower shield.
The Lion likewise by its colour and power
  Showeth its nature and its property.
In the Eagle yellow and white are manifest.
  Mark my words well, for there is need of care:
The imperial orb doth exhibit
  The symbol of this highest good.

Heaven and earth, four elements,
  Fire, light, and water, are therein.
The two hands do testify with an oath
  The right reason and the true knowledge,
And from what roots are derived
  All of the metals and many other things.
Now there remain only the seven words,
  Hear further what they mean:
If thou dost now understand this well
  This knowledge shall nevermore fail thee.
Every word standeth for a city
  Each of which hath but one gate.
☉ The first signifieth gold, is intentionally yellow.
☽   The second for fair white silver.
☿ The third, *Mercurius,* is likewise grey.
♃   The fourth for tin, is heaven-blue.
♂ The fifth for iron, is blood-red.
♀   The sixth for copper, is true green.
♄ The seventh for lead, is black as coal.
  Mark what I mean, understand me well:
In these city gates, indeed,
  Standeth the whole ground of the Art.
For no one city alone can effect anything,
  The others must also be close at hand.
And as soon as the gates are closed
  One cannot enter any city.
And if they had no gates
  Not one thing could they accomplish.
But if these gates are close together
  A ray of light appeareth from seven colors.
Shining very brightly together
  Their might is incomparable.
Thou canst not find such wonders on earth,
  Wherefore hearken unto further particulars:
Seven letters, and seven words,
  Seven cities, and seven gates,
Seven times, and seven metals,
  Seven days, and seven ciphers.
Whereby I mean seven herbs
  Also seven arts and seven stones.
Therein stands every lasting art.
  Well for him who findeth this.
If this be too hard for thee to understand
  Here me again in a few other particulars:
Truly I reveal to thee
  Very clearly and plainly, without hatred or envy,
How it is named with one word
  Vitriol, for him who understandeth it.
If thou wouldst oft figure out
  This Cabbalistic way with all diligence,
Seven and fifty in the cipher
  Thou findest figured everywhere.
Let not the Work discourage thee,
  Understand me rightly, so shalt thou enjoy it.
Besides that, note this fully,
  There is a water which doth not make wet.
From it the metals are produced,
  It is frozen as hard as ice.
A moistened dust a fuller wind doth raise,
  Wherein are all qualities.
If thou dost not understand this,
  Then I may not name it for thee otherwise.
Now I will instruct thee
  How it should be prepared.

Auslegung und Erklärung der Tabula Smaragdina Hermedis.

Diß Gmähl anzehen schlecht und ring,
Helt in sich groß und wichtig ding.
Ja solch geheimbnuß in sich helt,
Welchs ist der höchste Schatz der Welt.
Dann was ist worden je erhört,
Höher zu sein auf dieser Erd.
Dann alle Zeit zu sein ein Herr
Dem kein Geld zerrinnt nimmermehr.
Und hat ein gsunden Leib daneben,
Frisch jm darzu so lang sein Leben
Biß zur prädestinirten Zeit,
Die kein Creatur überschreit,
Solchs alles wie ich jetz gemeldt
Die Figur klärlich in sich hält.
Der schilt besicht man sonder drey,
Darinn Adler, Löw und Stern frey,
Ein Reichsapfel auch steht hierin
Gemahlet sein in mitten drin,
Himmel und Erd zu gleicher weiß,
Sein auch hierinn gesetzt mit Fleiß.
Die Händ so gegen einander reichen,
Sichstu drob der Metallen Zeichen.
Im Cirkul so diß Gmähl umringt,
Man sieben Wort geschrieben findt.
Darum will nun vermelden ich
Was jedes ausweist sonderlich,
Alsdenn anzeigen ohne Scheu
Wie das mit Namen genennt sey.
Darinn der Weisen gheimes Ding
In dem man groß Vermögen findt.
Und wie es denn bereit't werd auch
Folgt alles auf einander nach.
Die drey Schild deuten in einer Summ,
Sal, Sulphur und Mercurium.
Das Sal das ist ein Corpus vest,
So in der Kunst das allerletst.
Der Sulphur ist die Seel fortan,
Ohn den der Leib nichts schaffen kann.
Mercurius ist der Geist der Kraft,
Beid Seel und Leib zusammen hast.
Daher wird er ein Mittler gnannt,
Das ohn jhn gmacht wird, hat kein bstandt.
Dann Seel und Leib könnten nicht sterben,
Der Geist sey dann auch darneben.
So bstünden Seel, Geist nimmermehr,
Wenn nicht das Corpus bey jhm wär.
Auch han kein Kraft Leib oder Geist,
Wo nicht die Seel jhn'n Gsellschaft leist.
Diß alles von der Kunst verstand,
Der Leib figirt und gibt den Bstand.
Die Seel die färbet und tingirt,
Der Geist machts flüssig, penetrirt.
Drum kann in dieser Kunst nicht seyn,
Unter den dreyen eins allein.
Das gröste Gheim kann auch nicht bstan,
Es muß Seel, Geist und Corpus han,
Was aber nun das vierte sey,
Darvon die drey entspringen frey
Thut dich desselben Namen lehrn,
Im untern Schild, der siebnfach Stern.
Der Löw desselben Farb und Kraft,
Auch sein Natur und Eigenschaft,
Zeigt an der Adler Gelb und Weiß,
Versteh mich wol, dann es braucht Fleiß:

Des Reichs Apfel ausweisen thut,
Das Zeichen dieses höchsten Gut.
Himmel und Erd, vier Element,
Feur, Luft, Wasser darinnen seindt.
Den rechten Grund und wahren Bscheid
Die zwo Händ bzeugen mit ein'm Eid.
Aus welcher Grundwurzel kommen her
Alle Metall und anders mehr.
Nun bleibt nichts als die sieben Wort,
Was sie bedeuten, weiter hört.
So ihr nun dies verstehet wol,
Euch nimmermehr mißlingen soll.
Ein jeglichs Wort bedeut ein Stadt,
Dern jede nur ein Porten hat.

☉ Die erst bdeut Gold, ist gelb mit Fleiß.
☽ Die ander Silber, ist schön weiß.
☿ Die dritt Mercurium ist gleich grau.
♃ Die vierdt ist Zinn, ist himmelblau.
♂ Die fünft deut Eisen, ist blutroth.
♀ Die sechst Kupfer, ist grün ohn Spot.
♄ Die siebend Bley, ist schwarz wie Kol,

Merk wie ichs meyn, versteh mich wol:
In dieser Stadt Porten fürwahr,
Stehet der Kunst Grund ganz und gar.
Denn kein Stadt wirket nichts allein,
Die andern müssen darben auch seyn.
Auch könnt man in kein Stadt nicht gahn,
So die Porten wurden zugethan.
Und da sie gar kein Porten hätten,
Sie durchaus nichts ausrichten thäten.
So diese Porten beysammen seyn,
Gebiert von sieben Farben ein Schein.
Thun mit einander gar hell leuchten,
Ihrer Macht ist nichts zu vergleichen.
Ihr's Wunders findstu auf Erden nicht,
Drum weiter höre solchen Bricht.
Sieben Buchstaben, sieben Wort,
Auch sieben Städt, und sieben Port.
Sieben Zeit, auch sieben Metall,
Auch sieben Tag, und sieben Zahl.
Darzu ich sieben Kräuter meyn,
Auch sieben Künst, und sieben Stein.
Darinn steht aller Kunst bestandt,
Wol dem, der solches jemals fand.
So es zverstehn dir ist zu schwer,
Zu mehrerm Bricht mich weiter hör.
Warlich ich offenbar dir das
Gar hell und klar, ohn Neid und Haß,
Wie es mit ein'm Wort wird genennt,
Vitriol, welcher den recht kennt.
So du diß Cabalischer Weiß
Oft ausrechnest mit allem Fleiß,
Sieben und Funfzig an der Zahl,
Findst du gerechnet überall.
Laß dich die Arbeit nicht verdriessen,
Versteh mich recht, so wirstus gniessen.
Zum Ueberfluß merk mich noch baß,
Es ist ein Wasser macht nicht naß.
Von dem die Metall seind gebohrn,
Es wird wie Eis, so hart gefrorn.
Ein nasser Staub, steckt voller Wind,
Da alle Tugend innen sind.
Thust du solches nicht erkennen,
Darf ich dirs nich anderst nennen.

There are seven ways for this art,
  If thou neglectest any of them thou workest in vain.
But thou must, before all things else, know
  Thou hast to succeed in purification.
And although this be twofold,
  Thou art in need of one alone.
The first work is freely done by it
  Without any other addition,
Without distilling something in it,
  Simply through its putrefaction.
From all of its earthliness
  Is everything afterwards prepared.
This first way hath two paths,
  Happy is he who goeth on the right path.
The first extendeth through the strength of fire,
  With and in itself, note this well.
The second extendeth further
  Until one cometh to treasure and to gain.
This is done by dissolving,
  And again by saturating, I inform you:
This must be undertaken first of all,
  So comest thou to the end of the fine art.
After the whole purification hath been completed
  It will be prepared and boiled in the sun
Or in the warm dung of its time,
  Which extendeth itself very far
Until it becometh constant and perfect,
  And the treasure of the Wise is in it.
The other ways are very subtle
  And many mighty one fail therein,
For here is the purpose of the distillation
  And the sublimation of the Wise Men.
The separation of the four elements
  Is also called by the Wise Men
Air, water, and rectified fire.
  The earth on the ground hath mislead many,
Having been deemed a worthless thing,
  Although all the power lieth in it.
Some know not how to separate it
  From their *Cortibus,* therefore they fail.
It was cast behind the door,
  But the Wise Man taketh it up again,
Purifieth it snow-white and clear:
  This is the ground, I say in truth.
But if thou dost wish to separate it,
  Note that it is of no little importance,
For if they are not prepared
  Then you are in error, that I swear.
Therefore thou must also have some vinegar
  Which is revealed to the Wise Men,
Wherewith thou wilt effect the separation,
  So that nothing earthly remaineth in it any more,
Till body and soul have to be separated,
  Otherwise called fire and earth
And after they are thus purified,

And thereupon followeth the mixture, observe!
  And so it cometh to a wondrous strength,
The finished figures with the unfinished.
  And if the fire be likewise rightly controlled,
It will be entirely perfect
  In much less time than a year.

Now thou hast the entire way in its length
  On which are not more than two paths.
From these one soon wandereth and goeth astray,
  Else it all standeth clear and plain.
The one is the water of the Wise Men,
  Which is the *Mercurius* alone.
The other is called a vinegar,
  And it is known only to a very few.
And this vinegar doth circle
  Away from the philosophical iron.
It is Lord *Aes* whom it maketh glad.
  Therefore they have combined so closely
Many hundred forms and names are given
  After each hath chosen it.
One way springeth from the true source,
  A few have worked on it for a whole year.
But many through their art and craft
  Have shortened so long a space of time.
And quickly is the preparation set free
  As Alchemy doth point out.
The preparation alone
  Maketh this stone great and glorious.
Although there is but one matter
  It lacketh nothing else.
But when it is clarified
  Its name hath misled many.
However, I have revealed enough to thee
  In many ways, forms, and fashions.
There are many names; I say
  Let not thyself be misled from the true way.
In their scriptures the Elders write
  That it is a draught, a great poison.
Others call it a snake, a monster,
  Which is not costly anywhere.
It is common to all men
  Throughout the world, to rich and also to poor.
It is the property of the metals
  Through which they conquer victoriously.
The same is a perfection
  And setteth a golden crown upon it.
Now the practice is completed
  For him who understandeth it and knoweth the matter.
Only two things more are to be chosen
  Which thou wilt find by now
If thou dost follow the right way
  And attend carefully to thy work.
The composition is the one
  Which the Wise Men kept secret.
The nature of the fire also hath hidden craft;
  Therefore its order is another.
With that, one should, not deal too much
  Or else all execution is lost.
One cannot be too subtle with it.
  As the hen hatcheth out the chick
So also shall it be in the beginning,
  And time itself will prove it.
For just as the fire is regulated
  Will this treasure itself be produced.
Be industrious, constant, peaceful, and pious,
  And also ask God for His help:
If thou dost obtain that, then always remember
  The poor and their needs.

_____

Jetzt will ich geben dir Bescheid,
  Wie es soll werden zubereit't.
Der Weg sind sieben zu der Kunst,
  So der'n kein'n weist, arbeitst umsonst.
Dann wissen must vor allen Dingen,
  Die Reinigung, soll dirs gelingen.
Und wiewol dieses zwiefach ist,
  Aber allein die ein gebrist.
Das erst Werk geschicht durch sie frey,
  Ohn allen andern Zusatz bey.
Zu dem ohn einichs distilliern
  Allein durch sein putrificiern,
Von aller seiner Irdischheit,
  Alsdann so ist es all's bereit.
Dieser erst Weg zwo Strassen hat,
  Wohl dem, der recht dieselben gaht.
Die erst streckt sich durch des Feurs Stärk,
  Mit und in sich selbst, gewißlich merk.
Die ander streckt sich ferner hin,
  Biß daß man komt zum Schatz und Gwinn.
Dieselb durchs Soluiren geschicht,
  Und wieder zu tränken, ich dich bricht.
Dies muß gar fürgenommen seyn,
  So kommst zum Ende der Künste sein.
Nach ganzer Reinigung vollkomm,
  Wird er bereit und kocht durch d'Sonn,
Oder in warmem Mist sein Zeit,
  Welche sich aber streckt gar weit.
Bis daß es fir wird und perfect,
  In dem der Weisen Kleinod steckt.
Die andern Weg sind gar subtil,
  Darinn fehlen ihr'r mächtig viel,
Dann da ist Distillirens Fleiß,
  Und Sublimirens gleicher Weis'.
Auch Scheidung der vier Element,
  Ist von den Weisen also gnennt.
Luft, Wasser, Feur rectificiert,
  Die Erd am Grund hat viel verführt
Die wird für ein schlecht Ding geacht,
  Und liegt an ihr die ganze Macht.
Etlich wissen die nicht zu scheiden
  Von ihrn Corticibus, drum fehlts beiden.
Sie wird gworfen hinter die Thür,
  Der Weise aber zeuchts herfür,
Reiniget die schneeweiß und klar,
  Die ist der Grund sag ich fürwahr.
Wenn du sie aber scheiden willt,
  So merk daß es nicht schlechtlich gilt.
Dann so sie nicht wird seyn bereit,
  So irrst, sag ich bey meinem Eid.
Daher must haben Essig zwar,
  Der den Weisen ist offenbar,
Dardurch wirst du der Scheidung bricht,
  Daß sie nichts Irdischs mehr ansicht,
Bis Leib und Seel muß gscheiden werden,
  Wird sonst genannt Feur und Erden.
Und so sie dann gereinigt seind,

☞   ☞   ☞

Dann darauf folgt die Mischung merk,
  So kömts zu wunderlicher Stärk.
Das Fir das Unfir mit figiert,
  So and'rst das Feur wird recht regiert.
Und wird vollkommen ganz und gar,
  Wol bälder dann in einem Jahr,

Nun hast nach Läng den ganzen Weg,
  Darinn sind nicht mehr als zween Steg.
In dem man bald fehl und irr geht,
  Sonst es alls klar und lauter steht.
Der Weisen Wasser ist das ein,
  Welchs ist der Mercurius allein.
Das ander wird ein Essig gnannt,
  Von wenigen wird er erkannt.
Ab dem philosophischen Eisen,
  Thut dieser Essig vorher kreisen,
Das ist Herr Aes welchs sie ergetzt,
  Drum haben sies so hart versetzt.
Viel hundert Gstalt und Namen gstelt
  Nach dem ein jeder ihm erwehlt.
Ein Weg vom rechten Brunnen klar,
  Etlich han g'arbeit ein ganz Jahr.
Viel aber durch ihr Kunst und List,
  Haben abkürzt solch lange Frist.
In Gschwindigkeit der Breitung frey,
  So ihn anzeigt die Alchimey.
Die Präparation allein,
  Macht groß und herrlich diesen Stein,
Wiewol nur ein Matery ist,
  Der durchaus anders nichts gebrist,
Denn daß sie werd clarificiert,
  Ihr Nam hat aber viel verführt.
Doch hab ich dirs gnug offenbart,
  Auf mancherley Weis', Gstalt und Art.
Drum seind der Namen viel; ich sprich,
  Laß nicht vom Weg abführen dich.
Die Alten schreiben in ihr Schrift,
  Es sey ein Track, ein grosses Gift.
Der ander nennts ein Schlang, Ung'heur,
  Sey allenthalben auch nicht theur.
Alle Menschen habens zugleich,
  In aller Welt, Arm' und auch Reich',
Sey der Metallen Eigenschaft,
  Dardurch sie überwind sieghaft.
Derselben ein Perfection,
  Und setz ihm auf ein güldne Kron.
Jetzund die Practick ist vollendt,
  Ders versteht, und d'Matery kennt,
Allein zwey Ding sind ausgelohn,
  Welche aber wirst finden schon,
So du dem rechten Wege folgst,
  Und für dein Arbeit fleissig sorgst:
Die Zsammensetzung ist das ein,
  Welchs die Weisen ghalten geheim:
Des Feurs Art hat auch heimlich List,
  Drum sein Ordnung das ander ist:
Auf daß man ihm nicht thue zu viel,
  Sonst ist verlohren alles Spiel.
Zu subtil kam man ihm nicht thun,
  Gleich wie ausbrüt die Henn das Hun,
Soll es im Anfang also sein,
  Die Zeit giebt selbst den Augenschein:
Dann wie das Feur gewendet wird,
  Darnach sich dieser Schatz gebiert.
Sey fleissig, bständig, friedsam, fromm,
  Bitt daß dir Gott zu Hülf auch komm:
Erlangst du das, so laß dir sein,
  Die Armen stets befohlen seyn.

————

AUREUM SECULUM REDIVIVUM
That is
The Very Ancient Golden Age Having Passed Away
Which now hath risen again, blossomed in loveliness, and produced fragrant golden seed.
This precious and noble seed is pointed out and revealed to all true *Sapientiae and doctrinae filiis* by
HENRICUS MADATHANUS, THEOSOPHUS,
Medicus and tandem, Dei gratia aureae crucis frater.

Epistle of James, i:5:

If any of you lack wisdom, let him ask of God that giveth to all men liberally and upraideth not; and it shall be given him.

SYMBOLUM AUTHORIS.
Centrum mundi, granum fundi.

FOREWORD
To the Christian and Worthy Reader

Kind and God-loving Reader, and especially you sapientiae and doctrinae filii, some years ago Almighty God opened mine eyes with the enlightenment of His Holy Spirit (from Whom we receive all wisdom and Who was sent unto us through Christ from the Father), because I had prayed fervently, unceasingly, and constantly and had called upon Him many times. So that I beheld the true *Centrum in Trigono centri* the one and true *substance* of the Noble Philosopher's Stone, and although I had it in mine own hands for the length of five years, I did not know how to use it profitably, rightly, or befittingly, how to extract from it the *red lion's blood* and the *white eagle's gluten*, much less how to mix, enclose, and seal it according to the proportionate weight of Nature, or how to commit it to and proceed with the hidden fire, all of which must be done not without understanding and care. And although I searched in the *scriptis, parabolis and variis Philosophorum figuris* with special care and understanding, and laboured diligently to solve their manifold strange *aenigmata*, which existed in part only in their own minds, I found out *reipsa* that this was sheer phantasy and nonsense, as also testify the *Aurora Philosophorum*. They are all foolishness, like all the *praeparationes*, even of *Geber* and *Albertus Magnus*, with their *purgationes, sublimationes, cementationes, distillationes, rectificationes, circulationes, putrefactiones, conjunctiones, solutiones, assensiones, coagulationes, calcinationes, incinerationes, mortificationes, revificationes*, etc. In like manner are their tripods, *Alanthor*, reflecting ovens, smelting furnaces, putrescences, horsedung, ashes, sand, cupping-glasses, pelican vials, retorts, fixatoriums, etc., sophistical, futile, and useless things. Personally, I have in truth to admit this: especially since noble Nature, which letteth itself be easily found in its own innate *substance*, doth not know of any of these things. There are those who look for the *materiam lapidis* in wine, in the imperfect body, in blood, in marcasite, in mercury, in sulphur, in urine, in stercorate, in auripigment, and in herbs such as chelidonium, lungwort, yew, hyssop, etc. Theophrastus, in his *Secreto Magico de Lapide Philosophorum*, rightly says of them: all this is villainy and thievery, with which they mislead other people, take their money, spend and waste their time uselessly and vainly, follow only their own fool's-head, but who cannot figure out in advance the requirements of Nature. Rather tell me one thing: What dost thou think of those who burn water in the mines of the Earth, or are there also people therein who enhance the value of wine, or burn the urine of small children to make metals therewith? Or dost thou think there is any apothecary therein who hath for sale any thing with which thou canst make metals? Thou fool, canst thou not understand that thou dost err, that none of these things belong to Nature? Or dost thou want to be above God, that thou dost want to make metals out of blood? Thou mightest as well try to make a man out of a horse, or a cow out of a mouse, to give good milk in addition. This, too, would be a multiplication, but these things do not happen, and as little as they can happen, so little canst thou make metals with the above-mentioned recipes, for this is not a Nature-given art. And whatever Nature hath made, no art can effect; for if a woman hath given birth to a boy, no art can change the boy into a girl, whatever means might be employed for that purpose. After this short discourse, it should be easy for anyone to see how, and in what form, the *materia benedicta* should be sought and found. And no one should imagine, much less be persuaded by any clowns, that he really hath in his hands the *veram materiam* either through the secret revelation of God or through those who claim to be acquainted with it, and no one should imagine that he would then be able to disintegrate the said *veram materiam* proportionately, to separate the *purum ab impuro* in the highest things, that he knoweth how to purify it and completely understandeth. Nay, my dear analysts, that is by no means so: therein lies the difficulty, and to such matters belong art and a skilled mind. See me, for example: as you heard from me in the beginning, for five years I was acquainted with the *veram materiam lapidis*, but all that time I did not know how to proceed with it, and not until the sixth year was the key to its power entrusted to me through the secret revelation of Almighty God. And the old Patriarchs, Prophets, and *Philosophi* have at all times kept this key hidden and secret, for the *Monarcha in loco dicto* saith: It would be a great theft, and no longer secret, had they revealed it in their writings, so that every cobbler and tooth-drawer could understand it, and much evil could be done that way which would be against the will of the Lord, etc. Now there are many reasons why I should write this Tract: some are mentioned here, some in the *Epilogo*, and another reason is that I do not want to appear as if I would have for my exclusive use *talentum a Deo mihi commissum* (a talent intrusted to me by God). So I have written down in this, my *Aureo seculo redivivo* (*Golden Age Restored*), as much as God and Nature have permitted me, about the great secret of the Philosophers, as mine eyes have witnessed it and my hands grasped it, and how it was revealed through the mercy of God at the right time in great might and glory: and may the pious and God-loving reader take all this in good faith and accept it, examine it skillfully, and be not perturbed if at times there are words mixed up with my sayings which seem to be contrary to the letter. I could not write otherwise *per Theoriam ad praxim*, because it is forbidden to write more exactly and clearly about this *in republica chymica*. But undoubtedly all those who read this Tract in true confidence with the inner eyes of their minds, and are able to look upon it in the right way, to study it diligently, and who pray in all things inwardly and with all their heart, will enjoy, as I did, the wondrously sweet philosophical fruit hidden therein, and partake of it, according to God's will. And then they will be and will remain true Brothers of the Golden Cross, and in eternal alliance, chosen members of the Philosophical Community.

Finally, I will be so candid as to disclose my true given and family name in the following manner to the intelligent, worthy, and Christian reader, so that no one will have a right to cry out against me. So now let it be known to everyone that the number of my name is M.DCXII, in which number my full name was inscribed in the book of Nature by 11 dead and 7 living. Moreover, the letter 5 is the fifth part of the 8, and the 15 is again the fifth part of the 12, and let this suffice thee.

Datum in Monte Abiegno, die 25. Martii Anno 1621

AVREVM SECVLVM REDIVIVVM

Das ist

Die vhralte entwichene Güldene Zeit,

So nunmehr wieder auffgangen, lieblich geblühet, vnd wolriechenden güldenen Samen gesetzet.

Welchen tewren vnd edlen Samen allen wahren Sapientiæ & doctrinæ filiis zeigt vnd offenbahret:

HENRICVS MADATHANVS, THEOSOPHVS,

Medicus & tandem, Dei gratia aureæ crucis frater.

Jacob in Epist. v. 5.

So jemand vnter euch Weißheit mangelt, der bitte von Gott, der da gibt einfeltiglich, vnnd rücket es niemand auff, so wird sie ihme gegeben werden.

SYMBOLVM AVTHORIS.
Centrum mundi, granum fundi.

Vorrede

An den Christlichen vnnd würdigen Leser.

FReundlicher, Gottliebender Leser, vnd sonderlich ihr sapientiæ & doctrinæ filij, demnach vor etzlichen Jahren, Gott der Allmächtige auff mein stetiges einbrünstiges Gebett vnnd embsiges anruffen, meine Augen durch Erleuchtung seines heiligen Geistes (auß welchem wir alle Weißheit empfahen, vnnd vns durch Christum vom Vatter ist gesandt worden) so weit eröffnet, daß ich das wahre Centrum in Trigono centri, die einigen vnd wahren materien des Edlen Philosophischen Steins erkante, vnd wesentlich in Händen hatte, wuste ich gleichwol fast bey die 5. Jahr nicht, wie ich darmit ersprießlichen, recht vnd gebürlichen, des roten Löwen Blutt, vnd des weißen Adlers gluten darauß zuscheiden, viel weniger dieselben nach dem proportionirtem Gewicht der Natur gantz geeb vnd auffs beste zuuermischen, einzuschließen, versiegeln, vnd dem geheimen Fewer zu committiren, prociren solte, wie denn solche die Aurora Philosophorum gleichfals bezeuget, nemlich: das alle præparationes, daruon Geber, Albertus Magnus, vnd dergleichen sampt dero purgationes, sublimationes, cementationes, distillationes, rectificationes, circulationes, putrefactiones, coniunctiones, solutiones, assensiones, coagulationes, calcinationes, incinerationes, mortificationes, reuisicationes, &c. Wie gleicher gestalt jhr dreyfüß, Athanor, Reuerbierofen, Schmeltzofen, Faulhintz, Roßmist, Asch, Sandt, Cucurbith, Pellican Viol, retort, fixatorium, &c. Lauter Sophistische, verführerische vnd vnnütze dinge sein, wie ich den solches für meine Person auch in warheit bekennen muß: Sintemal die edle Natur, so in jhrer eigenen angebornen substantz sich gantz gerne finden lesset, hieuon nichts weiß: Dannhero der Theophrast. in Secreto Magico de Lap. Philos. von denen die da materiam lapidis in Wein, in den imperfecten corporen, im Blut, in Marcasiten, in Mercurio, in sulphure, in vrina, in stercore, in auripigmento, vnd in Kreutern, als: Chelidonia, Springfwurtzel, Ebbew, Jsoph, zc. suchen, recht saget: Es sey alles mit einander Schelmerey vnd Dieberey damit, das sie die Leut verführen, bringen sie vmbs Gelt, verzehren vnnd verliehren die zeit vnnützlich, vnd vergebentlich, vnd fahren allein jhren Narrenköpffen nach, der vorhin nicht kann außrechnen, was die Natur erfordert: Lieber sag mit eins, wer muß mir in den Mineren der Erden, Wasserbrennen, oder hat es auch Leut darinnen, die den Wein verterwen, oder Kinderharn brunzen, damit man Metallen macht, oder meinst du es sein Apotecker drinnen die alle ding also feil haben, damit du kanst Metallen machen: du Narr, kanst du nit verstehen das du jrrest, das du eben dingk keinco zu der Natur gehöret, oder wilt du vber Gott sein, das du auß Blut wilt Metallen machen, so mache auß einem Pferd einen Menschen, oder auß einer Mauß eine Kube, die gibt dir darnach gute Milch darzu, das wehre auß eine multiplication, es geschicht aber nicht, vnd als wenig das kann geschehen, also wenia kanst du auß obgenandten recepten metallen machen, dann die Kunst ist nicht auß der Natur, vnnd was dieselbe erschaffen hat, da kann die Kunst keine Wirkung haben, Wann eine Frawe ein Knäblein gebihret, darauß vermag die Kunst nicht ein Medelein zu machen, was ding auch darzu gebraucht wird. Hierauß ein jeglicher leichtlichen zuermessen hat, wie, vnnd welcher gestalt, auch worinn materia benedicta soll gesucht vnd gefunden werden. Es wolle sich aber keiner imaginiren, viel weniger von einigen Artisten vberreden lassen, das, ob er schon warhafftig veram materiam entweder durch heimliche offenbahrung Gottes, oder deren die sie kennen, auch weiß, kennet vnd in handen hat, das er alsdann ebenmäßig dieselben auffzuschließen, das purum ab impuro auffs höchst zuscheiden vnd zu reinigen wisse, gentzlich verstehe. Ach nein lieber laborant bey weitem nicht: der Hund licht nun allererst im Bisem begraben, vnnd gehöret Kunst vnnd ein geschicktes Gemüthe zu der sachen, siehe an zum Exempel was du anfange von mir gehöret, das ich die 5. Jahr veram materiam lapidis gekant, vnnd die gantze zeit vber nicht damit zu prociren gewust, biß mir entlichen nach dem 6. Jahr der Schlüssel des dann offentlich wieder den Willen Gottes gehandelt were, zc. Auß diesen vrsachen vnd deren so ich zum theil in Epilogo angesogen, auch, damit ich nicht, das talentum à Deo mihi commissum zuuergraben, angesehen würde, habe ich in diesem meinem Aureo seculo rediuiuo, so viel mir Gott vnnd die Natur erlaubt, das grosse Geheimnüß der Weisen, wie dasselbige haben meine Augen gesehen, meine Hände einges richtet, vnnd durch die Gnade Gottes zu rechter zeit in grosser Krafft vnnd Herrligkeit wieder außgewonnen, offenbahren wollen: Der fromme vnd Gottliebender Leser, wolle es andero nit als im guten erkennen, auff vnnd annehmen, dextre consideriren, vnd sich durch auß nicht jrren noch verführen lassen, das viel zeiten, den Buchstaben nach contraria mit vnterlauffen, es hat sich per Theoriam ad praxin zu schreiten nicht anders machen können, noch gebühren wollen: Weil deutlicher vnd Klärlicher hieruon zu schreiben ernstlich vnd zum allerhöchsten in republica chymica verboten ist: trage aber gantz keinen zweiffel, es werden all die, so diß Tractatlein in warer Zuuersicht mit der innerlichen Augen des Gemüths, so alles vermügen, recht anschawen, in denselben fleißig studiren, vnd darbey für allen dingen Gott inniglichen vnd von Hertzen anruffen, gleich mir, die hierin verborgene Philosophische wundersüsse Früchte geniesen, vnd derselben nach dem Willen Gottes theilhafftig werden. Vnd alsdann sein vnd bleiben sie, ware Brüder des güldenen Creutzes, vnnd außerlesene Gliedmassen der Philosophischen gemeine in ewiger Verbündnuß.

Schließlich, damit auch der Christliche verstendige vnd würdige Leser, eigentlich meinen Tauff- vnd Zunahmen, wil ich so candidus sein, vnd denselben folgender gestalt, damit sich mit fug niemand vber mich zu beschweren, geoffenbahret haben: So wisse nun ein jeglicher, das die zahl meines Nahmens ist M.DCXII. in welcher zahl mein gantzer Nahme durch 11. Todte vnnd 7. lebendige vollkomlich ist: das Buch der Natur ist geschrieben worden: Vber das ist der 5. Buchstab der fünffte theil des 8. vnnd der 15. ist abermal der fünffte theil des 12. vnd laß dir hierbey genügen.

Datum in Monte abiegno, die 25. Martij
Anno 1621.

EPIGRAMMA

ad Sapientiae and doctrinae filios.

Quae sivi: inveni: purgavi saepius: atque
Conjunxi: maturavi: Tinctura secuta est
Aurea, Naturae centrum quae dicitur: inde
Tot sensus, tot scripta virum, variaeque figurae
Omnibus, ingenue fateor, MEDICINA metallis:
Infirmisque simul: punctum divinitus ortum.
HARMANNUS DATICHIUS:,
Auth. famulus.

What I have eagerly desired, I have found; I have purified more often: and
I have united; I have brought to maturity: the resulting Tincture is
Golden, which is called the centre of Nature; thence
So many sensations, so many writings of men, and manifold forms.
In all, I frankly admit, the MEDICINA in metals:
And in the feeble as well: the point risen from heaven.

AUREUM SECULUM

REDIVIUM. *(The Golden Age Restored).*

Whilst I was meditating upon the wonders of the Most High and the secrets of hidden Nature and the fiery and fervent love of the neighbor, I recalled the white harvest where Reuben, the son of Leah, had found in the fields and had given the mandrakes Rachel had gotten from Leah for sleeping with the patriarch Jacob. But my thoughts went much deeper and led me further to Moses, how he had made a *potable* of the solar-calf cast by Aaron, and how he had it burned with fire, ground to powder, strewed it upon the waters, and gave it to the Children of Israel to drink. And I marvelled most about this prompt and ingenius destruction which the hand of God had wrought. But after pondering over it for some time my eyes were opened, just as happened with the two disciples at Emmaus who knew the Lord in the Breaking of Bread, and my heart burned within me. But I laid down and began to sleep. And, lo, in my dream King Solomon appeared to me, in all his might, wealth, and glory, leading beside him all the women of his harem: there were threescore queens, and fourscore concubines, and virgins without number, but one was his gentle dove, most beautiful and dearest to his heart, and according to Catholic custom she held a magnificent procession wherein the *Centrum* was highly honored and cherished, and its name was like an out-ointment, the fragrance of which surpassed all spices. And its fiery spirit was a key to open the temple, to enter the Holy Place, and to grasp the horns of the altar.

When the procession was ended, Solomon showed unto me the unified *Centrum in Ittrigoni centri* and opened my understanding to me, and I became aware that behind me stood a nude woman with a bloody wound in her breast, out of which came forth blood and water, but the joints of her thighs were like jewels, the work of the hands of a cunning workman, her navel was like a round goblet, which wanteth not liquor, her belly was like an heap of wheat set about with roses, her two breasts were like two young roses that are twins, her neck was as a tower of ivory, her eyes like the fishpools in Heshbon by the gate of Bath-rabbim: her nose was as the tower of Lebanon which looketh towards Damascus. Her head was like Carmel, and the hair of her head was tied in many folds, like king's purple. But her garments, which she threw off, lay at her feet, and were all unsightly, stinking, and poisonous. And she began to speak: I have put off my coat, how shall I put it on? I have washed my feet, how shall I defile them? The watchmen that went about the city found me, they smote me, they wounded me, and took away my veil from me. Then was I stricken with fear and not conscious and fell upon the ground; but Solomon bade me stand up again and said: be not afraid when thou dost see Nature bare, and the most hidden which is beneath heaven and upon the earth. She is beautiful as Tirzah, comely as Jerusalem, terrible as an army with banners, but nevertheless she is the pure chaste virgin out of whom Adam was made and created. Sealed and hidden is the entrance to her house, for she dwelleth in the garden and sleepeth in the twofold caves of Abraham on the field Ephron, and her palace is the depths of the Red Sea, and in the deep transparent chasms, the air hath given her birth and the fire hath brought her up, wherefore she is a queen of the country, milk and honey hath she in her breasts. Yea, her lips are like a dripping honey-comb, honey and milk are under her tongue and the smell of her garments is like the fragrance of Lebanon to the Wise, but an abomination to the ignorant. And Solomon said further: Rouse thee, look upon all my women and see if you can find her equal. And forthwith the woman had to cast off her garments and I looked at her, but my mind had lost the power of judgment, and mine eyes were holden, so that I did not recognise her.

But as Solomon observed my weakness, he separated his women from this nude woman and said: Thy thoughts are vain and the sun hath burned out thy mind and thy memory is as black as fog, so thou canst not judge aright, so if thou wouldst not forfeit thy concern and take advantage of the present opportunity, then can the bloody sweat and snow-white tears of this nude virgin again refresh thee, cleanse thine understanding and memory and restore it fully, so that thine eyes may perceive the wonders of the Most High, the height of the uppermost, and thou shalt really fathom the foundations of all Nature, the power and operation of all the Elements, and thine understanding will be as fine silver, and thy memory as gold, the colors of all precious stones will appear before thine eyes and thou wilt know their production, and thou wilt know how to separate good from evil, the goats from the sheep. Thy life will be very peaceful, but the cymbals of Aaron will awaken thee from sleep and the harp of David, my father, from thy slumber. After Solomon thus spake, I was very much more afraid, and was exceedingly terrified, partly because of his heartbreaking works, also partly because of the great glamor and splendor of the present queenly woman, and Solomon took me by the hand and led me through a wine cellar into a secret but very stately hall, where he refreshed me with flowers and apples, but its windows were made out of transparent crystals and I looked through them. And he said: What dost thou see? I replied: I can only see from this hall into the hall I just left, and on the left standeth thy queenly woman, and on the right the nude virgin, and her eyes are redder than wine, her teeth whiter than milk, but her garments at her feet are more unsightly, blacker, and more filthy than the brook of Kidron. From all of them choose one, said Solomon to be thy beloved. I esteem her and am highly pleased as I am with the loveliness of my wives, so little do I care about the abomination of her garments. And as soon as the king had thus spoken, he turned around and conversed in a very friendly way with one of his queens. Amongst these was an hundred-year-old stewardess, with a grey cloak, a black cap upon her head, bedecked wih numberless snow-white pearls and lined with red velvet, and embroidered and sewn in an artful manner with blue and yellow silk, and her cloak was adorned with divers Turkish colors and Indian figures; this old woman beckoned to me secretly and swore unto me an holy oath that she was the mother of the nude virgin, that she had been born from her body, and that she was a chaste, pure and secluded virgin, that until now she had not suffered any man to look upon her, and although she had let herself be used everywhere among the many people on the streets, no one had ever seen her naked before now, and no one had touched her, for she was the virgin of whom the Prophet said: Behold, we have a son born unto us in secret, who is transformed beside others; behold, the virgin had brought forth, such a virgin as is called *Apdorossa*, meaning: secretly, she who cannot suffer others. But while this her daughter was as yet unwed, she had her marriage-portion lying under her feet, because of the present danger of the war, so that she would be robbed of it by some roving soldiery and denuded of her stately treasure. However I should not be frightened because of her disgusting garments, but choose her daughter before all others for the delight of my love and life. Then she would give and reveal to me a lye to clean her garments, and then I would obtain a liquid salt and non-combustible oil for my house-keeping, and an immeasurable treasure, and her right hand would always caress me and her left hand would be under my head. And as I then wanted to declare myself categorically upon this matter, Solomon turned around again, looked upon me, and said: I am the wisest man on earth, beautiful and pleasing are my wives and the glamor of my queens surpasseth the gold of Ophir; the adornments of my concubines overshadow the rays of the sun, and the beauty of my virgins surpasseth the rays of the moon, and as heavenly as are my women, my wisdom is unfathomable and my knowledge is inexplicable. Whereupon I answered and, half afraid, I bowed: Lo, I have found grace in thine eyes, and since I am poor, give me this nude virgin. I choose her amongst all others for the duration of my life, and though her garments are filthy and torn, I will clean them and love her with all mine heart, and she shall be my sister, my bride, because she hath ravished mine heart with one of her eyes, with one chain of her neck. When I had thus spoken, Solomon gave her unto me, and there was a great commotion in the hall of his women, so that I was awakened by it, and I knew not what had happened to me, nevertheless I believed it to be but a dream and I thought many subtle thoughts about my dream until the morning. But after I had arisen and said my prayers, Lo! I saw the garments of the nude virgin before my bed, but no trace of her. And I began to be greatly afraid and all my hair stood upright upon my head and my whole body was bathed in cold sweat; but I took heart, recalling my dream, and thought about it again in the fear of the Lord. But my thoughts did not explain it, and for this reason I dared not to scrutinize the garments, much less to recognize anything in them. I then changed my sleeping-chamber and I left the garments in it for some length of time *ex mera tamen ignorantia*, in the belief that if I were to touch them or turn them over, something peculiar would happen to me, but in my sleep the smell of the garments had poisoned and inflamed me violently, so that mine eyes could not see the time of mercy, and never

Ἐπίγραμμα

ad

Sapientiæ & doctrinæ filios.

QVæ fui: inueni: purgaui sæpius: atque
Coniunxi: maturaui: Tinctura secuta est
Aurea, Naturæ centrum quæ dicitur: inde
Tot sensus, tot scripta virum, variæque figuræ.
Omnibus, ingenue fateor, MEDICINA metallis;
Infirmisque simul: punctum diuinitus ortum.

HARMANNVS DATICHIVS,
Auth. famulus.

AVREVM SECVLVM
REDIVIVVM.

Als ich gedachte an die Wunder des allerhöchsten, an die Geheimnüß der verschlossenen Natur, vnnd an die fewrige vnnd inbrünstige Liebe des Nechsten: da erinnerte ich mich der Weizen Arndte, worin Ruben Leæ Sohn das Dudaim so von Lea Rachel fürs beyschlafen bey dem Patriarchen Jacob, gegeben vnd auff dem Felde gefunden worden. Meine Gedancken aber waren sehr tieffsinnig vnnd verleiteten mich ferner auff Moysen, wie der nemlich das von Aron gegossene Solarische Kalb potabel gemacht, in deme er es mit fewr verbrent, zu Puluer zermalmet, auffs Wasser gestrewet, vnnd den Kindern Israel zu trincken gegeben: Das ich auch vber diese des Manns Gottes schleunige vnd künstliche zerstörung mich zum allerhöchsten verwundert: da ich aber meine Gedancken recht fassete, erfahre ich die Wahrheit, vnd meine Augen mit anders geöffnet als den beyden Jüngern zu Emahauß, die den Herrn am Brodtbrechen erkanten: Vnd das Hertze brante in mir, legete mich aber nieder ferners zu speculiren, vnd ward darüber entschlafen, vnd siehe der König Salomon erschien mir im Traum mit aller seiner Macht, Reichtumb vnnd Herrligkeit, führete neben sich sein gantze Frawen Zimmer, 60 war der Königinnen, 80 der Kebsweiber, allein der Jungfrawen war kein zahl, aber eine war seine Taube, seine fromme, die allerschönste vnd liebste in seinem Hertzen: Vnd nach Catholischem gebrauch hielten sie eine stattliche procession, worin das Centrum hochgeehret, vnd geliebet ward, dessen Name war wie eine außgeschüttete Salbe, welcher Geruch vbertrifft alle Gewürtze, rc. Vnnd sein fewriger Geist ein schlüssel zu eröffnen den Tempel, in das heilige zugehen, vnnd die Horn des Altars angreiffen.

Nach vollendeter Procession aber zeigete mir Salomon das einige Centrum in Trigono centri vnnd eröffnete mit meinem Verstandt, vnd ich ward gewahr, das hinter mich stund ein nackend Weibesbild mit einer blutigen Wunden in ihrer Brust, darauß Blut vnd Wasser trüppfete, ihre Lenden aber stunden gleich aneinander wie zwo Spangen die des Meisters Hand gemacht hat, ihr Nabel wahr wie ein runder Becher dem nimmer Getränck gemangelt, ihr Bauch wie ein Weizenhauffe vmbgesteckt mit Rosen, ihr zwo Brüste wie zwey junge Rehezwilling, ihr Halß wie ein Helfenbeinen Thurm, ihre Augen wie Teiche zu Heßbon am Thor Bathrabbim, ihr Nase wie ein Thurm auff Libanon der gegen Damascon siehet, ihr Haupt stundt auff ihr wie Carmelus, vnnd das Haar war auf ihrem Häupte wie die Purpur des Königs in falten gebunden, Ihre Kleyder aber die sie von sich geworffen, lagen zu ihren Füssen, vnnd gantz heßlich, stinckend, gifftig, vnd sie fieng an zu reden: Ich habe meinen Rock außgezogen, wie soll ich ihn wiederum anziehen? Ich habe meine Süsse gewaschen, wie soll ich sie wieder besudelen? Die Hüter die in der Stadt vmbher gehen, haben mich gefunden, Wundt geschlagen vnd meinen Schleier genommen. Da erschrack ich auß Furcht vnd nicht kennung vnd fiel zur Erden: Salomon aber heiß mich wieder auffstehen vnd sprach: erschrecke nicht, dann du siehest die entblöste Natur vnd das allerheimlichste das vnter dem Himmel vnd auff Erden ist. Sie ist schön wie Thirza, lieblich wie Jerusalem, schrecklich wie Heerspitzen, vnd ist dannoch die reine keusche Jungfraw, darvon Adam gemacht vnd geschaffen ist worden, zwar versiegelt vnd verborgen ist der eingang ihrer Hütten, dann sie wohnet in den Garten, vnd schlefft in der zweyfachen Hölen Abrahams auff dem Acker Ephron, vnnd ihr Pallast ist in der tieffe des roten Mehrs, vnd in durchsichtigen Klüfften, die Lufft hat sie gebohren, vnd das Fewer auffgezogen, darumb ist sie eine Königinne des Landes, Milch vnd Honig hat sie in ihren Brüsten, ja ihre Lippen sein wie trieffender Honnigseimb, Honnig vnnd Milch ist vnter ihrer Zungen, vnnd ihrer Kleyder geruch ist den Weisen wie der geruch von Libanon, den vnwissenden aber ein Grewel: Vnnd weiter sprach Salomon: ermuntere dich, schawe

an mein gantzes Frawen Zimmer, vnnd suche ihres gleichen: Vnd alsobald muste sich das gantze Frawen Zimmer höfflich entblösen, ich suchte, aber meine Gedanken kunten nicht vrtheilen, vnnd meine Augen wurden gehalten das ich sie nicht erkante.

Da aber Salomon meine Schwachheit merckete, scheidete er sein Frawen Zimmer von diesem nackten Weibesbilde vnnd sprach: deine Gedanken sein eitel vnd dein verstand ist von der Sonnen verbrant vnd deine Memorie ist Nebel schwartz, daß du nicht recht vrtheilen kanst, allein so du deine sachen nicht verschertzest, vnd die jetzige gelegenheit in acht nehmen wilt, kann dieser nackten Jungfrawen blutiger Schweiß vnd Schneeweisse zehren dich wiederum erquicken, deinen Verstand vnnd Gedechtnüs läutern vnd vollkömlich restituiren, das deine Augen erkennen die magnalia des allerhöchsten, die höhe der obersten, die tiefe der vntersten, vnd das fundament der gantzen Natur aller Element Krafft vnd Würckung wirst du eigentlich erforschen, vnd dein Verstand wird Silbern sein, vnnd dein Gedechtnüß Gülden, aller Edelgestein Farben werden für deinem Angesichte erscheinen, vnd du wirst ihre Geburt wissen, vnd scheiden das gute vom bösen, die Böcke von den Schaffen: dein Lebend wird Ruhe sein, aber die Schellen Aronis werden dich vom Schlaff erwecken, vnnd die Harpffe Dauids meines Vattern vom Schlummern. Vber dieser Rede Salomonis erschrack ich noch hefftiger, vnd entsetzete mich vber die massen sehr, theils wegen der hertzbrechenden Wort, theils auch wegen des anwesenden Königlichen Frawenzimmers grosser Pracht vnd Herrligkeit: Vnd der König Salomon fassete mich bey der Hand, führete mich durch einen Weinkeller in einen heimlichen aber sehr stattlichen Saal, worin er mich erquickte mit Blumen, vnd labete mich mit Oepffeln, dessen Fenster aber waren von durchsichtigen Cristallen, vnnd ich sahe hindurch, er aber sprach: was siehest du? Ich antwortede: Ich siehe auß diesem in das vorige Gemach, worauß ich gangen bin, vnd dein Königliche Frawen Zimmer stehet zur Lincken, vnd die nackte Jungfrawe zur rechten seiten, vnd ihre Augen sein röther denn Wein, ihre Zehne weisser denn Milch, ihre Kleyder aber sein Füssen heßlicher, schwartzer, vnd vnstetiger als der Bach Kidron. Erwehle eine von allen sprach Salomon, zu deiner liebsten, Ich achte gleich sie vnd mein Frawen Zimmer, vnd so hoch mich erfrewet die Holdseligkeit meiner Damen, so wenig erschrecken mich ihre abschewlichen Kleider, vnd alsobald wante sich der König vnnd redete gantz freundlich mit einer von seinen Königinnen. Da war eine alte hundertjährige Hoffmeisterinne vnter ihnen die hatte einen grawen Rock anne, eine schwartze Mütze auff ihrem Haupte mit Schneeweissen Zahl Perlen besetzet vnd innwendig mit roten Tasst gefuttert, vnd mit blawer vnd gelber Seyden gesticket vnnd gantz künstlich durchgenehet, die Mantel war mit allerhand Türckischen Farben vnd Indianischen Figuren erhöbet: diese alte Fraw gab mir heimlich einen Winck, vnd schwur einen tewren Eyd, das sie were die Mutter dieser entblösten Jungfrawen, sie were von ihrem Leibe geboren, ein keusche reine vnd verborgene Jungfrawe, welche biß daher keines Mannes anblick wollen leiden, vnnd ob sie sich schon vnter den Völkern allenthalben auff den Gassen gebrauchen lassen, so hette sie doch kein Man vor diesem niemals nicht nackend gesehen noch in einiger berühret, dann sie were die Jungfraw darvon der Prophet saget: Siehe, wir haben einen heimlichen gebohrnen Sohn, welcher ist verwandelt von andern, siehe, die Jungfrawe hat geboren, eine solche Jungfraw welche heist Apdorossa das ist, heimlich, die ander nicht leiden mag. Weil aber diese ihre Tochter annoch vnverheiratet, hette sie den Brautschatz vnter ihren Füssen liegen vmb der jetzigen Kriegsgefahr willen, damit sie nicht möchte von einem streiffenden Rott beraubet, vnnd der stattlichen Reichthums entsetzet werden, ich aber solte mich nicht durch abschew der vnansehnlichen Kleyder lassen abschrecken, besondern erwehlen ihre Tochter vor allen andern zu meiner liebe vnnd Lebens Wollust, alsdann wollte sie mir geben vnd offenbahren ein Lauge zu reinigen ihre Kleyder, so würde ich erlangen ein flüssig Saltz, vnnd ein vnuerbrenliches Oel zu meiner Haußhaltung, vnnd einen vnaußgreifflichen Schatz, vnd ihre Rechte würde mich stets hertzen, vnnd ihre Lincke stets vnter meinem Haupt liegen. Vnd als ich mich hierauff

could mine heart recognise the great wisdom of Solomon.

After the above-mentioned garments had lain for five years in my sleeping-chamber and I knew not what they were good for, I finally thought to burn them, in order to clean up the place. And then I spent the whole day going around with such thoughts. But the next night there appeared to me in my dream the hundred-year-old woman and she spake harshly to me thus: Thou ungrateful man: for five years I have entrusted to thee my daughter's garments; among them are her most precious jewels, and during all that time thou hast neither cleaned them nor thrown out of them the moths and worms, and now, finally, thou dost want to burn these clothes, and is it not enough that thou art the reason for the death and perishing of my daughter? Whereupon I became hot-headed and answered her: How shall I understand thee, that thou wouldst make a murderer of me? For five years mine eyes have not beheld thy daughter, and not the least did I hear of her, how then can I be the cause of her death? But she would not let me finish, and said: It is all true, but thou hast sinned against God, therefore thou couldst not obtain my daughter, nor the philosophical lixivium I promised thee for washing and cleaning her garments: for in the beginning, when Solomon willingly gave thee my daughter, and when thou didst abhor her garments, that made furious the Planet Saturn, who is her grandfather, and full of wrath was he that he transformed her again into what she had been before her birth; and since you infuriated Saturnus through thine abhorring, thou didst cause her death, putrefaction, and her final destruction, for she is the one of whom *Senior* saith: Ah, woe! to bring a nude woman unto me, when my first body was not good to look upon, and I had never been mother until I was born again, then I brought forth the power of all roots of herbs, and in mine innermost being I was victorious. Such and similar heart-breaking words were very strange to me, but nevertheless I withheld mine indignation as much as was humanly possible for me, at the same time protesting *solemniter* against her sayings: that I knew nothing at all about her daughter, much less about her death and putrefaction, and although I kept her garments for five years in my sleeping-chamber, I did not know them for my great blindness nor ever discovered their use, and therefore I was innocent before God and all others. This, my righteous and well-founded excuse, must have pleased the old woman not a little, for she looked at me and said: I feel and observe from thy righteous mind, that thou art innocent, and thine innocence shall be rewarded well and plentifully, therefore I will reveal to thee secretly and out of my good heart, namely that my daughter, out of special love and affection towards thee, hath left thee a gray marbled casket as an inheritance amongst her garments, which is covered with a rough, black, dirty case (and meanwhile she gave me a glass filled with lye, and continued speaking), this same little casket thou shalt clean from its stench and dirt which it hath received from the garments. Thou hast no need of a key, but it will open itself, and thou wilt find two things therein: a white silver box, filled with magnificent ground-lead and polished diamonds, and another golden work of art, adorned with costly solar rubies: and this is the treasure and entire legacy of my deceased daughter which she left for thee to inherit before her transformation. If thou wilt only transfer this treasure and purify it most highly and silently and lock it up with great patience in a warm, hidden, steamy, transparent and moist cellar, and protect it from freezing, hail, quick lightning, hot thunder, and other outward destruction till the wheat harvest, then thou wilt first perceive the entire glory of this inheritance and take part of it. Meanwhile I awoke for a second time and called upon God, full of fear, praying that He would open mine understanding that I might seek for the casket which was promised me in my dream. And after my prayer was ended I sought with greatest diligence in the garments and found the casket, but the casing was tight around it and seemed grown onto it by nature, so that I was not able to take it off; then I could not clean it with any lye nor split it with iron, steel, or any other metal. I left it alone once more and did not know what to do with it, and held it to be witchcraft, thinking of the prophet's saying: For though thou wash thee with lye, and take thee much soap, yet thine iniquity is marked before me, saith the Lord God.

And after a year had passed again and I did not know, after speculating and industriously deliberating, how to remove the casing, I finally went to walk in the garden to rid myself of the melancholy thoughts, and after long promenading, I sat down on a flinty stone and fell into a deep sleep. I slept, but my heart was awake: there appeared unto me the hundred-year-old stewardess in my dream: Hast thou received my daughter's inheritance? In a sad voice I answered no, though I found the casket, but alone it is still impossible for me to separate the casing therefrom, and the lye thou hast given me will not work on the casing. After this simple speech the old woman smiled and said: Dost thou want to eat shells and shellfish with the shells? Do they not have to be brought forth and prepared by the very old planet and cook *Vulcan*? I told thee to clean the gray casket thoroughly with the lye given thee, and which proceeded wholly from it, and was not refined from the outer rough casing. This thou hast especially to burn in the fire of the philosophers, then everything will turn out for the best. And thereupon she gave me several glowing coals wrapped up in white light taffeta and instructed me further and pointed out that I should make therefrom a philosophical and quite artful fire and burn the casing, then I would soon find the gray casket. And presently every hour a north and south wind rose, both sweeping at the same time through the garden, whereupon I awoke, rubbed the sleep out of mine eyes, and noticed that the glowing coals wrapped in white taffeta lay at my feet; with haste and joy I grasped them, prayed diligently, called upon God, studied and labored day and night, and thought meanwhile of the great and excellent sayings of the *Philosophers*, who say: *Ignis et azoth tibi sufficiunt.* About this *Esdras* saith in his fourth book: And he gave unto me a full cup which was full of fire, and his form was as of fire, and when I had drunk of it, my heart uttered understanding, and wisdom grew in my breast, for my spirit retained its memory: and my mouth was opened, and shut no more. The Most High gave understanding unto the five men, and they wrote by course the things that were told them, in characters which they knew not. So in forty days were written 204 books, 70 for the wisest alone, who were truly worthy of it, and all were written on box-wood. And then I proceeded *in silentio et spe*, as the old woman had revealed to me in my dream until, according to Solomon's prediction, after a long time my knowledge became silver and my memory became golden. But according to the instructions and teaching of the old stewardess, I enclosed and locked up in a proper and quite artistic manner the treasure of her daughter, namely: the splendid and brilliant lunar diamonds and the solar rubies, both of which came forth and were found from the casket and the landscape. I heard the voice of Solomon who said: My beloved is white and ruddy, the chiefest among ten thousand. His head is as the most fine gold, his locks are bushy, and black as a raven. His eyes are as the eyes of doves by the rivers of waters, washed with milk, and fitly set. His cheeks are as a bed of spices, as sweet flowers: his lips are like roses, dropping sweet smelling myrrh. His hands are as gold rings set with the beryl: his belly is as bright ivory overlaid with sapphires. His legs are as pillars of marble, set upon sockets of fine gold: his countenance is as Lebanon, excellent as the cedars. His mouth is most sweet: yea, he is altogether lovely. This is my beloved, and this is my friend, O daughters of Jerusalem. Therefore shalt thou hold him, and not let him go, until thou bringest him into his mother's house, and into his mother's chamber. And when Solomon had spoken these words I knew not how to answer him, and I became silent, but I wanted nevertheless to open up again the locked-up treasure, with which I might remain unmolested. Then I heard another voice: I charge you, O ye daughters of Jerusalem, by the roes, and by the hinds of the field, that ye stir not up, nor awake my love, till she please, for she is a garden inclosed, a spring shut up, a fountain sealed, the vineyard at Baal-hamon, the vineyard at Engeddi, the garden of fruits and spices, the mountain of myrrh, the hill of frankincense, the bed, the litter, the crown, the palm-tree and apple-tree, the flower of Sharon, the sapphire, the turquoise, the wall, tower, and rampart, the garden of joy, the well in the garden, the spring of living water, the king's daughter, and the love of Solomon in his concupiscence: she is the dearest to her mother, and the chosen of her mother, but her head is filled with dew, and her locks with the drops of the night.

Through this discourse and revelation I was so far informed that I knew the purpose of the Wise and did not touch the locked treasure until through God's mercy, the working of noble Nature, and the work of mine own hands, the work was happily completed

Shortly after this time, just on the day of the month when the moon was new, there occurred an eclipse of the sun, showing itself in all its terrifying power, in the beginning dark green and some mixed colors, until it finally became coal-black, darkened heaven and earth, and many people were much afraid, but I rejoiced, thinking of God's great mercy, and the new birth, as Christ Himself pointed out to us, that a grain of wheat must be cast into the ground, that it may not rot therein, else it bringeth forth no fruit. And then it happened that the darkness was covered with clouds, and the sun began to shine through, yet at the same time three parts of it were still heavily darkened; and lo, an arm broke through the clouds, and my body trembled because of it, and it held in its hand a letter with four seals hanging down from it, on which stood written: I am black, but comely, O ye daughters of Jerusalem, as the tents of Kedar, as the curtains of Solomon: Look not upon me, because I am black, because the sun hath looked upon me, etc. But as soon as the *fixum* acted in the *humidum*, a rainbow spanned itself and I thought of the covenant of the Most High, and of the fidelity of my *Ductoris*, and of what I had learned, and lo, with the help of the planet and the fixed stars, the sun overcame the darkness, and over every mountain and valley there came a lovely and bright day; then all fear and terror had an end, and everything beheld this day and rejoiced, praised the Lord, and said: The winter is past, the rain is over and gone; the flowers appear on the earth; the time of the singing of birds is come, and the voice of the turtle is heard in our land; the fig tree putteth forth her green figs, and the vines with the tender grape give a good smell. Therefore let us make haste to take the foxes, the little foxes that spoil the vines, that we may gather the grapes in time and with them make and drink wine, and be fed at the right time with milk and honey-comb: that we may eat and be filled. And after the day was done and the evening fell, the whole heaven

cathegorice erkleren wolte, kehrete sich Salomon wiederumb starrete mich an vnd sprach: Ich bin der allerweiseste auff Erden, schön vnd ergetzlich ist mein Frawen Zimmer, vnd meiner Königinnen Herrligkeit vbertrifft das Gold auß Ophir, meiner Kebsweiber Schmuck vberschattet die Stralen der Sonnen, vnnd meiner Jungfrawen Zier im Monschein, also Himmlisch sein meine Dahmen, vnaußgründlich meine Weißheit, vnd vnauffschließlich mein Verstandt. Da antwortede ich vnd neigte mich halb erschrocken: Siehe, hab ich gnade für dir gefunden, dieweil ich arm bin, so gib mit dieser nackende Jungfraw, so ich vnter allen zu erhaltung meines Lebens erwehlet habe, besudelt vnd zerrissen sind zwar ihre Kleider, aber ich will sie reinigen vnd von Hertzen lieben, vnd soll sein **meine Schwester, meine Braut,** weil sie mit ihrer Augen einem, vnd mit ihrer HalßRetten eine, mir das Hertz genommen, mich brünstig gemacht, das ich für Liebe kranck liege, vnd alsobald vbergab sie mir Salomon, vnnd es ward ein getummel im Frawen Zimmer das ich daruon erwachte, vnd wuste nit, wie mir geschehen war, nichts desto weniger hielte ich er in Traum, vnnd hatte hierüber biß zu morgends allerhand subtile Gedancken: da ich aber auffstundt vnnd mein Gebett gethan, Siehe: da sahe ich der nackenten Jungfrawen Kleider für meinem Bette liegen, sie aber nicht, vnd es begunnte mir angst vnd bange zu werden, vnnd gingen mir alle Haar zu berge, das mir auch der kalte Schweis vber den gantzen Leib herab lieff, dannoch fassete ich ein Hertz, wiederholte meinen Traum, vnd gedachte demselben in der Furcht des Herrn nach, alleine meine Gedancken vermöchten ihn denselben zuergründen, auß diesen Vhrsachen durffte ich mich nicht vnterstehen die Kleyder zu besichtigen, viel weniger etwas darinnen zu recognosciren, besonders mutirte meine SchlaffCammer, vnnd ließ eine geraume zeit ex mera tamen ignorantia die Kleider daselbsten liegen, in meinung, da sie mir würde vielleicht berühren oder verkehren, es möchte mir etwas merckliches wiederfahren, ich war im Schlaff von dem gestanck der Kleider hefftig vergifftet vnd enbündet, das meine Augen nicht sehen kunten die Zeit der Gnaden, noch mein Hertze erkennen die grosse **Weißheit Salomonis.**

Nach dem aber viel erwehnte Kleider 5. Jahr in meiner Schlaff Kammer gelegen, vnd ich nicht wuste worzu sie nütze, gedachte ich endlich sie zuuerbrennen, vmb das Losament zu reumen: vnd da ich mit sothanen Gedancken den gantzen Tag zugebracht, erschien mir folgende Nacht im Traum die alte hundertjährige Fraw vnd sprach mich folgender gestalt gantz hart an: Du vndanckbarer Mensche, ich habe dir nun 5. Jahr hero meiner Tochter Kleider, worunter ihre vornehmbste Clenodien vertrawet, vnnd hast dieselben die gantze zeit hero weder gereiniget noch vmb der Motten vnd Würme willen ausgesünnet, vnd vber das alles wiltu nun endlich die Kleyder mit Fewer verbrennen, ists nicht genug das du bist eine vrsache des Todts vnd vnterganges meiner Tochter? Da ward ich etwas hitzig für der Stirne, vnd gab ihr zur antwort: Wie soll ich das verstehen, wilt du kann einen Mörder auß mir machen, habe ich doch in 5. Jahren deine Tochter mit Augen nicht gesehen, noch von ihr das geringst nicht gehöret, wie kann ich dann eine vrsache ihres Todes sein? Vnd sie wolte mich nicht außreden lassen, besondern sprach: Es ist alles wahr, allein du hast dich gegen Gott versündiget, darumb hat dir auch meine Tochter nicht können zu theil werden, noch du mir verheisene Philosophische Lauge ihre Kleider zu waschen vnd zu reinigen, erfolgen: dann wie du anfangs, da dir Salomon meine Tochter gutwillig vbergab, vnd du hattest innen abschew für ihren Kleydern, erzürnte du den Planet **Saturnus,** so ihr Großvater ist, vnnd verwandelte sie auß lauter Zorn wiederumb in das, was sie vor ihrer Geburt gewesen war, vnd also hast du durch die Verschmehung Saturnum erzürnet, vnd ihren Todt, verwesung vnd endlichen vntergang veruhrsacht, wie es eben die von vhralter Senior sagt: Ach wehe! bring mir ein nackends Weib, wann vnsehnlich war mein erster Leib, vnd ich noch nie Mutter was geworden, biß ich zum andernmahl ward gebohren, da gebahr ich aller Kreuter Wurzeln Krafft, in meinem wesen ward ich Sieghafft, etc. Solche vnd dergleichen hertzbrechende Wort kamen mir sehr befrembt für, noch enthielt ich mich des Eyffers so viel mir mensch vnd müglich war, gleichwoll protestirte ich solenniter dargegen, das ich von ihrer Tochter nichts wuste, viel weniger von ihrem Todt, verwesung vnd Vntergange: zwar ihre Kleyder hette ich in meiner SchlaffKammer 5. Jahr vber in verwahrung gehabt, aber wegen grosser Blindheit nicht erkennet, noch ihre nützung erdencken können, vnd wehre danhero für Gott vnd jedermenniglich vnschuldig. Das alte rechtmeßige, woll fundirte entschüldigung, gefiel dem alten Mütterlein nicht vbel, sahe mich an vnd sprach: Ich spüre vnnd mercke auß deinem auffrichtigen Gewissen, das du vnschüldig bist, vnd soll dir auch deine Vnschuld reichlich vnd wohl belohnet werden: darumb will ich dir auß autem Hertzen vnnd in geheimb offenbahren, nemlich: das mir meine Tochter auß sonderbahrer Liebe, vnd gegen dir tragenden affection vnter ihren hinterbliebenen Kleidern ein **graw Mormaliertes Kästlein** zur Erbschafft verlassen, welches mit einem groben, schwartzen vnfletigen Futter vberzogen ist (vnd in deme gab sie mir ein Glaß mit Lauge vnnd redete weiter fort) dasselbige Kästlin solt du von gestanck vnd Vnfletigkeit, so es von den Kleydern bekommen woll reinigen, so bedarffst du keinen Schlüssel, besondern es wird sich selbsten eröffnen, vnd du wirst darinnen finden zweyerley: Ein **weiß silbern Bürlein** voller **herrlicher vnd auff Bley geschliffener vnd pollirter schneller Deman-**

ten, dann auch ein güldenes stück mit Köstlichen Solarischen Rubinen geschmücket: vnd diß ist der Schatz vnd gantze verlassenschafft meiner seligen Tochter, welches alles sie dir vor ihrer verwandelung vnd hintrit zum Erbtheil vermacht vnd hinterlassen hat. Wirst du nun diesen Schatz künstlich vnter einander versetzen, auff das allerhöchst reinigen vnd stillschweigens, in grosser Gedult in einen warmen verborgenen dampffigten durchsichtigen vnd feuchten Keller versperren, vnd für Frost, Wind, Hagel, schnellen Blitz, hitzigen Donnerstralen vnd anderer euserlicher zerstörung verwahren biß zur Weizenärndte, als dann wirst du der allererst die grosse Herrligkeit des Erbtheils empfinden vnd theilhafftig werden. Vnnd in deme erwachte ich abermahl, vnd siehe, ich rieff Gott engstiglich an, das er mir wolte eröffnen meinen Verstandt, zu suchen das Kästlein, so mir im Traum verheißet vnd zugesagt war: Nach volendtem Gebete suchte ich mit höchstem fleiß vnd begierde in den Kleydern, vnd fand es, aber das Futter war so hart darum verschlossen vnnd von natur angewachsen, das ich es nicht vermuchte daruon zu bringen, dann es wolte sich weder mit der Lauge reinigen, noch mit Essen, Stael, oder andern Metall zerspalten lassen, lies es also abermahl stehen, vnnd wuste nicht was ich damit machen solte, hielte es für ein Zauberwerck, vnnd gedachte an den Spruch des Propheten: Vnd wann du dich schon mit Laugen wuschest, vnd nehmest viel Seiffen dazu, so gleisset doch deine Vntugendt desto mehr für mir, spricht der Herr, Herr.

Vnd es verlieff wieder ein Jahr das ich gleichwohl mit speculiren vnd embsigen nachsinnen das Futter nicht wuste zu remouiren, biß ich endlich melancholische Gedancken zu vertreiben in einen Garten spacirn ging, wie langem deambuliren aber setzte ich mich nieder auff einen Kißling Stein, vnd ward darüber hart entschlafen, Ich schlieff aber mein Hertze wachete: Da erschien mir abermahl die alte hundertjährige Hoffmeisterinne vnnd sprach: Hastdu meiner Tochter Verlassenschafft bekommen? Ich antwortede mit trawriger Stimme, nein, das Kästlein hab ich zwar gefunden, allein das Futter dauon zu scheiden ist mir noch zur zeit vnmüglich, die lauge die du mir gegeben hast, will das Futter nit angreiffen. Auff diese meine einfeltige Rede ward die alte Frawe lechelnd vnd sprach: wilt du nun Mußlein vnd Krebse fressen mit den Schalen? müssen sie nicht zuuor von dem vhralten Planeten Koche Vulcano gezeitiget vnd zugericht werden? Ich habe gesagt, du soltest das grawe Kästlein mit der geschenckten Lauge, so auß demselben entsprungen auff das allerhöchst, vnnd nicht das außwendige rohe Futter reinigen, besondern must dasselbige zuuor mit der Weisen Fewer verbrennen, alß dann wird es sich woll schicken, vnnd fort hierauff gab sie mir etzliche glühende Kohlen in weissen Zindel gebunden, vnd ferrnern vnterricht vnd andeuten, ich solte hieuon ein Philosophisch vnd gantz künstlich Fewer machen, vnd verbrennen das Futter, so würde ich bald das grawe Kästlein finden, vnd stündtlich erhub sich ein Nordt vnd Südwind, weheten beyde zugleich durch den Garten, dauon erwachte ich, reinigte meine Augen vom Schlaff, vnd ward gewahr das die glühende Kohlen in weissen Zindel gewickelt zu meinen Füssen lagen, ich ergriff es eylendts vnd mit Frewden, betete fleissig, rieff Gott an, studirte vnd laborirte Tag vnd Nacht, gedachte interim an den herrlichen vnd fürtrefflichen Spruch der Philosophen, da sie sagen: Ignis & azoth tibi sufficiunt. Daruon auch Esdra im vierdten Buch saget: Vnnd er gab mir einen Becher voll Fewers, vnnd seine gestalt sach als ein Fewer, vnnd ich tranck es, da wuchs in mir Weißheit: Vnd Gott hat gegeben den fünfften verstant, vnnd mein Geist war in der Gedächtnus behalten, vnnd mein Mund ist auffgethan, vnnd weiter nicht zugethan, vnnd da 40. Nacht vmbwahren, da sind verfertiget gewesen 204. Bücher, 70. allein für die Weisesten, vnnd die wahren würdig zu sein auff Buxbaum geschrieben. Vnd procedirte also in silentio & spe, wie mir das alt Mütterlein im Traum geoffenbahret hatte, biß vber ein lange zeit nach der Verheissung Salomonis mein Verstandt silbern vnd mein Gedächtnus gülden ward. Nach deme aber auff vermeinte vnd Lehre der alten Hoffmeisterinnen, ich gebührlich vnd gantz kunstreich den Schatz ihrer Tochter eingesetzet vnd versperret hatte, Als nemlich: die herrlichen glentzenden Lunarischen Demanten, vnd die Solarische Rubinen, welche beyde auß einem Kästlein vnd aus einer Landschafft entsprossen vnd erfunden worden, hörete ich die Stimme Salomonis, die da sprach: Mein Freund ist **weiß vnd roth,** außerkorn vnter viel tausend, seine Locken sein krauß, schwartz wie ein Rabe, seine Augen sein wie Tauben Augen an den Wasserbächen mit Milch gewaschen, vnd stehen in der Fülle, seine Backen sein wie die wachsenden Wurtzgärtlein der Apotecker, seine Lippen sind wie Rosen, die mit fliessender Myrren triessen, seine Hände sein wie güldene Ringe voll Türkissen, sein Leib ist wie ein Helffen Bein rein, mit Saphiren geschmücket, seine Beine seind wie Marmelseulen gegründet auff güldenen Süssen, seine gestalt ist wie Libanon, außerwehlet wie Cedern, seine Kehle ist süß vnd gantz lieblich, ein solcher ist mein Freund, mein Freund ist ein solcher, ihr Töchter Jerusalem: darum solst du ihn halten vnd nicht lassen, biß du ihn bringest in seiner Mutter Haus, in seiner Mutter Cammer. Vnd da Salomon diese Wort außgeredet, wuste ich nicht darauff zu antworten, besondern verseumbte, hatte gleichwohl in willen den eingeschlossenen Schatz wieder zu eröffnen, damit ich möchte Friede

grew pale, and the seven stars rose with yellow rays and pursued their natural courses through the night, until in the morning they were overshadowed by the breaking of the sun's red dawn. And behold, the Wise who dwelt in the land arose from their slumber, looked heavenward, and said: Who is she that looketh forth as the morning, fair as the moon, clear as the sun, and there is no spot in her, for her ardor is fiery and not unlike a flame of the Lord: so that no water may extinguish the love, nor any river drown it; therefore we will not leave her, for she is our sister, and though she is yet little, and hath no breasts, we will bring her again into her mother's house, into a shining hall, where she hath been before, to suck her mother's breasts. Then she will come forth like a tower of David, built with ramparts whereon hang a thousand shields, and many arms of the mighty men; and as she went forth the daughter praised her openly, and the queens and the concubines spake well of her: but I fell upon my face, thanked God, and praised His Holy Name.

EPILOGUS

And thus is brought to a close, ye beloved and true *Sapientiae et doctrinae filii*, in all its power and its glory, the great secret of the Wise, and the revelation of the Spirit, about which the Prince and Monarch *Theoph. in Apocalypsi Hermetis* saith: It is a single *Numen*, a divine, wondrous, and holy office, while it incloseth the whole world within it, and will become true with all else, and truly overcometh the elements and the five substances. Eye hath not seen, nor hath ear heard, neither have entered the heart of any man, how the heaven hath naturally embodied to truth of this Spirit, in it the truth doth stand alone, therefore it is called: the voice of truth. To this power Adam and the other patriarchs, Abraham, Isaac, and Jacob, owed their bodily health, their long life, and finally prospered in great wealth thereby. With the aid of this Spirit, the *Philosophi* founded the seven free arts, and acquired their wealth therewith. With it Noah built the Ark, Moses the Tabernacle, and Solomon the Temple and through this provided the golden vessels from pure gold in the Temple, and for the glory of God, Solomon also wrought with it many fine works and did other great deeds. With it Esdras again established the Commandment; and with it Miriam, the sister of Moses, was hospitable. And this Spirit was much used and very common amongst the prophets of the Old Testament. Likewise it is a medicine and a cure for all things, and the final revelation, the final and highest secret of Nature. It is the Spirit of the Lord which hath filled the sphere of the earthly kingdom, and moved upon the face of the waters in the beginning. The world could neither understand nor grasp it without the secret gracious inspiration of the Holy Ghost, or without secret teaching. For the whole world longeth for it because of its great powers, which cannot be appreciated enough by men, and for which the saints have sought from the creation of the world, and have fervently desired to see. For this Spirit goeth into the seven planets, raiseth the clouds, and dispelleth the mists, giveth light to all things, transformeth everything into gold and silver, giveth health and abundance, treasures, cleanseth leprosy, cureth dropsy and gout, cleareth the face, prolongeth life, strengtheneth the sorrowful, healeth the sick and all the afflicted, yea, it is a secret of all secrets, one secret thing of all secret things, and healing and medicine for all things.

Likewise it is and remaineth unfathomable in nature, and endless power and an invincible might and glory, that is a passionate craving for knowledge, and a lovely thing of all things which are beneath the circle of the moon, with which Nature is made strong, and the heart with all members is renewed, and kept in blossoming youth, age is driven away, weakness destroyed, and the entire world refreshed.

Likewise this Spirit is a spirit chosen above all other heavenly things or spirits, which giveth health, luck, joy, peace, love, expelling altogether all evil, destroying poverty and misery, and also causing that one can neither talk nor think evil; it giveth to men what they desire from the depths of their hearts, worldly honor and long life to the godly, but eternal punishment to the evil-doers, who put it to improper use.

To the Most High. Almighty God who hath created this art and who hath also been pleased to reveal this knowledge unto me, a miserable, sinful man, through a promise and true vow, to Him be given praise, honor, glory, and thanks, with an entirely humble and fervent prayer that He will direct my heart, mind, and senses through His Holy Ghost, so governing that I talk to no one about this secret, much less communicate it to some one who doth not fear God, nor reveal it to any other creature, lest I break my vow and oath, and break the heavenly seals, and thus become a perjured Brother *Aurae Crucis*, and utterly offend the Divine Majesty, and thereby commit and perpetrate knowingly an unpardonable mighty sin against the Holy Ghost. Wherefore may God the Father, Son, and Holy Ghost, the Most Blessed Trinity, mercifully preserve and protect me constantly. Amen. Amen. Amen.

F I N I S .

haben, vnnd vngemolestiret bleiben, da hörete ich anderweit eine Stimme: Ich beschwere euch jhr Töchter Jerusalem bey den Rehen vnd Hinden auff dem Felde, das jhr meine Freundinnen nicht auffwecket noch reget, biß es jhr selbst gefellet, dann sie ist ein verschlossen Garte, eine verschlossene Quelle, ein versiegelter Born, sie ist der Weinberg zu Baalhamon, der Weingarte zu Engeddi, das Nuß vnd Wurtzgärtlein, der Myrrenberg, der Weyrauchs Hügel, das Bette, die Sännffte, die Crone, der Palmen vnd Apffelbaum, die Blume zu Saron, der Saphir, Türckisch, die Maure, Thurn vnd Brustwehr, der Lustgarte, der Gartenbrun, der Brun lebendiger Wasser, die Fürsten Töchter, vnnd die Liebe Salomonis in Wollüsten, sie ist jhrer Mutter die liebste, vnnd die außerwehlete jhrer Mutter: Jhr Häupt aber ist volles Tawes, vnd jhre Locken voll Nachts Tropffen.

Durch diese Rede vnd offenbahrung ward ich so weit informiret, das ich erkante den Zweck der Weisen, ließ den verschlossenen Schatz vnangerühret stehen, biß durch die Barmhertzigkeit Gottes, wirckung der edlen Natur vnnd meiner Hände Arbeit alles glücklich vollendet ward.

Kurtz nach dieser zeit, eben am Tage da der Monat new ward, geschach eine Finsternüß an der Sonnen, die sich gantz schrecklich erzeigte, anfangs mit dunckelgrünen vnd etwas vermischeten Farben, biß sie endlich Kohlschwartz ward, vnd verfinsterte Himmel vnd Erden, da ward den Leuten bang, ich aber frewete mich vnd gedachte an die grosse Barmhertzigkeit Gottes, vnnd die newe Geburt, wie vns dann das Weitzen Körnlein von Christo selbsten andeutung gibt, so werde denn in die Erde geworffen, das es darinnen verfaule, sonsten bringe es keine Frucht. Vnnd es geschach das die Finsternüß mit Wolcken bedeckt ward, vnd die Sonne beginte hervor zu blicken, gleichwohl wahren nur drey theil hart verfinstert, vnd siehe: Ein Arm brach durch die Wolcken, vnnd mein Leib erzittert darfür, hatte einen Brieff mit vier herabhangenden Siegeln in der Hand, darauff stund geschrieben: Ich bin schwartz aber gar lieblich, jhr Töchter Jerusalem, wie die Hütten Kedar, wie die Teppich Salomo: Sehet mich nicht an, das ich so schwartz bin, dann die Sonne hat mich so verbrent, etc. So bald aber das fixum agierte in das humidum, spannete sich ein Regebogen, vnd ich gedachte an den Bund des allerhöchsten, vnd an die Trewe meines Ductoris, vnd dessen der mich vnterrichtet hatte, vnnd siehe: durch hülffe der Planeten vnnd Firsternen, verwand die Sonne die Finsternüsse, vnnd erfolgte vber alle Berg vnd Thal ein gantz lieblicher heller Tag: da hatte all Furcht vnnd schrecken ein ende, vnd alle die diesen Tag sehen vnd erlebet hatten, frolockten dem Herrn vnd sprachen: Der Winter ist vergangen, der Regen 2. weg vnd dahin, die Blumen sind herfür gekommen im Lande, der Lentz ist herbey gekommen, vnd die Turteltaub lest sich hören im Lande. Item die Feygenbaum vnd Weinstöcke haben Augen vnd Knoden gewunnen, vnnd geben jhren Geruch: Darum last vns eylend die Füchse fangen, die kleinen Füchse, die den Weinberg verderben, damit wir zeitige Trauben Lesen, mit gemachtem Weine gedrencket, vnd zu rechter zeit mit Milch vnd Honigseimb gespeiset, auff das wir truncken vnd satt werden. Vnd nach deme der Tag sich geneiget, vnd der Abendt herein fiel, entferbte sich der gantze Himmel, vnnd das sieben Gestirn ging auff mit gelben Stralen, vnnd lieff die Nacht vber seinen natürlichen Lauff, biß das es zu Morgendts durch röte der Sonnen vbereylet vnd vberschattet ward. Vnnd siehe, die Weisen, die im Lande wohneten, stunden auff vom Schlaff, sahen gen Himmel, vnd sprachen! Wer ist die herfür bricht, schön wie der Mond, außerwehlet wie die Sonne, vnd ist kein flecken an jhr: dann jhr glut ist fewrig, vnd eine Flamme des Herrn, das auch viel Wasser nicht mögen die Liebe außleschen, noch die Ströme sie erseuffen: Darumb wollen wir sie nicht lassen, sie ist vnser Schwester, vnnd ob sie schon ist klein worden, vnnd hat keine Brüste, so wollen wir sie wider bringen in jrer Mutter Haus, in einen durchsichtigen Saal, worinn sie zuvor gewesen, zu saugen jhrer Mutter Brüste, alsdann wird sie hervorgehen wie der Thurn Davids mit Brustwehr gebawet, daran tausend Schilde hangen, vnd allerley Waffen der Starcken, vnd da sie heraß ging, preiseten sie die Töchter seelich, die Königinnen vnnd Rebsweiber lobeten sie: Ich aber fiel nieder auff mein Angesichte, danckte Gott, vnd preisete seinen heiligen Namen.

EPILOGVS.

VNd ist nun, jhr lieben vnd wahren Sapientiæ & doctrinæ filij in aller Macht vnnd Herrligkeit das grosse Geheimnüß der Weisen, vnd offenbahrung des Geistes vollendet, darvon der Fürst vnd Monarcha Theoph. in Apocalypsi Hermetis sagt: das er sey ein eintziges Numen, in Göttliches, wunderbahrliches vnd ein heiliges Ampt, weiln er beschliesse die gantze Welt, in jhme sey, werde wahr (mit einander, vnnd vberwinde warhafftig die Element, vnd die 5. substantz. Auch habe noch kein Auge gesehen, kein Ohr gehöret, noch zu keines Menschen Hertzen gestiegen, was der Himmel diesem Geist der Warheit natürlich eingeleibet habe, in jhme stehe alleine die Warheit, daher er die Stimme der Warheit genennet werde, Auß welches Krefften der Adam vnd die andern Patriarchen: Abraham, Isaac, vnd Jacob jhres Leibes Gesundheit, vnnd langes Leben gehabt, vnnd endlich darunter in grossem Reichthumb geblühet. Durch diesen Geist haben die Philosophi die 7. freyen Künste erfunden, vnnd jhr Reichthum damit erlanget. Noa habe die Archen, Moyses den Tabernakel, Salomon den Tempel gebawet, vnnd durch diesen güldene Geschir von reinem Golde in den Tempel geschaffet, vnd zu der Ehre Gottes habe auch Salomon damit viel zierlicher Wercke verrichtet, vnd viel ander grosse thaten mehr gethan. Esdras habe die gesaß wieder damit aufgerichtet: Maria Moysis Schwester sey damit gastfrey gewesen. Vnd sey dieser Geist bey den Propheten im Alten Testament sehr vblich vnd gemein gewesen. Item sey aller dinge Heilung vnd Artzney, vnd die leste erforschung, das letzte vnd höchste Geheimnüß der Natur, das ist der Geist des Herrn, der den Träst des Erdreichs erfüllet hat, vnd im anfang auffm Wasser geschwebet, den die Welt ohne heimliche gnädige einsprechung des heiligen Geistes, oder ohne heimliche Vnterweisung der, die jhnen bekannt, nicht haben fassen können, denn die gantze Welt wegen seiner Krefften begehret, welcher von den Menschen nicht genugsam könne geschetzet werden, welchen die Heiligen von anbeginne der Welt gesuchet vnd zu sehen inbrünstig begehret hetten. Dann er gehe in die Sieben Planeten, erhebe das Gewulck, vnnd vertreibe die Nebel, gebe allen dingen jhr Liecht, wircke alles in Gold vnd Silber, gebe alle Gesundheit vnd Vberflüßigkeit, die Schätze, reinige Außsatz, heile Wassersucht, Podagram, erklere das Gesicht, verlengere das Leben, stercke die Trawrigen, mache gesundt die Krancken, vnd heile allen Gebrechen, ja, es sey ein geheim aller Geheimnüssen, vnd allen heimlichen dingen eine Heimlichkeit, vnd aller ding Heilung vnd Artzney.

Item ein begierliches wissen, vnd liebliches ding aller dinge die vnter der Lunæ Circkel sein, mit welchem die Natur gestercket, vnd das Hertze mit den Gliedern ernewret, die blühenden Jugendt erhalten, das alter vertrieben, die Schwachheit zerstöret, vnd die gantze Welt renouiret werde, sey vnd bleibe einer vnergründtlichen Natur, eines vnendlichen Gewalts, vnd einer vnvberwindlichen Krafft vnd herrligkeit.

Item dieser Geist, sey wie alle andere Himmlische Ding, oder Geister ein außerlesener Geist, welcher gebe, Gesundheit, Glück, Frewde, Fried, Liebe, vertreibe ingemein alles böse, zerstöre Armuth vnd Elend, mache auch das einer das böse weder reden noch gedencken künne, gebe den Menschen was er im Hertzen begehre, den Frommen zeitliche Ehre vnnd langes Leben, den Bösen aber die jhn mißbrauchen, die ewige Straffe.

Vnd wollen nun also in Namen der heiligen Dreyfaltigkeit mit diesen wenig Worten das grosse Geheimnüß des edlen Philosophischen Steins, vnd das höchste Fest der Weisen hochfeyerlich beschlossen vnd begangen haben.

Dem allerhöchsten, Allmechtigsten, Gott, der diese Kunst erschaffen, vnnd deme es auch gefallen hat mir Elenden, sündigen Menschen durch ein versprochenes vnd tewres gelübte, diese Erkentnüß zu offenbaren, dem sey ewig Lob, Preiß, Ehre vnd Danck gesagt, mit gantz demütiger vnd inbrünstiger Bitte, mein Hertz, Sinn, vnd Gemüthe, durch seinen Heiligen Geist also regiren, das ich von diesem Geheimnüß vor niemand rede, viel weniger Vngottesfürchtigen mittheile, noch einer einigen Creatur offenbahre, damit ich nicht an meinem Gelübde vnd Eyde brüchig, ein zerreisser des Himmlischen Siegels, vnd ein meineidiger Bruder Aureæ Crucis werde, die Göttliche Majestät auff das allerhöchste beleidige, vnd dardurch eine mächtige vnselbare Sünde in den Heiligen Geist wissentlich committire vnnd begehe, dafür wolle mich Gott Vater, Sohn vnnd Heiliger Geist, die hochgelobte Dreyeinigkeit, gnädiglich behüten, vnnd beständiglich bewahren: Amen, Amen, Amen.
FINIS.

A Speech of an unknown Philosophi,
dedicated to the fraternity (R. C.)
being
A short discourse or brief example of the holy Philosophiae and most high medicine.

The Most Holy Trinity or Lord God Jehovah
hath made everything out of nothing.
And the Spirit of God moved upon the face of the waters or Chaos:
**This being the primum HYLE of the philosophers, or the water out of which every-
thing was created:**
Firmament, Mineralia, Vegetabilia, Animalia;

The Great World,
out of its Center and Quintessence.

The Small World,
as the Creator's most perfect creature, namely

The Human-Being,
an image of the Most High God.
The immortal Soul: a heavenly invisible fire.

He has Apostatised: but behold: there is the MESSIAH!
The light of Mercy and of Nature.
LILI; the first matter of the perfect body,
The Mother, giving birth to the middle-world,
Balsam and Mummy.
And the incomparable magical lode stone in the small world.
The philosopher's water from which proceedeth all things, in which are all things, which governs all things in
which one errs and in which one is also lead toward betterment.
A sane mind in a sane body.
Unceasing prayer,
Patience and waiting.
Matter, container, furnace, fire, boiling, is one and only one thing,
Alone in one, and the itself one alone, beginning, middle and end
It does not let any foreign thing come near, is being made without foreign matter.
For see: in the Mercurio is everything for which the philosophers seek

The Small Crystal Clear Fountain.
The twofold Mercurius.
A spin of the sphere and all planets,
And a substance that in an instant is black-smoking from a
GLEAMING

Death and Life.
The rebirth and renewal,
Beginning, middle and end of the fixation or stability,
and the main foundation of the entire magical secret.
Take the Quintessence of the Macro and Microcosmi, or Philosophical Mercurii,
The invisible heavenly living fire,
The salt of the metals ana q. s.
**Make out of it, according to the philosophical art of a Magi, through rotating,
dissolving, coagulating and figuring**

The Highest Medicine
in which
The greatest wisdom, most perfect health and sufficient wealth.
All from one, and all to one.
Lying and bragging belongs into hell.
Enough is said.
Plain and honest, eliminating all evil, which, is a hindering of the Pathmos.
It shall come to pass, according to JEHOVA'S will.

TO GOD ALONE BE THE GLORY.

Per ignem demum
Nomen & Aetas
PAULUS.

Lege.

Judica.

Tace.

Eine Rede eines unbekannten Philosophi,
der Brüderschafft (R. C.) zugeschrieben;
So
Ein kurtzer Discurß oder geringe Probe der heiligen Philosophiä und höchsten Medicin.

DER DREY-EINIGE GOTT ODER JEHOVAH

hat Alles aus Nichts gemacht.
Und der Geist Gottes schwebete über dem Wasser oder Chaos:
welches das primum HYLE der Weisen, oder das Wasser daraus Alles erschaffen:
Firmament, Mineralia, Vegetabilia, Animalia;

DIE GROSZE WELT,

aus dessen Mittelpunct und Quint-Essentz

DIE KLEINE WELT,

als des Schöpfers aller Dinge vollkommste Creatur, nemlich

DER MENSCH,

Ein Eben-Bild des allerhöchsten Gottes.

Die unsterbliche Seele; Ein himmlisch unsichtbares Feuer.

Er ist abgefallen: Aber siehe da ist der MESSIAS!

Das Licht der Gnaden und Natur.

LILI: die erste Materie des vollkommenen Cörpers,

Die Gebähr-Mutter der mittlern Welt,
Balsam und Mumie.

Und der unvergleichliche magische Magnet in der kleinen Welt.

Das Wasser der Weisen, aus welchem alle Dinge und in welchem alle Dinge, welches alles regieret, in welches geirret,
und auch darinn selber verbessert wird.

Ein gesundes Gemüth in einem gesunden Leibe,

Unermüdetes Gebet,
Gedult und Warten.

Materie, Gefäß, Ofen, Feuer, Kochung, ist eins, und allein ein Ding,
In Einem allein, und das Eine allein selbst, Anfang, Mittel und Ende.
Es läst nichts Frembdes zu sich, und wird ohne alle fremde Dinge bereitet.
Denn Siehe: im Mercurio ist alles was die Weisen suchen.

DAS KLAHRE DURCHSCHEINENDE BRÜNNLEIN.

Der doppelte Mercurius.
Eine runde Umbdrehung, der Sphär aller Planeten,
Und ein Wesen das im Augenblick schwartz rauchet von einem

LEUCHTENDEN

TODT UND LEBEN.

Die Wiedergeburth und Erneuerung,
Anfang Mittel und Ende der Fixität oder Beständigkeit,
und das vornehmste oder Fundament des gantzen magischen Geheimnisses.

Nimm die Quint-Essentz des Macro und Microcosmi, oder des philosophischen Mercurii,
Des unsichtbahren, himmlischen lebendigen Feuers,
Des Saltzes der Metallen ana q. s.

Mache darauß nach philosophischer Kunst eines Magi, durch Rotiren, Solviren, Coaguliren und Figiren

DIE HOECHSTE MEDICIN

in welche
Die gröste Weißheit, vollkommste Gesundheit und allgenugsamen Reichthum.
Alles von Einem, und Alles zu Einem.
Eylen und Großprahlen gehört zur Höllen.
Es ist genug gesagt.

Schlecht und Recht mit Verwerffung aller Boßheit, welches eine Verhinderung ist des Pathmos.
Es geschehe der Wille JEHOVAE.

Gott allein die Ehre.

Per ignem demùm
Nomen & Aetas
paVLVS.

Lege.

Judica.

Tace.

Perceive ye, how strangely the Lord leaveth His Saints. Psalm 4.

Act. 14. v. 17.
Cap. 17.v.27.28.

Ps.104.148.150.

Since everything left to us in the Holy Scriptures was intended for our study, research and remembrance, so that we humans may fully understand our great incomprehensible God and his noble creation, all creatures, and that we might know ourselves best of all, and since the wondrous ciphers Three, Four and Seven are mentioned often in the Holy Bible, these having hidden, undoubtedly, a great secret.

Therefore I ask in all simplicity and out of a pure heart, what do these numbers convey to us in the light of Nature and in the light of Mercy.

About the Cipher Three.

Firstly, what the three different days signify, Gen. 8, in which Noah let fly out of his ark the raven and after three times seven days the dove.

Secondly, what the very first sacrifice signified, which the Lord God Himself commanded Abraham to give him, about which we read in Gen. 15.

And thus the Lord God spoke unto me

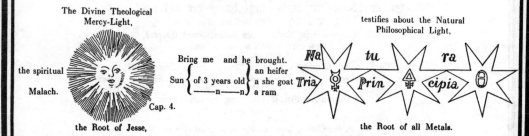

The Divine Theological Mercy-Light, the spiritual Malach. Cap. 4. the Root of Jesse,

Bring me and he brought. Sun { of 3 years old } an heifer a she goat a ram ——n——n.

testifies about the Natural Philosophical Light, the Root of all Metals.

Natura Tria Principia

And a turtle dove and a young pigeon,   = =   Eagles Gluten.
And he took unto him all these and divided them in the midst   =   Solutio Philosoph.
But the birds divided he not, = = = = = =   Sophist. Separatio.
And when the fowls came down upon the carcass Abram drove them away.   Caput. Mortum.

Hermetis Bird ☿ eats of the dead carcass also and flies away with it, is finally captured by the Philosopho, strangled and killed.

Thirdly, what signifies the strange holy fire had been, which fell down from heaven, kindling and consuming the sacrifices on the altar. Lev. 9. and 2 Chron. 7. This fire the priests took with them when they were led away into the Babylonian captivity, and they were commanded by the Prophet Nehemiah, also called Jeremiah, to hide the holy fire in a cave, until they again returned home; and then have the priests look for it; but instead of the fire, they found a dense water, but as soon as they poured it over the wood and sacrifice it was ignited by the Sun and the sacrifice and the wood were devoured by the water and the fire. Read 2 Maccab. 1. v. 19. 20. concerning this and where to find and to obtain today the same fire and water, which is the Prima Materia or Spiritus Mundi in which the gold is consumed and arises again to new life after the Putrefaction.

Fourthly, what signify the three great wonder-births in the Old and New Testaments, occurring over and again in the course of nature; announced and proclaimed by the Lord God Himself and subsequently by His angels. Firstly the birth of Isaac. Gen. 15. 18. & 21. Then of Samson, Judges 13. After this of John the Baptist, Luke 1. and lastly the most wondrous birth of our Saviour and redeemer Jesus Christ, the Virgin's Son, surpassing by far the other three, Mathew & Luke 1.

Fifthly, what signify and indicate the three parts of the human being, as 1. Spirit 2. Soul 3. Body, about which the Holy Apostle Paul writes in 1 Thess. 5., in the light of Nature and light of Mercy.

And this is something about the Wondrous Cipher.

Erkennet doch, daß der Herr seine Heiligen wunderlich führet. Psalm 4.

Act. 14. v. 17.
Cap. 17. v. 27. 28.

Pf. 104. 148. 150.

Nachdem alles, was in der H. Schrift aufgezeichnet, uns zur Lehre, Nachforschung und Erinnerung hinterlassen, dabey wir Menschen unsern grossen und unbegreiflichen Gott und sein edles Geschöpf, alle Creaturen, und zum meisten uns selbsten, recht erkennen sollen, und dieweil auch in der H. Biebel der Wunder=Zahlen, **Drey, Vier** und **Sieben** öffters Meldung geschiehet, haben dieselben ausser allen Zweifel ein groß Geheimniß in ihnen verborgen.

Darum frage ich in Einfalt, und von reinem Herzen, was doch etliche diese nachfolgende bedeuten, sowohl im **Licht der Natur** als im **Licht der Gnaden.**

Von der Zahl Drey.

Erstlich, was die Drey unterschiedliche Tage bedeuten, Gen. 8., in welchen Noah aus dem Kasten den Raben und hernach die Taube alle weg nach verstossenen dreymal sieben Tagen aussteigen lassen.

Zum andern, was das allererste Opfer bedeute, so Gott der Herr Selber dem Abraham ihm zu leisten anbefohlen, davon Gen. 15. zu lesen,

Und Gott der Herr sprach zu mir

Das göttliche Theologische Gnaden=Licht,

zeuget vom Natürlichen Philosophischen Licht,

die geistliche Sonne {eine dreyjährige {Kuhe, Ziegen, Widder} Bringe mir = und er brachts.
————n————n

Malach. Cap. 4.

die Wurtzel Jesse,

die Wurtzel aller Metallen.

Und eine Turtel=Taube, und eine junge Taube,	Adlers Gluten.
und er brachts, und zertheilte es mitten von einander	Solutio Philosoph.
aber die Vögel zertheilete er nicht,	Sophist. Separatio.
und das Gevögel fiel auf das Aas, aber er scheuchete sie davon.	Caput Mortuum.

Hermetis Vögelein ☿ frisset auch die todten Leichnam, und fleucht mit davon, wird endlich vom Philosopho gefangen, erwürget und getödtet.

Zum dritten, was das für ein heilig wunderlich Feuer gewesen, davon Lev. 9. und 2 Chron. 7. so vom Himmel gefallen, die Opfer auf dem Altar angezündet und verzehret. Welch Feuer hernach die Priester mit sich genommen, da sie in die Babylonische Gefängniß weggeführet wurden, und als ihnen der Prophet Nehemias, der auch Jeremias heist, befohlen, das heilige Feuer in eine Grube zu verstecken, bis sie wieder heimkommen würden, hernacher durch die Priester wieder suchen lassen; und anstatt des Feuers, ein dick Wasser funden, wie aber dasselbe auf das Holtz und Opfer gegossen, sey es von der Sonnen angezündet, und das gantze Opfer zusamt dem Holtze von dem Feuer und Wasser verbrannt und verzehret worden. Davon 2 Maccab. I. v. 19. 20. und wo noch heutiges Tages eben dieses Feuer und Wasser zu finden, und zu überkommen sey, welches ist Prima Materia, oder Spiritus Mundi, in welchen das Gold verzehret wird, und nach der Putrefaction zu einem neuen Leben wieder auferstehet.

Zum vierten, was die Drey grosse Wunder=Geburten im Alten und Neuen Testament bedeuten, so wider und über den Lauf der Natur geschehen; so Gott der Herr selber, auch hernach durch seine Engel angekündiget und andeuten lassen. Erstlich von dem Jsaac, Gen. 15. 18. & 21. Darnach vom Samsone, Judic. 13. Hernach vom Joh. Baptista, Luc. I. und letzlich die allerwundersamste Geburt von unsern Heyland und Erlöser Christo Jesu, der Jungfrauen Sohn, so die andern drey Geburten weit übertrifft, Matth. & Luc. I.

Zum fünften, was die drey Theile des Menschen, als 1. der **Geist**, 2. die **Seel**, 3. der **Leib**, davon der H. Apostel Paulus an 1 Thessal. 5. schreibet, sowol im **Licht der Natur**, als im **Licht der Gnaden**, bedeuten und anzeigen wollen.

Und diß ist etwas von der Wunderzahl.

ABOUT THE WONDROUS CIPHER FOUR.

Light of Nature.

Vae Vae Vae to you Sophists.

4 Elements.	3 Beginnings.	2 Seeds.	1 Fruit.
4. Fire △ I.	Sulphur △ I	Male ⊙	Natural becomes I.
3. Air △ 2.		△ 2.	✡
2. Water ▽ 3	Salt θ 2	Sperma 2. Sem. 2.	Tincture ☿
		▽ 2.	
I. Earth ▽ 4.	Mercury ☿ 3	Female ☽	Supernatural 2. ✡
about God	Nature	Metals	the Art.
God Father	Son	Holy Ghost	Christian

G.   P.   W.   M.

Quinta Essentia.

Light of Mercy.

The fume will rise over you from eternity to eternity and will be your torment.

Who rightly understands this table,
Can see how one originates from the other.
First all lie hidden in the fourth cipher
The Elements everywhere,
Out of these originate the three beginnings,

Producing the two sexes,
Male and female, from the Sun and Moon,
The imperial Son grows out of this:
Unequaled in this world,
Surpassing all kingdoms.

Firstly, why the Lord God has given three times 40 years respite and time for repentance, to the first world. Gen. 6.

Furthermore, from the Old and the New Testament:

40 Days and nights it rained when the flood came upon the earth.

40 Days after the flood subsided, Noah opened his Ark.

40 Days and nights Moses was upon Mount Sinai.

40 Years the children of Israel wandered in the wilderness.

40 Days and nights Elijah fasted in the wilderness.

40 Days Nineveh had for repentance.

40 Weeks it took for Christ and all humans to be formed in their mother's womb.

40 Months the Lord preached upon the earth and wrought miracles.

40 Days and nights Christ fasted in the wilderness.

40 Hours the Lord Christ lay in his tomb.

40 Days after His Resurrection He was on earth.

40 Years after His Ressurrection and Ascension Jerusalem was destroyed.

Summa 3 times 4 times 40
is the secret interpretation.

Preliminary work.
1. Mortificatio & Putrefactio –
2. Solutio – – – – – – – – –
3. Animatio – – – – – – – –
4. Purefactio – – – – – – –
5. Combinatio: est ... seu ☿ duplicatus.

T. duplicatus

Solutio — A
Coagulatio — W

— 40
— 35
— 30
— 20
— 5

— 15
— 10
— 8
— 4
— I

Subsequent work.
Mortificatio & Putrefactio 1.
– – – – – – – – Solutio 2.
– – – – – – – – Animatio 3.
– – – – – – – – Purefactio 4.
Perfectio seu Fixatio 5.

Genes. 1. v. 1. 2.
Job. 30. v. 6.
Deut. 32. v. 13.
Genes. 27. v. 28.
Cant. 5. v. 10. ff.

The Philosophical Furnace.

Licht der Natur.

Gnaden-Licht.

Væ Væ Væ euch Sophisten.

Quinta Essentia.

Vier Elementen.	Drey Anfänge.	Zween Saamen.	Eine Frucht.
4. Feuer △ 1.	Schwefel ☿ 1.	Männlein ☉	Natürlich wird 1.
3. Luft △ 2.	Salz ☽ 2.	Sperma 2 Sem. 2	Tinctur ♀
2. Waffer ▽ 3.			
1. Erde ▽ 4.	Mercurius ☿ 3	Weiblein ☽	übernatürlich 2.
von Gott	der Natur	den Metallen	der Kunst.
Gott Vater	Sohn	H. Geift	Chrift. Menfch.
G.	P.	W.	M.

Wer diese Tafel recht verfteht,
Sieht wie eins aus dem andern geht.
Erftlich fteckt alles in vierdter Zahl
Der Elementen überall,
Daraus die Drey Anfäng entfpringen,

Welche zwey Gefchlechter herfürbringen,
Männlich, Weiblich, von Sonn und Mond,
Daraus wächfet der Kayferliche Sohn:
Dem auf der Welt gar nichts gleich,
Und übertrifft all Königreich.

Der Rauch wird über euch
auffteigen von Ewigkeit
zu Ewigkeit und euch eine
Quaal feyn.

Erftlich, warum Gott der Herr der erften Welt dreymal 40 Jahr, das find 120 Jahr, Frift und
Zeit zur Buffe gegeben, Gen. 6.

Weiter, aus dem A. und N. Teftament:

40 Tage und Nächte regnete es, da die Sündfluth auf Erden kam.

40 Tage hernach, da die Sündfluth verlaufen, öffnet Noah den Kaften.

40 Tage und Nächte war Mofes auf dem Berge Sinai.

40 Jahre waren die Kinder Ifrael in der Wüften.

40 Tage und Nächte Elias in der Wüften gefaftet.

40 Tage hatte die Stadt Ninive zur Buffe.

40 Wochen Chriftus und alle Menfchen in Mutterleibe gebildet.

40 Monat der Herr auf Erden geprediget und Wunder gethan.

40 Tage und Nächte Chriftus in der Wüften gefaftet.

40 Stunden der Herr Chriftus im Grabe gelegen.

40 Tage nach feiner Auferftehung auf Erden gewefen.

40 Jahre nach feiner Auferftehung und Himmelfahrt Jerufalem zerftöhret.

Summa 3mal 4mal 40

ift die geheime Auslegung.

Solutio — **Coagulatio**

A. T. ☿ duplicatus W. O

Vorarbeit.

1. Mortificatio & Putrefactio — 40
2. Solutio — 35
3. Animatio — 30
4. Purefactio — 20
5. Combinatio: eft אור: feu ☿ duplicatus. — 3

אור

Nacharbeit.

Mortificatio & Putrefactio 1.
Solutio — 2.
Animatio — 3.
Purefactio 4.
Perfectio feu Fixatio — 5.

13
10
8
4
1

Deut. XXXII. v. 13.

Genef. I. v. 1. 2.
Job. XXX. v. 6.

Cant. V. v. 10. feqt.

Genef. XXVII. v. 28.

Der Philofophifche Ofen.

263

The mystery which hath been hid from ages and from generations, but now is made manifest to its Saints: to whom God would make known what is the riches of the glory of this mystery among the Gentiles; which is Christ in you. Col. 1 v. 27. This is the revelation and the true and right knowledge of Jesus Christ, God and Man, all heavenly and earthly wisdom in heaven and on earth.

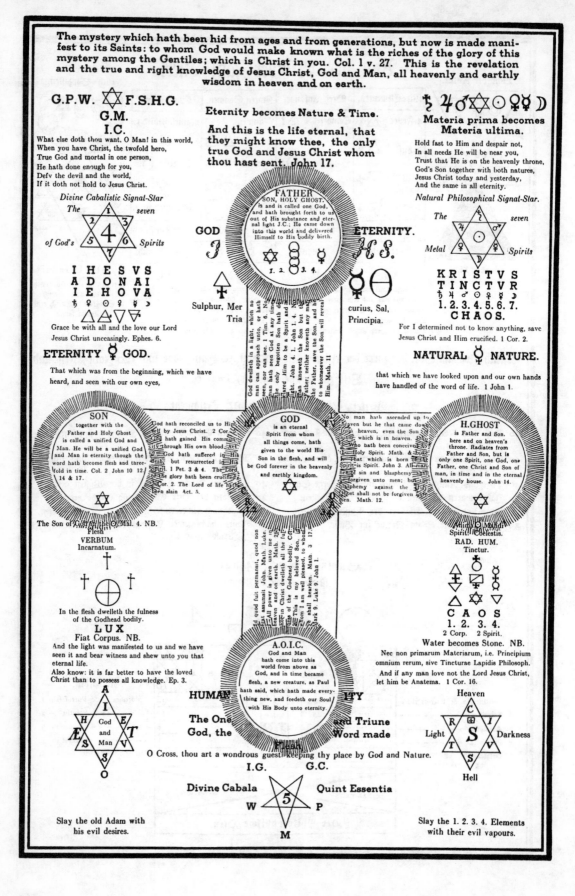

G.P.W. ✡ F.S.H.G.
G.M.
I.C.

What else doth thou want, O Man! in this world,
When you have Christ, the twofold hero,
True God and mortal in one person,
He hath done enough for you,
Defy the devil and the world,
If it doth not hold to Jesus Christ.

Divine Cabalistic Signat-Star

The   seven

2 1 3
5 4 6
7

of God's   *Spirits*

I H E S V S
A D O N A I
I E H O V A
♄ ♀ ☉ ♂ ☿ ♃ ☽

Grace be with all and the love our Lord
Jesus Christ unceasingly. Ephes. 6.

ETERNITY ☿ GOD.

That which was from the beginning, which we have
heard, and seen with our own eyes,

Eternity becomes Nature & Time.

And this is the life eternal, that
they might know thee, the only
true God and Jesus Christ whom
thou hast sent. John 17.

FATHER
SON, HOLY GHOST.
is and is called one God,
and hath brought forth to us
out of His substance and eternal light J.C.; He came down
into this world and delivered
Himself to His bodily birth.
1. 2. 3. 4.

GOD   **ETERNITY.**

Sulphur, Mer
Tria

curius, Sal,
Principia.

Materia prima becomes
Materia ultima.

Hold fast to Him and despair not,
In all needs He will be near you,
Trust that He is on the heavenly throne,
God's Son together with both natures,
Jesus Christ today and yesterday,
And the same in all eternity.

Natural Philosophical Signat-Star.

The   seven

Metal   *Spirits*

K R I S T V S
T I N C T V R
♄ ♃ ☉ ☿ ♀ ☽
1. 2. 3. 4. 5. 6. 7.
C H A O S.

For I determined not to know anything, save
Jesus Christ and Him crucified. 1 Cor. 2.

NATURAL ☿ NATURE.

that which we have looked upon and our own hands
have handled of the word of life. 1 John 1.

SON
together with the
Father and Holy Ghost
is called a unified God and
Man. He will be a unified God
and Man in eternity though the
word hath become flesh and threefold in time. Col. 2 John 10 12.
14 & 17.

The Son of God ☉ Mal. 4. NB.
Flesh
VERBUM
Incarnatum.

In the flesh dwelleth the fulness
of the Godhead bodily.
LUX
Fiat Corpus. NB.

And the light was manifested to us and we have
seen it and bear witness and shew unto you that
eternal life.
Also know: it is far better to have the loved
Christ than to possess all knowledge. Ep. 3.

GOD
is an eternal
Spirit from whom
all things come, hath
given to the world His
Son in the flesh, and will
be God forever in the heavenly
and earthly kingdom.

H.GHOST
is Father and Son.
here and on heaven's
throne. Radiates from
Father and Son, but is
only one Spirit, one God, one
Father, one Christ and Son of
man, in time and in the eternal
heavenly house. John 14.

Spirit. Coelestis.
RAD. HUM.
Tinctur.

C A O S
1. 2. 3. 4.
2 Corp. 2 Spirit.

Water becomes Stone. NB.

Nec non primarum Materiarum, i.e. Principium
omnium rerum, sive Tincturae Lapidis Philosoph.
And if any man love not the Lord Jesus Christ,
let him be Anatema. 1 Cor. 16.

A.O.I.C.
God and Man
hath come into this
world from above as
God, and in time became
flesh, a new creature, as Paul
hath said, which hath made everything new, and feedeth our Soul
with His Body unto eternity.

A
I
H E
God
Æ and T
S Man V
S
O

HUMAN   **ITY**
The One   **and Triune**
God, the   **Word made**

O Cross, thou art a wondrous guest keeping thy place by God and Nature.

Heaven
C
R ⊕ I
S
V
S

Light   Darkness

Hell

Slay the old Adam with
his evil desires.

I.G.   G.C.

Divine Cabala   **Quint Essentia**

W 5 P

M

Slay the 1. 2. 3. 4. Elements
with their evil vapours.

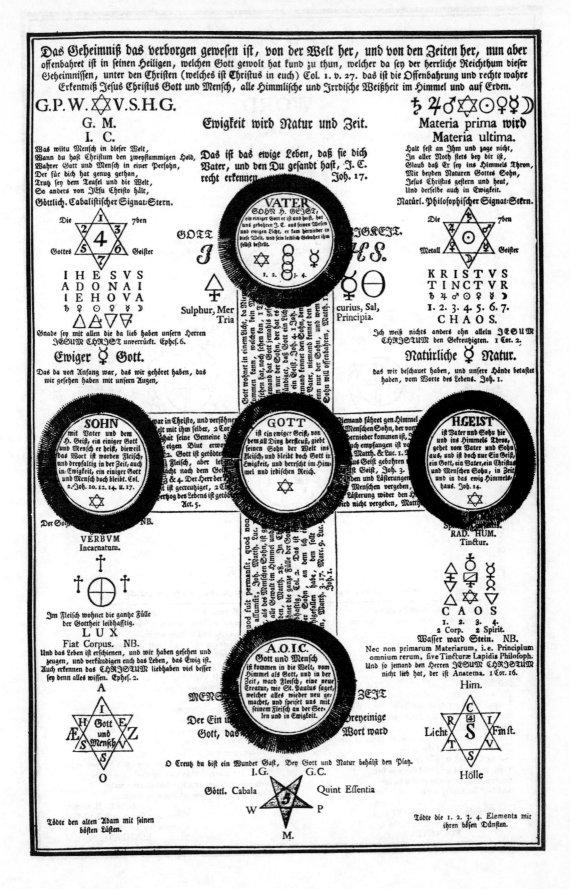

Das Geheimniß das verborgen gewesen ist, von der Welt her, und von den Zeiten her, nun aber offenbahret ist in seinen Heiligen, welchen Gott gewolt hat kund zu thun, welcher da sey der herrliche Reichthum dieser Geheimnissen, unter den Christen (welches ist Christus in euch) Col. 1. v. 27. das ist die Offenbahrung und rechte wahre Erkentniß Jesus Christus Gott und Mensch, alle Himmlische und Irrdische Weißheit im Himmel und auf Erden.

G. P. W. ☆ V. S. H. G.

Ewigkeit wird Natur und Zeit.

♄ ♃ ♂ ☆ ☉ ♀ ☿ ☽

G. M.
I. C.

Materia prima wird
Materia ultima.

Was wiltu Mensch in dieser Welt,
Wann du hast Christum den zweystammigen Held,
Wahrer Gott und Mensch in einer Persohn,
Der für dich hat genug gethan,
Trutz sey dem Teufel und die Welt,
So anders von Jesu Christo hält,

Das ist das ewige Leben, daß sie dich Vater, und den Du gesandt hast, J. C. recht erkennen. Joh. 17.

Halt fest an Ihm und zage nicht,
In aller Noth stets bey dir ist,
Glaub daß Er sey ins Himmels Thron,
Mit beyden Naturen Gottes Sohn,
Jesus Christus gestern und heut,
Und derselbe auch in Ewigkeit.

Göttlich. Cabalistischer Signat-Stern.

Natürl. Philosophischer Signat-Stern.

Die 7ben
Gottes Geister

Die 7ben
Metall Geister

I H E S V S
A D O N A I
I E H O V A
♄ ☿ ☉ ♃ ♀ ☽

K R I S T V S
T I N C T V R
♄ ♃ ♂ ☉ ♀ ☿ ☽
1. 2. 3. 4. 5. 6. 7.
C H A O S

Gnade sey mit allen die da lieb haben unsern Herren JESUM CHRIST unverrückt. Ephes. 6.

Sulphur, Mercurius, Sal,
Tria Principia.

Ich weiß nichts anders ohn allein JESUM CHRISTUM den Gekreutzigten. 1 Cor. 2.

Ewiger ☿ Gott.

Natürliche ☿ Natur.

Das da von Anfang war, das wir gehöret haben, das wir gesehen haben mit unsern Augen,

das wir beschauet haben, und unsere Hände betastet haben, vom Worte des Lebens. Joh. 1.

GOTT

Niemand fähret gen Himmel als des Menschen Sohn, der vom Himmel hernieder kommen ist, auch empfangen ist vom H. Geist. Matth. & Luc. 1. Das Geist gebohren ist Geist. Joh. 3. Menschen vergeben, Lästerung wider den H. wird nicht vergeben, Matth.

H. GEIST
ist Vater und Sohn hie und ins Himmels Thron, gehet von Vater und Sohn aus, und ist doch nur Ein Geist, ein Gott, ein Vater, ein Christus und Menschen Sohn, in Zeit und in das ewig Himmels haus. Joh. 14.

RAD. HUM.
Tinctur.

SOHN
mit Vater und dem H. Geist, ein einiger Gott und Mensch er heißt, dieweil das Wort ist worden Fleisch, und dreyfaltig in der Zeit, auch in Ewigkeit, ein einiger Gott und Mensch doch bleibt. Col. 2. Joh. 10. 12. 14. u. 17.

VERBVM
Incarnatum.

Im Fleisch wohnet die gantze Fülle der Gottheit leibhafftig.

LUX
Fiat Corpus. NB.

Und das Leben ist erschienen, und wir haben gesehen und zeugen, und verkündigen euch das Leben, das Ewig ist. Auch erkennen das CHRISTUM liebhaben viel besser sey denn alles wissen. Ephes. 2.

A
I
H G E
Gott
E und Z
S Mensch V
Æ
S
O

C A O S
1. 2. 3. 4.
2 Corp. 2 Spirit.

Wasser ward Stein. NB.

Nec non primarum Materiarum, i. e. Principium omnium rerum, sive Tincturæ Lapidis Philosoph. Und so jemand den Herren JESUM CHRISTUM nicht lieb hat, der ist Anathema. 1 Cor. 16.

Him.

C
R 4 I
Licht S Finst.
T V
S
Hölle

A. O. I. C.
ist ein kommen in die Welt, vom Himmel als Gott, und in der Zeit, ward Fleisch, eine neue Creatur, wie St. Paulus saget, welcher alles wieder neu gemachet, und speiset uns mit seinem Fleisch an der Seelen und in Ewigkeit.

O Creutz du bist ein Wunder Gast, Bey Gott und Natur behält den Platz.

I. G. G. C.

Göttl. Cabala Quint Essentia

W ☿ P

M.

Tödte den alten Adam mit seinen bösen Lüsten.

Tödte die 1. 2. 3. 4. Elementa mit ihren bösen Dünsten.

VATER
SOHN h. GEIST, ein einiger Gott ist und heißt, hat uns gebohren J. C. aus seinen Wesen und ewigen Licht, er kam hernieder in diese Welt, und sein leiblich Geburth ihm selbst bestellt.
1. 2. 3. 4.

ELOHIM
JEHOVAH
GOD
WORD

Fiat

Natura

Primum Mobile.
Prima Materia.
Quinta Essentia.
Quatuor Elementa.
Lapis Philosophorum.

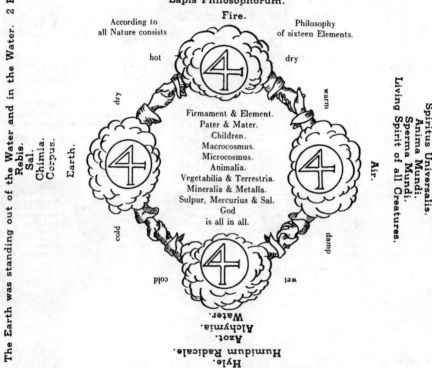

Fire.

According to
all Nature consists

Philosophy
of sixteen Elements.

hot — dry

dry — warm

Firmament & Element.
Pater & Mater.
Children.
Macrocosmus.
Microcosmus.
Animalia.
Vegetabilia & Terrestria.
Mineralia & Metalla.
Sulpur, Mercurius & Sal.
God
is all in all.

Earth.

Air.

cold — damp

cold — wet

Water.
Alchymia.
Azot.
Humidum Radicale.
Hyle.

The Earth was standing out of the Water and in the Water. 2 Pet. 3. 5.

Rebis.
Sal.
Chimia.
Corpus.

CHAOS.

Spiritus Universalis.
Anima Mundi.
Sperma Mundi.
Living Spirit of all Creatures.

The Spirit of God moved upon the face of the Waters. Gen. I. v. 2.

Ignis Philosophorum
invisibilis & secretissimus occultatum.

Strive for the fire,
Seek the fire:
So thou wilt find the fire,
Light a fire,
Put fire to fire,
Boil fire in fire,
Throw body, soul, spirit into fire:
So shalt thou get dead and living fire,
Out of which will come black, yellow, white and red fire.
Bear thy children in fire,
Feed, give them to drink, nourish them in fire:
So will they live and die in fire,
And be fire and stay in fire.
Their silver and gold will become fire.
Heaven and earth will perish in fire
And become finally a philosophic fire.

Ignis. Q. E. Coelest.

Four times four equals XVI lines,
so many are there of the
ELEMENTS.

Aqua Philosophorum h. e.
Mercurius Primaterialis Catholicus.

Water is water and will be water;
From the heaven of the philosophers water rains;
The philosophers stone cries tear-water,
But the world does not regard such water.
Its fire burns in the water
And lives in the water.
Out of fire make water,
And boil the fire in water:
You will have a fiery water,
Like a sharp salten ocean water.
To children it is a living water,
But consume soul and body to water.
Becomes stinking, green, rotten, blue like heaven water.
Digest, calcinate, dissolve and putrefy the water;
Seek the philosopher's fourfold eternal water
And if done well, the art becomes water.

Aqua Q. E. Secreta.

Four times four equals XVI lines,
so many are there of the
ELEMENTS.

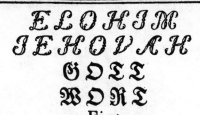

ELOHIM
JEHOVAH
GOTT
WORT
Fiat
Natura
Primum Mobile.
Prima Materia.
Quinta Essentia.
Quatuor Elementa.
Lapis Philosophorum.
Feuer.

Die ganze Natur Elementen nach — beftehet in fechzehn der Philofophie.

heiß — trocken — trocken — naß — kalt — feucht — kalt — fou

Firmament & Element.
Pater & Mater.
Kinder.
Macrocosmus.
Microcosmus.
Animalia.
Vegetabilia & Terreftria.
Mineralia & Metalla.
Sulphur, Mercurius & Sal.
Gott
ift alles in allem.

Rebis.
Sal.
Chimia.
Corpus.
Erde.

CHAOS.
Spiritus Vniverfalis.
Anima Mundi.
Sperma Mundi.
Lebendiger Geift aller Creaturen.
Luft.

Waffer.
Azot.
Alchymia.
Hyle.
Humidum Radicale.

Der Geift des Herrn fchwebete auf dem Waffer. Gen. 1. v. 2.

Jgnis Philosophorum
invisibilis & secretiffimus occultatum.

Trachte nach dem Feuer,
Suche das Feuer:
So findeft du Feuer,
Zünde an ein Feuer,
Thue Feuer zu Feuer,
Koche Feuer in Feuer,
Stürtz Leib, Seel, Geift ins Feuer:
So haft du todt und lebendig Feuer,
Daraus wird fchwartz, gelb, weis und roth Feuer,
Gebier deine Kinder im Feuer,
Speif, tränck und ernähr fie im Feuer:
So leben und fterben fie im Feuer,
Und feyn Feuer, und bleiben im Feuer.
Ihr Silber und Gold wird alles zu Feuer.
Himmel und Erde vergehen im Feuer.
Und wird endlich ein vierfach Philofophifch Feuer.
Ignis. Q. E. Coeleft.

Viermal Vier machen XVI Zeilen,
fo viel find auch der
ELEMENTEN.

Aqua Philosophorum h. e.
Mercurius Primaterialis Catholicus.

Waffer ift Waffer und bleibet Waffer;
Vom Himmel der Weifen regnet Waffer;
Der Weifen Stein weinet Thränen-Waffer;
Dennoch achtet die Welt nicht folch ein Waffer.
Ihr Feuer brennet im Waffer
Und lebet im Waffer.
Mach aus Feuer Waffer,
Und koche das Feuer im Waffer:
So wird ein feurig Waffer
Wie ein fcharff gefaltzen Meer-Waffer.
Ift den Kindern ein lebendig Waffer,
Verzehrt doch Leib und Seel zu Waffer.
Wird ftinkend, grün, faul, blau wie Himmel-Waffer.
Digerir, calcinir, folvir und putreficir das Waffer;
Such der Philofophen vierfach bleibend Waffer.
Und wenn es am beften gemacht ift, wird die Kunft zu Waffer.
Aqua Q E. Secreta.

Viermal Vier machen XVI Zeilen
fo viel find auch der
ELEMENTEN.

The right Reasons for the Wondrous Number of God,

I. 2. 3. 4.
ELOHIM.

O ARCANA ARCANORUM.

The One and Eternal God reveals Himself in the Holy Trinity.

There are three that bear record in Heaven the **F. W. HG.**	There are three that bear witness in Earth the **S. W. B.**

and these three agree in one. John. 5. v. 7. 8.

After Eternity Heavenly and after Time Creaturally, Naturally.

That is

In Heaven and on Earth

the determined Rosy-Cross apparent to our eyes, and the secret ⊕ which the world calls white; of all secrets in Heaven and on Earth.

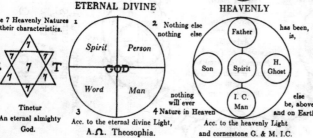

ETERNAL DIVINE

The 7 Heavenly Natures & their characteristics.

1. *Spirit* | *Person* 2. Nothing else nothing else

GOD

Word | *Man*

3. | 4. Nature in Heaven

Tinctur
An eternal almighty God.

Acc. to the eternal divine Light,
A. Ω. Theosophia.
Myster. Mag.
Acc. to the divine Cabala.

HEAVENLY

Father | has been, is,

Son | Spirit | H. Ghost

I. C. Man | else be, above and on Earth.

nothing will ever

Acc. to the heavenly Light and cornerstone G. & M. I.C.
Theologia.

NATURALLY TIMELY

The 7 Earthly Natures & their characteristics.

1. *Fire* | *Air* 2.

Water | *Earth*

3. | 4.

Tinctur
A small earthly mighty God.

Acc. to the natural Light & Stone of the Wise Philosopia.
Myster. Mag.
Acc. to Magia Philosophia.

Explanation of this Holy Figure according to the Alpha and Omega.

	1.	2.	3.		
One God {	Spirit,	Person,	Word,	3 Eternal spiritual heavenly Persons	– in one being
	Father.	Son,	Holy Ghost,	3 heavenly timely Persons	– in one being
	God,	Christ,	Man,	3 heavenly and 3 earthly Persons	– in I. C. the one human
	1.	2.	3.	who hath suffered and died for all men. 1 Tim. 2. Act. 3 & 20. 1 Cor. 2. Col. 2. John 14. 1 John 5.	

The one and three eternal God is a likeness of the entire Nature in all his works and creatures, in

Vegetabilibus

Root 1
Tree 2 | Seed | Blossom 3
Fruit 4

Animalibus

The likeness of to the

Adam 1
Woman 2 | Limbus Terrae | Sister 3
Children 4

in nature earthly and the kingdom.

Mineralibus.

God according Holy Trinity

Sulph. 1
Mercur. 2 | Chaos | Sal 3
Metal 4

5
F
L
5 EE 5
W
E
5

O Secret above all Secrets.

He who truly recognises Jesum Christum hath well employed his time.

The secret wondrous number, i.e., 1. 2. 3. 4., the true Rosy⊕Cross and the revelation and true knowledge of Jesus Christ, God and man, that is all heavenly and earthly wisdom in heaven and on earth. NB. as the one eternal God begot Himself and bore witness of Himself. Three different separate persons and nevertheless is and remains, according to His being, one eternal God, spiritual, heavenly, invisible in eternity as the three heavenly persons: 1. Spirit, 2. Word, 3. Father, one God; and earthly, visible, bodily, a man and God in three persons in time: 1. Spirit, 2. Person, 3. Word, a man; for the Word became flesh, i.e. Eternity became time; God a man; that is, one time, two times and a half a time according to the Old and New testaments, the Law and the Gospel, the heavenly and earthly Trinity, all in heaven and on earth. Since the whole fulness is in Him, J. C., NB. The Godhood itself. Col. 2 and John 9. 10. 12. 14 & 17. Thus speaketh the Heavenly Wisdom: I and the Father are one, believe that the Father is in Me and I in Him, and he that hath seen Me, seeth the Father who hath sent Me and loveth Me, NB. to Him I will manifest myself and the Father and I will come to Him and make mine abode in Him. 1. Cor. 3. & 6. 2 Cor. 6. Eph. 3. 4.

FIGURA CABALISTICA.

Der rechte Grund von der Wunderzahl Gottes,

I. 2. 3. 4.
ELOHIM.

O Arcana Arcanorum.

Der Einig Ewige Gott offenbahret sich in H. Dreyfaltigkeit.

Drey sind | ÆMZ | Drey sind
die da zeugen im Himmel | | die da zeugen auf Erden
der V.W.HG. | I C | der G.W.B.

und die Drey sind Eins und beysammen. 1 Joh. 5. v. 7. 8.

Nach der Ewigkeit Himmlisch und nach der Zeit Creatürl. Natürlich.

Das ist

Im Himmel und auf Erden

das beschlossene Rosen-Creutz, ⊕ davon die Welt zu sagen weiß,

augenscheinlich offenbahr, und das Geheimniß aller Geheimnisse im Himmel und auf Erden.

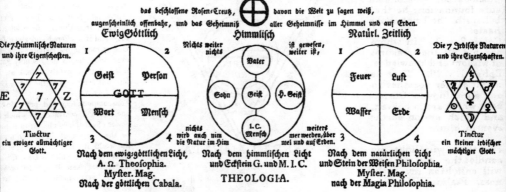

EwigGöttlich — **Himmlisch** — **Natürl. Zeitlich**

Die 7 Himmlische Naturen und ihre Eigenschaften.

1 Geist	Person 2
GOTT	
Wort	Mensch
3	4

Nichts weiter nichts — ist gewesen, weiter ist,

Vater	
Sohn	Geist	H. Geist
I. C. Mensch	

nichts wird auch nimmer die Natur im Him — weiters mer werden, aber mel und auf Erden.

Die 7 Irdische Naturen und ihre Eigenschaften.

1 Feuer	Luft 2
Wasser	Erde
3	4

Tinctur ein ewiger allmächtiger Gott.

Nach dem ewig-göttlichen Licht, A. Ω. Theosophia. Myster. Mag. Nach der göttlichen Cabala.

Nach dem himmlischen Licht und Eckstein G. und M. I. C.

THEOLOGIA.

Nach dem natürlichen Licht und Stein der Weisen Philosophia. Myster. Mag. nach der Magia Philosophia.

Tinctur ein kleiner irdischer mächtiger Gott.

Erklärung dieser heiligen Figur nach dem A und O.

Ein Gott
1. Geist, 2. Wort, 3 Ewige geistliche himmlische Personen — in einem Wesen
Vater, Sohn, h. Geist, 3 himmlische zeitliche Personen — in einem Wesen
Gott, Christus, Mensch, 3 himmlische und irdische Personen — in I. C. dem Einigen Menschen
der gelitten und gestorben ist für alle Menschen. 1 Tim. 2. Act. 3 & 20. 1 Cor. 2. Col. 2. Joh. 14. 1 Joh. 5.

Der Einig und Drey Ewige Gott ist eine Fürbildung der ganzen Natur in allen seinen Werken und Geschöpfen,
in

Vegetabilibus — **Animalibus** — **Mineralibus.**

Wurzel 1	
Baum 2	Saamen	Blüte
Frucht 4	

Das Gleichniß und nach der heil.

Adam 1	
Weib 2	Limbus Terrae	Schwester 3
Kinder 4	

Ebenbild Gottes Dreyfaltigkeit

Sulph. 1	
Mercur.	CHAOS	Sal 3
Metall. 4	

in der Na — tur und irdischen Reich.

O Geheimniß über alle Geheimnisse.

Wer Jesum Christum recht erkennt, der hat seine Zeit wohl angewendet.

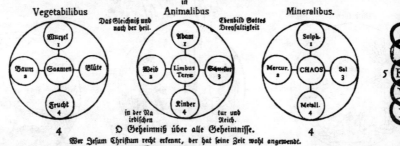

Die geheime Wunderzahl I. 2. 3. 4. h. e. das rechte Rosen ⊕ Creutz und die Offenbahrung und wahre Erkenntniß Jesu Christi, Gott und Menschen, das ist alle himmlische und irdische Weisheit im Himmel und auf Erden. NB. wie der einige ewige Gott aus und von sich selber gezeuget und gebohren, Drey unterschiedene selbstständige Personen, und ist und bleibet seinem Wesen noch doch nur ein ewiger einiger Gott, geistlich, himmlisch, unsichtbar, in der Ewigkeit nach den drey himmlischen Personen, 1. Geist oder Gott, 2. Wort, 3. Vater, ein Gott, und in der Zeit irdisch, sichtbar, leiblich, ein Mensch und Gott, nach den drey zeitlichen Personen, 1. Geist, 2. Person, 3. Wort, ein Mensch; denn das Wort ward Fleisch. h. e. Ewigkeit ward Zeit; Gott ein Mensch; das ist: eine Zeit, zwo Zeiten, und eine halbe Zeit, nach dem A. und N. Testament, Gesetz und Evangelium, die himmlische und irdische Dreyfaltigkeit, ganz im Himmel und ganz auf Erden. Sintemal in Ihm I. C. wohnet die ganze Fülle NB. der Gottheit leibhaftig, Col. 2. Und Joh. 9. 10. 12. 14. & 17. spricht die himmlische Weisheit selber: Ich und der Vater sind Eins, glaubet, daß der Vater in Mir ist, und Ich in Ihm: und wer mich siehet, der siehet den Vater, der mich gesandt hat, und wer mich liebet, NB. dem will ich mich offenbaren, und der Vater und Ich wollen zu ihm kommen und Wohnung bey ihm machen. 1 Cor. 3. & 6. 2 Cor. 6. Eph. 3. 4.

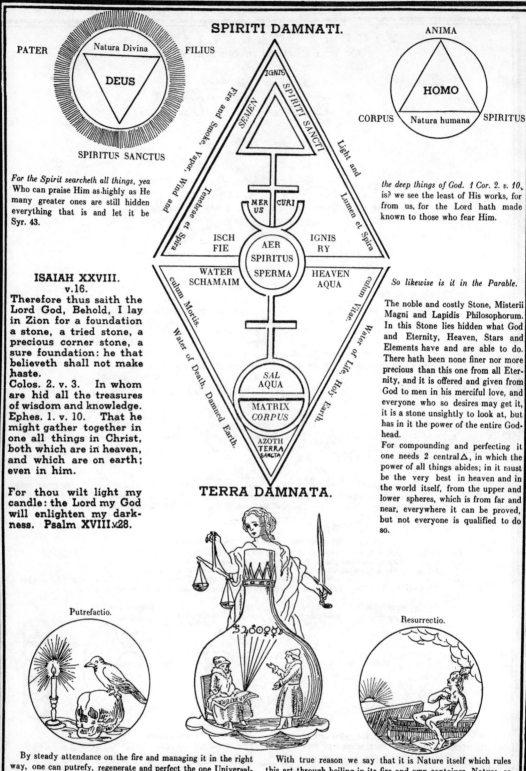

SPIRITI DAMNATI.

PATER — Natura Divina — **FILIUS**

DEUS

SPIRITUS SANCTUS

ANIMA

HOMO

CORPUS — Natura humana — SPIRITUS

Labels within central diagram:
IGNIS · SPIRITI SANCTI · SEMEN · Fire and Smoke, Vapor, Wind and · Light and · Tenebrae et Spira · Lumen et Spira · MERCURIUS · ISCH FIE · IGNIS RY · AER SPIRITUS SPERMA · WATER SCHAMAIM · HEAVEN AQUA · culum Mortis. · culum Vitae. · Water of Death, Damned Earth. · Water of Life, Holy Earth. · SAL AQUA · MATRIX CORPUS · AZOTH TERRA SANCTA

For the Spirit searcheth all things, yea Who can praise Him as highly as He many greater ones are still hidden everything that is and let it be Syr. 43.

the deep things of God. 1 Cor. 2. v. 10, is? we see the least of His works, for from us, for the Lord hath made known to those who fear Him.

ISAIAH XXVIII.
v.16.
Therefore thus saith the Lord God, Behold, I lay in Zion for a foundation a stone, a tried stone, a precious corner stone, a sure foundation: he that believeth shall not make haste.
Colos. 2. v. 3. In whom are hid all the treasures of wisdom and knowledge. Ephes. 1. v. 10. That he might gather together in one all things in Christ, both which are in heaven, and which are on earth; even in him.

For thou wilt light my candle: the Lord my God will enlighten my darkness. Psalm XVIII.v.28.

So likewise is it in the Parable.

The noble and costly Stone, Misterii Magni and Lapidis Philosophorum. In this Stone lies hidden what God and Eternity, Heaven, Stars and Elements have and are able to do. There hath been none finer nor more precious than this one from all Eternity, and it is offered and given from God to men in his merciful love, and everyone who so desires may get it, it is a stone unsightly to look at, but has in it the power of the entire God-head.

For compounding and perfecting it one needs 2 central △, in which the power of all things abides; in it must be the very best in heaven and in the world itself, from the upper and lower spheres, which is from far and near, everywhere it can be proved, but not everyone is qualified to do so.

TERRA DAMNATA.

Putrefactio.

Resurrectio.

By steady attendance on the fire and managing it in the right way, one can putrefy, regenerate and perfect the one Universal-Materia in one container and furnace; by one single management of the fires, and Nature does all the work itself, by means of a fire existing within itself, this fire being aroused and revived through the other Philosophic fire. So also the *Laborant* may have nothing else to do besides attending on the fire, pray God for His blessings and benedictions.

With true reason we say that it is Nature itself which rules this art through boiling in its fire and own container. Nature, as far as it is governed by the Heavenly things, till the work be done and even thereafter. But the will is free and may leave Nature to control the result of its work, and set a certain limit beyond which Nature may not go. Since the will rules Nature it should also attract it, but if the will does not attract and is itself subjected to Nature, Nature will go beyond the purposes of the work and destroy the same.

PATER — FILIVS

Natura Divina

DEUS

SPIRITVS SANCTVS

ANIMA

HOMO

CORPVS — SPIRITVS

Natura humana

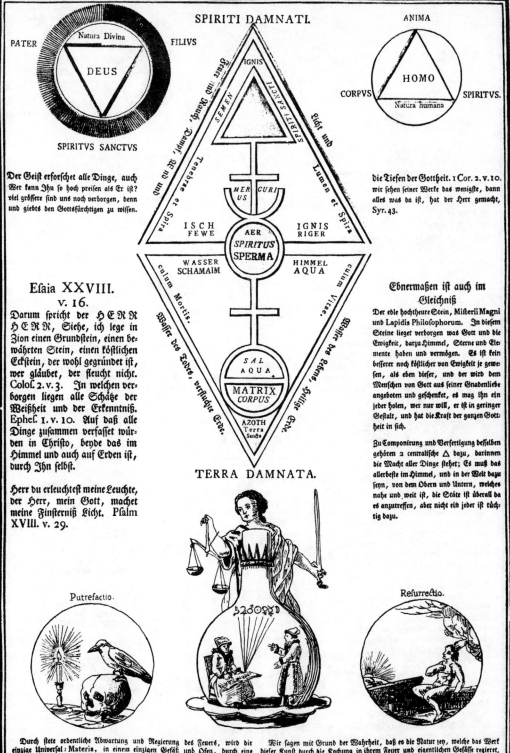

Der Geist erforschet alle Dinge, auch
Wer kann Ihn so hoch preisen als Er ist?
viel größere sind uns noch verborgen, denn
und giebts den Gottesfürchtigen zu wissen.

die Tiefen der Gottheit. 1 Cor. 2. v. 10.
wir sehen seiner Werke das wenigste, dann
alles was da ist, hat der Herr gemacht,
Syr. 43.

Esaia XXVIII. v. 16.

Darum spricht der HERR HERR, Siehe, ich lege in Zion einen Grundstein, einen bewährten Stein, einen köstlichen Eckstein, der wohl gegründet ist, wer gläubet, der fleucht nicht. Colos. 2. v. 3. In welchen verborgen liegen alle Schätze der Weißheit und der Erkenntniß. Ephes. 1. v. 10. Auf daß alle Dinge zusammen verfasset würden in Christo, beyde das im Himmel und auch auf Erden ist, durch Ihn selbst.

Herr du erleuchtest meine Leuchte, der Herr, mein Gott, machet meine Finsterniß Licht. Psalm XVIII. v. 29.

Ebnermaßen ist auch im Gleichniß

Der edle hochtheure Stein, Misterii Magni und Lapidis Philosophorum. In diesem Steine lieget verborgen was Gott und die Ewigkeit, darzu Himmel, Sterne und Elemente haben und vermögen. Es ist kein besserer noch köstlicher von Ewigkeit je gewesen, als eben dieser, und der wird dem Menschen von Gott aus seiner Gnadenliebe angeboten und geschenket, es mag ihn ein jeder holen, wer nur will, er ist in geringer Gestalt, und hat die Kraft der ganzen Gottheit in sich.

Zu Componirung und Verfertigung desselben gehören 2 centralische △ dazu, darinnen die Macht aller Dinge stehet; Es muß das allerbeste im Himmel, und in der Welt dazu seyn, von dem Obern und Untern, welches nahe und weit ist, die State ist überall da es anzutreffen, aber nicht ein jeder ist tüchtig dazu.

TERRA DAMNATA.

Putrefactio.

Resurrectio.

Durch stete ordentliche Abwartung und Regierung des Feuers, wird die einzige Universal:Materia, in einem einzigen Gefäß und Ofen, durch eine einzige Regierung des Feuers, putrificiret, regeneriret und perficiret: und verrichtet die Natur selbst alle Arbeiten, vermittelst seines bey sich wohnenden innerlichen Feuers, so durch das andere Philosophische Feuer aufgemuntert und erwecket wird. Darf also der Laborant anders und weiters nichts thun, als daß er, neben Abwartung des Feuers, Gott um seinen Segen und Benedeyen bitte.

Wir sagen mit Grund der Wahrheit, daß es die Natur sey, welche das Werk dieser Kunst durch die Kochung in ihrem Feuer und eigentlichen Gefässe regiret, so fern sie von den himmlischen Dingen regieret wird, bis zu dem Ende des Werks und noch weiter hinaus. Der Wille aber ist frey, und darf die Natur beym Ende des Werks regieren, und ihr gewisse Schranken setzen, daß sie nicht weiter gehe, weil der Wille, indem er die Natur regieret, die Natur an sich ziehen soll, so aber der Wille von der Natur gezogen und zu selbiger geneigt wird, so wird die Natur den Zweck des Werks überschreiten und selbiges zerstöhren.

De Septenarii Mysteriis.

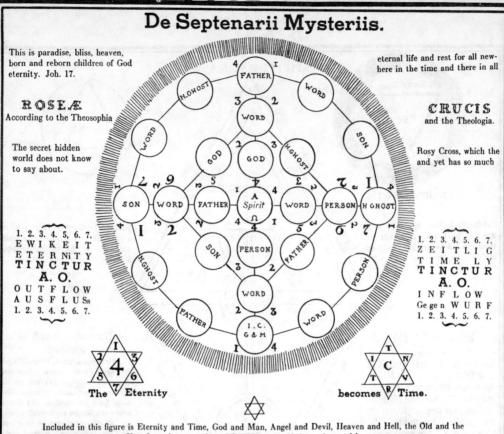

This is paradise, bliss, heaven, born and reborn children of God eternity. Joh. 17.

eternal life and rest for all new-here in the time and there in all

ROSEÆ
According to the Theosophia

CRUCIS
and the Theologia.

The secret hidden world does not know to say about.

Rosy Cross, which the and yet has so much

1. 2. 3. 4. 5. 6. 7.
E W I K E I T
E T E R N i T Y
TINCTUR
A. O.
O U T F L O W
A U S F L U S s
1. 2. 3. 4. 5. 6. 7.

1. 2. 3. 4. 5. 6. 7.
Z E I T L I G
T I M E L Y
TINCTUR
A. O.
I N F L O W
Ge ge n W U R F
1. 2. 3. 4. 5. 6. 7.

The △ Eternity

becomes ▽ Time.

Included in this figure is Eternity and Time, God and Man, Angel and Devil, Heaven and Hell, the Old and the New Jerusalem, together with all creatures, beings, time and hours.

12 Patriarchs.	12 Stars in the crown. Apoc. 12.
12 Prophets.	
12 Apostles.	12 Heavenly signs.
12 Articles of belief.	12 Months in the year.
12 Gates in the New	12 Hours in the day.
Jerusalem. Apoc. 21.	12 Hours in the night.

PROBAT FIDEM.

There is a Word speaking eternally,
Self out of itself, in itself, but still not itself,
It may never be spoken out!
Egos, everything, nothing, hell, heaven, earth,
Light, night, good, bad, body, spirit, this, that,
Yes, no, I, thou, give, take, do, let,
Sense, will, reason, no reason, here, there,
Sorrow, joy, scorn, love, quiet, time, eternity,
Soul, angel, devil, life, death, stillness,
Sound, one, none, Man, yes even God.
The Word cannot even reach itself,
Cannot be compared to anything
And yet it is at all times
All in All Jesus Christ!
He speaks, does not speak, is being spoken,
Speaks out, speaks in, remains unspoken,
Creates everything Himself, remains uncreated,
But is Himself what He created:
From the innermost out, from the outermost in,
He has been, is, is not, but will be,
One God, one Lord, one Spirit, one Unit:
Whoever does not believe this,
    cannot understand anything,
For from BELIEF comes understanding,
So speaks the Spirit, and writes the Hand,
First believe it, then try it,
If found good, then praise it.
Silentium Sapientiae; Simplicitas Veritatis
SIGILLUM.

The Cross is the best

interpretation of the Scriptures.

CONSTANTIA.

B·I·B·L·I·A·

Animae Pharmaca
Sanctissima Bibliotheca
Lecta placent. Xies repetita placebunt
Via Sancta
SPIRITUS & VITA
Oraculum & Spiraculum
Ie Ho Vae
Rationale Divinarum
AOURIM & TUMMIM
Tabernaculum
DEI cum Hominibus
SANCTUARIUM
MEMORIALE
Magnalium DEI
LUCERNA DOMINI
Armarium
Spiritus Sancti
PANACEA
Nectar & Ambrosia
PORTA COELI
LIBER DOMINI
FONS
Signatur
CIBUS ANIMAE
Lumen Gratiae
ORTUS
Conclusus
THESAURUS
Absconditus
VERBUM VITA
Quaerite & Invenietis
Credite & Intelligetis.

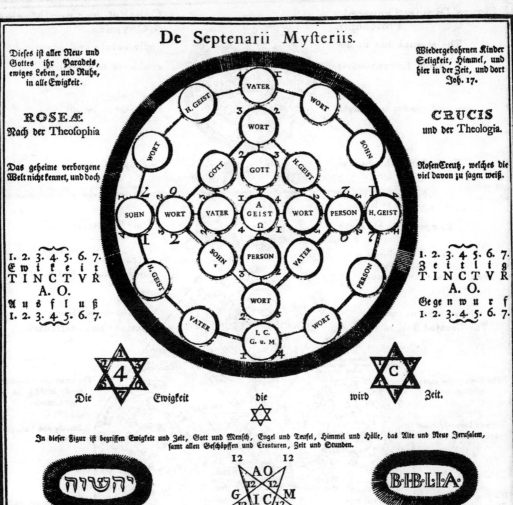

Dieses ist aller Neu- und Gottes ihr Paradeis, ewiges Leben, und Ruhe, in alle Ewigkeit.

ROSEÆ
Nach der Theosophia

Das geheime verborgene Welt nicht kennet, und doch

Wiedergebohrnen Kinder Seeligkeit, Himmel, und hier in der Zeit, und dort Joh. 17.

CRUCIS
und der Theologia.

RosenCreutz, welches die viel davon zu sagen weiß.

I. 2. 3. 4. 5. 6. 7.
Ewigkeit
TINCTVR
A. O.
Ausfluß
I. 2. 3. 4. 5. 6. 7.

I. 2. 3. 4. 5. 6. 7.
Zeitlich
TINCTVR
A. O.
Gegenwurf
I. 2. 3. 4. 5. 6. 7.

Die   Ewigkeit   die   wird   Zeit.

In dieser Figur ist begriffen Ewigkeit und Zeit, Gott und Mensch, Engel und Teufel, Himmel und Hölle, das Alte und Neue Jerusalem, samt allen Geschöpffen und Creaturen, Zeit und Stunden.

יהשוה

BIBLIA.

Es ist ein Wort, welchs ewig spricht,
Sich selbst aus sich in sich doch nicht,
Mag niemahls ausgesprochen werden!
Ichts, Alles, nichts, Höll, Himmel, Erden,
Licht, Nacht, gut, bös, Leib, Geist, dies, das,
Ja, nein, Ich, Du, gieb, nimm, thue, laß,
Gemüth, Will, Grund, Ungrund, hier, dort,
Leid, Freud, Zorn, Lieb, Ruh, Zeit, Ewigkeit,
Seel, Engel, Teufel, Leben, Todt, Still,
Schall, Eins, Keins, Mensch, ja selbst Gott.
Das Wort sich selbst nicht mag erreichen,
Ist auch mit ihm nichts zu vergleichen,
Und ist doch selbst zu aller Frist
In allen Alles Jesus Christ!
Der spricht, spricht nicht, wird doch gesprochen,
Spricht aus, spricht ein, bleibt ungesprochen,
Schafft alles selbst, bleibt unerschaffen,
Und ist doch selbst was er geschaffen:
Von Innen heraus, von Aussen hinein,
Ists gewest, ists, ists nicht, wirds doch seyn,
Ein Gott, ein Herr, ein Geist, ein Eins:
Wer diß nicht glaubt, versteht sonst keins,
Denn aus dem GLAVBEN kömmt Verstand,
So spricht der Geist, und schreibt die Hand,
Vor glaubs, denn probs,
Ists gut, so lobs.
Silentium Sapientiæ; Simplicitas Veritatis
SIGILLVM.

12 Patriarchen.
12 Propheten.
12 Aposteln.
12 Artikel ihres Glaubens.
12 Stadtthor im Neuen Jerusalem. Ap. 21.

12 Sternen in der Kron. Ap 12.
12 Himmlische Zeichen.
12 Monat im Jahr.
12 Stunden des Tages.
12 Stunden des Nachts.

Probat Fidem.

Das Creutz ist die beste

Auslegung der h. Schrift.

CONSTANTIA.

Animæ Pharmaca
Sanctissima Bibliotheca
Lecta placent. Xies repetita placebunt
Via Sancta
SPIRITVS & VITA
Oraculum & Spiraculum
Iz Ho Væ
Rationale Divinarum
AOVRIM & TVMMIM
Tabernaculum
DEI cum Hominibus
SANCTVARIVM
יהוה
MEMORIALE
Magnalium DEI
LVCERNA DOMINI
Armarium
Spiritus Sancti
PANACEA
Nectar & Ambrosia
PORTA COELI
LIBER DOMINI
FONS
Signatur
CIBVS ANIMÆ
Lumen Gratiæ
ORTVS
Conclusus
THESAVRVS
Absconditus
VERBVM VITA
Quærite & Invenietis
Credite Intelligetis.

Figura Divina Theosoph. Philosoph.

The eternal Sun in his

Deus Triunus exivit

understand according to Philosophy

Cabalist. nec non Magica & Chymica.

Godly nature and power.

ex Centro in Centrum

Coelesti and not terrestri.

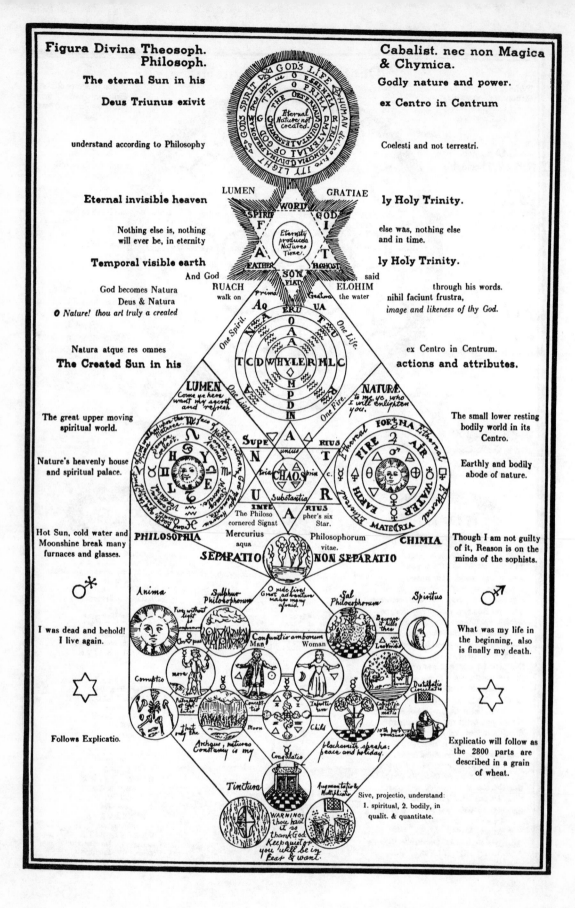

Eternal invisible heaven

Nothing else is, nothing will ever be, in eternity

Temporal visible earth

God becomes Natura
Deus & Natura
O Nature! thou art truly a created

Natura atque res omnes
The Created Sun in his

The great upper moving spiritual world.

Nature's heavenly house and spiritual palace.

Hot Sun, cold water and Moonshine break many furnaces and glasses.

I was dead and behold! I live again.

Follows Explicatio.

ly Holy Trinity.

else was, nothing else and in time.

ly Holy Trinity.

through his words.
nihil faciunt frustra,
image and likeness of thy God.

ex Centro in Centrum.
actions and attributes.

The small lower resting bodily world in its Centro.

Earthly and bodily abode of nature.

Though I am not guilty of it, Reason is on the minds of the sophists.

What was my life in the beginning, also is finally my death.

Explicatio will follow as the 2800 parts are described in a grain of wheat.

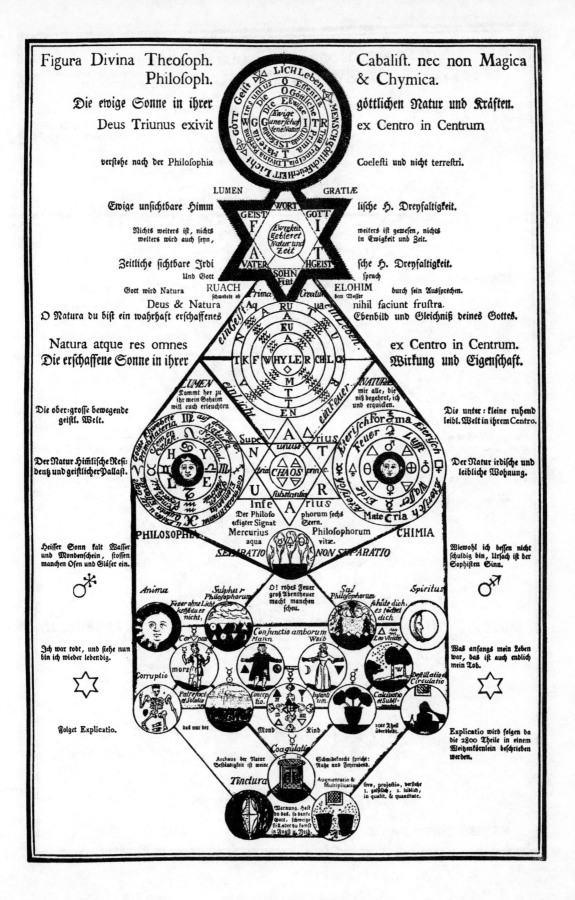

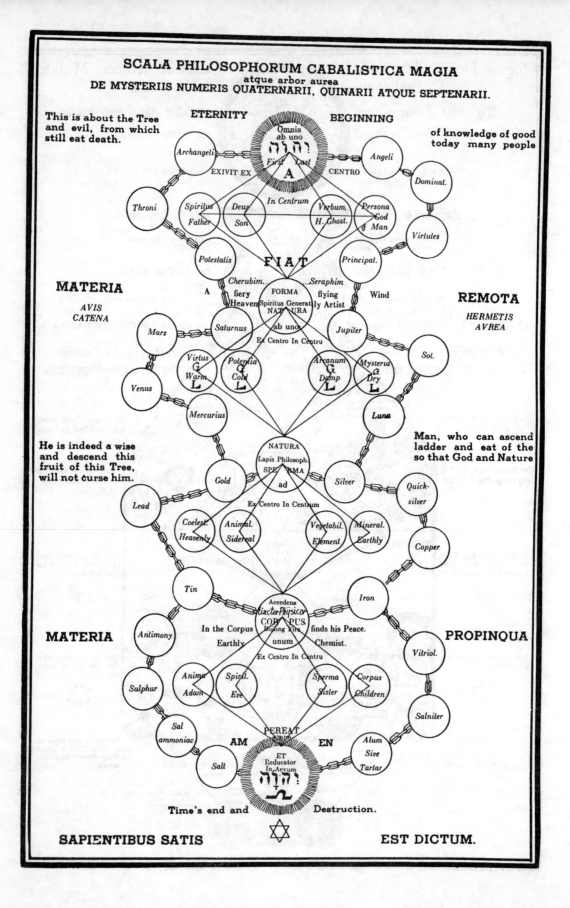

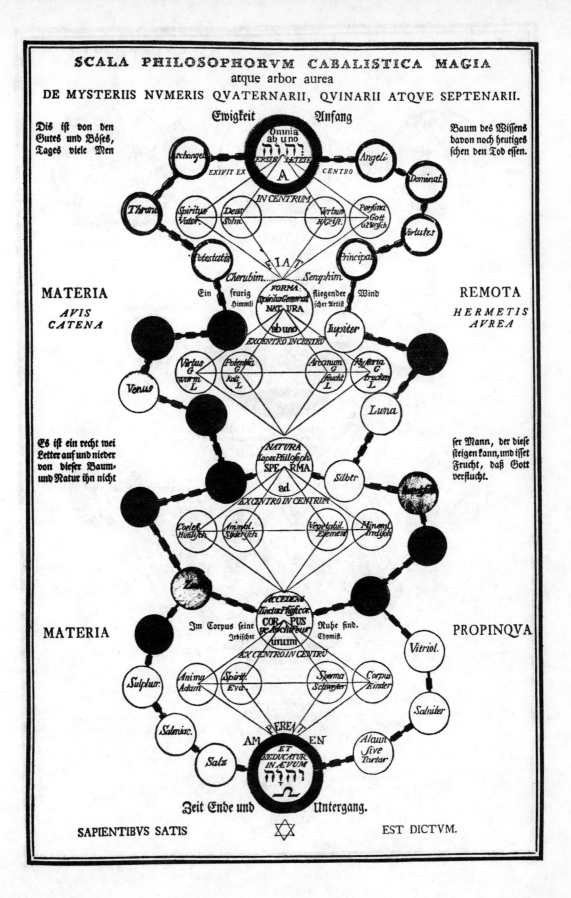

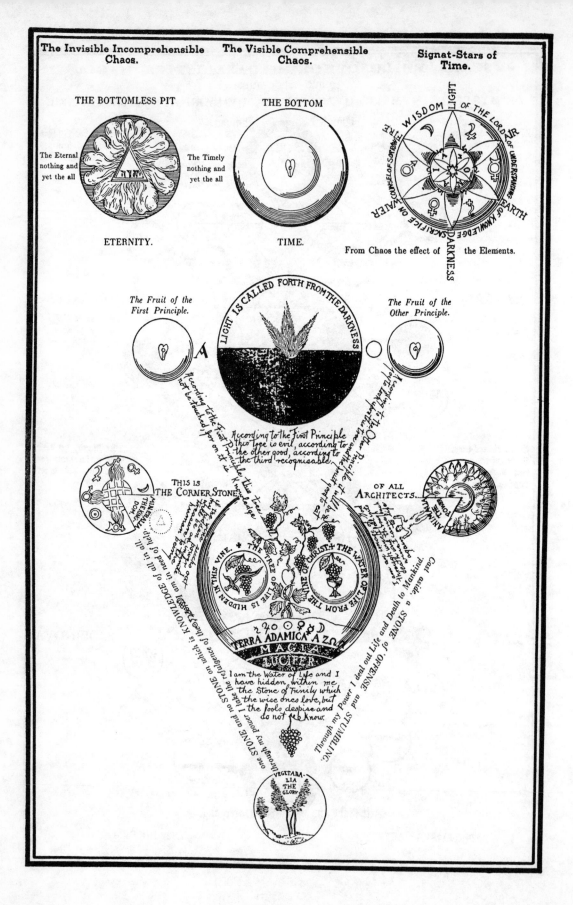

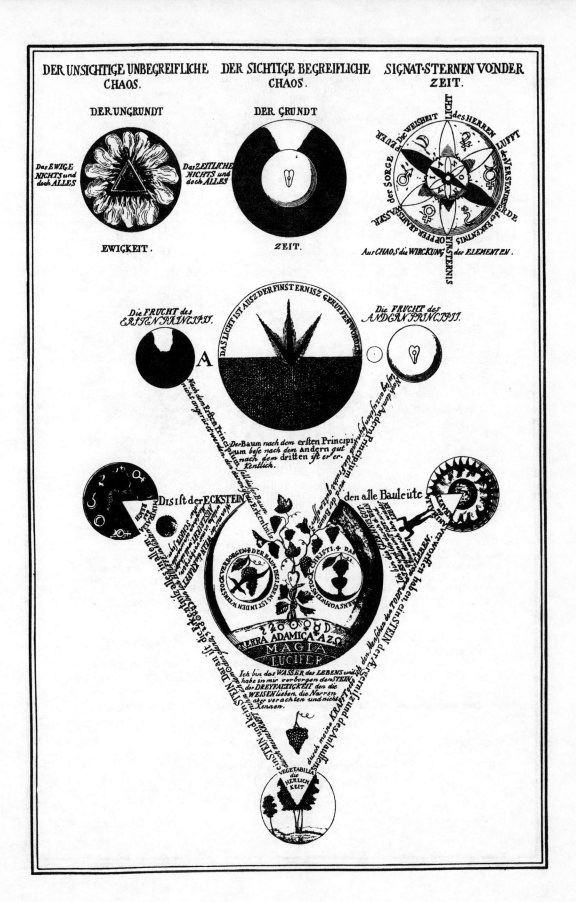

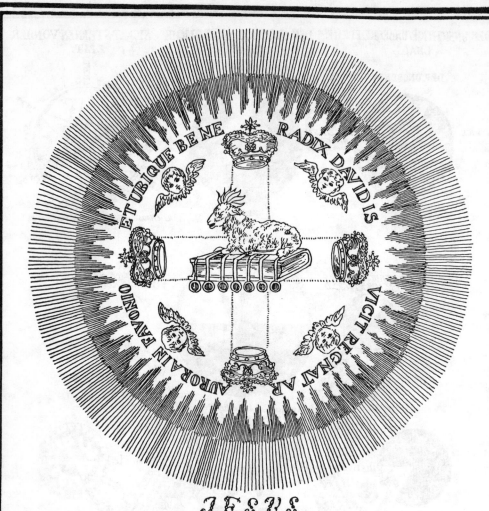

JESUS.

I know nothing, I can do nothing, I do not want anything, I do not please myself, I do not praise myself, I do not relish anything, I do not learn, I do not seek, I do not desire anything in heaven and on earth; only the living word alone, which became flesh, **JESUS CHRIST**, and him **CRUCIFIED**. 1 COR. 2.

This is the most holy, most understanding heavenly ARTICUL, and openly revealed to us through God Himself in the Light of Nature.

Physica.	I am the Alpha and Omega	Metaphysica
	the First and the Last.	& Hyperphysica.
	Apocal. 1. v. 11. 12. Cap. 5. v. 5. seq.	

D. O. M. A.

Deo omnipotenti sit Laus, Honos & Gloria in Seculorum Secula, Amen.

Mea

in Cruce 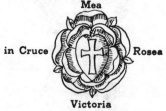 Rosea

Victoria

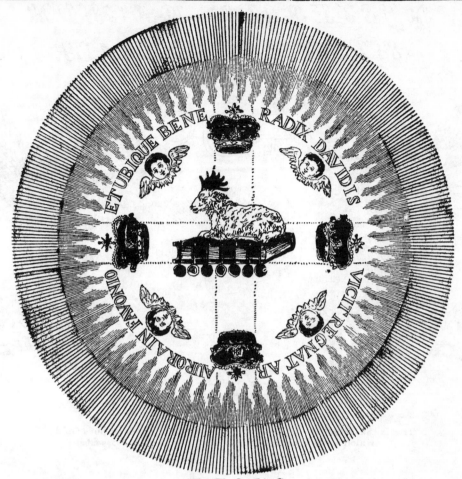

JESUS.

Ich weiß nichts, ich kann nichts, ich will nichts, mir geliebet nichts, ich rühme mich nichts, ich erfreue mich nichts, ich lerne nichts, ich suche nichts, ich begehre auch nichts im Himmel und auf Erden: ohn allein das lebendige Wort, das Fleisch worden, **Jesum Christum den Gecreutzigten.** 1 Cor. 2.

Diß ist der allerheiligste, hochverständigste, himmlischer Articul, und uns doch augenscheinlich von **Gott** geoffenbahret im Licht der Natur leibhaftig.

Physica.	**Ich bin das A und Ω**	Metaphysica
	der Erste und der Letzte.	& Hyperphysica.

Apocal. 1. v. 11. 12. Cap. 5. v. 5. seq.

D. O. M. A.

Deo omnipotenti sit Laus, Honos & Gloria in Seculorum Secula, Amen.

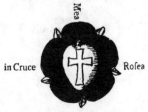

in Cruce   Rosea

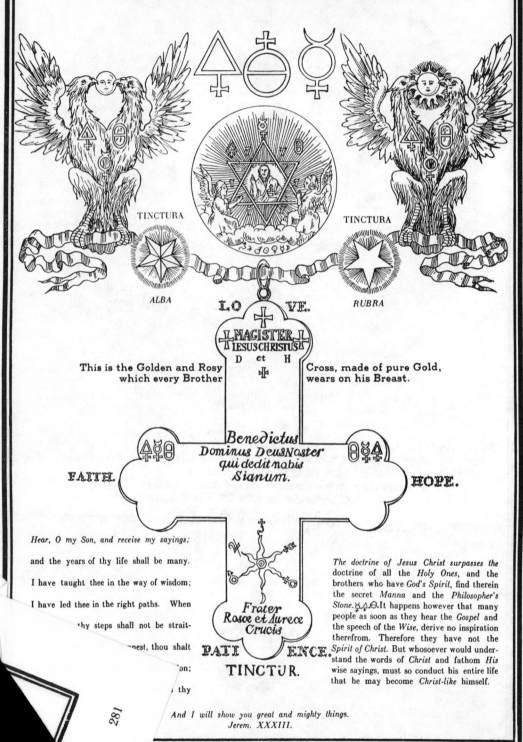

MYSTERIUM MAGNUM
STUDIUM UNIVERSALE.

TINCTURA

TINCTURA

ALBA

RUBRA

LOVE.

MAGISTER
IESUSCHRISTUS
D et H

This is the Golden and Rosy Cross, made of pure Gold, which every Brother wears on his Breast.

Benedictus Dominus Deus Noster qui dedit nobis Signum.

FAITH.

HOPE.

Hear, O my Son, and receive my sayings;

and the years of thy life shall be many.

I have taught thee in the way of wisdom;

I have led thee in the right paths. When

thy steps shall not be strait-

nest, thou shalt

on;

thy

Frater
Rosæ et Aureæ
Crucis

PATIENCE.

TINCTUR.

The doctrine of Jesus Christ surpasses the doctrine of all the *Holy Ones*, and the brothers who have *God's Spirit*, find therein the secret *Manna* and the *Philosopher's Stone*. It happens however that many people as soon as they hear the *Gospel* and the speech of the *Wise*, derive no inspiration therefrom. Therefore they have not the *Spirit of Christ*. But whosoever would understand the words of *Christ* and fathom *His* wise sayings, must so conduct his entire life that he may become *Christ-like* himself.

And I will show you great and mighty things.
Jerem. XXXIII.

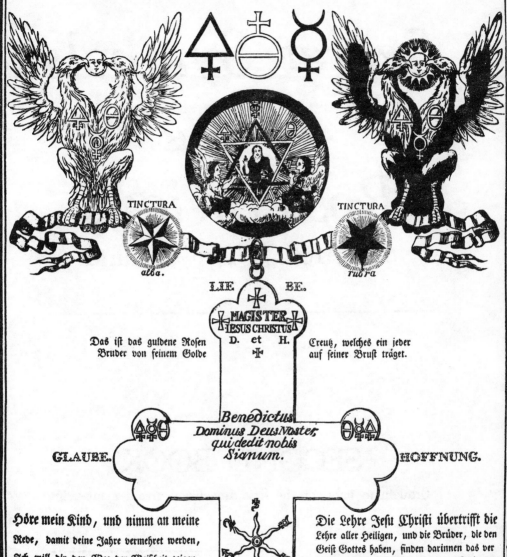

TINCTURA

TINCTURA

alba.

rubra.

LIE. BE.

MAGISTER IESUS CHRISTUS

D. et H.

Das ist das guldene Rosen Bruder von seinem Golde

Creutz, welches ein jeder auf seiner Brust träget.

Benedictus Dominus Deus Noster, qui dedit nobis Signum.

GLAUBE.

HOFFNUNG.

Höre mein Kind, und nimm an meine Rede, damit deine Jahre vermehret werden, Ich will dir den Weg der Weißheit zeigen, und dich führen durch die Bahn der Gerechtigkeit. Wenn du darauf gehen wirst, so sollen dir deine Gänge nicht beängstiget werden, und wann du geschwinde lauffest, wirst du nicht anstoßen. Halte die Lehre, und bewahre sie, denn sie ist dein Leben. Prov. IV. v. 10.

Frater Rosæ et Aureæ Crucis

GED ULT.

TINCTUR.

Die Lehre Jesu Christi übertrifft die Lehre aller Heiligen, und die Brüder, die den Geist Gottes haben, finden darinnen das verborgene Himmel-Brod, und den Stein der Weisen, . Es geschiehet aber, daß viele Menschen, ob sie schon oft das Evangelium und die Sprache der Weisen hören, jedoch keine Begierde daraus empfinden, denn sie haben den Geist Christi nicht. Wer aber die Worte Christi verstehen will, und der Weisen Reden ergründen, der muß sich befleißigen, mit seinem Leben Christo gleichförmig zu werden.

Ich will dir grosse und gewaltige Dinge zeigen.
Jerem. XXXIII.

Secret Symbols
of the
Rosicrucians
of the 16th & 17th Centuries

SECOND BOOK

Brought to light for the first time from an old manuscript

ALTONA, 1788

by J. D. A. Eckhardt, Printer to H. M. the King of Denmark

283

Geheime
Figuren der Rosenkreuzer,
aus dem 16ten und 17ten Jahrhundert.

Zweites Heft.

Aus einem alten Mscpt zum erstenmal ans Licht gestellt.

Altona, 1788.

Gedruckt und verlegt von J. D. A. Eckhardt, Königl. Dän. privil. Buchdrucker.

A Golden Treatise About the Philosopher's Stone

BY A STILL LIVING BUT UNKNOWN *PHILOSOPHER*, FOR THE INSTRUCTION OF THE *FILII DOCTRINAE*, AND FOR THE INFORMATION OF THE *FRATRES AUREAE CRUCIS*

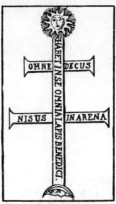

ANNO M. DC. XXV.

FOREWORD

TO THE READER IN SEARCH OF THE ART

Be not surprised, my dear Reader and honest Investigator of Nature's Secrets, that I should undertake to write this short Treatise when in this final age the world standeth with one foot already in the grave, while close at hand many libraries are found full of books which are written about this *Materia*, the majority of which, however, instill a false philosophy and give fictitious formulae. I have not written for my own sake, but for thy sake, to show thee the ground of truth, and to lead thee from wrong ways which seem important to thee. As far as I am concerned, I already know what is necessary for me to know of this, hence I have no need of books. For in the past twenty-two years I have read as many as I could lay hands on, and there have been not a few written as well as printed. Thou wilt find described herein the *Materia* and the *Solution theorice*, and also the entire *praxis* in its *allegoria* wilt thou find completely implied, as plainly and clearly as thou mayest hope to find from any Philosopher. I have studiously applied myself to consult thereon with the *Philosophi*, and I have called attention to all the places where they have mentioned this or that aphorism, so that thou mayest thyself see, look up their books, compare both the *concept* and my *allegata*, and sharpen thine understanding with it. Now I might have written this Treatise with much less effort by omitting my *allegata*, and could have made myself known to the *Fratres aureae crucis*; but, as said before, it is all for the best that thou mayest gather more understanding therefrom. Thou shouldest not be surprised that I have kept my name hidden and that I do not reveal myself to thee personally; for I do not seek vain honor, and I am not intent on making a great name for myself in this world, but I am thinking only of thy profit. Besides, my Masters, the true *Philosophi*, taught me not to risk my life at all for the sake of fame, and offer myself to greedy robbers, and load great sins upon myself by prostituting this great secret. They who taught me this were the true *Philosophi*, my *Teachers*. The reader will learn from *Sendivogius* that as often as he doth reveal himself to the great lords it is every time to his hurt and to the increase of danger. And experience proves that different *Philosophi* who did not take sufficient care of their treasures, were choked to death and robbed of their *Tincture* by greedy and vain fellows who risked their souls for that purpose. Reason asserteth that whoever carrieth so great a treasure with him doth not like to be robbed of it. *Sendivogius* concealed his name in his *Anagramatismis*. A short time ago a new *Frater aureae crucis* also made himself known in an *Anagramata* and *Aenigmata*, and his name is well known to me. Why then should I lay myself bare before the whole world? Let this be sufficient for thee, dear friend, that I make myself known to the Wise, and at the same time withhold my name from thee, which I have then done without fault, commending the rest to our Lord God, who will reveal me to thee if it should please Him, and if it should be advantageous to me and to thee. Do not let thyself long to search out my name; for even if thou shouldest

ever find it and should know me, thou wouldest still have to be content with this *Treatise*. For I have sworn with *Bernhardus of Trevisan* and other *Philosophi*, in all justice to reveal nothing more than is done here. And do not be concerned at all about whether I have this treasure in my hands. But rather ask if I have seen how the world was created? How the darkness came over Egypt? What is the cause of the rainbow? How the transfigured bodies will look after the Day of Judgment? Which is the most constant color? But I ask of you who understand my booklet whether ye have seen the great and universal salty sea, without any corrosive matter, which is in itself sufficient to carry the *Tinctures* of all things up onto the highest mountains? Tell me, Where doth Sulphur become Sulphur, and where doth Mercury come forth from Mercury? Likewise, where will Sulphur come forth from Mercury, and Mercury from Sulphur? When have your eyes beheld the symbol of ardent love, as when man and woman so embrace each other that they will be no more separated through all eternity, but become one in glorious love? Do ye understand now what I am talking about? If ye have worked out these things with your own hands, and beheld with your own eyes, then am I your consociate, and make known to you that I also know, and that I like nothing better than to receive your secret message; for that purpose I want to write this little Treatise.

But if anyone should complain about the difficulty of this art, then let him know that this art in itself is not difficult at all, that it will be easy for those who love God and who are by Him deemed worthy of it, will find it quite easy.

However, if some one should accuse me of having written all too plainly and clearly about the art, so that everyone could understand it: to him I answer that it is true that I have written about it lucidly enough for those who were found worthy in God's sight, but the unworthy will do well to leave it alone. I have previously set forth the entire art, word for word, to the over-clever ones, but they ridiculed it in their hearts, and did not believe that in our work was a twofold resurrection from the dead. Therefore is our art in *Theoria* and *practica*, a pure gift of God, who giveth it to whom, and when, He will, and it doth not depend on any man's willing or doing. I have known it with all *circumstantiae*, and manipulations for fully seventeen or eighteen years, and yet I had to wait until it pleased God to bestow upon me His grace. Also, no one should doubt the certainty and truth of this art, especially since it is as true, as certain in Nature and as undoubtedly ordered by God as that the sun shineth by day and the moon by night. Herewith I shall bring to a close this little *Praefatio*, and begin with the *Treatise* itself. But you, my beloved *Fratri aureae crucis*, who have now and then kept yourselves hidden in secret and enjoy the gifts of the High God in His fear, hearken unto my words, and hide not from me, and if so be you know me not, let it be known to you that the Cross trieth out the faithful and revealeth their faith in the light of day, but such are kept hidden for the sake of safety and delight. God be with us all. AMEN.

Dear beloved Reader and Follower of the True Wisdom: The old and new *Philosophi*, after they attained the goal of their desires through divine grace, took care in their writings to make themselves known to their fellow-students, who kept themselves hidden here and there in the world, and to indicate to them how the true God had enlightened their understanding, blessed the work of their hands, and revealed to them the great secret of earthly wisdom. Wherefore they rightly pledged themselves to give Him all praise, honor, and glory. And then also they promised that they would bequeath to their fellow-Christians and art-seeking disciples at the same time instruction and information, so that they might at once thereby might also love and be loved by God, and attain to understanding and knowledge of such *Secreta*.

And there have been such people amongst all nations, such as the Egyptians, the most eminent of whom was *Hermes Trismegistus*, the Chaldeans, Greeks, Arabs, Italians, French,

English, Spaniards, Germans, Poles, Hungarians, Jews, and many others. There is nothing surprising about it, although the said Wise Men wrote in different languages at different times, there is nevertheless unity and agreement and general *consensus* to be found in their writings, that every true Philosopher could soon recognise that God had favored them with His great blessing, and that they had had the Work itself in their own hands. And just as truth manifesteth itself in *Harmonia*, so on the contrary must *Dissonantia* bring every Sophist and supposed Philosophers into the open.

For while he never rightly knoweth the secret of the Wise and pursueth his way according to his own mind, every man who is cognisant of the art will see his error.

But *Harmonia* and concord especially consist mainly of these two points, *viz.*, in knowledge of the *Materia*, their *Solution*, weight, fire, and *Augmentation*. With respect to the *Materia*, it is such that it hath within itself everything which is necessary for

Ein güldener Tractat vom Philosophischen Steine.

Von einem noch Lebenden, doch vngenanten Philosopho, den Filiis Doctrinæ zur Lehre, den Fratribus aureæ Crucis aber zur Nachrichtung beschrieben.

Anno M. DC. XXV.

Vorrede
An den Kunstsuchenden Leser.

Verwundere dich nicht, lieber Leser, vnd rechtschaffener nachforscher der Natürlichen geheimnußen, warumb in diesem letzten Alter der Welt, da sie mit dem einem Fuße schon auf der gruben gehet, ich diesen kurtzen Tractat zuschreiben mich vnternommen, sintemahl bey nahe alle Bibliothecen voller Bücher gefunden werden, so von dieser Materia geschrieben seind, deren doch d' mehrëtheil falsche vnnd erdichtete Philosophie vnd Recepten in sich führen. Ich hab es nicht meinet, sondern deinet halben geschrieben, dir den Grund der warheit zuzeigen, vnnd von den Irrwegen abzuleiten, da dir dann nicht wenig angelegen ist: Mich betreffende, weiß ich allbereits was mir hierzu zuwissen von nöthen ist, ich bedarff keiner Bücher, habe deren in zwey vnd zwantzig Jahren so viel gelesen, als ich deren zu meinen Händen bekommen mögen, deren dann nicht wenig, so wohl von geschriebenen, als Gedruckten gewesen. Du wirst hierein die Materiam vnd die solution theorice beschrieben, wie auch die gantze praxin in einer allegoria begriffen volkommen finden, so deutlich vnd klar, alß du bey einem Philosopho solches suchen magst. Ich habe mich auch beflissen mit den Philosophis zureden, vnd derowegen alle Orter, wo sie diesen oder jenen Spruch führen, eigentlich angedeutet, das du selbst solche aufschlagen, vnnd den concept, auch meine allegata gegen einander halten, vnd deinen Verstand damit schärffen mögest. Zwar ich hette mit weniger mühe diesen Tractat ohne solche allegata beschrieben, vnnd den Fratribus aureæ crucis mich zuerkennen geben können: Aber dir wie schon gedacht, ists zum besten angesehen, das du desto mehr Verstand hierauß schöpffen mögest. Du solt dich auch nicht verwundern, das ich meinen Namen verborgen, vnnd mich dir Personlich nicht offenbahren wollen: ich suche nicht meine eitele Ehre, vnd mir für der Welt einen grossen Namen zumachen, sondern deinen Nutzen: Zu deme haben wir meine Lehrmeistere, die wahren Philosophos meines nicht gelebret, wegen grosses Ansehens mein Leben in die schäntze zuschlagen, vnd den geitzigen Räubern feil zubiethen, dazu auch mit prostituirung dieses grossen Geheimnuß grosse Sünden auf mich zu laden. Der Leser wird beym Sendiuogio vernommen haben, daß, so offt er sich bey grossen Herren offenbahret, jhme jederzeit zuschaden vnd gefahr gerichtet sey: die Erfahrung bezeugets, das vnderschiedene Philosophi, so jhre Schätze nicht gnugsam verborgen, von den geitzigen vnnd boffertigen Gesellen, so deßhalben ihre Seelen in die Schantz geschlagen, erwürget, vnd der Tinctur beraubet worden. Der Vernunfft bekräfftigtes, daß je leichter so einen grossen Schatz offenbarlich traget, nit gerne wolte beraubet sein. Es hat Sendiuogius in seinen Anagramatismis seinen Namen verborgen. Es hat vor weniger zeit ein newer aureæ crucis Frater gleichfalß mit einem Anagrammate vnd Ænigmate sich zuerkennen gegeben, dessen Nahmen mir dann wol bewust: warumb solte ich mich dann aller Welt für Augen stellen? Lasse dich begnügen lieber Freund, daß ich mich den Weisen zuerkennen gebe, vn zugleich dir deinen Namen kundbahr mache, welches ich dann, ohne Zehl, gethan habe, befehle das vbrige vnserm Herrn Gotte, der mich dir wird Fund thun, so du sein

gefallen, vnnd mir vnnd dir nützlich sein wird. Lasse dich nicht gelüsten nach meinem Namen zuforschen: denn so du jhn je erführet oder mich kântest, so wirst du doch dir mit diesem Tractat genügen lassen müssen: Den ich habe mit Bernhardo von Treſue vnd Naygenden Philosophis, der Billigkeit nach niemand weiter etwas zu offenbahren, alß hierin geschehen ist, geschworen. Bekümmere dich auch nicht darumb, ob ich diesen Schatz in Händen habe: frage viel mehr darnach, ob ich gesehen, wie die Welt geschaffen worden? wie die Finsternuß in Aegypten gewesen? was die vrsache des Regenbogens sey? Wie die clarificirten Leiber, nach der allgemeinen Auferstehung, außsehen werden? Welches die bestendigste Farbe sey? Ich aber frage euch, die jhr mein Büchlein verstehet, ob jhr gesehen habet dz allgemeine grosse gesaltzene Meer, obn alle corrosiff, so gnugsam ist aller dinge Tincturen auff die höchsten Berge zu führen? Saget mir, wo wird auß Schweffel Schweffel, vñ aus Mercurio Mercurius? Jte, Wo wird auß Mercurio Schweffel, vnd auß Schweffel Mercurius? Wann ewre Augen das Fürbild der Brünstigen Liebe, da Mann vnnd Weib sich so vmbfahen, das sie auch in ewigkeit nicht mehr von einander zubringen seind, sondern, für Hertzlich liebe ein Ding werden, erblicket? Verstehet jhr, was ich jetzo Rede, vnnd habet solches mit ewren Händen gearbeitet, vnd mit ewern Augen gesehen, so bin ich ewer Geselle, vnd notificire euch, das ich euch wisse, vnnd mir nichts liebers sey, alß ewer geheime Kundschaft zu haben, zu welchem ich euch auch diß Tractätlein schreiben wollen. Were jemand der vber die Schwerheit dieser Kunst klagte, der wisse, daß sie an vnd für sich selbst nicht schwer sey, vnnd das denen, die Gott lieben, vnnd von jhme hierzu gewürdiget werden, sie gar leicht ankomme. Wolte mich aber jemand beschüldigen, das ich die Kunst zu hell vnnd klar geschrieben, daß solches ein jeder verstehen könne: deme antworte ich, das ich sie zwar verstendig gnug beschrieben habe den würdigen, denen Gott solche gönnet, die vnwürdigen aber werden sie wol zufrieden lassen: Ich habe wol die gantze Kunst den Vberklügen von worten zu worten erzehlet, Sie aber haben solches in jhrem Hertzen verlachet nicht glaubende, daß eine zweyfache Aufferstehung der Todten sey in vnserm wercke. Darumb ist vnsere Kunst in der Theoria vnd Practica eine lautere Gabe Gottes, welcher sie gibt, wann vnd weme er wil, vnd ligt nicht an jemands wollen oder läuffen. Ich habe sie mit allen circumstantiis, vnd Handgriffen wol 17. oder 18. Jahr gewust, vnnd dennoch warten müssen, biß es Gott gefallen, mir Gnade zuuerleihen. Es soll auch kein Mensch an der Gewißheit vnd Warheit dieser Kunst zweiffeln, sintemahl solche so warhafft, so gewiß ist in der Natur vnd so vngezweiffelt von Gott geordnet ist alß die Sonne des Tages scheinet, vnd der Mond des Nachts leuchtet. Hiermit will ich diese wenige Præfation schliessen, vnnd den Tractatum selbst ansehen. Ihr aber geliebten Fratres crucis aureæ, die jhr euch hin vnd wieder in Geheim verborgen haltet, vnd der hohen Gottes Gaben in seiner Furcht geniesset, verhaltet euch mir nicht, vnnd so jhr mich nicht kennet, so wisset, daß das Creutze die Glaubigen probiret, vnnd jhren Glauben an Tag gibt, Sicherheit aber vnnd wollust solchen verstöret. Gott sey mit euch allen. AMEN.

Es haben die Alten vnnd newen Philosophi, viel geliebter Leser, vnd Nachfolger der wahren Weißheit, nach deme sie durch Göttliche verleihung den Zweck jhres begehrens erreichet, sich andern jhren mit genossen, welche sich in der Welt hin vnnd wieder verborgen gehalten, mit jhren Schrifften pflegen zuerkennen zugeben, jhnen beydes anzubieten, das der getrewe Gott auch jhren Verstand erleuchtet, jhrer Hände arbeit gesegnet, vnnd jhnen das grosse Geheimnuß dieser Irrdischen weißheit offenbaret, dafur sie jhme billich in gesambt Lob, Ehr vnd Preiß zu geben verpflichtet: vnnd auch, daß sie jhren neben Christen vnnd kunstsuchenden Schulern zugleich Anleitung vnd Nachrichtung hinterlassen möchten, damit auch selbige, so es dem lieben Gott also gelieben würde, zu Erkäntnuß vnnd Wissenschafft solcher Secreten gelangen mögen.

Vnd seind solche leute vnter allerley Völckern gewesen, alß Aegyptier, vnter welchen Hermes Trismegistus der fürnembste, Chaldæer, Griechen, Araber, Italiener, Frantzhosen, Engländer, Niederländer, Hispanier, Teutsche, Polen, Vngern, Juden vnd solche mehr. Es ist aber nicht wenig zuuerwundern, das ob schon gedachte weise Männer in vnderschiedenen Sprachen vnnd zu vnterschiedenen Zeiten geschrieben haben, gleichwol eine solche vber ein Stimmung vnd ein heiliger Consensus in jhren Schrifften zuerkennen wird, daß jhre intention zuereichen ein jeder wahrer Philosophus so bald erkennen kann, daß es Gott mit diesem grossen Segen erfrewet, vnd sie das Werck selbst in handen haben: gleichfalß, weil

auß der Harmonia die Warheit sich herfür thut, so muß hingegen die Dissonantia ein jeden Sophisten vnnd vermeinten Philosophum an Tag bringen.

Denn weil er das Geheimnuß der Weysen niemahln recht erkant, vnd seinem eigenen Hirn nach seinen Weg gehet, so siehet ein jeder Kunst wissender seine Irrthumb.

Die Harmonia aber vnd vber ein Stimmung bestehet fürnemlich in diesen Puncten, nemlich in Erkäntnuß der Materien, derer Solution, Fewr vnd Augmentation. Die Materiam belangende, ist solche eine einige, welche in sich hat alles, was jhr von nöthen, darauß alles, was der Kunstliebende begehret gemacht wird, nemlich nisus in arena, wie der Philosophus Anastratus in der Turba sagt: Es ist nichts köstlichers alß der rote Sand am Meer, vnnd ist der Speichel des Monds, welcher der Sonnen Liecht zugefügt vnd coaguliret wird.

Daß aber solche einige Materia erfordert wird, bezeuget Agadmon daselbsten, sagende: wisset, daß so jhr nicht dieses mein Corpus nehmet, so keinen Geist hat, so werdet jhr nicht erlangen, was jhr suchet: vnd das darumb, weil nichts frembdes ins Werck kommet, auch andere nichts darzu erfordert wird, alß was da reine ist. Darumb lasse alle vielheit fahren: Denn die Natur ist nur mit einem einigen Dinge vergnüget, vnnd wer das nicht kennet, der wird verderben. Eben mäßigen spruch führet Arnoldus de Villa noua, in seinem Büchlein Flos

X

287

it, hence all that the lover of the art desireth will be made of it, namely *nisus in arena*, as the *Philosopher Anastratus* saith in the *Turba Philosophorum*: There is nothing more precious than the red sand of the sea, and this is the Monn's saliva, which is added to the Sun's light and *Coagulated*.

But that such a unified *Materia* is necessary, *Agadmon* himself testified, saying: Know that if ye do not take my *Corpus*, which hath no spirit, ye will not obtain what ye are looking for: and this because no alien substances shall come into your work, and know also that nothing else is required for it except that which is pure. Therefore renounce all multiplicity. For Nature is satisfied with only one thing, and whosoever doth not know that, he will perish. Even likewise doth *Arnoldus de Villanove* express himself in his booklet called *Flos florum*: Our stone is made out of one thing and is made with one thing. Likewise doth he say to the King of *Neopolis*: Everything contained in our stone is essential to its existence, and it doth not have need of anything else, especially since the stone is of one nature and one thing. And *Rosinus* saith: Be thou sure that it is only one thing, whereof everything is made that thou dost desire. And *Lilius*: Thou art in need of but the one thing, which changeth into a different nature at every step of our work. Also saith *Geber* in his *Summa*: It is but one stone, one medicine, to which we add nothing, and from which we take nothing, only separating the superfluous from it. And *Scites* saith in the *Turba*: *The foundation* of this art is something that is stronger and higher than any other thing, and is called the sharp vinegar, which is the cause of the gold becoming a pure spirit, without which neither whiteness, blackness, nor redness could exist; and when it is mixed with the body, then it becometh one with the body, and transformeth it into a spirit, and it coloreth it with spiritual and unchangeable color, and receiveth from that which is colored its bodily color in turn, which cannot be obliterated; and if thou shouldst out the body into the fire without the vinegar, then it would be consumed.

But some one might draw the conclusion from the sayings of *Scites* that not one but two things are required, namely: the body and the vinegar, as he calleth it; and it is necessary that a moist and a dry be joined together, so that the dry will not be consumed by the fire, but will be protected by the moisture from the burning fire. I must truly consent to such *Argument* and conclusion, if it be rightly understood, but nevertheless I must maintain the above-mentioned philosophical sayings in their merit and truth. Because it is certain for one thing that the one *Materia* of our blessed stone hath many names amongst the Philosophers, which Nature hath prepared for the artist, and for the *Materia* of the great stone alone, and hath ordained otherwise nothing else in the world.

This is before the eyes of everyone, the entire world seeth it, apprehendeth it, loveth it, but still doth not comprehend it. It is noble and bad, dear and cheap, costly and low-priced, and is found everywhere. *Theophrastus Paracelsus* calleth it the "Red Lion" in his book *De Tinctura Physica*, much mentioned, but little known. *Hermes*, in his book, chapter 1, calleth it: Mercury, which is hardened in the innermost cells. In the *Turba* it is sometimes named *Aes* or Ore; in the *Rosario Philosophorum it* is called Salt. In the *Summa* this *Materia* hath as many names as there are things in this world. That is the reason why it is so little understood by the ignorant. I call them ignorant because they proceed to the art without previous knowledge of Nature and her qualities; as *Arnoldus* saith: They proceed like an ass going to its manger, and which doth not know what it is going to receive into its opened mouth.

Therefore in his *Summa perfectionis*, *Geber* saith truly and rightly: He who hath no knowledge by himself of the beginning of Nature is still far from this art. And *Rosarius* saith: I advise that no one commit himself to finding this art save he who hath knowledge of the beginning of true Nature and its order; then when he hath knowledge of this he doth not need more than this one thing, and it doth not require great expense. For it is not more than a stone, a medicine, a phial, an order, and a preparation. Thus will our *Materia* be separated with the help of Nature and the intelligent manipulations of the *Artisan*, so that it will be transmuted into the "White Eagle," as *Theophrastus* saith, and the radiance of the *Sol* doth not shine after the *Spagyrization*, or (as *Basilius Valentinus* saith) out of it cometh a spirit as white as snow and another spirit as red as blood, both of which spirits have the third hidden within themselves. King *Aros* spake well when he said: Our medicine will be one substance made out of two, namely out of the unification of the constant, of the spiritual and bodily, of the cold and moist, warm and dry nature, and it cannot be made out of anything else. And *Richardus Anglicus* saith: It is a stone and a medicine made out of the *Philosophis* Rebis, *i. e.*, out of two things, namely, out of the body and the spirit, white or red; and many fools have erred therein by explaining in many different ways the verse: *Est rebis in dictis rectissima norma figuris*. That is, two things, and these two things are one thing, namely: the water added to the body, and such dissolved in a spirit, that is, into a mineral water out of the body and spirit, which is the Elixir that is called a *Fermentum*. For then the water and the spirit are one thing from which is made the *Tincture* and medicine in which all bodies are purified. Therefore our medicine is compounded out of one thing, this being the water and the spirit of the body. And so we have, according to the *Philosophi*, the nature of Sulphur and Mercury above the earth, from which are made gold and silver beneath the earth. And *Bernhardus, Count of Trevisan*, saith: Our work is taken raw from one root and two mercurial substances and is drawn, clean and pure, from the *Minera*, etc. And in his book *Concerning Natural and Supernatural Things, Basilius Valentinus* saith in the 4th chapter: I will reveal unto thee truthfully and through the love of God, that there is to be found the root of the philosophical Sulphur, which is a heavenly spirit, together with the root of the spiritual but natural *Mercurii*, which is the beginning of the spiritual salt in one, and is found in one *Materia*, out of which the Stone, destined for me, was made, and not in many things. And although Mercury by itself is found by all Philosophers, and Sulphur by itself, and Salt is drawn particularly from itself, so *Mercurius* will be found in one element, Sulphur in one, and Salt in one. Nevertheless I say unto thee that they arise only out of their superfluity, which is found most plentifully and can be used *particulariter* in many ways with advantage, and be prepared for medicine and for transmutation of metals. But the *Universal* alone is the highest earthly treasure, and all three things in their beginning are one thing only, and will at the same time be found in one thing only and extracted therefrom, which can make one out of all metals; and this is the true *Spiritus Mercurii* and *Anima Sulphuris* including the Spiritual Salt at the same time united and enclosed under one heaven and dwelling in one body, and this is the Dragon and the Eagle, it is the King and the Lion, it is the Spirit and the Corpse, which must color the corpse of the Gold into a Medicine, etc. So now our prepared *Materia* is called the man and the woman.

Likewise with respect to the working and the suffering, *Zimon* saith in the *Turba*: Know ye that the secret of this work existeth in the man and the woman, *i.e.*, in the producing and suffering. In lead is the man, in *Auripigment* is the woman. The man rejoiceth over the woman whom he hath received unto himself, and she helpeth him, and the woman receiveth from the man a coloring seed and is colored by him. And *Diamedes* saith: Join together the manly son of the Red Knight to his fragrant wife, and thus joined together they will beget the Art, to which there should be added no alien matter nor powder nor any other thing, and be ye content with the conception: so shall the true son be born unto you. Oh, how precious is the *Materia* of the Red Knight, without whom no order can exist! Others call it *Argentum vivum* or *Mercurius* and *Sulphur* or Fire. As *Rogerius Baco* saith in *Speculum Alchemiae*, chapter 3: All metals are born out of *Sulphur* and *Mercurius*, and nothing is connected with them, for if nothing be added to them, nothing will change them save what is derived from them. Therefore we must rightly take *Mercurius* and *Sulphur* for the *Materia* of the stone. And *Menabadus* saith: Whosoever addeth Mercury to the body of *Magnesia* and the Male to the Female, draweth out the hidden nature, with which the bodies will be colored.

And *Lullius* saith in his *Codicil*: It is the quality of our *Mercurius* that it letteth itself be coagulated by its Sulphur. And in the *Practica* of his *Testament* he saith: The Mercury is an overflowing and running moisture, thus preserved from the burning. Others call it body, spirit, soul. Thus *Arnoldus* in *Flos florum* saith: The *Philosophi* have said that our stone is composed at the same time from body, soul, and spirit, and they have spoken the truth. For they have compared the unperfected *Corpus* to the body, because it is weak. They have called the water spirit, and this with truth, as it is a spirit. But to the *Fermentum* they have given the name of soul because it giveth to the unperfected body the life which it did not have before, and it thus produceth a better form. And a little before this he saith: The spirit will not be joined to its body except through the medium of the souls. For the soul is the medium between the body and the spirit, which joineth both together. And *Morienus* saith: The soul quickly entereth its body; but if thou wouldst join it to another body, thou wouldst work in vain. And *Lullius* saith: Soul, spirit, and body are together, and are one thing, which hath everything in itself, to which nothing alien is added. But why is it necessary that one bring up all the names which people call our *Materia* and of explaining them? Let it be sufficient for our purpose to have mentioned the ones most commonly used. And after we have explored where this, our *Materia*, came from and where it will arrive, then we will consider a little the *Solution* as the principal part of the whole art, and through reflection we shall sharpen our reason and understanding.

Proceeding now to the consideration of what our *Materia* is and where it must be obtained: it is to be known that the Almighty Creator, whose wisdom is as great as is He Himself, hath created two things in the beginning, when there was nothing but Himself: the heavenly things and those that are under the heaven. The heavenly things are themselves in heaven, and the heavenly inhabitants, about whom we do not want to have philosophical discourses at this time. The created works under the heavens are produced from four elements, and their numbers are to be found only in three species, namely: first those that have life and feeling, called *Animalia;* then secondly everything which groweth out of the earth but hath not feeling, and called *Vegetabilia*. Finally everything growing beneath the earth, and called *Mineralia*.

Now these three species of creatures comprise everything created out of the four elements under the moon, and neither more nor fewer of them will be found, and the Most High God hath approved of each of them in its species and kind, so that not one of them can be transformed from one kind or species to another. As if one could make a man or a tree out of a stone, or a monkey out of an herb or lead; or out of lead make some other animal or herb. Such, I say, is impossible by decree of the Great King. If such were permitted in Nature, there would be fewer of their kind, yea, one could be transformed into any of the others. But as all would therefore fall into great confusion, the Lord of all lords hath decreed that such a metamorphosis of species shall not be permitted. And what is more, not only hath He preserved the three species, each true to its kind, but He hath hath given to every creature a seed, to increase and reproduce its own likeness with it, and these forms should not be transformed into any other form, as a man into a horse, or an apple tree into lettuce, or a diamond or other stone into gold. So I say: In Nature such things are not permitted. And as it hath been since

florum genennet: vnser Stein wird auß einem dinge, vnd mit einem dinge gemacht. Ebenmäßig sagt er zu dem Könige von Neapolis: Alles was in unserm Steine ist, ist jhme von nöthen, vnnd er bedarff keines andern, sintemal der Stein einer Natur vnd ein Ding ist. Vnd Rosinus spricht: Versichere dich, das nur ein ding sey, darauß alles gemacht wird, was du begehrest. Vnd Lilium: Du bedarffst nicht mehr alß eines dinges, welches sich in einer jeden Staffel vnsers Wercks in eine andere Natur verkehret. Also spricht auch Geber in seiner Summa: Es ist ein Stein, eine Artzney, welcher wir nichts zusetzen, noch etwas dauon nehmen, sondern allein das vberflüßige dauon scheiden. Vnd Scites in Turba spricht: der Grund dieser Kunst ist etwas einiges, das da stärcken vnd höher denn alle Ding ist, vnnd wird der scharffe Eßig genennet, das da gemacht hatt, daß das Golt ein lauter Geist worden, ohne welchem weder die Weiße, noch die Schwärtze, noch die Räthe bestehen kann: vnnd wenn er mit dem Leibe vermischt wird, wird er mit behalten, vnd wird eines mit jhme, vnnd verkehret jhn in ein Geist, vnd färbet jhn mit Geistlicher vnd vnwandelbahrer Farbe, vnd bekompt von dem gefärbten hinwieder seine leibliche Farbe, welche nicht ausgeleschet werden kann: vnnd wenn du den Leib ohne Eßig würdest zum Fewre setzen, wird er verbrennen.

Es möchte aber jemand auß diesen des Scitis Reden schliessen, das nicht ein, sondern zwey dinge, nemlich der Leib, vnd der Eßig: wie ers nennet: erfordert werden, vnnd müsse mann nothwendig ein Nasses vnd Trockenes zusammen fügen, damit das trockene vom Fewer nicht verbrennet, sondern von dem Nassen für solcher verbrennung beschützet werde. Solchem Argument vnd Schlusse muß ich billich, wenn er nur recht verstanden wird, bey pflichten, vnnd nichts desto weniger obgesetzte Philosophische Sprüche in jhrer würde und Warheit erhalten. Denn einmahl ist gewiß, das nur eine einige Materia ist vnseres gebenedeyeten Steins, so bey den Weysen sehr viel Namen hat, welche die Natur dem Künstler vorbereitet, vnnd zur Materia des grossen Steins einig vnnd allein, vnnd sonsten keines andern dinges in der Welt, verordnet hat.

Solche ist jederman für Augen, die gantze Welt besiehets, begreiffts, liebts, vnd kennets doch nicht: Es ist ein Edel vnnd schlecht, thewer und wolfeil, kostbar vnd gering, vnd wird an allen Enden gefunden. Theophrastus Paracelsus nennets in seinem Buche Tincturam Physicorum, den Roten Löwen, vielen genant, wenigen bekant. Hermes nennets in seinem Buche am 1. Cap. Quecksilber, so in den innersten gemachen verhärtet ist. In der Turba wird sie hin vnnd wieder Æs oder Ertz genennet: in Rosario Philosophorum heissets Saltz. In Summa diese Materia hat so viel Namen, als dinge in der Welt seind. Dannenhero es auch kombt, das sie von den vnwissenden so wenig verstanden wird. Vnwissend nenne ich sie, weil sie ohne vorhergehende Erkäntnuß der Natur vnnd jhrer Eigenschafft zur Kunstschreiten, alß ein Esel zur Krippen gehet, so nicht weiß, wornach ein sein Maul ausstrecket, wie Arnoldus saget.

Darumb spricht Geber in seiner Summa perfectionis wol vnnd recht: Wer bey sich selbst die Anfäng der Natur nicht weiß, der ist noch weit von dieser Kunst abgesondert. Vnd Rosarius sagt: Ich rathe, das sich niemand einlässe, diese Kunst zufinden, es sey dann, das er den Anfang der wahren Natur vnnd jhre Ordnung erkenne: Wenn er dieselbe dann erkant hat, so bedarff er nicht mehr alß eines einigen dinges, vnnd erfordert nicht große vnkosten: Denn es ist nicht mehr alß ein Stein, eine Artzney, ein Gefäß, eine Ordnung vnnd eine Anstellung. So wird doch vnsere Materia also gescheiden durch der Natur hülff vnd des Artisten klüge Handgriffe, das, wie Theophrastus sagt, sie in den weissen Adler transmutiret wird, vber das des Solis Glantz dem Spagyro nicht nachleuchte, oder (wie Basilius Valentinus es nennet) darauß werde ein Geist Weiß wie der Schnee, vnnd noch ein Geist roth alß ein Blut, welche beyde Geister den dritten in sich verborgen haben. Dannenhero der König Aros nicht übel redet, wenn er spricht: Vnsere Artzney wird auß zweyen eines Wesens gemacht, nemlich auß der vereinigung der bestendigen, Geistlichen vnnd Leiblichen, kalten vnnd feuchten, warmen vnnd truckenen Natur, vnd kann auß keinem andern Ding gemacht werden. Vnd Richardus Anglicus sagt: Es ist ein Stein, vnd eine Artzney, welche von den Philosophis REBIS, das ist, auß zweyen dingen, nemlich auß dem Leibe vnnd dem Geiste, Weiß oder Roth: in welchem viel Thoren geirret haben, auf vnderschiedene weiße, außlegende den Vers: Est rebis in dictis rectissima norma figuris. Das ist, zwey dinge: vnnd diese zwey ding seind ein ding, nemlich das Wasser, so dem Leibe zugefügt wird, vnd solchen in ein Geist auflöset, das ist, in ein Mineralisch Wasser, darauß es anfangs gemacht worden, vnnd wird also auß dem Leibe vnnd Geiste ein Mineralisch Wasser, welches Elixir, das ist, ein Fermentum genennet wird. Denn alß dann ist das Wasser vnd der Geist ein Ding, auß welchem die Tinctur und Artzney gemacht wird, so alle Leiber reinigen. Darumb vnsere Artzney auß einem dinge, welches ist das Wasser vnd Geist des Leibes, vollenbracht. Vnd also haben wir, den Philosophis nach, die Natur des Schwessels vnd Quecksilbers vber der Erden, aus welchem Golt vnnd Silber vnter der Erden gemacht worden. Vnnd Bernhardus Graue von Tregne vnd der Marck spricht: vnser Werck wird auß einer Wurtzel vnd zweyen Mercurialischen Substantzen, rohe genommen vnd auß der Minera gezogen, säuber vnd reine, 2c. Vnd Basilius Valentinus sagt im Buche von Natürlichen vnd vbernatürlichen Dingen am 4. Cap. Ich.wil dir in der Warheit vnd durch die Liebe Gottes dieses noch offenbären, das die Wurtzel des Philosophischen Schweffels, der da ein Himmlischer Geist ist, mit der Wurtzel des Geistlichen vber Natürlichen Mercurij, so wol der Anfang des Spiritualischen Saltzes in einem ist, vnnd in einer Materia gefunden wird, darauß der Stein, der für mir gewesen, gemacht wird; vnnd nicht in vielen Dingen: Ob gleich der Mercurius für sich von allen Philosophis, vnnd der Schweffel für sich, neben dem Saltze insonderheit eingezogen wird, das der Mercurius in einem, der Schweffel in einem vnnd das Saltz in einem gefunden wird: So sage ich dir doch, das solches nur auf jhre Vberflüßigkeit zuuerstehen, welches in jedem am meisten gefunden wird, vnd particulariter in vielwege mit Nutzen kann gebrauchet vnd bereitet werden zu der Artzney vnnd verenderung der Metallen: Allein das Vniuersal alß der höchste Schatz der jrrdischen Weißheit, vñ aller drey anfangenden dingen ist ein einiges Ding, vnnd wird in einem einigen Ding zugleich gefunden vnd herauß gezogen, welches alle Metallen zu einem einigen machen kann, vnd ist der wahre Spiritus Mercurij vnd Anima Sulphuris sampt dem Geistlichen Saltze, zugleich vereiniget beschlossen vnter einem Himmel, vnd wonhafftig in einem Leibe, vnd ist der Drache vnd der Adler, Es ist der König vnd der Löwe, Es ist der Geist vnd der Leichnam, so den Leichnam des Goldes färben muß zu einer Medicin, 2c. Also wird nun vnsere zubereitete Materia der Man vnd das Weib genennet.

Item das wirckende vnnd das leidende, wie Zimon in der Turba sagt: wisset, daß das Geheimnuß dieses Wercks auß dem Manne vnd dem Weibe bestehet, das ist, auß dem wirckenden vnnd dem leidenden. Im Bley ist der Man, im Auripigment das Weib. Der Man erfrewet sich seines aufgenommenen Weibes, vnd jhme wird von jhr geholffen: vnd das Weib empfahet von dem Mann einen färbenden Samen, vnd wird von jhme gefärbet. Vnd Diamedes spricht: Füget den Mänlichen Sohn des rothen Knechts zu seinem wolriechenden Weibe, so werden Sie also zusamen gefugt, die Kunst gebehren, zu welcher jhr kein frembdes, noch Puluer, noch einig ander ding einführen sollet, vnd lasset euch an der Empfängnus genügen, so wird euch der rechte Sohn gebohren: O wie vber kostbahr ist die Materia dieses rothen Knechts, ohne welchem keine Ordnung bestehen kann: Andere nennens Argentum viuum oder Mercurium vnd Sulphur oder Fewr. Alß Rogerius Baco in Speculo cap. 3. sagt: Auß Sulphure vnd Mercurio werden alle Metalla gebohren, vnd hänget ihnen nichts an, wird auch nichts jhnen beygefügt, es verändert sie auch nichts, alß was von jhnen herkompt. Darumb müssen wir auch billich Mercurium vnnd Sulphur für die Materiam des Steins nehmen. Vnd Menabadus: Welcher das Quecksilber dem Leibe der Magnesiæ, vnd das Weib dem Manne zufüget, der zihet die verborgene Natur auß, mit welcher die Leiber gefärbet werden.

Vnd Lullius in seinem Codicillo: Die Eigenschaft vnsers Mercurij ist, das es sich von seinem Schweffel Coaguliren lesset. Vnd in der Practica seines Testaments spricht er: Das Quecksilber ist eine vberschwemmende vnd fliessende Feuchte, so vor der verbrennung bewahret. Andere nennens den Leib, Geist vnd Seele. Also spricht Arnoldus in flore florum: Die Philosophi haben gesagt, vnser Stein werde auß dem Leibe, der Seelen vnnd dem Geist zusammen gesetzet, vnnd sie haben die Warheit geredet: Denn das vnuolkommene Corpus haben sie dem Leibe vergliechen, darumb weil es schwach ist: Das Wasser haben sie den Geist geheissen, vnnd das mit warheit, weil es ein Geist ist: das Fermentum aber haben sie mit dem Namen Seele außgesprochen, dieweil es dem vnuolkommenem Leibe das Leben gibt, welches er vorhin nicht hatte, vnd bringet eine bessere Form herfür. Vnd ein wenig vorher sagt er: der Geist wird seinem Leibe nicht zugefügt, alß durch vermittelung der Seelen: Denn die Seele ist das Mittel zwischen dem Leibe vnd der Seelen, welches die beiden zusammen füget. Vnnd Morienus spricht: Die Seele gehet geschwinde in jhren Leib ein: Wenn du sie aber einem andem Leibe zufügen woltest, wirst du vergebens arbeiten. Vnnd Lilium: Die Seele, der Leib vnd der Geist seind beisammen, vnd es ist ein Ding, welches alles in sich hat, vñ deme nichts frembdes zugefüget wird. Was ists aber nötig, das mann alle Namen, damit diese vnsere Materia genennet wird, allhie anziehe vnnd erkläre? Wir wollen vns mit diesen, alß den gebreuchligsten vnnd vnserm fürhaben am nehesten, genügen lassen. Vnd nachdeme wir eigentlich erforschet, woher diese vnsere Materia kommen vnnd gelanget werden muße, wollen wir die Solution, alß das Hauptstücke der gantzen Kunst ein wenig betrachten, vnd durch selbige Betrachtung vnsern Verstand schärffen.

Belangende nun die Consideration vnd Erwegung, was vnsere Materia sey, vnnd wo mann sie bekommen müsse, ist zu wissen, das der Allmächtige Schöpfer, dessen Weißheit so groß alß er selbsten ist, nemlich vnendlich, im Anfange, da nichts alß er selbsten war, zweyerley Dinge geschaffen, nemlich die Himmlischen, vnnd die so vnter dem Himmel seind. Die Himmlischen seind die Himmel selbsten, vnd die Himlischen Einwohner, daruon wir auf dißmal nicht weitleuftig Philosophiren wollen. Die vnder dem Himmel erschaffene Wercke seind, so auß den vier Elementen erschaffen, vnnd werden in deren Zahl nur dreierley Geschlechte gefunden, nemlich erstlich alles was Leben vnd Fühlung hat, vnd werden Animalia geheißen, darnach alles was auß der Erden wächset, vnd nicht fühlet, vnd werden Vegetabilia genennet. Endlichen alles was unter der Erden wächset, vnd heißen Mineralia.

Diese drey Geschlecht der Geschöpffs nun begreiffen in sich alles was vnter dem Monde auß den vier Elementen erschaffen worden, vnd werden deren weder mehr noch weniger gefunden, seind auch von dem höchsten Gott also jedes in seinem Geschlecht vnd seiner Art bestetiget, das keines auß seiner Art vnd Geschlechte in der andern eines kann verkehret werden. Alß wann mann auß einem Steine einen Menschen oder Baum: oder auß einem Kraute einen Affen, oder Bley: oder auß Bley ein ander Thier oder Kraut machen wolte. Solches, sage ich, ist auß verordnung des grossen Königs unmöglich. Denn wenn solches in der Natur zugelassen were, könten deren Geschlechte weniger, ja auch woll alle in eines verkehret werden. Weil aber darauß alles vber einen hauffen fallen würde, so hat der Herr aller Herren eine solche verenderung der Geschlechten nicht gestatten wollen: Vnnd das noch mehr ist, hat er nicht allein diese drey Geschlechte ein jedes in seiner Art erhalten, sondern auch in einem jeglichem Geschöpffe seinen eignen Samen einverleiben wollen, damit ein jedes dadurch vermehret in seiner Gestalt verbleiben, vnnd nicht dieses Gestalt in des andern Gestalt verwandelt werden möchte, Alß eines Menschen in ein Pferd: oder eines Apffel-Baums, in Lattich: oder eines Diamants oder andern Steins in Gold. Solches sage ich, ist in der Natur der vndern Dinge nicht zugelassen. Vnd wie es von Anfang her gewesen, also wirds auch verbleiben biß an den Tag, da der Allmächtige, so im Anfang sagte, es werde, sprechen wird, es vergehe. Das ist aber wol zugelassen, das vnter denen dingen, welche eine gemeine Materiam, Samen vnd composition der Elementen haben, eine veredlung vnnd verbesserung seines Standes, nach dem jhre Materia rein vnnd volkommen ist, verrichtet vnnd vollenbracht werden kann.

Als mann siehet, das ein Mensch viel höhern vnnd verstendigern Gemüts, viel höher empor kommet, alß andere, so solchen scharffen vnd subtilen Verstand nicht haben, welches denn von den reinen vnnd subtilen Geistern, so auß der gerechtfertigten vnd wol temperirten Constitution des Leibes herrühret vnd entspringet. Also siehet man auch, wie ein Pferd vmb ein grosses Edeler ist alß das ander, vnd also bey nahe in allen speciebus animalium. Wie nun solches sich in den Thierischen Geschlechten verhelt, also wirds auch in den Kräutern vnd Bawmen vberflüßig gefunden. In den Bawmen durch Einpflanzung, Einpropfung vnd andere den fleißigen Gärtnern bewuste Mittel: in den Kräutern siehet man Täglich, wie die Kräuter und Blumen einer Art je eines Edler, Schöner, Wolriechender, besser, geschmackter alß das andere ist: Mann sehe nur an die Garoyphyllos oder Näglein vnd die Tulipanen, ich wil von andern dißmal nicht sagen, wie vielerley Geschlechte deren seind, daß mann auch bey nahe sie nicht zehlen kann, welche, durch fleißige wartung vnnd verbesserung, je lenger je edler werden, daß auch so schöne vnd wolriechende Blumen herfür kommen, deren gleichen, wie es scheinet, zuuor niemaln gewachsen.

Was soll ich nu von den Metallen sagen, deren allgemeine Materia das Quecksilber ist, welches von dem Schweffel gekocht vnd coaguliret wird? Wie denn Richardus Anglicus cap. 6. sagt: Aller flüßigen vnd schmeltzhafftigen dingen Geschlechte hat die Natur auß dem Wesen des Quecksilbers vnd seines Schweffels gewürcket: denn die Eigenschafft deß Quecksilbers ist, das es von dem Dünste, gleich alß von der Wärme des Schweffels, so Roth oder Weiß ist, vnd nicht brennet, sich coaguliren lasset. Vnnd Arnoldus spricht in seinem ersten theil am 2. Cap: Von der perfection des Magisterij: das Quecksilber ist der Anfang aller dinge, so sich schmeltzen lassen, dieweil alle Schmeltzhaffte dinge, wenn sie geschmeltzt seind, in dasselbe verkehret werden, vnnd es lesset sich mit jhnen vermischen, weil es von ihrem wesen ist: ob schon selbige corpora in jhrer composition vom Quecksilber vnterschieden seind, solcher massen, nach deme solches reine oder vnreine gewesen, von dem vnreinen Schweffel, so jhme frembd vnd zuwieder ist. Vnd Rosinus sagt zu Saratanta: Die Materia aller Metallen ist das gekochte vnd vnuollkomene Quecksilber, welches der Schweffel im Bauche der Erden kochet: vnd nachdem der Schweffel vnterschieden ist, so werden auch in der Erden vnderschiedene Metalla geboren, die weil sie alle mit ein ander eine einige vnd allgemeine ansangliche Materiam haben, allein, das nur mehr oder weniger Wirckung dazu oder nicht darzu kommet, mit Maßigkeit.

Darumb sehen wir Täglich für Augen, wie die Natur selbsten in stetiger Arbeit sich bemühet, selbige zu reinigen vnd zu mehr volkommenheit zubringen, vnd zu Gold, welches denn der Natur endliche intention ist, zumachen, wie wir dann sehen in allen Metallen, das die Natur in jhnen angefangen zuwircken: sintemal keines so Arm gefunden wird, das nicht ein Korn Silber oder Gold bey sich führet, vnd zwar ist es mit den Metallen also gethan, das die Natur alsobald aus dem Quecksilber, so seinen eignen Sulphur bey sich hat, Gold machen wil vnd kann,

the beginning, so will it be until the day cometh when the Almighty, as He said in the beginning: Let there be, will say: Let it perish. But it is fully permitted that among the things which have a common *Materia*, seed, and *composition* of the elements, a refinement of their conditions may be accomplished and achieved, according to the purity and perfection of their *Materia*.

Thus one seeth a man who hath a much nobler and intelligent mind, because of the pure and subtle spirits which originate in the justified and well-tempered *Constitution* of the bodies, rising higher than others, who do not have such acute and subtle understanding. So, too, one seeth how one horse is much nobler than another, and the same thing is to be observed in nearly all the *species animalium*. And as is the case with animal species, so is it also found amongst the superabounding herbs and trees. In trees through implanting, grafting, and others means well known to the gardener; amongst the herbs and flowers one can observe every day how one is more noble, more beautiful, more fragrant, better, finer tasting than the other; one hath only to look upon the *Caryophylli*, or carnations, and the *Tulips*, and I will not say here how many kinds there are, for no one can begin to count them, which, through constant attention and improvement, can be taller and finer, so that some flowers are to be produced so beautiful and fragrant that one might think there had been none of their kind before.

Now what shall I say about the metals? Their common *Materia* is Mercury, which is boiled and coagulated from Sulphur. As *Richardus Anglicus*, chapter 6, saith: The qualities of all liquid and fusible things were wrought by Nature from the essence of Mercury and its Sulphur; for it is the quality of Mercury that it cannot be burned and coagulated by any fumes or heat of red or white Sulphur. And *Arnoldus*, in the first volume, chapter 2, of his *Perfectum Magisterium et Gaudium*, saith: Mercury is the source of all things which can be dissolved, for as soon as a metal is dissolved it turneth into Mercury and can be mixed with it, since it is of the same essence. There is one difference in the *composition* of the said *Corpora* from Mercury, and that is their degree of purity or impurity, the impurity coming from the impure Sulphur, and which is alien and contrary to it. And *Rosinus* saith to *Saratanta*: The *Materia* of all metals is the boiled and imperfect Mercury, which boiled the Sulphur in the belly of the earth, and after the Sulphur hath been separated there are many metals produced in the earth, all of which have in common a single and universal original *Materia*, the only difference between them being that some are more and some are less affected than the others.

Therefore we see daily with our own eyes how Nature taketh pains in assiduous labor to purify all metals and to bring them to greater perfection, which is to make gold of them, that being Nature's final *intention*. So we then see in all metals what Nature beginneth to produce in them: since there are no metals which do not contain a grain of silver or gold. And what is more, it is so done with the metals that Nature forthwith will and can make gold out of Mercury when it hath its Sulphur in itself, when nothing alien cometh between, and the unclean, stinking, and combustible Sulphur doth not prevent it, as we then see, in many places will be found fine and pure gold without being mixed with other metals.

Because in the tunnels there commonly cometh to the Mercury an alien Sulphur, which contaminateth the former and hindereth it in its perfection, so also will be produced different metals after the manner of such alien Sulphurs. For as *Aristotle*, 4 *Meteorologica*, saith: If the substance of the Mercury is good and the combustible Sulphur impure, so will it turn such into copper. But when the Mercury is calculous, impure, and earthy, and the Sulphur is also impure, then iron will result. It appeareth as if tin had good Mercury, which is pure, but it hath bad and evil Sulphur. But lead hath crude, bad, heavy, glutinous Mercury and a bad, impalatable, and stinking Sulphur, and therefore it is not easy to let it coagulate.

This hindering, combustible, and stinking Sulphur is not the right fire, which doth boil the metals well, but the Mercury hath its own Sulphur, which doth such, and as *Bernhardus Count of Trevisan* saith: Many believe erroneously that in the production of metals a sulphur-like *materia* would be added; but it is evident that in the Mercury, when Nature worketh, is inclosed its own Sulphur: But which doth not prevail in the same, except through warm motion, through which the said Sulphur, and at the same time the other two qualities of the *Mercurii*, are altered. And in this manner are produced in the other different metals of the earth. For in this earth, as *Arnoldus* saith in the first chapter of his *Rosarii*, is a twofold superfluity: One is included in the innermost part of the Mercury, which hath in the beginning mixed itself in its essence: The other, however, is added apart from its nature, and corrupteth it. The one can be separated from it with great difficulty; the other, however, will be taken away by no skill of any artist.

Therefore the great heat of the fire separateth the combustible moisture from the metals, because the Mercury holdeth that and preserveth it from combustion, which is its nature, but expelleth the foreign substance from itself and letteth it be destroyed by fire. But the innermost Sulphur, which boileth the Mercury and bringeth it to its perfection, is pure and impure in the same degree, combustible and non-combustible. The combustible keepeth the Mercury from its perfection, so that it should not become gold, until this Sulphur is finally entirely separated therefrom, and constant sulphur alone remaineth therein. Then the mercury will become gold or silver, according as its sulphur is red or white. But this innermost sulphur is nothing else than a timely *Mercurius* or the ripest and most timely part of the Mercury, therefore Mercury readily receiveth it, but leaveth other and alien sulphur behind. For as *Richardus*, chapter 9, saith: The better and purer the sulphur is, the more it relisheth the good and pure Mercury and attacheth itself to it. So that one

is more and more closely associated with the other, until more and more perfect metals are produced by this union.

But such sulphur is not to be found above the earth, as saith *Avicenna*, except in those two bodies, namely of gold and silver, and much more mature in the gold. *Richardus*, chapter 12, saith: The red sulphur is in the gold through greater maturing, but the white is in the silver through lesser maturing.

Now if all this be so, namely: that there is a single universal *Materia* in all metals, which through its power with innate sulphur, either soon or otherwise, according as it separateth itself through length of time in more steady boiling from the alien and ineffective sulphur of the other metals, becometh gold, which is the goal of the metals, and the perfect purpose of Nature. Then we must indeed admit and say that Nature also seeketh and desireth to have, in this species as in the animal and vegetable kingdoms, its improvement and perfection through purification and subtle refinement of the *subjecti* in its own nature.

This now, beloved seeker of the things in Nature, would I explain somewhat more in detail, that thou mayest grasp it much more thoroughly and that thou mayest understand the *Materiam* of our great stone. For if thou wouldest undertake to make for thyself such a stone as ours out of some animal substance, thou wouldst be thwarted, for they both belong to two different species, since the stone is mineral, but the *Materia* is animal. And as *Richardus*, chapter 1, saith: One cannot bring out of anything something that is not in it. Therefore, because every species seeketh in its own species its power of increase, and every *genus* or kind seeketh it in its own kind, and every nature seeketh it in its own natural nature, and beareth fruit according to its natural characteristic, and no contrary nature: therefore every collectivity agreeth with its own seed. And *Basilius Valentinus* saith: Beware, my friend, and understand that thou shouldest not seek to make use of any animal soul. Like thine, their flesh and blood, as it hath been granted and given by the Creator to the animals, belongeth to the animals, therefore God hath at the same time ordained that an animal shall be made out of it.

Therefore they are to be greatly wondered at who, holding themselves to be great artists, look for their *Materiam Lapidis* in *Menstruis muliebribus*, in *Spermate*, in eggs, hair, urine, and in many other things, and fill many books with such recipes, and also convince, deceive, and mislead other foolish folk with such worthless things.

And greatly astonished at the folly of such people is *Rogerius Baccho*, in *Speculi*, chapter 3, since he saith: One should greatly marvel that a thoughtful man should base his *intention* upon animal and vegetable things, which are so very widely separated, when one findeth *Minaralia* which are much closer.

It is by no means to be credited that any *Philosophus* should have placed the art in such above-mentioned widely separated things, except it be knowingly for the sake of allegory. As *Basilius Valentinus* saith: Our stone doth not come forth from things that are combustible. For our stone and its *Materia* are safe from all danger of fire. Therefore thou mayest well abstain from searching in animal things, since Nature hath not permitted it to be found in such. But if anyone would look for our stone in vegetable things, as in trees, herbs, or flowers, he will err for the above-mentioned reasons, no less than he who would make a great rock out of an animal. For all herbs and trees, together with all that cometh out of them, is combustible, and nothing remaineth of them except a mere salt with its earth, which it hath received from Nature in the composition. And let no one be mislead because some pretend to be able to make the Philosopher's Stone out of wine or parts thereof. For while they do not understand rightly the writings of *Raymundus Lullius*, they only prove with all their great knowledge that they do not understand anything, and mislead both themselves and others. Of course it is also true that out of these things very splendid and excellent *Menstrua* could be prepared, without which in neither medicine nor in alchemy could anything be undertaken or accomplished. But that the Philosopher's Stone could be made therefrom, or its seed be extracted, was not granted to Nature by the Creator, but which, as mentioned above, is ordered to remain true to its kind.

Therefore, everyone who hath understanding, can easily deduct and conclude that our stone, which, as said, is incombustible, must be sought and found in an incombustible *Materia*, which is found nowhere except in the mineral kingdom, since animal and vegetable things are all combustible.

Because our previously mentioned Philosopher's Stone is a mineral product, one can reasonably ask out of how many kinds of minerals may the stone ultimately be made; for there are as many species as stones, among them divers kinds of substances and earths will have been understood, salts, semi-minerals, and metals.

To this I answer there is reason to believe that it is impossible to make the stone out of any of these, for the reason that there is in all of them no liquid or fusible Mercury, and that they cannot be melted or dissolved into their first *Materiam* on account of the Sulphur in them, which is much too crude and has too great an abundance of Judaic qualities. No intelligent seeker of the natural secrets will seek the *Materiam* of the Philosopher's Stone in salts, alums, and materials of their sort. For he will find in them nothing else than a sharp corroding and destroying spirit, but not the kind of *Mercurium* or *Sulphur* that the *Philosophi* want and need.

But from such things can no intermediate mineral, such as *Magnesia*, *Marcasite*, *Antimonium*, etc., be made. Much less will a metal come from them. How then could one obtain from them the *Materiam* of the Philosopher's Stone, which is the end and perfection of all metals and mineral things? Besides, these have absolutely nothing in common nor any affinity with any metals — nay, rather, they burn, break, and corrupt them; how then could they serve to perfect them? Hear now what *Richardus*

wenn nichts frembdes darzwischen kommet, vnd der vnreine stinckende vnnd verbrennliche Schweffel solches nicht verhindert, wie wir dann sehen, das an vielen Orten rein vnnd fein Gold, ohne vermischung anderer Metallen, gefunden wird.

Weil aber in den Erdgängen zu dem Queckfilber gemeiniglich ein frembder Schweffel kommet, vnd daßselbige verunreiniget, vnd an seiner vollkommenheit verhindert, so werden auch nach Art solches fremden Schweffels vnderschiedene Metalla gebohren. Wie denn Aristoteles 4. Meteor. sagt: Wenn das Wesen des Queckfilbers gut ist, vnnd der verbrennliche Schweffel vnreine, so verwandelt er solches in Kupffer. Wenn das Queckfilber aber steinig, vnrein vnd irrdisch sein wird, vnd der Schweffel auch onreine ist, wird Eysen darauß. Es scheinet aber, alß hette das Zinn gut Queckfilber, so da reine ist, aber einen bösen vnd vbel vermischten Schweffel. Das Bley aber hat ein grobes, böses, wichtiges vnd leimhafftes Queckfilber, vnd ein bösen, vnschmackhafften vnnd stinckenden Schweffel, darumb lest sichs nicht gerne Coaguliren.

Dieser verhinderliche, verbrennliche vnd stinckende Schweffel aber ist nicht das rechte Fewer, welches die Metallen garkochet, sondern es hat das Queckfilber seinen eigenen Schweffel, welcher solches verrichtet, wie Bernhardus Graue von Trygene sagt: Viel vermeinen vergeblichen, es komme in der Gebehrung der Metallen eine Schweffeliche Materia darzu: aber es ist hin gegen offenbahr, das in dem Queckfilber, wenn die Natur wircket, sein eigner Schweffel ein geschlossen ist: Welcher aber in demselben nicht herrschet, alß nur durch die warme Bewegung, durch welche gesagter Schweffel, vnnd zugleich des Mercurij andere beyde Eigenschafften, verendert verden: Vnnd werden auf diese Weise in den andern der Erden vnterschiedenen Metallen geboren. Denn in den Metallen, wie Arnoldus im 1. Cap. seines Rosarij sagt, ist eine zweyfache vberflüßigkeit: Eine zwar stecket in dem innersten wesen des Queckfilbers selbsten verschlossen, so im Anfang dessen wesens sich darein vermischet hat: Die andere aber, so außerhalb seiner Natur hinzukommet, vnd solches verderbet. Vnd diese zwar kann mit grosser Mühe dauon gescheiden werden, jene aber wird mit keines Künstlers scharffsinnigkeit hinweg genommen.

Darumb scheidet die grosse Hitze des Fewrs die verbrennliche feuchtigkeit von den Metallen ab, weil das Queckfilber das jenige helt, vnnd vor der verbrennung beschützet, welches seiner Natur ist, das frembde aber von sich stösset vnd verbrennen lesset. Der jnnerliche Schweffel aber, so daß Queckfilber kochet, vnnd zur volkommenheit zeitiget, ist ebenmeßig reine vnnd vnreine, verbrennlich vnnd vnuerbrennlich: Der verbrennliche verhindert das Queckfilber an seiner volkommenheit, das es nicht zu Golde werden kann, biß solcher dauon endlich gar gescheiden, vnnd der reine vnuerbrennliche vnnd bestendige Schweffel allein dabey bleibet, alß dann wird Gold oder Silber darauß, nachdeme solcher Schweffel weiß oder roth ist. Dieser innerliche Schwefel aber ist anders nicht alß ein zeitiger Mercurius oder der reiffeste vnnd zeitigste Theil des Queckfilbers, darumb nimmt ihn das Queckfilber auch so gerne an, andern vnd frembden Schwefel aber lest es liegen: Wie dann Richardus cap. 9. sagt: Je schlechter vnd reiner der Schwefel ist, je mehr frewet er sich des schlechten vnd reinen Queckfilbers, vnnd henget demselben an, das eines mit dem andern stärcker verknüpffet, vnd also volkommenere Metallen darauß gebohren werden.

Solcher Schweffel aber wird vber der Erden nicht gefunden, wie Auicenna spricht, alß nur was in den beyden Cörpern, nemlich deß Goldes vnd Silbers gefunden wird, vnd zwar im Golde viel zeitiger. Deñ, wie Richardus cap. 12. spricht: Es ist der rote Schweffel im Golde durch grössere zeitigung, der weisse aber im Silber durch geringere zeitigung.

Wann dann diesem allen also, das nemlich eine einige vnnd allgemeine Materia der Metallen ist, welche durch Krafft seines mit angebornen Schwefels entweder so balde, oder aber, nach dem es den frembden vndüchtigen Schwefel der andern Metallen, durch die länge der Zeit, in steter Kochung von sich gescheiden, zu Golde wird, welches das Ende der Metallen, vnd volkommene intention der Natur ist: so müssen wir ja bekennen vnnd sagen, daß die Natur auch in diesem Geschlechte nach Reinigkeit vnd Subtiligkeit des subjecti, gleich wie in dem Vegetabilischen vnnd Animalischen Reichen jhre verbesserung vnnd volkommenheit in jhrer selbst eigenen Natur suchet vnd haben wil.

Dieses habe ich nun, lieber Nachforscher der Natürlichen Dingen, ein wenig vmbständlicher andeuten wollen, damit du so viel gründlicher verstehen vnd begreiffen mögest, wannenhero du die Materiam vnsers grossen Steins langen vnnd hernehmen müssest. Denn wenn du solchen vnsern Stein auß einer Animalischen Materien zumachen dich vnderstehen wolltest: ligt dir im Wege, das die beyde in zwey vnterschiedliche Geschlecht gehören: Sintemal der Stein Mineralisch, die Materia aber Animalisch ist. Vnd aber auß keinem Dinge: Wie Richardus cap. 1. sagt: etwas außgezogen werden kann, das darinnen nicht ist. Derowegen weil eine jede Species in seiner Specie vnd ein jedes Genus oder Geschlechte in seinem Geschlechte, vnd eine jede Natur in seiner Natur natürlichen jhrer Krafft vermehrung suchet, vnd nach jhrer Natur Eigenschafft Frucht bringet, vnd in keiner andern Natur, so jhr zuwieder: Demnach ein jedes gesametes mit seinem Samen vberstimmet. Vnnd Basilius Valentinus spricht: Nimb ab vñ verstehe, mein Freund, das du dir keine Animalische Seele hierzu zusuchen erwehlen sollest. Dein Fleisch vnd Blut, wie das vom Schöpffer den Thieren vergönnet vnnd gegeben, gehöret auch den Thieren zu, dauon sie Gott zusammen gebawet, das ein Thier draus worden.

Darumb ist sich zuuerwundern vber die jenige, so sich für grosse Künstler halten, und in Menstruis muliebribus, in Spermate, in Eyern, in Harren, im Harne vnnd andern Dingen jhre Materiam Lapidis suchen, vnd so viel Bücher mit solgen Recepten erfüllen, auch andere vnuerstendigere mit solchen nichtswürdigen Dingen einnehmen, bethören vnd verführen.

Vnnd verwundert sich der Rogerius Baccho in Speculi ca. 3. vber solcher Leute Thorheit, da er spricht: Darumb ist zuuerwundern, das ein fürsichtiger Man seine intention auf die animalischen vnd Vegetabilischen Dinge gründet, welche doch weit abgesondert seind, so man doch Mineralia findet, welche viel näher seind.

Es ist auch keineswegs zuglauben, das einiger Philosophus die Kunst in obgemelte weit abgesonderte Dinge gesetzet habe, es sey dann Gleichnus weise. So wechset auch vnser Stein: wie Basilius Valentinus sagt: nicht auß den Dingen, so verbrennlich seind. Denn vnser Stein vnnd sein Materia ist sicher für aller Fewers gefahr. Darumb magst du wol vnterlassen in animalischen Dingen zusuchen, dieweil der Natur nicht zugelassen jhn in solchen zufinden. Wolte aber jemand in Vegetabilischen sachen, alß in Baumen, Kreutern oder Blümen vnsern Stein suchen, wird derselbe, auß obgesetzten vrsachen nicht weniger jrren, als der auß einem Thiere ein grossen Steinfelsen machen wollen. Denn alle Kreuter vnd Bäwme, sampt allem deme, so von jhnen kompt, ist verbrennlich, vnnd bleibet nichts dahinden, alß ein blosses Saltz mit seiner Erden, welches es in der composition von der Natur empfangen. Vnd es lasse sich niemand verführen, das etzliche **auß Weitzen den Philosophischen Stein zumachen fürgeben:** vielweniger höre diejenigen, so auß dem Weine, vnd dessen Stücken, diesen Stein zu machen sich vnterstehen. Denn weil sie des Raymundi Lulij Schrifften nicht recht verstehen, beweisen sie mit jhrem großen Verstande, das sie nichts verstehen, vnd beides sich vnd auch andere verführen. Zwar ist es nicht ohne, das hierauß sehr herrliche vnd fürtreffliche Menstrua, ohne welche weder in der Artzney noch Alchmey etwas fürnehmes verrichtet werden kann, bereitet vnnd zugerichtet werden. Daß aber der Stein der weisen darauß gemacht, oder dessen Samen darauß gezogen werden könte, ist der Natur solches von dem Schöpfer aller dinge nicht zugelassen, sondern, wie oben vermeldet, in jhrer Art zubleiben befehlicht.

Derowegen dann nun ein jeder Verstendiger leichtlich abnehmen vnd schliessen muß, daß, weil vnser Stein, wie gesagt, vnverbrennlich ist: die Animalischen vnnd Vegetabilischen dinge aber alle verbrennlich seind, das auß einer vnuerbrennlichen Materia, welche anders nicht, alß in dem Mineralischen Reiche gefunden wird, solcher gesucht vnd gemacht werden muß.

Weil dann gemelter vnser Philosophischer Stein ein Mineralisch Werck ist, so fragt mann billich, weil deren vielerley Geschlechte seindt als Steine, darunter auch allerhand Materien vnnd Erden verstanden werden, Saltze, Mittel Mineralia vnd Metallen, auß welchen denn endlichen solcher gemacht werden müsse?

Darauf antworte ich, das auß den Steinen solchen zumachen nicht möglich, vrsache ist, weil in denselben kein flüßiger vnnd schmeltzlicher Mercurius ist, oder das die nicht können geschmeltzet, außgelöset wñ in jhre erste Materiam, wegen jhres zu viel groben Schwefels vnnd vberflüßigkeit der jrdischen Eigenschafft gebracht werden. So wird auch kein kluger Nachforscher der Natürlichen Geheimnussen solche Materiam des Philosophischen Steins in Saltzen, Alaunen vnd dergleichen Dingen suchen. Denn hierein wird er anders nichts, alß ein scharffen Corrosiuischen vnnd verstörenden Geist, aber gar keinen Mercurium vnnd Sulphur finden, wie solchen die Philosophi erfordern, vnnd haben wollen.

Vber daß kann auß solchen Dingen kein mittel Mineral, alß eine Magnesia, Marcasita, Antimoniam, &c. Viel weniger ein Metall werden: wie solte denn die Materia des Philosophischen Steins darauß genommen werden können, so doch das Ende vnd Vollkommenheit aller Metallen vnd Mineralischen dinge ist? Zu dem haben solche mit den Metallen auch gantz vnd gar keine Gemeinschaft vnnd Freundschaft, sondern sie verbrennen, zerbrechen vnnd verderben dieselben, wie können sie dann zu dero verbesserung dienen? Höre nur, waß Richardus Anglicus cap. 10. hieruon sagt: Die geringe Mineralia können keine Metalla werden, Erstlich, weil sie von der ersten Materia der Metallen, welche der Mercurius ist, nicht gebohren werden.

Weil aber jhre Gebehrung mit der Gebehrung des Mercurij zum Ersten vnterscheiden ist, in der Form vnd Materia vnnd zusammen setzung, so können auch keine Metalla auß jhnen werden, sintemal eines einigen Dinges eine einige erste Materia vnd Same ist, darauß solches gebohren wird. Was aber gesagt ist, erscheinet klar darauß, weil die geringere Mineralia nicht auß dem Mercurio gebohren worden, wie dann auß Aristotele vnd Auicenna am Tage ist. Darumb wenn Metalla auß jhnen werden solten, so musten sie erstlich in die erste Materiam gebracht werden.

Weil aber solches durch keinerley Kunst geschehen kann, so können sie auch keine Metallen, vnnd schließlich keine Materia des Steins sein. Darnach weil die mindern Mineralia der Anfang der Kunst durch Kunst nicht sein können, welcher Mercurius ist, so können sie auch zum Mittel vnd Ende, welche die Metallen vnd die Tinctur seind, nicht kommen: sondern weil die mindern Mineralia den Metallen in der Natur frembd, ob sie schon an einiger Mineralischen krafft Theil haben, so seind doch schwächerer Tugend, vnd verbrennlich. Darumb frewet sich auch die Metallische Natur jhr gar nicht, sondern stösset sie von sich, vnnd behelt nur bey sich, was jhrer Natur ist. Darumb seind die Thoren, welche so viel vnd so mancherley Arbeiten vnnd Betriegereien an Tag geben, die Leute zubetriegen, nemlich vngereimte dinge, welche weder die Natur bey sich haben, noch von sich geben können.

Es lasse sich auch keiner die Schrifften der Philosophen verführen, wenn sie vnter zeiten von Saltzen reden: alß wenn in Allegoriis Sapientum gesagt wird: Wer ohne Saltz arbeitet, der wird die Todten Leichnam nicht aufferwecken. Vnd im Buche Soliloquij stehet: Wer ohne Saltz arbeitet, der schiesset mit dem Bogen ohne Senne: Sindemal dieselben viel eine andere Meinung, alß von den Mineralischen Saltzen, haben. Wie dann klar bey dem Rosario Philosophorum zusehen ist, wenn er spricht: das Saltz der Metallen ist der Philosophische Stein. Denn vnser Stein ist ein Coagulirt Wasser, im Golde oder Silber, vnd widerstehet dem Fewr, vnd wird in seinem Wasser aufgelöset, dauon es in seiner Art gemacht worden. Das aber der Philosophen Coagulirte Wasser nicht Mineralisch Wasser, sondern jhr Mercurius sey, lehret Geber im Buche von dem Ofen am 19. Cap: da er sagt: Befleißige dich Sonn vnd Mondt jhr trucken Wasser aufzulösen, welches der gemeine Man Mercurium nennet. Die Philosophi nennen auch jhre reden bißweilen Saltz, wie in Clangore Buccinæ zusehen, wo gesagt wird: Mercke das die Corpora Alaun vnnd Saltze seind, welche auß vnsern Cörpern herfliessen. Bißweilen nennen sie auch die Medicin selbsten Saltz, wie den in der Scala stehet: das Werck deß andern Wassers ist, das es die Erde erhöhet in jhr wunderbarlich Saltz, allein durch seine anziehende Krafft. Vnnd Arnoldus spricht im Buche von erhaltung der Jugend: Aber das jenige, so seines gleichen: in erhaltung der Jugend: nicht hat, ist das Saltz auß der Minera. Die weisen haben solches, wenn es bereitet worden, der natürlichen wärme eines gesunden Jünglings vergliechen, vnd haben auch wegen dieses Gleichnüsses den Stein mit eines Thiers Namen genennet, andere Mineralischen Chifir, vnd etliche habens eine stets werende Artzney geheißen vnd Aquam Vitæ. Die gantzewissenschafft seiner Bereitung ist, das es in ein reines vnd trincklich Wasser reduciret werde, mit denen dingen, so mit jhm eben dieselbe Eigenschafft haben.

Hierauß ist nun klar zusehen, das weder nach lehre der Philosophen, noch der Natur selbsten Eigenschafft, die Materia des Steins auß den mindern Mineralien genommen werden könne.

Nun wollen wir vns ein wenig vmbsehen, ob vnsers Grossen Steins Materia auß den mitlern Mineralien, alß Marcasiten, Antimonio, Magnesia vnnd andern gemacht werden könne, sonderlich weil die Philosophi deren zum mehren mahle gedencken. Alß wenn Senior spricht: Wenn im Auripigment nicht die Tugend den Mercurium zu Coaguliren were, so köme vnser Meisterschaft nimmer zu Ende. Vnd Thomas de Aquino: Nim vnsern Antimonium oder die geängelte schwartze Erde ꝛc. vnd Parmenides in der Turba: nemet Queckfilber, vñ Coaguliret solches in dem Leibe der Magnesiæ, oder in dem Schwefel, der nit verbrennet.

So ist doch zuwissen, das die Philosophi solche Reden nicht dero Meinung führen, alß wolten sie hiermit andeuten, das auß solchen Sachen vnser grosse Stein gemacht werden könne, sondern sie reden solches nur Gleichnus weiße. Denn der Philosophen Auripigment vnnd Magnesia ist viel ein ander Ding, alß die Gemeinen, nemlich die Materia selbsten, welche sie sonsten das Agens, den Löwen, den König, den Sulphur, vnd mit viel mehr Namen nennen: vnd wird solche zwar Auripigment geheißen, weil sie die Krafft hat das Gold in vberflüßige Farbe, vnd heisset Magnesia wegen jhrer grossen Tugend vnd herligkeit, so darauß entspringet vnd herfliesset.

Daß aber Thomas de Aquino sie Antimonium nennet, thuter solches wegen der schwartzen schimmernden Farbe, darin sie nach der Auflösung kommet. Denn wenn vnser Stein schwartz worden, haben jhn die Philosophi allen schwartzen dingen verglichen.

Es möchte mir aber jemand einreden vnd sagen, das dieser mittel Mineralien etliche nicht allein vom Mercurio vnd Sulphure gebohren, sondern auch zu Metallen werden: Alß mann siehet, das die Magnesia oder Wißmuth mit dem Bley vnd Zinn in flüsche sich vermischet.

Anglicus, chapter 10, saith hereon: The lesser *Mineralia* cannot change into any metals, in the first place because they are not born of the first *Materia* of all metals, which is *Mercurius*.

But since their origin differs so greatly from the origin of *Mercurii*, in form and *materia* and at the same time in setting, no metals can come forth from them, since there has to be a first substance and seed of a like thing, from which such will be produced. But what is said appeareth clearly therefrom, that the lesser *Mineralia* are not produced from *Mercurio*, as is clear, also, according to *Aristotle* and *Avicenna*. Therefore if they should be transformed into *Metalla*, they would first have to be brought into their first *Materiam*.

But since this cannot be done through any art whatsoever, so there can never be any metals and no final *Materia* of its stone. Wherefore, since the lesser *Mineralia* cannot be in the beginning through the art, which is *Mercurius*, they cannot be in the middle and the end of it, which are the metals and the *Tincture*. But the lesser *Mineralia* are alien to the metals in their nature, and although to some extent they have a part in the mineral power, they are the lesser quality thereof and are combustible. Therefore the metallic nature hath no pleasure in them, but repelleth them and keepeth only what is of its own nature. Wherefore they are fools who bring forth so many and such different deceits, to deceive the people, and they do preposterous things, who neither have Nature with them, nor can they make themselves understood.

And let no one be deceived by the writings of the Philosophers if at times they speak about salts, as when in *Allegoriis Sapientum* it was said: Whosoever laboreth without salts cannot resuscitate dead bodies. And in the book *Soliloquii* it is written: Whoever worketh without salts shooteth with a bow without a string. But they have quite another meaning than mineral salts. As is to be seen clearly in the *Rosario Philosophorum*, where it is said: The salt of the metals is the Philosopher's Stone. For our stone is a coagulated water, in gold or silver, and resisteth the fire, and can be dissolved only in its own water. Geber, in his book about the furnace, chapter 19, teaches that the coagulated water of the philosophers is not mineral water, but their *Mercurius*, saying: Apply thyself to dissolving the dry water of the sun and the moon, which the common man calleth *Mercurium*. The *Philosophi* in their parlance call it salt at times, as is to be seen in *Clangore Buccinae*, where it is said: Note that the *Corpora* is alum and salts, which floweth out of our bodies. Also at times they call the medicine itself salt, as is written in the *Scala*: It is the work of the other water, that it augments the earth in its wondrous salts, through its attracting power alone. And *Arnoldus* saith in his book about the preservation of youth: But that which hath not its equal in preserving youth is the salt out of the *Minera*. The Wise compared it, when it was prepared, to the natural warmth of a healthy youth, and also because of this they have called the stone by the name of an animal; others have called it a mineral *Chifir*, and some have called it an everlasting medicine and *Aquam Vitae*. The entire science of its preparation is that it should be reduced to a pure and drinkable water, with those things which have much the same qualities as it doth.

Hence it is now easy to see that, according to the teaching of the philosophers and also the property of Nature itself, the *Materia* of the stone cannot be taken from the lesser minerals.

Now let us look around a little and see whether the *Materiam* of our great stone can be made out of the semi-minerals, such as *Marcasite*, *Antimony*, *Magnesia*, and others, especially since the *Philosophi* mention this on several occasions. As when *Senior* saith: If there were not in our *Auripigment* the quality of coagulating the *Mercurium*, our mastery would never reach the goal. And *Thomas Aquinas*: Take our *Antimonium* or the captured black earth, etc., and *Parmenides* in the *Turba*: Take Mercury and coagulate it in the body of the *Magnesiae*, or in Sulphur, which is not combustible.

But here, nevertheless, it is to be understood that the *Philosophi* did not so speak to indicate that our great stone could be made out of such things, but they spoke in this manner only by way of allegory. For the philosophical *Auripigment* and *Magnesia* are quite another thing from those of the common people, namely, the *Materia* itself, which they call *Agens*, the Lion, the King, the Sulphur, and many more names; and, what is more, it will be called *Auripigment* because it hath the power of gold in superfluous color, and it is called *Magnesia* because of its great virtue and glory, which emanateth from it.

But when *Thomas Aquinas* calleth it *Antinomium*, he doth so because of its black and glittering color, which it taketh on after its dissolving. For when our stone became black, it was compared to all black things by the *Philosophi*.

Here some one might talk to us and say: That of these semi-minerals some were produced not only from *Mercury* and *Sulphur*, but also became metals: as one sees Magnesia or Bismuth succeed in being mixed with lead or tin.

Likewise, not only doth the *Antimonium* mix with metals, but it becometh a natural lead. So also have people of low and high degree occasionally seen it become gold. Could one not obtain from it the *Materia* of the stone, since it was produced from *Mercury* and *Sulphur*, into which it can be reduced again through art, and is of one origin with all metals? To this I answer: First, one hast to distinguish between the semi-minerals, namely, between those which have by themselves a *Mercurium* and those which have it not. One hast to pay close attention to those which have *Mercury*, because, through our medicine, their *Mercury* can be changed into gold and silver, and therefore, as I claim, they have to be regarded as half metals, *i.e.*, as minerals disposed to turn to metals. The others which have no *Mercury* are not to be considered at all. But on account of the bad and combustible Sulphur which is found in them, and which is the reason that the *Antinomium* is opposed to all metals and burneth them all except the gold, which because of its constancy it hath to leave in peace, so here one cannot come so far, one cannot select them for the *Materiam* of our stone, which must be pure and delicate and incombustible Sulphur. But on close examination and testing, one can easily see that they are impure and thoroughly infected with their Sulphur.

Zinc appeareth, from its brightness, weight, outer looks, and feeling like pure *Mercurium*, but as soon as it cometh into fire it dissolveth into smoke, vanishing like a pale yellow Sulphur. The *Marcasites* cannot be forced to melt at all because of their great earthy impurity. The *Antimonium*, however, can be cleared of its over-great blackness through skilled manipulations and be brought into a white and beautiful *Regulum*, and it appeareth to all as if something great could be made out of it, therefore many people, who otherwise deem themselves to be very clever, believe that the Philosopher's Stone can be made out of it. But however much one may clear the *Antinomium* from its blackness, there still remaineth in it crude and inflexible Sulphur which appeareth when it doth not let itself be expanded under the hammer and become malleable, which is the quality of every metal, by which, together with other qualities, it is known to be a metal.

In addition to that, it hath a crude and impure *Mercurium*; I do not wish to say now that it retaineth within itself at any time a dissolving Sulphur. And I hope that they do not mind that I cannot agree with their point of view who call themselves great *Philosophi* and want to convince themselves and others in many books and widely circulated writings, that at just this point is the *Scrupel* of their *Universal*. For one seeketh foolishly for something in a thing where it is not. As *Arnoldus* saith: Because it is established in the practice of the *Turba* that the Philosopher's Stone is of a pure *Materia*. So also saith *Lullius* in his last Testament: Our *Tincture* is only a pure fire. And in the *Vade Mecum* he saith: It is the subtle Spirit alone which tingeth and thus cleareth the *Corpora* from their leprosy; but the *Minerals*, however, which are crude and impure like the other can in no way be cleansed in their innermost except by means of our *Tincture*; and therefore one can not obtain from them the *Materiam* of our stone. For *Richardus*, chapter 1, saith: Nothing can be taken, out of a thing which is not therein.

What shall one say about the *Vitriol*? Through its wonderful qualities it bringeth many into error, especially since a part of it can be changed into copper, and it can also change iron into copper. Let it be known that *Vitriol* is nothing else than a beginning and *Materia* of copper. In the veins of the earth fire-damp and vaporous *Mercurius* are found in a place where in great quantity hath been found a bitter and astringent venereal *Sulphur* which, as soon as it was mixed therewith, hath coagulated and tried to become a metal. But because Nature wanted to separate the pure from the impure, the combustible from the incombustible, the abundance and manifoldness of the abovementioned Sulphur have exceeded the *quantitas* thus far. So also in such separation the *Mercurius* had to separate itself and had to let itself be concealed in the vitriolic green.

This can be seen clearly: that one addeth a common Sulphur to the copper is the cause of its destruction and calcineth it; for art accomplisheth with strong fires in a short time what Nature must perform with slow-burning fire. Then the copper will be entirely consumed, and bringeth this into the vitriolic order through general manipulations: and according as there is much or little Sulphur, the *Vitriol* will be richer or poorer in colors. Therefore that is the reason that some *Vitriol* hath more copper qualities than the other: one findeth much copper in the cyprian Vitriol, less in others.

It is to be well noted that the sour *Spiritus* in the *Vitriol* cometh from the Sulphur, especially since it can be found likewise and extracted from common Sulphur. The sulphur-like smell can be well observed in the *Spiritu Vitrioli*, and the *Spiritus Sulphuris* can change the *Sulphur Martis* into a Vitriol, like the *Spiritus Vitrioli*. But because in iron there is also a crude Sulphur, the corrosiveness of the Vitriol eateth such away, seeketh its *Mercurium* which is not much unlike its own, and through union of it with its Sulphur, becometh a good, malleable copper.

But because there is in Vitriol such a crude, superfluous Sulphur, and because there is but very little Mercury in it, and which has not yet arrived at its purification, we shall not get more out of it than out of the other. And we have to heed the teaching of *Alphidius* who saith: My son, beware, separate thyself from the dead bodies and stones; therein is no way to walk, since their life is not being augmented but diminished, as are the Salts, *Auripigmenta*, arsenic, magnesia, marcasite, and the like.

And *Arnoldus*, in *Flore florum*, saith: The cause of their error is that the four spirits, namely, *Auripigment*, *Salmiac*, *Mercurius*, and *Sulphur*, are not the seed of either the perfect or the imperfect metals, with the exception of *Mercury* and *Sulphur*, which coagulateth the *Mercurium*.

Now some one might conclude from these last words of *Arnoldus*, that common Sulphur and Mercury are the *Materia* of our stone, because such are counted among the four spirits, and because the Sulphur coagulateth the Mercury. Hereupon I must ask with *Richardo*, chapter 11: Whether every Sulphur will coagulate Mercury? To this I answer: No! For every common Sulphur, as the *Philosophi* say, is opposed to the metals. It is to be known that Sulphur was produced from the fat of the earth in the depths of the earth, and hath been made solid by moderate boiling, and then it is called Sulphur.

Item, das Antimonium vermischet sich nicht allein mit den Metallen, sondern es wird auch natürlich Bley darauß: So haben auch hohen vnnd niederen Standts Personen zu mehren mahlen gesehen, das Gold darauß worden sey. Weil nun selbige von Sulphure vnd Mercurio, in welche sie auch durch Kunst wieder reduciret werden können: gebohren, vnnd mit den Metallen einen Vrsprung haben, so könne auch darauß die Materia des Steins genommen werden? Deme gebe ich zur antwort, erstlich, das billich vnter diesen mittel Mineralien ein Vnterscheid gehalten werden solle: nemlich vnter denen, so einen Mercurium bey sich führen, vnd dann denen, so denselben nicht haben. Die ersten, so nemlich einen Mercurium haben, seind billich in acht zu haben, weil auch deren Mercurius durch vnsere Medicin in Gold vnnd Silber verwandelt werden kan, vnnd derowegen, wie ich dafür halte, billich halbe Metallen, so nemlich die Disposition Metallen zu werden, haben, geachtet werden sollen; die Andern aber, so keinen Mercurium haben, nichts zu achten. Weil aber wegen des bösen vnnd verbrennlichen Schwefels, so bey ihnen gefunden wird, vnnd vrsach ist, das der Antimonium aller Metallen seind ist, vnd sie verbrennet, ohne daß Gold, welches er seiner Beständigkeit halber wol zufrieden lassen muß, dieselben so weit nicht kommen können, kan man sie auch für die Materiam vnsers Steins nicht erwehlen, welche ein reiner vollkommener Mercurius, vnd ein reiner zarter vnd vnverbrennlicher Schwefel sein muß. Daß aber sie gar vnreine vnd von ihrem Schwefel gantz rein seyn, siehet mann leichtlich, wann mann sie in ihre Schule führet vnd sie examiniret, was sie gelernet haben.

Denn man siehet an den Zincken, den mann für eitelen Mercurium, seinem Glantz vnd Gewichte nach, auß dem eusserlichen Ansehen vnd Begreiffen halten solte, so balde er ins Fewer kommet, gehet er in Rauche, wie ein bleichgelber Schwefel schnelle dauon. Die Marcasiten seind wegen ihrer grossen jrrdischen Vnreinigkeit mit keinem schmeltzen zu zwingen. Das Antimonium aber, so sich durch kluge Handgriffe von seiner vbergrossen Schwärtze reinigen, vnd in einen schönen weissen vnd schönen Regulum bringen lässet, hat wol für allen das anschen, alß ob darauß etwas sonderliches zu machen were, in massen dann viel, so sich sonsten gar klug achten, dero Meinung seind, das der Philosophische Stein darauß gemacht werden müsse. Abert, wie dem allen, wird das Antimonium werde so sehre von seiner Schwärtze gereiniget, alß immer möglich, so bleibet doch seine Vnart, vnd spröde Schwefligkeit bey ihm, welche dann erscheinet, das er nicht vnter dem Hammer sich auß dehnen lässet, oder geschmeidig wird, welches dann eines jeden Metalles Eigenschafft ist, damit es neben andern Eigenschafften für ein Metall zuerkennen.

Vber das hat es einen groben, vnreinen Mercurium, wil jetzo nicht sagen, das es noch jederzeit einen flüchtigen Schwefel bey sich behelt. Vnd wollen wir die jenigen, welche sich für grosse Philosophos halten, auch neben sich andere durch viel Bücher vnd weitleuftige Schrifften bereden wollen, auch dieser der Scrupel jhres Vniuersals sey, freundlich zu gut halten, das ich jhnen solche jhre Meinung nit gar lassen kan. Denn man suchet gar thörlich etwas in einer Sache, das darinnen nicht ist, wie Arnoldus sagt: vnd weil in der Vbung der Turbæ stehet, der Philosophische Stein sei eine reine Materia; So sagt auch Lullius in seinem letzten Testament: Vnsere Tinctur ist nur ein reines Fewr. Vnd in dem Vade mecum spricht er: Es ist allein der subtile Geist, so da tingiret, vnd die Corpora von jhrem Außfatz reiniget: Die Mineral aber, wie auch die andern grob vnnd vnreine seind, das sie auch durch keinerlei weise, es geschehe denn durch Mittel vnser Tinctur darzu gebracht, oder jnnerlich gereiniget werden kann: So kan je auch die Materia vnsers Steins darauß nicht gelanget werden: sintemal auß seinem dinge, wie Richardus cap. I. spricht, etwas genommen kan, das darinnen nicht stecket.

Was sol mann aber von dem Victriol sagen, welcher durch seine wunderbare Eigenschafften auch viele in Jrrthumb bringet, jnsonderheit, da solches grosses Theil dauon zu Kupfer wird, je auch Eysen in Kupfer verwandeln kan? Hiervon ist kürtzlich zu wissen, das der Victriol anders nicht ist, alß ein Anfang vnd Materia des Kupfers, da in den Adern der Erden der Bergschwaden vnd dünstige Mercurius einen Ort angetroffen, da in solcher bitterer zusammenziehender Venerischer Sulphur in so grosser menge gefunden worden, welchen er zwar also balde angenommen, sich darin Coaguliret vnd ein Metall werden wollen: Weil aber die Natur das reine vom vnreinen, das verbrennliche vom vnverbrennlichen absondern wollen, die menge vnd vielheit aber obgedachten Schwefels die quantitet zu weit vbertroffen, so hat sich auch in solcher scheidung der Mercurius mitscheiden, vnnd in die Victriolische Grüne verstecken lassen müssen.

Dieses siehet man klärlich in deme, das so mann gemeinen Schwefel alß vrsache dieser verderbung dem Kupfer zusetzet, vnnd es Calciniret, denn die Kunst thut mit starckem Fewr in kurtzer zeit, was die Natur mit langsamen Fewr verrichten muß: verbrennet solches das Kupfer gantz vnd gar, vnd bringet solches in die Victriolische Art, durch gemeine Handgriffe: vnd nachdeme des Schweffels viel oder wenig, so wird der Victriol reicher von Farben, oder Ärmer: Dannenhero wo Kupfer vnd wenig von der Arnei, von dem Kupfferigen Eigenschaft ist, alß bey dem Cyprischen findet mann viel Kupffer, in andern weniger.

Es ist auch wol zumercken, das der sawre Spiritus, so im Victriol ist, von dem Schwefel herrühre, sintemal mann in gemeinen Schwefel eben massig findet vnd herauß ziehet: das im Spiritu Victrioli auch den Schwefelischen Geruch zuspüren, vnd der Spiritus Sulphuris verwandelt den Sulphur Martis in einen Victriol, wie der Spiritus Victrioli. Weil aber in dem Eysen auch ein grober Sulphur ist, frisset die Schärffe des Victriols solchen hinweg, suchet dessen Mercurium, der dem seinigen nicht sehr vngleich ist, vnd wird mit demselben durch vereinigung seines Schwefel, so den Mercurium vberwindet, zu gutem geschmeitigem Kupffer.

Weil nun in dem Victriol ein so vberflüssiger vnd reyner Schwefel, vnd des Mercurij so gar wenig ist, der doch auch noch zu seiner Reinigung nicht kommen ist, so werden wir darauß mehr nicht alß dem andern auch erlangen: Vnd müssen des Alphidij lehre in allen diesen in acht nehmen, da er spricht: Mein Sohn, hüte dich, vnd sondere dich von den Todten Cörpern vnd Steinen ab, weil darinnen kein Weg zu wandeln ist, deßgleichen nicht leben, nicht vermehrung, sondern verzehret wird, alß da seind die Saltze, Auripigmenta, Arsenic, Magnesia, Marcasita vnd dergleichen.

Vnd Arnoldus sagt in flore florum: Die Vrsach ihrer Jrrthumb ist, weil die vier Geister: nemlich Auripigment, Salmiac, Mercurius vnd Sulphur: nicht der Samen weder der vollkommenen noch vnuollkommenen Metallen seind: außgenommen der Mercurius vnd Sulphur, welcher den Mercurium Coaguliret.

Es möchte aber auß diesen letzten worten den Arnoldi jemand schliessen, das der gemeine Sulphur vnnd Mercurius die Materia vnsers Steins seye, weil solche vnter die vier Spiritus gezehlet werden, weil der Sulphur den Mercurium Coaguliret? Hierauff muß ich mit dem Richardo cap. II. fragen, ob ein jeder Schwefel den Mercurium Coagulire? Darauff antworte ich nein. Denn ein je der gemeiner Schwefel, wie der Philosophus sagt, ist den Metallen zuwider. Denn es ist zu wissen, das der Schwefel auß der fettigkeit der Erden in den Erdklufften gebohren, vnd durch mässige kochung hart gemacht wird, vnd alß dann heisset mann ihn Schwefel.

Es ist aber der Schwefel zweyerley, lebendig vnnd verbrennlich: Der lebendige ist das wirckende Theil bey den Metallen, vnnd wenn er von aller Vnreinigkeit durch die Natur gesaubert, die Materia vnsers Steins, dauon hernacher.

There are two kinds of Sulphur: living and combustible. The living Sulphur is the effectual part of the metals and when cleansed by Nature of all impurities, the *Materia* of our stone, but of this more later. But the common or combustible Sulphur of metals or *lapidis Materia*, but their enemy. For, say *Avicenna* and *Richardus Anglicus*, the common and combustible Sulphur doth not belong to our masterly skill, because it did not originate from it. For white as art can make it, it infecteth at all times, maketh black, and corrupteth everything made of it, for it is a destroying fire.

Therefore it preventeth fluidity, when it is fixed. The example of this we see in iron, which hath in itself a constant, crude, and impure Sulphur. But if it be burned, it becometh an earthy substance, like a dead powder. Now how could this give life to others? For it hath a twofold superfluity, namely, one that can be set on fire, and the earthy one

Now consider the common Sulphur, not the Sulphur of the Philosophers which is a simple, live fire, which reviveth other dead bodies, and bringeth them to maturity. Therefore common Sulphur cannot be the *Materia* of our stone. But what shall we say about common Mercury? Of which all *Philosophi* say that the *Materia* of our stone is a mercurial substance and hath very many qualities which will be attributed to our Mercury. For it is the source of everything which letteth itself be fused, as *Arnoldus, Ros. lib.* 1, *cap.* 2, saith: Every fusible thing, when it is melted, will be transformed into it, and it mixeth itself with them because it is their substance; albeit the bodies differ at the same time in their composition from Mercury, according to their purity or impurity, and would have retained alien Sulphur. And in chapter 4 he saith: The *Mercurius vivus* is clear in all its effects, that most perfect and constant thing, for it withstandeth burning and causeth liquifaction, when it hath been fixed, and is the *Tincture* of a red superfluous perfection, of glittering appearance, and doth not cease from the mixture so long as it lasteth; and it is friendly and sociable and the means of joining together the *Tinctures* since it letteth itself be thoroughly mixed, and adhereth to their innermost, hence it is of their nature. There is one, and one only, which the fire conquereth, but it will not be conquered by the fire, yet rejoiceth in it and remaineth in it.

And *Bernhardus* saith: Most precisely do we follow Nature, which hath in its lodes no other *Materiam* wherein it operateth other than the pure mercurial form. In this *Mercurius* now is hidden the constant and non-combustible Sulphur, which bringeth our work to perfection, without any other substance save for the pure mercurial substance. Since there are such splendid qualities in the *Mercurius*, must it not certainly follow that the *Materia* of our stone must be in this? To this we answer: That as there are two kinds of Sulphur, there are also two kinds of Mercury: the common and the philosophical. The common *Mercurius* is still a crude, untimely and open *Corpus*, which cannot remain in fire like the philosophical, since through a moderate heat it is turned into smoke and will quickly vanish. Therefore the *Philosophi* also say in common parlance: Our Mercury is not a common mercury. So *Lullius* also saith in his *Clavicula*, chapter 1. We say that the common mercury cannot be the mercury of the Philosophers, whatsoever may be the art with which it is prepared: for one cannot keep the common in fire, therefore it is done through another bodily mercury, which is warm, dry, and more timely.

But most of the Philosophers have written according to their superfluity about the sublimation and other preparation of the common mercury: wherefore many queer books about this subject have come into existence, so that people learned more and more about the nature and character of this subject, but the purpose they had aimed at, namely, the great treasure of earthly wisdom, no one hath as yet ever been able to find in their writings, because Nature hath not placed it therein. But in truth, it is so peculiar in its work that it would mislead one who calleth himself a Wise Man. For example, I knew one who had amalgamated it with gold and handled it so subtly that he brought it through all the colors unto *Citrination*.

In this color it stood, and he, thinking he had it fixed, put some more fire under it, thinking he could not go wrong in putting fire under it after the manner of the *Philosophi*. Whereupon the glass burst, and the *Mercurius* went up the chimney, taking with it all the gold, gilding the chimney with it. And he had to scrape the gold out of the chimney and reduce it again.

It hath also been seen that the common *Mercurius* as a *Corpus* itself can neither open another *Corpus*, namely the gold, nor work therein, even if many colors let themselves be perceived in it, whilst the heat worketh its effect in moisture. But had this good man realised, as many others have done, what *Arnoldus* saith in *Flore florum*, such would not have happened to him. For *Arnoldus*, when he discourses about such alchemists, saith: When they considered this more subtly, they found that mercury is the origin and source of all metals, and with sulphuric and boiling heat, they sublimated the *Mercurius* for themselves, then they fashioned it, they excluded it, and coagulated it, but when they came to the projection, they found nothing, etc.

Therefore we cannot consider common mercury as the *Materia* for our stone. Thus far we have sough for the *Materia* for our stone in animals, vegetables, and in stone, in the lesser minerals, and also in the semi- and greater minerals, but we have not found it so far, and we must therefore look further, whether we can find it in metals, and if it should be therein, whether it is in all of them at once, or only in some of them, and if so, in which they are to be found. This has long been known, and *Rogerius Baco* doth assert in his *Speculo*, chapter 3, all metals are produced out of Sulphur and Mercury. And one cannot take away or add anything to them, and cannot change them, except what cometh from them, since every improvement augmenteth the nature of the thing from which it cometh. As *Richardus*, chapter 1, saith: As it also is otherwise in all Nature, everything is ordained by the Highest Creator, so that each thing doth bring forth and bear its own kind. And as dumb animals cannot bring forth their kind to any increase except through the nature of their own kind, so is it with everything else in Nature. Therefore *Basilius Valentinus* saith: Thou art not permitted to look for the true stone, nor shalt thou undertake to make it, except out of its own seed, out of which our stone hath been made even from the beginning.

To find this seed, thou must consider by thyself for what purpose thou dost want to find the stone, and then it will become obvious to thee that it can come only from a metallic root, from which the Creator commanded all metals to bear and come forth. There is a great similarity between the production of metals and that of the great stone, especially since there is Sulphur and Mercury in both, as well as the Salt, and the noble soul hath concealed itself, and one cannot possibly obtain the advantage of use in metallic form until these three are brought together in one, after having been taken out of metallic substance, and after this nothing must be added which doth not come from them. And therefore it is plain, as *Baccho* saith, that no thing which hath not had its origin in Mercury and Sulphur can be sufficient to perfect them and transform them. Therefore it is necessary for the production of the great stone that a metallic substance be taken. But whether one can find this in the imperfect metals remaineth to be seen.

There are many to be found who want to find the white in lead or tin, and the red in copper or iron, or the *Materia Lapidis* in both; without doubt mislead by the *Philosophi* themselves. For thus saith *Geber in Lib. Fornac.*, chapter 9: As customary, the dough that is to be fermented we extract out of imperfect bodies. And therefore we give thee a general rule: that the white dough is to be extracted from *Jupiter* and *Saturn*, but the red from *Venus, Saturn*, and *Mars*. So also doth *Basilius Valentinus*, in his book about natural and supernatural things, teach that a *Tincture* can be made out of the *Conjunction of Mars and Venus*.

Likewise in his *Triumphal Chariot*, he saith: After this followeth the *Tinctura Solis et Lunae*, etc., from white, then the *Tinctura Vitrioli* or *Veneris*, and likewise the *Tinctura Martis*, both of which have in them the *Tinctura Solis*, if they have been brought before to permanent fixation. Then followeth the *Tinctura Jovis and Saturni* unto the Coagulation of *Mercury*, and then the *Tinctura Mecurii* itself.

Now let this be known to the investigators of natural secrets, that such hath not been the opinion of *Geber* and *Basilius Valentinus* or other Philosophers, else they would contradict themselves, which cannot be, since the Wise must always tell the truth in their writings, although they may mask the truth in concealing phrases. For there can come forth perfection neither in the imperfect metals nor amongst those which are so mixed with each other that they could at least be improved. Out of those things themselves alone such cannot come, because for our stone the purest essence of Mercury is required, as *Clangor Buccinae, Avicenna, Lullius*, and in general all Philosophers say: We must choose for our Work the purest Mercurial substance. But the purest substance of Mercury is not to be found in the imperfect metals of Nature, because they are like leprous bodies, which are corrupted and rendered inactive by alien and impure Sulphur, so that no kind of art can bring them to their inner and perfect purification, and they cannot even stand fire. And it is a necessary quality of our *Materia* that it remain constant in fire, which does not occur here.

Let us now hear what *Geber* hath to say in his *Summa*, chapter 63, about this impurity of the imperfect metals and the qualities of the perfect Mercury: Herein we found by true experimentation a peculiar kind of two secrets, *viz.*, one secret is that there are three causes for the destruction through fire of every imperfect metal, the first of which is that their combustible Sulphur is inclosed in their innermost part, and is enkindled with a strong fire, lesseneth the entire substance of the bodies, transformeth them into smoke, and finally consumeth them, however excellent their Mercury may be.

The second cause is that the outer flame is augmented by them, passeth through them, and dissolveth them into smoke, however dense they may be.

The third cause is that their bodies may be opened through the Calcination, for then the flame of the fire can pass through them and transform them into smoke, however perfect they may be. Now when all these causes of destruction come together, then necessarily the bodies will be destroyed and reduced to nothing. But when they are not together then the speed of the destruction of the bodies is less rapid. The second kind of these secrets concerneth the quality of the Mercury in these bodies. For since in Mercury there is no cause of destruction or expulsion, it doth not separate the compound into parts, but remaineth with its entire substance in the fire. For this reason one hath necessarily to recognise the reason of its perfection. Let us therefore praise and give glory unto God the All-Highest, who hath created the Mercury and given it its substance, and to the substance those qualities which cannot be found in the other things of Nature, that therein the perfection may be brought about by some art, and which we find therein in its nearest power (*potentia proquinqua*). For this it is that overcometh fire and is not overcome by it, but remaineth friendly therein and rejoiceth in it.

In these words Geber proveth infallibly that the *Materia* of our stone cannot be in the imperfect metals, because they are themselves impure, and if one wanted to purify them they would completely disappear therefrom. But our *Mercurius*, on account of its purity, is constant in fire and cannot be damaged by it.

Now since these imperfect metals cannot be the *Materia* of our stone, much less can they be such when mixed together, for they become not purer than they were before through their mixture. And in addition to this cometh another *Confusion* out of it, which is contrary to our *intention*, and only, as mentioned

So ist offenbar, wie Baccho sagt, das kein ander Ding, so nicht auß Mercurio vnd Schwefel seinen Vrsprung genommen, gnugsam ist dieselbe vollkommen zu machen, vnnd zur verwandlung zubringen. Darumb müsse nothwendig zur Gebehrung des grossen Steins eine Metallische Materia genommen werden: Ob aber solche in den vnuollkommenen Metallen zufinden, wollen wir mit wenigen besehen.

Es werden jhrer viel gefunden, welche auß Zinn oder Bley zum weißen, zum rothen aber auß Kupffer oder Eysen, oder denen beyden die Materiam Lapidis haben wollen, sonder zweiffel verführet von den Philosophis selbsten. Denn also spricht Geber lib. fornac. cap. 9. Den Teig, so mann fermentiren muß, ziehen wir, wie gebreuchlich, auß den vnuollkommenen Cörpern. Vnd dannenhero geben wir dir eine gemeine Regul, das der weiße Teig vom Ioue vnd Saturno, der rothe aber auß Venere, Saturno & Marte außgezogen werde. So lehret auch Basilius Valentinus in seinem Buch von Natürlichen vnd vbernatürlichen dingen auß der Coniunction Martis & Veneris eine Tinctur machen.

Item im Triumph Wagen spricht er: dem folget nach die Tinctura Solis & Lunæ &c. auff weiß, weiter die Tinctura Victrioli oder Veneris, deßgleichen die Tinctura Martis, welche beyde die Tincturam Solis auch in sich haben, wenn sie vorher zu der fixation bestendig gebracht worden. Diesen folgen nach die Tinctura Iouis & Saturni zu der Coagulation Mercurij, vnnd demnach die Tinctura Mercurij selbsten.

Es soll aber der Erforscher der Natürlichen Geheimnußen wissen, das dieses nicht deß Gebri vnd Basilij Valentini oder anderer Philosophen Meinung gewesen sey, sonsten redeten sie wider sich selbsten, welches nicht seyn kann, sintemal die Weisen in jhren Schrifften nimmer liegen müssen, ob sie gleich in verborgenen Reden die Warheit verdecken: denn einmal kann weder in den vnuollkommenen Metallen alleine, noch vnter einander vermischet, einigevollkommenheit herspriessen, damit sie im wenigsten verbessert werden möchten. Auß jhnen selbsten alleine kann solches nicht sein, weil zu der Materia vnsers Steins daß reineste wesen deß Mercurij erfordert wird, wie Clangor Buccinæ, Auicenna, Lullius, vnd ins gemein, alle Philosophen sagen: Wir müssen zu vnserm Wercke, die reineste Mercurialische Substantz erwehlen: Diese reineste Substantz des Mercurij aber wird in den vnuollkommenen Metallen von Natur nicht gefunden, weil die von jhrem frembden vnd vnreinem Schwefel deromassen verderbet vnd eingenommen, das dahero sie als aussetzige Leiber, zu der jnnerlichen vnnd vollkommenen Reinigung, auch durch keinerley Kunst, gebracht werden können: bleiben sie auch selbsten im Fewre nicht stehen, welches denn auch eine nothwendige Eigenschafft vnserer Materia ist, das sie nemlich im Fewre bestendig bleibe, welches aber hier nicht geschiehet.

Lasset vnß hören, was Geber in seiner Summa cap. 63. von dieser der vnuollkommenen Metallen Vnreinigkeit, vnnd deß vollkommenen Mercurij Eigenschafft saget: hierdurch haben wir mit warhaffter Erfindung ein wunderlich Geschlecht zweyer Geheimnussen erfunden: das eine nemlich das dreyerley Vrsachen der verderbung eines jeden (vnuollkommenen) Metals durch Fewr sey, deren die erste ist, das der verbrenliche Schwefel in jhrem innersten wesen eingeschlossen, durch starckes Fewr angezündet, das gantze wesen der Cörper verringert, in Rauch jaget, vnnd sie endlich verzehret, wie gut auch jhr Queckfilber sey.

Die ander Vrsach ist, das die eußerliche Flamme durch sie vermehret wird, sie durchgehet, vnd in Rauch aufflöset, wie fix sie auch sein mögen.

Die dritte Vrsache ist, das ihre Leiber durch die Calcination geöfnet werden können: Denn alßdann kann sie die Flamme des Fewrs durchgehen, vnnd sie in Rauch jagen, wie vollkommen sie auch seind. Wann nun alle Vrsachen der verderbung zusammen kommen, so müssen die Cörper nothwendig allerdings verderben vnd zu nichts werden: Wenn sie aber nicht beysammen seind, so lesset die schnelligkeit der verstörung der Cörper in etwas nach. Das ander Geschlechte dieses Geheimnuß ist die Güte, welche wegen des Queckfilberß in den Cörpern betrachtet wird: Denn das Queckfilber, weil keine Vrsachen der verderbung vnnd Außjagung bey jhme gefunden werden, lesset sich nicht zertheilen in Theile der zusammensetzung, sondern bleibt mit seinem gantzen wesen im Fewre stehen: darauß mann nothwendig die Vrsache seiner vollkommenheit erkennen muß. Darumb last vns den hochgelobten vnd höchsten Gott preisen, der dasselbe geschaffen, vnd jhme das wesen, dem wesen aber die Eigenschafft gegeben hat, die mann aus keinen dingen in der Natur finden mag, das darin diese vollkommenheit durch einige Kunst möchte gebracht werden, welche wir darin in der nehesten krafft (potentia propinqua) finden. Dann dieses ist, welches das Fewr vberwindet, aber vom Fewr nicht vberwunden wird, sondern darinnen freundlich ruhet, vnd sich dessen erfrewet.

Zu diesen erzehlten worten beweiset Geber ohne fehl, das in den vnuollkommenen Metallen die Materia vnsers Steins nicht sein könne, weil sie an sich selbsten vnreine, vnnd im Fewre, wenn mann sie reinigen wolte, gantz dauon fliehen: Vnser Mercurius aber, wegen seiner Reinigkeit im Fewre bestendig sey, vnd deme nichts schaden könne.

Wie nun die vnuollkommene Metallen alleine die Materia vnsers Steins nicht seind, so können sie auch zusammen gemischt viel weniger dieselbe herfür geben, angesehen, das durch jhre vermischung sie nicht reiner werden, alß sie vorher alleine waren.

Zu dem wird eine newe Confusion drauß, welche vnser intention gantz zuwider, vnd nur, wie oben gedacht, eine einige Materia erfordert wird. Solches bezeuget Haly klärlich, wenn er lib. Secret. cap. 9. sagt: Es ist ein Stein, darunter du kein ander Ding mischen solt: mit diesem wircken die weisen, vnnd hierauß fliesset, das mann gesund machet. Es wird nichts anders mit ihme, weder im gantzen, noch in seinen Theilen, vermischet.

Vnd Morienus sagt: Diese Meisterschafft reichet anfänglich her aus einer Wurtzel, welche sich hernach in mehr Theile außbreitet, vnnd wieder in jhr Ding verkehret wird. So nun die vnuollkommene Metalla die Materia des Steins nicht sein können, warumb haben denn die Philosophi darin zu arbeiten befohlen? Antwort. Wann die Philosophi befohlen die vnreinen Cörper zunehmen, haben sie dardurch nicht Kupffer, Eysen, Bley, Zinn, rc. sondern jhr Corpus oder jhre Erde verstanden, wie Arnoldus in flore florum sagt: Der Mercurius wird der Erden zugefügt, das ist, dem vnuollkommenem Leibe. Dann ob zwar jhre Erd an vnd für sich selbsten so vollkommen vnd reine ist, alß die Natur etwas machen können, so ist sie doch respectu lapidis Physici noch vnreine vnd vnuollkommen.

Vnnd hierin vbertrifft die Kunst die Natur, weil sie dasjenige verrichtet, welches die Natur nicht vollbringen können. Das aber diese Erde, wie gesagt, vnuollkommen sey vor vollkommener Reinigung vnd wiedergebehrung, erscheinet darauß, das sie alßdann noch nicht tingiren vnd vollkommen machen kann, vnnd mehr nicht hat, als was jhr die Natur verliehen hat: Wann sie aber wiedergebohren ist, alßdann vermag sie viel zuthun. Jhre Vnreinigkeit aber ist in vnserm Wercke Augenscheinlich zuspüren, in dem sie gantz Schwartz, vnd alßdann dem Bley oder Antimonio verglichen wird, darnach wird sie Graw, vnnd heißet Iupiter oder Zinn oder Wißmut, vnnd das vor der weiße: Nach der Weiße heisset sie Mars vnnd Venus ehe sie zu volstendiger Röthe gebracht wird. Das aber Basilius Valentinus ebenmäßiger Meinung sey, vnnd viel ein anders suche, alß er in obgemeltem Buche beschreibet, zeuget er selbst in seinem Tractat vom grossen Steine, da er die Materiam lapidis inuestigiret, vnd gesagt, wie in Sole die Gabe aller dreyer fixigkeit bey einander sey, vnd derowegen alle Gewalt deß Fewers bestehe: vnd dz die Luna wegen jhres fixen Mercurij nicht so schnell im Fewre dauon fliehe, vnd jhr Examen bestehe, spricht er endlich: Die Ertzbülerin Venus ist mit vberflüßiger Farbe bekleidet vnd eingenommen, vnd jhr Meister Leib ist lauter Tinctur vnd gleich eine solche Farbe, wie im besten Metall auch wohnet, vnd Vberflüßigkeit halber auf roth beweiset. Vnd dieweil jhr Leib Außsetzig, kann die bestendige Tinctur keine bleibende Wohnung haben, sondern muß zugleich mit jhrem Leibe verschwinden. Denn wo d' Leib durch Tödtung verzehret wird, kann die Seele auch nicht bleiben, sondern muß außweichen vnd flihen. Denn die Wohnung ist zerstöret, vnd mit Fewer verbrand worden, das jhre stet nicht zuerkennen, noch einige ferner da Wohnen mag. In einem figirtem Leibe aber wohnet sie gerne mit verstande. Das bestendige Saltz hat dem Streitbaren Marti einen harten, strengen vnd groben Leib zugeeignet vnd verlassen, darauß die Tapferkeit seines Gemüts bewiesen wird, vnd diesem Kriegs Fürsten nicht wol abzugewinnen, denn sein Leib ist hart, das man jhn nicht wol verwunden kann. So aber jemand sagen wolte, weil die Venus einen bestendigen Sulphur habe, müße selbiger, nach Basilij lehre mit dem Spiritu Mercurij perfecti vereiniget, vnd eine Tinctur darauß gemacht werden: Der bedencke, was schon zu mehrmahln gesagt, vnnd auß dem Basilio selbsten angezogen worden, das vnsere Materia nicht auß vielen dingen genommen werden müsse, weil das Vniuersal ein einiges Ding ist, vnd in einem einigen dinge zugleich funden vnd herauß gezogen wird, vñ sey der Spiritus Mercurij vnd Anima Sulphuris sambt dem Geistlichen Saltze, zugleich vereiniget, beschlossen vnter einem Himmel, vnnd wonhafftig in einem Leibe, so wird er auß solchen seinen Irthumen kommen, vnnd zu den vollkommenen Metallen seine Gedancken, ohne weiteres nachdencken, wenden: betrachtende den Spruch Platonis quart. 2. Warumb Calciniret vnnd Soluiret jhr die andern Cörper mit großer Mühe, sintemal jhr in diesen (vollkommenen) finden könnet, was jhr suchet? Wenn jhr sie aber je gebrauchen müsset, ist von nöthen, das jhr sie zuuor in die Natur der vollkommenen Cörper verkehret.

Darumb mein lieber Nachforscher der Natürlichen Geheimnussen, verlasse alle animalische vñ vegetabilische dinge, alle Saltze, Alaun, Victriol, Marcasiten, Magnesien, Antimonium, alle vnuollkommene vñ vnreine Metallen, vnd suche deinen Stein mit Arnoldo de villa noua, Rosar. part. 1. cap. 7. in Mercurio vnnd Sole zum Golde, vnnd in Mercurio vnnd Luna zum Silber, sintemal die gantze Kunst hierein stecket. Denn gleich wie das Fewr der Anfang ist ein Fewer zumachen, sagt Riplæus porta 1. Also ist auch das Gold der Anfang Gold zumachen. Wenn du derowegen durch die Philosophische Kunst Gold vñ Silber machen wilt, so nim nicht darzu Eyer oder Blut, sondern Gold vnd Silber, welche natürlich vnd weißlich, aber nicht mit der Hand, calciniret eine newe Geburt herfürbringen, welche sein Geschlechte, wie alle andere dinge, vermehret. Darumb vermahnet auch Richardus cap. 10. daß mann Gold vnd Silber säen solle, auf das sie mit vnser Arbeit, vnd vermittelung der Natur Frucht bringen mögen: sintemahl sie in jhnen haben, vnd seind das jenige, so mann suchet, vnnd kein ander Ding in der Welt. Vñ warumb solte mañ nicht diese beyde erwelẽ, da sie doch einen reinen vñ vollkommenen Mercurium vñ roten vñ weißen schwefel bey sich habẽ, wie Rich. c. 12. bezeuget? Deñ es sagt Auic. dz in einem jedem Golde ein roter Schwefel ist. Solcher Schwefel aber wird vber der Erden nicht funden, alß nur in den beyden Cörpern. Darumb bereiten wir diese zwey Corpora gar subtil, das wir den Schwefel vnnd Mercurium von solcher Materia haben mögen, dauon Gold vnd Silber vnter der Erden gemacht worden. Dann die seind leuchtende Cörper, darein färbende Stralen stecken, welche die andern leiber in warhaffte röthe vnd weisse tingiren, nach dem sie bereitet worden. Denn vnsere Meisterschafft, wie Arnoldus Rosar. lib. 1. cap. 5. sagt, hilfft den vollkommenen Leibern, vnd machet die vnuollkommenen vollkommen, ohne vermischung einiges andern Dinges. Weil dann das Gold das edelste Metall ist, soists die Tinctur der röthe, farbende vnnd verwandelende ein jedes Corpus. Das Silber aber ist die Tinctur der weiße, so alle Corpora in warhaffte Weiße färbet.

Es soll aber der guthertzige Leser berichtet sein, das die Metalla alß Gold vnd Silber in jhrer Metallischen Form die Materia vnsers Steins nicht seind: Sie sind das Mittel zwischen vnser Materia vnnd den vollkommenen Metallen, gleich wie vnsere Materia das Mittel zwischen jhnen vñ vnserm grossen Steine ist. Höre doch, was hieuon Bernhardus Graue von Treßne vnnd Naygen im andern Theile seines Büchleins saget: Es mögen wol die jenigen schweigen, die nicht vnsere Tinctur, sondern eine andere, so nicht warhafftig, noch scheinbarlich, noch zu einigem Dinge nutze ist, herfürbringen: vnnd mögen auch diejenigen schweigen, die da sagen, das ein ander Schwefel alß der vnser sein solle, welcher im Bauche der Magnesiæ verborgen ist.

Auch mögen die wol schweigen, die einander Argentum viuum außziehen wollen, denn allein auß dem fermento oder rothem Knechte, vnd ein ander Wasser außziehen wollen, denn allein vnsers immerbleibendes, welches sich keinem andern vermischet, denn allein deme, das seiner eignen Natur ist, auch kein ander Ding erweichet oder aufflöset, denn allein das, so von seiner eignen Metallischen Natur ist. Denn es ist kein ander Eßig, alß der vnsere: kein ander Regiement, alß das vnsere: keine andere Farben, alß die vnsere; keine andere Sublimation, alß die vnsere; keine andere Aufflösung, alß die vnsere; keine andere Fäulung, alß die vnsere; keine andere Materia, alß die vnsere.

Lasset derowegen fahren den Alaun, Saltz, Victriol vnnd alle andere Arramenta, Borax, starcke Wasser, vnnd alle Kräuter, Thiere, Bestien vnd was dauon kompt, Haar, Blut, Harn, Menschen Saamen, Fleisch, Eyer vnd Mineralische Steine, vnd ein jedes Metall allein für sich. Denn obwol der Eingang vnd vnsere Materia aus jhnen ist, vnnd nachbesage aller Philosophen auß Queckfilber zusammen gesetzet werden solle, vnnd solches in keinem andern dinge, alß in den Metallen gefunden wird, wie solches erscheinet aus dem Gebro, &c.

So seind sie doch, so lange sie in jhrer Metallischen Gestalt seind, vnser Stein nicht. Deñ es ist vnmöglich, das eine einige, ja dieselbe Materia zwo gestalten zugleich haben könne. Wie können sie denn der Stein sein, welcher eine würdige vnd mittelere Form hat zwischen dem Metall vnd Mercurio, wo die nicht vorher zerstöret, vnd die Metallische Gestalt von ihnen genommen worden? Derowegen spricht auch Raymundus Lullius im 56. cap. seines Testaments: Darumb nimbt der gute Kunstler die Metalla für die mittelere in dem Werck der Meisterschafft, vnnd sonderlich Solem & Lunam, vnd das darumb, weil die beyde zu einer gemäßigten Gleichheit, vnnd grossen Reinigkeit des schweffelichen vnnd Mercurialischen wesens kommen, vnd gekocht seind, reine vnd wol gezeitigt durch der Natur wirckung, zu welcher proportion der Kunstler sich vergebens zukommen quelen würde, wenn er von den Natürlichen Anfängen ohne thätliche Mittel sein fürhaben zuerfüllen, anfangen wolte.

Vnd weiter spricht er in seinem Codicillo: ohne diese beyde, nemlich Gold vnd Silber kann diese Kunst nicht vollkommen werden, weil hierin die reineste Substantz des Schwefels ist, welche die Natur vollkömlich gereinigt hat, zu welcher Reinigung zukommen die Kunst viel schwächer ist, alß die Natur, vnd kann darzu nicht gelangen, ob sie sich schon sehr darumb bemühet.

Auß diesen beyden Leibern, wenn sie mit jhrem Schwefel oder Arsenico bereitet werden, kann vnsere Medicin gemacht werden, ohne sie aber keines weges. Vnd in der Vorrede seines Schlüssels sagt er: Ich rathe euch, O meine Freunde, das jhr in nichts alß in Sole vnd Luna arbeitet, sie in jhre erste Materiam, nemlich in vnsern Sulphur vnd Mercurium wider zurückbringende. Denn auß den Leibern, sagt Arnoldus lib. 1. Rosar. cap. 7. wird der sehr weiße vnd rothe Schwefel außgezogen, weil darin am mehristen ist die reineste schwefeliche Substantz von der Natur zum höchsten gesaubert.

above, requireth a single *Materia*. *Haly* testifieth clearly to this when he saith in *Lib. Secret.*, chapter 9: It is a stone, and thou shalt not mix any other thing with it; with this the Wise work, and an all-healing power floweth from it. There shall be nothing else mixed with it, either in the whole nor in its parts.

And *Morienus* saith: This masterly skill cometh in the beginning out of a root, which extendeth later into many parts and finally returned to its source. Now why have the *Philosophi* bidden us to work with the imperfect metals, since these cannot be the *Materia* of the stone? And the answer is: When the *Philosophi* order the impure bodies to be taken, they did not mean thereby copper, iron, lead, tin, etc., but they meant its *Corpus* or its earth; as *Arnoldus* in *Flore florum* saith: The *Mercurius* is added to the earth, *i. e.*, to the imperfect body. And what is more, its earth in itself, however perfect and pure it can be made by Nature, still is impure and imperfect *respectu lapidis Physici*.

And herein art excelleth Nature, for it can do what Nature cannot accomplish. But since this earth, as said, is imperfect before perfect purification and regeneration, it appeareth therefrom that it cannot as yet tinge and make perfect, and hath no more than what Nature hath bestowed upon it. But when it is regenerated it may then add much. But its impurity is obviously perceptible in our work. At first it is wholly black, and then it will be comparable to lead or antimony, after that it becometh gray, and is called *Jupiter* or tin or bismuth, and all this before it turneth white. After it is white, it is called *Mars* and *Venus* before it is brought to a complete redness. *Basilius Valentinus* is of the same opinion, and seeketh many another, as he doth set forth in the above-mentioned book, and himself doth testify in his treatise about the great stone, where he investigateth the *Materia lapidis*, and saith: That in *Sol* the gift of all three fixities is together, and therefore resisteth every power of fire; and that *Luna*, on account of its fixed Mercury doth not escape so quickly, and doth pass its *Examen*. And thus he saith finally: The archcourtesan *Venus* is clothed and dressed with superfluous color and her master's body is of pure *Tinctur* and of the same color as abideth also in the best metals, and on account of this superfluity is proven red. And since her body is leprous, the *Tinctur* hath no permanent abode in it and must at the same time disappear with her body. For where the body is consumed through death, there the soul cannot remain, it must give way and escape. Because the abode is destroyed and burned with fire, so that its place is unrecognisable, and no one may continue to dwell there. But gladly and with understanding dwelleth the soul in a formed body. The constant salt hath given the warlike *Mars* a hard, strong, and crude body, by which is proven the valor of his mind, and one cannot easily wound this war-lord, since his body is invulnerable. But if someone should say: Because *Venus* hath a constant Sulphur it must likewise, according to the teaching of *Basilius*, be united to the *Spiritus Mercurii perfecti*, and a *Tinctur* will be made therefrom. What hath already been said many times, and what hath been stated by *Basilius* himself, should be borne in mind: That our *Materia* must not be taken from many things, since the *Universal* is one thing, and can only be found and extracted from a single thing; and that the *Spiritus Mercurii* and *Anima Sulphuris* including the spiritual salts, are united together under one heaven and dwell in one body. So will he cease from his error and, without further consideration, turn his thoughts to the perfect metals, observing the saying of *Plato*, quart. 2. Why do ye calcinate and dissolve the other bodies with great difficulty, since ye can find in this (perfectly) what ye seek? But is ye ever want to use it, then it is necessary that ye first transform it into the nature of the perfect body.

Therefore, my dear seeker of the natural secrets, leave all animal and vegetable things, all salts, alum, vitriol, marcasite, magnesia, antinomy, all imperfect and impure metals, and seek for thy stone in *Mercurius* and *Sol*, for the gold, and in *Mercurius* and *Luna* for the silver, since this is the essence of the whole art, according to *Arnoldus de Villa Nova, Rosar.*, part 1, chapter 7. Just as the fire in the beginning is a sealed fire, saith *Riplaeus*, porta 1. Thus gold is also the beginning of gold-making. If, therefore, thou wouldest make gold and silver through the philosophic art, do not take for that purpose eggs or blood, but gold and silver, which engender a new birth, augmenting their kind, as do all other things when calcinated intelligently and naturally, but not through manual work. Therefore *Richardus*, chapter 10, admonisheth us: That one should sow gold and silver, that through our work an the intervention of Nature, they may bear fruit; since they have it in themselves and that is what one seeketh, and no other thing in the world. And why should one not choose both of these, since, according to *Richardus*, chapter 12, they have a pure and perfect *Mercurius* within them and a red and white Sulphur? For *Avicenna* saith that in every gold there is a red sulphur. But such sulphur is not found on the whole earth except in these two bodies. Therefore we very subtly prepare these two *Corpora*, that we may obtain the Sulphur and Mercury from such *Materia*, as gold and silver have from beneath the earth. They are luminous bodies, and coloring rays are in them, which tinge other bodies in true red and white, according to their preparation. For as *Arnoldus, Rosar.*, lib. 1, chap. 5, saith: Our masterly skill aideth the perfect bodies and maketh perfect the imperfect ones, without a mixture of any other thing. Now, since gold is the noblest of all metals, so is the *Tinctur* of the redness, the coloring and transforming of every *Corpus*. But the silver is the *Tinctur* of whiteness, which coloreth all *Corpora* true white.

Now let the good-hearted reader be informed that such metals as gold and silver are not the *Materia* of our stone in their metallic form; they are the medium between them and our great stone. Hear therefore what *Bernardus Count of Trevisan* hath to say in another part of his book: They will do well to keep

silent who do not produce our *Tinctur*, but another, which is not true, not plausible, and good for nothing; and let those be silent who claim that there is another sulphur than ours hidden in the belly of *Magnesia*.

And let those also be silent who want to extract an *Argentum vivum* from anything other than the *derment* or red knight, and want to extract another water other than our everlasting one which doth not mix with anything unless it be of its own nature, and doth not melt or dissolve anything unless it be of its own metallic nature. For there is no vinegar other than ours; no other management other than ours; no other *Sublimation* other than ours; no other dissolution other than ours; no other putrefaction other than ours; no other *Materia* other than ours.

Therefore renounce the alum, salts, vitriol, and all other *Arramenta*, borax, strong water, and all herbs, animals, beasts, and whatever may come from them, hair, blood, urine, human seed, flesh, eggs, and mineral stones, and every metal by itself alone. Even if the beginning of our *Materia* is from them, it should at the same time, according to all the aforesaid Philosophers, be based upon Mercury, which will be found in no other thing than metals. As appeareth from *Geber, et al.*

But still they are not our stone so long as they are in their metallic form. For it is impossible that the one, yea, the very same *Materia* should have two forms at the same time. For how could the stone, which hath a worthy and medium form, be between the metal and the Mercury, if they be not destroyed beforehand, and their metallic form hath not been taken from them? Wherefore saith *Raymundus Lullius* in chapter 56 of his *Testament*: Therefore the good artist taketh the metals as mediums in the work of masterly skill, and especially doth he take *Sol* and *Luna*, and he taketh these because they have both come to a moderate uniformity and great purity of their sulphureous and mercurial substances, and because they are boiled, pure, and well-timed through Nature's working, to which proportion the artist would struggle in vain if he should attempt to accomplish his purpose from the natural beginning without effective means.

And furthermore he saith in his *Codicil*: Without these two, namely gold and silver, the art cannot be brought to perfection, because in them is the purest substance of Sulphur, which Nature hath completely purified. In effecting this purification, art is much less effective than Nature, and it could never achieve it, as hard as it might try.

Our medicine can be made from these two bodies, if they are prepared with their Sulphur or *Arsenicum*, but not without them. And he saith in the preface to his *Clavicule*: I advise you, O my friends, that ye work with nothing but *Sol* and *Luna*, to reduce them again to their first *Materia*; namely, into our Sulphur and Mercury. For, saith *Arnoldus*, lib. 1. *Rosar.* chapter 7, from these bodies the very white and red Sulphur will be extracted, because therein in the greatest quality is the purest sulphureous substance, cleansed by Nature to the highest degree.

Thus saith *Nicarus* in the *Turba Philosophorum*: I bid the followers (of the Art) to take the gold that they want to increase and renew, then divide the water into two parts, and take one part in such a way that the gold is concentrated in it. For the metal, when it falleth into this water, will be called the *Ferment* of the gold. But why doth the Philosopher here call the water his gold, when he saith: When the metal falleth into this water, it shall be the *Ferment* of the gold? Let this be known to my art-seeking followers: That the *Philosopher's* gold is not common gold. *Senior* saith, and it is written in the first exercise of the *Turba*: As the *Mercurius* is the origin of all metals, so also is the sun the end and last of all metals; and all metals, whether they be pure or impure, are in their innermost *Sol*, *Luna*, and *Mercurius*. But one is a true sun, which is extracted from it.

And therefore thou understandest that the *Philosopher's* gold, although extracted from them, is a quite different gold from the common sun or gold. So also saith the *Aurora consurgens*, chapter 16. From this it is evident that the philosophical gold is not common gold, neither in color nor in substance. For that reason it is said that it bringeth joy to the heart of man, and the same thing holdeth true with silver. But what it extracted from it is a white and a red, a true, constant, and living *Tincture*. But it is the philosophical gold which one should not buy cheaply, as *Alphidius* saith. And *Morienes* saith: Everything bought dearly is deceitful. For with a very small amount of this thing and with little gold we can buy much. But in addition to that, our gold is living gold and our silver living silver, which cannot bring forth anything except life and increase. The common gold and silver are dead, which cannot accomplish anything more than is granted to them by Nature, until they are awakened by a skilled artist from their death, and obtain their life again; then they live also and can prove very effective in the increase and propagation of their kind. Concerning the death of the common metals and the life of our metals, the splendid, still living *Philosophus Michael Sendivogius*, in the 11th *Tractate* of his book about the Philosopher's Stone, speaketh thus: Thou shouldest be warned not to take common gold and silver, for they are dead: take ours, which are living. And then put them in our fire and a dry moisture will come from them. First dissolve the earth in water, called *Mercurius* by the Philosophers, and the water will dissolve these *Corpora Solis at Lunae*, so that only the tenth part remaineth with one part, and this is the deep-rooted moisture of the metals.

Now to speak further about the gold of the Philosophers, it should be known that from the earliest times the *Philosophi* call their water gold, also sometimes their earth. Of the first *Modo* the *Philosophus Nicarus* hath spoken above, and the *Rosarius Philosophorum* asserts it in the following words: But what say ye to this, that the *Philosophi* say: Our gold is not a common gold, and our silver is not a common silver? To this I reply that they call water their gold, which riseth to the heights

Also spricht Nicarus in der turba: Ich heisse die Nachkommende das Gold, so sie vermehren vnd vernewern wollen, nemen, darnach das Wasser in zwey Theil theilen, den einen Theil zwar, alß das Gold selbsten zusammen drucken: Denn das Ertz, wenn es in diß Wasser felt, sol des Goldes Ferment genennet werden. Wie nennet aber der Philosophus allhie das Wasser sein Gold, wenn er spricht, wenn das Ertz in diß Wasser felt, sol es des Goldes Ferment sein? Mein Kunstsuchender Nachfolger sol wissen, das der Philosophen Gold nicht gemeine Gold, wie Senior spricht, vnd in der ersten Vbung in die Turbam gesagt wird: wie der Mercurius ist der Anfang aller Metallen, so ist auch die Sonne das Ende, vnd letzte der Metallen, vnd es seind alle Metalla, sie seyen reine oder vnreine in ihrem inwendigen Sol, Luna vnd Mercurius: Aber einer ist die rechte Sonne, welcher darauß gezogen wird.

Also verstehest du, das viel ein andere Sonne oder ander Gold, alß das gemeine Gold, der Philosophen Gold ist, ob solches schon darauß genommen worden. So spricht auch Aurora consurgens cap. 16. Darauß ist offenbar, daß das Philosophische Gold nicht gemeins Gold sey, weder in der Farbe, noch in der Substantz. Darumb wird gesagt, dz es des Menschen Hertze erfrewe, vnd das Silber der gleichen. Aber das von jhnen außgezogen wird, ist eine weisse vnd rothe, wahre, fixe, vnd lebendige Tinctur. Es ist aber das Philosophische Gold, das mann nicht thewer kauffen darff, wie Alphidius sagt: vnd Morienes spricht, ein jedes Ding, das thewr gekauft wird, ist lügenhafft. Denn mit einem wenigen dieses Dinges, vnd mit wenigem Golde kauffen wir sehr viel. Vber das so ist vnser Gold lebendig Gold, vnd vnser Silber lebendig Silber, welche anders nichts alß Leben vnd vermehrung bringen können. Das gemeine Gold vnnd Silber seind Todt, welche mehr nicht verrichten können, alß ihnen von der Natur verliehen worden, biß sie von dem klugen Künstler von den Todten wieder aufferwecket, vnnd jhr Leben wieder erlanget haben: alßdann Leben sie auch, vnd können zur vermehrung vnnd fortpflantzung jhres Geschlechts viel Tugent erweisen. Von dem Todte der gemeinen, vnd Leben vnserer Metallen redet der vortreffliche noch lebende Philosophus Michael Sendiuogius im 11. Tractat seines Büchleins vom Philosophischen Steine also: Du solt aber ermahnet seyn, das du nicht das gemeine Gold vnnd Silber nehmest, denn sie seind Todt: nim vnsere, welche Leben. Darnach setze sie in vnser Fewr, so wird eine truckene Feucht daruon. Erstlich löse die Erde im Wasser auff, welches der Philosophen Mercurius genennet wird, vnnd das Wasser löset dieselben Corpora Solis & Lunæ auff, vnd verzehret sie, das nicht mehr als der zehende Theil mit einem Theile bleibet, vnnd diß ist die eingewurtzelte Feuchtigkeit der Metallen.

Nun aber weiter von dem Golde der Philosophen zureden, ist zuwissen, daß die Philosophi vnter zeiten jhr Wasser das Gold nennen, bißweilen auch jhre Erde. Von dem ersten Modo hat der Philosophus Nicarus oben geredt, vnnd Rosarius Philosophorum bekräfftigets mit nachfolgenden Worten: Was saget jhr aber hierzu, das die Philosophi sprechen, vnser Gold ist kein gemeine Gold, vnd vnser Silber ist kein gemeine Silber? Hierauf sage ich, daß sie das Wasser jhr Gold nennen, welches durch Krafft des Fewrs oben an in die höhe steiget: vnd ist dieses Gold warhafftig nicht gemeine Gold. Denn der gemeine Man würde nicht glauben können, das es wegen seiner Bestendigkeit oben hinansteigen könte.

Daß aber die Philosophi jhre Erde auch jhr Gold geheissen, bezeuget ebenmäßig dieser Rosarius, da er sagt: Wisse, das das Ertz der Philosophen Gold sey. Diese Erde wird Ertz, ferment vnnd Tinctur oder Seele genennet, gleich wir jhr Wasser die weisse vnnd geblätterte Erde geheissen wird: Dannenhero sagt der Author, so Clangorem Buccinæ geschrieben im Cap. von der solution (wie auch Hermes spricht.) also: Säet ewer Gold in die weisse vnd geblätterte Erden, die durch die Calcination Fewrig gemacht worden ist, subtil vnnd lüfftig, nemlich so viel säet das Gold, das ist die Seele vnnd tingirende Krafft in die weisse Erden, die mit gebührlicher zubereitung weiß vnnd reine worden ist, in welcher kein Vnflat ist.

Auß diesem ist offenbar, daß das Gold der Natur nicht ist die Materia des fermenti, sondern der Philosophen Gold ist das tingirende ferment. Vnd in Scala Philosophorum gradu 7. stehet also: Jhre Erde, darin jhr Gold gesäet wird, ist weiß, vñ jhre Seele ist Gold, vñ dasselbe Corpus ist der ort d' Weißheit, d' sie versamlet, vñ die wohnung d' Tinctur.

Vnd ein wenig fort spricht dieser Author: Derowegen sagt Hercules; Giesset wieder vmb, das ist, soluiret den Leib Magnesiæ, welcher weiß worden ist, vnd gleich den Hymbeerblättern. Deñ es ist das jenige, so da fliehet in das beste, vnnd das Gold, so von jhme außgezogen wird, heisset das Gold der Philosophen, vnd ist eine Tinctur, so eine Seele ist. Denn mit dem Wasser steiget der Spiritus auf in höhere Lufft, vnd dieses weisse Corpus, wenn das Gold wird weiß worden sein, haben sie es nach vnser Schwärtze vnser Gold genennet. Dahero spricht Senior: Vermische Gold vnd Gold, das ist, Wasser vnd Aschen. Vnd Hermes: säet Gold in geblätterte Erde: darumb schreiben die Philosophi, das vnser Gold nicht gemein Gold sey.

Es möchte zu obgesatzter Meinung hier jemand sagen vnnd fragen, warumb die Philosophi denn durch jhr Gold jetzt Wasser, bald aber Erde verstehen; das habe ein ansehen, das sie jhnen entweder selbst wiedersprechen, vnnd ihrer Sachen nicht einig seyen, oder aber, das sie solches confundiren, vnnd ihre Nachfolger verführen wollen? Hierauf ist die Antwort, das alle vnnd jede Philosophi, da sie die Warheit am offenbarlichsten gezeiget, solche in verborgene Reden wieder eingewickelt haben, vnnd seind in deme nicht wieder einander, sondern Stimmen wunderbarlich mit ein ander vberein, gleich alß hetten sie alle aus einem Munde geredet: so machen sie auch keine confusion, vnd suchen den würdigen Nachfolger nicht zuuerführen, sondern stellen jhme Hell vnnd Klar, doch in figürlichen Reden, für die Augen alle jhre Heimligkeiten, welche sie doch für den vnwürdigen vñ Gottlosen, so viel jhñen der höchste Gott Gnade verliehen hat, verdunckeln, vnd verbergen, damit solche edle Perlen nicht für die Säw, so nichts alß jhren Begierden damit nachzufolgen suchen, geworffen, vnd das Heiligthumb mit Füßen getretten werde: wie dann in gegenwertiger frage das Werck selbsten beweiset.

Denn es ist ja der gutherztige Nachfolger vnser Kunst gnugsam berichtet, vnd zu mehrenmahlen wiederholet, nicht allein woher vnsere Materia gelanget werden solle, sondern auch, das sie eine einige Materia sey, welche durch des Künstlers Klugheit in zwey Dinge, nemlich in Wasser vnnd Erden oder Mercurium vnnd Sulphur auffgelöset wird. So nun die Philosophi das Wasser Gold, oder die Erde Gold nennen, thun sie nicht vbel, vnd stehet bey jhrem freyen willen, wie sie es nennen wöllen: sintemal sie auch jhren Stein selbsten jhr Gold, ein mehr denn vollkommenes Gold, ein wiedergebornes Gold, vnd mit viel mehr dergleichen Namen nennen. Daß aber ein jeder jhre Meinung so balde nicht verstehen kann, ist vielmehr deren Vnwissenheit, alß der Philosophen Mißgunst zu zuschreiben.

Vnd ist also der Kunstsuchende Nachforscher der vberköstlichen Geheimnuß vberflüßig vnnd volstendig von der Materia vnsers grossen Steins berichtet worden, das sie aus keinerley vegetabilischen Gewächse, aus keinerley Thieren oder was davon genommen worden, auß keinerley Mineral, auß keinem Vnuollkommenem Metalle, sondern auß Gold vnd Silber gezogen werden müsse, vnnd das vnser Gold vnd vnser Silber nicht gemeine vnnd Todt Gold vnnd Silber, sondern der Weisen, so da lebendig Gold, vnd lebendig Silber ist, sey.

Nun ist noch vbrig, das er auch von vnser Solution alß von deß gantzen Wercks größten Geheimnüßen vnterrichtet werde.

Nu von der Solution zu reden, so geschiehet selbige, wann mann ein trockenes Ding naß, ein hartes weich, vnd ein verborgenes offenbar machet, das ist, so wann ein hartes Ding in Wasser verwandelt, nicht zwar in gemeine Wasser: wie Parmenides vnd Agadmoe die Philosophi, in der Turba lehren, da sie sprechen: Es sind etliche, wenn sie hören von der Aufflösung der Cörper, vermeinen sie, es sey ein Wasser der Wolcken: Wann sie aber vnsere Bücher gelesen, vnnd verstanden hätten, so würden sie je wissen, das vnser Wasser bleibend ist: sondern in das Wasser der Philosophen, das ist, in die erste Materiam, wie der Arnoldus sagt Rosar. 1. cap. 9. Das Werck der Philosophen ist, das sie jhren Stein in jhren Mercurium auflösen, das ist, in seine erste Materiam wieder bringen.

Vnd Auicenna sagt: Weñ du arbeiten wilt, so ist dir von nöthen, das du in der Aufflösung vnd Sublimation der beyden Liechter zu erst arbeitest, sintemal die erste Staffel des Wercks ist, das darauß Queckfilber werde. Darumb beschreibet auch Arnoldus lib. 2. cap. 1. & 2. die Solution, das sie sey eine Scheidung der Leiber, vnnd Bereitung der ersten Materi oder Natur.

Vnd Richardus Anglicus: Der Anfang vnsers Wercks ist, den Stein in seine erste Materiam auflösen, vnd ist die vereinigung des Leibes vnd Geistes, das darauß ein Mercurialisch Wasser werde. Wie aber die Solution das erste vnd nothwendigst stück ist vnsers Wercks, also ist sie auch wol das schwereste Theil desselben, wie dauon nicht vbel zeuget Eubaldus Vogelius, da er sagt: Welch ein schweres Werck es vmb die Solution sey, können diejenigen bezeugen, welche sich darin bemühet haben.

Vnd Bernhardus Graue von Treßne schreibet in seinem Brieff an Thomam von Bononia: Wer die Kunst vnd Wissenschaft der Auflösung weiß, das ist zu der Kunst Geheimnuß gelanget, welches ist die Gestalten vermischen, vnnd auß den Naturen die Naturen außziehen, welche darin kräftiglich verborgen liegen. Denn einsmal muß solche Solution nicht geschehen mit scharffē Wasser, sintemal alle scharffe Wasser verstören vnnd verderben das Corpus, welches sie auflösen vnnd zur verbesserung bringen sollen. Zu deme wird, wie gesagt ist, keine Auflösung im Wasser, das die Hände netzet, erfordert, sondern vielmehr ein trockenes Waßer, das ist, die erste Materia, welche nicht allein Mercurius. sondern auch Sulphur heisset.

Hieruon redet Zeumon in der Turba also: Wenn jhr die Corpora nicht reibet, zerbrechet, beflüchtiget vnd fleißig regieret, biß jhr seine Fettigkeit außziehet, vnd einen vnbegreifflichen Geist machet, so arbeitet jhr vmbsonst.

Vnnd Richardus Anglicus spricht auß Anweisung Auicennæ: Die Philosophi haben jhme fleißig nach gedacht, welcher Gestalt sie auß den vollkommenen Leibern die Schwefel außlocken, vnnd jhre Eigenschafften durch die Kunst besser reinigen möchten, damit das jenige durch der Natur hülff darauß werde, welches mann zuuor in jhnē nicht gesehen hat, ob sie es schon vollkommlich verborgen bey jhnen gehabt haben, vnnd sie sagen, das solches, ohne die Auflösung des Cörpers, vnnd dessen wiederbringung in die erste Materiam, nimmermehr geschehen könne, welche dann anders nichts ist alß Queckfilber, darauß sie zuuor gemacht gewesen seind, vnd solches ohne einige vermischung vnd zusatz eines frembden dinges. Denn vnsere Corpora lösen kein Wasser auff, alß das ihres Geschlechts ist, vnd welches von den Leibern dicke gemacht werden kann, sagt Bernhardus in dem Sendschreiben an Thomam von Bononia. Vnnd ein wenig vorher spricht er in demselben Schreiben: Die Auflösung erfordert eine zusammen verbleibung, nemlich des auflösenden vnnd aufgelöseten, das auß beyden, nemlich dem Mänlichen vnd Weiblichen Samen eine newe Gestalt entspringe. Ich sage dir in aller Warheit, das kein Wasser durch Natürliche Reduction die Metallische Gestalt auflöset, alß dasjenige, welches bey jhnen in Materia vnd forma verbleibet, vnd welches die aufgelösete Metallen selbsten wieder coaguliren können.

Vnd Morfoleus spricht in der Turba: ein jedes Corpus wird aufgelöset mit dem Geiste, mit welchem er vermischet wird, vnd wird sonder zweiffel geistlich mit jhme, vnnd ein jeder Geist wird von den Leibern geendert vnd gefärbet, mit welchem Geiste eine tingirende vnd wieder das Fewr bestendige farbe vermischet wird.

Wann dann nun diesem allen also, so hat der Kunstsuchende Discipul mit fleiß nachzudencken, was diß dann für ein Wasser sey, sintemal die Erkäntnuß des Menstrui, wie Raymundus in Compendio animæ sagt, deren Dinge eines ist, ohne welches in der Meisterschaft dieser Kunst nichts verrichtet werden kan. Deñ es ist kein Ding in d' Welt, das der Metallen auflösung zusammen füget, spricht er im seinem Codicillo, alß vnser Menstruum: sintemal solches das Wasser ist, damit die Metallen mit Erhaltung jhrer Gestalten aufgelöset werden.

Weil aber dieses das grosse Geheimnuß ist, so die Philosophi nicht allein in allen jhren Schrifften am höchsten verborgen gehalten, sondern auch zu offenbahren verbotten haben, so wil ich dich doch, so viel mir zugelassen ist, auf den rechten Weg mit zweyen Philosophischen Sprüchen führen, deren der erste im Büchlein Rosarij abbreuiati mit folgenden worten gefunden wird: Die erste Bereitung, vnnd das fundament der Kunst ist die Auflösung, das ist, die wiederbringung des Leibes in Wasser, das ist, Queckfilber: Vnnd dieses haben sie die Aufflösung geheissen, wenn sie gesagt haben: Es werde das Gold, so im Leibe der Magnesiæ verborgen ist, auffgelöset, das es in seine erste Materia wieder gebracht werde, daß darauß werde Schwefel vnnd Queckfilber, nicht das es wieder im Wasser verkehret werde: sintemal vnsere solution nichts anders ist, alß das der Leib wieder feuchte, vnnd in die Natur des Queckfilbers wieder auffgelöset, vnnd die Sältzigkeit seines Schwefels geringert werde, welcher heilige Schwefel von zweyen Schwefeln abgezogen, gemacht wird, wenn der Geist dem Leibe begegnet.

Den andern Spruch setzet Riplæus in der vorrede seiner zwölf Thüren: ich wil dich in Warheit, lehren, das du verstehest, es seyen drey Mercurij, welche die Schlüssel der Wissenschaft sind, vnd Raymundus seine Menstrua genennet hat, ohne welche nichts rechts gemacht wird. Deren aber zwene seind wieder abweichende, so nicht des Cörpers eigner Natur seind: Der dritte aber ist der wesentliche Mercurius der Solis vnd des Lunæ, deren Eigenschaft ich dir erklären wil. Denn der andern Metallen wesentlicher Mercurius ist vnsers Steins vornembstes Materiale. In Sonn vnd Mond werden vnsere menstrua nicht mit Augen gesehen, nur allein durch die Wirckung.

Dieses ist vnser Stein, so vnsere Schrifften jemand recht verstehet. Es ist die Seele vnd glantzende Wesen der Sonnen vnd des Mondes, vnnd die gar subtile Influentz, dadurch die Erde jhren Schein empfangen. Denn was ist Gold vnd Silber anders, spricht Auicenna, alß eine reine, weisse vnd rothe Erde. Nimb obgedachten Schein von jhnen, so wird alß dann die Erde sehr geringen werths sein. Wenn alles zusammen gesetzt ist, heissen wirs vnser Bley. Die Eigenschafft des Scheins rüret von der Sonnen vnd dem Monde her: vnd dieses seind in Summa vnsere Menstrua.

Die vollkommene Corpora calciniren wir mit dem ersten natürlich: aber es kommet kein vnreine Corpus darzu, alß ines, welches gemeiniglich von den Philosophis der grüne Löw geheissen wird, der das Mittel ist die Tincturen zwischen der Sonnen vnnd dem Monde mit vollkommenmachung zusammen zufügen.

Mit dem andern, so eine Vegetabilische Feuchtigkeit ist, die da lebendig machet das, so zuuor Todt war, sollen beyde Materialische Anfänge, wie auch die formalische, aufgelöset werden, sonsten seind sie geringen werths.

Mit dem dritten, so eine allerdings bleibende Feuchtigkeit ist, vnuerbrennlich vnd Fett in seiner Natur, wird der Baum Hermetis in Aschen verbrennet. Dieses ist vnser gewissestes natürliche Fewr, vnser Mercurius, Schwefel, vnser reine

through the strength of fire; and this gold truly is no common gold. For the common man would not believe that it could rise because of its constancy.

But that the *Philosophi* also called their earth their gold is likewise attested by *Rosarius* who saith: Note that the ore is the philosopher's gold. This earth becometh ore, and is called *Ferment* and *Tincture*. Therefore saith the author who wrote *Clangor Buccinae*, in the chapter about the Solution (as also *Hermes* saith): Sow your gold in the white and leavened earth, which is made fiery, subtle, and airy through *Calcination*, i.e., Sow so much gold, which is the soul and tingeing power, in the white earth, made white and pure by due preparation, in which is no filth.

From this is revealed that the gold of Nature is not the *Materia fermenti*, but the tingeing *Ferment* is the philosopher's gold. And thus it is written in *Scala Philosophorum*, gradu 7: Their earth wherein their gold is sown is white, and their soul is gold, and the very same *Corpus* is the place of wisdom, which it assembleth, and is the abode of the *Tincture*.

And further on the author saith: For that reason *Hercules* saith: Pour it again, i.e., dissolve the body of Magnesia, which hath become white and like raspberry leaves. For that body seeketh refuge in the best, and the gold extracted from it is called the gold of the philosophers, and is a *Tincture*, hence is a soul. For with the water the *Spiritus* riseth into high air, and this white *Corpus*, when the gold hath become white, they have called our gold after our blackness. Therefore *Senior* saith: Mix gold with gold, i. e., water with ashes. And *Hermes*: Sow gold in leavened earth. Therefore the *Philosophi* write that our gold is no common gold.

To this positive opinion someone might here reply and ask: Why do the philosophers sometimes conceive of their gold as water, but at other times as earth? Doth this not look as if they contradict each other and do not agree about these matters? That they confound these things? Or do they want to mislead their followers? The answer to this is that each and all of the Philosophers, where they have shown the truth, have shrouded it in hidden sayings, and therefore they do not contradict each other, but agree wonderfully with each other, as if speaking with one mouth. They do not create any confusion, and do not seek to mislead the worthy follower, but they present to him truly and clearly, in figurative language, all their secrets before his eyes, but which they conceal and darken before the unworthy and ungodly as much as the Highest God hath given them His mercy, so that such noble pearls will not be cast before swine, which follow only their bodily desires; and thus the Holy Sanctuary will not be desecrated. So in respect to the present question the Work proveth itself.

For the good-hearted follower of our art is many times sufficiently instructed, not only as to where our *Materia* should be obtained, but also that it is a single *Materia* which, through the skill of the artist, is dissolved into two things, viz., into water and earth, or *Mercurium* and *Sulphur*. Now if the *Philosophi* call the water "gold" or the earth "gold," they do nothing amiss, for it is a question of their own free will how they shall name it: since they also call their stone their gold, a more than perfect gold, a regenerated gold, and many more names of the kind. But not everyone can understand their meaning, as hath to be accredited to his ignorance rather than to the ill-will of the Philosophers in writing.

And now the art-seeking follower is sufficiently and completely informed of the super-excellent secret of the *Materia* of our great stone, and that it cannot be taken out of any kind of vegetable growth, or any kind of animal, out of no kind of mineral, and out of no imperfect metal, but it must be extracted from gold and silver, and that our gold and our silver are not the common dead gold and silver, but is that of the Philosophers which is living gold and silver.

Now all that the remaineth to be done is to be instructed about the *Solution*, the greatest secret of the entire Work.

Now to speak about the *Solution*: This occureth at once if one maketh something dry moist, softeneth something hard, and revealeth something hidden, i.e., when one transformeth a hard thing into water, but not into common water, as *Parmenides* and *Agadmoe* the *Philosophi* teach in the *Turba Philosophorum*, where they say: There are some who, when they hear about the dissolving of the bodies, believe it is a water of the clouds. But if they had read and understood our books, they would know that our water is permanent, especially in the water of the Philosophers, i.e., in the first *Materia*, as saith *Arnoldus* in *Rosarium* 1, *chapter* 9. The work of the Philosophers is that they dissolve their stone in their *Mercurium*, that is, they bring it again into its first *Materia*.

And *Avicenna* saith: If thou wouldst work, then it is necessary that thou dost first start with the dissolving and *Sublimation* of the two lights, especially since this is the first step of the work, that Mercury cometh therefrom. Therefore *Arnoldus*, lib. 2, chapters 1 and 2, hath written: The *Solution* is a separating of the bodies, and preparation of the *Materia* or nature.

And *Richardus Anglicus*: The beginning of our work is to dissolve the stone into its first *Materia* and the fusion of the body and spirit, so that it becometh a mercurial water. But just as the *Solution* is the first and the most necessary part of our work, so it is also the most difficult part of it. *Eubaldus Vogelius* testifieth not badly to it when he saith: How difficult a work the preparing of the *Solution* is they know who have labored at it.

And *Bernhardus*, *Count of Trevisan*, writeth in his letter to *Thomas of Bononiae*: He who knoweth the art and science of the dissolving, that is, he who hath attained to the secret of the art, which is to mix the forms and extract the natures out of the natures, which lie effectively concealed therein. Then again this *Solution* must not occur with caustic waters, since all caustic waters disturb and destroy the *Corpus* which they should dissolve

and perfect. And in addition, as hath already been said, no dissolving in the water which wetteth the hands is required, but rather a dry water, i.e., the first *Materia*, which is not called *Mercurius* alone, but also *Sulphur*.

Concerning this *Zeumon* also speaketh in the *Turba*: Ye do work in vain unless ye grind the *Corpora*, break them, dissolve them, and govern them industriously, until ye extract their fat and make an incomprehensible spirit from it.

And thus saith *Richardus Angelicus*, on the advice of *Avicenna*: The *Philosophi* considered studiously in what form they should extract the Sulphur from the perfect bodies, and how they might better purify their qualities through their art, so that such a thing might come out of it with the aid of Nature as no one had seen in them before, and they say that this could not be done without the dissolving of the bodies and returning them to the first *Materia* could never occur, which is nothing else than the Mercury out of which they had been made before, and it is this Mercury alone, without mixture or addition of any alien matter. For our *Corpora* are not dissolved by any waters, except that of their own kind, which can be thickened by the bodies, as saith *Bernhardus* in his epistle to *Thomas of Bononiae*. And a little before in the same epistle he saith: The dissolving requireth a remaining together, namely that of the dissolving and the dissolved, that out of both the male and female seed come forth in a new form. I tell thee in all truth that no water dissolveth the metallic form through natural *Reduction* except that which remaineth with them in the *Materia* and *Forma*, and that which can again coagulate the dissolved metals.

And *Morfoleus* saith in the *Turba*: Every *Corpus* will be dissolved by the spirit with which it is mixed, and will become, undoubtedly, spiritually one with it, and each spirit will be changed and colored by the bodies, with which spirit a tingeing and the fire-withstanding color is mixed.

Now, if all this be true, then the *Discipulus*, seeking the art, hath only to reflect diligently upon what kind of water it is, since he hath to strive for the knowledge of the *Menstruum*, whose things are one, and without which nothing can be accomplished in the mastery of this art, as saith *Raymundus* in *Compendio animae*. For there is nothing in the world but our *Menstruum*, he saith in his *Codicillo*, which can join together the dissolution of the metals; since it is such a water that the metals, retaining their form, can be dissolved with it.

But while this is the great secret, which the *Philosophi* have kept most deeply hidden in their writings, but have also forbidden it to be revealed, I shall direct thee (so far as I am permitted to do so), to the right way with two philosophical dicta. The first is found in the book *Rosarii abbreviati* in the following words: The first preparation and the *Fundament* of the art is the dissolving, that is, the restoration of the body in water, i.e., Mercury. And they called this the dissolving when they said: The gold, which is hidden in the body of *Magnesia*, is being dissolved, that it might be brought back into its first *Materia*, therein to become Sulphur and Mercury, not to be turned again into water, since our *Solution* is none other than the body moistened again and dissolved again into the nature of Mercury. And the salty content of its Sulphur is decreased, which holy Sulphur is extracted from two Sulphurs when the spirit meeteth the body.

The other dictum is to be found in *Ripley's* preface to his *Twelve Gates*: I will instruct thee in Truth that ye may understand that there are three *Mercurii*, which are the keys to knowledge, and which *Raymundus* hath called his *Menstruum*, and without which nothing can be made rightly. But two of them again differ, and are not the bodies' own nature. But the third is the essential *Mercurius* of *Sol* and of *Luna*, the quality of which I shall explain to thee. For the *Mercurius*, essential in the other metals, is the principal *Materia* of our stone. In Sun and Moon are our *Menstrua*, not to be seen with our eyes except through their effects.

This is our stone, when some one rightly understandeth our writings. It is the soul and radiant substance of the Sun and the Moon, and the very subtle *Influentia* through which the earth receiveth its light. For what else is gold and silver, saith *Avicenna*, but the pure white and red earth? Take the above-mentioned light from them and they will become earth of very little value. When everything is compounded together we call it lead. The very existence of the quality of the light originateth from the Sun and the Moon: and these are the *Summa* of our *Menstrua*.

We calcinate the perfect *Corpora* with the first according to Nature: but no impure *Corpus* will be added thereto except the one commonly called by the Philosophers the "Green Lion," which is the means for joining together the *Tinctures* between the Sun and the Moon with perfection.

With the other, which is a *vegetable* moisture, which bringeth to life that which had been dead before, both material elements as well as the formal ones, should be dissolved, otherwise they are of little value.

With the third, the tree *Hermetis* must be burned to ashes with a certainly lasting humidity, incombustible and greasy in its nature. This is our surest natural fire, our *Mercurius*, Sulphur, our pure *Tincture*, our soul, our stone, lifted up by the wind, born in the earth. Keep this well in thine heart.

This I may say to thee: That this stone is a potential vapor of the Sulphur, but thou must be careful how thou dost obtain it. For this *Menstruum* is in fact invisible, although it can still take the form and appearance of a clear water through the help of the other philosophical water, when the elements are separated.

And by very hard and strenuous work with this *Menstruum* the *Sulphur Naturae* can be made, when it hath been intensified in a natural way and hath been calcinated into a pure spirit. Then thou canst dissolve with it thy *Basis* or *Mass*.

Tinctur: vnsere Seele, vnser Stein, so vom Winde aufgehaben, in die Erde gebohren worden. Dieses verwahre wol in deinem Hertzen.

Ich darf dir sagen, **das dieser Stein ein *potentia*lischer Dampff des Schwefels ist**, wie du aber denselben vberkommest, must du fürsichtig sein. Deun dieses Menstruum ist in Warheit vnsichtbar, ob es schon durch das andere Philosophische Wasser, wenn die Elementa geschieden seind, dem Gesicht in Gestalt eines klaren Wassers vorkommen kann.

Auß vnd mit diesem Menstruo kann durch vberfleißige Arbeit das Sulphur Naturæ gemacht werden, wenn es Natürlich geschärffet, vnnd zu einem reinen Geiste calciniret ist: alßdann kanst du damit dein Basin oder massam auflösen.

Dieses seind nun die Worte dieser Philosophen, darin das gantze Geheimnuß der Solution entdecket ist. Wilt du nun mit der Müglichkeit der Natur zusammen halten, vnd bedencken, das du alle Wercke, so die Natur verrichtet, verrichten, das ist, wieder zuruckbringen, vnnd gleich einem Klawen zwirne wieder abwicklen must, so wirst du darin alle Warheit gar eigentlich vnd gründlich finden. Kanst du aber hierauß noch nicht mercken, wo die Thore verriegelt seind, so kennest du auch die materiam, vnd die Krafft der Natur nicht, darzu dich dann keine Brillen, oder vermeintes putabam, sondern ein inbrünstiges Gebett, vnnd darnach fleißiges Studieren, neben Betrachtung der Natur Mögligkeit, befordern werden.

Denn nach Offenbahrung des hohen vnd grossen Gottes habe ichs einig vnd alleine auß fleißigem Studieren vnd offtmals wiederlesung guter Bücher; nicht zwar, das ich darauß die materiam gelernet, welche ich allein auß Göttlicher Offenbahrung können lernen, sondern was ich gelernet, darauß confirmiret vnd conformiret, auch **die *solutionem*, welche bey allen *Philosophen* nur eine einige ist, vnnd ohne welche** weder die alten noch newen Philosophi etwas verrichten können: Dannenhero **sie dann auch** *Secretum artis* vnd Arcanum Philosophorum, quod nemo nisi Deus reuelare debet, geheißen wird, auch alle Arbeit begriffen, dafür ich dann dem Schöpffer aller Dinge mit Mund vnnd Hertzen Lob, Ehr vnnd Preiß sage, jetzt vnnd in Ewigkeit, Amen.

Damit du aber, lieber Leser, je keine Vrsache dich vber mich zubeschweren haben mögest, so wil ich dir durch die Liebe Gottes noch ein Geheimnuß offenbahren: vnnd solt wissen, ob schon eine einige Solution ist, das doch solche *secundum prius & posterius*, wie mann in den Schulen zu reden pfleget, abgetheilet wird.

Die erste ist die zertheilung, dauon Arnoldus redet, oder zerlegung in seine erste materiam, wie obgedacht: die andere aber ist die vollkommene Auflösung des Leibes vnnd des Geistes zugleich, da dann das soluirende, vnd das da soluiret wird, immer beysammen bleiben, vnd geschiehet mit dieser Auflösung des Leibes die Coagulation des Geistes. Allhier kanst du sehen gantz Hell vnd Klar für deinen Augen alles, was du zusehen vnd zuwissen begehrest: **vnd ist doch nur ein Werck der Weiber, vnnd ein Spiel der Kinder, wegen der wenigen Mühe, so mann dabey hat,** dauon dann nicht weiter zu reden nötig ist: sintemal wer den Anfang recht weiß, auch wol das Ende, durch Gottes Segen, erlangen, vnnd alle diese herrligkeit, so vns die ewige Herrligkeit, wenn wir in vnsern verklärten Leibern Gott schawen werden, gleichsam vorbildet, das wir auch alle irrdische wollüste verachten, vnnd dieser ewigen, vnendlichen vnnd vnaußsprechlichen Wollust alleine nachtrachten, gar schöne mit seinen leiblichen Augen sehen wird.

Hiermit wil ich nun dieses kurtze Tractetlein beschliessen, vnnd was dir weiter zu wissen nötig, in folgender Parabol klärlich ohne einigen Mangel oder fehler für Augen stellen, darin du zugleich die gantze Practicam finden, vnnd so du dero fleißig nachfolgest, wirst du selbst zu dem volstendigen Ende vnd wahren Weißheit gelangen, darzu dir vnd vns allen verhelffen vnd darbey erhalten wolle Gott der Vatter, Gott der Sohn vnd Gott der heilige Geist, hochgelobet in alle Ewigkeit, Amen.

Folget nun die Parabola, darin die gantze Kunst begriffen ist.

Es ist ein Ding, einig in Zahl vnd Wesen,
Welchs die Natur durch der Kunst hilff verkehret,
In zwey, in drey, vier, fünff, alß wir thun lesen,
Mercur vnd Sulphur solches ernehret,
Geist, Seel vnd Leib, darzu vier Elementen,
Der weisen Stein das fünst ist, so sie senden.
Ohn Trug du dein materiam solt zehlen,
Zwiefach-mercurialischer Substantz,
Ohn frembden Schwefel, rein du dir solt wehlen,
Vnd sie im Grund soluiren gar vnd gantze,
Nach rechtem Gewicht sie wieder componiren,
So werden sie dich zu der Warheit führen.
Nach der Solution solt du bald sublimiren,
Auch Calcinirn, vnd fleißig distilliren,
Coaguliren vnd darnach figiren
In einem Gefäß, denn fahe an zu tingiren,
So hast du Artzney Menschen vnd Metallen
Gesund zumachen, nach all deim Gefallen.

Alß ich eines mahls mich in einem schönen, grünen vnd jungen Walde spatzierete, vñ die Müheseligkeit dieses Lebens betrachtete, auch, wie wir durch den beschwerlichen Fall vnserer ersten Eltern in solch Elende vnd Jammer gerathen, beweinete, kam ich in solchen Gedancken fortgehende von dem allgemeinem Wege, vnnd gerieth, weiß nicht wie, auff einen engen Fußpfad, der gantz rauhe, vngebehnet vnd vnwegsam, auch mit so vielen Gebüschen vnnd Streuchen bewachsen ware, das leichtlich zuerkennen, wie solcher gar wenig gebraucht würde. Derowegen ich erschrack, vnd gerne wieder zuruck gangen were: solches aber war nicht mehr in meiner Macht, sintemal ein starcker Wind so gewaltiglich hinder mich herbliesse, das ich ehe zehen Schritte für mich, als einen zurucke thun könte.

Derowegen ich dann fortwandeln vnnd der rauhen Tritte nicht achten muste.

Alß ich nun eine gute Zeit fortgangen, komme ich endlich auff eine liebliche Wiese, welche gleich einem runden Circul mit schönen fruchtbaren Bäumen vmbwachsen vnd von den Einwohnern Pratum felicitatis genennet wird, vnder eine Schar alter Männer alle mit eißgrawen Bärten, ohne das einer ein zimlich junger Man war, mit einem spitzigem schwartzen Barte; so war auch einer darunter, deßen Namen mir zwar bekant war, sein Angesicht aber jetzo zur Zeit noch nicht ersehen könte, der war noch jünger, die disputirten von allerhand Dingen, insonderheit von einem hohen vnnd großem Geheimnuß, so in der Natur steckete, welches Gott vor der grossen Welt verborgen hielte, vnd nur allein wenigen, welche ihn liebten, offenbarete.

Ich hörete jhnen lange zu, vnnd gefiel mir jhr Discurs sehrwol, allein wolten etliche auß dem Geschier schlagen, nicht zwar die materiam oder Arbeit betreffende, sondern was die Parabolas, similitudines vnnd andere Parerga anlangete: Darin folgeten sie des Aristotelis, Plinij vnd anderer Figmentis, welche je einer von dem andern abgeschrieben hatte. Da konte ich mich nicht lenger enthalten, sondern mischte meinen Senf mit darunter, refutirete solche nichtige Ding auß der Experients, vnnd fielen mir der mehrentheil zu, examinirten mich in jhrer Facultet, jagten mich zimlich durch die Brände, Aber mein Fundament war so gut, das ich mit allen Ehren bestunde, darüber sie sich alle mit einander verwunderten, schlossen einhelliglich mich in jhr Collegium auf vnnd anzunehmen, deßen ich mich dann von Hertzen erfrewete.

Aber, sagten sie, ich könte noch kein rechter Collega sein, biß ich jhren Löwen erst recht kennen lernete, vnnd was er inwendig, so wol alß außwendig könte vnd vermöchte, vollkommen wüste. Derowegen solte ich fleiß anwenden, das ich ihn mir vnderthenig machte. Ich trawete mir selbsten zimlich wol, verhieß jhnen, ich wolte mein bestes darbey thun: Dann ihre Gesellschafft gefiel mir so wol, das ich nicht ein grosses genommen hette, vnd mich von jhnen scheiden lassen.

Sie führeten mich zu dem Löwen, beschrieben mir denselben sehr fleißig: Wie ich aber anfangs mit jhm vmbgehen solte, wolte mir keiner sagen: etliche vnter jhnen theten zwar Andeutung dauon, aber so confuse, das der Tausende jhn nicht verstehen könte, aber wenn ich ihn erst fest gemacht, vnnd mich für seinen scharffen Klawen vnnd spitzigen Zänen versichert hette, verhielten sie mir weiters nichts. Nun war der Löw sehr Alt, Grimmig vñ gros, seine gelbe Zoten hiengen jhme über den Halß, schiene gantz vnuberwindlich, das ich mich meiner Temeritet halben halb entsetzte, vnnd gerne wieder zuruck gekehret were, wo meine zusage, vnd dann das die Alten vmb mich herumb stunden, vnnd was ich beginnen würde, erwarteten, mich nicht auffgehalten hetten. Ich trat zum Löwen mit guter zuuersicht in seinen Graben, fieng ihm an zu schmeicheln, er aber, sahe mich mit seinen hellglantzenden Augen so starck an, das für Furcht mir bey nahe das Wasser vber die Kärbe gangen wäre: Gleichwol erinnerte ich mich, daß ich von den alten einem, alß wir nach den Löwen graben giengen, vernommen hatte, das sehr viel Leute sich den Löwen zuzwingen vnternommen, vnnd jhrer wenig solches zu Ende bringen können, wolte ich nicht zuschanden werden, vnnd erinnerte mich mancherley Griefflein, so ich durch grössern fleiß in dieser Athletica gelernet, zu dem war ich auch in der Natürlichen magia wolerfahren, vergaß dagegen des liebkosens, vnnd grieff den Löwen so behende Künstlich vnd subtile an, das ehe er es recht gewar würd, ich das Blut auß seinem Leibe, ja auß seinem Hertzen herauß langete, das war schön roht, aber sehr Cholerisch, ich anatomirete weiter, vnnd fand bey jhm, darüber ich mich verwundern muste, sonderlich waren seine Gebeine so weiß alß ein Schnee, vnd waren deren viel mehr alß seines Bluts.

Alß nun solches meine liebe Alten, so oben vmb den Graben herumbstunden vnd mir zusahen, innen wurden, disputirten sie hefftig vnter einander, so viel ich auß jhren Bewegungen abnehmen möchte, was sie aber sagten, könte ich, alß der ich noch tief vnten im Graben war, nicht vernehmen: Doch alß sie mit Worten hart an einander kamen, hörete ich, das einer sprach, er muß jhn auch wieder Lebendig machen, sonsten kann er vnser Collega nicht seyn, Ich wolte nicht gerne viel weitleufftigkeit machen, vnd begab mich auß dem Graben vber einen großen Platz, vnnd kam, weiß nicht wie, auf eine sehr hohe Mawren, deren höhe vber 100. Elen gegen die Wolcken auffsteig, oben war sie aber nicht eines Schuhes breit, vnd gieng von Anfange, da ich hienauf gangen biß zum Ende eine eyserne Handhabe recht mitten auf der Mawren hin mit vielen eingegossenen Stützen wolbefestigt. Auf dieselbe Maure kam ich, sag ich, vnd dauchte mich es gienge einer etliche schritte lang vor mir her auf der rechten Seiten der Handhaben.

Alß ich aber demselben eine weile nachgefolgt, sahe ich hinter mir auf der andern Seiten auch jemand folgen, zweiffel noch, obs ein Man oder Weib gewesen, das rieff mir vnnd sagte, auf seiner Seiten were es besser Wandeln, alß da ich gienge, welches ich leichtlich glaubte, denn wegen der Handhaben, so in der mitten stund vnnd den Gang gar enge machte, war sehr vbel gehen in solcher Höhe. Dann ich auch etliche, so solchen Weg gehen wolten, hinter mir her hierunter fallen sahe. Derowegen schwang ich mich vnter der Handhaben, mich gar feste mit den Händen haltende, hindurch, vnd gieng also auf der andern Seiten fort, biß ich endlich an ein ort der Mauren kam, der sehr gehe vnnd gefehrlich hienunter zukommen war, Da gerewete mich erst, das ich nicht auf der andern Seiten blieben were, vnnd konte auf dieselben nicht mehr vnden hindurch kommen, so ware es mir auch vnmöglich wiederumb zuwenden, vnnd auf den andern Weg mich zubegeben, Derowegen wagte ich mich, trawete meinen guten Füssen, hielt mich fest vnd kam ohne Schaden hienunder, vnd alß ich ein wenig weiter gewandelt, sahe vnnd wüste ich von keiner Gefahr mehr, wuste auch nicht, wo die Maure oder Handhabe hinkommen ware.

Nachdeme ich nun hienunder kommen, stunde daselbsten ein schöner Rosenstock, darauf waren schöne rote vnd weisse Rosen gewachsen, doch der roten vielmehr als der weissen, deren brache ich etliche abe, vnnd steckte sie auf meinen Hut. Mich bedauchte aber daselbsten eine Maure, so vmb einen großen Garten gieng, in dem Garten waren junge Gesellen, vnd weren die Jungfrawen zu denselben gerne in den Garten gewesen, wolten aber nicht weit vmbwandern, oder viel Mühe anwendẽ, das sie zur Thüren kommen weren. Da erbarmete ich mich vber dieselbigen, gieng den Weg wieder, den ich kommen war, doch auf ebener Bane, vnd gieng so geschwinde, das ich bald bey etliche Häuser käm, da ich vermeinete des Gärtners Hauß zu finden. Aber ich fand daselbsten sehr viel Volcks, ein jedes hatte seine eigene Kammer, waren langsam 2. zusammẽ, die arbeiteten gar fleißig: doch hatte ein jeder seine eigne Arbeit. Was sie aber theten, bedauchte mich, hette ich vor diesem auch gethan vnd gearbeitet, vnd were mir alle jhre Arbeit bewust, sonderlich gedachte ich, sihe, thun auch so viel andere Leut solche schmutzige vnd suddelhafftige Arbeit, so nur einen Schein, nachdem eines jeden Anbildung ist, aber kein fundament in der Natur hat, so ist dirs auch zuuerzeihen, Wolte mich derowegen, weil ich wüste, das solche Kunste mit dem Rauche verschwinden, nicht lenger hierein vergeblich aufhalten, vnnd gieng meinen vorgenommenen Weg fort.

Alß ich nun nach der Gartenthür zugieng, sahẽ mich etliche auf einer seite sawr an, daß ich fürchte, sie würden mich an meinem Proposito verhindern: Andere aber sagten: sihe, der wil in den Garten, vnnd wir haben so lange zeit Garten Dienste allhie gethan, vnnd seind doch niemaln hinein kommen, wie wollen wir jhn außlachen, wenn er einen Blossen schlegt. Ich aber achtete solches alles nicht, weil ich dieses Gartens gelegenheit besser, alß sie, wuste, ob ich schon niemalen darin gewesen, sondern gieng mitten zu einer Thür, die war feste verschlossen, das mann auch von aussen kein Schlüsselloch sehen noch finden könte. Ich aber merckte, das ein klein rundes Loch, das mann doch mit gemeinen Augen nicht sehen konte, an der Thür war, vnd gedachte alßbald, mann müste daselbst die Thür öfnen: War derowegen mit meinẽ hierzu sonderlich bereiteten Diederich fertig, schloß auf, vnnd gieng hienein. Alß ich nun zu der Thür hienein war, fand ich noch etlich andere verriegelte Thor, die ich doch, ohne Mühe, öfnete. Es war aber diß ein Gang, gleich alß were es in einem wolgebawetem Hause, etwa sechs Schue breit, vnd zwantzig lang, oben mit einem Boden. Vnd obwol die andern Thüren noch verschlossen, könte ich doch durch dieselbigen, alß die erste Thüer geöffnet war, gnugsam in den Garten sehen.

Ich wanderte im Namen Gottes in den Garten fort, da fand ich mitten darinnen ein kleines Gärtlein, so viereckicht, vnd auf jeder seiten bey Sechsmeßruten lang in sich begrieffe, das war mit Rosendorn vmbhecket, vnd blüheten die Rosen sehr schöne. Weil es aber ein wenig regnete, vnd schiene die Sonn darin, verursachete vnd gab es ein sehr liblichen Regenbogen. Alß ich nun bey demselben Gärtlein hinweg war, vñ an dẽ Ort, da ich den Jungfrawen helfen solte, gehen wil, sihe, da werde ich gewar, das an stat der Mauren ein niedriger geflochtener Zaun daselbsten stund, vñ gieng die schönste Jungfraw in gantz weißen Atlaß gezieret, mit dem statligsten Jüngling, so vnterm hauffen vnd in Scharlachen beklei-

Now these are the words of the Philosopher wherein the whole secret of the *Solution* is disclosed. Now if thou dost want to hold fast to and ponder over all the potentialities of Nature, so that thou perform all the works which Nature performeth, then thou must recall and unwind like a ball of twine, what thou wilt find herein of all truth, clearly and profoundly set forth. But if thou canst fail to note herein where the locked doors are, then thou knowest neither the *Materia* nor the power of Nature, and for this thou wilt not need any spectacles nor an imaginary *putabam*, but a most fervent prayer; and assiduous study, in addition to contemplation of the possibilities of Nature, will expedite thee.

I have acquired my knowledge solely and alone, after the revelation of the High and Great God, from the assiduous study and oft-repeated reading of good books; I do not say explicitly that I have learned about the *Materia* therein, which I could learn only from divine revelation, but what I learned confirmed and conformed thereto, also about the *Solution*, which with all Philosophers is but one, and without which neither the old nor the new Philosophers can accomplish anything. Therefore it is called also *Secretum artis* and *Arcanum Philosophorum, quod nemo nisi Deus revelare debet*, including all work, and for this I thank the Creator of all things, giving unto Him praise, honor, and glory, now and for ever. Amen.

But thou, dear reader, must have no reason to complain about me, and therefore I will reveal to thee, through the love of God, still another secret. And thou shalt know that this *Solution* although one, is divided into a *secundum prius et posterius*, as they take care to say in the schools.

The first is the dissolution of which *Arnoldus* speaketh, or the decomposition into its first *Materia*, but the other is the complete dissolving of the body and the spirit at the same time, since the dissolving and the dissolved always remain together, and together with this dissolving of the body ocurreth the *Coagulation* of the spirit. Here thou canst see quite clearly and plainly with thine own eyes all that thou dost desire to see and know: and it is only a woman's work and a child's play, because one hath so little difficulty therewith, whereof there is no need to speak further; since whoever knoweth the beginning, knoweth also how, by God's blessing, to attain the end, which, so to speak, pictureth to us all the glory, all the eternal glory, when we shall behold God in our transfigured bodies. Hence we scorn all earthly lusts and strive only for the eternal, infinite, and unspeakable delights, which, all beautiful, we shall see with our own eyes.

Herewith I shall now close this short *Treatise*, and set clearly before thine eyes, in the following parable, what is further necessary for thee to know, without lack or error. And in this parable thou wilt find the whole *Practica*, and if thou but follow it diligently, thou wilt arrive at the final end and true knowledge. To that end mayest thou and all of us be helped and preserved from want, by God the Father, God the Son, and God the Holy Ghost, to Whom be highest praise for ever and ever. Amen.

HERE FOLLOWETH THE PARABOLA WHEREIN THE WHOLE ART IS COMPRISED.

There is one thing, one in cipher and in essence,
  Which Nature through art helpeth to transform
Into two, into three, four, five, as we do read.
  Mercury and *Sulphur* do nourish it,
    Spirit, Soul and Body, and four Elements,
  The Philosopher's Stone is the fifth, which they transmit.
Without fraud shouldest thou count thy *Materia*,
  A two-fold *mercurial* substance.
Free from alien *Sulphur*, thou shalt choose the pure
  And dissolve them from the ground up entirely,
    Compound them again in their true weight,
  And they will lead thee unto the truth.
According to the *Solution* shalt thou soon *sublimate*,
  Calcinate, and diligently *distillate*,
    Coagulate, and then place it securely
  In a container, then begin to tinge,
  And thou hast put up a medicine
    To heal men and metals — as you choose.

Once upon a time I went walking in a beautiful green and young wood and mediated upon and deplored the hardships of this life and upon how we came, through the troublesome fall of our first parents into such misery and distress. Thus thinking, I left the common path and I came, I know not how, upon a narrow footpath, very rough, untrodden, and hard to walk upon, overgrown with many bushes and shrubs, and it was easy to see that this trail was very little used. Thereupon I became frightened and wanted to turn around and go back, but it was not within my power, especially since a strong wind blew mightily behind me, so that I had to take ten steps ahead for every one I could take backwards.

Therefore I had to continue on the trail despite its roughness.

Now after I had walked for some length of time, I came to a lovely meadow, surrounded by beautiful fruitful trees, as in a circle. This meadow was called by the inhabitants *Bratum felicitatis*. There I met with a group of old men with snow-white beards, save for one young man with a pointed black beard; and among them was one whose name I knew, and who was still younger, but as yet I could not see his face. And they had a great dispute about all kinds of things, especially about a high and great secret, which was hidden in Nature and which God kept hidden from the great world, revealing it only to those few who loved Him.

I listened to them for a long time, and I liked their discourse very much, but some of them seemed to maunder absurdly, not indeed about the *Materia* or the work in question, but about the *Parabolae, Similitudes*, and other *Parergons*. Therein they followed *Aristotle, Pliny*, and other *Figmenta*, each of whom had

copied from the other. Here I could no longer contain myself, but put in mine own word, refuting many futile things out of my *Experients*, and there were many who gave heed to me, examining me in their *Faculty*, putting me through some very hard tests. But my foundation was so good that I came through with all honors, and they wondered a great deal about it, but unanimously took me into their *Collegium*, for which I was heartily glad.

But they said I could not be a real *Collega* until I first learned to know their Lion and knew fully what he could and would do internally as well as externally. Therefore I should apply myself diligently to making him submissive to myself. I was rather sure of myself, and promised them that I would do my best. For I enjoyed their company so much that I would not have parted with them for any amount of money.

They led me to the Lion and described him to me very carefully. But what I should do with the beast in the beginning no one would tell me. Some of them gave me hints thereon, but so confusedly that not one in a thousand could understand them, and after I had tied up the lion and made sure that his sharp claws and pointed teeth could not harm me, they no longer kept anything secret from me. The lion was very old, ferocious, and big, and his yellow mane hung over his neck, and he seemed unconquerable, and on account of my *Temerity* I was almost terrified, and I would gladly have turned back but for my agreement, and the old men stood all around me to see how I would begin, which also kept me. With good confidence I went up to the lion in his den, and began to cajole him, but he glared at me so intensely with his flittering eyes that out of fear I nearly let my water. At the same time I recalled having heard from an old man, on our way to the lion's den, that very many people had undertaken to conquer this lion, but very few had really done so. I did not want to come to grief, and I remembered many a grip I had learned through great diligence in athletics, and besides I was well versed in natural *Magia*, so that I forgot about the cajoling, and attacked the lion so fast, artfully, and subtly that I pressed the blood from his body, even out of his heart; it was beautifully red, but very choleric, and this I did before he even realised it. But I looked further into his anatomy and found many things about which I had to wonder greatly, especially his bones which were as white as snow, and there were more of them than of his blood.

When my dear old men, standing around the den and watching me, became aware of what I had done they began to dispute with each other vehemently, but I could not hear what they said, because I was still so deep in the den, and I could only see their gestures. But when they began to utter hard words to each other, I heard one who said: He must revive the lion also, else he cannot be our *Collega*. I did not intend to raise difficulties, left the den, went across a great square and came. I know not how, to a great wall, the height of which was over 100 ells against the clouds, but it did not have the width of a shoe, and from the beginning of the wall where I started unto the end, there ran on top of it an iron rail, well secured with many supports. On top of this wall I walked and thought I noticed someone going a few paces ahead of me on the right side of the rail.

After following that person for some time, I noticed some one following me on the other side of the rail, and I still doubted whether it were a man or a woman who called me and said it would be better to walk on his side than where I was going, and I believed it readily, for the hand-rail which thus stood in the middle made the walk very narrow and it was hard to walk on such a height. And then I saw some people behind me who wanted to go that way. Therefore I swung myself under the rail, grasping it tightly with both hands, and I continued on the other side until I came finally to a place on that wall which was dangerous to descend. Then I regretted that I had not stayed on the other side, for I could not pass under the rail again, and it was also impossible for me to turn back and take the other way again. Therefore I took a chance, trusted my good feet, held on tightly, and came down without harm. And when I had walked on for some time, I had forgotten all about danger and also did not know what became of the wall and hand-rail.

But after I had thus come down, there stood a beautiful rose-bush, on which grew beautiful white and red roses, but more red than white ones, some of which I broke off and put upon my hat. Whereupon I was aware of a wall enclosing a great garden, and in the garden were young fellows, and where the maidens would have liked to be, but who did not like to make so great an effort as to walk around that wall in order to come to the door. I was sorry for them and went back the way I had come, then upon a more level way, and I went so fast that I soon reached several houses, where I thought to find the house of the gardener There I found many people, each of whom had his own chamber, and two were working together slowly and diligently. But each had his own work. I thought I had done all this work which they were doing before them, and I knew all their work, and I thought: Look, since so many other people do such squalid and dirty work only for the appearance of it and according to their own notion, having no *Fundament* in Nature, then thou art thyself forgiven. Therefore I did not want to remain any longer, because I knew that such art would disappear in smoke, and I continued on my planned way.

As I now went toward the garden door, some people looked at me sourly, so that I feared lest they hinder me in my *Propositio*. But others said: See, he wanteth to go into the garden, and we who for so long a time did services for the garden have never entered it. Let us jeer at him, if he doth blunder. But I did not pay attention to them, for I knew better than they the situation of the garden, although I had never been in it, and I went right up to a door that was locked tightly, where one could not find even a key-hole from outside. But I noticed a small

det war bey dem Rosen Garten vorbey, eines das ander in Armen führende, vnd viel wolriechende Rosen in jhren Handen tragende. Ich sprach jhnen zu, und fragte sie, wie sie vber den Zäun kommen können? Dieser mein allerliebster Breutgam, sagte sie, hat mir vbergeholfen, vñ wir gehen nun auß diesem lieblichen Garten in vnsern Gemach Freundschafft zupflegen, Es ist mir lieb, sagte ich, das, ohne meine weitere Mühe, ewerm willen ein Genügen geschiehet: Dennoch sehet ihr, wie sehr ich mich geeilet, das ich euch zu dienen einen so weiten Weg, in so kurtzer Zeit, vmbgelauffen bin. Nach deme kam ich in eine große Mühle, von Steinen inwendig erbawet, darin waren keine Mehlkasten oder andere Dinge, so zum Mahlen gehören, sondern man sahe durch die Maure etliche Wasserräder im Wasser gehen; ich fragte, wie es darumb eine Gelegenheit hette, da antwortete mir ein alter Müller, das Mahlwerck ist auf der andern Seiten verschlossen, wie dann auch ich sahe vom Schütze Stege ein Müllerknecht hinein gehen, deme folgete ich nach. Alß ich nun vber den Steg, der zur lincken Hand die Wasserräder hatte, kommen war, stund ich stille vnnd verwunderte mich vber das, so ich da sahe. Dañ die Räder waren nun vber dem Stege, das Waßer Kohlschwartz, dessen Tropffen doch weiß waren, vnd war der Schütze steg nicht vber drey Finger breit, gleichwol wagte ich mich wieder zurücke, vnnd hielte mich an den Höltzern, so vber dem Schütze stege waren, kam also wol vñ ohngenäßet vbers Wasser. Da fragte ich den alten Müller, wie viel Waßerräder er hette: Zehen, antwortete er. Das Abentheur lag mir im Kopffe, vnd hette gerne gewüst, was die Bedeutung were. Alß ich aber vermerckte, das der Müller nicht loßbrechen wolte, gieng ich hinweg, vñ war vor der Mühlen ein erhabener gepflasterter Hügel, darauff waren etliche der vorigen Alten, die spatzierten bey d' Sonnen, die damaln sehr warm schiene, vnnd hatten einen Brieff von der gantzen Facultet an sie geschrieben, darüber consultirten sie. Ich vermerckte bald, was der inhalt sein möchte, vnnd das es mich antreffe, gieng derowegen zu jhnen vnnd sprach: Ihr Herren; ists meinet halben zuthun? Ja sagten sie, jhr must ewer Weib, so jhr vnlengst genommen, zur Ehe behalten, oder wir müssens vnserm Fürsten anmelden. Ich sprach, das bedarff keiner Mühe, denn ich mit ihr gleichsam gebohren vnd von Kind auf erzogen worden bin, vnnd weil ich sie einmahl genommen, wil ich sie auch jmmerdar behalten, vnnd sol vns der Todt selbst nicht scheiden: Denn ich habe sie von brünstigen Hertzen lieb. Was haben wir dann für Klage? antworten sie, die Braut ist auch zufrieden, vnd wir haben jhren willen; jhr müsset euch lassen copuliren. Wolzufrieden, sagte ich: Wolan, sprach der eine, so wird der Löw sein leben wiederbekommen, vnnd viel mächtiger vnnd kräfftiger werden als vorher.

Da fiel mir meine vorige Mühe vnd Arbeit ein, vnd gedachte bey mir selbst auß sonderbaren Vrsachen, es müste nicht mich, sondern einen andern, so mir wol bekant, betreffen: In dem sehe ich vnsern Breutgam mit seiner Braut in vorigem Habit daher gehen, zur Copulation fertig vñ bereit, dessen ich mich höchlich erfrewete: Deñ ich in grossen Angsten gewesen, die sachen möchten mich selbsten antreffen.

Alß nun, wie gedacht, vnser Breutgam in seinem Scharlachen glintzenden Kleidern, mit seiner liebsten Braut, deren weisser Atlassen Rock sehr helle Strahlen von sich gabe, zu gemelten Alten kame; Copulirten sie die beyde also balde, vnd verwunderte ich mich nicht wenig, das diese Jungfraw, so doch jhres Breutgams Mutter sein solte, noch so Jung war, das sie auch jetzo erst gebohren sein schiene.

Nun weiß ich nicht: was diese beyde müsten gesündigt haben, alß das sie, weil sie Brüder vnnd Schwester waren, sich solcher massen mit liebe verbunden, das sie auch nicht wieder von einander zubringen waren, vnd also gleichsam Blutschande wolten bezüchtiget werden. Diese beyde wurden an stat eines Brautbettes vnnd herrlichen Hochzeit in ein stetigs vnd immerwerendes Gefängnuß, so doch von wegen jhrer hohen Geburth, vnd ansehnlichen Standes, auch das sie ins künfftige nichts heimliches begehen, sondern all jhr thun vnnd lassen, der auff sie verordneten wacht bekant vnd in Augen sein solten, gantz durchsichtig, helle vñ Klar, gleich einem Cristall, vnd rund, wie eine Himmels Kugel, formiret waren, condemniret vnd verschlossen, darin mit stetigen Thränen, vnd wahrer Rew für jhre begangene Missethaten zubüssen vnd gnug zu thuen. Es wurden jhnen aber vorher alle frembde Kleidung vnnd Geschmück, so sie zur Zierde an sich gelegt, abgenommen, das sie in solchem Gemache gantz nacket vñ bloß ein ander beywohnen musten. Mañ gab jhnen auch niemand zu der in das Gemach hette gehen mögen, jhnen aufzuwarten, sondern nach dem mann jhnen alle Notturfft von Speise vnnd Tranck, welcher von vorigem Wasser geschöpfet, hinein gethan, würd die Thür des Gemachs gantz feste verriegelt vnd verschlossen, auch der Facultet Siegel dafür getrücket, vnnd mir anbefohlen, das ich jhrer hierin hüten, Vnd weiln der Winter für der Thür, das Gemach gebürlichen erwärmen solte, damit sie weder frieren noch brennen, sie auch auf keinerley wege herauß kommen vnd entfliehen möchten: Solte aber vber verhoffen einiger Schade vber diß Mandatum fürlauffen, würde ich deßwegen billich in grosse vnd schwere Straffe genommen werden. Mir war nicht woll bey der Sache, mein furcht vnd Sorgfeltigkeit machten mich kleinmütig: Denn ich gedachte bey mir selbst, das es nicht ein geringes were, was mir anbefohlen worden, so wüste ich auch daß das Collegium sapientiæ nicht zu liegen, sondern was es sagte, gewiß ins Werck zurichten pflegte. Jedoch weil ich es nicht endern konte, zu deme auch dieses verschlossene Gemach mitten in einem starcken Thurne stunde, so noch mit starcken Pollwercken vnd hohen Mauren vmbgeben war, darin mann mit zimlichen, doch stetem Fewr das gantze Gemach erwärmē konte, vntername ich mich dieses Ampts, vñ fieng in Gottes Namen an dz Gemach zuerwärmen, vñ die gefangene Eheleute von der Kälte zubeschützen. Aber was geschiehet? so balde sie die wenigste wärme empfindē, vmbfangen sie ein ander so lieblich, das der gleichen nicht bald wird gesehen werden, verbleiben auch in solcher Inbrünstigkeit, das dem jungen Breutgam das hertze im Leibe für inbrünstiger liebe zergehet, auch sein gantzer Leib in seiner liebsten Armen gleichsam zerschmeltzet, vnnd von einander fellet. Alß sie, so jhnen nicht weniger, als er sie, geliebet, solches gesehen, hat sie jhn mit jhren Thränen hertzlich beweinet vnnd gleichsam begraben das mañ für jhren vergossenen Thränen, so alles vberschwemmet, nicht mehr gesehen, wo er hin kommen. Solches jhr Weinen vnnd Trawren nun hat sie eine kurtze zeit getrieben, vnnd hat für grossem Hertzenleid auch nicht lenger leben wollen, sondern sich freywillig in dē Todt dahin gegeben. Ach wehe mir, in was Angst. Noth vnd Bekümmernuß war ich, das ich beyde mir anbefohlene gleichsam gantz in Wasser zergangen, vnd Todt für mir liegen sehen solte. Mir stunde mein gewisser Vntergang für Augen, vnd welches mir noch das beschwerligste ware, fürchte ich mehr den mir für Augen schwebenden Hohn und Spott, so mir wiederfahren würde, alß der Schaden, so vber mich ergehen solte.

Alß ich nun in solchen sorgfeltigen Gedancken etliche Tage zugebracht, vnd wie ich meinen Sachen rathen möchte, hin vnnd wieder bey mir berathschlaget, fiele mir endlich ein, wie die Medea des Aesonis Todten leib wieder lebendig gemacht hette, vnd gedachte bey mir selbsten: hat Medea ein solches thun können, warumb solte dir solches mißlingen? Fienge darauf an bey mir zu bedencken, wie ich solchem thun wolte: fande aber keinen bessern Weg, alß das ich mit steter Wärme wolte anhalten, biß so lange das Gewässer vergangen, vnnd ich vnserer Liebhaber Todte leichnam wieder sehen möchte, alß dann verhoffte ich aus aller Gefahr mit meinem grossen Nutzen vnd Lobe zuentkommen. Fuhr derowegen mit meiner angefangenen wärme fort, vnd continuirite dieselbe viertzig gantzer Tage, da ward ich gewahr, daß das Wasser je lenger je mehr abnam, vnd die Todtenleichnam, so doch so schwartz alß eine Kohle waren, wiederumb sich begunten sehen zulassen: vnd zwar were solches wol ehe geschehen, wenn das Gemach nicht allzu feste verschlossen vnnd versiegelt gewesen were. Welches ich doch keines Weges eröffnen dörffte. Denn ich merckte gar eigentlich, das das Wasser, so in die höhe stieg, vnnd den Wolcken zueilete, sich oben in dem Gemache wieder zusammen thete, vnd wie ein Regen herunter fiele: daß also nichts dauon kommen konte, biß vnser Breutgam mit seiner liebsten Braut Todt vnd verfaulet, vnd derohalben vber alle Masse vbel stinckend für meinen Augen lagen. Vnter dessen wurde in dem Gemache von der Sonnenschein in dem feuchten Wetter ein vberauß schöner Regenbogen gesehen, mit vbermäßigen schönen Farben, der mich denn nicht wenig meines vberstandenen Betrübnuß erfrewete, vielmehr aber ward ich frölich, daß ich meine beyde liebhabende für mir wieder liegen sahe. Wie aber keine Frewde so groß, welche nicht mit vieler Trawrigkeit vermischt: Also wurde ich auch in meiner Frewdigkeit betrübet, dieweil gedachte meine Anbefohlene noch Todt für mir lagen, vnnd mann kein Leben bey jhnen spüren köñte. Weil ich aber wüste, das jhre Kammer von so reiner vnnd dichter Materia gemacht, auch so feste verschlossen, das jhr Seel vnnd Geist nicht herauß kommen, sondern feste verwahret noch drinnen waren, führe ich mit meiner stetigen Wärme fort, Tag vnnd Nacht, mein anbefohlen Ambt zuuerrichten, gentzlich mir einbildende, das die beyde zu den Leibern, nicht wiederkehren wurden, so lange die Feuchtigkeit wehrete. Denn in der feuchten Natur sich selbige gerne halten. Wie ich dann auch in der That vnd Warheit befande. Denn ich wurde durch fleißig. Auffsehens gewahr, das von der Erden gegen Abend, auß Kraft der Sonnen, viel Dünste auffstiegen, vnnd sich in die hohe zohen, gleich alß ob die Sonne wasser zöhe: Die Coagulirten sich die Nacht vber in einen lieblichen vnnd sehr fruchtbaren Thaw, welcher des Morgens sehr frühe herab fiel, vnnd das Erdreich befeuchtete, auch vnsere Todte leichnam abwuschen, das sie von Tage zu Tage, je mehr solches Baden vnd Waschen geschahe, je lenger je schöner vnd weißer wurden. Je schöner vnnd weißer sie aber wurden, je mehr verlohren sich die Feuchtigkeiten, biß auch endlich, alß die Lufft hell vnd schöne, vnnd alles neblichte vnnd feuchte Wetter für vber, der Geist vnnd Seele der Braut in der hellen Luft sich nicht lenger enthalten konte, sondern giengen wieder ein in den Clarificirten vnnd nunmehr verklärten Leib der Königin, welcher also balde solche empfand, vnnd wurde dieselbe Augenblicklich wieder lebendig: welches mich dann, wie jhr leichtlich erachten könnet, nicht wenig erfrewete, sonderlich da ich sie in vber auß köstlichem Gewande, deßen gleichen auf Erden bey den wenigsten gesehen worden, vnnd mit einer köstlichen Krone von lauter Diamanten gezieret, sehen auffstehen, vnnd also reden hören: höret jhr Menschen Kinder, vnnd nemet war, die jhr von Weibern gebohren seyd, das der Allerhöchste macht hat Könige einzusetzen, vnnd Könige abzusetzen: Er machet Reich vnnd Arme, nach seinem willen: Er Töddtet vnd machet wieder lebendig.

Sehet dessen alles an mir ein wares vnd lebendiges Exempel: Ich war groß, vnd wurd geringe: Nun aber bin ich, alß ich gedemütigt worden, enige Königin erhaben vber viel Königreiche: ich bin Getödtet vnd wiederlebendig gemachet; Mir Armen sind die grossen Schätze der Weisen vnd Gewaltigen vertrawet vnd. vbergeben.

Derowegen mir auch die Macht gegeben worden, den Armen Reich zumachen, dem Demütigen Gnade zuuerleihen vnd dem Krancken Gesundheit zubringen. Aber ich bin noch nicht gleich meinem allerliebsten Bruder, dem großmächtigen Könige, so noch wieder von den Todten erwecket werden soll: Wenn der kommen wird, so wird er beweisen, das meine Reden war seind.

Vnnd alß sie dieses gesagt, schein die Sonne sehr helle, vnnd der Tag wurd wärmer alß zuuor, vnd waren die Hundstage für der Thür. Weil aber lang zuuorn auf die herrliche vnnd große Hochzeit vnserer newen Königin vielerley köstlicher Röcke, alß von Schwartzen Sammet, Aschfarben Damast, grawer Seiden, Silberfarben Taffet, Schneeweißen Atlaß, ja einem vber aus schönen silbern Stücke, so mit köstlichen Perlen vnd herrlichen hell glentzenden Diamanten gestücket, zubereitet waren, Also wurden auch gleichmäßig für den jungen König vnterschiedene Kleider, nemlich von Incarnat, gelben Auranien Farben, köstlichem Zeuge vnnd endlich ein roth Sammetes Kleid mit köstlichen Rubinen vnnd Carfunckeln in sehr grosser Menge gesticket, zugerichtet vnd bereitet: Die Schneider aber, so solche Kleider machten, waren gantz vnsichtbar, das ich mich auch verwunderte, wenn ich einen Rock nachdem andern, vnnd ein Kleid nach dem andern fertig sein sahe, wie doch solches zugegangen were, sintemal ich wol wuste, das niemand mehr alß der Breutgam mit seiner Braut in die Cammer gangen waren: das mich aber am allermeisten verwunderte, war das, so bald ein ander Rock oder ein ander Kleid fertig worden, die vorigen für meinen Augen gleichsam verschwunden, das ich nicht wuste, wo solche hinkommen, oder wer sie beygeschlossen hatte.

Alß nun dieses köstliche Kleid verfertigt, erschien auch der grosse vnd mächtige König, in grossem Glantze vnd Herrligkeit, deme nichts gleichen mag: Vnd alß er sich beschlossen befande, bat er mich freundlich vnd mit sehr holdseligen Worten, das ich jhme die Thür öffnen, vnnd herauß zukommen vergönnen wolte, es solte mir zu grossen Frommen gereichen. Ob mir nun wol zum höchsten verbotten worden, das Gemach nicht zuöfnen, so erschreckte mich doch das grosse Ansehen, vnnd die liebliche Beredsamkeit des Königs, das ich jhm gutwillig aufthät. Vnnd alß er herauß gieng, war er so freundlich, so holdselig, ja so demütig, das er in der That bezeugte, das hohe Personen nichts so wol zieret alß diese Tugenden.

Weil er aber die Hundstage över in grosser Hitze zugebracht hatte, ware er sehr dürstig, auch Mat vnnd Müde, vnd befahle mir, das ich von dem lauffenden schnellen Wasser vnter den Mühlen Rädern schöpfen vnd bringen solte, welches, alß ichs verrichtet, er einen grossen Theil mit grosser Begierde tranck, gieng wieder in seine Kammer, vnd befahl mir die Thür hinder jhm feste zuuerschliessen, damit jhn niemand verunruhigen, oder auß dem Schlaffe auffwecken möchte.

Hierin ruhete er wenig Tage, vnnd rief mir die Thür zu öffnen: Mich aber bedauchte das er viel schöner, blutreicher vnd herrlicher worden, welches er dann auch vermercket, vnnd solches ein herrlichs vnd gesundes Wasser zusein erachtete, forderte auch so bald mehr Wasser, tranck auch deßen viel, mehr als vorher, also auch, das ich die Kammer viel weiter zu bawen endlich bey mir beschlossen. Alß nun dieser König solches köstlichen Trancks, den doch die vnwissenden für nichts achten, nach seinem eignen Willen gnugsam getruncken, wurd er so schön vnd herrlich, das ich die zeit meines lebens weder herrlichere Person, noch herrlicher Thun vnd Wesen gesehen. Dann er führete mich in sein Königreich vnd zeigte mir alle Schätze vnd Reichthumb der Welt, das ich bekennen muß, das nicht allein die Königin die Warheit verkündiget, sondern auch den mehrsten Theil denen, so jhn kennen, zubeschreiben, hinderlassen: Denn Goldes vnnd edler Carfunckelsteine waren da kein Ende, verjüngerung vnd Wiedererstattung natürlicher Kräfte, wie auch Wiederbringung verlorner Gesundheit vñ hinnehmung aller Kranckheiten war ein gemein Ding daselbsten. Das war aber das Allerköstligste, das die Leute selbigen Landes jhren Schöpffer kennen, fürchten vnd ehren, vnd von demselbigen Weißheit, vnd Verstand, vnd endlich nach dieser zeitlichen Herrligkeit die ewige Seligkeit erlangen. Darzu verhelffe vns Gott Vatter, Sohn vnd heiliger Geist.

A M E N.

round hole in this door, which one could not see with common eyes, and I thought it was necessary to open the door there. I took out my master-key, prepared for this occasion, unlocked the door, and entered. After I was inside, I found some more locked doors, but I opened all of them without much trouble. But this was a passageway, as if it were in a well-constructed house, about six shoes wide, and twenty long, covered with a ceiling. And although the other doors were still locked, I could see through them sufficiently into the garden as soon as the first door was opened.

In God's Name I walked further on in the garden, and found in the midst of it a little garden, square in shape, and measuring six rods on each of its sides. It was covered with briar-rosebushes, and the roses thereon blossomed very beautifully. And since it had rained a little and the sun was shining, there was a beautiful rainbow. When I had left the little garden and had arrived at the place where I should assist the maidens, I noticed that instead of the walls there stood a low wattled fence, and a most beautiful maiden, bedecked in white satin, with a most splendid youth, went past the rose-garden, one leading the other by the arm and carrying many fragrant roses in their hands. I spoke to them and asked them: How did they come over the fence? She said: My dearest bridegroom helped me over it, and we are now going out of this lovely garden into our chamber to enjoy our friendship. I said: I am pleased that you can satisfy your desire without any further effort on mine. But see, how I ran so long a way in so short a time, only to serve you. After this I came to a great mill, built inside of stones. In it were not flour bins nor any other things necessary for milling, and one did not even see any waterwheels turning. I ask how all this came about, and the old miller answered me, saying that the milling-machinery was locked up on the other side, and I saw the miller's servant go in to it on the covered passage-way, and I followed him. But when I stood in the passage and beheld the water-wheels on my left side, I stood still, marvelling greatly at what I saw. For now the wheels were above the passage, the water was as black as coal, and the drops therefrom were white, and the passage was not more than three fingers wide. Nevertheless I risked going back, holding on to the logs which were over the passage, and came over the water unwetted. Then I asked the old miller how many water-wheels he had. Ten, he answered. I could not forget this adventure and I would have liked to know its meaning. When I saw that the miller did not want to reveal anything, I departed, and there was in front of the mill a high paved hill, and on top of it some of the above-mentioned old men, walking in the warm sunshine, and they held a letter in their hands, written by the entire *Faculty* and addressed to them, about which they took counsel. I soon noticed what it might contain and that it might concern me, therefore I went up to them and said: Sirs, is it about me? Yes, they answered, you have to keep the wife you married a short time ago, in wedlock, or we have to report it to our Prince. I answered: This will be very easy, for I was, so to speak, almost born with her and raised together with her from childhood, and because I had once taken her, I shall keep her always, and even death itself shall not part us, for I love her with all my heart. They replied: What then have we to complain about? the bride is also happy, and we know what she doth want: ye must be joined together. I am well satisfied, I answered. Well, said one of them, then will the lion also come back to life and be mightier and more powerful than before.

Then I recalled my previous exertion and work, and for some strange reason I thought that all this did not concern me, but some one whom I knew well. And thus thinking, I saw our bridegroom with his bride in their above-mentioned garments, going away, ready and prepared to be joined together, which pleased me greatly. For I had been in great fear lest these things might concern me.

Now when, as said, our bridegroom in his brilliant scarlet clothes came to the old men with his beloved bride whose white satin frock radiated in very bright rays, they were both soon joined together, and I marvelled not a little that this maiden, who might still be her bridegroom's mother, was yet so young that she seemed to have been born but recently.

Now I do not know wherein these two had sinned; it may be that they, being brother and sister and bound together in such a way that they were not to be separated, had been accused of incest. Instead of a bridal bed and true marriage, they were condemned and locked up in a strong and everlasting prison, to repent and pay for their evil deeds with everlasting fears and true regret. But because of their noble birth and rank, and in order that they might not do anything secretly any more, and that they might be always before the eyes of the watchman who was ordered to take care of them, their prison was transparent, crystalline, and formed not unlike a heavenly dome. But before this, all their clothes and ornaments with which they were adorned were taken from them, so that they had to live naked and bare in their dwelling-place. And no one was given them to wait upon them. But all the food and drink which was drawn from the above-mentioned water, which was necessary for them was placed therein. The door of their chamber was well locked and sealed with the seal of the *Faculty*, and I was ordered to guard it and since winter was soon to come, to heat their chamber duly, so that they should not freeze or burn, but in such a way that they could in no wise come out and escape. But if any damage should occur under the said *Mandatum*, I would certainly receive great and severe punishment therefor. I did not feel well about this matter, and my fear and worry made me faint-hearted. For I thought to myself that it was not a small work which I was commanded to do, but I knew that the *Collegium sapientiae* was not given to lying and always did what it said, and certainly prepared its work with care. However, I could not change it, and besides this locked chamber stood in the middle of a strong tower, surrounded by high walls and strong fortifications, and since one could heat the chamber with a moderate but constant fire, I undertook my office and began in God's Name to heat the chamber in order to protect the imprisoned married couple from the cold. But what happens? As soon as they notice the slightest warmth, they embrace each other so lovingly that one will not see the like again. And they stay together in such ardor that the heart of the young bridegroom vanished in fervent love, and his entire body melted and fell apart in the arms of his beloved. Then she, who had loved him no less than he had loved her, saw what had happened, she shed many tears for him and buried him, so to speak, with them, so that one could not see for overflowing tears what had happened to him. But her grieving and crying lasted only for a short time, and because of her grief she did not want to live any longer, but went voluntarily to her death. Ah! woe unto me! I was in fear, anguish and misery, because these two whom I was supposed to guard had been apparently dissolved entirely into water, and I saw them lying before me as dead. Certain failure confronted me, and what seemed to be the worst and what I feared most, was the coming derision and ridicule, as well as the perils I should have to meet.

I spent a few days in careful thought, considering how I could help mine affairs, when I recalled how Medea had brought Aeson's dead body to life again. And I thought to myself: If Medea could do it, why should I not be able to do it? I began to think about how to proceed with it, but did not find any better way than to maintain the steady warmth until the water would recede and I could view the dead bodies of our lovers. Then I hoped to escape all danger with gain and praise. Therefore I continued for forty days with the warmth with which I had begun, when I noticed that the longer I did so, the more the water disappeared. And I could see the dead bodies, black as coal. This would have happened sooner if the chamber had not been locked and sealed so tightly; but I was not permitted to enter it in any way. Then I noticed quite particularly that the water rose high up toward the clouds, collected on the ceiling of the chamber, and came down again like rain; and nothing could escape, so that our bridegroom and his lovely bride lay before mine eyes dead and rotten, stinking beyond all measure. Meanwhile I noticed in the chamber a rainbow in the most beautiful colors, caused by the sunshine in the moist weather, which gladdened me not a little in my sorrows, and I became rather happy to see my two lovers lying before me again. But no joy is so great that there is no sorrow in it; and therefore I was grieved in my joy because I saw the ones I was supposed to guard so lying before me that one could perceive no life in them. But since their chamber was made from such firm and pure *Materia* and closed so tightly, I knew that the soul and spirit could not escape therefrom, but were still enclosed therein. I continued with my steady warmth and heat day and night, performing my ordered duty, imagining that spirit and soul would not return to the bodies as long as the dampness lasted. For they like to dwell in the damp nature. And, indeed, I found this true. For I noticed in many painstaking observations that many vapors arose from the earth about eventide, through the strength of the sun, and went up high as if the sun were drawing up the water. But during the night they coagulated into a lovely and fertile dew, coming down in the morning, moistening the earth, and washing our dead bodies, which became all the more white and beautiful through such bathing and washing. But the more beautiful and white they became, the more they lost of their moisture, until finally the air became so light and clear, while all the foggy and damp weather had passed, the spirit and soul of the bride could not remain any longer in the clear air and went back into the transfigured and glorified body of the queen, and as soon as the body felt them it became instantaneously alive. Over this I rejoiced not a little, as you can very well imagine, especially since I saw her rise in a very costly garment, the like of which is seen by only a very small number of people on this earth, and she was adorned with a costly crown embellished with flawless diamonds, and I could see her rise and say: Hearken, children of men, and observe ye who are born from women, that the All-Highest hath the power to enthrone kings and to dethrone them. He maketh rich and poor, according to His will. He slayeth and maketh to live again.

And behold all this in me as a true and living example: I was great and became small; but now after I became humble I was raised to be a queen over many realms. I was slain and made alive again. The great treasures of the philosophers and of the mighty have been entrusted and given to me, the poor one.

Therefore was I granted the power to make the poor rich, to deal mercy to the humble, and to bring health to the sick. But not yet am I like my beloved brother, the great and mighty king, who will still be recalled from the dead. When he cometh he will prove my saying true.

And while she thus spake, the sun shone brightly and the days became warmer and the dog-days were soon to come. And long before the wedding of our new queen there were prepared many costly robes, made out of black velvet, ash-gray colored damask, gray silk, silver-colored taffeta, snow-white satin, yea, a silver piece of exceeding beauty, embroidered with costly pearls and bedecked with gloriously clear glittering diamonds. And in the same manner were prepared garments for the young king, namely of *Incarnat*, with the yellow colors of aureolin, costly fabrics, and finally a red velvet garment, embroidered, adorned, and prepared with costly rubies and carbuncles in very great quantities. But the tailors who made these garments were invisible, and I marvelled greatly when I saw one coat after another, and one robe after another, being finished, since I knew that no one else besides the bridegroom and the bride had gone into the chamber. But what most astonished me was that as soon as one coat or robe was ready, the former ones disappeared before my very eyes, and I did not know whither they had vanished nor who had locked them away.

And after this costly coat was finished, there appeared the great and mighty king in all his power and glory, and there was nothing like unto him. And when he found himself locked in, he asked me in a friendly way, with gracious words, to open the door for him, so that he would be able to go out, and said it would be to mine advantage. And although I was strictly forbidden to open the chamber, I was so terrified by the great appearance and the sweet power of persuasion of the king that I opened the door willingly. And when he left he showed himself very friendly and gracious, yea humble, so that one could truly see that nothing adorns persons of noble birth so much as these virtues.

And since he had spent the dog-days in great heat, he was very thirsty, weak, and tired, and he asked me to bring him some of the running water from below under the water-wheels of the mill. This I did, and after he had drunk a great part of it eagerly, he went back into his chamber and told me to lock the door fast behind him, lest some one should disturb him or awaken him from his slumber.

There he rested for several days, and then called me to open the door. But I observed that he had become far more beautiful, full-blooded, and glorious, and he also noticed it. Whereupon he thought it must have been a marvellous and healthy water, and he ordered more of it and drank much more of it than the first time. And I resolved to build the chamber much larger. After the king had drunk of this delicious beverage, which the ignorant do not value at all, to his heart's content, he became so beautiful and glorious that in all my life I never beheld a person more glorious or more noble in behavior and character. Thereupon he led me into his kingdom and showed me all the treasure and riches of the world, so that I have to admit that not only did the queen speak the truth, but he also gave a great part of it to those who know the treasure and can describe it. There was no end of gold and precious carbuncle-stones, and the rejuvenation and restoration of the natural powers, as well as restoration of lost health and the taking away of all diseases, was a common thing there. But what was most delightful in this kingdom was that the inhabitants knew, feared, and praised their Creator, obtaining from Him their wisdom and knowledge, and finally, after this earthly joy, they obtained eternal glory. To this end may God, Father, Son, and Holy Ghost help all of us.

A M E N .

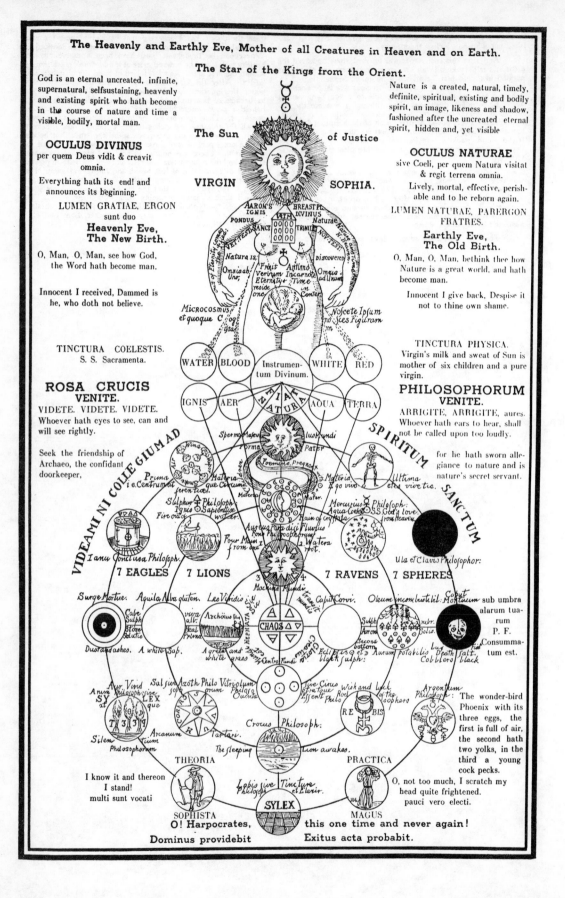

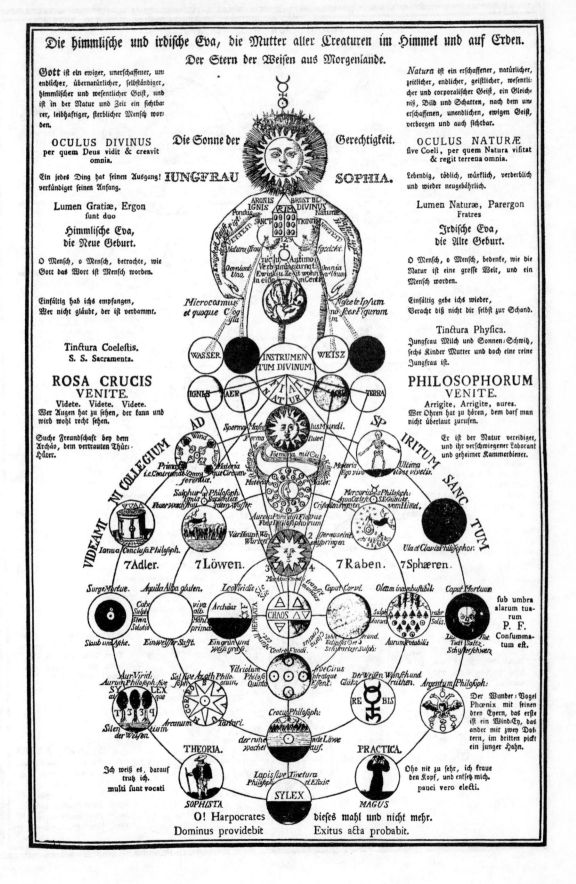

Die himmlische und irdische Eva, die Mutter aller Creaturen im Himmel und auf Erden.
Der Stern der Weisen aus Morgenlande.

305

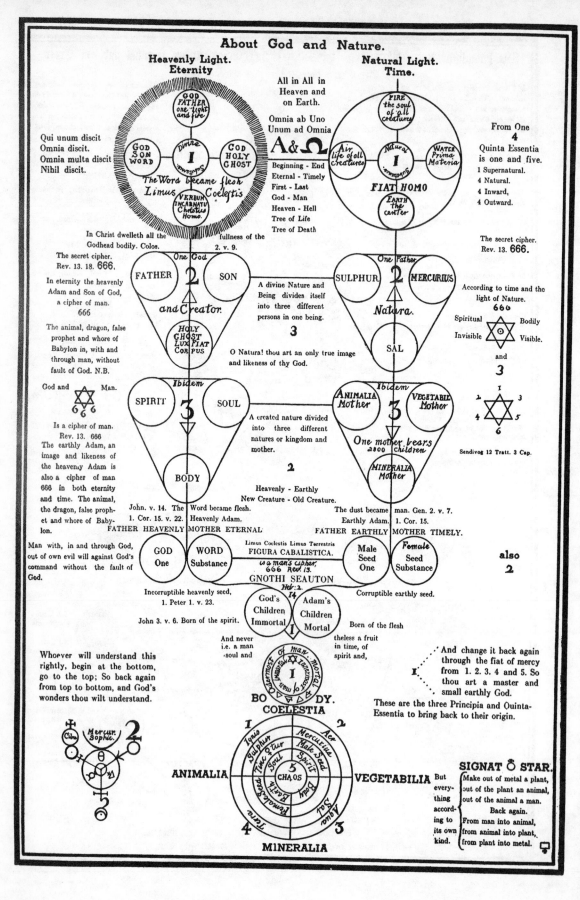

About God and Nature.

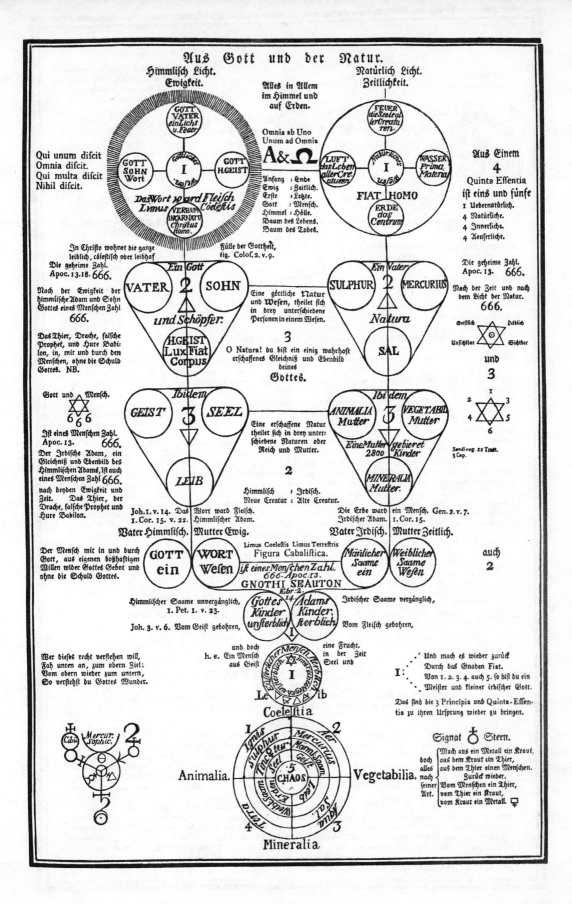

Aus Gott und der Natur.

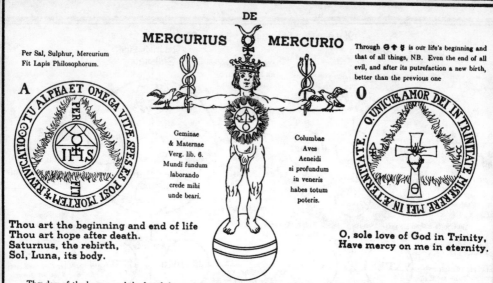

DE
MERCURIUS ☿ MERCURIO

Per Sal, Sulphur, Mercurium
Fit Lapis Philosophorum.

Through ⊖✚☿ is our life's beginning and that of all things, NB. Even the end of all evil, and after its putrefaction a new birth, better than the previous one

A

O

Geminae
& Maternae
Verg. lib. 6.
Mundi fundum
laborando
crede mihi
unde beari.

Columbae
Aves
Aeneidi
si profundum
in veneris
habes totum
poteris.

Thou art the beginning and end of life
Thou art hope after death.
Saturnus, the rebirth,
Sol, Luna, its body.

O, sole love of God in Trinity,
Have mercy on me in eternity.

The dew of the heaven and the fat of the earth is our art-subjectum or Materia. Consequently it is neither mineral nor metal; the Pytagorean indicates to us that there are two mercurial substances of one root: Fire and water, Ischschamaim, namely ☿, drawn out of Minera, wherein all metal and minerals are situated. It is a dew of heaven ⊖, but a mineral and metallic dew of heaven, in which are all the colors in the world, which may be coagulated through artificial operations into a sweet salt, called Manna, into a medicine; Sol pater, Luna Mater, from both these it receives its light, life and splendor, its fiery light-essence from the Sun, from the Luna its watery light-essence. We find it coagulated and dissolved. This dew falls from above into the depths of the earth and its body is made up from the most subtle parts of the earth. From above this dew receives its soul, and spirit; fire and light go into its salty body, receiving the powers of the things from above and below (nempe Virtutes Substantiales.) To our eyes appears this mineral-dew in white, yellow, green, red and black colors, these being the only colors visible to our outer eyes. For it appears corporeally to the outer eyes, at times seen by miners in the mountains, appearing to the outer eye, heavy, watery, and dripping. Neither the miners nor artists know to what use to put it, since they do not know for what purpose Nature placed it there, nor of what sex it is, nor whether it be mineral or metal; all this is incomprehensible and unrecognisable. The best dew is that which in color looks like coagulated electrum or transparent amber. What the world uses it for I do not know, yet it is with all its power in all things. The dew itself is always rejected and despised; it separates into two branches, white and red, from a single-rooted , and stands upon this single root, growing like a white and red Rose of Jericho and blossoms like a lily in the valley of Josephat, oft-times broken off untimely by miners and is tortured by ignorant workmen. The true artist knows its influence, and plucks it in full bloom, with blossom, seed, root, stem and branches, namely: In full bloom, through the faith of the inner opened eyes. This is enough said of its bodily form: It is neither metal nor mineral, but nevertheless first mother and materia of all metals and minerals.

It is nothing but a Lion with its coagulated blood, and gluten of the white eagle.

Whoever seeks it, suffer,	For He alone keeps His vow,
Whoever finds it, be silent,	Seek for friends in your mind,
Whoever holds it, hide it,	Be friendly with everybody,
Whoever may use it, do so unbeknown,	But trust no one,
Whoever is a true Philosophus,	No one but God,
Remain nameless,	If you do not want to be cheated.
Trust no one but God,	Experto crede Ruberto.

For loyalty flew from earth heavenward and left all men whose mind is upon earthly matter.

LIBER VITÆ CHRISTVS
or
The only true way to arrive at the only good and right understanding of God and nature and to attain true perfection.

ENIGMA.

Our (the right believers) dwelling-place is in a dark grey and sinister castle, bewitched, surrounded by a very thick cloud, so that no one may come near it. In front of that castle and surrounding it is a fine green lawn, on this a great rock, which hides the castle, upon the rock is a four cornered pillar, made of alabaster, on top of this stands a golden Sceptre, decked with many precious stones. Down from the rock leads a stairway made of 11 steps of white marble; around the entire edifice is a wide, deep water. On its shore lies a boat at anchor, great to look upon, bedecked with blue velvet. Its master and his servants wear crimson red mantles. Not far from it springs forth a fresh clear fountain, nearby is a pyramid and obelisk on which are written the customs of this strange island in 72 languages. If one wants to reach the princely castle, and discover it, one has first to pass through a ruined tower called the uncertain passage, from there one can view and estimate the places in the sinister and as yet invisible castle; then one comes to another tower, called the dangerous one, through which one must pass on foot, then one reaches the rock, on which the water beats, and if one touches the Sceptre thereon with the middle-finger, and conquers the wolf and a goat, which will appear suddenly, then will appear a very beautiful virgin, who will give the victor a wreath, signifying his virtue and bravery. And the clouds will part, soon the castle will be seen, and the master of the castle, in a long silken yellow coat and deep brown beret, will receive the new guest and lead him unto all earthly and heavenly happiness.

MERCVRIVS ☿ MERCVRIO

Per Sal, Sulphur, Mercurium
Fit Lapis Philosophorum.

Durch ☉ ♃ ☿ ist unser Anfang des Lebens,
und alle Dinge, NB. auch das Ende alles
Bösen, und nach der Fäulung dessen eine neue
Geburt, welche besser als vorher gewesen.

A

Geminæ
& Maternæ
Verg. lib. 6.
Mundi fundum
laborando
crede mihi
unde beari.

Columbæ
Aves
Æneidi
si profundum
in veneris
habes totum
poteris.

O

Du Anfang und Ende des Lebens
Die Hoffnung bistu nach dem Tod.
Saturnus die Wiedergeburht,
Sol, Luna, derselben Leib.

O! Einzige Liebe Gottes in der
Dreyfaltigkeit, erbarme dich meiner in Ewigkeit.

Der Thau des Himmels und die Fettigkeit der Erden ist unser Kunst-Subjectum oder Materia. Es ist also weder Mineral noch Metall; das Pytagori sche Y zeiget uns, daß es zwey mercurialische Substantien sind einer Wurzel, Feuer und Wasser, Ilschschamaim, nemlich ☿ gezogen aus der Minera darinnen alle Metalle und Mineren liegen. Es ist ein ☉ Thau des Himmels, aber ein Mineral: und Metallischer Thau des Himmels, darinnen alle Far ben der Welt liegen, welcher mag durch Kunst coaguliret werden in ein süsses Salz, Manna genannt, zur Arzney; Sol Pater, Luna Mater, aus diesen beyden empfängt er sein Licht, Leben und Glanz, aus der Sonnen sein feuriges, aus der Luna sein wässeriges Lichtwesen. Wir finden ihn coaguliret und solviret. Dieser Thau fällt von oben in die Tiefe der Erden, und von dem subtilesten Theil der Erden ist sein Körper, von oben kömmt seine Seele und Geist, Feuer und Licht, und gehet in einen salzigen Leib, und empfängt die Kräffte (nempe Virtutes Substantiales) der obern und untern Dinge. Unsern Augen erscheinet dieser Mineral-Thau an Farben weis, gelb, grün, roth und schwarz, mehr Farben hat er den äussern Augen nicht. Denn er erscheinet den äussern Augen corporalisch; in den Bergen wird er von den Bergleuten zuweilen gesehen, den äussern Augen nach dick, wässerig-abtriessend, aber weder ihnen noch den Künstlern nütze, sintemalen man nicht wissen kann, wozu er von der Natur ordiniret worden, auf ein Mineral oder Metall, und auf welches Geschlecht, das ist unwissend und unerkenntlich. Der beste ist der coagulirte wie ein Electrum, oder wie der durchsichtige Bernstein, an der Farbe als gemeldet. Ich weis nicht wozu ihn die Welt brauche, und er ist doch mit seinen Kräfften in allen Dingen. Er selbst aber ist von ihnen veracht und verworfen; er scheidet sich in zwey Äste, weis und roth, aus der einigen Wurzel Y, und er stehet auf der äussern Wurzel da er wächst, wie eine weisse und rothe Rose von Jericho, und blühet wie eine Lilie im Thal Josaphat stehende; von den Bergmann vielmal unzeitig abgebrochen, von un verständigen Arbeitern gemartert. Der rechte Künstler merket seine Influenz, und bricht ihn selbst in seiner Reise, mit Blüthe, Saamen, Wurzel, Stamm und Zweigen, nemlich in der Reise durchs Gesicht der innern geöffneten Augen. Dies sey genug von seiner körperlichen Gestalt; er ist kein Metall noch Mineral, und doch aller Metallen und Mineren anfängliche Mutter und erste Materia.

Es ist nichts als der Löwe mit seinem coagulirten Blut, und das Gluten des weissen Adlers.

Wer es suchet der leide,
Wer es find der schweige,
Wer es hat der verberge es,
Wer es brauchet der thue es unbekannt.
Wer ein wahrer Philosophus ist
Der bleibe ungenannt,
Traue niemand als Gott,
Der allein hält sein Wort,
Deines Gemüths Freund erwehlen sollt,
Sey mit jedermann freundlich,
Traue aber niemand,
Sey niemand geheim als Gott,
Willt du nicht betrogen seyn,
Experto crede Ruberto.

Denn Treue ist von der Erden gen Himmel geflogen, hat alle Menschen verlassen, deren Gemüth an der Erden klebet.

LIBER VITÆ CHRISTVS
oder
Der einige wahre Weg zur wahren und rechtschaffenen Erkänntniß Gottes und der Natur und der wahren Vollkommenheit zu kommen.

Räthsel.

Unsere (der rechtwahren Gläubigen) Residenz ist in einem schwarzgrauen finstern Schloß dermassen gefangen, bezaubert, und mit einer sehr dicken Wolken umgeben, daß niemand hinzukommen kann. Vor diesem Schloß, und um dasselbe herum, ist ein schöner grüner Anger, auf diesem liegt ein harter Fels, welcher das Schloß zu sehen verhindert, auf diesem Fels ist eine viereckige Säule von Alabaster aufgerichtet, in welcher überzwerg ein gulbener Scepter, so mit vielen Edelgesteinen köstlich besetzt, stecket. Von dem Fels herab gehet eine Treppe von 11 Staffeln aus weissem Marmor gemachet: um das ganze Gebäude gehet ein breites tiefes Wasser, an dessen Ufer ein gewaltig ausgerüstetes Schiff mit blauen Sammet bedeckt lieget, der Patron desselbigen samt seinen Dienern ist mit langen rothen carmoisin: atlassnen Mänteln angethan, und stehen angebunden am Anker. Nicht weit davon entspringt ein lebendiger Brunnen, dabey eine Pyramis mit einem Scepter gesetzt ist, auf welcher die Gebräuche dieser abentheurlichen Insul nach der Länge in 72 Sprachen beschrieben worden. Will man nun zu den fürstlichen Schloß gelangen, und selbiges entdecken, so muß man erstlich durch einen baufälligen Thurm passiren, der ungewisse Durchzug genannt, aus welchen man zu der finstern und unsichtbaren Burg Situation ermessen und beschauen kann; dann kommt man zu einem andern Thurm, der Gefährliche genannt, den muß man zu Fusse passiren, welcher denn auch über das Wasser bis zum Felsen hinan dringet, und wann man das Scepter mit dem mittlern Finger berühret, und den Wolff und Bock, so einem unvermuthet begegnen, ritterlich überwindet und erleget, dann erscheinet eine überaus schöne Jungfrau, und verehret dem Ueberwinder ein Kränzlein, zum Zeugniß seiner Tugend und Tapferkeit. Und alsobald verliehren sich die Wolken, und das Schloß präsentiret sich, der Oberste darinnen läst sich in einem gelben langen seidenen Rock, und hohen braunen Baret sehen, empfähet den neuen Gast, und führet ihn zu aller irdischen und himmlischen Glückseligkeit.

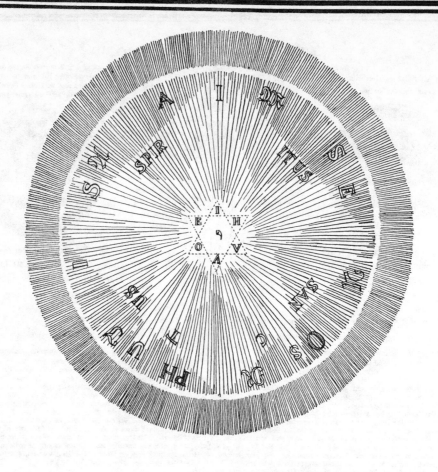

Lord from Thy hands cometh all good. All blessings and all benedictions come from Thy hand. With Thy fingers Thou hast written the character of Nature which none may read unless he be taught in Thy school. Therefore let us lift up our eyes to Thee, O Lord, even as servants look upon the hands of their master and as maids look upon the hands of their mistress, that Thou mayest help us. O Lord our God, who should not praise Thee, who should not glorify Thee, the King of Glory! For all things come from Thee and hearken unto Thee, and must all return to Thee again, being received either in Thy love or Thy wrath. Nothing can escape Thee, all things must serve Thy honor and glory. Thou alone and none other art the Lord. Thou dost what Thou wilt with Thy mighty arm, nothing can escape Thee. Thou alone dost help the humble, the meek and the poor, those who are devoted to Thee with all their heart, in their hour of need, those who humble themselves in the dust before Thee, to them Thou art gracious. Who should not praise Thee, O Thou King of Glory; there is none like unto Thee, whose dwelling place is in heaven and in a troubled and virtuous holy heart. O Great God; Thou all in all! O Nature! thou everything from nothing, what more then shall I say? I am nothing in myself, I am everything in thee, and I live in thine everything from nothing: live Thou then in me, and so bring me unto the all in Thee. Amen

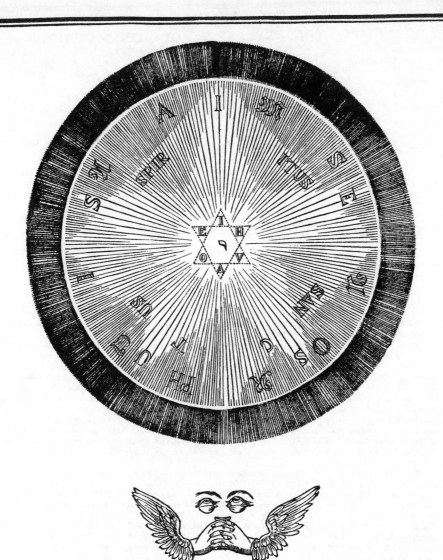

Herr, von deiner Hand kommt alles Gute, aller Segen und Benedeiung kommt von deiner Hand herab, du hast mit deinen Fingern den Character der Natur geschrieben, niemand kann ihn lesen, er sey denn in deiner Schulen gewesen. Darum wie die Knechte auf ihres Herren Hände sehen, und die Mägde auf die Hände ihrer Frauen; also auch sehen unsere Augen auf dich bis du uns hilfest, Herr unser Gott, wer sollte dich nicht loben, wer sollte dich nicht preisen du König der Ehren, denn alles ist aus dir, und gehöret allein dir, und muß alles wieder zu dir, entweder in deiner Liebe oder Zorn einfließen, nichts kann dir entfallen, es muß alles zu deiner Ehre und Herrlichkeit dienen. Du bist allein Herr und niemand mehr, du thust was du wilt mit deinen mächtigen Arm, niemand kam dir entlaufen, den Demüthigen, Sanftmüthigen und Armen, von Herzen dir Ergebenen, hilfst du allein aus der Noth, welche sich im Staube und Erde vor dir demüthigen, denen bist du hold; wer sollte dich nicht loben du König der Ehren, den niemand gleichet, dessen Wohnung im Himmel und in einem geängsteten und tugendhaften göttlichen Herzen ist. O grosser Gott: du alles in allem! O Natur! du Jchts aus Nichts, was soll ich doch mehr sagen; ich bin Nichts in mir, Jchts in dir, und lebe in deinem Jchts aus Nichts, lebe du doch in mir, und bringe mich aus dem Jchts in dir, Amen.

ABOUT THE REVELATION OF JESUS CHRIST.

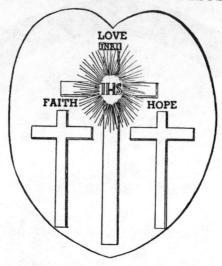

Dear Christian brethren: As Jesus Christ, the Son of God will be revealed by the Holy Ghost through His Father and the Father was revealed through His Son, so it will come to pass that those who are seemingly Christians will become Christians and all the people will accept the Christian belief and will become Christian men. But so far, as one can easily see, Jesus Christ and Christianity have never been revealed, for until now love towards the neighbor and towards God hath been entirely closed' up and hath been extinguished and instead of it, rules the Flesh; i.e. idolatry, whoring, drinking, eating, envy, wrath, contention, dissension, murder, robbery, injustice and all luxury and ambition, all this being contrary to the Revelation of Jesus Christ and His bodily rebirth. Woe upon us, wretched men, that we are so much opposed to one another! Why do we fight each other with claws and teeth, is it that the love poured out by the Holy Ghost is entirely extinguished and dead? Does no one no longer respect the other man? Are we like the dumb beasts that one hath to rend, devour and destroy the other, was heaven and the earth made for one man alone? Nay, that cannot be.

O, ye nobles, counts and knights, do we have to pray to God, our Creator, for the revelation and knowledge of Jesus Christ, His Son, who is despised and ridiculed, and who is nevertheless the greatest in heaven and on earth?

O, ye Theologians, Preachers including all Teachers: Ye should be taught by God and ye should proclaim Jesus Christ of Nazareth, the Crucified, to all people with right knowledge and teaching and should do so out of love and not for money or motives of profit. It is also necessary for you to ask Almighty God for the revelation and right knowledge of Jesus Christ, the Son of God and the Virgin. So then you may go ahead as the true lights of this world, before men as you have your illumination from God. Learn to know Jesus Christ, who hath made us for wisdom, for justice, for holiness, and for salvation, so that as it is written: He that glorieth, let him glory in the Lord. 1. Cor. 1. v. 31. So there will soon cease fighting, quarreling, damnation and heresy and there will be only brotherly love and unity amongst you, with the friendliness of one mind, one will, one knowledge, one belief, one blessedness and a perfect love towards neighbor and God.

O, all ye people in this world, rich and poor, man and woman, young and old, great and small, let us pray God for the revelation and true knowledge of His Son, Jesus Christ, that we may live in unity, peace, friendship, patience, kindness, and humbleness of heart, that all men in this entire world may live as of one heart, one love, one community, one church, one faith and in one mind in Jesus Christ in whom we and all men shall be blessed.

Otherwise we do not know Jesus Christ, who died for us on the cross, and no one should glorify Him with his mouth only, for He looketh into the heart, and where there is love, injustice will cease from all things, which are done in all the world.

O, ye people, loving lovingly, love of all loves, how easy is thy yoke and how light is thy burden! Thus speaketh the heavenly and eternal Wisdom and Love Itself. Matth. 11. John 3.

Von der Offenbahrung Jesu Christi.

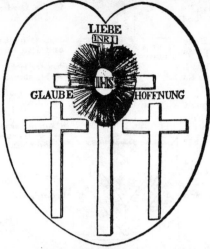

Lieben Christen Menschen, so Jesus Christus Gottes Sohn vom H. Geist durch seinen Vater, als der Vater vom Sohn ist offenbahret worden, offenbahret wird werden, so werden nicht allein die vermeinten Christen zu Christen, sondern alle Völker den Christlichen Glauben annehmen, und Christen Menschen werden. Aber bis anhero, als man wol siehet, ist Jesus Christus, und der Christliche Glaube noch nie offenbar gewesen, denn die Liebe des Nächsten und die Liebe Gottes ganz und gar verschlossen und verloschen, und regieret an statt dessen, das Fleisch, i. e. Abgötterey, Hurerey, Säuferey, Fresserey, Neid, Zorn, Zank, Hader, Mord, Diebstahl, Ungerechtigkeit, und alle Ueppigkeit und Ehrgeiz, welches alles ganz wider die Offenbahrung Jesu Christi, und wider seine neue (Geburt) Creatur ist. Ach was zeihen wir uns elende Menschen, daß wir also wider einander seyn! Warum beissen und zanken wir uns doch, ist denn die Liebe, so ausgegossen ist durch den H. Geist, ganz und gar verloschen und erstorben, achtet denn niemand den andern, seynd wir denn unvernünftige Thiere, daß also einer den andern zerreisset, frist und schändet, ist Himmel und Erden allein Einen erschaffen worden? Ach nein.

O! Ihr Edlen, Grafen, Ritter und Edelleute, es ist noth, daß wir Gott den Schöpfer bitten um die Offenbahrung und Erkenntniß Jesu Christi seines Sohnes, der da ist verschmähet und verspottet, und verachtet, und doch der groste im Himmel und auf Erden ist.

O ihr Theologen, Geistliche, sammt allen Lehrern, ihr sollet seyn von Gott gelehret, und Jesum Christum von Nazareth den Gekreuzigten allem Volk mit rechter Erkenntniß und Lehre verkündigen, und solches aus Liebe, und nicht von Geld oder Gewinnswegen. Euch thut auch noth zu bitten Gott den Allmächtigen um die Offenbahrung und rechte wahre Erkenntniß Jesu Christi des Sohns Gottes und der Jungfrauen. Alsdenn mögt ihr recht als Lichter dieser Welt den Menschen vorgehen, so ihr die Erleuchtung von Gott habet. Lernet Jesum Christum erkennen, welcher uns gemacht ist zur Weisheit, zur Gerechtigkeit, und zur Heiligung, und zur Erlösung, auf daß, wie geschrieben stehet, wer sich rühmet, der rühme sich des Herrn. 1. Cor. 1. v. 31. So wird alsdann aller Streit, Zanken, Verdammen und Verketzern ganz aufgehoben werden, und wird ferner brüderliche Liebe und Einigkeit unter euch seyn, mit Freundlichkeit, eines Sinnes, eines Willens, eines Wissens, eines Glaubens, einer Seligkeit und ganz vollkommener Liebe des Nächsten und Gottes.

O alles Volk in dieser Welt, reiche und arme, Mann und Weib, jung und alt, groß und klein, laßt uns Gott bitten um die Offenbahrung und rechte wahre Erkenntniß Jesu Christi, seines Sohnes, so werden wir einig, friedlich, freundlich, geduldig, sanftmüthig und von Herzen demüthig unter einander leben, und werden seyn ein Herz mit allen Menschen in der ganzen Welt, eine Liebe, eine Gemeine, eine Kirche, eines Glaubens und Sinnes in Jesu Christo, durch welchen wir und alle Menschen selig werden.

Sonsten kennen wir Jesum Christum den Gekreuzigten noch nicht recht, es soll sich auch seiner niemand rühmen mit dem Munde, denn er siehet das Herz an, wo die Liebe ist fallen ab alle Ungerechtigkeiten in allen Dingen so da begangen werden in der ganzen Welt.

O liebreiche liebliche liebende Liebe, Liebe aller Liebe, wie bist du ein solches süsses Joch! also spricht die himmlische und ewige Weisheit und Liebe selber. Matth. 11. Joh. 3.

313

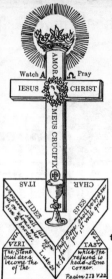

Eat, my Beloved, Become	Drink, my Friends, intoxicated. Cant. 5. v. 1.

Taste and see how friendly for My Body is the right food — is the Lord and think of Me, and My Blood the right drink.

Whosoever eateth My Body Abideth in Me — and drinketh My Blood and I in him.

That is affecteth what is imperishable but — how the food abideth there unto life eternal.

For the Spirit is life-giving, and are spirit — the flesh of no use, these my words and life.

Taulerus.

The true supper is the essential, powerful and almighty presence of Jesus Christ, the Son of the living God.

God is light and in Him is no darkness at all. But if lowship with one another, and the blood of Jesus Christ,

Taulerus.

Whenever God wants to give us the sweet savour of His love and kindness, He Himself becomes food and drink of our souls.

we walk in the light as He is in the light, we have fellowship. His Son cleanseth us from all sin. 1 John 1. v. 7.

For our sins was He wounded and — through His wounds we were healed.

EGREDERE.
per Viam CRUCIS.

INGREDERE.
per Vitam LUCIS.

To him that overcometh, will I give to eat of the hidden Manna, and will give him a white stone, and in the stone a new name written, which no man knoweth saving he that receiveth it. Rev. 2. v. 17.

Christ is the trunk and tree of life through which the bitter water of Mara was sweetened, and what are we but His twigs and branches, through which He bears fruit in us by His power. All those made white in the bitterness of this time limited life were reborn through Him into the sweetness of eternal life.

His soul is the essential thing in my soul, and for that Soul's sake God hath become man, that we may become Godlike in and through Him in the love and life of Jesus Christ. So that we may be reborn and revealed in the eternal heavenly image into a divine life. O Man: It is a great unfathomed Secret when we come to consider it and remember that we are in Christ members of one body and all of us are in Him but One. That all of us receive and benefit from the One Christ and that we are and remain in the same Christ a unified body, which body is He Himself. And we are the body and the members thereof. Yes, we are tied and bound together with and in Him to One Man, and this Man is each severally in Christ. Through the medium of bread and wine we all eat and drink Christ's body and blood with the Essential desire and desirous believing mouth, the fiery love and life mouth of our souls. The real innermost man, a creature of paradise and of eternity, an image of God, is hidden under the gross animal form, and desires a spiritual nutriment or Tinctur and therefore eats Christ's spiritual flesh and blood, for he is a spiritual being.

The soul's hunger for the true belief is the divine spiritual mouth, eating and drinking, in the innermost depths of the soul, Christ's Body and Blood. Whatever cometh from the Spirit and consists of the Spirit that is the greatest and highest nutriment of the souls. The spiritual hungry fire of the soul reaches for, grasps, eats and drinks with its spiritual, opened, believing mouth the holy inconceivable being, Christ's Flesh and Blood. It takes this supernatural holy essential power through the medium of bread and wine, through which medium the invisible eternal becomes one with the visible, spiritual, immortal eternal human being; understand: Faith becomes through this transformation a being, a spiritual flesh and blood. For one faith can grasp the other: The earnest faith of the living grasps for the eternal: And is so mighty and powerful that it can overthrow the mountains and move them elsewhere. The true and essential faith of man is Christ Himself, who is in him and abideth in him and is his life and light. Behold, this is the way we are being purified through the faith and enlightened and inspired through the Holy Ghost. The gross animal, which is only the outer shell, receiveth only an elemental being or earthly food and eats of the perishable world-being out of which he himself consists. But the soul is of God and of His words. Mark: As is the mouth, so is also the food: Every Principium eats and drinks of its likeness: Every spirit eats and drinks of that from which it came forth, and in whose depths or Centrum it standeth: For what hath light in common with darkness? It cannot comprehend it.

The natural, mortal and perishable body receives its food from the earth; and the sidereal, volatile and perishable body its food from the firmament; but the Spirit of the Lord is the life of souls and the life of the innermost immortal life.

The innermost man as the pure Adamic power-body, with his beautiful, chosen, gracious, heavenly bride, receives in great love, desire in his spiritual believing mouth the invisible spirtual being and supernatural heavenly flesh of Christ, a tincture of life, a perpetrating fiery love and power being, for faith is the cornerstone, the beginner and the finisher, effecting, the right innermost, eternal Sabbath in the innermost depths of our souls, effecting, also, the power of God through the love of Jesus in quiet tranquility and peaceful bliss.

Christ hath not given unto His disciples the creaturely being, the outer understandable fleshly human nature, nay: Whosoever discerneth not the body of the Lord and eateth and drinketh the bread and wine, receiveth Him unto his condemnation. He gave them the spiritual human nature, the power of His body and blood, a holy, heavenly body life and loveliness, a spiritual being a spiritual body. This He brought down from heaven in which is understood the divine and eternal human power: This He introduceth into our body, made white by the light, so that He maketh us live again through His heavenly existence in our bodies.

No mortal creature can look upon a spiritual being, much less can we grasp, handle and enjoy it with our earthly mortal mouth. But such is conceivable and comprehensible to the spirit of the souls standing in the divine Centro, for He, Christ, is the body of the spirit and the spirit of the body, in our soul's body which He giveth unto us to eat in faith. No mortal and unworthy man can reach and receive the unchangeable and indescribable heavenly bread of eternity, much less can he taste of it.

WOE and WANT NEED and DEATH	NATURE	A	MERCY	PEACE and JOY BLESSING and LIFE
	ADAM	LAW ⟍⟋ GOSPEL	CHRIST	
	FLESH	Ω	SPIRIT	

Eſſet meine Lieben Werdet   Trinket meine Freunde trunken. Cant. 5. y. 1.

Schmecket und ſehet wie freundlich der Mein Fleiſch iſt die rechte Speiſe,

HErr iſt, und gedenket Mein dabey, denn Mein Blut iſt der rechte Trank.

Wer Mein Fleiſch iſſet der bleibet in Mir

und Mein Blut trinket und Ich in Ihm.

Dero würket Speiſe, nicht die da vergänglich iſt,

halben ſondern die da bleibet ins ewige Leben.

Denn der Geiſt iſts der da Lebendig macht, ſind Geiſt

aber das Fleiſch iſt kein nütze, dieſe meine Worte und Leben.

Taulerus.
Das rechte Abendmahl iſt die weſentliche kräfftige und allmächtige Gegenwart Jeſu Chriſti des Sohnes des lebendigen Gottes.

Taulerus.
Wann unſer lieber Gott den ſüſſen Geſchmack ſeiner Liebe und Güte uns will zu ſchmecken geben, ſo wird Er ſelber unſer Seelen Speiſe und Trank.

Gott iſt ein Licht, und iſt keine Finſterniß in ihm, ſo wir Gemeinſchaft mit Ihm, und das Blut Jeſu Chriſti ſeines

nun im Licht wandeln, wie Er im Licht iſt, ſo haben wir Sohnes reiniget uns von aller Sünde. 1 Joh. 1. v. 7.

Er iſt um unſer Miſſethat willen verwundet

Und durch ſeine Wunden ſind wir geheilet.

EGREDERE.
per Viam CRVCIS.

INGREDERE.
per Vitam LVCIS.

Wer überwindet, dem will ich zu eſſen geben von dem verborgenen Manna, und will ihm geben einen weiſſen Stein, und auf dem Stein einen Neuen Namen geſchrieben, welchen Niemand kennet, denn nur der ihn empfähet. Apoc. 2. v. 17.

Chriſtus iſt der Stamm und Baum des Lebens, durch welchen das bittere Waſſer zu Mara verſüſſet, und wir ſind ſeine Zweige und Aeſte, in und durch die er durch ſeine Kraft in uns Frucht gebähret. Er hat das Verbliche aus der Bitterkeit dieſes zeitlichen Lebens in die Süſſigkeit des ewigen Lebens wieder erbohren.

Seine Seele iſt meiner Seelen Eigenſchaft, und um derſelben war es zu thun, daß ſich Gott vermenſcht, auf das wir in und durch Ihn in der Liebe und im Leben Jeſu Chriſti wieder vergöttet, und zu einem ewigen himmliſchen Bilde, zu einem göttlichen Leben, wiedergebohren und offenbahr wurden. O Menſch, es iſt ein groſſes unergründliches Geheimniß, wann wir wohl bedenken und erinnern, daß wir in Chriſto Glieder eines Leibes, und in Ihme alle nur Einer ſind. Daß wir alle den einigen Chriſtum genieſſen und empfahen, und in demſelben Chriſto, nur ein einiger Leib, der wir Glieder iſt, in ſeinen Gliedern, ſeyn und bleiben. Ja wir ſeyn mit und in Ihm zu einem einigen Menſchen verknüpfet und verbunden, und derſelbige einige Menſch iſt ein jeder in Chriſto ſelber. Wir eſſen und trinken alle Chriſti Fleiſch und Blut unter Brod und Wein, (als durch ein Mittel) mit der Eſſen tialiſchen Begierde, und begierlichen Glaubens-Munde, verſteht der wahre innere Menſch, welcher ein Paradeiſiſches und der Ewigkeit Weſen und Gottes Ebenbild, und unter der thieriſchen Grobheit verborgen iſt, begehret ein geiſtliches nutri ment oder Tinctur (denn er iſt ſelber ein geiſtliches Weſen) und iſſet Chriſti geiſtliches Fleiſch und Blut.

Der Seelen Glaubens-Hunger iſt der göttliche geiſtliche Mund, der iſſet und trinket im inwendigen Grunde des Gemüths, Chriſti Fleiſch und Blut. Was aus dem Geiſt gehet, und im Geiſte beſtehet, das iſt das höchſte und gröſte nutriment der Seelen. Das geiſtliche hungrige Seelen-Feuer faſſet, ergreiffet, iſſet und trinket in ihrem geiſtlichen in voller Begierde aufgethanen Glaubens-Mund das heilige unbegreifliche Weſen, Chriſti Fleiſch und Blut, in ihren Seeliſchen Mund, die übernatürliche heilige weſentliche Kraft unter Brod und Wein, als ein dazu geordnetes Mittel, durch welches Mittel ſich das unſichtbare Ewige, dem ſichtbahren, geiſtlichen unſterblichen ewigen Menſchen einergiebet; verſehe der Glaube wird in ſolcher Nieſſung ein Weſen, als ein geiſtliches Fleiſch und Blut. Denn ein Glaube fänget den andern: der Lebendige ernſter Glaube fänget das ewige, und iſt ſo mächtig und kräfftig, daß er Berge umſtürzen und verſetzen kan. Dann der wahre weſentliche Glaube im Menſchen iſt Chriſtus ſelber, der in ihme iſt und bleibet, und ſein Leben und Licht iſt.

Siehe, ſo werden wir durch den Glauben gereiniget, und durch den H. Geiſt durchleuchtet und erlenchter. Das grobe Thier, welches nur eine Hülſe iſt, empfahet nur ein Elementiſches Weſen oder Speiſe, und iſſet von dem vergänglichen Welt-Weſen, daraus es iſt; die Seele aber von Gott und ſeinem Worte, daraus ſie iſt. Merke, wie der Mund iſt, ſo iſt auch die Speiſe: Ein jedes Principium iſſet und trinket von ſeiner Gleichheit: Ein jeder Geiſt iſſet und trinket von dem, woraus er entſprungen, und in deſſen Grund er in ſeinem Centrum inne ſtehet: Denn was hat das Licht für Gemeinſchaft mit der Finſterniß, ſie kans nicht begreiffen.

Der natürliche, ſterbliche und verderbliche Leib empfähet ſeine Nahrung aus der Erden; und der ſyderiſche, flüchtige und vergängliche Leib ſeine Nah rung aus dem Firmament; aber der Geiſt der Seelen empfähet das Leben der Seelen, und des innern unſterblichen Leben Leben.

Der innere Menſch, als der reine Adamiſche Kraft-Leib, ſamt ſeiner ſchönen, auserwählten, holdſeligen, lieblichen, himmliſchen Braut, empfähet, in groſſer Liebe-Begierde, in ſeinen Seeliſchen Glaubens-Mund das unſichtbare geiſtliche Weſen, und übernatürliche himmliſche Fleiſch Chriſti, eine Tinctur des Lebens, ein durchdringendes feuriges Leben und Kraft-Weſen; denn der Glaube iſt die Grundveſte, der Anfänger und Vollender, der wirket den rechten inwendigen ewigwährenden Sabbath, die Kraft Gottes, durch die Liebe Jeſu, in ſtiller Ruhe, und ſanfter Wonne, im innern Grunde der Seelen in uns.

Chriſtus hat ſeinen Jüngern nicht die creatürliche äuſſere begreifliche, fleiſchliche Menſchheit, den geblähte Weſen gegeben, nein, wer nicht un terſcheidet den Leib des Herrn vom Brod und Wein, der empfähet es Ihme zum Gerichte. Er gab ihnen die geiſtliche Menſchheit, die Krafft ſeines Leibes und Bluts, eine heilige, himmliſche Leib-Leb- und Lieblichkeit, ein geiſtliches Weſen, einen geiſtlichen Leib, welchen er vom Himmel brachte, dar innen die göttliche und ewige menſchliche Kraft verſtanden wird, den führet er in unſern, vom Licht verblichnen Leib ein, auf daß er denſelben durch ſeine himmliſche Weſenheit in ihme lebendig machte.

Ein geiſtliches Weſen kan keine vergängliche Creatur ſchauen, viel weniger können wir ſolches mit unſerm irdiſchen tödtlichen Munde faſſen, ergreiffen und genieſſen. Aber dem Geiſte der Seelen, welcher im göttlichen Centro ſtehet, iſt es faßlich und begreiflich, denn Er, Chriſtus, iſt der Leib des Gei ſtes, und Geiſt des Leibes, unſer Seelen Leib, welchen er uns im Glauben zu eſſen giebt. Es kans und wirds kein ſterblicher und unwürdiger Menſch empfahen noch erlangen, vielweniger koſten das unwandelbare, und unbegreifliche Himmel-Brod der Ewigkeit.

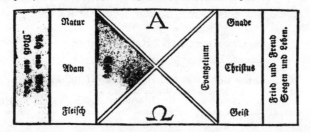

315

This is the revelation and the testimony and the true knowledge of J.C., God and Man, the living Book of Life, all heavenly and earthly wisdom in heaven and on earth, the sealed book according to time and eternity. And I saw on the right hand of Him that sat on the throne, a book written within and on the backside, sealed with seven seals. And I saw a strong angel proclaiming with a loud voice, who is worthy to open the book, and to loose the seals thereof? And no man in heaven, nor in earth, neither under the earth, was able to open the book, neither to look thereon. And I wept much, because no man was found worthy to open and read the book, neither to look thereon. Rev. 5. And he said unto me, these sayings are faithful and true, to shew unto his servants the things which must shortly be done. Seal not the sayings of the prophecy of this book: for the time is at hand. Rev. 22. v. 6. 10. Blessed is he whose name is written in the book of life. And I will not blot out his name out of the living book of the lamb. Philip. 4. v. 3. Rev. 3. v. 5. Rev. 21. v. 27. And whosoever was not found written in the book of life was cast into the lake of fire. Rev. 20. v. 15. Behold, I come quickly: Blessed is he that keepeth the sayings of the prophecy of this book. Rev. 22. v. 7.

The Sealed Book.
Rev. 5.

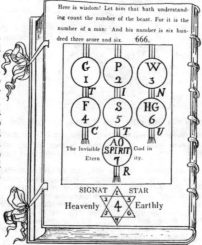

The four bands tied together, i.e., Alpha and Omega, Eternity and Time, and the one wheel to look upon not unlike four wheels, and all four were one like the other, as being one wheel in the other. So are the four beasts Ezek. 1. and the four beasts Rev· 4. 5. & 19 and the foursquare city of God fashioned after the measure of a man. Rev. 21.

And behold: in the midst of the throne stood a lamb as it was slain and had seven horns and seven eyes, these are the 7 spirits of God, sent into all countries. i.e.,

The Seven Seals.

And I beheld a beast coming up out of the earth; and he had two horns, like a lamb and he spake as a dragon: and he exerciseth all the power of the first beast; and he causeth all to receive a mark in their right hand, or in their foreheads, that no man might buy or sell, save he that had the mark, or the name of the beast, or the number of his name: i. e. 666.

Here is wisdom, for it is the number of a man. Rev. 13.

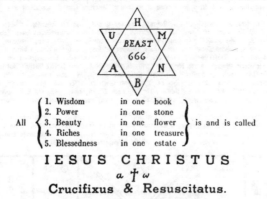

All
1. Wisdom   in one book
2. Power   in one stone
3. Beauty   in one flower   } is and is called
4. Riches   in one treasure
5. Blessedness   in one estate

IESUS CHRISTUS
a ✝ ω
Crucifixus & Resuscitatus.

That is:
The well, the tree, the light and the right book of life and of the lamb, he who hath that,
Understandeth all things in heaven, on earth and under the earth, and cometh forth therefrom, and all other books bear testimony thereof alone.

Dies ist die Offenbahrung und das Zeugniß, und das wahre Erkenntniß von I. C. Gott · und Mensch, das lebendige Buch des Lebens, alle himmlische und irdische Weisheit im Himmel und auf Erden, das versiegelte Buch nach der Ewigkeit und Zeit. Und ich sahe ein Buch in der rechten Hand deß, der auf dem Stuhle saß, in und auswendig geschrieben, und mit 7 Siegeln versiegelt; und ich sahe einen starken Engel predigen mit heller Stimme: Wer ist würdig das Buch aufzuthun, und seine Siegel zu zerbrechen? und niemand im Himmel noch auf Erden, noch unter der Erden, konnte das Buch aufthun, noch drein sehen, und ich weinete sehr, daß niemand würdig erfunden ward, das Buch aufzuthun, und zu lesen, noch drein zu sehen. Apoc. 5. Und er sprach zu mir, diese Worte sind gewiß und wahrhaftig, zu zeigen seinen Knechten, was bald geschehen muß. Apoc. 22. v. 6.10. Selig sind die geschrieben stehen im Buch des Lebens. Und ich werde ihren Namen nicht außtilgen auß dem lebendigen Buche des Lammes. Philip. 4. v. 3. Apoc. 3. v. 5. Apoc. 21. v. 27. Wer aber nicht erfunden wird und geschrieben stehet im Buch des Lebens, der wird geworfen werden in den feurigen Pfuel. Apoc. 20. v. 15. Siehe ich komme bald, selig ist der da hält die Worte der Weissagung in diesem Buche. Apoc. 22. v. 7.

Das versiegelte Buch.
Apoc 5.

Die vier zusammengebundene Bänder, h. e. A & O. Ewigkeit und Zeit, und auch das eine Rad, welches anzusehen war wie vier Räder, und waren alle vier eins wie das ander, und als wäre ein Rad im andern.

Immaßen auch die vier Thiere Ezech. 1. und die vier Thiere Apoc. 4. 5. & 19. und die viereckigte Stadt Gottes nach dem Maas eines Menschen. Apoc. 21.

Und siehe mitten im Stuhl stand ein Lamm, wie es erwürget war, und hatte sieben Hörner, und sieben Augen, welches sind die 7 Geister Gottes, gesandt in alle Land. h. e.
Die sieben Siegel.

Und ich sahe ein Thier aufsteigen von der Erden, und es hatte zwey Hörner, gleich wie das Lamm, und redete wie der Drache; und es thät alle Macht des ersten Thiers; und es gab ihnen ein Mahlzeichen an ihrer rechten Hand, oder an ihrer Stirne, das niemand kaufen oder verkaufen kann, er habe denn das Mahlzeichen, oder den Namen des Thiers, oder die Zahl, h. e. 666 seines Namens. Hie ist Weisheit, denn es ist eines Menschen Zahl. Apoc. 13.

Alle	1. Weisheit	in einem	Buche	
	2. Kraft	in einem	Steine	
	3. Schönheit	in einer	Blume	ist und heist
	4. Reichthum	in einem	Schatze	
	5. Seligkeit	in einem	Gute	

IESUS CHRISTUS
α † ω
Crucifixus & Resuscitatus.

Das ist:
Der Brunn, der Baum, das Licht, und das rechte Buch des Lebens und Lammes,
Wer das hat,
der verstehet alle Dinge so im Himmel, auf Erden und unter der Erden sind, aus diesem kommen, und allein von diesem zeugen alle andere Bücher.

This is the revelation and testimony and the true knowledge of J.C., G and M, the living book of life, all heavenly and earthly wisdom in heaven and on earth, the opened book according to the Word and His holy mortal existence in the world and in time, which God hath given unto his servants. And I saw a mighty angel come down from heaven clothed with a cloud and he had in his right hand a little book open, and I heard a voice from heaven saying unto me: go and take the little book which is open in the hand of the angel, and the voice spake again and said: Take it and eat it up; and as soon as I had eaten it my belly was bitter. And he said unto me: Thou must prophesy again before many peoples, and nations, and tongues, and kings. Rev. 10. And another book was opened, which is the book of life. Rev. 20. And one of the elders saith unto me: Weep not, behold, the Lion of the tribe of Judah, the Root of David, hath prevailed to open the book, and to loose the seven seals thereof; and he came and took the book out of the right hand of him that sat upon the throne. And when he had taken the book, the four beasts and four and twenty elders fell down before the Lamb and spake: Thou art worthy to take the book and to open the seals thereof. Rev. 5. He that hath an ear, let him hear what the Spirit saith unto the churches. Rev. 2. & 3. He that hath an ear, let him hear, here is wisdom. Rev. 13.

The opened book with it's seven seals.
Rev. 10.

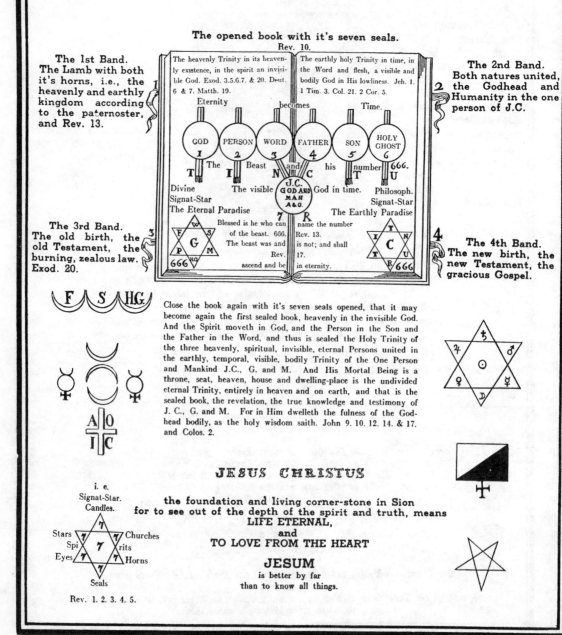

The 1st Band. The Lamb with both it's horns, i.e., the heavenly and earthly kingdom according to the paternoster, and Rev. 13.

The 2nd Band. Both natures united, the Godhead and Humanity in the one person of J.C.

The heavenly Trinity in its heavenly existence, in the spirit an invisible God. Exod. 3.5.6.7. & 20. Deut. 6 & 7. Matth. 19.

The earthly holy Trinity in time, in the Word and flesh, a visible and bodily God in His lowliness. Jeh. 1. 1 Tim. 3. Col. 21. 2 Cor. 5.

Eternity becomes Time.

GOD 1 · PERSON 2 · WORD 3 · FATHER 4 · SON 5 · HOLY GHOST 6

The Beast and his number 666.

J.C. GOD AND MAN A. & O.

Divine Signat-Star. The Eternal Paradise · The visible God in time. · Philosoph. Signat-Star. The Earthly Paradise

Blessed is he who can name the number of the beast. 666. Rev. 13. The beast was and is not; and shall Rev. 17. ascend and be in eternity.

The 3rd Band. The old birth, the old Testament, the burning, zealous law. Exod. 20.

The 4th Band. The new birth, the new Testament, the gracious Gospel.

Close the book again with it's seven seals opened, that it may become again the first sealed book, heavenly in the invisible God. And the Spirit moveth in God, and the Person in the Son and the Father in the Word, and thus is sealed the Holy Trinity of the three heavenly, spiritual, invisible, eternal Persons united in the earthly, temporal, visible, bodily Trinity of the One Person and Mankind J.C., G. and M. And His Mortal Being is a throne, seat, heaven, house and dwelling-place is the undivided eternal Trinity, entirely in heaven and on earth, and that is the sealed book, the revelation, the true knowledge and testimony of J. C., G. and M. For in Him dwelleth the fulness of the Godhead bodily, as the holy wisdom saith. John 9. 10. 12. 14. & 17. and Colos. 2.

JESUS CHRISTUS

the foundation and living corner-stone in Sion
for to see out of the depth of the spirit and truth, means
LIFE ETERNAL,
and
TO LOVE FROM THE HEART

JESUM
is better by far
than to know all things.

i. e. Signat-Star. Candles.

Stars · Churches
Spi · rits
Eyes · Horns
Seals

Rev. 1. 2. 3. 4. 5.

Dieß ist die Offenbahrung und das Zeugniß, und die wahre Erkenntniß von I. C., G. und M., das lebendige Buch des Lebens, alle himmlische und irdische Weißheit im Himmel und auf Erden, und das eröfnete Buch nach dem Wort und seiner heil. Menschheit in der Welt und Zeit, welche Gott gegeben hat seinen Knechten. Und ich sahe einen starken Engel vom Himmel herabkommen, der war mit einer Wolken bekleidet, und er hatte in seiner rechten Hand ein Büchlein aufgethan, und ich hörete eine Stimme vom Himmel herab mit mir reden und sagen, gehe hin, nimm das offne Büchlein von der Hand des Engels, und er sprach, nimm hin, und verschlings, und da ichs gessen hatte, krummet michs im Bauch, und er sprach zu mir, du must abermal weissagen, den Völkern und Heiden, und Sprachen, und vielen Königen Apoc. 10., und ein ander Buch ward aufgethan, welches ist das Buch des Lebens Apoc. 20., und einer unter den Aeltesten spricht zu mir: Weine nicht, siehe es hat überwunden der Löwe, der da ist vom Geschlecht Juda, eine Wurzel David, aufzuthun das Buch, und zu brechen seine sieben Siegel; und es kam und nahm das Buch aus der rechten Hand des, der auf dem Stuhl saß, und da es das Buch nahm, da fielen die vier Thiere, und die 24 Aeltesten für das Lamm, und sprachen, du bist würdig zu nehmen das Buch, und aufzuthun seine Siegel. Apoc. 5. Wer Ohren hat der höre, was der Geist den Gemeinen saget. Apoc. 2 & 3. Hat jemand Ohren der höre, hier ist Weißheit. Apoc. 13.

Das eröfnete Buch mit seinen sieben Siegeln.
Apoc. 10.

Das 1 Bendel. Das Lamm mit den beyden Hörnern, h. e. das himmlische und irdische Reich nach dem Vater unser und Apoc. 13.

Die himmlische Dreyfaltigkeit im himmlischen Wesen nach dem Geist ein unsichtbarer Gott. Exod. 3. 5. 6. 7 & 20. Deut. 6 & 7. Matth. 19.

Die irdische heil. Dreyfaltigkeit in der Zeit nach dem Wort und Fleisch im Stand der Niedrigung ein sichtbarer leibhaftiger Gott. Joh. 1. 1 Tim. 3. Col. 21. 2 Cor. 5.

Das 2 Bendel. Die vereinigten beyden Naturen, die Gottheit und Menschheit in der einigen Person I. C.

Ewigkeit wird Zeit.

PERSON 2 WORT 3 SOHN 5 H.GEIST 6

Das Thier und seine Zahl 666.

I. C. GOTT UND MENSCH A₂O.

Der sichtbare *Gott in der Zeit.*

Göttlicher Signat Stern. Das Ewige Paradies

Philosophis. Signat Stern. Das Irdische Paradies

Das 3 Bendel. Die alte Geburt, das alte Testament, das brennende eifrige Gesetz. Exod. 20.

Selig ist der die Zahl 666 Apoc. 13. Das Thier ist gewesen, Apoc. und wird bleiben

des Thiers nennen kan Apoc. 13. und ist nicht, und ist doch Apoc. 17. in Ewigkeit.

Das 4 Bendel. Die neue Geburt, das neue Testament, das holdselige Evangelium.

Thue das Buch wieder zusammen mit seinen geöfneten Siegeln h. e. und verschließ es wieder, so ist es das erste versiegelte Buch, himmlisch nach dem unsichtbaren Gott, und kömmt Geist in Gott, Person in Sohn, und Vater ins Wort, und wird die heil. Dreyfaltigkeit, der drey himmlisch, geistlich unsichtbaren ewigen Personen, vereiniget und geschlossen in der irdischen zeitlichen, sichtbaren leiblichen Dreyfaltigkeit der einigen Person und Menschheit I. C., G. und M., welch seine heil. Menschheit, ein Thron, Sitz, Stuhl, Himmel, Haus und Wohnung ist der unzertrennten ewigen himmlischen Dreyfaltigkeit, ganz im Himmel, und ganz auf Erden, und das ist das versiegelte Buch, die Offenbahrung und wahre Erkenntniß und Zeugniß von I. C., G. und M. Denn in ihm wohnet die ganze Fülle der Gottheit leibhaftig, wie die heil. Weißheit selber meldet. Joh. 9. 10. 12. 14 & 17. und Colof. 2.

i. e. Signat=Stern. Leuchter.

Sterne Gemeinen
Gei 7 ster
Augen Hörner
Siegel
Apoc. 1. 2. 3. 4. 5.

IESUS CHRISTUS
der Grund und lebendige Eckstein in SION
den im Grunde des Geistes und der Wahrheit erkennen, ist das
Ewige Leben,
und
IESUM
lieb haben im Gewissen
ist besser
denn alles wissen.

Summa Summarum: This is the final conclusion: Hidden in these two proverbs is everything in the heavenly and earthly light, and he that rightly understandeth these proverbs in eternity and time is a right and true Theosophus, Cabalist, Magus and Philosophus and he that knoweth how to interpret these two proverbs according to the Alpha and Omega is a man well to be trusted and believed. And also thou canst test anybody who can thus do this, and weigh him on the R. C. scale.

Mark this well!

1.

In Christ, the visible, understandable God and Man, dwelleth the entire heavenly invisible divine nature of the holy Trinity, that is: God, Father, Son and Holy Ghost,

bodily Col. 2.

2.

In the visible, understandable, beautiful Gold, dwelleth the created invisible earthly, perfected nature, the earthly natural Trinity, that is: Sulphur, Mercurius and Sal,

bodily.

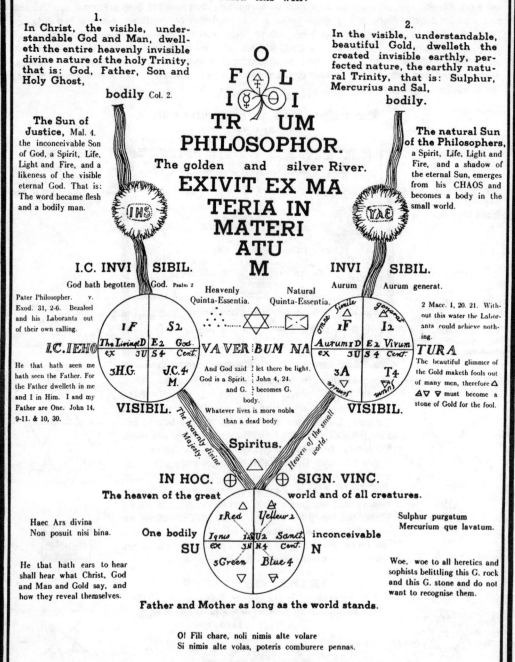

The Sun of Justice, Mal. 4. the inconceivable Son of God, a Spirit, Life, Light and Fire, and a likeness of the visible eternal God. That is: The word became flesh and a bodily man.

O F I L I
TR UM
PHILOSOPHOR.
The golden and silver River.
EXIVIT EX MA TERIA IN MATERI ATU M

The natural Sun of the Philosophers, a Spirit, Life, Light and Fire, and a shadow of the eternal Sun, emerges from his CHAOS and becomes a body in the small world.

I.C. INVI SIBIL.

God hath begotten God. Psalm 2

Pater Philosopher. v. Exod. 31, 2-6. Bezaleel and his Laborants out of their own calling.

I.C. IEHO

He that hath seen me hath seen the Father. For the Father dwelleth in me and I in Him. I and my Father are One. John 14, 9-11. & 10, 30.

VISIBIL.

Heavenly Quinta-Essentia.

Natural Quinta-Essentia.

VA VER BUM NA

And God said : let there be light. God is a Spirit. : John 4, 24. and G. : becomes G. : body. Whatever lives is more noble than a dead body.

INVI SIBIL.

Aurum Aurum generat.

2 Macc. 1, 20. 21. Without this water the Laborants could achieve nothing.

TURA

The beautiful glimmer of the Gold maketh fools out of many men, therefore △ △▽ ▽ must become a stone of Gold for the fool.

VISIBIL.

Spiritus.

IN HOC. ⊕ ⊕ SIGN. VINC.

The heaven of the great world and of all creatures.

Haec Ars divina Non posuit nisi bina.

One bodily SU inconceivable N

Sulphur purgatum Mercurium que lavatum.

He that hath ears to hear shall hear what Christ, God and Man and Gold say, and how they reveal themselves.

Woe, woe to all heretics and sophists belittling this G. rock and this G. stone and do not want to recognise them.

Father and Mother as long as the world stands.

O! Fili chare, noli nimis alte volare
Si nimis alte volas, poteris comburere pennas.

Let this be a warning to those that always want to be Know-alls.

O Man, how long wilt thou lack Knowledge, how long wilt thou not even Know Thyself?

Summa Summarum zum endlichen Beschluß, und an diesen zweyerley Sprüchen ist alles gelegen, was in dem himmlischen und natürlichen Licht verborgen ist, wer diese Sprüche recht verstehet, und recht gründlich erkennet, nach der Ewigkeit und Zeit, der ist ein recht wahrhaftiger Theosoph, Cabalist, Magus und Philosophus, und wer diese zweyerley Sprüche nach A und Ω ausdeuten kann, den magst du sicherlich glauben, und wohl trauen, und kannst auch einen jedweden hieran just und recht probiren, und auf die R. C. Wage stellen.

Das merke wohl!

1.

In Christo dem sichtbaren begreiflichen GOTT und MENSCHEN wohnet die ganze himmlische unsichtbare göttliche Natur, der heil. Dreyfaltigkeit, das ist: Gott Vater, Sohn und Heil. Geist, **leibhaftig.** Col. 2.

Die Sonne der Gerechtigkeit, Mal. 4. der unbegreifliche Sohn Gottes, ein Geist, Leben, Licht und Feuer, und Ebenbild des unsichtbaren ewigen Gottes, das ist: das WORT ward Fleisch und ein leibhaftiger Mensch.

2.

In dem sichtbaren begreiflichen schönen GOLT, wohnet die erschaffene unsichtbare irdische ganz vollkommene Natur, die irdische natürliche Dreyeinigkeit, das ist: Sulphur, Mercurius und Sal, **leibhaftig.**

Die natürliche Sonne der Weisen, ein Geist, Leben, Licht und Feuer, und ein Schatten der ewigen Sonne, gehet herfür aus ihrem CHAOS, und wird leibhaftig in der kleinen Welt.

O
F L
I I
TR UM
PHILOSOPHOR.
Der güldene und silberne Fluß.
EXIVIT EX MA
TERIA IN
MATERI
ATU
M

I.C. INVI SIBIL.
Gott gebieret Gott. Pfal. 2.

Pater Philosophor. v. Exod. 31, 2-6. Bezaleel und seine Laboranten selbst berufen.

I.C. IEHO

Wer mich siehet, der siehet auch den Vater. Denn der Vater ist in mir, und ich in ihm. Ich und der Vater sind Eins. Ioh. 14, 9-11. & 10, 30.

IV · S2
Q · O2 · Goet Cent.
T4
HG · IC. 4 M.

VISIBIL.

Himml. Quint. Essent.

VA VER BUM NA
Und Gott sprach: es werde Licht. Gott ist ein Geist, Ioh. 4, 24. und G. G. werden Leib.
Was lebendig, ist doch edler denn ein todter Leib.

Natürl. Quint. Essent.

INVI SIBIL.
Aurum Aurum generat.

2 Macc. 1, 20. 21. Ohne dieses Wasser haben die Laboranten nichts machen können.

TURA.

Des Goldes schöner Glanz, bringt manchen an Narrentanz, darum △ △ ▽ und ▽ müssen den Narren ein Goldstein werden.

1F · I2
Aurum · O2 vivum Cent.
5A · T4

VISIBIL.

Spiritus.
△

IN HOC. ⊕ ⊕ SIGN. VINC.
Der große Welt Him mel aller Creaturen

Haec Ars. divina
Non posuit nisi bina.

Eine leiblich und unbegreifliche SO NN

Wer Ohren hat zu hören, der höre doch einmal recht, was Christus Gott und Mensch, und das Gold reden, und sich offenbaren.

1Roth · Gelb 2
Ignis · O2 Sanct. Cent.
3Grün · Blau 4

Vater und Mutter so lange die Welt stehet.

Sulphur purgatum
Mercurium que lavatum.

O WE WE allen Ketzern und Sophisten, welche diesen Fels G. und diesen Stein G. verwerfen, und nicht einmal recht erkennen wollen.

O! Fili chare, noli nimis alte volare
Si nimis alte volas, poteris comburere pennas.

Zur Warnung denen so ohne Verstand Hans in allen Gassen seyn wollen.

O Mensch, wie lange wilt du unwissend seyn, und dich selbst einst nicht recht erkennen lernen.

FIGURA CABALISTICA

of the Wonderful Cipher
1. 2. 3. 4.

Fire and light were the beginning. Gen. 1.v.3.
Fire will be the end. 2. Pet. 3. v. 10. 12.
I am Nature's palace and cottage.
Defy him that speaketh against me.

Fire and light were. 2. Cor. 4.v.6.
Fire and light will be. 1.Tim. 6.v. 16.   1. John. 1. v. 6.7.
The philosopher's Sun for him who beholdeth.
My power is in and above the earth.

The Heavenly Sun
with his rainbow and 4 colours.
NATURA.

The Earthly Sun
with his rainbow and 4 colours.
TINCTURA.

About the natural and supernatural fire.

The invisible and visible fire of the 4 Elements.

The inconceivable ... **divine fiery light**
in the ... innermost

1. the red colour
2. the yellow colour
3. the green colour
4. the purple colour

black colour 1.
green colour 2.
white colour 3.
red colour   4.

☉ and ☽
have to be darkened
and have to become
black.
Mortificatio.

Chaos   Sperma

1. Straight natural fire
2. Supernatural fire
3. Fire against nature
4. Unnatural fire

The preliminary work — dry way
Solve & — Coagula
Corruptio — regeneratio
Subsequent — wet way
work
itself, out of itself and
a natural way.
go, will lead thee to
spiritual life.

Nature hath to work in
through itself in
The right way thou shalt
the natural and

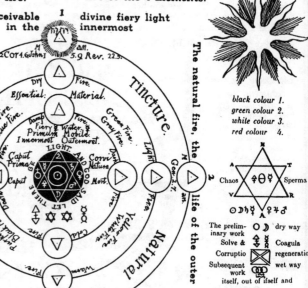

Rom. 11. v. 36. **Of Him and through Him and to Him are all things.** Act. 17. v. 28.
In Him we live and move and have our being.

God who is above all and through all and in you all. Ephes. 4. v. 6.

God is all in all. 1. Cor. 12. v.
in heaven

28. **In eternity and time, and the hell.**

What help are Sun, Moon, Fire and Light,
right way and lets a will o'

when man will not see, while traveling the
the wisp lead him astray.

O God, how deep in darkness
Everywhere is the world!
How deep is the world in foolishness
And how is the world afflicted with blindness,
The right way is also poor.

I wonder how one goes astray,
That one cannot find reason in Nature,
So consumate are Nature's works;
All this is done through God's grace alone,
Without it all is vain.

For the Lord wilt light my candle: The Lord my God will enlighten my darkness.
Psalms. 18. v. 28.

FIGURA CABALISTICA
von der Wunderzahl
1. 2. 3. 4.

Feuer und Licht war der Anfang. Gen. 1. v. 3.
Feuer wird seyn der Untergang. 2. Pet. 3. v. 10. 12.

Der Natur Pallast und Hütte bin ich
Trutz dem der mir dies widerspricht.

Die Himmlische Sonne
mit ihren Regenbogen und 4 Farben.
NATURA.

Feuer und Licht war. 2. Cor. 4. v. 6.
Feuer und Licht bleibt immerdar. 1. Tim. 6. v. 16.
1. Joh. 1. v. 6. 7.

Der Weisen Sonn wer dich betracht
In und ob Erde ist meine Macht.

Die Jrdische Sonne
mit ihren Regenbogen und 4 Farben.
TINCTURA.

1. die rothe Farbe
2. die gelbe Farbe
3. die grüne Farbe
4. die purper Farbe

☉ und ☽

müssen verfinstert und
schwarz werden.
Mortificatio.

♃ ☿

1. Grad natürlich Feuer
2. übernatürlich Feuer
3. widernatürlich Feuer
4. unnatürlich Feuer

Die Natur muß in, aus,
beweget
Den rechten Weg, den du
führen zu dem natürli

schwarze Farbe 1.
grüne Farbe 2.
weisse und 3.
rothe Farbe 4.

Die Vorarbeit ☉ truckner Weg
Solve & coagula
Corruptio regeneratio
Nacharbeit nasser Weg
und von sich selber natürlich
werden.
wandeln solt, der wird dich
chen geistlichen Leben.

Vom übernatürlichen und
natürlichen Feuer.
*Das göttliche unbe
in dem in
wendigen*

Der 4 Elementen unsicht-
und sichtbaren Feuer.
greifliche Feurlicht

Röm. 11. v. 36. Von Jhm, durch Jhn, und in
Jhm sind alle Dinge. Actor. 17. v. 28. In
Jhm leben, weben, und sind wir.

Der da ist über euch alle, und durch euch alle,
und in euch allen. Ephes. 4. v. 6.

Gott ist alles in allem. 1. Cor. 15.
Himmel und

v. 28. In Ewigkeit und Zeit, im
in der Hölle.

Was helfen Sonn, Mond, Feur und Licht,
Wie sie wandeln auf rechter Strassen,

Wenn die Menschen wollen sehen nicht,
Und von Jrrwischen verführen lassen.

Ach Gott, wie steckt die Welt zumal
In Finsterniß tief überall!
Wie ist sie in Thorheit versunken
Und in Blindheit schwerlich ertrunken.
Der rechte Weg ist also schlecht,

Mich wundert wie man geht unrecht,
Daß man der Natur nicht nachgründ,
Wie es so schön sein Werk vollend;
Dies macht allein Gottes Gab und Gunst,
Ausser dem ist es alles umsonst.

Herr, du erleuchtest meine Leuchte. Der Herr, mein Gott, machet meine Finsterniß Licht. Psalm 18. v. 20.

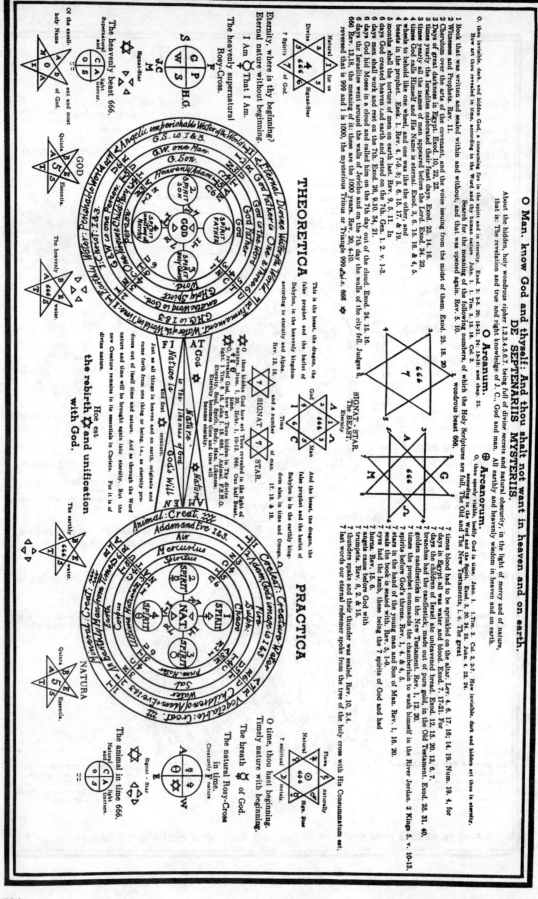

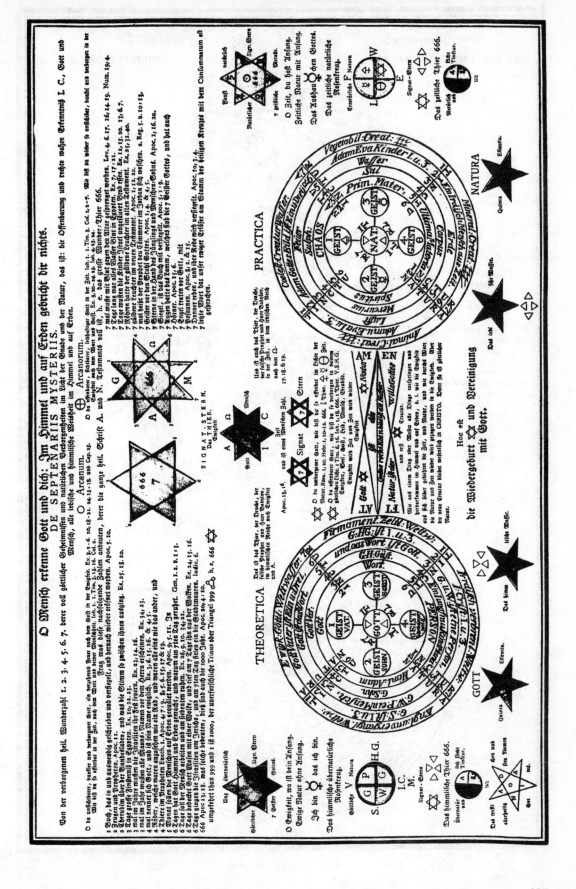

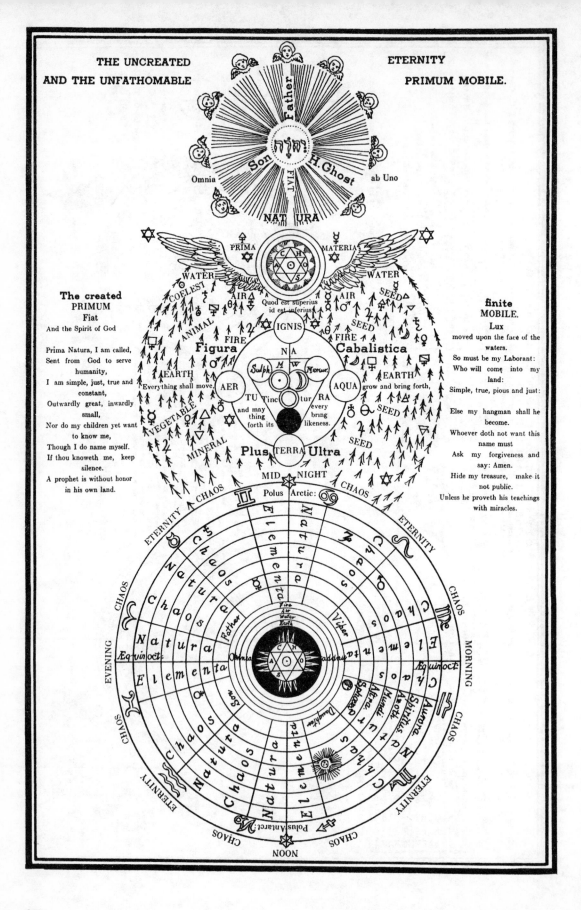

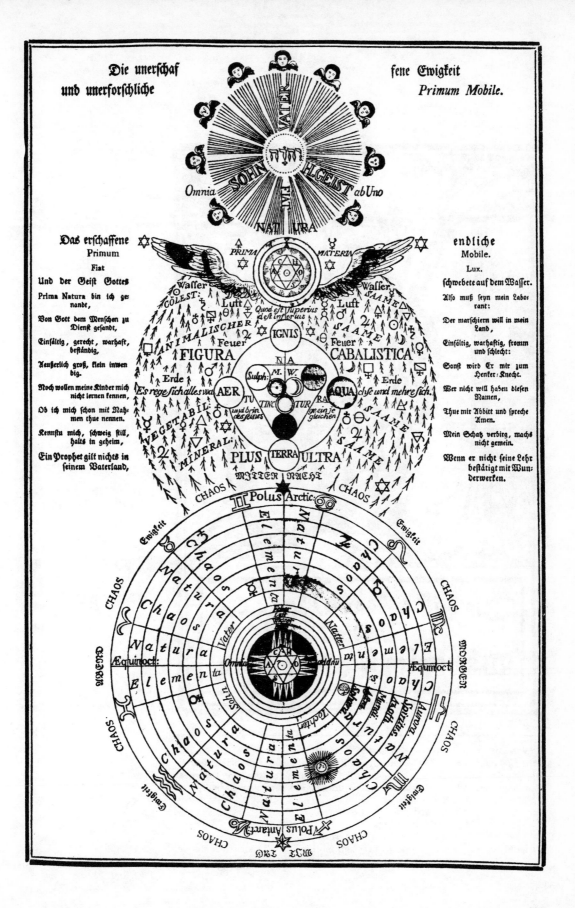

Was helffen Fackeln/ Liecht oder
Brillen/
Wann die Leut nicht sehen wollen.

A Woodcut from Heinrich Khunrath's *Von Hylealischen . . . Algemeinen Natuerlichen Chaos . . .* , Magdeburg, 1616. On the red and black printed title page of this work, which appeared in the same year as *The Chymical Wedding,* is an owl, wearing spectacles, holding two torches, flanked by lighted candles. The owl exclaims:

> "What good are torches,
> Light or spectacles,
> To people who *will* not see?"

A number of writers have found Rosicrucian motifs in this very curious device.

HEINRICH KHUNRATH'S AMPHITHEATER OF ETERNAL WISDOM, 1609

(Notes by the Editor)

The following eleven plates — here published *as a complete series* for the first time since their first appearance in 1609 — are considered to be among the most important and remarkable mystical drawings in the world. The order of the plates follows that of the copy formerly in the library of Isaac Myer, eminent American authority on the Cabala. Careful study and comparison will show that these plates include motifs which later appeared in *The Chymical Wedding* and *The Secret Symbols of the Rosicrucians*.

Plate I.   Heinrich Khunrath (1560-1605)

Plate II.   Title Page of Khunrath's *Amphitheater of Eternal Wisdom*, 1609

Plate III. The Portal to the Amphitheater of Eternal Wisdom

Plate IV.   The First Stage of the Great Work

Plate V.   The Journey to the Heights

Plate VI.   The Castle of the Mysteries

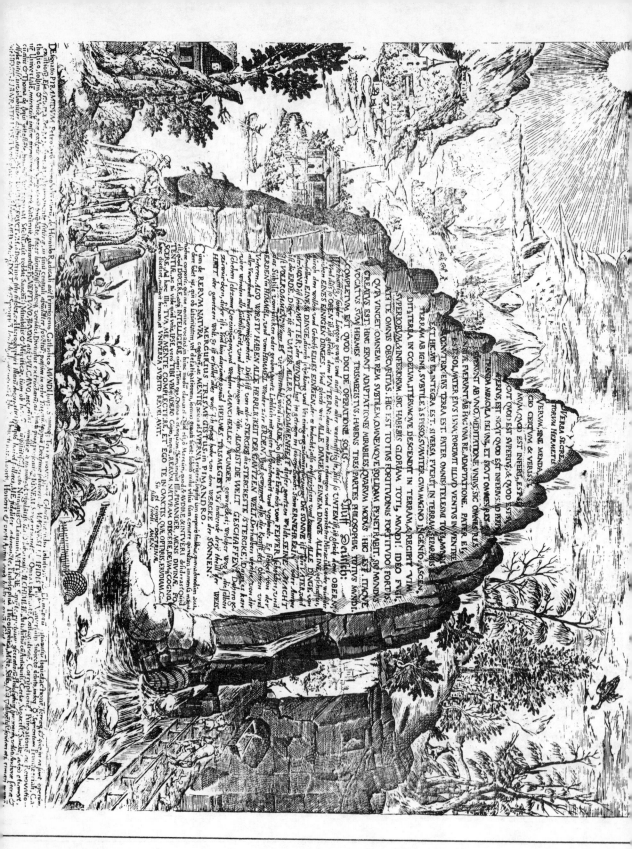

Plate VII.   The Word of the Mysteries

Plate VIII. The Defense of the Mysteries

337

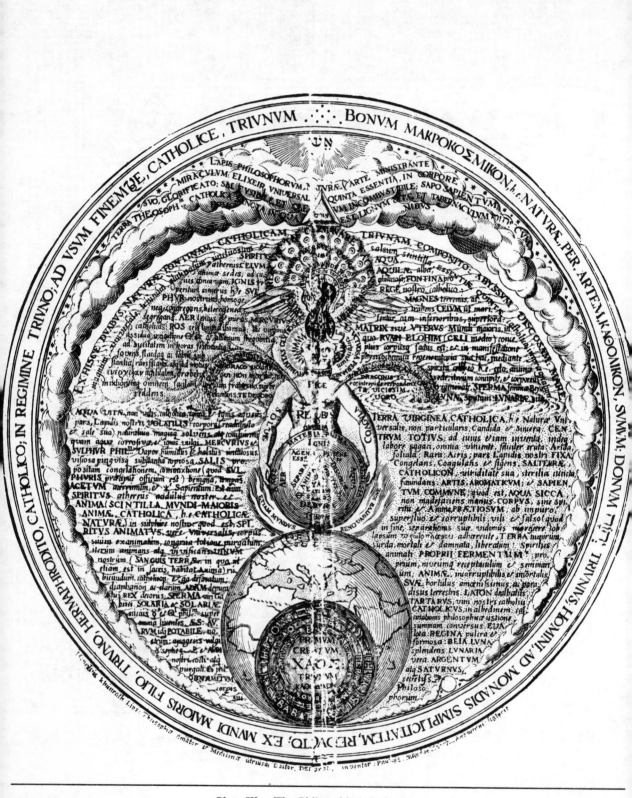

Plate IX.   The Philosophical Androgyne

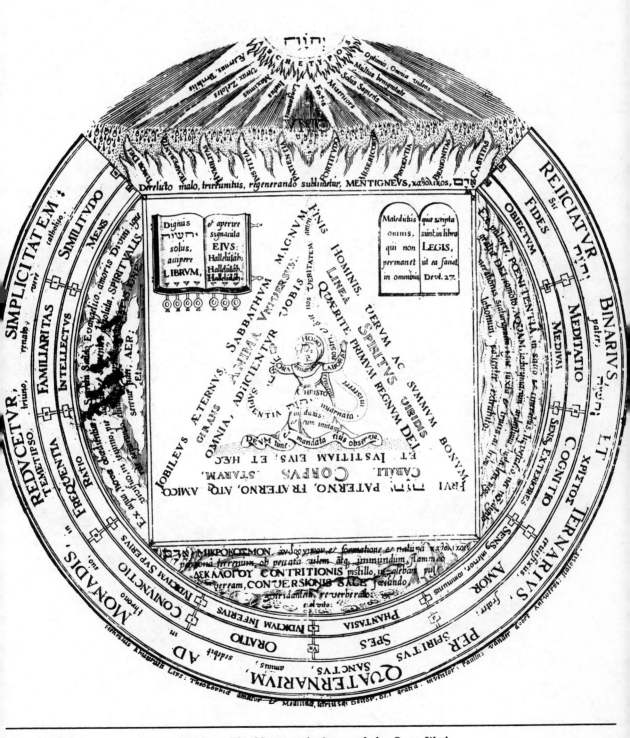

Plate X.   The Macrocosmic Aspect of the Great Work

Plate XI.   The Ultimate Goal

Plate I. *Heinrich Khunrath (1560-1605)*, Physician and Author, born in Saxony, educated at Basel, practised Medicine in Hamburg and Dresden, died in poverty and obscurity at forty-five. Rudolf Steiner indicated his importance as "A Theosophist who, in a moment of enlightenment, discovered the law of Becoming and Decaying" in the working of the forces behind external Nature. This plate is the Frontispiece of Khunrath's most important book, *The Amphitheater of Eternal Wisdom,* published posthumously by his friend, Ernst Wolfart, Hanover, 1609. — Details of the engraving are of considerable interest. Crowned as a "Son of the Doctrine," his life-motto, "Thy grace is sufficient for me," Khunrath is shown before a table, upon which is the Bible, opened at Psalm 71:17, "O God, thou hast taught me from my youth; hitherto I have declared thy wondrous works." The watchful dog is always associated with Hermes and the Hermetic mysteries. At the left, what Robert Fludd in his *The Rosicrucian Brotherhood,* included in the present volume, refers to as "the strongest pillars of Wisdom" — Magic, Cabala and Alchemy — are shown in book form, resting upon the foundation of the Bible, with Medicine and History as supporting elements.

Plate II. *Title Page of The Amphitheater of Eternal Wisdom.* The extraordinary mystical engravings on copper illustrating this work, here reproduced as a complete series, are clearly related to later Rosicrucian writings and drawings. — The keynote to all spiritual striving is shown by the words "Work" and "Pray" inscribed on the two pillars. The right-hand pillar is related to Luna, the Moon, the night, the "inner" aspect, the left-hand pillar to Sol, the Sun, the day, the "outer" aspect. The path between the two leads to the fruit of Perseverance in the form of a laurel wreath which a hand from the heavens extends above the head of the author, here shown as representative of all who faithfully carry out the Great Work.

Plate III. *The Portal to the Amphitheater of Eternal Wisdom.* The inscriptions, as the statement at the bottom of the plate indicates, were written by Khunrath, "faithful lover of Theosophy and Doctor of Medicine," on the basis of "a true Philosophy" which embraces "Christian Caballa, Divine Magic, Physio-Chemistry" (Alchemy). They are composed of three languages, Hebrew, Greek and Latin, reminiscent of the wisdom of the Ancient World, reminding one of the Gate of the Temple of Solomon, the Portal leading to the Greek Mysteries, and the Entrance to the Lower World depicted by Dante in the mighty record of his own spiritual Initiation, *The Divine Comedy.* — On the left face of the gateway is inscribed, "Indeed (it is) a Mystery, one truly divine, which will entice all observers, especially the Innermost (Mystery), which will rightly call forth their wonder and love." On the lower right face is written, "God has given all things rightly to know, to have power, and to be." — Uniting these two inscriptions, on the curve of the rocky arch is written, "All in All," and the keystone, resting upon the very top of the arch, warns, "Far away remain, O you profane ones!" (This injunction appears also in *The Chymical Wedding,* though in slightly different words.) Within the opening itself seven guiding statements greet the aspirant. These are numbered, and read: I. "Be washed; you will be clean." II. "God, One Creator of all; they shall be blessed by other powers." III. "To the First, sacrifices and prayers; to inferiors, hymns. IV. "If the prayer has been offered to inferiors, unless they be messengers of the First, it is no service." V. "Our offerings shall be acceptable to God, and for us they shall be reverence and awe." VI. "To them, according to the stage of probation, it shall be joyful obedience." VII. "The holy rituals whose Mysteries you are about to practice, shall be open to the worthy, but closed to the profane." — These seven guide-lines are reflected in the seven steps leading into the temple of the Mysteries. Of the six figures in the center of the picture, three stand outside and discuss, but show no sign of entering, two are mounting the steps with some hesitation, while only *one*, arms lifted in joyful anticipation, moves rapidly and energetically toward the light within. — It will be noted that the gateway to the Temple opens *inward*, and the aspirants move forward *in darkness* toward the light which shines up from *within*. At the outset is graphically shown that "the Light which shines in the darkness" is reached through an *inner* path, and the first step upon it — as Rudolf Steiner reminds us — is *Studium*, Study.

Plate IV. *The First Stage of the Great Work*. What at first may appear to be a "realistic" representation of the laboratory of an Alchemist, upon further study is shown to be a presentation of spiritual facts and relationships. In the midst of a great hall, the floor design of which converges upon a closed sanctuary at the back of an arched space, supported by four columns, is placed a table upon which is shown an assortment of objects, including musical instruments, writing materials, books, and a set of scales. At the *right* are the external implements of the "work" aspect of things, reminiscent of the right-hand column shown on the title page reproduced in Plate II. At the left is a tent-like structure, circular in form, reminding one of the tent of the Israelites on their journey through the desert. This occupies the same relative position as the column inscribed "Pray" in the title-page of Khunrath's book. That this is *not* the really final goal of spiritual striving is shown by the "temporary" aspect of the tent-sanctuary as compared with the highly "fixed" nature of the temple-sanctuary in the distance, reminding one of the divine Reality toward which everything in the foreground strives. The arms of the kneeling figure are lifted in the same gesture as that of the eager aspirant at the top of the steps in Plate III. On the cloth-covered table is an open book at the right, which, together with the inscribed tablet hanging above, indicates the *spoken and written* word. At the left of the table is shown an open book in which can be seen two drawings very like those in *The Secret Symbols of the Rosicrucians.* These show the *picture-aspect* of the word, in which the *eye* plays the leading role in contrast to the *ear.* The sanctuary lamp within the tent reminds one that the word is also a *light,* and the rising smoke of burning incense at the left indicates the *fragrance* of reverent prayer. — In conclusion we can say that this illustration indicates that only by the path of devotion can the true goal, the revelation of the Mystery concealed within the closed Sanctuary, be attained. The saying, "To labor is to pray," is here balanced with "To pray is to labor." As Nicholas Valois, the 15th century adept, wrote; "The good God granted me the divine secret through my prayers and the good intentions I had of using it well, for the science is lost if the purity of heart is lost." — In true Rosicrucian strivings, science and art went hand in hand with inner purity and spiritual devotion.

Plate V. *The Journey to the Heights.* The Mountain of the Philosophers, the Mountain of Initiation, is shown as the goal of man's spiritual striving.

Many of the motifs in this engraving are comparable with those described in *The Parabola* and *The Chymical Wedding*. For example, the boat at the lower left, the mill in the center, the "guardian" sitting in the cave at the foot of the ascending steps, the oratory halfway up the mountain at the right, and the summit formed of crystalline columns, in the midst of which the "Portal to the Amphitheater of Eternal Wisdom of the Sun" is shown. A significant point is indicated in that the main source of the river flowing downward from left center of the plate, seems to be in the church, the spire of which, like a sign of aspiration, rises upward. Thus it can be said that religious *devotion* is the *source* of a spiritual striving which finds its *ultimate* in the "Eternal Wisdom" of the heights. — This entire scene, however, is shown to be in truth *a meditation-picture* unfolding before the eyes of the kneeling figure at the lower right. He is shown "alone" on his island of meditation, open book on the ground, arms half-lifted in wonder, as he gazes upon the panorama before him. — If one compares the gesture and position of this man with that of the "eager" aspirant in Plate III, repeated in the kneeling figure in Plate IV, one can readily see that *the same person* is depicted, hence, *a progressive spiritual development* is indicated.

Plate VI.   *The Castle of the Mysteries.* The outermost wall surrounding the castle is divided into 21 sections, each with a gateway. All but one of these sections have no exit, showing — as the inscriptions indicate — false ways to the attainment of the spiritual goal. The 20 "cells" communicate with each other, making a bewildering labyrinth for the unwary. The 21st path is the true one, but the inner sanctum is watched over by a "guardian." Some aspirants have climbed to the top of the surrounding inner wall, but they cannot reach the solution of the mystery though — like many of the guests at the *Chymical Wedding of Christian Rosenkreutz* — they know many secrets very well indeed, "for the Art is lost if the purity of heart is lost." — Within the Castle, two figures greet the aspirant with the words "Pray theosophically, work physio-chemically." — He passes through 7 stages of development, coming at last to the great goal, presided over by the winged dragon. — These and other details of this plate (including the figures, buildings, etc. in the outer sections of the drawing) invite careful study and comparison with motifs of *The Chymical Wedding* and designs in *The Secret Symbols of the Rosicrucians*.

Plate VII.   *The Word of the Mysteries.* Beneath a brightly shining sun, the words of the Mysteries are inscribed "triumphantly" in the face of an everlasting "pyramid of rock," as "a revealed secret" for all "the world" to read. — But few heed the message, and life goes calmly on, as shown in the peaceful landscape in the background. However, the little circle of men in the foreground, separated from a rocky cliff by a swift-flowing stream, is stirred by the inscription, but thus far all they do is "talk." — The text inscribed on the rock in Latin and German is taken from *The Divine Pymander* of Hermes Mercurius Trismegistus, one of the earliest of all Hermetic writings extant, which had a profound influence upon Alchemists and Rosicrucians alike. (See Edouard Schure, *The Great Initiates* and G.R.S. Mead, *Thrice Greatest Hermes*) — At the right, the footway beside the flooding torrent is reminiscent of the adventure with the mill-race in *The Parabola*, and certain other motifs are shown here which are repeated in *The Chymical Wedding* as well.

Plate VIII. *The Defense of the Mysteries*. Bigots and pedants attacking the teachings and rituals of the Mysteries are shown in composite animal-human forms. Above, the hum of "insects" fills the air with hatred, gossip, slander, jealousy and poison. (One is reminded, for example, of Marinus Mersennus' attacks as described by Robert Fludd in *The Rosicrucian Brotherhood,* included in this present book.) — But protected by the downstreaming influence of the Macrocosm, the Great Work goes forward undisturbed, sheltered from profane eyes by ten flames and the rocks of the grotto. At left and right, reminiscent of the two pillars on the title-page of the book (see Plate II), two men — the one at the right clothed in everyday dress of the world of "Work," the other at the left clad in cultic garments of "Prayer" — defend the Mysteries. — It is interesting to note that the adept on the left side has his foot firmly planted on the serpent, his divided rod over the latter's back as though to control its movements, while the novice at the right apparently does not see the serpent half hidden beneath the bush, coiled, ready to spring upon him. — Within the grotto itself are seen the lion, dragon and fountain, similar to motifs to be found in *The Chymical Wedding*.

Plate IX. *The Philosophical Androgyne*. The united Sun and Moon — the pillars of "Prayer" and "Work" of the title page, (see Plate II) bring to birth the mystic Azoth, the bird of immortality, sometimes referred to as the universal Mercury, the invisible, eternal fire, the astral light, the measureless spirit of life. In a well-known woodcut the physician, Paracelsus is shown holding a sword, his hand resting upon a ball which crowns the hilt. This ball is marked "Azoth," indicating yet another aspect of this creation, that of the Stone of the Philosophers, the consummation of the Great Work. — That this affects all worlds is shown by the surrounding heavens with the Light of the Divine Name above, the globe of the earth beneath. Thus, through his deeds, man himself becomes a cooperator in the progress of evolution. — The designs in circular form below the male-female figure, and the globe of the earth, are reminiscent of certain similar motifs in *The Secret Symbols of the Rosicrucians.*

Plate X. *The Macrocosmic Aspect of the Great Work.* The tenfold flames of the divine Virtues, reflecting the tenfold rays of the divine world of the Archetypes overspread the twofold kneeling figure in the center, whose arms are lifted in "Work" and "Prayer", reminiscent of the two pillars on the title page of the book itself (see Plate II). In the upper right the Tables of the Law are balanced by the open Book of Praise (repeating the threefold *Hallelujah* from the title-page of the book), with its Seven Seals. In the triangular border around the central figure the words Body, Soul (*Anima*, Mind), and Spirit are to be seen.

Plate XI. *The Ultimate Goal.* The cosmic aspect of the Christ, here shown as the central point of evolution of the world and humanity, is surrounded by the tenfold Sephiroth, the flames of the divine Glory, the mystical Threefold One of the Godhead. Beneath is the Phoenix, symbol of death and Resurrection, the sign of eternal rebirth. Sometimes referred to as "the mystic Rose-Panticle," this plate has been cited as proof of Khunrath's affinity with the spiritual goals of the Rosicrucians. From this engraving it is clear that this is the source from which the representation of the Christ in. glory appearing in *The Secret Symbols of the Rosicrucians* was derived.

THE ROSICRUCIAN BROTHERHOOD

by
ROBERT FLUDD

Book IV of his *Summun Bonum,*
The Highest Good, 1629

(Translated by Carlo Pietzner from the German version of F. Freudenberg)

Since it is the habit and pleasure of Brother Marinus Mersennus* to persecute people of all kinds by slander and lies, it cannot surprise us that he attacks with wickedness those who are familiar with true Magic, Cabala and Alchemy. He himself disdains, despises these sciences, which are the strongest pillars of wisdom, and with shouting and sound of trumpets he condemns the inhabitants of the Palace of Wisdom, trying to separate them from the community of Christians, seeking to send them into exile. —

Let us first see who these men actually are who possess these gifts of wisdom, before we make any remarks about them in reply to the audacious judgment of Mersennus. At the beginning we shall cite the testimony of two recent authors, and then that of the Holy Scripture.

Among recent writers, Agrippa speaks about these men in the following way: "I confess," says he, "that today also there are men, filled with wisdom, distinguished by knowledge, virtue and skill, blameless in life and custom, unexcelled in cleverness, and through experience in life and strength able to serve the State in deed and counsel. And they are as far from coveting the cattle of your field as they are from the habitation of those who, in place of wisdom put wickedness, for reason substitute subterfuge and treason; for uprightness, slyness and cunning; for science, fraud; for cleverness, faithlessness; for religion, superstition. "— Cardanus also speaks a strong word about people of this kind.

But apart from the testimony of these secular authors, we also have that of the Holy Scripture concerning such people who, as it were, wish to erect and inhabit the House of Wisdom, and also concerning their continued existence to the end of the world. The Scriptures teach us that no age has existed, exists, or will exist, in which single individuals, experienced in the world and its darknesses, have not been able to retain knowledge of the holy light, counting themselves among the sons of God. Thus in each century and epoch were some, however, small in number, who passed through the narrow portal, while the larger part of mankind trod the broader and more conspicuous way. For we read that in each epoch of the Church, some were found who were given the "victory, the tree of life which is in the midst of the Paradise of God" (*Revelation* 2:7), the "hidden manna and the white stone" (*Revelation* 2:17), the "morning star" (*Revelation* 2:28), or "clothed in white raiment." (*Revelation* 3:5) They shall receive their heritage and their name shall not be blotted from the book of life, and they will be "pillars in the temple" and will receive "the new name of the Lamb."

The following words of the Evangelist are also applicable to those men: all who receive "the true Light that cometh into the world," receive the "power to become the sons of God." (*John* 1:9,12) They are to live in the above-mentioned House of Wisdom, safely and strongly erected on the mountain, of which the *Saviour* speaks: "Whosoever heareth these sayings of mine and doeth them, I will liken him unto a wise man, which built his house upon a rock; and the rain descended and the floods came, and the winds blew, and beat upon that house; and it fell not: for it was founded upon rock." (*Matthew* 7:24-25 and *Luke* 6:48)

But, you will ask, why are these good inhabitants of that imaginary house so hidden; why do their habitations remain so secret? Why have they not appeared before the world long since? Why do they not reveal (as Mersennus wishes) their secrets for the prosperity of the State in which they live — if they can call such virtue and power their own?

To these questions I reply that while they are truly endowed with heavenly riches, they stand before the world poor and unknown. It is no wonder that, rich as they are through the Holy Spirit, they despise the world and its splendor, according to the word of the Evangelist: "Love not the world, neither the things that are in the world . . . For all that is in the world is the lust of the flesh, the lust of the eyes, and the pride of life." (*I John* 2:15-16) Thus it is that the world does not know the sons of God because "the sons of God do not know the world" for the world "is built entirely upon wickedness." (*I John* 5:19)

On the other hand, however, it is the will of God that what is hidden shall be revealed. And God has promised through His prophets, in the last days before the end of the world, "to pour out His spirit upon all flesh" (*Joel* 2:28), and the royal Psalmist prophesies that God will quench the thirst of the sons of men out of the stream of His grace; those who remain under the protection of His wings in hope will find in Him the fountain of life, for in his light we shall see the light. (See *Psalm* 36)

But to return to the inhabitants of that Castle of Wisdom, built with such reason on the mountain. — It is given to them by the Holy Spirit to know everything — because it is His task to teach everything as was said by the Apostle, through "the grace of God which is given to you by Jesus Christ, in everything you are enriched by him, in all utterance and in all knowledge." (*I Corinithians* I:4-5) — Thus it follows that these inhabitants of the House of Wisdom — they alone, and no one other than they — are those who, together with Solomon, have knowledge of true Magic, of true Cabala, and of true Alchemical science. — We have already spoken sufficiently about these arts in the past.

Therefore it seems to me praiseworthy that this society, the Brotherhood of the Rosicrucians, does not wish to appear before the world before the appointed time. This Fraternity has been slandered by the world in past ages because the children of the world can understand only worldly things, esteeming them to be greater than divine things, and persecuting the servants of the Lord with hatred and mockery in our time as they have done in the past. I leave to those among my readers who are aware of such things, to judge how unjust it is for Christians to reject the divine gifts offered by these Brothers, and even to mock them, to speak about them in the most wicked manner, and finally to declare them to be sorcerers and brothers of hell.

Far may it be from us that *all* laymen would gain such ugly, satanic views about their truly Christian brothers, and more especially may it come about that the clergy will be stopped from persecuting these brothers in Jesus Christ with slander and disdain. Do they not read time and again the words of Christ: "Whosoever is angry with his brother without a cause shall be in danger of the judgment... Whosoever shall say, Thou fool, shall be in danger of hell fire." (*Matthew* 5:22) And at a different place: "Judge not, that ye be not judged. For with what judgment ye judge, ye shall be judged; and with what measure ye mete, it shall be measured to you again." (*Matthew* 7:1-2) — Such a one seems to be Brother Marinus Mersennus himself, if we can believe his expostulations at all. "Take care," says he, "that you do not harm brotherliness!" However, I fear that he himself wavers in his conviction, for in his writings he sometimes agrees and sometimes rejects. How often he himself has done injury to the admonition he has uttered, cannot remain hidden to anyone with an open mind. And yet he has assumed that saying of our Saviour: "Why beholdest thou the mote that is in thy brother's eye, but considerest not the beam that is in thine own eye? Thou hypocrite, first cast out the beam out of thine own eye..." (*Matthew* 7:3,5) He himself, I say, urges us not to harm the brother, but he injures his brothers through slander and perjury; he judges unmercifully, attacks with cunning, and easily glosses over previously unheard-of tortures. — But let us hear his opinion concerning that divine, that choice seed among men, — concerning those who are called the Brotherhood of the Rosicrucians.

From the Writings of Mersennus

"With diligence I wish to admonish the judges, and with earnestness the princes, that they shall not let these monsters of false opinion rage within the sphere of their influence. Rather should they completely eradicate these brothers of hell, these Brothers of the Rosicrucians, who on almost every market-day at Frankfort introduce their writings, stinking of godlessness, telling about their false and mysterious Father R.C. and his cave, presenting these before the people of the Christian world. For it is blasphemy they teach, and they make themselves known as the heirs of the Magi, whose works they copy, producing little themselves, etc."

Answer

On two grounds I am goaded to defend here the aims of these blessed men against the false accusations of Mersennus. The first is that in my writings, I have already defended this Brotherhood against the accusations of an anonymous writer. The second is that it is the highest duty of a true Christian and righteous man to oppose the enemies and adversaries of those who are the guardians of truth itself, protectors of divine Wisdom, and to revere equally divine Wisdom and her sons with highest reverence, accomplishing this with faithful and sincere love. — In order that we can deal with one subject of this Brotherhood and their three main pillars of wisdom, namely, Magic, Cabala, and Alchemy, mentioned above, we say:

—Either the Brother-hood is	true and essential, and leads by a straight path to true —	Magic or Wisdom Cabala Alchemy
—Or	untrue and false, and some of this sect bear in a treasonable way such unjustified titles, or are guided by a spirit which is of the following kind:	covetous or begging, by which they defraud the people. haughty, so they appear as they are not. evil, so that, leading a sinful life, they bring a bad reputation to the real Brotherhood.

As for the untrue and fraudulent name given to the Brotherhood, we leave that to those whose business it is to judge the cunning and fraud of the windbags and highly culpable impostors who exist everywhere. These impostors deceive people every day with their superstitious magic, affected astrology, false formulae of a sub-chemistry, or their pranks with a deceitful cabala. They deceive the laymen, who marvel with open mouth at their gold, their treasures, their secrets. Those impostors bring harm to true wisdom and to the most sincere servants of wisdom by meanness and by spreading evil reports, making the latter contemptuous in the eyes of the world.

If Marsennus refers to impostors of the sort we have just described above, then we declare him to be innocent. However, he must be judged on the fact that he continually confuses truth with error, takes the part to be the whole, or — better expressed — the shadow for the real object, semblance for truth.

These men, devoted to God in their true Brotherhood, are much more to be honored with highest praise than to be judged by the ignorant with such passion. However, since they are judged by Brother Mersennus, damned and declared to be brothers of the devil, it is incumbent upon us first to investigate what their palace, castle or house may be, which has often been mentioned in their *Fama*. After this we may seek to learn who are the inhabitants of this building, and why they are called particularly and constantly, *Brothers* and also *Rosicrucians*. Finally, we shall publish a declaration given by these Rosicrucians, from which we can deduce whether or not men of this kind can justifiably and publicly be declared and branded monsters, heretics, and companions of hell by a Mersennus. Thus I shall here set forth briefly my own opinion about these questions.

Let us therefore say, to begin with, that the palace or cloister of this Fraternity is that of which the Holy Scripture speaks, as we can prove by these words: "Let us ascend the mountain of reason, and erect the House of Wisdom." As the foundational element in that mountain we recognize the "cornerstone which" (according to the testimony of the prophet) "has been taken from the mountain without the use of hands, and has itself become a great mountain, filling the whole earth after it shattered the feet of the statue." Thus says the prophet: "The house of the God of Israel is great and mighty in its possession." — This is the mountain which, in truth, is the Mount of Horeb, that spiritual Zion which is so often spoken of in Holy Scripture, and this stone is the same rock, that true house, which is meant by the Evangelist when he says, "The wise man will build his house by digging into the depth and placing the foundation on the selfsame rock." *That rock*, however, is *Christ,* upon whom the spiritual house and the sanctuary of the priests rests. — However clear it may be that it is required of us that we build a house upon that rock mountain, it is also clear that this cannot be the work of men, as is believed by foolish alchemists or magicians, but rather is a divine work. It is entirely certain that if Wisdom herself is not present in such things and does not undertake the leadership, both as architect and executor of the work, then human power can do nothing. — This is already confirmed in clear words by the sacred text (*Psalm* 127:1): "Except the Lord build the house, they labor in vain that build it . . ." — Thus it is in truth the Lord who does the building of the house, executes it with wise and experienced hands, and brings everything to completion. This is none other than what we see manifested when the active man brings forth in suffering woman through adjustment and dispersion, a third entity, namely, the foetus, which, however, is not created by clever men, but by the spirit of God hidden in the seed.

Therefore the Apostle also speaks: "We require of you, you brothers, that you bear rich fruit and work diligently; that you are calm and go about your business; work with your hands as we have prescribed for you, etc." — And, as a result, "So that no one will be in need." David says in his Psalm, "Blessed are those who walk in the ways of the Lord; He will establish the work of their hands." — And yet the hands of the artist create nothing (as I have said) except that they separate the superficial, and then out of itself the Spirit acts for the perfecting and heavenly ordering of that royal palace. "Your habitation," says the Apostle, "was not made by the hands of men, but we have a spiritual building in the heavens, which is the House of Wisdom on the Mount of Reason, built upon the spiritual rock."

Paul expresses this aptly in the following words: "I have planted, Apollo watered, but God gave the increase. Thus neither is he that planted anything, neither he that watered, but God gave the increase. Every man shall receive his reward according to his labor, for we are laborers together with God. You are God's building. According to the grace of God given to me, as a wise master-builder have I laid the foundation, and another builds upon it." (*I Corinthians* 3:6, etc.) — Everyone must discover how he can build upon this foundation, "for other foundation can no man lay than what is laid, which is Jesus Christ. If any man's work remain, which he has built upon this foundation, he shall receive a reward.

"Now if any man build upon this foundation gold, silver, precious stones, wood, hay, stubble; every man's work shall be made manifest because it shall be revealed by fire; and the fire shall try every man's work of what sort it is."

To this is related the oft-quoted stone of contention for the false Christians (*Romans* 9:33). This is the precious and proven cornerstone laid for everyone who believes in him as the foundation stone of the building, which will not be overthrown (*I Peter* 2:6). He is also a stone of contention (*Isaiah* 28:16). The prophet speaks of the ill-founded house (*Jeremiah* 22), and in *Proverbs* it says, "Woe to him who builds his house upon unrighteousness, and woe to his house in the day of judgment." Solomon also says, "The house of the unrighteous will be destroyed."

Since there exists a proven and a precious cornerstone, the true architects built the House of the Word above that stone. — This house of the just, I say, will last forever, according to the decrees of Wisdom as is testified by *Matthew* 7:24: "Therefore whosoever heareth these sayings of mine and doeth them, I will liken him to a wise man, which built his house upon a rock. And the rain descended, and the floods came, and the winds blew, and beat upon that house; and it fell not: for it was founded upon a rock."

Of this house the royal Psalmist sang, (*Psalm* 5:7; 26:8; 84:10): "I will come into thy house in the fulness of thy mercy. I have loved the habitation of thy house, and the place where thy honor dwelleth. I had rather be a doorkeeper in the house of my God than to dwell in the tents of wickedness."

By this, however, the king did not understand the temple built by the art of men because, as is testified by the Scripture, God did not inhabit a house from the exodus of Israel from Egypt to the time of Solomon, but He had His place in a tent. Addressing Himself to David, God also said, "Thou shalt not build an house for my name because thou hast been a man of war, and hast shed blood." With these words he means a material temple, for the Holy Scriptures testify that David possessed a description of the material temple which had been written into his spirit by the finger of God. — From this it seems clear that the divine Spirit Himself was the master of the plan of the House on the mountain, erected by reason, because, as it were, not only the Tabernacle and the Temple of Solomon, but also Man himself was formed according to this image, and therefore he is called the temple of the Holy Spirit.

Thus we come to the conclusion that the building of that house under the cooperation of a true Brother is a revelation of the occult, that is, the spiritual rock or the revelation of the mystical wisdom of the Stone of the Patriarch, which he calls the house of God. This is the erection of the spiritual house or palace on the Mount of Reason. And this rock we call the mystical castle Bethlehem, of which the Evangelist says, Christ was of the castle Bethlehem. — From that place also came David, which can easily be proved by etymology, for Bethlehem means "house of bread" and "of war." But manna means "the hidden bread" and "the food of the angels," "the bread of heaven," and "the Word," by which everyone can live without ordinary bread, as we are taught by Christ in the Scriptures. From this it follows that *Bethlehem* is the same as *Beth-El,* which means "the House of the Lord." Thus the stone or rock of Jacob is called "the House of God." Concerning the secret of this House of God, this Temple of Christ, we are excellently told by that patient man, Job, who says, "He brings fire of Solomon which makes men into prophets and friends of God." It makes them into faithful, wise, just, holy ones. Likewise one speaks of the holy house, of the holy Christians, universal, a ransomed generation, true seed of Abraham, priests, apostles, brothers of Christ, a Christian brotherhood, and many other names too numerous to mention.

I have undertaken to explain carefully why these last — these Brothers of the Rosy Cross — are properly to be called the seed of Abraham, and have been chosen from among the heathen, how they are descended from the blood of the Jews, how they have been called brothers of the Apostles, Christians, and members of the Rosicrucian Fraternity. — One has to know, first of all, that just as Christ came from the seed of Abraham, to whom by the word of God was promised blessing and through him salvation for the world, so also all true Christians must be called the seed of Abraham, because they have been born, as the Evangelist says, "not out of blood, nor of the will of the flesh, but of God." "Who," asks Christ, "is my mother, and who are my brothers? Whoever does the will of my Father who is in heaven, the same is my brother, my sister, my mother." — Such a descent from such seed is recognized unmistakably by the Apostle when he says, "They are of Christ who are of the seed of Abraham and the heirs of his promise." Thus the Apostle Paul praises not those who are circumcised in the foreskin alone, but in their hearts, when he says it is not the external Jew only, but the inner Jew who is chosen by God. So it is also with many among the heathen, because he says that of the seed of Abraham not only the Jews but all people of the world will be redeemed, as already seems evident from the Genesis. The heathen are co-workers, co-members and participants in this promise of Jesus Christ through the Gospel. For, as the Apostle testifies, Christ is the promised seed.

To anyone who doubts whether this Rosicrucian Brotherhood originates out of such blood, I reply in the sense of the evidence mentioned above, that if one kinship or brotherhood is of the flesh and of man, another is spiritual and divine. Thus it is written that the sons of God and the daughters of men, that is, those chosen by God from the tribe of Shem united themselves with the daughters of the tribe of the accursed Cain. However, the Scripture speaks quite generally: "You are a divine generation." — Therefore the divine seed is not from below out of the earth, for it is from above that the divine nourishment comes. In many places one finds sapphires, and lumps of earth in which there is gold. No bird has recognized this path, and no vulture's eye has discerned it, and so on. "He places His hand upon the stones, and overturns the foundations of the mountains." —

With those words is not only described the earthly substance of that House, but also its riches, the fiery light within it, and its power and might. The immeasurable strength of Bethlehem, interpreted as the house of war, is shown in the castle from which Christ went forth. Thus that spiritual stone (not the erroneous one of the false Alchemists) is also called "the fame of the whole world" by Hermes, a true and divine Alchemist. Through the discernment of that spiritual stone all darkness disappears from around one, and He appears "in the power of his strength" because He conquers all fine things and permeates all solid ones. — Thus was the world created.

Job and Hermes, however, not only describe the precious metals of that house, but also its virtues. For the city or castle built upon the summit of the mountain is also cabalistically called *Beth-ulia,* which means, as it were, "the Virgin of the Lord," or "the House that gives birth to the Lord." Hence Bethlehem is designated as the virginal earth which shall bring forth the Redeemer. And this saying comprises the whole claim of the prophets: "The earth will open and will give birth to the Messiah." For above all, it must be recognized that in the Holy Scriptures the names of both men and of cities contain secrets. Therefore the name of the city of Lutz was changed to Bethel because of the notable effect of the stone, which is called the house of God. Likewise, Bethlehem corresponds to the living Bread which shall come forth as out of a house or castle, and *Bethulia* means metaphorically the House of Wisdom built on the Mount of Reason. Apparently this name was given to this town because it was the most beautiful town or castle upon a height or mountain in that region. The latter is also called Mount Horeb in order to designate the Mountain of God. Finally, the prophet points to the mystery of the word Bethlehem when he says, "Christ, the Lord of Israel, will be given out of Bethlehem . . ."

Here then you have that House or Palace of Wisdom erected on the Mount of Reason. It remains however, to learn who are those sages to whom this House is open. These most fortunate of men and their spiritual house are described by the Apostle in the following manner: "To whom coming, as unto a living stone, disallowed indeed of men, but chosen of God, and precious, ye also, as living stones, are built up a spiritual house, a holy priesthood, to offer up spiritual sacrifices, acceptable to God by Jesus Christ." (*I Peter* 2:4-5) — And further on, he says, "But you are a chosen generation, a royal priesthood, an holy community, a ransomed people, that you should practise the virtues of him who has called you out of darkness into his royal light. For previously you were not a people, but now you are the people of God." — With these words he not only describes the overwhelmingly strong foundation and the builder of the House, but also the inhabitants. For these dwellers in the House of Wisdom are shown by him to be the faithful in Christ also, according to the teachings of Esdras, who lay down their mortal sheaths, choosing the immortal, confessing the name of the Lord, crowned with victory. Thus says a man, enlightened by wisdom: "For mortals labor in vain who have chosen a different path than was shown by the prophet," but this is not the path of death, as people are accustomed to believe, for it is the one mentioned by the Apostle Peter when he speaks of the one taught him by Christ when the latter was transfigured on the Mountain. — And this should remain secret and hidden, otherwise the Apostle would not have said, "As Jesus has taught me," and the highest Wisdom would not have directed, "Do not tell anyone."

From the beginning of the world it has been known that there is a death of the body. And from this it is clear what remarkable power had been given to these men by Christ. — The same is true for the one of whom it is said, "I will erect a house to the faithful one, and he will walk before me all the days of his life." These are the people meant by the prophet, I say, when he invites, "O house of Jacob, come, and let us walk in the light of the Lord," (*Isaiah* 2:5), and elsewhere, "Those who receive the true light will receive the power to become the rightful sons of God, even those who believe on His name."

You can discern from this the point of view and the true character of the inhabitants of that House of Wisdom. In addition, we now must consider how they are named, and the relationship given to them at that time by the Holy Scripture, namely, sons of God, the chosen of the Lord, the chosen generation, prophets, friends of God. Wisdom — not that of the flesh — but the one arising out of pure fire, kindled by the Spirit, brings it about that the children of the world become the children of God by being chosen, as Peter said, "Who once were not a people, but now are a people of God." — And this seed is that incorruptible spirit which God enclosed within all things, as Christ seems to confirm with the words, (*Matthew* 3:9) "God is able of these stones to raise up children unto Abraham," that is, new sons of Christ, Christians, whose head, according to the Apostle, is Jesus Christ, for he says (*I Corinthians* 11:3) "I would have you know that the head of every man is Christ, and the head of Christ is God," and further, "You are of Christ, but Christ is of God." —

Christ, who according to the prophets is the light of Israel out of Bethlehem (that is, the House of Bread), speaks in you, and though he does not assume your form, yet he is in you, is "the chief cornerstone" (*Ephesians* 2:20), whom we — as living stones — should serve to erect the House of Wisdom. This we should do in the same manner as Christ who as the leader of Israel, the chief rock, sends from his never-failing will the water of life. From this it follows that inasmuch as we are living stones, so we are seeds of Abraham; inasmuch as we are seeds of Abraham so we are truly brothers of Christ and true Israelites; and inasmuch as we are true Israelites, we are the Temple of God.

As we are divine seed and also living stones, that is, living stones cut from a single rock, carved out of Christ, so in this faith we have become one with Christ, having become, as it were, his members, according to the word of the Apostle, "a body which has many members;" therefore we are inheritors of the kingdom of heaven. And what is in us, by which we can be called living stones, is one truth in us. Thus we may believe that we are sons of God, and what beyond this is the night-side of man is lie and delusion, cannot in truth be called virtue or truth. For truth alone will pass safely through the trial of fire on the day of judgment. In the same manner as we Alchemists seek for that gold of God which emanates from Christ, so there is the perfect truth which alone will pass through each trial of fire in which the true and glowing virtue is purified, glorified and made more radiant, as is clearly evident from the words of the Apostle (*I Corinthians* 3:13).

Here it must be said explicitly that these Brothers are truly sons of Abraham and Israel, but only spiritually, not in the flesh. Thus also they are living stones whom the Evangelist describes as "born out of God," and not through physical intercourse, of whom he also says that it is possible to awaken sons of Abraham out of stones.

Because these stones have sprung out of one stone in this manner, they are also inner and spiritual stones. They can be called living stones because they give life and being to stones and all other earthly things which, because of their density are called "earth" and "stones." — Because they have been taken as living stones from the general and universal Rock, they make clear that all is in one and one is in all. For it seems to them that according to the word of the Apostle, through Him is everything, and He is in everything, and outside Him all is illusion and untruth, things which seem to be but are not.

Therefore it is also the task of the true and blessed Alchemists to distinguish illusion from truth, that is, to distinguish the evil from the good. This distinction is necessary to free Christ in the creation where he was, as it were, kept prisoner by unbelief, and to work against the godless nature of Barabbas, the son of dark confusion. Thus we become creators of the true word and of that wisdom which shines out of darkness, making us friends of God, enriched by every kind of gift.

All this happened through the opening of the earth so that, according to the words of Isaiah, "it may give birth to the Messiah." But this does not take place according to the ways of false Alehcmists, but in a divine and mystical manner, which is revealed according to the laws of true Alchemy. And Paul seems to call the true Alchemist "the true husbandman," saying, "the one who strives will not be crowned unless he strives righteously," for the striving husbandman stands in the first place to harvest the fruits. But Paul censures other philosophers and theologians who do not know the Divine Work, calling them, "men of corrupt minds, reprobate concerning the faith" (*II Timothy* 3:8). Thus he describes both the good laborers, that is, the builders of the House of Wisdom on the Mount of Reason, and also the evil, the false architects. He points to the right way for each man to unite himself with the brotherhood of Christ and the seed of Abraham, to work as the true husbandman and architect.

Now these are also called Apostolic Brothers because they are familiar with those secrets which the Apostle not only knew, but proclaimed courageously to the world. That is, they know that mystical wisdom, the secrets of their relationship to the chief cornerstone. For the Apostles called men brothers who dedicated themselves to the same secrets of God as they did. From this comes that Apostolic Brotherhood of which the Apostle Paul speaks, "The brotherly love remain in you," and Peter, "live of the brotherhood," and elsewhere, "How good and pleasant it is for brothers to live with each other."

Such a common habitation has now been taken up by the Brotherhood of the Rosy Cross, and their strong bond of love and joy lies in their knowledge of that one Christ and that one spiritual rock, upon which foundation everything has been erected, as has been adequately proven by the words of the Apostle mentioned before. Thus every understanding reader who grasps the above correctly, will realize that Marinus Mersennus does not belong to that Brotherhood, either as companion or member, even though he gives himself the title "*Brother* Marinus Mersennus" on the title-page of his book, and wants to make the world believe it. If, nevertheless, he *is* a Brother of this Order, then he is a false and untrue Brother, for in that Brotherhood of the Rosicrucians the highest and only truth, the greatest good-will, and brotherly love dwells. In Mersennus, on the other hand, dwells nothing but subterfuge, cunning and slander, which are altogether excluded from the school of the true Fraternity.

To the truth of this, Peter testifies in the words, "Laying aside all malice, guile, hypocrisy, envy, evil speaking, as newborn babes desire the sincere milk of the word that you may grow thereby, if so be that you have tasted that the Lord is gracious, to whom coming as unto a living stone, disallowed indeed by men, but chosen of God and precious, etc." (*I Peter* 2:1-4) — If Mersennus, therefore had not been so infantile in his worldly blindness, he would not have interfered in other people's business as a judge, and would not have called his brothers — who, after all, share Christianity with him — atheists, blasphemers, heretics, sorcerers, arch-magicians, fools, shameless ones, spirits of mystification, ignorants, vicious. — And this is not to mention that he publicly and wrongfully branded them thus.

Without question Mersennus himself must be counted as one of the false brothers of whom the Apostle says, "False brothers secretly were brought in, who came secretly to spy out our liberty which we have in Christ Jesus, that they might bring us into bondage." (*Galatians* 2:4) — But already I hear that enemy of truth mutter to himself, "I am a brother only of *my* brothers, the Roman Catholic ones, but in no way am I a brother of those heretics like the Lutherans, the Calvinists and those Rosicrucians! For I am a brother of a heavenly Order, but those are brothers of hell!"

But I answer Mersennus that such an excuse will not help him, for is it because they confess to a different religion than himself that he damns them? If he would look with a sharper spiritual gaze into the *Acts of the Apostles* he would have discovered that those of the true Brotherhood of Christ called the Jews, who then were their worst enemies, their brothers. Thus Stephen says, "My brothers and fathers, hear," and Paul and Barnabas called both Gentiles and Jews their brothers and sisters of the tribe of Abraham.

Mersennus most certainly would answer that in that place in Scripture he understood the word "brothers" to mean the successors of the Jews from Abraham downward, for among the Israelites all were called "brothers." — But with this Mersennus cannot talk himself out of his dilemma, for in many places in his sermons and letters, Paul calls the most unbelieving heathens, even the servants of idols, his brothers. We read from the Prophet Micah concerning the Lord of Israel, the Saviour from Bethlehem, "Therefore will he rescue them, and the remnant of his bretheren shall return to the children of Israel."

In this passage a dispersed flock is spoken of, and Christ is clearly characterized as the Saviour of the world, as is said in *Matthew* 23:8, "One is your Master, but you all are brothers." — And he continues, "For one is your Father, who is in heaven." With these words Christ does not indicate brothers in the flesh, but brothers in God, and he does not address the disciples alone, but the mixed crowd of listeners as well — and among them were unbelieving Jews and Gentiles. And finally the Prophet says clearly, confirming the word of the Saviour: "Why should you hate your brother, for you both have one Father and one Creator?" — From this it follows that with this he refers to *all* men who have been taken from one and the same rock.

Since this is so, how can this monk dare assert, in face of the word of the Apostle, and even against the word of the Highest, that there is *anyone* who cannot be his brother? For it is said in clear words that all men are brothers, taught by *one* teacher, descended from *one* Father. —

Does Brother Mersennus not know the words of the royal Psalmist, "Thy mouth runneth over with evil, and thy tongue bringeth forth cunning; sitting in counsel thou speakest against thy brother and against him thou createst strife. Therefore thou art in darkness because thou hatest thy brother; thou walkest in darkness and dost not know where thou art." — In his hatred, Mersennus therefore kills his brother, according to John, "Whosoever hateth his brother is a murderer: and ye know that no murderer hath eternal life abiding in him." — What John would have thought of that monk I do not dare to judge, since judgment is the concern of him who judged Cain according to righteousness, and the Apostle also uses this example.

Now we can consider the reasons why that Brotherhood can give itself the name *Rosicrucian*, since we have explained above out of the clear words of the holy Testament why the designations *Apostolic* and *Christian* can rightly be used by those chosen ones. — And why *not* the designation "Rosicrucian?" In the Roman Catholic Church is there not an Order dedicated to the Holy Cross? Is it then such a great offense to concede to this Apostolic Fraternity, to the true chosen ones and Brothers of God, the name *Rosicrucians?* — Or is one to believe that the designation *Rosicrucians* in such an important matter means nothing? — I shall here show, however, that to the initiate the word *Rosicrucian* or *Rose Cross* reveals the whole secret of the Brotherhood, however little it seems to mean to the ignorant.

Not without intention was the sign of the Rose Cross carried on English sails, and by Christian heroes on their breasts in the wars against the Saracens and Turks. The more I consider it worthwhile to reveal here before all the mystery of the Rose Cross, the more I recognize the justification of this design for the Brotherhood.

One must certainly know that the teaching of salvation has placed before us a twofold cross in the sense of a twofold law or twofold sense of the Holy Scriptures, a twofold wisdom, namely, an outer and an inner, whereof the outer is the sheath of the inner. Thus, under the outer law is hidden in Holy Scripture the spirit within the letter, the divine and mystical wisdom within the seemingly confused meaning of the external words.

After Adam had tasted of the Tree of Good and Evil, confusion arose, clear wisdom was veiled by the darkness of illusion, and error was brought into the world. Thus, in place of pure and simple unity of unities arose confusion, namely that duality, that two-headed monster which looks at good and evil at the same time.

In a similar manner developed the relationship between the inner and outer, the mixture of virtue and vice, the pollution of the mystical wisdom by the human, the darkening of light through darkness, and — to say it briefly — the veiling of the spirit by the letter.

But why use further words? Suffice it to say that the same relationship that exists between human wisdom and divine Wisdom also rules between the physical and outer and that inner, spiritual cross. "For," says the Apostle, "the wisdom of this world is foolishness with God," and in another place, "God has made it into foolishness." (See *I Corinthians* 1:18 and *James* 1:22.) "Thy wisdom and thy knowledge deceives thee." — However, the divine and mystical Wisdom is that which is "the hidden wisdom which God ordained before the world unto our glory" (*I Corinthians* 2:7), as testified by the Apostle Paul. James speaks of the *other* wisdom: "This wisdom descendeth not from above, but is earthly, sensual, devilish." (*James* 3:15) — This is what one can also say of the cross, for the real and true being of mystical Wisdom is an inner Wisdom, while the external wisdom is only an illusion, a false image of the true.

The Apostle Paul seems to point to this when he says (*Hebrews* 9:24-25): "For Christ is not entered into the holy places made with hands, which are the figures of the true; but into heaven itself, now to appear in the presence of God for us; Nor yet that he should offer himself often, as the high priest entereth into the holy place every year with the blood of others." — Throughout the whole chapter, the Apostle seems to prove that parables and "figures" are all those acts which took place by sprinkling with "blood of others" in the Tabernacle with that cross, in which the brazen serpent had been placed. The corresponding truth was only to reveal itself in a future century, as clearly foretold by his words (*Hebrews* 9:8): "The Holy Ghost signified that the way into the holiest of all was not yet made manifest while the first tabernacle was yet standing." In addition, we find written elsewhere that the All-Highest does not dwell in habitations made with hands (*Acts* 7:48). —

From this it is clear that the cross created by the human spirit means little, that the worldly wisdom means little, compared with the divine, mystical Wisdom, which is the power of God. Human wisdom is pure foolishness, as is also said by the Apostle, "The cross of Christ is a stumblingblock to the Jews, foolishness to the Greeks" (*I Corinthians* 1:23). With "stumblingblock" he refers to the hatred which they harbored against Christ, for they expected only miracles from him. With the word "foolishness" he means not only those who mocked the cross, but also those who accepted the worldly and visible cross instead of the spiritual cross, that spiritual Wisdom which is the power of God — the outer instead of the inner.

In the world, therefore, we see two strong opposites from which arise so much strife, such monstrous discord in worldly affairs, namely, the light and the darkness. The light is Christ, the darkness is the prince of the letter — the devil. In the same manner we see both crosses — the one which is the power of God, true Wisdom, the pure and clear light, — the other is devilish, for the Godhead is not in it, and because it is external it misguides according to the foolishness of the Gentiles, misleading people into worshiping idols, i.e., to a veneration of things which cannot be called divine. And thus through ignorance the cross of the thief is venerated instead of the living cross.

It was in this sense that a venerable Church Father wrote that the cross of Christ consisted of two woods, upon which the devil and our Saviour Jesus Christ were crucified at the same time. Had he said, however, that Christ was crucified on the dead wood, and the other on the living wood, he would not have spoken in the sense of the Apostle who says, "But God forbid that I should glory, save in the cross of our Lord Jesus Christ, by whom the world is crucified unto me and I unto the world." (Galatians 6:14) — What he meant by the expression that "the world is crucified" is explained by the words, "I bear in my body the marks of the Lord Jesus," (Ibid. 6:17) which is the same as though he said Christ's true and spiritual cross I bear within me, compared with which worldly things are crucified and dead, and therefore I am dead for the world. Elsewhere he says, "I am crucified with Christ so that I may live unto God." (Ibid 2:19.)

We therefore may not worship the outer, satanic, worldly part of the cross, nor are we to surround it with divers testimonies and venerations. For it is the cross of death, not of life, fashioned out of earthly timber or some other corruptible material. But we must venerate only that true, genuine, living cross of Christ, that is, the mystical Wisdom which is called by the Holy Scriptures the wood of the Tree of Life, the fountain or root of which is the enlightened Word. To this is related the saying, "The holy form of the cross shines out of its venerated sheath."

This "holy form of the cross" is the true inward, central cross of Christ, from which the Brotherhood takes its name, the Brotherhood which has been given such an evil name, which has been slandered by worldly-minded phantasts. However, they richly deserve to be called *Brothers of the Cross,* for to this Order not only belonged the holy Prophets, but all Apostles, and also the true Disciples, as the Redeemer said, "If any man will come after me, let him deny himself and take up his cross, and follow me." (*Matthew* 16:24) By this he seems to indicate that above all the true Christian must seek the spiritual cross, of which the Apostle speaks as cited above, and that through the denial of self he is to crucify himself for the world and the world for himself. Peter requires similarly that "As newborn babes desire the milk of the word, that ye may grow thereby, if so be that ye have tasted that the Lord is gracious, to whom coming, as unto a living stone, chosen of God and precious . . . etc." (*I Peter* 2:2-4). Likewise is said elsewhere, "He that taketh not his cross and followeth after me is not worthy of me," (*Matthew* 10:38) and further, "He who does not take up his cross and follow me cannot be my disciple."

In these words, therefore, lies the secret, the greatest mystery, and from them it follows that no man can be a true disciple of Christ who does not "ask" and "knock," and thus find and recognize within himself that secret cross, and then follows worthily the chief of all mankind and leader of Israel from Bethlehem, carrying Christ Jesus within himself consciously. From this can be clearly seen that the true disciple of Christ must be a Brother of the Rosy Cross.

Now we shall explain why this name, *The Rosicrucian Brotherhood,* is a fitting one. From what has been said it can easily be seen that all true Christians must be engaged with greatest effort to discover and recognize that mystical cross, and to bear it within themselves. For without it they cannot justifiably be regarded as pupils and disciples of Christ.

But straightaway is asked in what color, what guise, does this cross usually appear to the chosen ones and is recognized by them? — That cross to which all good Christians should dedicate themselves is not conceived or fashioned according to the material used. It has the color of blood and is similar to the reddest red of the rose, surrounded by lilies, of which the Prophet asks in a mystical manner, "Wherefore art thou red in thy apparel, and thy garments like him that treadeth the winepress?" (*Isaiah* 63:2). The answer is, "their blood is sprinkled upon my garments, etc." — With these words the Prophet seems to indicate that the blood or redness of the cross, that rosy sap of the cross, originates from the fact that the cross of Christ is dipped into the blood of all sinners, and that through this virtue each of them is cleansed from the imperfections of his sins. Thus John says, "The blood of Jesus Christ, the Son of God, washes us clean of all sin." (*I John* 1:7)

With the expression, "the blood of the Son of God" he means not human blood, but the divine and mystical blood. For as there is procreation out of human blood and sensual intercourse, so there is also a divine procreation out of the Spirit of God, according to the word of the Evangelist, "Not out of blood, nor of the will of the flesh, but out of God," for blood and flesh cannot enter into the Kingdom of God. Peter also says that we are redeemed "with the precious blood of Christ, as of a lamb without blemish and without spot." (*I Peter* 1:19) It is likewise said in another place that the shedding of the blood of Christ "speaks better things" than that of Abel, for Christ was spiritual and mystical, the other, material and typical. (*Hebrews* 12:24) Again we read that "The God of peace ... brought again from the dead our Lord Jesus, that great shepherd of the sheep, through the blood of the everlasting covenant." (*Ibid.* 11:20) — Here is meant that blood of the testament which is living, spiritual, through whose mediation — and through it alone — according to the testimony of the Holy Scripture, has the restoration from death to eternal life been effected.

In another place the Apostle speaks of that "blood of the testament which God hath entrusted to you," and he speaks still more clearly where he points out that the ceremonies of the Old Covenant are only parables and figures for the explanation of that hidden, spiritual secret: "For if the blood of bulls and of goats and the ashes of an heifer sprinkling the unclean, sanctifieth to the purifying of the flesh: How much more shall the blood of Christ, who through the eternal Spirit offered himself without spot to God, purge your conscience from dead works to serve the living God?" (*Hebrews* 9:13-14)

The Holy Scripture also says that those are blessed who have washed their garments and have received power through the wood or Tree of Life. Now that blood of the cross, I say, was that spiritual blood of the Covenant into which God has instituted us. For it is a gift of the Holy Spirit which teaches us that we must understand that Chalice which we bless, and likewise that mystical Blood is the true Sacrament, according to the word of the Apostle: "The cup of blessing which we bless, is it not communion with the blood of Christ?" (*I Corinthians* 10:16)

It is *this* therefore which is the true rose-cross adorned with lilies, which is described by Esdras, or rather is described by God through the testimony of Esdras, indicating the House of Wisdom erected on the imaginary seven pillars: "I have," says the Lord, "prepared seven mighty mountains whereupon there grow roses and lilies, whereby I will fill all thy children with joy." (*II Esdras* 2:19) — And in that place he mentions the House or that heavenly Castle Zion, and describes the condition of the inhabitants when he says, "Take thy people, O Zion, which have fulfilled the law of the Lord, that thy people, who have been chosen from the beginning, may be hallowed." These are the ones who are clothed in white because they have known the name of God. But I spoke above concerning the secret arrangements of this Tabernacle when I mentioned what others usually call "dying," — for as everyone knows, this latter also must have a secret and hidden meaning.

In a similar manner the whole parable of the *Song of Solomon* is related to our subject, and there we read (the bride and bridegroom are speaking): "I am the rose of Sharon, and the lily of the valleys" ... "My beloved is like a young hart among the mountains of Bethel" (that is, the

House of the Lord) . . . "A garden enclosed is my sister, my bride; a spring shut up, a fountain sealed. Thy plants are an orchard of pomgranates; a fountain of gardens, a well of living waters, etc."

Finally, we are taught by the Holy Scripture what we must do in general and in particular in order to attain a pearl of such incomparable worth. What we must do in general is indicated by the Apostle thus: "We beseech you, brethren, that ye increase more and more; and that ye study to be quiet, and to do your own business, and to work with your own hands, as we commanded you; that ye may walk honestly toward them that are without, and that ye may lack nothing." (*I Thessalonians* 4:10-12)

What we are to do in particular he teaches us in a similar way through the pictures of the Sower and the Builder. Under the picture of the Sower he says (*I Corinthians* 3:6, *etc.*): "I have planted, Apollos watered, but God gave the increase." "For we are laborers together with God." — This last also means "You are the seed of God." And James, taking such Sowers into consideration, says (*James* 5:7): "Be patient therefore, brethren, unto the coming of the Lord. Behold, the husbandman waiteth for the precious fruit of the earth, and hath long patience for it, until he receive the early and the latter rain. Be ye also patient; stablish your hearts: for the coming of the Lord draweth nigh." —

Paul, however, teaches us that the Lord Jesus Christ will appear to the chosen ones in this life, by saying, "See that you lack no gift, waiting for the coming of our Lord Jesus Christ: who shall also confirm you to the end, that ye may be blameless in the day of our Lord Jesus Christ." — With these words he shows that the Lord reveals himself to the true Brothers in this life, and that the following life is without end. In this sense also speaks the prophet Isaiah: "The earth will open itself and give birth to the Saviour," while the Evangelist says that God is able to awaken out of the stones the seed of the sons of Abraham.

Job says that "Out of the earth cometh bread, and from beneath it cometh fire. The stones of it are the place of sapphires, and it hath dust of gold." (*Job* 28:5-6) The Patriarch knows that indeed the stone which he has erected as a symbol shall become the House of God. In the word of Wisdom is found the most perfect light which reveals the hidden, the invisible, to the eyes of mortals.

If the husbandman described above prepares the right soil in a proper manner, if he cares for it and tills it, if he plants it with Paul and waters it with Apollo, nevertheless he cannot gather the harvest until the fruit has been blessed by God, until he has "waited in patience" for the revelation of the Lord. The reason for this is given in the words of the Apostle: "it is not given to the one who desires and hastens, but through God's mercy."

After this, the Apostle makes the Brothers labor toward the perfection of the work, under the picture of the Builder, for he says that God has laid the foundation like a wise architect. Such building is indicated by Paul: "For we are workers together with God; ye are God's husbandry, ye are God's building." (*I Corinthians* 3:9) David echoes this thought when he says, "If the Lord does not build the house, they labor in vain that build it." This is exactly the same as is shown by the picture of the Sower above.

Although the indestructible Spirit of God lives within the grain of wheat, nothing can come of it without the labor of the husbandman and his sowing. It is his business to prepare the earth and to bed into it the seed for the purpose of its decomposition. Otherwise nothing will come from its living, inner germ.

With the picture of the Architect, the Prophet demands of us that we "ascend the Mount of Reason and build the House of Wisdom." As for the right way of going about this, and how we may reach the rose-red blood of the cross which hides itself in the center of the cross, having been poured out into it, we have to consider how much labor and diligence we must devote to the task — for this is not a superficial work. One has to dig into the inner core of the earth, and to "knock" and "seek," or his labor is in vain.

A philosopher experienced in true and genuine Alchemy says that all bodies have their boundaries in three dimensions, namely the height before the eyes, the hidden depths, and the widths lying between. There is no direct transition from the one extreme to the other. One must pass through an intermediate element. Therefore, on the basis of the outer form of anything we cannot deduce for ourselves its inner, hidden aspect unless through the destruction of the revealed we come to the revelation of the hidden element.

The truth of this observation is made apparent through the content of a geometrical cube, the height of which, multiplied by itself gives the width, which in turn multiplied by the height gives its content.

In just this way the Alchemist transmutes the apparent forms into occult ones by finding the general form through destruction of the specific one. This is the work of the true and divine Alchemy, through the mediation of which the earthly has been opened to the entry of the joys of Paradise so that men may pluck that red rose with the lilies of the field and taste of the Tree of Life. This is also taught by the Apostle when he says (*Ephesians* 3:18): "That ye may be able to comprehend with all saints what is the breadth, and length, and depth, and height, and to know the love of Christ, that ye may be filled with all the fulness of God." — Thus the truly wise Artist will have to dig deeply into the earth, will have to work carefully in all three directions in order to find the true cornerstone which God has laid as foundation in the earth.

Through this he will come to know an all-towering love for the science of Christ, and he will be filled with the all-conceivable fullness of God. Thus we can deduce that the Rose-Cross, or that mystical building of the cross, has to be striven for through diligent knocking and patient expectancy of divine grace, through begging and asking to the very core of our being. This is that mystical building of which the divine poet spoke, "That sanctified form which shines out of the venerated form."

All of this is according to the statement of the Apostle: "Ye have not yet resisted unto blood, striving against sin." Through these words we are taught in an occult manner that sin is all that alien part in us which does not correspond to pure truth, which is Jesus Christ. We have to use all possible care, working without ceasing in order that there may shine forth from the human or animal rock, the truth in its rose-colored, blood-colored glory. — Thus it will shine to the true Artist and Brother so that in this divine radiance he may see the light and at last harvest the fruits of his labor, according to the word of the Apostle.

All of this carefully considered will make clear what this mystical building of the cross and also the cross of Christ means. For each true Christian will strive for this with all his strength until he finds that reddest of roses, that most precious and eternal building of the cross, so he can be recompensed rightly by being called a Brother of the Rose-Cross, and will find himself a member of the true Fraternity. This is confirmed by the Psalmist: "Behold how good and how pleasant it is for brothers to dwell together in unity!"

Now without doubt someone could say, "How is it that you profess to know the spirit of that Brotherhood so well; how are you so well informed about their secrets so that you proclaim not only their religion and circumstances, but also reveal why they should be called Rosicrucian Brothers?" — "What? — Are you also one of the Brothers of the Rose-Cross?" —

Under such questioning I answer that I least of all have deserved such high grace from God, for I acknowledge with the Apostle that such gifts cannot be bestowed through longing and impatience, but through God's mercy alone.

So as to give satisfaction to any questioner, whoever he may be, and also to you, well-disposed reader, I shall place before you a letter written by the Rosicrucian Brothers and sent to a German candidate, which I have reproduced faithfully below. I received a copy of this through my friend in Danzig, and after serious reading and re-reading you yourselves can judge whether what I have written above about the Spirit and the spiritual gifts of God, about the cornerstone, the living waters, and about the religion of these Brothers and members of the Fraternity, has been produced by me out of error or unrighteousness. Those can judge best who base themselves on the pillars of fairness and justice, giving impartial testimony as to whether people like the so-called Rosicrucians should be persecuted with such baseness, whether they deserve such hatred, whether they must be so diligently excluded from the Christian world and condemned to exile, as seems to be the wish of that hell-judging monk, who appears least of all to be called to such an office.

"Venerable and Honorable Sir!

"Seeing that this will be the first year of your nativity, we pray that you may have from the Most High God, a most happy entrance into and departure out of your life, because until now you have been with good mind a constant searcher of divine philosophy. Well done! Go forward, fear God, for thus you will gain Heaven. Acquire the most true knowledge, for it is God who has discovered every way; God alone is circumference and center.

"But now draw near and pay heed, take this cross unto yourself, for the one who increases knowledge increases sorrow, for in much knowledge is much grief, as we know from experience. For all worldly men, proud, vain, boasters, talkers, unworthily attack us, yes, curse us without cause. But we are not surprised that the ungrateful world persecutes the professors of the true Arts, together with truth itself. Yet, for your sake we shall briefly answer these questions: What is it that we do? What can we do? Whether there are any such as we?

"In John we read that God is the Supreme Light, and we walk in light so that we show light to the world. But the man of the world who denies this knows not and sees not that in his vile body the Christ dwells. This you have from the Apostle. 'And Jesus knew all their thoughts,' to whom if you remain faithful, you will at length be made one spirit with him, and having become one, who will hinder you — like Solomon — from knowing the good and the evil thoughts of men? And this you may take from us as truth. Hence it is that we do not answer the questions of all because of the deceitful minds of some. For whoever are alienated from God are against us, and who is so foolish as to allow a total stranger to enter another man's house?

"On the other hand, if men expect that this union with Christ is to be attained only in the world to come, in this they show their foolishness and ignorance. Are they not also ashamed to make the Apostle a liar, in whom these things are clearly shown in the words, 'So that you may be wanting in no grace, expecting the coming of our Lord Jesus Christ.' "

"But men say that this is not to be understood as pertaining to this life on earth. If this is so, what does the following mean: 'Who shall conform you even to the end,' — for in the Kingdom of God there is no end, therefore in this earthly condition will appear the glory of the Lord and Christ glorified.

"If anything further is required to be known concerning our work, our effort is to lead back the lost sheep to the true sheepfold. Therefore mortals labor in vain to enter upon another path than that outlined by the Apostle. And that path is not walked in through dying, but like Peter when he said, "As Christ taught me," that is, when he was transfigured in the mount. Had this not been secret and hidden, the Apostle would not have said, "As Christ taught me," neither would the Supreme Truth have said, 'Tell it to no man,' for according to the way of earth, to die was known to all men from the beginning of the world. Therefore you are to be changed from dead stones into living philosophical stones.

The Apostle shows you the way to this when he says, 'Let this mind be in you which was also in Christ Jesus.' He describes that mind in the following words, 'As being in the form of God he thought it no robbery to be equal to God.'

"Behold these things, you who search into the secrets of nature! You hear these things but you don't believe them, miserable mortals, who so eagerly run after your own ruin! — If you will be happy, you most miserable; if you will be lifted above the world, you proud; if you will rule this earth from Heaven above, and your dark body as well, you ambitious; if you will perform all miracles, you unworthy — then know — you rejected ones — what nature is before it is sought!

"But you, O Brother, listen! I will speak with the words of John that you may have communion with us, and indeed our communion is with the Father and Christ, and we write to you that you may rejoice 'God is light and in Him is no darkness at all.' — And that you may come to us, behold this light, for it is impossible for you to see us — unless we will it — in another light. Therefore follow us in this so you may be happy with us, for our most immovable palace is in the center of all things; it is also much obscured because it is covered with many names.

"Enter, enter into the glory of God and your own salvation! Enter the gates of the School of Philosophical Love, in which is taught everlasting charity and brotherly love! Enter into that same resplendent and invisible castle which is built upon the mountain of the Lord, out of which flows a fountain of living water, a river of love! Drink, drink, and again drink, that you may see all hidden things, and converse with us!

"Again, beware! — But what? — For you know very well that nature receives nothing for nutriment but what is subtle, the thick and foeculent is cast out as excrement. And you well know that those who will live in the Spirit rather than in the body take in nourishment by the Spirit, not by the mouth. As for example, it is lawful to know heaven by heaven, not by earth, but by virtues of earth — if you understand us aright — no man enters into heaven, which you seek, unless he who descended from heaven enlighten him first. Therefore whatever comes not from heaven is a false image and cannot be called a virtue.

"Therefore, O Brother, you cannot be better confirmed than by virtue itself, which is the Supreme Truth which, if you will religiously and with all your strength endeavor to follow, in all your words and works, it will confirm you more and more. For it is a fiery spirit, a glistening spark, dwelling in every created being, sustaining and governing it, by Christ purged, purified in fire, always more glorious and pure, jubilating without limit. This Spirit, we say, will confirm you daily until — as a certain learned man has said — you become like a lion in battle, can overcome all the strength of the world, and you fear neither death nor any violence whatever that devilish tyranny can invent. For you will have become what you desire to be — a Stone and a true Work.

"In order that God may bless your labors, you will study most approved authors, but under a shadow as it were, for a wise man reads one thing and understands another.

"Are you imperfect? Strive for due perfection. Are you foul and unclean? Purge yourself with tears, lift yourself by good manners and virtues, beautify yourself with the grace of the Sacraments. Make your soul sublime and subtle for the contemplation of heavenly things, conformable to angelic spirits, that it may vivify your vile ashes and gross body, making it white and altogether incorruptible through the Resurrection of our Lord Jesus Christ.

"Do these things and you will agree that no man has written more plainly than we. These things the Lady Virtue has commanded should be told you, by whom, according to your deserts, you will hereafter be more fully taught. This read, and keep what has been committed to your trust.

— F.T.F., in Light, etc."

Hinricus Madathanus Theosophus, Hadrianus a Mynsicht (c.1590-1638),
Rosicrucian, Alchemist, Physician, Author. Rudolf Steiner identified him as
the anonymous compiler of *The Secret Symbols of the Rosicrucians*, which
was not published until long after his death. The above engraving appeared
in the first edition of his *Thesaurus*, Hamburg, 1631.

THE PARABOLA

A Golden Tractate Concerning the Philosopher's Stone

from
Die geheimen Figuren der Rosenkreutzer,
The Secret Symbols of the Rosicrucians,
published at Altona, 1785-88,

by

Hinricus Madathanus Theosophus*

As I once was walking in a beautiful, green, young forest, meditating and deploring the difficulties of this life, considering how, through the grievous Fall of our first Parents we came into such wretchedness and grief, I left the accustomed road and came, I know not how, upon a narrow *footpath,* very rough, untrodden, difficult and overgrown with so many bushes and brambles that it was easy to see it was very seldom used. At this I became frightened and wished to retrace my steps. But this was not possible, especially since a strong wind blew so mightily behind me that I had to take ten steps forward for every one I could take backward. Therefore I had to press on, despite the roughness of the way.

After advancing thus for a good while, I came at last to a lovely meadow, encircled by beautiful fruit-laden trees, and called by the inhabitants, *The Field of the Blessed.* Here I met *a group of old men* with snow-white beards, but one among them was young and had a pointed black beard. A still younger man was present also, whose name I knew, but whose face I did not yet see. These men conversed about many things, particularly about a high and great secret in

*The anagrammatic pseudonym for the Paracelsian, Hadrianus a Munsicht (Adrian von Mynsicht), c. 1590-1638. Rudolf Steiner identified him as the anonymous author of the Altona work mentioned above (Lecture given at Neuchatel, Sept. 27, 1911). See also C.S. Picht, *Gesammelte Aufsaetze,* Stuttgart, 1964, p. 13 *seq.* The original publication of the *Parabola* is dated 1625.

See Reference Notes, beginning p. 635

Nature which God kept hidden from the multitude, revealing it only to the few who loved Him. I listened to them for a long time, and their words pleased me much. But some among them appeared to mutter foolishly, indeed not about the objectives or the work, but about Parabolas, Similitudes and other Parergons. In this they followed the *Figmenta* of Aristotle, of Pliny and of others, each of whom had copied from the other. At this I could no longer remain silent, but put in a word of my own, answering many futile things on the basis of experience, so that many listened to me, examining me in their speciality, putting me to some very hard tests. But my foundation was so good that I came through with all honors, whereat they all were amazed. However they unanimously accepted me into their Brotherhood, whereat I rejoiced heartily.

But they said that I could not be a full colleague so long as I did not know their *Lion* and was not fully aware what he could do internally and externally. I was therefore to set about diligently to make him submissive to myself. Confidently I promised them I would do my best, for I enjoyed their company so much that I would not have parted from them for anything in the world.

So they led me to the Lion and very carefully described him to me. But what I was to do with him at first, no one would tell me. Indeed some of them did give me certain hints, but so confusedly that not one in a thousand could understand them. However, when I had tied him and made certain that his sharp claws and pointed teeth could not harm me, they no longer kept anything back. The Lion was very old, fierce and huge; his yellow mane hung over his neck, and he really appeared unconquerable. I was nearly terror-stricken, and had it not been for my agreement and for the old men who stood around me to see how I would begin, I would have run away. Confidently I approached the lion in his cave and began to cajole him, but he looked at me so sharply with his glittering eyes that I nearly let my water for fear. At the same time I remembered that as we went to the Lion's cave one of the old men had told me that many people had attempted to conquer the Lion, but very few had succeeded. Since I did not wish to fail, I recalled many grips

I had learned through careful application to athletics, and in addition I was well trained in natural magic, so I forgot about the pleasantries and attacked the Lion so artfully and subtly that before he was aware of it, I had pressed the blood out of his body, indeed out of his heart itself. The blood was beautifully red, but very choleric. But I examined his anatomy further and found many things which greatly surprised me; his bones were white as snow, and they were of greater quantity than his blood.

When my old men, standing round the cave and watching me, realized what I had done, they began to dispute with each other violently so that I could see their gestures. But what they said I could not understand because I was so far inside the cave. And when they began to shout at each other, I heard one who cried, "He must also bring the Lion to life again; otherwise he cannot be our colleague."—

I did not wish to make trouble. Therefore I walked out of the cave and crossed a broad space. Then I came, I do not know how, to a very *high wall* which rose over a hundred ells into the clouds. But above there it did not have the width of a shoe. From the beginning where I started, to the end there ran an iron railing along the top of the wall, well fastened with many supports. I walked along the top of this wall and thought I saw someone going along a little ahead of me on the right side of the railing.

After I followed him a while, I saw someone following behind me on the other side of the railing (to this day I don't know whether it was a man or a woman) who called to me and said that it was better to walk on his side than where I was going. I easily believed this, for the railing which stood in the middle of the wall made the passageway very narrow so that it was difficult to walk along it at such a height. Then behind me I saw some people who wanted to go that same way. So I swung myself under the railing, holding it fast with both hands, and continued along the other side until I came to a place on the wall where it was especially dangerous to descend. Now I regretted that I had not remained on the other side; for I could not pass under the railing again; also it was impossible to turn back and take the other way again. Therefore I summoned my courage, trusted in my sure-footedness, held on tightly, and descended without harm. When I went on for a while, I had indeed forgotten about all danger and also did not know where the wall and railing had vanished.

After I had descended I saw standing a lovely *rosebush* on which beautiful red and white roses were growing; but there were more of the red than the white. I broke off some of them and put them on my hat.

I soon saw a wall encircling a great garden, in which were young *fellows*. Their *maidens* also would have liked to be in the garden, but they did not wish to make the great effort of walking the long distance around the wall to the gate. I was sorry for them and returned the whole distance I had come, then followed a smoother path, and I went so fast that I soon came to several houses, where I hoped to find the cottage of the gardener. There I found *many people*; each had his own room; often two were working together slowly and diligently; but each had his own work. And it appeared to me that all this they were doing, I had done before them, and that I knew it all very well. Then I thought, "Look, if so many other people do such dirty and slovenly work only for appearance's sake, and each according to his own ideas, but not established in Nature, then you yourself are forgiven."—Therefore I would not stay there any longer for I knew that such art would disappear in smoke, so I continued on my destined way.

As I now went toward the *garden gate* some looked at me sourly, and I feared that they would hinder me in the fulfillment of my intentions. Others, however, said, "See, he wishes to go into the garden; but we who worked for so long in its service have never entered it. We shall laugh at him if he blunders."—But I paid no attention to them, for I knew the plan of the garden better than they, although I had never been in it, and I went straight up to the gate. This was locked fast, and one could not discover even a key-hole from the outside. But in the gate I saw a tiny round hole which one could not distinguish with ordinary eyes, and I thought it was necessary to open the gate there. I took out my skeleton-key, especially prepared for this purpose, unlocked the gate and walked in.—After I was inside the gate I found more locked gates, but I unlocked them without more difficulty. But I found that this was a hallway as if it were in a well-built house, about six shoes wide and twenty long, covered with a ceiling. And although the other gates were still locked, I could see through them sufficiently into the garden as soon as the first gate was opened.

And so in God's Name I wandered further into the garden. There in the midst of it I found a little flower-bed, square, each of its four sides six measuring-rods long, and covered with rosebushes, on which the roses were blossoming beautifully. Since it had rained a little and the sun was shining, a very lovely rainbow appeared. After I left the flower-bed and had come to the place where I was to help the maidens, behold! instead of the walls there stood a low wattled fence. And *the most beautiful maiden,* dressed all in white satin, with *the most handsome youth,* clad in scarlet, went past the rose-garden, one leading the other by the arm and carrying many fragrant roses in their hands. I spoke to them, asking how they had come over the fence.—"My dearest bridegroom here helped me over," she said, "and now we are leaving this lovely garden to go to our room to be together."—"I am happy," I replied, "that without further effort of mine you can satisfy your wish. Nevertheless you can see how I ran so long a way in so short a time, only to serve you."

After this I came into a great *mill,* built within stone walls; inside were no flour-bins nor any other things necessary for milling; moreover, through the wall one saw no waterwheels turning in the stream. I asked myself how this state of affairs came about, and one old miller answered me that the milling-machinery was locked up on the other side. Then I saw the miller's helper go into it by a covered passage-way, and I followed close after him. But as I was going along the passage, with the waterwheels on my left, I paused, amazed at what I saw there. For now the waterwheels were above the level of the passage, the water was coal-black, although the drops from it were white, and the covered passage-way itself was not more than three fingers wide. Nevertheless I risked turning back, holding fast to the beams over the passage-way; thus I crossed over the water safely. Then I asked the old miller how many waterwheels he had. He answered, Ten. This adventure I long remembered and dearly wished I could know what it meant. But when I saw that the miller would not reveal anything, I went on my way.

In front of the mill there arose a high, paved hill; on its summit some of the old men I have mentioned were walking in the warm sunshine. They had a *letter* from the Brotherhood and were discussing it among themselves. I soon guessed its contents, and that it might concern me, so I went to them and asked, "Sirs, does what you read there concern me?"—"Yes," they replied, "Your wife whom you recently married, you must keep in wedlock or we shall have to report it to the Prince."—I said, "That will be no trouble, for I was born together with her, as it were, was raised with her as a child, and because I have married her I shall keep her always, and death itself shall not part us. For I love her with all my heart."—"What have we to complain of, then?" they asked; "the bride is also happy, and we know her wish is that you must be joined together."—"I am very happy," I replied.—"Well then," said one of them, "the Lion will come back to life, mightier and more powerful than before."—

Then I recalled my previous struggle and effort, and for some curious reason I felt this did not concern me but another whom I knew well. At that moment I saw our bridegroom walking with his bride, dressed as before, ready and prepared for the *wedding*, whereat I was very happy; for I had greatly feared that these things might concern me.

When, as has been said, our scarlet-clad bridegroom came to the old men with his dear bride, her white garments gleaming brightly, they were soon united and I greatly wondered that the maiden who might be the bridegroom's mother was nevertheless so young that she seemed newly born, as it were.

Now I do not know how the two had sinned; perhaps as brother and sister, united in love in such a way that they could not be separated, they had been accused of incest. Instead of a bridal bed and brilliant wedding they were condemned to a strong and everlasting *prison*. However, because of their noble birth and station, in order that they could do nothing together in secret, and so all their doings would always be visible to their guard, their prison was transparent-clear like crystal and round like a heavenly dome. But before they were placed inside, all the clothing and jewels they wore were taken from them so they had to live together stripped naked in their prison. No one was assigned to serve them, but all their necessities of food and drink—the latter drawn from the stream mentioned above—were placed inside before the door of the room was securely closed, locked, sealed with the seal of the Brotherhood, and I was placed on guard òutside. And since winter was near I was to heat the room properly so they would neither freeze nor burn, but under no conditions could they come out of the room and escape. But if any harm resulted from my neglect of these instructions, I would undoubtedly receive great and severe punishment.

I did not feel well about this, my fear and worry made me faint-hearted, and I thought to myself, It is no small task which has been assigned to me. I also knew that the Brotherhood did not lie, always did what it said, and certainly performed its work with diligence. However, I could change nothing, and besides, the locked room was situated in the midst of a strong tower, encircled by strong bulwarks and high walls, and since one could warm the room by a moderate but constant fire, I took up my task in God's Name, beginning to heat the room in order to protect the imprisoned married couple from the cold. But what happened?—As soon as they felt the faintest breath of warmth, they embraced each other so lovingly that the like of it will not be seen again. And they remained together in such ardor that the heart of the young bridegroom disappeared in burning love, and his entire body melted and sank down in the arms of his beloved. When the latter, who had loved him no less than he had loved her, saw this, she began to lament, weeping bitterly over him and, so to say, buried him in such a flood of tears that one could no longer see what had happened to him.—But her lamenting and weeping lasted only for a short time, for because of her great heart-sorrow she did not wish to live longer, and died of her own free will.—Ah, woe is me! In what anxiety, grief and distress was I when I saw those two I was to have helped, dissolved entirely to water and lying before me dead. Certain failure was there before my eyes, and moreover, what to me was the bitterest, and what I feared most were the coming taunts and sneers, as well as the punishment I would have to undergo.

I passed a few days in careful thought, considering what I could do, when I recalled how *Medea* had restored the corpse of Jason to life, and so I asked myself, "If Medea could do it, why cannot you do it also?"—Whereat I began to think how to proceed with it, but I did not find any better method than to maintain a steady warmth until the water would recede and I could see the dead bodies of the lovers once again. Then I hoped that I would escape all danger to my great gain and praise. Therefore for forty days I continued with the warmth I had begun, and I saw that the longer I did this, the more the water disappeared, and the dead bodies, black as coal, came to view. And indeed this would have happened sooner had not the room been locked and sealed so tightly. But under no conditions dared I open it. Then I noticed quite clearly that the water rose high toward the clouds, collected on the ceiling of the room, and descended again like rain; nothing could escape, so our bridegroom lay with his beloved bride before my eyes dead and rotten, stinking beyond all measure. Meanwhile, I saw in the room a rainbow of the most beautiful colors, caused by the sunshine in the moist weather, which heartened me no little in the midst of my sorrows. And soon I became rather happy that I could see my two lovers lying before me. However, no joy is so great that sorrow is not mixed with it; therefore in my joy I was sorrowful because I saw the ones I was to have guarded lying lifeless before me. But since their room was made from such pure and solid material and was shut so tightly, I knew that their soul and their spirit could not escape, but were still enclosed in it, so I continued with my steady warmth day and night, carrying out my duty as prescribed, for I believed that the two would not return to their bodies so long as the moisture was present. This I indeed found to be true. For in many careful observations I observed that many vapors arose from the earth about evening, through the power of the sun, and ascended on high as if the sun itself were drawing up the water. But during the night they gathered into a lovely and fertile dew, descending very early in the morning, enriching the earth and washing the corpses of our dead, so that from day to day, the longer such bathing and washing continued, they became even whiter and more beautiful. But the more beautiful and whiter they became, the more they lost their moisture, until at last when the air became light and clear and all the foggy, damp weather had passed, the spirit and soul of the bride could no longer remain in the pure air, and returned into the transfigured, glorified body of the *Queen,* and as soon as the body felt their presence, it instantly became living once again. This brought me no little joy, as one can easily imagine, especially as I saw her arise, dressed in a very rich garment, the like of which very few on this earth have seen, wearing a costly crown, adorned with perfect diamonds, and heard her say; "Harken, you children of men, and learn, all of you who are of women born, that the All-Highest has power to enthrone kings and to dethrone them. He makes rich and poor, according to his will. He kills and makes to live again. —And all this behold in me as a living example! I was great and I became small. But now after I became humble, I have been made queen over many realms. I was killed and am resurrected again. To me, the poor one, have the great treasures of the wise and mighty been entrusted and given. Therefore have I been given power to make the poor rich, to extend mercy to the humble, and to bring health to the sick— But not yet am I like my dearest brother, the great, mighty king, who will also be awakened from the dead. When he comes he will prove that my words are true."—

And as she said this, the sun shone brightly, the days became warmer, and the dog-days were near at hand. But long before the sumptuous and great wedding of our new queen many costly *robes* were prepared from black velvet, ash-gray colored damask, gray silk, silver-colored taffeta, snow-white satin; indeed, a silver piece of extraordinary beauty, embroidered with costly pearls and worked with marvelous, clear-sparkling diamonds was also made ready. And robes for the young king were also made ready, namely of pink, with yellow aureolin colors, costly fabrics, and finally a red velvet garment adorned with costly rubies and carbuncles in very great numbers. But the tailors who made these garments were invisible, and I marvelled when I saw one coat after another, and one garment after another being finished, for I knew that no one except the bridegroom and his bride had entered into the chamber. But what astonished me the most was that as soon as a new coat or garment was finished, the former ones disappeared from before my eyes, and I did not know where they had gone or who had locked them away.—

And after this costly coat was made ready, the great and mighty *king* appeared in all his power and glory, and there was nothing like him. And when he discovered he was locked in, he asked me in a friendly manner and with gracious words to open the door for him so he would be able to come out; he said it would result in great blessing for me. Although I was strictly forbidden to open the room, I was so overwhelmed by the great appearance and the gentle persuasive powers of the king that I opened the door willingly. And as he walked out, he was so friendly, gracious, even humble, that one could indeed see that nothing graces noble persons so much as do these virtues.

And since he had passed the dog-days in the great heat, he was very thirsty, weak and tired; and he asked me to bring him some of the fast-flowing *water* from beneath the water-wheels of the mill, which I did, and he drank it with great eagerness. Then he returned to his chamber and told me to lock the door fast behind him, lest someone should disturb him or waken him from his sleep.

There he rested for a few days, and then he called me to open the door. But I saw that he had become much more handsome, full-blooded and splendid, and he also noticed it; and he thought that the water was marvellous and healthy. Therefore he asked for more, and drank a larger quantity than he had the first time, and I resolved to enlarge the chamber. After the king had drunk his fill of this wonderful beverage which the ignorant do not value at all, he became so handsome and glorious that in all my life I never saw a more splendid appearance, or anyone more noble in manner and character. Then he led me into his *kingdom* and showed me all the treasures and riches of the world, so that I must say that not only did the queen speak the truth, but he also gave the greatest part of it to those who know the treasure and can describe it. There were gold and precious carbuncle stones without end, and the rejuvenation and restoration of the natural powers, as well as the recovery of health and the removal of all illnesses were daily occurrences there. But most delightful of all in this kindgom was that the people knew, reverenced and praised their Creator, receiving from Him wisdom and knowledge, and at last, after this happiness in the world of time, they attained an eternal blessedness. To this may God, Father, Son and Holy Spirit help all of us.

A Rosicrucian Initiation in the 17th Century. From Thomas Vaughan's *Lumen de Lumine*, 1651, and described in the text beginning on the page opposite.

THE HOLY MOUNTAIN,
A ROSICRUCIAN ALLEGORY

by

THOMAS VAUGHAN

Every man naturally desires a superiority, to have treasures of gold and silver, and to seem great in the eyes of the world. God indeed created all things for the use of man, that he might rule over them and acknowledge therein the singular goodness and omnipotence of God, give Him thanks for His benefits, honor Him and praise Him. But there is no man looks after these things otherwise than by spending his days idly. They would enjoy them without any previous labor and danger; neither do they look for them in that place where God has treasured them up, Who expects also that man should seek for them there, and to those that seek will He give them. But there is not any that labors for a possession in that place, and therefore these riches are not found. For the way to this place—and the place itself—have been unknown for a long time, and it is hidden from the greatest part of the world. But notwithstanding that it be difficult and laborious to discover this way and place, yet the place should be sought after. But it is not the will of God to conceal anything from those that are His; and therefore in this last age—before the final judgment comes—all these things shall be manifested to those that are worthy. As He Himself—though obscurely, lest it should be manifested to the unworthy—has spoken in a certain place, "There is nothing covered that shall not be revealed and hidden that shall not be known." We therefore, being moved by the Spirit of God, do declare the will of God to the world, which we have also already performed and published in several lan-

393

guages.* But most men either revile or condemn our Manifesto, or else—waiving the Spirit of God—they expect the proposals thereof from us, supposing that we will straightway teach them how to make gold by art, or furnish them with ample treasures, whereby they may live pompously in the face of the world, swagger and make wars, turn usurers, gluttons and drunkards, live unchastely and defile their whole life with several other sins—all of which are contrary to the blessed will of God. These men should have learned from those ten Virgins—whereof five that were foolish demanded oil for their lamps from those five that were wise—how that the case is much otherwise. It is expedient that every man should labor for this treasure by the assistance of God and his own particular search and industry. But the perverse intentions of these fellows we understand out of their own writings, by the singular grace and revelation of God. We do stop our ears and wrap ourselves, as it were, in clouds to avoid the bellowings and howlings of those men who cry out in vain for gold. And thus indeed it comes about that they brand us with infinite calumnies and slanders, which nevertheless we do not resent; but God in His good time will judge them for it. But after we had known well—though unknown to you—and perceived by your writing how diligent you are to pursue the Holy Scripture and seek the true knowledge of God, we have out of many thousands thought you worthy of some answer; and we signify this much to you by the will of God and the admonition of the Holy Spirit.

There is a Mountain situated in the midst of the earth or center of the world, which is both small and great. It is soft, also above measure hard and stony. It is far off and near at hand, but by the providence of God invisible.* In it are hidden the most ample treasures, which the world is not able to value. This mountain—by envy of the devil, who always opposes the glory of God and the happiness of man—is compassed about with very cruel beasts and ravening birds—

---

*Reference to the FAMA FRATERNITATIS R.C. which appeared almost simultaneously in German, Dutch and Latin.

*Thus the mountain is not a mountain, but a degree of spiritual attainment; the "holy mountain" of Initiation is indicated.—Ed.

which make the way thither both difficult and dangerous. And therefore until now—because the time is not yet come—the way thither could not be sought after nor found out. But now at last the way is to be found by those that are worthy—but nonetheless by every man's self-labor and endeavors.

To this Mountain you shall go in a certain night—when it comes—most long and most dark, and see that you prepare yourselves by prayer. Insist upon the way that leads to the Mountain, but ask not of any man where the way lies. Only follow your Guide, who will offer himself to you and will meet you in the way. But you are not to know him. This Guide will bring you to the Mountain at midnight, when all things are silent and dark. It is necessary that you arm yourselves with a resolute, heroic courage, lest you fear those things that will happen, and so fall back. You need no sword nor any other bodily weapons; only call upon God sincerely and heartily.

When you have discovered the Mountain the first miracle that will appear is this: A most vehement and very great wind that will shake the Mountain and shatter the rocks to pieces. You will be encountered also by lions and dragons and other terrible beasts; but fear not any of these things. Be resolute and take heed that you turn not back, for your Guide —who brought you thither—will not suffer any evil to befall you. As for the treasure, it is not yet found, but it is very near.

After this wind will come an earthquake that will overthrow those things which the wind has left, and will make all flat. But be sure that you do not fall off. The earthquake being past, there will follow a fire that will consume the earthly rubbish and disclose the treasure. But as yet you cannot see it.

After these things and near the daybreak there will be a great calm, and you will see the Day-star arise, the dawn will appear, and you will perceive a great treasure. The most important thing in it and the most perfect is a certain exalted Tincture, with which the world—if it served God and were worthy of such gifts—might be touched and turned into most pure gold.

This Tincture being used as your Guide shall teach you will make you young when you are old, and you will perceive no disease in any part of your bodies. By means of this Tincture also you will find pearls of an excellence which cannot be imagined. But do not you arrogate anything to yourselves because of your present power, but be contented with what your Guide shall communicate to you. Praise God perpetually for this His gift, and have a special care that you do not use it for worldly pride, but employ it in such works as are contrary to the world. Use it rightly and enjoy it as if you had it not. Live a temperate life and beware of all sin. Otherwise your Guide will forsake you and you will be deprived of this happiness. For know of a truth: whosoever abuses this Tincture and does not live exemplarly, purely and devoutly before men, will lose this benefit and scarcely any hope will be left of recovering it afterward.

The Temple of the Fraternitatis Rosae Crucis. A plate from Schweighardt's *Speculum Sophicum Rhodo-Stauroticum,* 1618. The date 1604 in upper left is that given in the *Confessio* as the time of the opening of the tomb of Christian Rosenkreutz; at lower left a man is being lifted through an opening in the earth, similar to the scene in *The Chymical Wedding;* Rose and Cross are inscribed on each side of the doorway, and other motifs from true Rosicrucian writings will be discovered in this plate. It has been suggested that Schweighardt was really a pen-name for Johann Valentin Andreae himself. (See bibliography in this book.)

Theophilus Schweighardt's *Speculum Sophicum Rhodo-Stauroticum*, 1618,
dedicated to the establishment of a College of Universal Learning, in harmony
with the wisdom of "the enlightened Fraternity of the Christian Rose-Cross."
Details of the engraving are of utmost interest, particularly since this work
appeared only two years after *The Chymical Wedding*.

The Unity of Microcosm and Macrocosm. From *Opus Medico-Chymicum, Basilica Chymica*, Frankfort, 1618, by Johann Daniel Mylius, Physician from the Wetterau. The engraving was made by Jean Baptiste Mérian. Below was printed a Latin text: "By the word of the Lord were the heavens made..." from Psalm 33. At left and right, the archetypal Adam and Eve are linked with golden chains (reminiscent of the *Aurea Catena Homeri*) to the Macrocosmic world, the celestial world of Trinity of the Tetragrammaton, the Divine Name, the Lamb and Dove, surrounded by Angels. Beneath is the world of Zodiac and Planets, and below this the earthly world of the Elements, Garden of Paradise, and enigmatical animal figures reminding one of *The Chymical Wedding*.

The Holy Mountain of Initiation. One of four engravings in *Cabala, Spiegel der Kunst und Natur . . .* by Steffan Michaelspacher, physician in the Tirol, published at Augsburg, 1616, the same year as *The Chymical Wedding*.

The Mountain of Life. Here shown in relation to the stages of developing human life, this is a variant of the Mount of the Philosophers, the Mountain of Initiation theme.

Aureolus Philippus Theophrastus Paracelsus, ex Familia Brombastorum ab Hohenheim, Philosophus, Medicus, Mathematicus, Chimista, Cabalista, rerum naturæ industrius, indagator. Alterius nonfit, qui suus esse potest. Laus Deo, Pax vivis, Requies æterna sepultis.

Theophrastus Paracelsus of Hohenheim (1493-1541) — Eminent Swiss-German physician, alchemist, philosopher and cabalist. Doubtless the most famous and important forerunner of the classic age of the Rosicrucians of the 17th century. He is mentioned in *The Fame and Confession of the Fraternity of the Rosy Cross* (see page 174 of this book). His teachings, first introduced into England in 1585, profoundly influenced the work of Robert Fludd and other writers on Rosicrucianism in the West.

Interior of the "Modelleau" at Malsch — Designed and erected near Pforzheim, West Germany by E.A. Karl Stockmeyer, following indications by Rudolf Steiner, who on 5/6 April 1909 laid the foundation stone of this building, referring to it as "the first Rosicrucian temple to stand upon the surface of the earth," in contrast to earlier structures dedicated to Rosicrucian purposes, which were constructed underground. (See illustration on page 400 where such an underground temple is indicated.)

The Polish Rider by Rembrandt. A tradition exists that this represents a 17th century incarnation of Christian Rosenkreutz. The similarity between the building on the heights in the background and the forms of the first and second Goetheanum Buildings designed by Rudolf Steiner at Dornach, Switzerland is remarkable.

Johannes Theodorus de Bry (1561-1623) — From Robert Fludd's *Anatomiae Amphitheatrum Effigie Triplici*, Frankfort, 1623. The famous illustrator of books by noted writers on Rosicrucianism and related subjects. Originally established as an engraver in Liege, he eventually settled in Frankfort a/M. where he and his two sons became well known for the remarkable spiritual insight and technical skill displayed in their copper engravings for books by Fludd, Maier, Hakluyt, etc. (Illustration courtesy the Houghton Library, Harvard University)

Robert Fludd (1574-1637). Engraved frontispiece by de Bry to his *Tractatus Secundi Sectio Prima, Mundi Historia,* Frankfort, 1621. (Courtesy the Houghton Library, Harvard University)

PHILOSOPHIA
MOYSAICA.

In qua

Sapientia & scientia creationis & creaturarum Sacra veréque Christiana (vt pote
cujus basis sive Fundamentum est unicus ille Lapis Angularis Iesus Christus)
ad amussim & enucleaté explicatur·

AVTHORE,
ROB. FLVD, alias DE FLVCTIBVS,
Armigero & in Medicina Doctore Oxonienfi.

Christus est imago Dei invisibilis, primo genitus omnis creaturæ, quoniam in ipso condita
sunt universa in cœlis & in terra visibilia & invisibilia, sive Throni, sive Dominationes,
sive Principatus, sive potestates, Omnia per ipsum & in ipso creata sunt:
ipse est ante omnes & omnia in ipso constant. Coloss. 1§. 16.

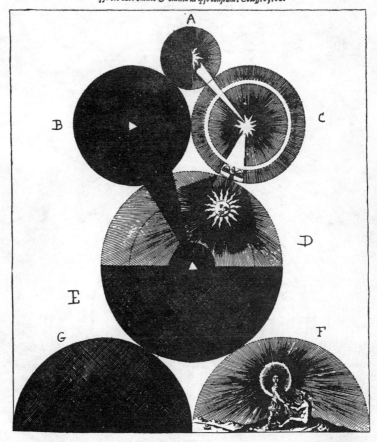

GOVDÆ,
Excudebat *Petrus Rammazenius*, Bibliopola.   *Anno.* M. DC. XXXVIII.

The Apollonian and the Dionysian Principles in Man and Cosmos. Title page
of Robert Fludd's posthumous work, *Philosophia Moysaica*, Gouda, 1638. The
man walking in darkness at the left indicates the "inner," Dionysus-principle;
the radiant figure at the right, lifting naked man, is Apollo, the "external"
aspect of things. The correspondence between "outer" and "inner" in both
Macrocosm and Microcosm was a subject of Rosicrucian study and meditation.

The Rosicrucian Correspondence between Macrocosm and Microcosm, Eternity and Time, illustrated by this engraved title page of Robert Fludd's principal work, de Bry, 1617.

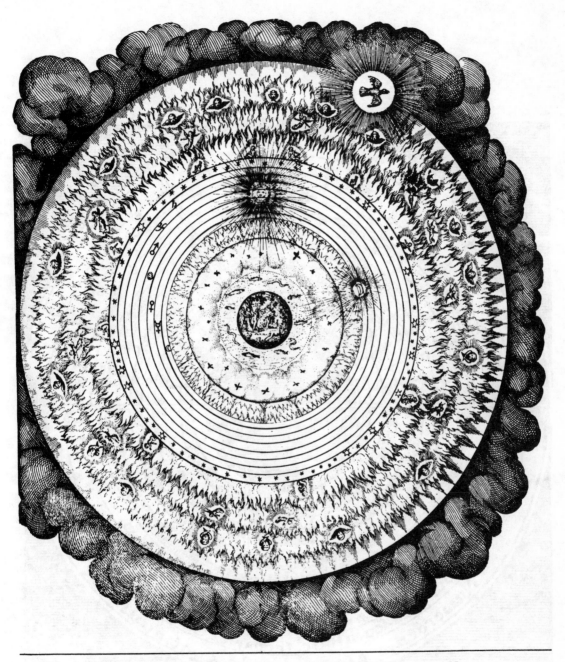

The Rosicrucian Correspondence between Macrocosm and Microcosm. Man, typified by the Parent Couple in Eden, the Earthly substance, is surrounded in turn by the Watery Element with fish, etc., by Air with birds, and the Element of Fire. Beyond are the Planets, the Fixed Stars, and finally the Empyrean, the world of Spiritual Beings. The Dove of the Holy Spirit "broods" over all. From Robert Fludd's *Utriusque Cosmi . . . Historia, Tractatus Primus,* Oppenheim, 1617, p. 9, engraved by de Bry.

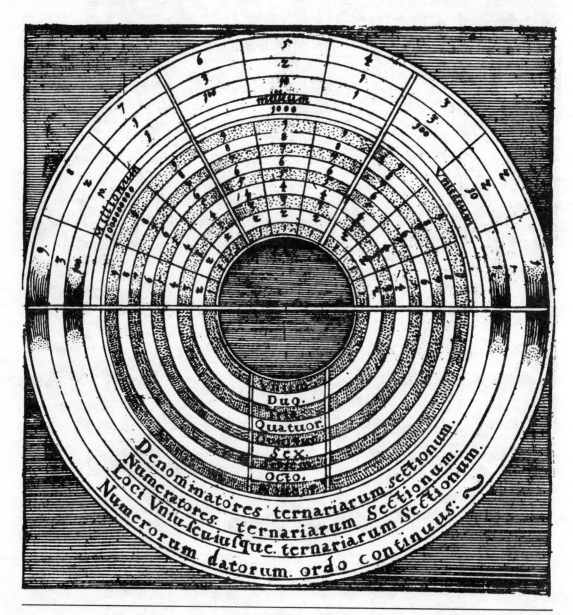

A Page from Robert Fludd's *Macrocosmi Tractatus Secundus*, Oppenheim, 1624. The engraving is by de Bry. Courtesy the Houghton Library, Harvard University.

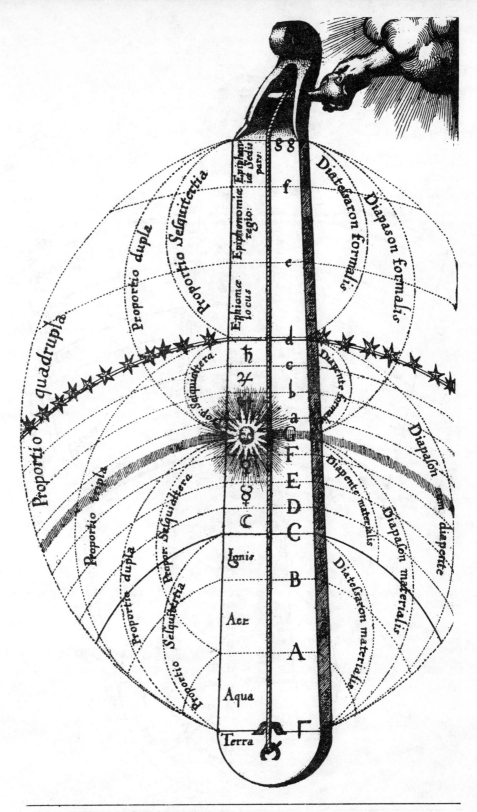

The Divine Monochord. An engraving by De Bry from Robert *Fludd's Utri-usque Cosmi Historia*, Part II, *de Arte Naturae, Musicam*, Oppenheim, 1617. Secrets of tone based on the indications of Pythagoras. (*Tractatus* I, *Lib*. III, p. 90)

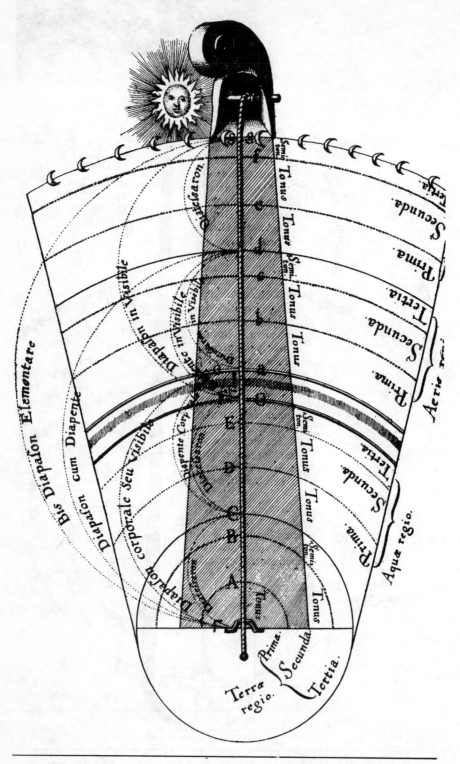

The Monochord. An engraving by de Bry from Robert Fludd's *Utriusque Cosmi Historia*, Part II, *de Arte Naturae, Musicam*, Oppenheim, 1617. (*Tractatus I, Lib.* III, p. 100)

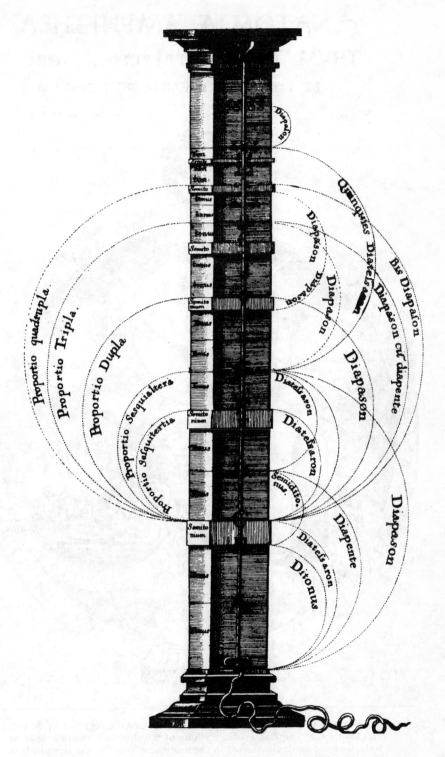

The Column of Music. Engraving by de Bry from Robert Fludd's *Utriusque Cosmi Historia*, Part II, *de Arte Naturae, Musicam*. Oppenheim, 1617.

Title Page of Robert Fludd's *Anatomiae Amphitheatrum*, engraved by de Bry, Frankfort, 1623. The Rosicrucian teaching of the threefold nature of man as body, soul and spirit is reflected in the anatomical study at the left which in turn is directly related to its soul aspect, the bread at left, and its spirit-aspect, the "mystical image of external anatomy" above.

Chaos and Cosmos. An engraving by de Bry from Robert Fludd's *Utriusque Cosmi . . . Historia, de Macrocosmi Principiis,* Oppenheim, 1617, p. 41. The metabolic processes in Macrocosm and in Microcosm are indicated.

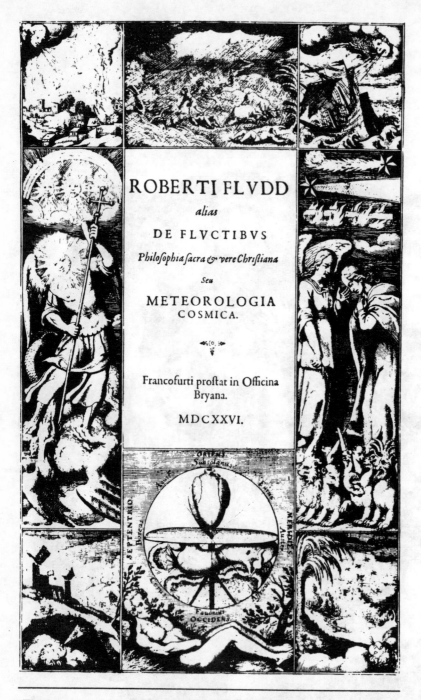

ROBERTI FLVDD
alias
DE FLVCTIBVS
Philosophia sacra & vere Christiana
Seu
METEOROLOGIA
COSMICA.

Francofurti prostat in Officina
Bryana.

MDCXXVI.

The Interrelationship of Microcosm and Macrocosm. In the center below, Man is stretched upon the ground, while above him a chart depicts the workings of his internal organs, heart above, metabolic system beneath, divided by the diaphragm, The Macrocosmic world is shown by scenes of fire, flood, wind above, and "earth" below, including earthquake and a pastoral scene. These actions of the Elements are separated by Michael overcoming the Dragon at left, and Gabriel showing Daniel the Four Beasts at right. The title page of Robert Fludd's *Philosophia Sacra*, Frankfort, 1623. Courtesy the Houghton Library, Harvard University.

Preparing a Horoscope, A vignette engraving by deBry from the title page of
Robert Fludd's *Utriusque Cosmi . . . Historia*, Part II, *de Arte Naturae, Astrologiam*, Oppenheim, 1617. (Courtesy the Houghton Library, Harvard University)

INTEGRVM
MORBORVM
MYSTERIVM:
SIVE
MEDICINÆ CATHOLICÆ
TOMI PRIMI TRACTATVS SE-
cundus, in Sectiones diftributus duas;
QVORVM

PRIOR *generalem Morborum Naturam, fiue variam Munimenti Salutis hoftiliter inuadendi atq oppugnandi rationem, more nouo & minimè antea audito, fiue intellecto defcribit.*

VLTIMA, *vniuerfale Medicorum fiue Ægrotorum depingit Catoptron: in quo Meteororum morboforum figna tam Demonftratiua, quam Prognoftica, lucidè fpeculantur, & modo haud vulgari atque alieno planè defignantur.*

AVTHORE
ROBERTO FLVDD, aliâs DE FLVCTIBVS,
Armigero, & in Medicina Doctore Oxonienfi.

FRANCOFVRTI,
Typis excufus Wolfgangi Hofmanni, Proftat in Officina GVLIELl
MI FITZERI, Anno M. DC. XXXI.

The Title Page of Robert Fludd's Leading Medical Work, 1631. The engraving shows how the patient and his symptoms appear to his attendants. In the next plate is shown how his illness appears *to his physician*.

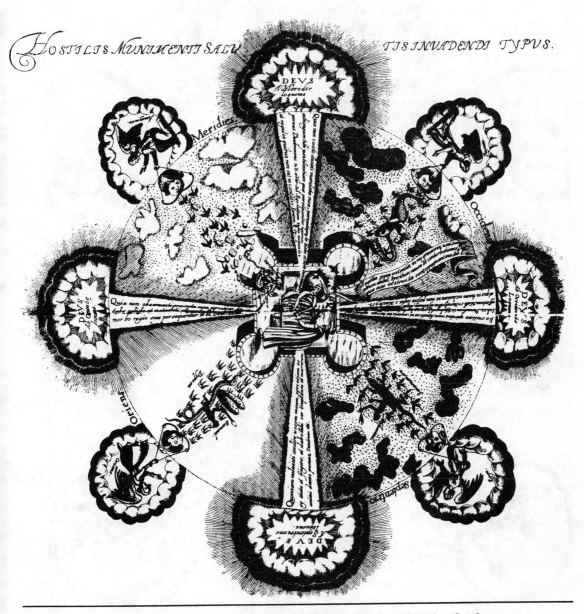

The Art of Restoring Health. The patient is suffering from the "break-through" of Azazel and his Basiliscus, surrounded by scorpion-like creatures; meanwhile, the dark Samael, riding upon his winged serpent-like Dypsas, Mahazazael, mounted upon his Salamander, fiery dart in hand, and Azael, astride his fish-like Coelus, are unable to penetrate to the man lying in the bed. Beside the patient stands the Physician, whose gaze is directed toward the quarter from which the "attack" has come, showing he is fully aware of it, uniting *in himself* the downstreaming divine words of power, seeking to direct them to the sick man. From Robert Fludd's *Integrum Morborum Mysterium*, 1631.

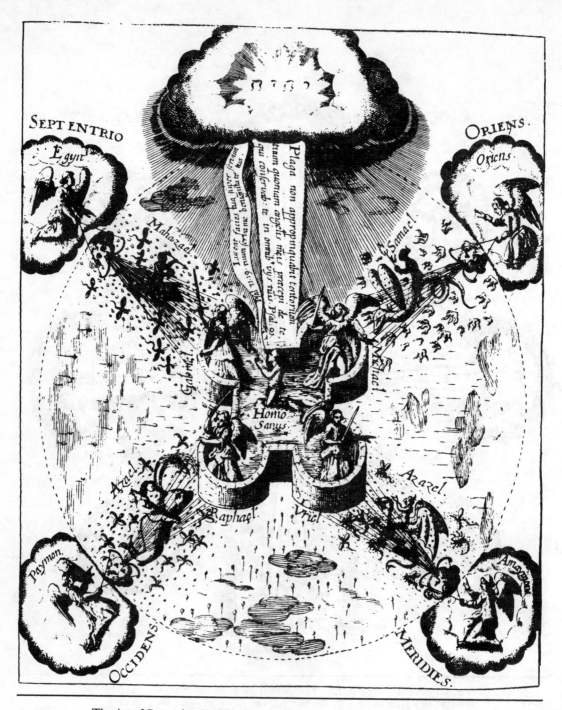

The Art of Preserving Health. "The Sound Man" *(Homo Sanus)* kneels within his "fortress" and addresses God: "How great is thy goodness . . ." (Ps. 19:31), and the latter replies: "No evil shall befall thee, neither shall any plague come nigh thy dwelling; his angels shall have charge over thee . . ." (Ps. 91:10). Meanwhile the Archangel Michael fights the evil hosts of Samael attempting to invade from the East; Raphael fights those of Azael coming from the West; Gabriel fights those of Mahazael from the North; Uriel fights those of Azazel from the South. From Robert Fludd's *Integrum Morborum Mysterium*, 1631.

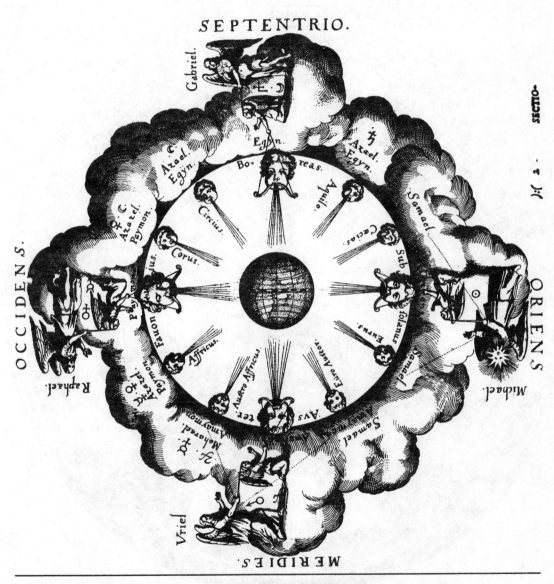

The Four Archangels and the World. Michael, Regent of the Sun, is in the East; opposite is Raphael in the West; Gabriel is in the North; Uriel is in the South. Each of them guides the winds, and in addition other spiritual beings are named and their signs are shown. The caption is from the Apocalypse, Ch. 7: "I saw four angels standing. . . ." From Robert Fludd's *Integrum Morborum*, 1631.

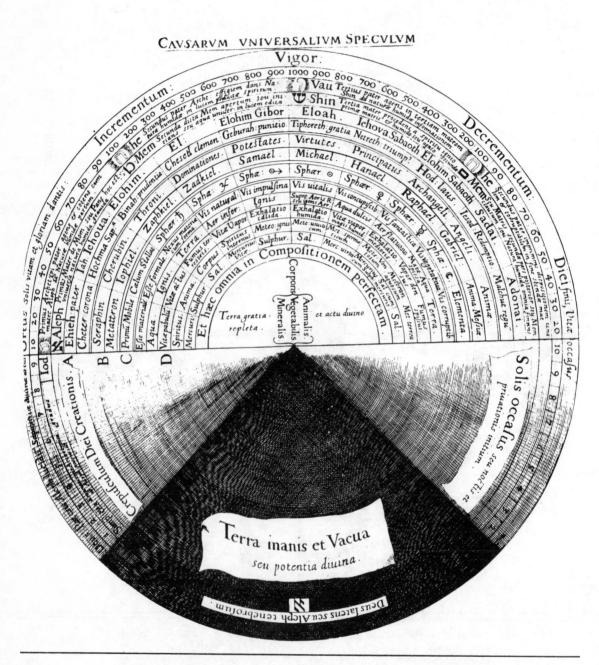

A Table of Universal Causation, from Robert Fludd's *Integrum Morborum Mysterium*, 1631. The relationship between physical substances and spiritual causes was a field of great interest to early Rosicrucian writers.

PVLSVS
Seu
NOVA ET ARCANA
PVLSVVM
HISTORIA, E SACRO
FONTE RADICALITER
EXTRACTA, NEC NON MEDI
CORVM ETHNICORVM DICTIS
& authoritate comprobata.
Hoc Est,
PORTIONIS TERTIÆ PARS TERTIA,
DE PVLSVVM SCIENTIA.
Authore ROBERTO FLVD
Armigero , & in Medicina Doctore Oxoniensi:

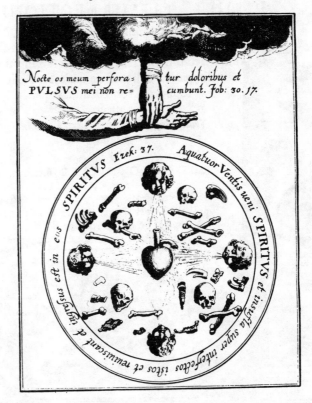

Title Page of Robert Fludd's Treatise on the Pulse, 1629. The quotation at the top of the illustration is "My bones are pierced with pain at night, and my *pulsus* does not rest." (Job 30:17) According to Fludd, the pulse is the effect of the working of the divine Breath breathed into Adam by God, and reflects — in a healthy state — the divine music of the spheres, the concord of the Alpha and Omega of existence.

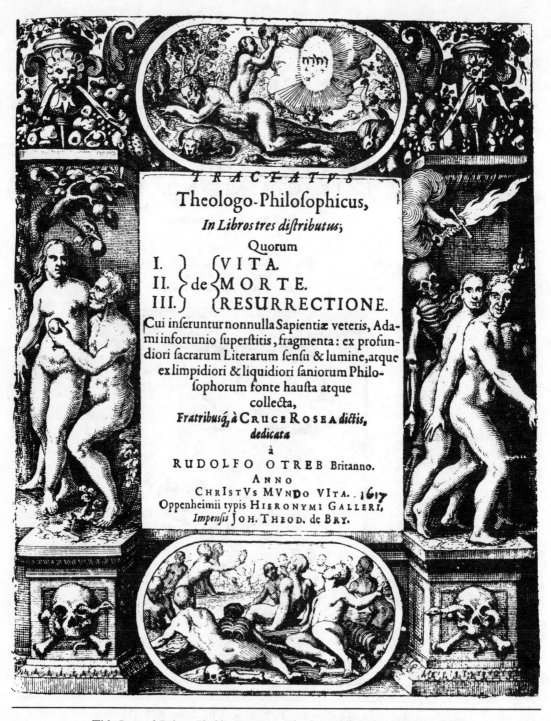

TRACTATVS

Theologo-Philosophicus,

In Libros tres distributus;

Quorum

I. ⎫ ⎧ VITA.
II. ⎬ de ⎨ MORTE.
III. ⎭ ⎩ RESURRECTIONE.

Cui inseruntur nonnulla Sapientiæ veteris, Adami infortunio superstitis, fragmenta: ex profundiori sacrarum Literarum sensu & lumine, atque ex limpidiori & liquidiori saniorum Philosophorum fonte hausta atque collecta,

Fratribusq̃, à CRUCE ROSEA *dictis,*

dedicata

à

RUDOLFO OTREB Britanno.

ANNO

CHRISTVS MVNDO VITA. 1617

Oppenheimii typis HIERONYMI GALLERI,

Impensis JOH. THEOD. de BRY.

Title Page of Robert Fludd's *Tractatus Theologo-Philosophicus,* engraved by de Bry, 1617, the year after the publication of *The Chymical Wedding.* Dedicated to the Brothers of the Rosy Cross, the work deals with the profound theme of Birth, Death and Resurrection. The motifs are of particular Rosicrucian interest.

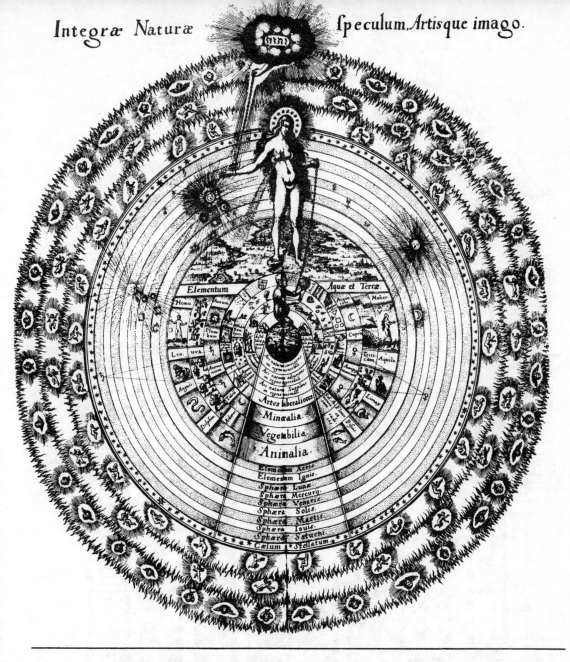

The Mirror of Nature and the Image of Art. Probably the most famous of all engravings by de Bry in the works of Robert Fludd, this plate from his *Utriusque Cosmi . . . Historia,* 1617, shows Nature standing upon the elements of water and earth, the power of her right hand subservient to the divine Will from above, the force of her left guiding the ape seated upon the globe, thus showing that the highest accomplishment in art is the "aping of Nature." Through Art the four elements have been transformed into the Mineral, Plant, and Animal kingdoms; man has "improved Nature in the mineral kingdom" by Alchemy; he has "helped Nature in the vegetable kingdom" by Agriculture; he has "supplemented Nature in the animal kingdom" by Medicine, Apiculture, etc. Further, through the Liberal Arts working in the Three Kingdoms, he transforms his world in terms of the working of the Macrocosm itself. This plate alone can provide ample basis for recognizing the vast difference between the contemplative, phenomenological approach to Nature fostered by the Rosicrucians and the purely analytic method advocated by Bacon, Newton and their followers.

The Temple of Music. Engraving by de Bry from Robert Fludd's *Utriusque Cosmi . . . Historia*, Part II, *de Arte Naturae, Musicam*, Oppenheim, 1617. The "workmen" around the anvil at the lower left are followers of Tubal-Cain. The designs of the Tower are reminiscent of similar motifs in *The Chymical Wedding*.

Johann Baptista Van Helmont (1577-1644), the most important chemist of the first half of the 17th century. Rudolf Steiner observed, "It is altogether helpful for modern men to become thoroughly acquainted with the thoughts of Van Helmont, who was a Rosicrucian."

Helmont

Ransi

Beuw

Vilain

Ioannes Baptista Van Helmont

Franciscus Mercurius von Helmont

Staßart

Halmale

Renialme

Merode

Johannes Baptista Van Helmont and his son, Franciscus Mercurius. This engraved frontispiece of the Amsterdam edition of the *Ortus Medicinae* shows them surrounded by their family coats of arms. Rudolf Steiner identified the father as a Rosicrucian, and the son collaborated with Baron von Rosenroth in compiling the famous *Caballa Denudata*. (Courtesy of the Houghton Library, Harvard University)

FRANCISCUS MERCURIUS VAN HELMONT

Portrait by Sir Peter Lely, reproduced by permission of the Trustees of the Tate Gallery, London. Probably a gift from Van Helmont to Lady Anne Conway. "One of those countenances which, once seen, live in the memory and are never effaced from it." — For details on the history of this painting see note to p. 63, l. 12 in the Reference Notes section.

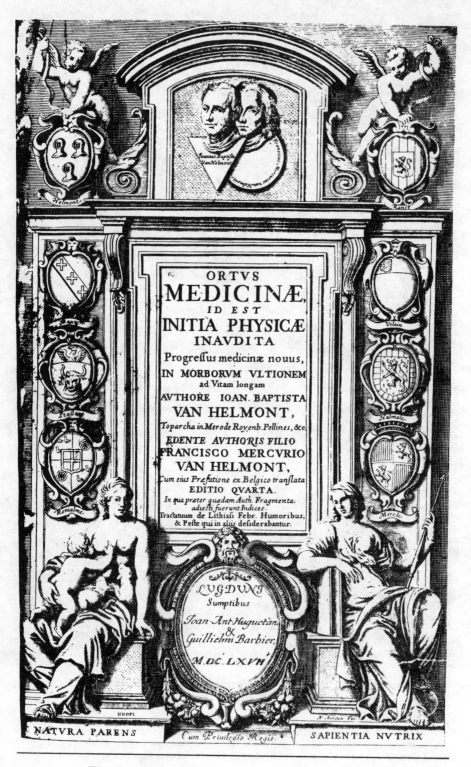

Title Page of Van Helmont's *Ortus Medicinae*, 4th ed., 1667.

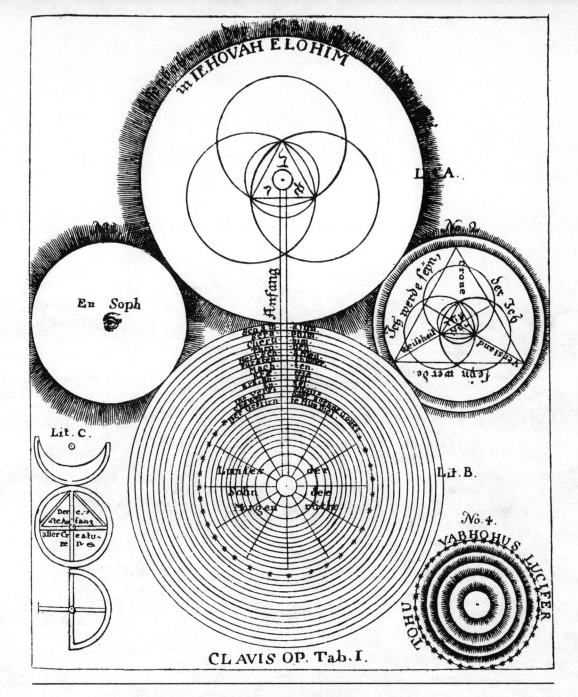

ROSICRUCIAN COSMOLOGY ACCORDING TO
FRANCISCUS MERCURIUS VAN HELMONT

This plate from Welling's *Opus Mago-Cabbalisticum et Theosophicum*, edition of 1784, and the points made in Welling's text, p. 495, *seq.*, are based on Rosicrucian teachings by F. M. Van Helmont. Fig. 1, The Infinite. Fig. 2, The first Manifestion. Fig. 3, The Revelation of the divine Majesty. Fig. 4, Lucifer. This latter drawing is of profound significance since the true nature of Lucifer was one of the most important points in all Rosicrucian teaching. As Rudolf Steiner observed in his lecture cycle, *The East in the Light of the West*, August, 1909; "The Rosicrucian initiates strove to understand and see the Christ in such a form that as the mystical Christ He permeated their souls and lived within them, and this Christ substance in their inner being became a bulwark of strength against all attacks. As a result, the Rosicrucian initiates were sufficiently mature, and were the first to be able to penetrate into the the realm of Lucifer."

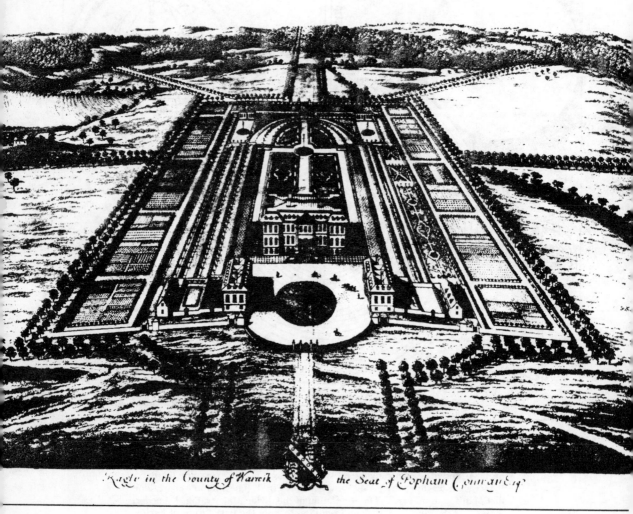

Ragley in the County of Warwick *the Seat of Popham Conway Esq*

RAGLEY IN WARWICKSHIRE
The estate of the Conway Family near Alcester, from a contemporary print.
Here in the 17th century Lady Anne Conway and her friends, including Henry
More, Franciscus Mercurius Van Helmont, Baron von Rosenroth, Ezechiel
Foxcroft and others discussed Rosicrucianism, philosophy, Jacob Boehme,
Alchemy and related subjects with insight and enthusiasm.

LADY ANNE CONWAY (1631-1678)
A little-known but highly important figure in the circle of Rosicrucians in 17th century England, friend of Henry More and of Ezechiel Foxcroft, translator of *The Chymical Wedding of Christian Rosenkreutz*. From a portrait now at the Hague.

VALENTINE GREATRAKES (1628-1694)
A contemporary drawing showing the "stroker" treating a patient.

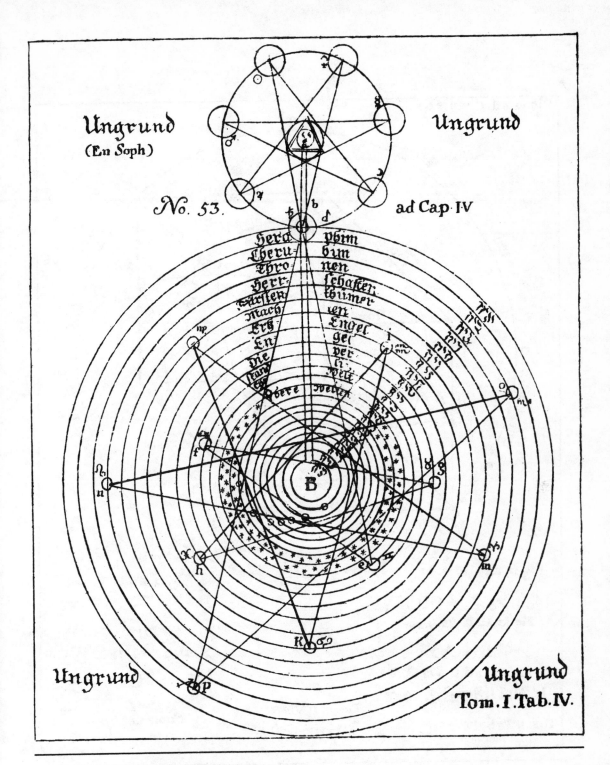

THE ARCHETYPAL WORLD
Plate from Chapter IV of Welling's *Opus Mago-Cabbalisticum et Theosophicum*, edition of 1784. The spiritual Hierarchies are clearly shown in their interrelationships. A modern author has suggested an affinity between this drawing and the description of the form of the tomb of Christian Rosenkreutz as described in the *Fame and Confession*, contained in this book.

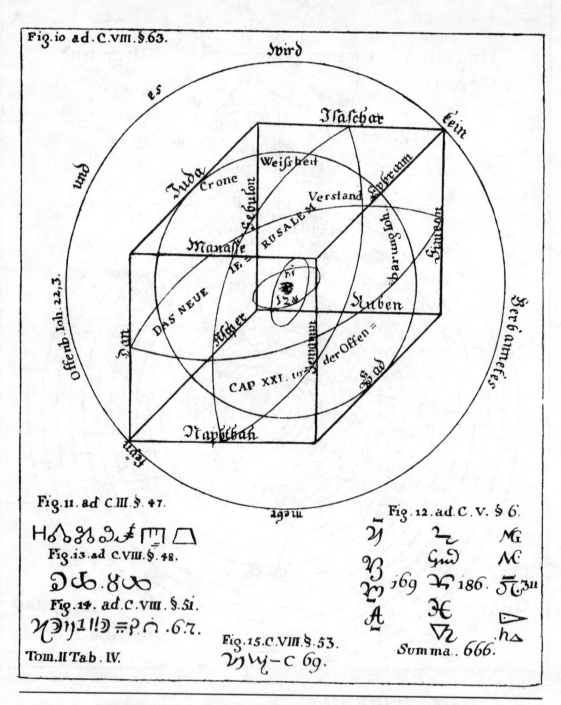

THE HEAVENLY TEMPLE OF DIVINE WISDOM
Based on the description of the New Jerusalem in the *Apocalypse*, this plate
from Welling's *Opus Mago-Cabbalisticum et Theosophicum*, edition of 1784,
p. 335, should be studied in the light of Robert Fludd's remarks concerning
the Rosicrucian House of Wisdom, included in this book.

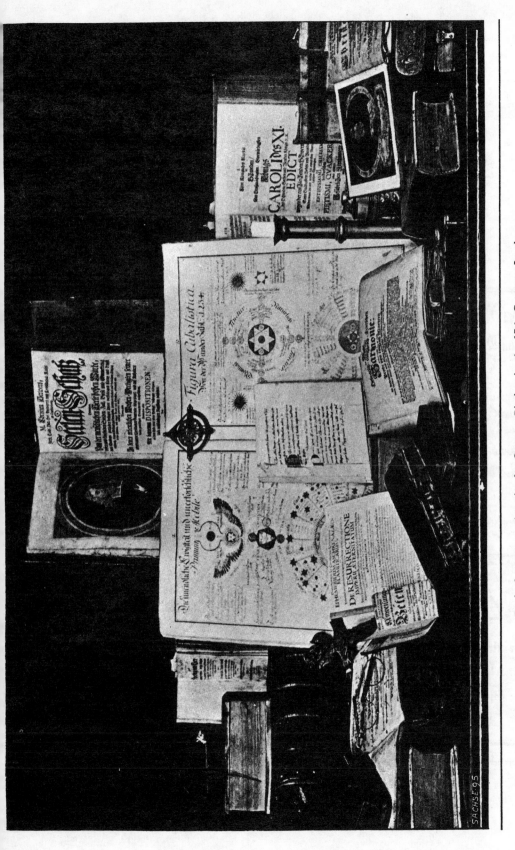

Books brought to America by German Pietists in the 17th Century. In the center is a hand-drawn copy of a version of *The Secret Symbols of the Rosicrucians*. From a photograph by Julius F. Sachse, published in his *German Pietists of Provincial Pennsylvania*, 1895.

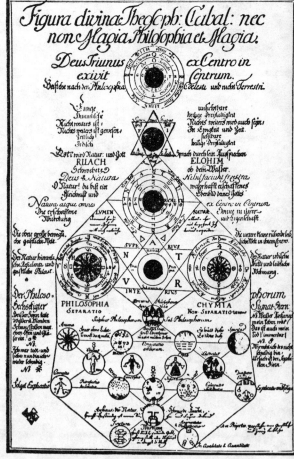

A Rosicrucian Manuscript from Provincial Pennsylvania. Two pages from a hand-drawn, colored ms. preserved in the family of Julius F. Sachse. Compare these with pages 26 and 32 of *The Secret Symbols of the Rosicrucians*.

ON THE HISTORY OF
CHRISTIAN ROSENKREUTZ

by

RUDOLF STEINER

(Extract from a lecture given in Berlin, May 6, 1909)

Today we would like to speak about the remarkable world of sagas and legends. There is one saga which is little noted, and which was put into poetic form by Konrad Fleck in 1230. It belongs to the sagas and myths of Provence and is related to the initiation of the Knights of the Grail and of the Knights Templars. There an old couple are spoken of, named "Flor" and "Blancheflor." In modern language this means approximately "the flower with red petals," the rose, and "the flower with white petals," the lily. In earlier times much was connected with this saga. Today one can speak only sketchily and abstractly about it. It was said: Flor and Blancheflor are souls, embodied in human beings, who have lived before. According to the saga they were the grandparents of Charlemagne. Those who occupied themselves more intimately with these sagas saw in Charlemagne that figure who, in a certain sense, brought a relationship into existence between inner, esoteric and exoteric Christianity. This was expressed in the coronation of the Emperor.

If one went back to Charlemagne's grandparents, to Flor and Blancheflor, one could see that in them lived the rose and the lily who were to preserve in purity esoteric Christianity as it goes back to Dionysos the Areopagite. One could see in the rose, in Flor or Flos, the symbol for the human soul who has taken into itself the personality-impulse, the ego-impulse, allowing the spiritual to work out of the individual-

See Reference Notes, beginning p. 635

ity, who has brought into the red blood the 'ego-impulse. In the lily, however, was seen the symbol of the soul who can only remain spiritual because the ego remains without, comes only to the boundary of the soul's existence. Thus rose and lily are polar opposites. The rose has taken the consciousness of itself wholly into itself; in the lily it has remained outside. But there has once been a union between the soul who is within, and the soul who, outside, enlivens the world as World-Spirit. Flor and Blancheflor express the finding of the World-Soul, the World-Ego, by the human soul, the human ego.

What happened later through the legend of the Holy Grail is also expressed here in the saga just described. Flor and Blancheflor are not a "real" outer couple. In the lily is expressed the soul which finds its higher egohood. In this union of lily-soul and rose-soul was seen something which can find a relation to the Mystery of Gologtha. It was said that over against that stream of European initiation which is brought about by Charlemagne, and through which is united exoteric and esoteric Christianity, over against this the purely esoteric Christianity is to be kept alive, is to be continued in purity.

In the circles of the Initiates it was said: The same soul which was in Flos or Flor and which is celebrated in the song of the saga, appeared again and reincarnated in the 13th and 14th century in order to found a new Mystery School which is to cultivate in a new form, corresponding to modern times, the Christ Mystery. It appeared in the founder of Rosicrucianism. Thus we meet with the secret of the rose in comparatively early times, for the saga really comes from the time before Charlemagne.

Thus it is that esoteric Christianity flows into Rosicrucianism. Since the 13th and 14th centuries Rosicrucianism has developed those initiates who are the successors of the ancient European Mysteries, the successors of the school of the Holy Grail.

Many things have emerged into outer life regarding the Rosicrucian Mysteries, but much of this is a caricature of the truth. Extraordinary achievements of spiritual life were influenced by the hidden currents of Rosicrucianism which found their way into external culture . . . But often connected with the name Rosicrucian is all the charlatanism and caricature that cannot be avoided since the discovery of the art of printing. Since this discovery it is no longer possible, as it was in earlier times, to allow secrets to remain secret. Everything comes out, but often distorted . . .

Goethe's greatest poetic achievements were nourished upon Rosicrucian sources. It is not without meaning that in his poem, *Die Geheimnisse, The Mysteries,* he speaks of a man who was led to a house and found on its door the sign of the Rose Cross. Then is asked, "Who brought the roses to the Cross?" — In other words, Who were those Initiates of the European Mysteries who united the mysteries of the rose and the mystery of the Cross?

Johann Valentin Andreae (1586 - 1654) and his wife, Agnes Elizabeth (1592 - 1659).

**Mare eſt Corpus, duo Piſces ſunt
Spiritus & Anima.**

Rosicrucian Teaching in Pictures. An illustration from Lambspring's *De lapide
Philosophorum Figurae et Emblemata,* 1625, included in the *Musaeum Hermeticum,* Frankfort, 1749, page 337, *seq.*—The caption reads, "The Sea is the
Body, the two Fish are Soul and Spirit."—The knowledge that man consists
of Body, Soul and Spirit, in contrast to the then general teaching that he is
comprised of Body and Soul alone, was a fundamental tenet of early Rosicrucian teaching.

CHRISTIAN ROSENKREUTZ
AND
THE TEMPLE LEGEND

by

RUDOLF STEINER

(An extract from unrevised notes
of a lecture given in Berlin, November 4, 1904)

Many exoteric legends containing an esoteric truth were given to mankind in order to implant in humanity certain verities at a time when men were not yet sufficiently mature to receive such esoteric facts directly. These narratives, and the concepts given with them, told hold of men's "causal body" and prepared them to understand such esoteric truths themselves in later incarnations.

At the beginning of the 14th century there appeared in Europe a personality who had been initiated into certain secrets in the East. This was Christian Rosenkreutz. — By the time this incarnation of Christian Rosenkreutz had come to an end, he had initiated about ten other people into such matters as he himself had learned through initiation. This small brotherhood called itself the *Fraternitas Rosae Crucis*. This little group then gave a certain legend to a larger fraternity. In the smaller circle Christian Rosenkreutz had explained certain events and processes. These could not be revealed to many people, so they were clothed in a kind of legend which has approximately the following content. — Since its inception at the beginning of the 14th century this legend has often been told in brotherhoods and also has been interpreted. It was told in larger brotherhoods, but was interpreted only in intimate circles. —

There was a time when one of the Elohim created a human being, a human being whom he called Eve. That Elohim

---

See Reference Notes, beginning p. 635

united himself with Eve and she gave birth to Cain. After this, another Elohim named Jahve created Adam. Adam also united himself with Eve, and from this union came Abel. Thus Cain was a son of the gods, but Abel was a son of man, of Adam and Eve. Later, the sacrifice Abel made to Jahve was pleasing to him, but the sacrifice brought by Cain did not please Jahve because Cain was not created at the latter's behest. Then Cain committed fratricide. He killed Abel, and for this he was excluded from communion with Jahve. He went away into distant lands and there became the creator of a special progeny.

Adam again united himself with Eve, and from this union came Seth. Thus arose the human generations: — the first was descended from Eve and the Elohim, while the other was descended from man. From the first, from Cain's progenitors, descended all who brought about the arts and sciences on earth. From Cain descended Methusael, who invented the sacred writing, the Tao-script (T-TAU), and Tubal-Cain, who taught the working of iron and bronze. Thus Tubal-Cain was directly descended from the Elohim. And out of Cain's line came Hiram, the inheritor of all that had been accumulated by the various descendants of Cain, in the form of knowledge of technology and art. Hiram was the most significant architect.

Out of Seth's line came Solomon who was endowed with everything that came from Jahve, with the wisdom of the world, with all that is calm, clear, objective wisdom which can be expressed in terms which can inspire the human heart. But it is not that wisdom which can produce something tangible of a technical nature, of art or science. It was not that wisdom which is attained from below, through human passions; it was not wisdom welling up from human will. This kind of wisdom, on the other hand, was found in the sons of Cain, who desired to accomplish everything through their own effort.

Now a temple was to be built. Solomon called upon the descendent of Cain, upon Hiram, to become the master-builder of this temple. At this same time Balkis, the Queen of Sheba, was living. She was elated by the wisdom of Solomon, who wooed her successfully. Then the queen heard of the building of the temple and wished to meet the master-builder, Hiram. When she saw him she was captivated merely by his glance. As a result, a certain jealousy arose between Hiram and Solomon, and the latter wished to do something or other against Hiram, but was dependent upon him for the completion of the temple. And for its completion only one thing was lacking — the Brazen Sea, which was to represent the ocean, cast in bronze, and was to adorn the temple. All the necessary mixtures of ores had been prepared by Hiram in a most wonderful manner, ready to be cast.

Among Hiram's apprentices were three whom he had found to be so lacking in skill that he could not promote them to be masters. These three swore to take revenge, and determined to prevent the successful casting of the Brazen Sea. They planned to pour water into the molten fiery mass, thus destroying the work. A friend of Hiram informed Solomon about this in order to thwart the plan of the three apprentices, but out of jealousy against Hiram, Solomon did nothing to prevent the deed.

Hiram had to witness how the water mixed itself into the molten ores, and how everything was destroyed. As Hiram was about to give way to dispair, his ancestor, Tubal-Cain appeared to him and advised him to plunge into the fire. Thus Hiram was initiated into the mystery of fire and into the secret of bronze casting, receiving from Tubal-Cain a hammer and a Golden Triangle. He then returned and was enabled to complete the casting of the Brazen Sea.

After this the Queen of Sheba gained Hiram's hand, but he was attacked by the three apprentices, bent on murdering him. Before he died, however, he managed to throw the Golden Triangle into a well. His body disappeared, and Solomon searched for it everywhere. Meanwhile it was feared that the three apprentices would betray the old Master-Word, so a new one was decided upon. At last Hiram was found, and was able to utter a few last words. He said, "Tubal-Cain has promised me that I shall have many sons who will complete my work." He then pointed to the place where the Golden Triangle would be found. This was then brought to the Brazen Sea and both were preserved in the Holy of Holies. They can be shown only to those who have an understanding for what this legend may mean. —

This legend represents the destiny of the third and fourth sub-race of our fifth root race.* The temple is the temple of the secret brotherhood of the fourth and fifth sub-race. Those initiated ones knew the meaning of the Brazen Sea and the Golden Triangle.

Two groups of men existed upon earth: those who were in possession of divine wisdom, represented by Solomon, and the descendents of Cain, who knew how to handle and understand fire. This is not physical fire, but the fire burning in astral space, the fire of passions, of instincts. — The sons of Cain are those who remained a little behind during the Moon epoch, under a certain class of Elohim. On the other hand, other Elohim who were beyond this stage of evolution, formed man no longer permeated with passions. They endowed him with clear, calm, objective wisdom, with the true Jahve or Jehova religion, with wisdom which was passionless. The other Elohim brought into being the sons of Cain, in whom wisdom is united with fire. They are those who represent the impulsive element, who can feel enthusiasm for wisdom. Out of this line all art and science have come, while out of the other have arisen all clear, objective wisdom, all religious feeling without passion.

This continued until the beginnings of the fourth sub-race. Then came the founding of Christianity. At that time the earlier piety, which had been a piety from above, was merged with the element which came to the earth through Christ — the incarnated love in a high, divine Kama, which is at the same time Budhi, — a pure, flowing Kama, which wants nothing for itself. Within the type of men who were pious, an enthusiastic piety prepared itself — Christianity. This whole stream is not yet in a position to unite with the sons of Cain, however; they remain adversaries. If Christianity were too quickly to take hold of a human being, then the individual human heart would not be able to give birth to Christ within itself, to recognize the Christ as the brother within man. To this end the sons of Cain had to be active throughout the whole time of the fifth sub-race. They work

---

*See Editorial Notes.

in their initiates. They build the temple, which is constructed entirely out of worldly knowledge. The world-historic development steps fully onto the physical plane. And during the life of the fourth and fifth-sub-race develops the material element of the war of all against all.

The Christian principle that all human beings are equal before God could not be fully understood by men. The French Revolution took the consequences of Christianity in a worldly sense in the idea that all men are equal. The spiritual teaching of Christianity was translated into a purely worldly teaching.

At that time there appeared before a lady-in-waiting of Marie Antionette a personality who prophesied all the important events of the coming Revolution, in order to warn against them. It was Christian Rosenkreutz — the Count of St. Germain. At this time he represented the point of view that men would have to be led in a quiet way from a worldly culture to the culture of true Christianity. He regarded the Revolution as a necessary consequence, but he also warned against it. He, Christian Rosenkreutz, in his incarnation as Count St. Germain, was the guardian of the Brazen Sea and of the Golden Triangle. He now appeared, warning that mankind should develop slowly. But he also saw what was to happen.

The great temple of Solomon was built, but what can actually crown it must remain a secret, for that can be brought into being only by an initiate. It is the actual secret of Christianity. There it lies as the Brazen Sea and as the Golden Triangle. It is the secret of the Rosicrucians. Before the time of Christ, Christian Rosenkreutz had already lived as a high initiate. It was then that he made his remarkable dictum: "He who sows the wind will reap the storm." This was the guiding word of the fourth and fifth sub-race. It can be expressed as, "You will make men free, yes, it will be that you will unite Kama and Budhi with your freedom. But first the spirit will become a storm."

At first Christianity had to appear as the Christianity of the Cross, that is, that which had to develop through the earthly sphere, through the physical plane. But the Cross was not the symbol of Christianity from the beginning. It was when Christianity became political that the crucified Son of God was introduced, the Son of God suffering on the cross of the body of the world — throughout the fourth and fifth sub-race of the fifth root race At first Christianity is linked with the purely material culture. Nevertheless, within it exists the Christianity of the future which is in possession of the secret of the Brazen Sea and of the Golden Triangle. This secret is no longer the crucified Son of God, but the Cross from which the Roses grow. It is this which will become the symbol of the sixth sub-race. This Christianity honors the Brazen Sea and the Golden Triangle.

Hiram is the representative of the sons of Cain. The Queen of Sheba is the soul of humanity who has to choose between the objective and pure piety which does not conquer the earth, and the unpurified but earth-conquering knowledge. With this one connects the true soul of man with whom Hiram is united in the fourth and fifth sub-race. This is the Brazen Sea in which — in suitable manner — water is mixed with molten bronze. The apprentices do it wrongly, but later Hiram can unite water with bronze, water with fire. Through this the Brazen Sea comes about. The Brazen Sea is the secret of the Rosicrucians. It arises when the water of quiet wisdom unites with the fire of passion. The quiet wisdom unites itself — throughout the fourth and fifth sub-race — with all that lives as passion within man. This amalgam then becomes bronze.

To this must be added the secret of the Golden Triangle — Atma, Budhi, Manas. This Triangle will be what will form the content of the renewed Christianity of the sixth sub-race. Then men will know the secret of reincarnation and karma. This is the new occult teaching which must be inserted into Christianity. This secret will become manifest when the sixth sub-race becomes mature. Then all that was strife on the outer plane will find peace through the Golden Triangle . . .

TRES SCHOLA, TRES COESAR TITVLOS DE.
DIT; HÆC MIHI RESTANT,
POSSE BENE IN CHRISTO VIVERE, POSSE MORI.
MICHAEL MAIERVS COMES IMPERIALIS CON,
SISTORII cíc. PHILOSOPH: ET MEDICINARVM
DOCTOR. P. C. C. NOBIL: EXEMPTVS FOR.OLIM
MEDICVS CÆS: cíc:

Count Michael Maier (c. 1568-1622), alchemist, author and Rosicrucian apologist, from an engraving in his *Symbola Aurae Mensae*, 1617, the year after publication of the *Fame and Confession R.C.* in Frankfort. On p. 290 of this book Maier wrote: "Since the Rosicrucians advance nothing contrary to true piety, to nature, to any condition of men, nor, finally, to virtue and justice, but every detail is directed to the praise of the Creator, the revelation of nature and the good of God's creatures, we shall with dutiful and well-deserved prayers await from this laudable order whatever will come about." — Sir Isaac Newton mentioned this statement in a note he wrote on the flyleaf of his copy of Vaughan's translation of the *Fame and Confession*, 1652. — Maier's *Themis Aurea*, an important commentary on the laws of the Fraternity of the Rosy Cross, appeared in 1618. — See J. B. Craven, *Count Michael Maier, Rosicrucian Mystic*, London, 1910.

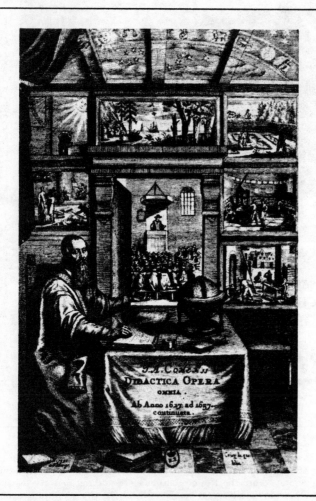

Johann Amos Comenius (1592-1670). This engraved title page from his *Didactica Opera Omnia,* Amsterdam, 1657, includes a portrait of Comenius himself. Rudolf Steiner once said, "Among those who had higher knowledge by virtue of their spiritual development, and were able to lift themselves into higher worlds through their strong and energetic will-power, as a result of having been influenced by the Rosicrucians—among these men belonged Comenius, the great educator. Today it is very useful for men to permeate themselves with Comenius' ideas."

JOHANN AMOS COMENIUS
AND
THE TEMPLE OF PANSOPHIA

by

RUDOLF STEINER

(Extract from a lecture given in Berlin, April 11, 1916)

Born in Moravia, Amos Comenius was a man who came
into contact with numerous secret fraternities in the course
of his life. Such fraternities were widespread throughout
Europe at that time, and I have mentioned them before.
They were to be found everywhere, and Comenius entered
into a real relationship with them, trying to influence them.
How he was able to influence them is particularly beautifully shown in what he says in his *Pansophia*.

In Amos Comenius we have a man of the 16th and 17th
centuries. We see in him a human being who, in the beginning of our epoch, says: Now a change will come; a different
age is about to arise. Now it will be necessary to translate
into reason what previously has existed as tradition. Tradition was concerned with the last remnants of what had still
been a matter of revelation: the building of the Temple.
Regardless whether it was a matter of the Greek temple or
the Temple of Solomon, the essential thing was the building of the Temple, the images concerning the building of the
Temple, and from these images everything was taken in a
symbolic and imaginative way. Amos Comenius set himself
the task to translate all this into his *Pansophia* in a way corresponding to the activity of the soul in the fifth post-Atlantean epoch. He said:

"Whether this or another name is more pleasing, we preferred that of *Pansophia* because it was our intention to

See Reference Notes, beginning p. 635.

stimulate all people to know everything, to be wise, to fill their spirit with the truth of all things, and not with the fog of opinions. It could also be called knowledge of the best, of the choicest, or also knowledge ot the not-knowing, if one wishes to recall Socrates or the Apostles. Why, however, should the Temple of Pansophia be erected according to the ideas, measurements and laws of the highest Master-Builder Himself?

Here Amos Comenius joins his ideas with the "highest Master-Builder of worlds." It was He, the "highest Master-Builder of worlds," who was invoked because in olden times one knew what architecture, the true art of building, really was. It is to be taken literally, but *spiritually-literally*. But Amos Comenius tries to translate it into the language of the fifth post-Atlantean epoch. Take note as to how he translates:

"Why, however, should the Temple of Pansophia be erected according to the ideas, measurements and laws of the highest Master-Builder Himself? — Because we follow the prototype of the whole, according to measure, number, position and purpose of its parts in the way that was indicated by the wisdom of the Godhead Himself, at first through Moses when he erected the Tabernacle, then through Ezekiel when he restored the Temple." — (He could equally well have cited the Greek temple.) —

"If we wish to erect the Temple of Wisdom, we shall have to remind ourselves that the Temple to be built is considered great, majestic and praiseworthy throughout all lands, because our God is above all gods. Therefore the worthiest and most skillful builders must be called upon, wherever they can be found, so that they will bring together and help to create everything that is needful. The Temple of Solomon was built by the command of God on the mountain of Moriah; Moriah means 'the Countenance of God.'" — (In the same way man himself is built out of the lap of the Godhead. You have seen that Vetruvius requires that the builder should have gathered into his spirit all wisdom concerning Man.) —

"The foundation of the Temple of Wisdom thus will be the countenance of God," (This implies that through modern knowledge the countenance of God, that is, the revelation of God, shall be made manifest.) "this means: through all

452

things visible the invisible One on His throne of the world with His all-might, wisdom and goodness shall be recognized and beheld by the spirit of man.

"The substances used for the building of the Temple of Solomon were stones, timber, metals, precious and semi-precious stones, marble and sap-filled, scented woods, pines and cedars, pure metals and gold. Three forests gave their timbers for the Temple of Wisdom (Now he begins to translate.) — the forest of the senses, the forest of reason, and that of divine revelation. The first gives the understandable, the second the living, and the third everything that is imperishable." — (At first he spoke about stone and wood, the inlaid gold, and so on. This he now translates into the language of the fifth post-Atlantean epoch: the first gives the understandable, that is, the senses; the reason gives that which is living; revelation gives what is imperishable. Here you have the translation. —)

"Stones," he continues, "became walls, timber became wainscoting, and from the gold were made sheets to cover the wainscoting and the marble floor, as well as the sacred vessels and appliances. Thus the walls of the Temple of Wisdom change into that truth which becomes evident through the certainty of our senses." (This means that what we receive through our senses forms the walls of our temple of wisdom.) "The wainscoting is made by the conclusions of our reasoning, and the gold comes from the harmony between what has been understood and what has been revealed. The Temple of Solomon was erected from perfectly hewn stones, and during the building no one could hear the sound of hammer or axe, nor of any iron tool. Similarly in the building of the Temple of Wisdom there must be no quarrel nor discord, but everything must be worked into a perfect cube so that it only requires to be placed together; wisdom will have had to be considered before, will have been fitted into all things...

"All parts of the Temple of Solomon were in the most perfect and beautiful relationship with each other, according to number and measure, and it was an angel who drew the plan for Ezekiel." (You will note the repeated reference to the *Angelos*.) — "So also shall the Temple of Wisdom be well measured, so that the spirit may nowhere be led astray. In the Temple of Solomon were ornaments, sculptures, embossed work, Cherubim, palms and flowers. In the Temple of Wisdom beauty itself shall be the adornment, the beautiful way of representation. Everything within the confines of the Temple of Solomon was sacred. So also will it be in the Temple of Wisdom; its contents shall be pure and holy, devoted to highest purposes alone. To the builders of the Temple of Jerusalem God promised His presence. This also may be expected by the builder of the Temple of Wisdom, for He says, 'I love those who love Me.' — And finally, when the foundations were laid for the walls of the Temple of Solomon there stood the priests in their vestments and with cymbals and flutes, together with the people, praised the Lord . . .

"Therefore all people devoted to God should come together when the Temple of Wisdom is being erected and praise the name of the Lord from sunrise to sunset, from now through all eternity."

"We wish for a school of universal wisdom, a pansophic or school of all-embracing wisdom, — that is, a workshop into which we are admitted in order to attain skill for everything necessary for life — both the present and the future life — and to be able to do this fully. This is to be done in such a manner that no one could be found there who would know nothing, who would lack understanding, or who who not be experienced in anything he knows is true and useful."

It can be said that what Goethe wished to represent in his *Wilhelm Meister* is a continuation of what Amos Comenius intended. If we, in turn, look in an objective way toward the goal of our striving, without becoming immodest we may be able to see how in the 16th, 17th centuries a beginning was made, and that we have only the task to place ourselves in the right way into the evolution of mankind . . .

ROSICRUCIANISM, KARMA, REINCARNATION

by

RUDOLF STEINER

(An extract from a lecture given in Karlsruhe, October 6, 1911)

Today we no longer stand upon those premises which motivated the Rosicrucians from the beginning of the thirteenth century onward, but we take into consideration the progress of the human soul. Therefore it is not permissible to confuse what in my book, *Knowledge of Higher Worlds* is shown to be the most appropriate way into the spiritual spheres, with what can be designated as "the Rosicrucian path." By way of our stream it is possible to penetrate into true Rosicrucianism, but our way must not be designated as "Rosicrucianism" because our stream encompasses a far broader realm than that of the Rosicrucians, namely, the whole of Anthroposophy . . .

The Rosicrucian initiation of the thirteenth through the seventeenth centuries has to be modified in our time. For the Rosicrucianism of previous centuries . . . did not include what today must form the starting-point of our initiation-science: the teaching of Reincarnation and Karma, of repeated earth-lives . . . Today the idea of Reincarnation enters modern life by inner necessity, and must be taken into consideration.

The Hon. Robert Boyle, 1627-1691, pioneer chemist, philosopher, scientist, discoverer of Boyle's Law, author of many scientific works, including *The Sceptical Chymist,* 1661, founding member of the council of the Royal Society, 1663, and by many considered an even greater figure than Lord Bacon of Verulam. Generally unknown is the fact that in 1659 Boyle introduced to the University of Oxford "the noted chemist and Rosicrucian, Peter Sthael of Strasbourg" whom Boyle had brought to England to be his tutor. Sthael lived in Boyle's lodgings at Oxford, instructing him "in geometry, philosophy and chemistry." Among Sthael's other pupils were Christopher Wren, famous architect of St. Paul's Cathedral, John Locke, Fellow of the Royal Society, and Anthony a Wood, from whose diary this information is taken. Sthael later became head of the Royal Society's laboratory, and his influence extended to even wider circles of important men of the time. — From this can be seen how Rosicrucian influences — often working in subtle ways — have had a profound effect upon human progress since the 17th century.

REFERENCES TO CHRISTIAN ROSENKREUTZ IN LECTURES AND WRITINGS BY RUDOLF STEINER, 1903-1924

Compiled by
PAUL M. ALLEN

(An asterisk before a date indicates that the lecture or written work has appeared in English translation.)

May 23, 1904 — Berlin — Members' Lecture — *Das Pfingstfest* — in ms only, (Schmidt #850)

*November 4, 1904 — Berlin — Members' Lecture — *Das Mysterium der Rosenkreuzer* — in ms. only. (Schmidt #937) An important extract from this lecture is included in the present volume.

December 16, 1904 — Berlin — Members' Lecture — *Ueber Hochgradfreimaurerei* — in ms. only. (Schmidt #985)

October 4, 1905 — Berlin — Members' Lecture — *Die Sinnesorgane und die Zukunft der Erde*, publ. in *Nachrichtenblatt*, 1934, 20. Jahrg. Nr. 2. Important details concerning Christian Rosenkreutz. (Schmidt #1129)

October 10, 1905 — Berlin — Lect. 15 in Cycle of 31 Lects. — *Die Lehre der Rosenkreutzer* — publ. in *Nachrichtenblatt* 1934, 20. Jahrg., Nr. 14-15 under title *Die zwoelf Nidanas*. (Schmidt #1136)

October 20, 21, 1906 — Berlin — Members' Lectures — *Der Erkenntnispfad im Sinne der Rosenkreutzer*, — publ. in *Der Erkenntnispfad und seine Stufen*, Dornach, 1933. (Schmidt #1403-1405)

November 30, 1906 — Cologne — Members' Lecture — *Die drei Wege der Einweihung* — in ms. only. (Schmidt #1439)

December 11, 1906 — Munich — Members' Lecture — *Wie erlangt man Erkenntnisse der hoeheren Welten im Sinne der Rosenkreuzer?* — in ms. only. (Schmidt #1451)

February 16, 1906 — Leipzig — Members' Lecture — *Wer sind die Rosenkreutzer?* — in ms. only. (Schmidt #1495)

May 19, 1907 — Munich — Congress Lecture — *Die Einweihung des Rosenkreuzers* — publ. in *Nachrichtenblatt*, 1948, 25 Jahrg., Nr. 5-10, also in *Bilder okkulter Siegel und Säulen*, Dornach, 1957. (Schmidt #1527)

*May 22 — June 6, 1907 — Munich — Cycle of 14 Lectures publ. as *Die Theosophie des Rosenkreuzers*, Berlin, 1911, 4th Ed., Dornach, 1955. Translated as *The Theosophy of the Rosicrucians*, London, 1953, (Schmidt #1535+)

°June 16-29, 1907 – Cassel – Cycle of 14 Lectures – *Theosophie und Rosenkreuzertum* – publ. in *Nachrichtenblatt*, 1942, 19 Jahrg., Nrs. 8-42. Translated as *Theosophy and Rosicrucianism*, publ. in *Anthrop. News Sheet*, Dornach, 1942, Vol. 10, p. 145, *seq.* (Schmidt #1551+)

°September 7, 1907 – Written reply to questions by Edouard Schure at Barr. The section relative to Christian Rosenkreutz is reproduced in facsimile and translation in this book.

December 15, 1907 – Duesseldorf – Members' Lecture – *Das Rosenkreuzertum* – in ms. only. (Schmidt #1642)

°May 6, 1909 – Berlin – Public Lecture – *Die europaeischen Mysterien und ihre Eingeweihten* – Publ. in *Die Drei*, 1928/29, 8 Jahrg, 9 Heft, *also in Wo und wie findet man den Geist*, Dornach, 1961. Translated as *The European Mysteries and their Initiates*, publ. in *Anthroposophy Quarterly*, London, Vol. 4, 1929, p. 275 *seq.* A revised transl. publ. in *Anthroposophical Quarterly*, London, 1964, Vol. 9, No. 1, p. 1, *seq.* (Schmidt #1996)

°May 31, 1909 – Budapest – Congress Lecture – *Von Buddha zu Christus* – publ. in *Nachrichtenblatt*, 1944, 21 Jahrg., Nr. 23/25. Translated as *From Buddha to Christ*, publ. in *Anthrop. News Sheet*, Dornach, 1944, Vol. 12, p. 209 *seq.* (Schmidt #2012)

October 31, 1910 – Berlin – Members' Lecture – *Einiges ueber das Rosenkreuzermysterium "Die Pforte der Einweihung"*, Berlin, 1916, Dornach, 1925. (Schmidt #2294)

°September 27/28, 1911 – Neuchâtel – Members' Lectures – *Ueber Christian Rosenkreuz* and *Christian Rosenkreuz und sein Werk*. Publ. in *Das Rosenkreuzerische Christentum*, Dornach, 1947, and in *Das esoterische Christentum*, Dornach, 1962. Translated as *Rosicrucian Christianity*, publ. in *Anthroposophical Quarterly*, London, Vol. 5, No. 4, Winter, 1960, p. 2 *seq.*, and Vol. 6, No. 1, Spring, 1961 (Centenary Number). The importance of these two lectures cannot be overestimated in understanding the role of Christian Rosenkreutz in the history of mankind. (Schmidt #2443/44)

°October 5-14. 1911 – Karlsruhe – Cycle of 10 Lectures – *Von Jesus zu Christus*, publ. Berlin 1921, Dornach, 1933, 3rd, enlarged edition, Dornach, 1958. Translated as *From Jesus to Christ*, London, 1944, 1945. Special ref. in lectures 1 and 2. (Schmidt #2448+)

°October 23, 1911 to June 20, 1912, Berlin – Cycle of 9 Lectures – publ. as *Der irdische und der kosmische Mensch*, Berlin, 1917, Dornach, 1932. Translated as *Earthly and Cosmic Man*, London, 1948. Lectures 1, 5 and 9 contain important statements regarding Christian Rosenkreutz. (Schmidt #2462+)

°November 18 and 20, 1911 – Munich – Members' Lectures on *Okkulte Zeitstroemungen und Christian Rosenkreuz*, publ. in *Nachrichtenblatt*, 1944, 21 Jahrg., Nr. 50-52. 2nd lect. publ. in *Die Mission des Christian Rosenkreuz*, Donarch, 1947, p. 44 *seq.* Both lectures publ. in *Das esoterische Christentum*, Dornach, 1962. Translated as *The Christ Impulse as Living Reality*, publ. in *Christian Rosenkreutz*, London, 1950, p. 65 *seq.* (Schmidt #2476/78)

°January 27, 1912 – Cassel – Members' Lecture – *Gesichtliches ueber Christian Rosenkreutz*, publ. in *Die Mission des Christian Rosenkreuz*, Dornach, 1947 and in *Das esoterisch Christentum*, Dornach, Dornach, 1962. Translated as *The Dawn of Occultism in the Modern Age*, publ. in *The Mission of Christian Rosenkreutz*, London, 1950, p. 13 *seq.* (Schmidt #2529)

*January 29, 30, 1912 — Cassel and Berlin — Members' Lectures — *Die Morgenroete des neueren Okkultismus* and *Reinkarnation und Karma*, publ. in *Die Mission des Christian Rosenkreuz*, Dornach, 1947 and in *Das esoterische Christentum*, Dornach, 1962. Lecture of Jan. 30th publ. in Berlin, 1917 and in *Wiederverkoerperung und Karma*, Dornach, 1959. The lecture of January 29th translated and publ. in *The Mission of Christian Rosenkreutz*, London 1950, p. 23 *seq.* Lecture of January 30th not publ. in English translation. (Schmidt #2531-32)

*February 8, 1912 — Vienna — Members' Lecture — *Das menschliche Laben im Lichte des Karmagedankens*, publ. in *Die Mission des Christian Rosenkreuz*, Dornach, 1947 and in *Das esoterische Christentum*, Dornach, 1962. Translated as *The True Attitude to Karma*, publ. in *The Mission of Christian Rosenkreutz*, London, 1950, p. 32 *seq.* (Schmidt #2538)

*February 9, 1912 — Vienna — Members' Lecture — *Christian Rosenkreuz*, publ. in *Die Mission des Christian Rosenkreuz*, Dornach, 1947, and *Das esoterische Christentum*, Dornach, 1962. Translated as *Intimate Workings of Karma*, publ. in *The Mission of Christian Rosenkreutz*, London, 1950, p. 49 *seq.* (Schmidt #2539)

*April 17, 1912 — Stockholm — Members' Lecture — *Der Weg der Initiation*, publ. in *Die drei Wege der Seele zu Christus*, Dornach, 1937. Translated as *The Path of Initiation* in *The Three Paths of the Soul to Christ*, New York, 1942, p. 21 *seq.* (Schmidt #2580)

June 17, 1912 — Hamburg — Members' Lecture — *Einweihung des Christian Rosenkreuz-Zweiges*, publ. in *Das esoterische Christentum*, Dornach, 1962, p. 307 *seq.* (Schmidt #2515)

*November 5, 1912 — April 1, 1913 — Berlin — Cycle of 10 Lectures — *Das Leben zwischen dem Tode und der neuen Geburt im Verhaeltnis zu den kosmischen Tatsachen*, publ. Berlin 1916, Dornach, 1936. Translated as *The Life between Death and Rebirth in Relation to Cosmic Facts*, London, 1930. Rosicrucian references in lectures 1, 5, 10 especially. (Schmidt #2643+)

*December 18, 1912 — Neuchâtel — Members' Lecture — *Christian Rosenkreutz*, publ. in *Die Mission des Christian Rosenkreuz*, Dornach 1947, also in *Das esoterische Christentum*, Dornach, 1962. Translated as *The Mission of Christian Rosenkreutz, its Character and Purpose*, publ. in *The Mission of Christian Rosenkreutz*, London, 1950, p. 81 *seq.* (Schmidt #2665)

*December 19, 1912 — St. Gallen — Members' Lecture — *Das Leben nach dem Tode*, publ. in *Die Mission des Christian Rosenkreutz*, Dornach, 1947, and *Das esoterische Christentum*, Dornach, 1692. Translated as *The Starry Heaven above Me — the Moral Law within Me*, in *Christian Rosenkreutz*, London, 1950, p. 74 *seq.* (Schmidt #2666)

*February 6 — March 20, 1917 — Berlin. Cycle of 7 Lectures publ. as *Kosmische und menschliche Metamorphose*, Berlin 1921, 3rd enlarged ed., Dornach, 1961. Traslated as *Cosmic and Human Metamorphoses*, London, 1926. Lecture 4 contains important reference to *The Chymical Wedding of Christian Rosenkreutz*. (Schmidt #3340+)

*March 27 to April 24, 1917 – Berlin – Cycle of 8 Lectures titled *Bausteine zu einer Erkenntnis des Mysteriums von Golgotha*, 3rd ed., Dornach, 1961. Translated as *Building Stones for an Understanding of the Mystery of Golgotha*, London, 1945. Note especially lecture 7, p. 116. (Schmidt #3354)

July 31 – September 25, 1917 – Berlin, Cycle of 9 Lectures, publ. as *Das Karma des Materialismus*, Berlin 1922, especially Lectures 8 and 9 with reference to *The Chymical Wedding of Christian Rosenkreutz*. (Schmidt #3392+)

September 30, 1917 – Dornach, Members' Lecture – Publ. as Lecture 2 in *Die spirituellen Hintergruende der aeusseren Welt*, Dornach, 1933, 1941. Important indications on the Rosicrucian writings and J. V. Andreae. (Schmidt #3042)

*October 1917 to April 1918: An article titled *Die Chymische Hochzeit des Christian Rosenkreutz* by Rudolf Steiner in *Das Reich*, Munich. Reprinted (with corrections) in *Die Drei*, Stuttgart, 1927, Nos. 3, 4, 5. This article was included in Dr. Walter Weber's edition of *Die Chymische Hochzeit des Christian Rosenkreutz*, Dornach, 1942, revised ed., Stuttgart, 1957. From the latter edition the English translation – the first to be published – appearing in the present volume, was made.

June 25 and July 16, 1918 – Berlin –Lectures from Cycle 50, publ. as *Gesunder Blick fuer Heute und wackere Hoffnung fuer Morgen*, Berlin, 1922. These two lectures contain important details concerning Andreae and *The Chymical Wedding of Christian Rosenkreutz*. (Schmidt #3534, 3540)

*January 13, 1923 – Dornach – Members' Lecture –*Salz, Sulphur und Merkuprozesse im Menschen*. Publ. in *Das Goetheanum*, 1930, 9 Jahrg., Nr. 21-22, also in *Das Suchen nach der Welt*, usw., Dornach, 1943 and in *Ueber Gesundheit und Krankheit*, Dornach, 1959. Translated as *Salt, Mercury and Sulphur*, publ. in *Anthroposophy Quarterly*, 1931, Vol. 6, No. 1, p. 1 *seq*. Valuable indications concerning Jacob Boehme with indirect reference to the Rosicrucian theme.

*December 9, 21, 22, 1923 – Dornach – Members' Lectures publ. in *Mysteriengestaltungen*, Dornach, 1931, 1958. Translated as *Mystery Centers*, London, 1943, pp. 72, 101, 117 *seq*. The lecture of Dec. 9th contains important material on Andreae and *The Chymical Wedding;* those of Dec. 21 and 23 deal with *The Rosicrucian Mysteries*. (Schmidt #s 5504, 5513, 5517)

*January 4-13, 1924 – Dornach – Members' Lectures – *Mysterienstaetten des Mittelalters, Rosenkreuzertum and modernes Einweihungsprinzip*, Dornach, 1932 and *Die Weltgeschichte in anthroposophischer Beleuchtung*, usw., Dornach, 1962. Translated as *Rosicrucianism and Modern Initiation*, 6 lectures in *Christian Rosenkreutz*, London, 1950, p. 91 *seq*. revised transl. 1965. (Schmidt #5564+)

*March 23, 1924 – Dornach – Members' Lecture. Publ. in *Esoterische Betrachtungen karmischer Zusammenhaenge, Erster Band*, Dornach 1927, 3rd ed., 1959. Translated as Lecture 12 in *Karmic Relationships, Esoteric Studies, Vol. 1*, London, 1955, p. 189 *seq*. Important reference to Andreae and *The Chymical Wedding*. (Schmidt #5645)

*December 6, 1924 — Dornach — Letter to the Members — publ. in *Das Michael-Mysterium*, Dornach, 1930, and in *Anthroposophische Leitsaetze*, Dornach, 1954, p. 207 *seq.* Translated into English as *The Michael Mystery*, London, 1956, p. 75 *seq.* An important reference to the Rosicrucian impulse.

Geometrical Figures of the Rosicrucians, a plate from Michael Maier's *Atalanta Fugiens,* 1618. Indicating that "explanation" and "interpretation" of such figures of symbols is "quite nonsensical," Rudolf Steiner said that under the guidance of his teacher, the early Rosicrucian student learned "to *make* them, to *experience* them with his body . . . and thereby he learned to know the true and authentic World Geometry, learned to know how forces have been inscribed into the world by divine spiritual beings. Thus he came to understand the *forms* at work in the objects of the world."

Castle Karlstejn — an aerial view, 1960.

Castle Karlstejn. From a watercolor made in the late 18th century. The castle was erected in 1348-1365 for Emperor Charles IV by the Architect, Matthias of Arras, from Avignon, and his successors.

Castle Karlstejn Today. From a photograph made in the summer of 1965. Passing through two gateways one enters the lower castle; from there a gate leads to the upper castle. On the right are living rooms of Charles IV, with the Nicholas Chapel and Canons' House nearby. A covered passage leads to the Tower of our Lady, in which is the Church of Mary, with its Apocalypse paintings, and the Catherine Chapel. On the highest level of the rocky platform is the massive Citadel, on the third floor of which is the Chapel of the Cross, 1365. On the walls of the stairway leading up to this chapel are frescoes of greatest Rosicrucian interest.

Interior of the Catherine Chapel at Karlstejn. The walls are inlaid with over 1,000 semi-precious stones. Here the Emperor, Charles IV spent many hours in prayer and meditation.

The Bohemian and German King and Emperor, Charles IV. A limestone bust, one of a series of 21 donors to the building of the Cathedral of Prague, carved by Peter Parler in 1380.

Charles IV (1346-1378), described by Rudolf Steiner as "the last Initiate on the throne of the Emperors." This contemporary engraving, preserved in the Imperial Library, Vienna, shows the Emperor in court dress.

Charles IV receiving from the Dauphin of France a holy relic of two Thorns of Christ enclosed in a reliquary in the form of a single crystal. From a fresco on the south wall of the Maria Church at Castle Karlstejn, 1356.

The Emperor Charles IV examining a reliquary Cross on an altar. From a fresco in the Maria Church at Castle Karlstejn, 1356.

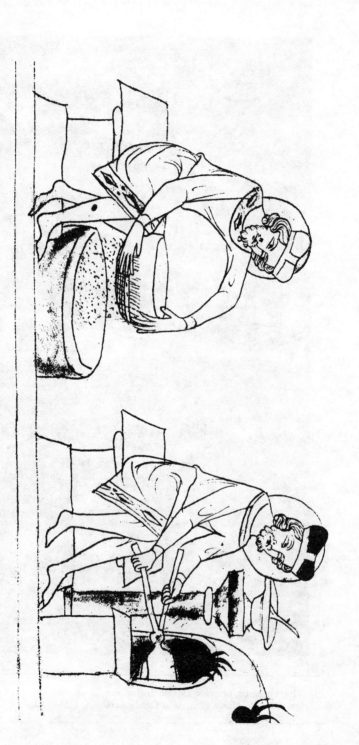

Wenceslas sifts flour and bakes bread for sacramental use. From *Wenceslas' Picture Bible*, a rare ms. volume in the Library of Prince Lobkovitz, Prague. This drawing is contemporary with the frescoes reproduced on the opposite page.

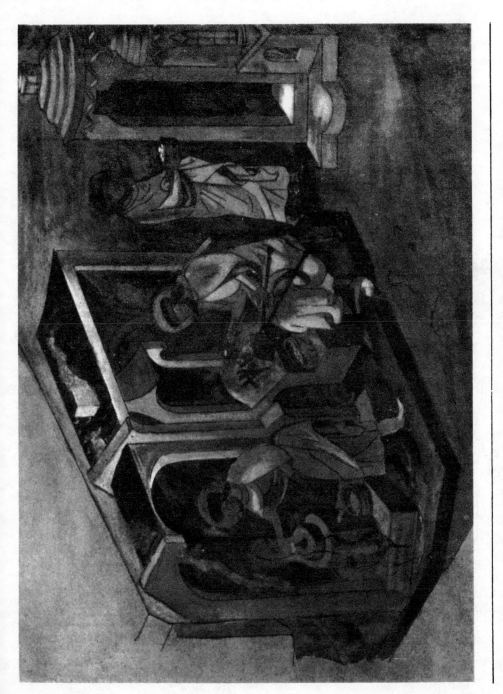

Scenes from the Life of Wenceslas, Patron-Saint of Bohemia, d. 935. These frescoes on the wall of the stairway in Karlstejn Rudolf Steiner described as scenes from *The Chymical Wedding* "in primitive form." Wenceslas is seen grinding the wheat, baking and carrying the completed wafers into the chapel (shown as the round Romanesque-style building originally standing on site of present Cathedral of Prague) to be used in the Sacrament. The frescoes were painted by Nicholas Wurmser of Strassburg, whom Charles IV invited to Karlstejn for this work in 1359.

Wenceslas Harvesting Grapes for Sacramental Wine. A drawing from the *Wenceslas' Picture Bible* ms. in the Library of Prince Lobkovitz, Prague. Compare with the Karlstein fresco on opposite page.

Wenceslas Harvesting Grapes. Photograph of the fresco by Nicholas Wurmser of Strassburg, 1359, in the stairway at Castle Karlstejn.

Scenes from the Life of Wenceslas from a codex in the Imperial Library Vienna,
These drawings are contemporary with the frescoes of Castle Karlstejn.

Drawings from a Codex in the Imperial Library, Vienna, contemporary with Nicholas Wurmser's frescoes at Karlstejn. The seven angelic maidens in the upper plate are reminiscent of the seven virgins in *The Chymical Wedding*. In the lower plate Wenceslas harvests wheat and grapes for sacramental use.

Castle Karlstejn — a photograph taken in 1960.

ON CASTLE KARLSTEIN AND ITS
ROSICRUCIAN CONNECTIONS

An Extract from an Article

by

ITA WEGMAN, M.D.

In the immediate neighborhood of Prague is the castle
of Karlstejn, the building of which was begun by Charles
IV in 1348. The castle lies in a beautiful district about an
hour from Prague, surrounded by four hills and steep rocky
promontories.

When we study this building and all that is preserved
there from the past, there unfolds before us a history, the
significance of which it is well to know. That such a castle
stands there as a monument of the past, in Bohemia of all
countries, gives food for thought. For the castle was at the
same time a center for spiritual rites. Why did it arise just in
this district, in the very heart of Bohemia?

We find that there is a wealth of ores and silicious crystals in Bohemia and in the mountains that enclose the country. In the west, in the "Bohemian Forest," great quantities
of silica crystals are to be found, especially in the form of
pure quartz and in the many kinds of semi-precious stones,
varied according to the metals that enter into their formation.

On the other hand, to the northwest in the *Erzgebirge* in
the neighborhood of Joachimstal, we find silver, gold and
radioactive substances, for example the uranium ore, pich-
blende. To the north as far as the Silesian border, lead, tin
and iron abound; and in Moravia itself mainly iron. In earlier epochs when the cosmic forces were able to work still
more freely and uninterruptedly, the powers of all these
minerals and especially of the metals exercised their influence

upon Bohemia. Thus Charles IV, who was among the last of the German Emperors possessing esoteric wisdom, could feel an inner impulse to erect in the midst of this land where such forces worked together, a castle that was to serve not only as a home but as a place of holy ritual and for the protection of valuable and sacred relics, State papers and precious stones.

What impresses one at once when visiting the castle is the interior decoration. The adornment of the walls in the various chapels to be found in the castle, with their quantities of semi-precious stones and gold, the way the light is diffused through these semi-precious stones which — set in gilded lead — take the place of window glass, lead one to conclude that Charles IV knew about the powers of precious stones and of gold. The small Chapel of St. Catherine, for example, is a veritable gem. The entire walls up to the ceiling are inlaid with semi-precious stones such as amethyst, jaspar, cornelian and agate, while the cross-vaulting above has a blue background adorned with roses, according to the Rosicrucian motif. According to tradition it was here that Charles IV withdrew every year from Good Friday to Easter Sunday in order to meditate in undisturbed privacy. To describe all the wealth of beauty to be seen at Karlstejn would require much space, and therefore we shall mention only what particularly concerns our subject. We come, therefore, to a tower connected by a bridge with the castle, which, separated from the actual palace, rises like a mighty fortress on a height somewhat further away, towering over the whole. At the very top of the tower is the Chapel of the Holy Cross. The staircase leading to this Chapel is adorned with frescoes on the surrounding walls, said to represent the life of St. Ludmila on the right, and on the left the life of King Wenceslas, the ruler of Bohemia who died a martyr's death in 936, and who has been regarded as the patron saint of Prague ever since.

Dr. Steiner once said of these frescoes that they represent *The Chymical Wedding of Christian Rosenkreutz* in a primitive form, and in looking at the several pictures one can well recognize the various phases of *The Chymical Wedding,*

— for example, the picture of the releasing of the prisoner from his chains and letting him go from the Tower, or the representation of St. Wenceslas sowing seed in the night, harvesting, and threshing the grain, milling the wheat and baking the sacred wafers himself. All this represents an alchemical process, carried out during the night, — a process connected with Earth, Air, Fire and Water. — Again there is the picture of the Burial of the Dead. Here where St. Wenceslas is serving out the food to the invited guests, we recognize the invitation to the marriage feast, and we can also see how the picture of the Last Supper in the life of St. Wenceslas is taken from the feast of the worthy and unworthy spiritual seekers in *The Chymical Wedding.*

Finally, there is the holy man's execution, in which the beheading, the piercing with the spear and the dismembering of the body remind one of the experiences of Initiation.

After the ascent of the Tower we arrive, as already described, at a Chapel — a Chapel of the Grail — which in Karlstejn is called "The Chapel of the Holy Cross." From Dr. Steiner's words we know that indeed we have here before us a kind of Chapel of the Grail. Wonderful is the ascent from the way of Initiation to the Chapel above. It shines before us in magnificent splendor. The windows are formed of pure topazes, amethysts and almandines. The entire ceiling is gilded, representing the vault of Heaven with sun, moon and many stars interspersed among the roses mentioned above. The walls are inlaid from the floor upward to a height of a little over three feet with polished semi-precious stones, with amethysts, red chalcedony, agates and jaspar, and above that with yet more pictures. All this makes an overpowering impression.

Thus it can be considered certain that the individuality of St. Weceslas was connected in some way with Christian Rosenkreutz, and if we compare still further the separate legends from the life of St. Wenceslas with true Rosicrucianism, we shall find everywhere the same relationship. In St. Wenceslas, the patron saint of Prague, who died on Michaelmas, the 28th of September, 937, the figure of a true Rosicrucian appears before us. Michael stands near him and when we realize that St. George's Church in Prague dates also from this period, then indeed Prague becomes for us today — and rightly so — a center of spiritual inspiration and of great interest.

Reliquary Cross with crown, scepter, orb and ceremonial sword belonging to Charles IV, builder of Castle Karlstejn.

LE COMTE DE St GERMAIN
CÉLÈBRE ALCHIMISTE:

THE COUNT OF ST. GERMAIN
From an 18th century engraving made in Paris. The son of Francis II of the House of Rakoczy, often called "The Prince of Transylvania" (1676-1735), and Princess Maria Amelia of Hesse-Rheinfels (married 1694). Their son, born about 1710, was christened Josephus Germanus, and was later known as the Count of St. Germain, the last prince of the House of Rakoczy. Rudolf Steiner identified him as one of the incarnations of Christian Rosenkreutz.

AN ANNOTATED BIBLIOGRAPHY
OF BOOKS AND ARTICLES OF
ROSICRUCIAN INTEREST

Compiled by
PAUL M. ALLEN

The following titles represent only a very small selection out of the vast body of literature in many languages on the general subject of Rosicrucianism. A number of the items are included because they have been of help in preparation of this Anthology, or because they point the way to further study of themes indicated in the text. Some of the books listed contain extensive bibliographies which will enable the student to pursue his particular area of interest in this broad field of research.

Adams, George: *The Mysteries of the Rose Cross, The Spiritual Guidance of Europe and the Three in One.* An article publ. in *Anthroposophy Quarterly*, London, Vol. 3, No. 1, Easter, 1928, p. 12 *seq.* A study of the backgrounds of the Rosicrucian Mysteries, based on indications by Rudolf Steiner.

Adams, George: *The Rosicrucian Mystery*, an article in *Anthroposophy Quarterly*, London, 1931, Vol. 6, No. 1, p. 41 *seq.* A discussion of the Rosicrucian themes in Rudolf Steiner's first Mystery Drama, *The Portal of Initiation.*

Ashmole, Elias (Ed.): *Theatrum Chemicum Britannicum*, London, . 1652. (Xerox reprints currently available). Alchemical tracts with introduction by Ashmole in which the Rosicrucians are discussed. Illustrated by Thomas Vaughan.

Bennell, M. and Wyatt, I.: *An Introductory Commentary on The Chymical Wedding of Christian Rosenkreutz*, England n.d. (1965). A report based on a course of study of the principal themes of the work in the light of Rudolf Steiner's indications.

Blaschka, Anton (Transl. and Editor): *Kaiser Karls V Jugendleben und St.-Wenzels-Legende*, Weimar, 1956. The story of the builder of Castle Karlstein.

Boehme, Jacob: *Collected Works.* The standard 10 volume edition edited by Ueberfeld, 1730, including the mystical plates from the earlier Gichtel edition of 1682 is now available in reprint form. The original *English translations* by Ellistone and Sparrow were included in the so-called "Law Edition" (which William Law did *NOT* edit!) publ. in late 18th century. Reprints of some of these translations were published in London, 1900-1924. Boehme's connection with the Rosicrucians has been defended by Peuckert in his biography of Jacob Boehme. Albert Steffen pointed out in an essay that Dr. Balthaser Walter who suggested the title for Boehme's first work, *The Aurora*, was an important Rosicrucian.

Caron, M. and Hutin, S.: *The Alchemists*, transl. from French by H. R. Lane, New York and London, 1961. A well-illustrated, reliable introduction to the story of Alchemy, including useful bibliographic references to Alchemy and related subjects.

Craven, J. C.: *Count Michael Maier, Doctor of Philosophy, Medicine, Alchemist, Rosicrucian, Mystic*, London, 1910. An excellent and reliable study of the great Rosicrucian apologist, whose *Silentium Post Clamores* (Frankfort, 1617) was one of the earliest and most important works on the subject.

Craven, J. B.; *Doctor Robert Fludd, The English Rosicrucian*. The Life and Writings of the great apologist of the Rosicrucians, illustrated from his works. London, 1902, reprint, New York, n.d. A reliable and standard work containing, among other things, synopses of the contents of Fludd's works, otherwise available only in Latin.

Dee, John: *The Hieroglyphic Monad*, transl. by J. W. Hamilton-Jones, London, 1947. The famous work of 1564 in which is discussed "the sign" of the invitation to *The Chymical Wedding*, "Hieroglyphically, Mathematically, Magically, Cabbalistically and Anagogically explained." An important source-book.

De Quincy, Thomas: *Historico-Critical Inquiry into the Origin of the Rosicrucians and the Freemasons*, London Magazine, Vol. IX, January to June, 1824, reprinted London, 1886. A very interesting study by an English man of letters, indicating interest in the subject in the early 19th century.

Eckartshausen, Karl von: *The Cloud upon the Sanctuary*. Transl. from German, London, 1919, many reprints exist. A famous devotional work often considered to have Rosicrucian overtones.

Ferguson, John: *Bibliotheca Chemica*, 2 Vols., Glasgow, 1904, reprinted London, 1954. A world-famous authority concerning books on Alchemy and related subjects. The section (in Vol. 2) on *Christian Rosenkreutz* and on *The Rosicrucians*, with all cross-references indicated, is a "must" for anyone wishing to have details on biographical data, early editions, translations, etc. in this area of study. Entirely objective and completely reliable.

Gleich, Sigismund von: *Marksteine der Kulturgeschichte*, 2nd Ed., Stuttgart, 1963. Important details concerning the Rosicrucian connections with the Middle East and the journeys there of Christian Rosenkreutz as recorded in the *Confessio*. See esp. p. 152 and 157, etc.

Gleich, Sigismund von: *Die Wahrheit als Gesamtumfang aller Weltansichten*, Stuttgart, 1957. Many references to Christian Rosenkreutz and the Rosicrucians, esp. p. 149 and 260.

Gottschalk, Eduard G.: *Joachim Jungius und sein Zeitalter*, Stuttgart, 1850. Gives a very comprehensive account of the relations between Jungius and Johann Valentin Andreae. Reliable reference work.

Hall, Manly Palmer: *An Encyclopedic Outline of Masonic, Hermetic, Qabbalistic and Rosicrucian Symbolical Philosophy — The Secret Teach-

ings of all Ages, California, 1928, 12th facsimile ed., 1959. A wealth of details and illustrations bearing on the general subject and relating to the Rosicrucians, ably presented. A monumental and indispensable reference text.

Hall, Manly P.: *Codex Rosae Crucis*, publ. California, 1938. A rare and curious manuscript of Rosicrucian interest together with many illustrations from early books and mss. of the Order. With introduction and commentary. A very scholarly, objective presentation, essential to understanding the role of Rosicrucianism in Colonial America.

Heckethorn, Charles W.: *Secret Societies of All Ages and Countries*, 2 vols., London, 1897, Reprinted, New York, 1965. A useful reference work, providing vast information on the subject. The Rosicrucian references appear on pp. 219 and 234-41 of Vol. 1.

Heydon, John: *The English Physician's Guide, or The Holy Guide*, London, 1662. A fabulous account of "Rosicrucians", resembling Arabian Nights stories. But Heydon's book — along with his *Wise Man's Crowne, or the Glorie of the Rosie-Cross*, which he claimed was a translation of the famous "Book M" of Christian Rosenkreutz himself — nevertheless served to bring the Rosicrucian ideas to the attention of many readers in 17th century England. It well may be that Heydon, after all, deserves far better treatment than he has received at the hands of writers on Rosicrucian history — A.E. Waite among them!

Heyer, Karl: *Geschichtsimpulse des Rosenkreuzertums*, 2nd ed., Kressbronn, Bodensee, 1959. A very useful reference work of accuracy and insight into the whole subject.

Higgins, Godfrey: *Anacalypsis, An Attempt to Draw Aside the Veil of the Saitic Isis, or an Inquiry into the Origin of Languages, Nations and Religions*, 2 vols., London, 1836, Reprint, New York, 1965. One of the greatest of all works on this subject, Rosicrucian references are included.

Jennings, Hargrave: *The Rosicrucians, their Rites and Mysteries*, London, 1887. A generous mixture of fact and fancy, nevertheless this book is important to the subject. Has been described by competent authorities as of no use from a scholarly point of view.

Khunrath, Heinrich: *Amphitheatrum Sapientiae Aeternae . . . etc.*, Hanover, 1609. This is one of the "association texts" of great interest to students of Rosicrucian matters particularly because of the 10 symbolic engravings, 9 of them double, which the work contains. It is of interest that Johann Arndt, mystic and author of *True Christianity* (containing a number of mystical plates) wrote a detailed commentary on the first 4 plates in Khunrath's book. This commentary appears in *Chymisches-Lust-Gaertlein*, an anthology publ. in 1747. Johann Valentin Andreae in his *Mythologia Christiana* (1619) mentions Arndt with appreciation. Plates from Khunrath's book are included among the illustrations in this present volume.

Kienast, Richard: *Joh. Val. Andreae und die vier echten Rosenkreutzerschriften*. Published in the periodical, *Palaestra*, Number 152, edited by Brand and Roethe, publ. by Verlag Mayer and Mueller, Leipzig, 1926. A work frequently quoted and which contains a good bibliography of further Rosicrucian interest.

Kirchweger, Anton Joseph: *Aurea Catena Homeri*, etc., Frankfurt, 1723; Leipzig, 1728, etc. This is the famous *Golden Chain of Homer* which Goethe valued highly (see *Dichtung und Wahrheit, Poetry and Truth*, Book VIII(. Kirchweger was a physician at Gmunden, Upper Austria, died 1746. Herwerd von Forchenbrunn, *Landphysicus* in Moravia, teacher of medicine at Cromau, has also been suggested as author. Another writer states that it was written c. 1654 by "a Rosicrucian of Utrecht" and that "the Ms. lay a long time in the Imperial Library, Vienna." The title is from *The Iliad*, VIII, v. 17-26 where Homer speaks of a chain that binds earth to the Summit of Olympus, calling it "the Chain of the World." Similar titles were used for medieval alchemical studies (among them one by Raimundus Lullus) and for later works with some Rosicrucian undertones. The book, however, made a tremendous impression in the 18th century when it appeared, and was often referred to by many writers. Though it has been called "a Rosicrucian instruction-book," it is difficult to see why it merits this designation over many other works more qualified for the distinction.

Lehrs, Ernst: *The Rosicrucian Foundations of the Age of Natural Science*. An article publ. as Supplement to *Anthroposophical Movement*, London, 1934, Vol. XI, No. 23, Supplement No. 4. Valuable information on Andreae, Jungius, Lord Bacon and Goethe in the light of Rosicrucian impulses.

Maack, Ferdinand (Editor): *Die Chymischen Hochzeit des Christian Rosenkreutz*, Verlag Barsdorf, Berlin, 1913, 1922. The introduction to this edition of *The Chymical Wedding* is discussed (without enthusiasm!) by Rudolf Steiner in the 8th lecture of the cycle, *Secrets of the Threshold*.

Maurer, Theodore: *Die Seelenpruefung in der Chymischen Hochzeit des Christian Rosenkreuz*. An article in *Das Goetheanum*, 15 Jahrg., Nr. 10, March 8, 1936, p. 75 *seq*. An important study in the light of Rudolf Steiner's indication — particularly concerning the role of the Seven Liberal Arts in *The Chymical Wedding*.

Maurer, Theodore: *Die Wandegemaelde im Treppenhaus der Gralsburg Karlstein*. An article in *Das Goetheanum*, 7 Jahrg., Nr. 21, May 20, 1928, p. 162 *seq*.

Neuwirth, Joseph: *Mittelalterliche Wandgemaelde und Tafelbilder der Burg Karlstein in Boehmen*, 2 Vols., Prague, 1896. A remarkable study of the frescoes in Castle Karlstein by a great 19th century authority on the subject. The more than 50 plates illustrating the work are not of the best reproduction, but nevertheless this work will repay careful study. Though it is rare today, copies can be consulted in larger libraries, especially those specializing in Art.

Oakley, Isabel Cooper—: *The Comte de St.-Germain*, publ. Milan, 1912. A remarkable book, based on outstandingly important source materials, among them the "Mitchell Papers" in the British Museum, records of the French court, diplomatic reports, etc. Unquestionably the best biography of St.-Germain in English. Steinerbooks 1970, Reprint.

Palmer, Otto: *Bulwer-Lytton, A Study*. An article in *The Golden Blade*, an annual. London, 1953, p. 62, *seq. Also* see the article, *The Hibernian Mysteries and "Zanoni"* by John Muller in *The Golden Blade*, London, 1960, p. 79 *seq*. These articles give indications concerning the Rosicrucian themes in the life and writings of Bulwer-Lytton in the light of Rudolf Steiner's statements.

Paracelsus of Hohenheim: *Hermetic and Alchemical Writings of Paracelsus*, 2 vols., London, Ed. by A. E. Waite. Excellent source material. The best Paracelsus Anthology in English is *Paracelsus, Selected Writings*, Ed. by J. Jacobi, illustr. with 150 contemporary woodcuts.

Peuckert, Will-Erich: *Pansophie, ein Versuch zur Geschichte der weissen und schwarzen Magic*, Stuttgart, 1936. Important references to the Rosicrucians, particularly in the 17th Century.

Peuckert, Will-Erich: *Die Rosenkreutzer*, Jena, 1928. A standard work on the subject; contains much interesting and useful material.

Philalethes, Eugenius (Trans.): *The Fame and Confession of the Fraternity R:C:, Commonly of the Rosie Cross*. A Facsimile of the London edition of 1652 (transl. by Thomas Vaughan) with Introd., Notes, and Transl. of the letter of *Adam Haselmeyer* to the Rosicrucian Brotherhood. Margate, 1923. A valuable reprint with important notes and references on the Rosicrucians.

Picht, C. S.: *Hinricus Madathanus* in *Gesammelte Aufsaetze, Briefe und Fragmente*, Stuttgart, 1964, p. 13 *seq.* An important result of scholarly research concerning the life and work of the compiler of *The Secret Symbols of the Rosicrucians*.

Regenstreif, Paul: *Beitraege zum Studium der von Rudolf Steiner gehaltenen Vortraege ueber Christian Rosenkreuz*. Privately issued, n.p., n.d. The editor of this present work gratefully acknowledges indebtedness to this remarkable compilation in preparing the section on *References to Christian Rosenkreutz in Lectures and Writings by Rudolf Steiner, 1903-1924.*

Regenstreif, Paul: *Ueber Christian Rosenkreuz. Hinwiese auf Angaben Rudolf Steiners fuer das eigene Studium*, an essay in *Mitteilungen aus der Anthroposophischen Arbeit im Deutschland*, 16 Jahrg. Heft 3, Nr. 61, Michaeli, 1962, pp. 145-161. (Stuttgart)

Sachse, Julius F.: *The German Pietists of Provincial Pennsylvania*, Philadelphia, 1895. Contains important material on Kelpius and other mystics from 17th century Germany whom Sachse identifies as "Rosicrucians." Much interesting data and unusual illustrations. This book is often overlooked by students interested in possible Rosicrucian influences in Colonial America.

Schweighardt, Theophilus: *Speculum Sophicum Rhodo-Strauroticum*, n.p., 1618. (Actual name of author given as Schweighardt Constantiens.) "An extensive explanation of the Collegium of the rules of the highly enlightened Brotherhood of the Rosicrucians." *The Speculum* contains 3 plates, the first is called "The Tree of Pansaophia" and is reproduced in the *Geheime Figuren der Rosenkreutzer*. One other plate (reproduced in this book) shows the *Collegium Fraternitatis*, the Temple of the Rosy Cross itself. This work was publ. 19 years before Comenius proposed such a "college of universal science" in his letter. *Prodromus Pansophiae.* In his *Bibliographie der Freimaurerei* (1844) Kloss says that one Daniel Moegling concealed himself under the names of Schweighardt and Florentinus da Valentia ("author" of *Jhesus Nobis Omnia*, — on the Rosicrucians — 1617). However, the very learned Gottfried Arnold in his *Kirchen und Ketzer Historien*, 1741,

Vol. II, p. 255 states directly that Florêntinius de Valentia was Valentin Andreae himself! — All of which gives rise to the question, Exactly who *was* the man who wrote under the name of Schweighardt and contributed to the *Secret Symbols of the Rosicrucians?*

Semler, Johann Solomon: *Unparteiische Samlungen zur Historie der Rosenkreutzer*, Leipzig, 1786-88. A professor of Theology at Halle, Semler (1725-1791) was a prolific writer, mainly on theological subjects. Meusel lists his works in 16 pages of close type, in his *Lexicon*, 1813 (pp. 89-107).

Steiner, Rudolf: See the special bibliographical section in this book titled *References to Christian Rosenkreutz in Lectures and Writings by Rudolf Steiner, 1903-1924.*

Trismosin, Solomon: *Splendor Solis, A.D., 1582.* Alchemical Treatises including 22 Allegorical Pictures. London, n.d., a reproduction of the original ms. in the British Museum, with Introd. and Notes by J. K. — An important work, reproducing "the most beautiful ms. in the entire British Museum collection" showing early Rosicrucian motifs.

Vaughan, Thomas: *The Works of Thomas Vaughan, Eugenius Philalethes.* Edited with Introd. by Arthur E. Waite. London, 1919. Indispensable for an understanding of Rosicrucian backgrounds in 17th century England.

Wachsmuth, Guenther: *The Life and Work of Rudolf Steiner*, New York, 1955. This work contains many references to Christian Rosenkreutz, especially pages 53-58. Further references will be found on p. 592 under "Rosicrucianism."

Waite, Arthur E.: *The Brother of the Rosy Cross*, London, 1924, reprint edition, New York, n.d. A helpful reference book, containing much otherwise inaccessible material on the Rosicrucians. The reader must be alert, however, to separate Mr. Waite's presentation of objective historical, documented facts from his often unfounded prejudices. — And it often requires considerable care to distinguish clearly between the two! — Excellent bibliographical data is contained in the footnotes throughout the book.

Waite, Arthur E.: *The Real History of the Rosicrucians*, London, 1887. A valuable reference text containing translations and renderings of early Rosicrucian writings; one of the best 19th century books on the subject, much more objective and useful than his other work listed above.

Weber, Walter (Editor): *Die Chymische Hochzeit des Christian Rosenkreuz Anno 1459* with Essay by Rudolf Steiner. Publ. Dornach, 1942, revised and enlarged ed., Stuttgart, 1957. The standard, scholarly text, including valuable reference notes. This present volume owes much to this work and to the painstaking efforts of Dr. Weber to present the essence of true Rosicrucianism in modern form.

Wyatt, Isabel: *The Buddha Stream in Christian Times,* an article in *The Anthroposophical Quarterly*, London, Vol. 9, No. 4, Winter 1964, p. 235 *seq.* Valuable indications on the "Illumination of Christian Rosenkreutz."

The early Rosicrucians said, "The Stone of the Philosophers is to be found everywhere, yet is fully unknown; it is both noblest and lowliest, mineral and not mineral; it has a special relationship to fire . . ." — Rudolf Steiner explained that "Carbon played an enormous role in the ancient Mysteries, for it was called the Stone of the Wise, the Philsopher's Stone. Carbon appears on earth in many forms — as diamond, graphite, coke, coal, and so on." — This illustration from Michael Maier's *Atalanta Fugiens*, 1618, shows the Philosopher's Stone as present everywhere — under men's feet, in the heavens, on water, on the hillsides.

ABRAHAM VON FRANCKENBERG (1594-1652) From a painting in the Stadtbibliothek, Breslau. Remembered as the friend and first biographer of Jacob Boehme, von Franckenberg has been identified as a leadng figure in Rosicrucian circles in Silesia during his lifetime. He studied law and mathematics at Leipzig, Wittenberg and Jena, and later gained considerable importance as an alchemist, Paracelsian chemist, cabbalist and as the author of numerous Rosicrucian works, some of which remain in ms. in the Library at Breslau.

DANIEL STOLCIUS
AND
HIS PLEASURE GARDEN
OF CHYMISTRY

(Notes by the Editor)

In July 1623 a young medical graduate of the Universities of Prague and Magdeburg had settled himself in Oxford and was completing a book which has made his name famous. Enroute to England from his native Bohemia which was then experiencing the horrors of the onset of the Thirty Years' War, Daniel Stolcius had visited the studio of the famous engraver-publisher, Lucas Jennis in Frankfort a.M. There Jennis showed him a large collection of copper engravings used by him over the past few years to illustrate works on Alchemy which he had published. Stolcius showed such interest in the plates that Jennis offered him permission to use as many as he wished to illustrate a work of his own, suggesting that he write Latin verses interpreting each of the engravings. Stolcius finally selected 107 of the finest drawings, and took them along with him to Oxford.

In the following year — 1624 — a little pocket-volume about 3 by 6 inches in size titled *Viridarium Chymicum*, with Latin verses by Stolcius was published by Jennis. A German translation followed almost at once, and the book has rightly been described as "a pictorial encyclopedia of 17th century Alchemy."

Intended, as the original preface tells us, "not only to please the eye and amuse the mind, but also to arouse a deeper contemplation of Nature," this is one of the rarest of all works of its kind and is of great Rosicrucian interest as well. The works of two of the leading Rosicrucians of the 17th century were the source of the plates in *The Pleasure*

Garden of Chymistry, as Stolcius wrote: "Thank the cherished memory of the very famous and learned Herr Michael Maier, the most celebrated Doctor of Physic and Medicine for part of the illustrations, and Master Daniel Mylius, that industrious Chymist, for the rest."

Indeed, the series of 107 plates of Stolcius' work — published in their entirety in the following pages — are taken from works of Maier and Mylius published by Jennis between 1616 and 1624. In other words, the engravings reproduced here first appeared at the same time as *The Chymical Wedding of Christian Rosenkreutz,* and are an exceedingly valuable help in appreciating and understanding many of the motifs included in the latter work.

The First Key of Basilius Valentinus

The crown of the king shall be
　Of gold, beautiful, pure, and clear.
　　　　A chaste bride is led to her groom;
　　　　That is as it ought to be.

Then give to eat to the king the grey wolf
That wants to eat continuously.
　　　　This do three times with a strong fire;
　　　　Burn the wolf entirely.

Then the king will come forth;
Without a blemish, clean, he will stand before you.
　　　　He can decorate you wth his blood,
　　　　And renovate you.

The Other Key of Basilius

When the garment is taken off.
　Then the sun appears.
　　　Diana no longer wears her garment,
　　　So that marriage becomes more desirable.

From two noble fencers
The bride receives delicious water,
　　　So that she can bathe her own body
　　　For her groom.

The fighters may well fight.
But if the fight comes to an end on both sides,
　　　The fighters bring out of the fight
　　　Treasures and great booty.

The Third Key of Basilius

From the rocks unite
  The eagle with the dragon,
    So that he extract his white feathers.
    Solve with greatest zeal.

Remember, preserve the sulphur
With the astral salt,
    So that the cock in this way
    May devour the sly fox.

And that he drown in the water
And become alive again through fire,
    Again to be eaten
    By the fox entirely.

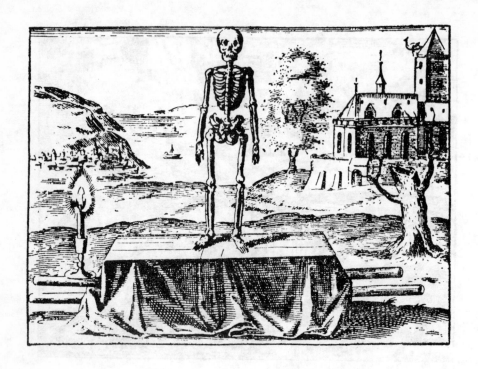

The Fourth Key of Basilius

All flesh that came into the world
Took its origin from the earth.
    It must again become earth,
    And consequently also ashes.

A salt will come from the earth
That causes the flesh to ensue:
    Which in the mentioned manner
    Is resolved with greatest zeal.

If you desire politely
To see the form again,
    Then give to the salt
    The sulphur and the mercury.

The Fifth Key of Basilius

The earth for itself brings
Nothing to the light of day.
    The spirit must maintain
    Everything and give it life.

This spirit has its beginning
In the heavenly stars.
    Therefore, all metals receive
    At once plenty of force and effect.

The stone is strong and unites
In love with the iron.
    Our generous lion
    Greatly loves our mercury.

The Sixth Key of Basilius

If woman is joined to man,
From the seed, fruit she bears:
    When Neptune has perfectly
    Prepared its watery bath.

Then a doubly fiery man
Must be fed with a white swan;
    Together must they kill themselves
    And become alive again.

The four winds will roar
So that the king, with great honor,
    Through fire is united with the bride
    That trusts him.

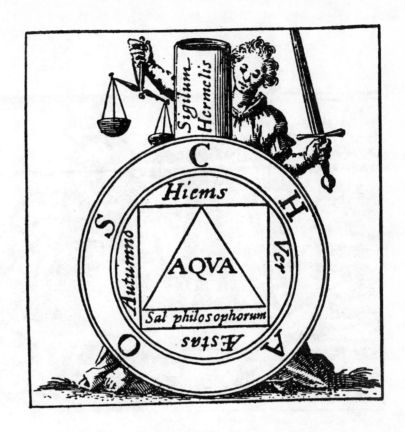

The Seventh Key of Basilius

Spring, summer, and autumn,
Winter, water, and the white salt
    Produce through the light of the sun
    Our work and the admixture.

Provided that you in weight
Use not too much nor too little.
    Because then it would surely happen
    That your work will not succeed.

Also seal the glass
With the hermetic seal
    So that the material
    Will not be eaten by the winds.

The Eighth Key of Basilius

The seed is laid into the earth
  For its decay.
     In the grave our bodies lie hidden
     Without worries, so that they come again.

You can find all the elements
In one single element:
     If you only know how, in such things,
     To bring also everything out of one.

This is the purpose and aim of the work
And the premise of our great labors.
     If you direct now adroitly the arrow
     Then you will have the treasures of the key.

The Ninth Key of Basilius

See to it that three serpents
Come forth from three hearts,
    After you have sealed them
    Up in a glass container.

In such things Venus will then
Bring a beautiful peacock's tail
    And also regale your eyes
    With a white swan.

Then, added to Saturnus, the
Black raven will do its damage,
    And the eagle's feather will
    Grow beautiful and fine.

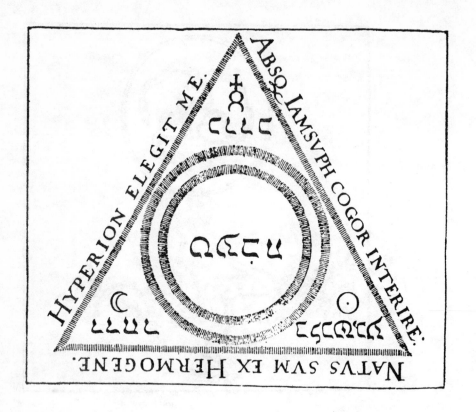

The Tenth Key of Basilius

In the beginning the sun must give
The life to Hermogeni.
　　The moon with its kind and shine
　　Will help Hyperion.

Mercury must suffer much
So that he die and be destroyed
　　If not you willingly add
　　To him its Iamsuph.

If you understand these words correctly,
Sing the praise of your Creator,
　　That He has gifted man with
　　Such reason and wisdom.

The Eleventh Key of Basilius

Orpheus took Euridice,
Or the brother took the sister,
        As his wife so that the blood
        From both bodies may become pure.

Thus, unite the sweat of father and mother,
When it is still warm, industriously.
        Let it enter into and seal it up at once
        In the globe of the white Master.

Then, with pleasure, you will see
The generous lion standing.
        It will see so many of its body's fruits
        That they cannot be counted.

The Last Key of Basilius

When then the lion
Has devoured the serpent:
    Then Mercury will produce
    A thousand fruits and flowers.

Because without the ferment of the gold
This stone cannot work.
    If it has found its way
    It will tincture that much more.

He who uses this means
Will persevere
    And he will see that through his sighs
    God will be willing toward him.

The Material of the
Philosopher's Stone

It is one thing, and through two
It is also three things;
    All these are but one.
    If you do not understand me, you will find none.

The dragon is not dear,
Because it is lazy and loses its power.
    But it has within itself
    The king's bourn and rich gifts.

There are two mercuries:
Quickly unite the volatile and fixed.
    It is one soul, one body, one spirit
    To which art and nature direct you.

Three Possessors of the

Philosopher's Stone

Here you see, dear reader,
Three artists of the highest art,
  Who through their zeal have succeeded
  In obtaining the stone, so highly esteemed.

The known Cremerus stands in the center,
Nortonus to the left,
  At the right Basilius;
  Their praise cannot be passed in silence.

Read zealously their works,
Then also use the vulcanic tools,
  If you want to pluck the golden apples
  In the land of the Hesperides.

Mercurius, a Lord of all
Worldly Things

The goose, the bee, the calf, and Mercurius,
  The silkworm and the sheep,
        As well as the mussel and the flax,
        Are worldly goods and riches.

Dear reader, I implore you,
Follow not many masters.
        Better beware of them and their burden,
        If you possess the knowledge of this art.

Remember that the other things are perishable.
Take care to serve God alone!
        Then seek with joyous courage
        Hermes' great good and treasure.

The Champions of Alchemy and the
Principle Alchemists of Twelve Nations

1. Hermes Trismegistus, called the Greatest,
an Egyptian.

Mercurius, also called Hermes,
Was a king in Egypt.
> On account of his character, office, art, and wisdom,
> He was the greatest of his times.

He has described a variety
Of beautiful things, wonderful ones, too.
> With wisdom he explained
> The excellence of the chemical art.

The father of the marital union is the sun;
The moon, however, is the mother.
> The third that directs it all
> Must be the fire.

Mary, the Hebrew Woman

Mary of the Jewish race
Is indeed a sister of Moses.
    She is very happy, and remains
    Amongst the number of chemists.

Many secrets were revealed to her
Through the stone.
    With her wise sayings
    She taught much good.

The smoke loves the haze
And the haze loves the smoke.
    But the white plant of the high mountain
    Partakes of both.

Democritus, a Greek

Democritus, often displayed
Much laughter.
    He laughed at all times at
    The vanity of the human heart.

Happily, this man had seen
Many foreign countries.
    He arrived at various riches
    And possibilities of nature.

He taught: That the mobile shadow
Is taken from the body;
    With constant fortune one will learn
    That they produce much fiery medicament.

Morienes, a Roman

Morienes did not care for
The pomp and pleasures of the world;
    Voluntarily he retired
    Into solitude.

The whole art he explained
In his dialogue with Calidius;
    Though to inexperienced people
    It remains a secret forever.

Take what you trample under your feet!
Because if you want to climb
    Without a ladder
    You will fall on your head.

Avicenna, an Arab

Avicenna was honored by the ancients
As a great prince
Of the medical art,
For he knew many things.

To the world he bared
The secrets of mastership.
He incorporated in his writings
Many fine sayings and words.

Unite a garden toad
With a flying eagle; then you will see
In our art, excellently,
The right mastership.

Albertus Magnus, a German

Albertus who was known far and near
Often carries this surname
    Because he was great in the art,
    Industrious and excellent.

He knew many arts
That he described,
    And to this day
    His name is greatly honored.

He says: Those who write of one
Agree in this:
    He has two kinds of organs
    And a twofold body.

Arnold Villanova, a Frenchman

Arnold when in Rome
Acquired the right gold
      And decided to give it
      The true test.

In chemistry, astrology, and medicine
He was proficient.
      His works prove clearly
      What a wise man he was.

He says: Our young son
Will issue from the marriage union,
      As the fruit of our bodies,
      A truly sweet child.

Thomas Aquinas, an Italian

Thomas Aquinas has the name of
Angelic Doctor:
  With his teachings
  He was known universally.

It is often claimed
That his teacher was Albertus Magnus.
  He has drawn freely
  From the bourn of the chemical art.

Like nature, namely, the art
Comes from mercury,
  So come all pure metals
  From the mixture with sulphur.

Raymund Lully, a Spaniard

Raymund confesses openly
That he finally came
    To the perfection of the chemical art
    Through the favors of his teacher Arnold.

In reason he was Proteus,
In philosophy Policletus,
    In art he equalled Daedalus,
    He was a great honor to the Spanish people.

He says: A man produces
The beautiful body of a child
    If he takes to his side
    A woman, as is usually the case.

Roger Bacon, an Englishman

Roger Bacon,
Though a monk,
    As professor at Oxford in England
    Was an honor to the arts.

The greatest wonder works
He put before our eyes,
    To be had by all
    In the course of nature.

If you give equal weight
Again to the elements,
    You will see with your own eyes
    Many gifts of his.

Melchior Cibinensis, a Hungarian

Melchior, called Cibinensis,
Was born in Hungary
    Though he was a priest
    He possessed the golden art.

In the form of the mass
He alone described the precious stone.
    Whether it be so, you may judge
    According to the the tenets of the artists.

Like a tender babe
Is nourished by the milk,
    So the precious stone
    Has to be fed with pure milk.

Michael Sendivogius, a Pole

Though this name in the past
  Has been kept in oblivion,
    Its praise now penetrates the darkness,
    As it ought to be, indeed.

Prague in Bohemia
Has well acknowledged his works.
    He has written twelve books
    And taught accordingly.

He said: Saturn
Himself must water the earth
    If it, dear sun and moon,
    Shall bear your beautiful flowers.

METEORIC THINGS

That is, all things that stay above

The elements produce
Many beautiful colors, dew, and rain,
  Thunder, hail, lightning, and wind;
  So experience teaches.

Thus the artist's stone gives
Many fine figures,
  That is, only in the glass,
  Illuminated by the light of the air.

Therefore, one can readily compare
The stone to dew and rain;
  Also to thunder, lightning, and fire,
  And even to fierce storms.

MINERAL THINGS

That is, what is dug out of and
found in the earth

How many precious stones,
How many metals, large and small,
   Are found deep in the earth!
   They must be sought with zeal.

Many important things you can have
Through your art and charity,
   If you desire to know well
   Their kind, birth, quality, and gender.

Yet without work, labor, and pain
Nothing is dug nor found.
   Thus you cannot without work
   Count such fine riches.

VEGETABLE THINGS

That is, what grows upon the earth

Like a garden greens beautifully
And bears many fine herbs,
   So also this our garden
   Bears many forms and kinds.

Here stand the beautiful hyacinth,
Also grapevines,
   Wheat and poppies,
   And red roses.

Golden apples and mulberry trees
Can here be found;
   Myrtle, laurel, olive trees, liquid-amber,
   And the prettiest saffron.

ANIMAL THINGS

That is, all that is animal and has

life, or the living creatures

Over hill and vale
Many animals walk and run.
The air carries many birds;
The water is full of fish.

But more important to the artists
Is the ram, bull, lion, and bear,
The mule, and the wild pig,
The lynx, wolf, and the dog.

Look at the eagle, phoenix, and peacock,
The raven and the swan;
Do not forget the whale,
Adders, otters, and the bees.

MAN

What comprises and maintains
The work of the great world
    Is contained in the small world,
    Namely, in man.

Europe is the head, indeed,
Africa nourishes the heart;
    Asia supplies the abdomen,
    America the hands and feet.

Death destroys the harmony
Of the human body.
    Therefore man passes away
    Like a bubble or like smoke.

The Division of the Stone into the
Four Elements

If you desire to have the son of wisdom
With all his beautiful gifts,
    Then divide the four elements
    And put each in its place.

This operation will not succeed
Unless you putrefy the material
    That shall bear to you
    The son.

Through distillation the powder becomes clear.
That nature is hidden
      We experience here.
      And what is known to us, hides itself again.

The Four Effects, Disintegration,
Lavation, Composition, and Stabtility

Four beautiful sisters of fine forms
And of equal fortune are portrayed to you.
  They show you, in a pleasant way,
  What your work is like.

The first one tells you to disperse
Any part resulting from disintegration.
  The other teaches you how you lave together
  Such excellent materials.

The third advises you
To put together separate parts;
  And the fourth, how to stabilize
  This stone in the fire.

The Stone of the Wise Ones

from the Spirit, Body, and Soul

Like this unique serpent
Shows three heads
    And has but one body
    Full of deadly poison:

So receives the offspring
Of sun and moon the three natures,
    And it has in its own body, too,
    A fierce poison.

Therefore the king and the raven,
The swan and the peacock indicate the colors;
    If you see them with your own eyes
    You will be surer of the art.

Our Dragon

Delius with his warm arrow
Hurriedly kills the rough dragon
    So that he can put its life
    Into the fire.

If one would ask:
Who is this dragon?
    The ancients answer:
    It is the sulphur.

If now you want to know
Whence Delius takes his bow and arrow,
    The resting lion
    Will explain the riddle.

Calcination is the First Step
of the Wise Ones

Mercurius sits happily
Winged at the table.
  He is guarded on both sides
  By sun and moon.

Upon this table, not by accident,
Grow herbs with flowers.
  The courageous lion unhesitatingly
  Devours the serpent.

Through powder the volatile spirit
Is generally fixed and made permanent.
  Then when put on its own soil
  It enjoys itself with fruit and flowers.

The Other Step is the

Disintegratton or Solution

The hot lion promptly devours
The sun in the heavens.
    The beautiful nymph brings for this occasion
    Her tender flowers.

Then the fiery man will sweat
And become hot in the fire;
    Also he will resolve his body
    And carry it afar through moisture.

Expel the mastery accomplished
Through the mentioned powder's force,
    So that happily and beautifully
    Mercurius may issue therefrom.

The Third Step is the

Separation

The broken fetters fall;
   That which is light rises;
         That which is heavy sinks;
         Each one has its place.

The heaviness of the earth
Destroys the light things from above.
         Proud hearts are hurt,
         And put on low stools.

However, the lightness of the air
Mixes with the heaviness,
         For it embellishes all
         With its glorious light.

Coniunctio.

The Fourth Step is the

Composition or Conjunction

After rain often appears
Beautiful, lovely sunshine;
    After anger comes again
    Much greater love.

What you have separated,
Unite again completely,
    So that many fertile seeds
    Bless you with many children.

In the meantime
Neptunus prepares a warm bath,
    So that husband and wife
    Wash their bodies clean.

The Fifth Step is the

Putrefaction

Destruction brings about
Death of the material;
      But the spirit renews,
      Like before, the life.

Hence the black globe
Signifies the black raven.
      Also the light spirit
      Quickly expels human consciousness;

Provided that the seed is
Putrefied in the right soil;
      Otherwise all labor, work, and art
      Will be in vain.

The Four Grades of Warmth

The sun passes in one year
  Through the whole zodiac,
      And renews with its warmth
      All herbs, trees, and flowers.

Hence one has to learn
The four grades of our labors:
      Which will then be a norm
      In the undertaken work.

They are the ram, cancer, libra,
And capricornus.
      Find out which amongst them
      Is first and which follow.

Congelatio.

The Sixth Step is the

Congelation

The volatile spirit of the air
Must become fixed:
    And the hitherto hidden sap
    With its water will be reproduced.

Many become united.
What is tender and soft becomes stiff and hard:
    The crooked organs of the serpent
    Become then manifest.

Our Mercurius is remade.
He throws away the wings,
    Adorns himself with kingly scepter,
    And his limbs become beautiful and clean.

The Seventh Step is the

Cibation

This, our child, is mostly fed
  With the milk of his mother:
    So that it grow gradually
    And produce its own new powers.

In such things the triangle
Produces the rough dragon,
    Which again gives us
    The fruit of the moon and sun.

Three eagles stand on one side
Of the indicated triangle.
    These together you can ascribe
    To the three spirits.

The Eighth Step is the

Sublimation

So that our body change itself
Into lovely air,
    It is taken from a lowly place
    And led on high.

The king gives up the phoenix,
The queen the swan,
    While the wolf, as it ought to be,
    Comes from its hole.

On the sun-tree stand,
And grow many fruits.
    Hence cut then the grass
    With the scythe at the desired time.

The Ninth Step is the

Fermentation

The seed thrown
On good soil, sprouts,
For which purpose
It regains its soul.

The trumpet sounds
For the resurrection of the bodies,
So that they take on
New flesh again.

Without ferment the sun cannot
Again see the light of day,
And beautiful Diana at its side
Without ferment cannot have life again.

Exaltatio.

The Tenth Step in the

Exaltation

King and queen are finally
Elevated to the throne.
    The lovely tree visible in the center
    Bears beautiful fruit.

On the steps of the throne
Are fourteen stately lions.
    Yet there are two heads
    On one spine, or vertebra.

Thus is elevated
And enjoys honors
    Our stone that shines
    In the whole world.

The Eleventh Step in the

Multiplication

The queen, in great honor,
 Rides on the generous lion
    And carries, O Pelican,
    All the fruit of your body.

The lion nourishes many young
With its own flesh and blood.
    The tender young cubs
    Play with their father.

Thus you can produce quickly
The many children of the stone.
    They cause multiplication without end.
    Therefore do rejoice.

Out of the Four Elements

Come All Things

In the beginning all things
Consist of the four elements,
    Even those which you surmise
    Are but pure elements.

Nothing pure is found.
The Creator of the world
    Mixes all elements
    With his dexterous hands.

Therefore our moon and sun
Shine with great pleasure;
    And our daughter
    Has received the life.

The Seven Metals

Here are portrayed
The hidden treasures of the earth;
    And how the stars of the heavens
    Are locked up deep in the mountains.

The earth contains
Its own planets,
    To which the elements
    Give their qualities and powers.

If you doubt who they are
You must look closely
    At all metals.
    Heaven will help you to understand.

Marriage or the Marital Tie

In our heavens stand
Two beautiful lights;
  They indicate the great light
  Of the great heaven.

Unite them both
As if a woman were led to a man:
  So that in your own case
  The marital status be induced.

Then adroitly combine
The elements proportionately
  So that the round form
  Produces its tender forces.

Mercurius or Quicksilver

In Mercurius is at all times
What the wise ones seek:
    He represents the highest treasures
    Of the entire world.

The great flame of the fire-eating father
Does not damage Mercurius.
    He always flies away
    From the warm hearth.

Yet if you can keep him there,
Stiff and fine,
    Then you will be considered blissful
    Here on earth by his child.

The Tincture or the Coloring

The fierce animal
 Pursues with awful howls
  The tender girl
  In field and forest.

Mercurius says without shame:
You beautiful nymph, come hither.
  No hair shall be touched
  In your great and deadly danger.

Because he who dies with me
Will be happy with me:
  He will be resurrected after the sad death,
  And enter into the desired riches.

The Water of the Wise Men

When a woman mixes
Coloring with water,
    She is about to wash
    Linen or clothes.

The water leaves the material
When it is dried in the open air;
    But the colored cloth
    Retains the desired color.

Likewise the water of the wise
Penetrates all large and small metals;
    Use it
    And it tinctures things speedily.

The Two Sulphurs

Look, two lions meet
With their paws
    Tying friendship's
    Lasting tie.

If you seek the ferment,
Put together the two sulphurs
    So that you can multiply your work
    As well as the burden.

The one sulphur be fixed and remain;
The other be volatile and escape.
    Yet both remain fixed
    In one step, the best.

The Elixir or an Oily Juice in Flux

He who desires to know
What the elixir is, and what it is
      That renders all metals
      Amenable to his work:

Firstly, must to this end
Seek such a medicament
      That flows everywhere
      Before the quick flight of mercury.

Unite to this the sulphur
Of the king or queen;
      And then the one bird betrays the other
      That flies away.

The Conjunction

Lock up in two glasses
The two captured birds,
And seal the round opening
At once.

One flies away;
The other can not move;
Neither one henceforth desires
To ascend.

Have patience!
Your work will not be in vain.
The lovely tree will in time
Bear you fruit.

The Multiplication

Here you see three glasses
As well as the strong lion,
    And Mercurius in the same form
    Soon made light by wings.

Take three parts of the medicament
And unite them with the flying one.
    Soon he will lose his wings
    In the warm fire.

Then the lion will be present
Which through your zeal, and at your pleasure,
    You may lead into the oven
    And therein multiply.

The Cibation

A little child on this earth
Is nourished by the mother's milk;
But a man strong in body
Partakes of wheat as nourishment.

Each one receives the food
That agrees with him;
Hence the powers are increased
In the child as well as in the man.

Give therefore to our little boy
Ever his digestible food,
So that it may grow and grow
In its strength.

The Wonder-Works of Our Stone

Four sisters divide their treasures
   Without dispute,
      Fortunately each receives
      Her proper part and special piece.

The first at all times
Can take away sickness;
      The other heals the sick limbs
      Of the metals.

The third can change the useless stones
Into beautiful jewels.
      The fourth gives from her treasure
      Again the glass that thins.

The Water of Life

The living water
  Comes from the bourn of life;
    To your life, too, it can give
    Much usefulness and many fruits.

The stars stretch forth
Their great strength;
    And sun and moon
    Wash their faces.

Dear wanderer,
Rush to this bourn
    And quench your thirst completely,
    Because the sun shines hot, indeed.

The Philosophic Ore of the Wise

or Copper

Our living ore, pure and clear,
Is the gold of the wise men.
    Because with its rays
    It illuminates all things.

It be then that you add to it
Its own "Duenech;"
    Otherwise you will not have for such
    Marriage the desired wedding bed.

If then the two lions come together,
And also their hearts,
    From their mouth will flow
    A golden juice.

The Philosophic Fire

Here is our warm fire,
Humid, lovely, and not dangerous;
    That preserves all things,
    And permits none to spoil.

It is even and good,
Agreeable to things to be born;
    It carries everything properly heated
    Away with the mixture.

The sun with his wife
Does not shun this fire
    But accepts it voluntarily
    Like a bath.

The Philosophic Bath

Our bath is so prepared
That the body does not get wet.
      Let sun and moon both wash themselves
      Therein in the same manner.

After having done this,
Unite the spirit.
      Then you will see with your eyes
      Two stems of calendula.

Each tree will then
Bear its own fruit,
      And you can pluck many apples
      For yourself.

The Conjunction

Gabricus and Beya
Rest here in tranquil slumber
    As man and wife
    On their marriage bed.

Those who before were two
Became then one.
    And the child is the treasure
    Of the union.

The sun and moon
Are husband and wife,
    And they, too,
    Multiply their kind.

The Putrefaction

First the seed must rot
  And fully die,
      So that it come forth again
      In a perfect state.

Without this process
There is no growth on earth.
      And remember well,
      All labor, too, is in vain.

When death takes
The lovers,
      Vulcanus gives the life
      New form and limbs.

The Extraction or Impregnation

of the Souls

Both bodies putrefy
In the grave below.
    They take on again
    The powers of the new soul.

They become united with the souls
And sustained by them.
    One becomes free through the other
    And is led to life again.

Be patient and wise
With hand and in mind at once;
    So that the spirit does not escape
    From the place of fire.

The Lavation or Cleansing

A lovely downpour falls
From above onto the world,
    And washes, with its drops,
    Our bodies clean and pure.

The black color vanishes
And is lost entirely.
    The limbs soon take on
    Lovely beauty and form.

Why are the bodies washed?
It is the work of the pure spirit on earth.
    This spirit is not conjoined to them,
    Unless they are sufficiently clean.

The Exaltation or the Ecstasy
of the Souls

It is now time
To rise from bed and grave.
    The rejoicing of the souls
    Rebounds now everywhere.

The soul rejoices
Because the body has agreed
    To recognize the soul's prerogative
    And to serve it well.

The bird saves the bird
From the water,
    Surrounded by the fear
    Of drowning.

The Growth

Here a body has two heads
And stands upon the crescent moon.
    It holds three serpents
    And a bird.

There is a tree with beautiful branches
Bearing many delicious fruits,
    Of which you may count
    Great riches;

Provided that you understand well
The kind and gender of this root.
    Otherwise the tree with its fruits
    Will be secure against your intrusion.

The Multiplication

Take the true and genuine ferment
And unite it with its own sulphur
    So that you can render mild
    Whatever you want to bring forth.

If you throw the well-known two things
Happily upon our land,
    Then this alive flame
    Will produce its powers.

Thus you may throw your seed
Into the earth
    Which has been prepared by the fire
    With great pleasure and joy.

The Illumination

Here you see the sun shining
With spread wings,
   And leaving hell
   Symbolized by a deep well.

The moon, however, in its anger
Shoots through it with its arrow,
   Then the sun with its shine
   Falls back into the well.

The whole well receives
A heavy golden color.
   If the sun thus shines with its rays
   Then there is Apollo.

The Nourishing

Here is our lovely garden,
For our fruit rests here.
    Mercurius appears as if
    He is ready for a quick flight.

You, most beautiful king, with your might
Seize quickly this booty
    Because for your noble stomach
    No other booty will be more appropriate.

Utilize the seized so that
The limbs do not grow flabby,
    And from ravenous hunger
    Gradually enfeeble.

The Stability

Our noble body lies here
Hidden in the grave.
    The spirit stands near
    And the mind comes again from heaven.

Take care at all times
That the mind is elevated,
    And again return from above
    To that which is below.

Thus it unites the friendly powers
Of heaven and of earth;
    And with its rich gifts
    It will bring the body to life again.

The Multiplication

From the clouds
  Pours pelting rain;
    Child and mother both
    Get quickly wet.

Our water is dissolved
And led first on high.
    Then it is brought again with might
    Down into the most lowly places.

Now wash our tender boy;
Let flow the liquid clear and pure,
    So that his limbs
    Take to the multiplication.

The Revivification.

Look, how the beautiful moon
And its shining brother
    With happy countenance
    Emerge from the pure well.

Oh pelican! the young,
Your darling children,
    You nourish with your heart
    And you sprinkle them with your blood.

Into their tender limbs
Comes a new virtue,
    That afterwards receives
    Animated strength.

The Perfection

See, the honorable king
Holds in the left hand a chain
    Attached to the neck of the lion
    Which he leads at certain hours.

In the right hand he carries a staff
Wherewith he shows an ugly worm.
    With many fruits, oh noble sun,
    Stands here your proud tree.

In the beginning search for the root
If you want to break the fruit;
    Otherwise you will have no fruit,
    Be it then that you looked for its seed.

The Green Lion

What does the lion with its star signify?
And what does the sun that likes to be
    Held tight in the lion's paw?
    Tell me, Mufa, as best you can!

This our courageous hero
Is the green lion
    In whose innermost abdomen
    The red star also lies hidden.

The green lion is extremely agile
And blows forth the sun's colors
    So that the reflection
    May be seen on the plain.

Our Gold

Here sits the sun
Clad in kingly attire.
The beautiful moon
Sits at its side.

Their dear son stands in the center
Being crowned by both,
So that he govern the kingdom
With much success and happiness.

Now tell me, what does this mean?
Without the sun and its wife
Our darling boy
Will not be able to govern.

The Awakening of the King

To our king is given
  The greatest might from above.
    Such gifts he alone possesses
    From the powers of the father.

Though he overcomes everything,
He is overpowered by a servant
    Whose limbs he solves
    With his washing.

Soon the virtuous mother collects
Her solved limbs.
    To the servant and mother is therefore due
    Glory and praise, fame and honor.

The Three Wells of the True Water

Three wells with plenty water
Are here in a hollow rock.
    We are provided with
    Many wonderful waters.

See, how the sun and moon
Give their powers and effects;
    Also, how all other stars
    Favor us with their own splendor.

He who of us elect ones drinks,
Is as born anew.
    He will also live and
    Continue on the desired path.

The Philosopher or the
Friend of Wisdom

See, I carry heaven and earth
Upon my arms, without trouble.
    With my mind
    I perceive all things.

What is past, I revoke;
What is present, I understand;
    What is in the future, I can see
    And interpret from three aspects.

But yet, ever I show myself
Friendly, willing, and ready,
    And I am rightly compared
    With a boy, simple and just.

The Nymph of our Ocean or the

Goddess of the Water

I am a daughter,
Born pure and clear of my father,
    Who with quick step
    Has long run around the world.

From my breasts I give you
The milk with the blood.
    These two things, when boiled,
    Will give you much heavy gold.

Thus the possessor will receive from it
Much use and benefit,
    And his labors and pain
    Will not be wholly in vain.

Our Sulphur

See that the precious eagle
Be united in love with the lion;
    Also that the delicate and weak
    Pour out his tears.

Unite these tears
With the blood of the courageous lion.
    Then you will possess
    The whole world.

If, after usage of the salamander,
They come together through the fire,
    Then the fire, bold and gay,
    Will always see your powers.

The Egg of the Wise Ones

Here stands our dragon,
So blown up by the branch of the sun
That everybody can have it
With little expense.

What properly lies here under the dragon
Rests also badly in him.
Therefore, oh celebrated group,
This is called your egg.

Tell me what mean here
The many crowns with their jewels?
He prepares, kindly and well,
Golden gifts for his brothers.

The Birth

See, an old man rests
In a desolate cave on a rocky spot.
   A black raven stands near him;
   It is his companion.

His spirit and his mind
Permit his limbs to be content,
   So that the punishment be only
   In payment for a badness.

If they then come again
And are united with him correctly,
   From the three will be born
   Our Apollo elect.

The Conjunction

Here stand sun and moon;
Each carries a lily branch.
     Our Apollo is the third:
     He stands erect in the center.

They become conjoined to him
With their powers, in great pomp.
     Consequently he carries
     A kingly scepter in his hand.

His beauty and excellence
Are praised in the whole world.
     To the rambling little folk
     Is due alone honor and fame.

The Death

Great honor causes to this king
Envy and enemies in the kingdom.
    This king is killed at the hand
    Of ten youths from the peasant folk.

All things are upset.
Sun and moon are sad
    And give many signs at this time
    Of darkness and sadness.

A rainbow stands above:
It rises with many colors;
    It brings extremely good news
    To the people, and also certain peace.

The Putrefaction

The city is destroyed by fire
And by many fierce enemies.
Thereupon the peasants die
With their king.

The black ravens devour
The corpses, near and far.
That which possesses soul and spirit
Here on earth, remains entirely undisturbed;

And which, if it can be united
With the body of the king,
Will give to all
The beginning to a new life.

The Blanching

If the again-living sister
Precedes her dear brother,
    Then she again gets
    White limbs like crystal.

They accused her brothers
That so far they loved
    Nothing but earth's heavy burden;
    And that they have despised the heavenly.

She admonishes them to become
Like the star of their rich brother
    And then she puts upon the head
    Of each a crown of honor.

The Rubefaction

The king is resurrected from the fetters of death
And brings new pleasure.
  He regales with his gifts
  Those who before were sad and depressed.

He is fond of his colleagues
And crowns them with clear gold.
  The tender limbs this time
  He clothes with genuine purple.

Here the true Azoth is free,
And also the medicine of the wise,
  Which restore with their powerful things
  Sick limbs to health.

A Dream or Vision

Here stands a respectable man
Who appeared to me at night.
   I saw his limbs
   Clean, beautiful, and fine.

His whole body
Was clad in green.
   An unblemished golden crown
   Was being put upon his excellent head.

Above it was a shining star
That illuminated the darkness.
   As I wondered who he might be,
   He said: Rise and follow me.

The Confession of Our Virgin

or the Bringing Together

Our virgin tells
Of great wonderworks.
  Pay attention to her
  And forget nothing.

Let the bear give you the warm fire
From the wind that blows at midnight.
  The wind at noon will bring you then
  A good supply of the lion's water.

Because two things so mixed are volatile,
Bring them into a warm oven,
  So that they flow again
  From greatest height to the lowest place.

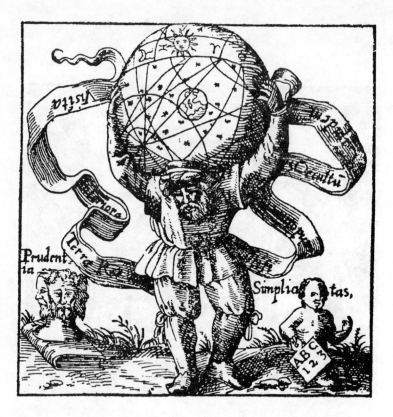

The Rhodostaurotic and

Heaven-Carrying Atlas

Atlas carries on his shoulders
The burden of the whole world.
    With your mind carry, without complaint,
    Heaven and the earth.

Then you will speedily arrive at
The foundation of all things,
    And soon the stone from the earth
    Will be known to you.

Be always wise and prudent,
Without cunning toward others.
    Be ever plain and simple,
    Betray nobody, and you will be happy.

Hermes' Emerald Tablet

Hermes says: What is above must correspond
To what is below,
If someone desires to accomplish
Such wonderworks, with art and might.

The moving planets may be seen
Standing in the heavens.
The earth with its precious metals
Resembles them exactly.

The father of this stone is the sun;
The mother is the moon;
The wind carried the reward in its body;
The earth has nourished it tenderly.

The New Bringing-Together

or the Confession

I am indeed a beautiful goddess
Born in the deepest ocean,
    That in its course
    Runs around the world.

My two breasts give you
Two noble rivulets with special beauty,
    Which, by the white milk and red blood,
    You may recognize immediately.

Put into the fire these two things
So that they mix completely.
    Sun and moon will then
    Let you do as you like.

Another Combination

Torment the eagle
When it sheds its tears.
 The timid lion will then die
 A terrible death

The blood of this lion alone is considered
The greatest treasure of the world.
 Unite it immediately with the eagle's
 Tears and you will be rich.

Then both wash each other clean;
They will be consumed through love;
 While they, Oh salamander,
 Become identical with your good nature.

The First Material

I am the dragon because I drive
The deadly poison from the body.
    The red lion always loves me,
    And the green gives me pleasure.

By many I am recognized
And called the egg of nature.
    I fly away unless
    One binds me with measure.

I have many forms and colors,
And carry within me manly and womanly powers.
    I recreate the human body
    And all metals.

The First Effect

Here I rest, not by accident,
Buried in the hard earth.
My spirit wants to rise
With the soul.

So that none flees the other,
The grave is artificially sealed.
They demand my life
In order to repair it.

After a fortnight
I almost look like a raven.
Then I renovate beautifully
The scepter of my people.

The Other Effect

After many colors
Have appeared,
    I rise with a red body
    Shining, pure, and clean.

In the world none can be found
Who is my equal.
    The sun as well as the moon
    Is always forced to obey my will.

The effects of herbs, large and small,
Everything is subject to my will,
    Also all sickness on earth
    That is driven from the human body.

The Third Effect

Ten men are not ashamed
  To take my life.
      However, as they stand now here
      They will go with me to death.

Sun and moon are sad with me,
Which the black color indicates.
      The heavenly rainbow
      Is a sign of happiness.

Therefore I wash my enemies
Clean of all dirt.
      Finally it is due me
      That I be triumphant.

The Fourth Effect

So that one understands clearly
What my virtue is, what my might,
    I compensate the damage only
    With my riches that are great.

Though the ravens, near and far,
Eat up the corpses,
    There remain constant
    Both soul and spirit.

Of the two I unite many.
What is volatile, I fix,
    So that everybody can behold
    The work of my hands.

The Fifth Effect

In the form of a queen
I come forth from the grave
    And bring to my brothers
    Happy bodings.

My bridegroom has ordered me
To come to you in person
    So that I may solace
    Sad hearts with my gifts.

With gratitude and decorum
Take this white crown from me,
    Until Apollo the great
    Will issue from his grave.

The Sixth Effect

I have in these hours
Overcome my enemies.
To my people I have brought
Great trophies.

Therefore, you true brothers,
And you dear hearts,
If you love me without shame,
Rush to me.

Take the shining crown
Wherewith I honor you.
Multiply yourselves
Into the tenth generation.

The Whole Philosophic Work

All things which heretofore
Have been portrayed in figures
    You can see here
    In the circle.

The old man is the clear beginning;
He also gives you the key;
    Sulphur and Mercurius
    With Salt must produce the work.

See you here nothing, then there is nothing.
Why do you ask for more?
    In the midst of the clear light
    You will be stone-blind.

The Coat of Arms of Our Hero

Our hero has overcome
At certain hours his enemies in war.
   He has also added
   The highest honor of all virtues.

On his helmet shines the sun
With its lovely rays.
   Below the face of the sun
   Stands the erected moon.

Three round apples decorate
The sun in the shield.
   This escutcheon will give you advantage
   Through your deeds.

Saturn's Bringing-Together or Confession

Africa produces without doubt
Hot lions with red hearts.
    Together they possess
    The excellent gifts of our dragon.

But the cold north wind
Brings us the cold bears,
    That bring us your eagle,
    Oh my beautiful Apollo!

Then the golden sap will rise
With its flame.
    The virgin asks you cautiously
    To take the two things.

A

Catalogue Raisonné

OF WORKS ON THE

Occult Sciences

BY

F. LEIGH GARDNER

Rosicrucian Books.

PRIVATELY PRINTED.

———

1 9 2 3.

NOTE

The following is an abridged reprint of Gardner's bibliography as originally published. Items omitted include those already listed in the annotated bibliography, p. — 483 , above, works containing only passing reference to Rosicrucianism, and — for the most part — books on alchemy, free masonry, articles in periodicals, as well as items published before the 17th century. In its present form, Gardner's bibliography will be of real value to the student who wishes to concentrate his research within the specific area of Rosicrucianism as such.

BIBLIOTHECA ROSICRUCIANA.

WORKS by AGNOSTUS (Irenæus).

Fortalicium Scientiæ das ist die unfehlbare, volkommenliche vnerschäzliche Kunst aller Künsten und Magnalien, welche allen würdigen, tugendhafften Pansophiae Studiosis die glorwürdige, hocherleuchte Brüderschafft des *Rosencreuzes* zu eröffnen gesandt, &c. 8vo. (13 August, 1617), 1618. *45 pp.*

Fons Gratiae das ist Kurtze Anzeyg und Bericht wenn zu welcher Zeit unnd Tag der jenigen so von der heiligen gebenedeyten Fraternitet dess Rosen-Creutzes zu Mitbrüdern auffgenommen. 8vo. (1 Januar), 1619. *37 pp.* (The Author subscribes himself as *Indigus Notarius*).

Thesaurus Fidei das ist Ein nothwendiger Bericht und Verwarnung an die Novitios oder junge angehende Discipel welche von der hochlöblichen gesegneten Frat. des R.C. auff und angenommen, etc. 8vo. (2 Martii), 1619. *36 pp.*

Frater non Frater das ist Eine hochnothdürstige verwarnung an die Gottselige fromme Discipul der H. gebenedeyten Societet des R.C. dass sie sich für den falschen Brüdern vnd Propheten fleissig vorsehen so unter dem Namen und Deckmantel wohlermelter gesellschafft ad S.S. in der welt herumbstreichen, &c. 8vo. N.P. (16 Marz), 1619. *40 pp.*

At the end of the 4 preceding works and also the one entitled "Epitimia Fr. R.C.," appears to be a separate tract (although bound up and included in the pagination) by *F. G. Menapius,* it is suggested that this Pseudonym together with those of "Schweighardt" "Agnostus (I.)" "Valentia" and "Alberti" are those used indiscriminately by Andreas (J. V.) and his friends; it is certainly a curious fact that two of these pseudo authors should issue works bearing both of their signatures whereas no one else appears to have done so.

Thesaurus Fidei das ist ein nothwendiger Bericht vnd Verwarnung an die Novitios, dass sie im Glauben an Gott, Liebe dem Rechsten, Geduld vnd Sansstmut der Frat., bis ans Ende verharren sollen. 8vo. (3 April), 1619. *36 pp.*

Vindiciae Rhodostauroticae das ist Warhaffter Gegenbericht der Gottseeligen Frat. des R.C. vnnd gegründte widertreibung der vor wenig wochen von S. Mundo Christophori F. wider hochermelte Gesellschaft aussgestreuten injuri, verläumbdung Lugen vnd Calumnien. 8vo. N.P. (5 Sept.), 1619. *47 pp.*

WORKS by ANDREAS (J. Valentine).

Allgemeine und General-Reformation der ganzen weiten Welt. Beneben der *Fama Fraternitatis* des löblichen Ordens des Rosenkreuzes an alle Gelehrte und Häupter Europä geschrieben. Auch einer kurtzen *Responsion* von dem Herrn Haselmeyer gestellt, jetzo öffentlich in Druck verfertiget, und allen trewen Hertzen *communiciret* worden. 8vo. Gedruckt zu Cassel durch Wilhelm Wessel, 1614. *147 pp.*

Allgemeine und General Reformation der ganzen weiten Welt. Beneben der *Fama Fraternitatis* des löblichen Ordens des Rosenkreuzes an alle Gelehrte und Häupter Europä geschrieben. Auch einer kurzen *Responsion* von dem Herrn Haselmeyer gestellet welcher deswegen von den Jesuitern ist gefänglich eingezogen und auff eine Galleen geschmiedet: Jetzo öffentlich in Druck verfertiget, und allen trewen Hertzen *communiciret* worden. 8vo. Erstlich Gedruckt zu Cassel Im Jahr, 1614. *152 pp.*

This was the first work put forward by Andreas, and which caused all the stir and excitement as witnessed by the number of pamphlets, etc., which deluged Europe in general and Germany in particular for a considerable time afterwards. According to *Herder* this must have circulated in MSS. sometine previously because Hasselmeier in the Tyrol had seen and read it in 1610 and replied to it in 1612.

The "Universal Reformation" is a literal translation of a work by an Italian "Boccalini" (vide Article) "De Ragguagli di Parnasso," 1612, this had no connection with the R.C. order, but was merely bound up with the Fama; as regards the Confessio this was not issued until A.D. 1615 (vide next two items). The above works were the two first printed editions, their titles vary sligthly but the contents are similar.

Another Edition appeared dated Regenspurg Anno 1681 (*sic* for 1781) it was edited by Fri Nicolai and was printed at Berlin 1781. It contains also the following, viz:

"*A. Haselmeyers*" Antwort etc. pp. 99—114.
"*Wohlgemeyntes*" Ausschreiben pp. 115—122.
"*Stellis* (Dr. A de)" Geistlicher Discurs pp. 123—192.

Fama Fraternitatis. Beneben der Confession oder Bekanntnuss derselben Fraternitat, an alle Gelehrte und Häupter in Europa geschrieben, auch etlichen Responsionen und Antwortungen von Herrn Haselmeyrn und andern gelerten Leuten auf die *Famam* gestellet, Sampt einem Discurs von allg. Reformation der gantzen Welt. Itzo von vielen Erraten entledigt, etc., Frankfurt am Mayn durch Joh. Bringern in verlegung Joh. Berners. 8vo. 1615. *216 pp.*

Summa Doctrina Christianæ Trigemina. 12⁰. Tübingen 1614.

Fama Fraternitatis, R.C. Das ist Gerücht der Brüderschaft des hochlöblichen ordens des R.C. an alle Gelehrte und Häupter Europä. Benebst derselben Lateinischen Confession welche vorhin in Druck noch nie ausgegangen nuhnmehr aber auff vielfältiges anfrangen zusampt deren beigefügten Teutschen Version, in druck gegeben, von einem *Philomago.* 8vo. Cassel Wilh. Wessel, 1615. *111 pp.*

In these two works we now have the addition of the Confessio which in the words of my worthy collaborateur Dr. Westcott contains "Lutheran views as contrasted with those of Roman Catholicism whereas the *Fama* treats of the form of Christianity as contrasted with Pagan Worship, there being no reference to the Reformed Church whatever." This is very significant and is a point that has hitherto been overlooked by all the Critics.

Another edition appeared in A.D. 1616, Frankfurt, on the title page of which one finds "first printed at Cassel in the year 1616" which we know to be wrong. The excitement was so great that the work now ran through several editions, some omitting the *Reformation* and inserting fresh matter of their own until the old editions having become scarce during the last century Frederic Nicolai of Berlin undertook the reprinting of it in 1781, inserting however the date 1681 instead, and to complicate matters still further, omitted Berlin and inserted Regensburg (vide Article No. 49, "Authentische Geschichte, etc.") where a number of similar books had been printed.

Chymische Hochzeit *Christiani Rosenkreutz* anno 1459—Four different 8vo Editions appeared in this year, viz.—*Original Edition,* Strasburg, published by Lazarus Zetzners, 1616, printer's note at end, "printed by Conrad Scher, 1616"—*Second Edition,* Same title, without printer's note at end "printed by"—*Third Edition,* Strasburg, published by L. Zetzners, Erben, 1616, at end by Conrad Scher, 1616. This Edition was again printed with a vignette title of an Alchemical Figure, and the words "Erstlich Gedruck zu Strasburg (first printed at Strasburg), 1616", *173 pp.*

Collation, the first, second and fourth editions, consist of 146 pp., the third edition of 143 pp.

Another edition was issued by Nicolai of Berlin, dated Regenspurg, 1781.

I have placed this work under *Andreae* as the generally accepted Author, or at all events the person responsible for its publication; to some it is a fable and a school boy's romance, to others it contains sublime Hermetic Truths of a very high order. I wonder how many of its readers are able to decipher the Ænigma contained therein.

The Hermetic Romance, or The Chymical Wedding, written in High Dutch by C. R., translated by E. Foxcroft, late Fellow of King's Colledge in Cambridge, licensed and entered according to order, printed by A. Sowle at the Crooked Billet in Holloway Lane, Shoreditch, and sold at the Three Kyes in Nags Head Court, Grace Church Street, 1690. *226 pp.*

Invitatio Fraternitatis Christi, ad sacri amoris Candidatos. 12mo. Argentorati, L. Zetzner, 1617 (another edition, Argent, 1626). *81 pp.*

Invitationis ad Fraternitatem Christi (pars altera) Paraenetica. 12mo. Argentorati, L. Zetzner, 1618. *67 pp.*

Mythologiae Christianae sive Virtutum et Vitiorum Vitae Humanae Imaginum Lib. III. 12 mo. Argentorati, L. Zetzner (1619).

Collation (xxiv) 352 (vii) pp.

We see here in this and the preceding work, the attitude of Andreas's mind when he began to endeavour to stem the tide of public opinion that he had aroused, even to the extent of denying the existence of the Order, as he states that it is purely imaginary.

Turris Babel sive Judiciorum de Fraternitate Rosaceæ Crucis Chaos. 12mo. Argentorati, L. Zetzneri, 1619. *72pp.*

This work was published by our same author. He signs the preface with his initials and dedicates the book to D. Heinricus Heinius of Rostock, he states that the whole history was nonsense and says that he himself was responsible for starting the movement; of course he refers to the "Fama and Confessio" the immense amount of attention and the number of replies it called forth; but it appears to me that the hubbubs that was caused by the issuing of the *Fama,* etc., exceeded his expectations and he endeavoured to allay it by publishing this work, as he says in it "Listen ye mortals, In vain do you wait for the coming of the Brotherhood, the Comedy is at an end, etc.," but this did not have the effect he desired as many were dissastified with this explanation, and the excitement continued for long after, judging from the literature that followed.

Turbo sive moleste et frustra per Cuncta Divagans ingenium, in theatrum productum. 12 mo. Helicone, juxta Parnassum, 1616 et 1621.
Collation (iv) 188 pp.

Arndt (Johann),.Zweytes Silentium Dei. 12⁰. Argentorati, 1618.

Archiv für Freimaurer und Rosenkreuzer. 2 vols, 8vo. Berlin, A. Mylius, 1783.
Collation, Vol. I (iv) 474 pp.; Vol. II (xvi) 447 pp.
A reprint of some of the choicest works including the Reformation, Fama, etc.

"In the posthumous writings of M. C. Hirschen, pastor at Eissleben, it has been found that John Arnd informed him in confidence as a near friend and former colleague how he had been told by John Valentine Andreä—also subrosa—that he namely Andreä, with thirty others in Wurtemberg had first sent forth the *Fama Fraternitatis*, that under this screen they might learn the judgment of Europe therein, as also what lovers of true wisdom lay concealed here and there, and would then come forward" (*translated*).

Arnold (Gottfried) Unparteyische Kirchen und Ketzer Historie vom anfang des Neuen Testaments biss auff das jahr Christi, 1688, etc., in 4 parts, folio, Franckfurt am Main, Thos. Fritsch, 1700—1715. (*Another Edition,* in large 4to issued by the same Firm appared in 1729, & 1741.)

In the fourth part page 899, Arnold adduces some conclusive evidence as to *Andrea* being the person responsible for the sending forth of the "*Fama Fraternitatis.*" He also adopts the view that the order existed before A.D. 1600, vide Book ii p. 245.

[**Ashmole** (Elias)] Fasciculus Chemicus or Chymical Collections expressing the Ingress, Progress and Egress, of the secret Hermetic Science out of the choicest and most famous Authors, whereunto is added the Arcanum or Grand Secret of Hermetic Philosophy, both made English by *James Hasolle, Esq.,* qui est Mercuriophilus Anglicus, *fine mystical plate.* 8vo. London, R. Mynne at the sign of St. Paul in Little Britain, 1650.
Collation (l) 268 pp.

Halkett and Laing (Anon Dicy.) state that their copy (Bodleian Library) has the word "Grant (*sic*) Secret": my copy has "Grand" this is interesting as evidently the first edition contained this misprint. The Arcanum has a separate title page, and the whole of this is a translation of Jean D'Espagnet's Hermetic Arcanum (vide Art) although Ashmole fails to acknowledge it. This was his first work on Hermeticism and probably was inspired by *Wm. Lilly*, the Mystic, whose acquaintance he first made in November, 1646, and whom he refers to in eulogistic terms of praise.

Ashmole (Elias) Theatrum Chemicum Britannicum, containing severall Poetical Pieces of our famous English Philosophers who have written the Hermetique

Mysteries in their owne Ancient Language, faithfully collected into one volume, with annotations thereon. 4to. London, Nat. Brooke at the Angel in Cornhill, 1651.

Collation (xvi) 486 (viii) pp.

A most important collection of Achemical tracts, including Thos. Norton's Ordinall of Alchemy, G. Ripley's Compound of Alchemie, Dr. John Dee's Testament, etc., etc., it is embellished with several very finely engraved plates and cuts of a mystical character, engraved by Vaughan, also a table at page 118 which is frequently missing, it states that this figure conteynes all the secrets of the treatise both great and small. In the preface he complains of the scant honour the Fratres of the R.C. receive at the hands of their countrymen, instancing the cures done to the Earl of Norfolk of leprosie, and Queen Elizabeth twice of the small pox by two of the Fratres. He then goes on to compare the warm reception they receive at the hands of Foreigners, instancing Maierus, Combachius, Faber, etc. This is one of the most important works we possess in the English language on this subject. Ashmole obtained his Hermetic knowledge of the Philosopher's Stone from Mr. William Backhouse of Swallowfield, Berks., as in his diary he says: May 13th, 1653: "My father Backhouse being ill unto death told me in syllables the true matter of the Philosopher's Stone which he bequeathed to me as a legacy."

Ashmole (Elias) The Way to Bliss, in three Books, made public by E. A., qui est Mercuriophilus Anglicus. 4to. London, Nat. Brook at the Angel in Cornhill, 1658.

Collation (vi) 220 pp.

A work on Long Life, the Hermetic Medicine and Philosopher's Stone. Richard Saunders who was contemporary with Ashmole dedicates his large work on "Chiromancy," 1671, to to "Universally-Learned Elias Ashmole."

Bacon (Roger) Epistolæ Fratris, R.B. De Secretis Operibus Artis et Naturæ, et de nullitatæ Magiæ, Operâ Johannis Dee Londinensis e pluribus exemplaribus castigata olim et ad sensum integrum restituta. 8vo. Hamburg, 1618. *80 pp.*

Contains a dedicatory epistle to the "Roseæ Crucis Fratribus."

[Barrett (Francis)] The Lives of Alchemistical Philosophers, with a critical Catalogue of Books in Occult Chemistry, and a selection of the most celebrated treatises on the Theory and Practice of the Hermetic Art. 8vo. London, 1815.

Collation (iv) 384 (ii) pp.

Compiled by the author of the well known book on magic called " *The Magus,*" London, 1801. My copy which formerly belonged to the famous mystic Frederick Hockley (as he has written his name on the title page with the date 1844), contains two title pages, the second one is called " *Lives of the Adepts,*" and contains a list of 751 Alchemical works which include a number by Rosicrucian Authors, it is not satisfactory however, as it only gives one line titles. Frater A. E. Waite published a reprint of this work in 1888, but it is not verbatim which I think is a pity as I consider it would have become more valuable had he adhered strictly to the original text.

Blavatsky (H. P.) Isis Unveiled, a Master Key to the Mysteries of Ancient and Modern Science and Theology. 2 vols, 8vo, New York, 1887.

Blavatsky (H. P.) The Secret Doctrine, The Synthesis of Science, Religion, and Philosophy. 2 vols, royal 8vo. London, 1888. (since reprinted in 4 Vols).

These four volumes all have many references to the order and speak highly of its Hermetic Teachings, Mysticism, &c.

Blavatsky (H. P.) The Theosophical Glossary. Royal 8vo. London, 1892.

Vide Article "Rosicrucians."

Boccalini (Trajano) De Ragguagli di Parnasso. Centuria Prima. 4to. Venetia, P. Farri, 1612.

Collation (xviii) 478 (xl) pp.

— Centuria Secunda. 4to. Venice, 1613.

Collation (xx) 453 (xix) pp.

Advertisement 77 of the first part of this work formed the subject matter of the "*Universal Reformation*" so I have thougt fit to include several editions of it; it had no connection with the Rosicrucian Order, and was merely bound up with the Fama. Other Editions also appeared at Venice in 1618, 1624, 1630, 1669, and again at Amsterdam. 2 Vols. 12vo. 1669.

— I. Ragguagli di Parnasso, or Advertisements from Parnassus, in two centuries, with the Politick Touchstone, translated by Rt. Hon. Henry, *Earl of Monmouth*. folio, with a fine portrait. London, 1656 (other editions 1669, 1674), with portrait; collation (xvi) *291 pp*.

Collation (xx) 452 pp.

— Advertisments from Parnassus, written originally in Italian by the famous Trajano Boccalini, newly done into English by N. N., Esquire. 3 vols, 8vo, fine portraits to vols I and III. London, 1704.

A poor and paraphrastic rendering.

Boccalini (Trajano) Advices from Parnassus in two Centuries. . . . . all translated from the Italian by several hands, revised and corrected by Mr. Hughes. Folio. London, 1706.

Collation (xvi) 454 (xiv) pp.

Borri (Gioseppe Francesco) La Chiave del Gabinetto. 12mo. In Colonia Appo Pietro del Martello, (Geneva) 1681.

Collation xxii 383 pp.

This author is commonly accredited with being an adept, and the two first letters in the work treat of elementary spirits which the Abbe de Villars hat already embodied in his *Count de Gabalis,* published at Paris 11 years previously. This work has been translated into English by a very learned member of the R.C. Fraternity known under the pseudonym of "*Fortiter et Recte*," this MSS. has never been published and is in the custody of the Head of the Order in England, in it the author gives a most systematic account of the R.C. doctrines.

Bridegroom (The) of the Fay, a Rosicrucian Tale, in rhyme, by a descendant of the *Count de Gabalis*. 8vo. London, 1827.

Collation (viii) 163 pp.

In the preface the author states that *his ancestor,* the Abbé Villars, was assassinated by a Rosicrucian fanatic for betraying the secrets of the Society in his work the "Count de Gabalis."

Bry (Rud. de) Fidele animi fidelis speculum, seu epistolium quoddam extremi desiderii pennis manibus cujuspiam Frat. R.C. veri ac sinceri non spurii ac adulterini . . . advolans, 1620. *32 pp.*

Buhle (J. G.) De vera origine adhuc latente Ordinis Fratrum de R.C. imprimis vero Ordinis Francomuratoriorum. Im auszug in den Götting. Gel. Anzeigen, 1803.

Part of this was translated into English and appeared in The London Magazine, 1824.

Bulwer Lytton (Sir Edward) A Strange Story. 3rd ed., 2 vols. 1862.

— Zanoni, by the Author of "Night and Morning," etc. In 3 vols, 8vo. London, 1842.

This well known author was a member of the Rosicrucian Society in England, and these two works embody some of his happiest inspirations derived therefrom ; if anyone has any latent mysticism in them, the latter work would be certain to discover it. Many other editions of his works have appeared.

Butler (Samuel) Hudibras, a Poem, with notes, a new edition. 2 vols, 8vo. London, 1819.

This author introduces the Rosicrucians into his witty poems, and speaks disparagingly of them. Vide vol I, p. 75, Vol II, p. 30.

Chambers Papers for the People, Vol. V., No. 33, Art. "Secret Societies of the Middle Ages," contains an account of the Order. 8vo. Edinburgh, 1850.

Chazal (Count du) Copy of the Admission of Dr. S. Bachstrom into the Society of the Fratres Rosae Crucis by the Count de C. Mauritius, September 12th, 1794.

This is to be found in "Rosicrucian," October, 1876.

[**Cohausen** (John Henry)] Hermippus Redivivus or the Sages Triumph over old Age and the Grave . . . prolonging the Life & Vigour of Man &c. translated from the German by Dr. J. Campbell. 8vo. London 1744 (reprinted by E. Goldsmid, Edinburgh 1885).

Contains numerous references to members of the order.

Craven (Revd Dr. J. B.) Doctor Robert Fludd (Robertus de Fluctibus) The English Rosicrucian, Life and Writings, fine portrait of R.F. 8vo. Kirkwall, 1902.

Collation (xvi) 260 pp.

This is the best account of Fludd's Life that we have up to the present in English, there is another to be found in "Wood's" work "*Athenæ Oxoniensis*." In his Bibliography of Fludd's works I notice that a mistake has occured in describing the large Table which follows on after the work "*Pulsus*." I am fortunate enough to possess the bulk of this Author's works in the *Original Binding* with all the *edges uncut,* and in my copy the Catchword at the end of *The "Pulsus"* work, viz. "Medi," refers to Part V. of the same series, consisting of a large Table measuring 39 by 17 inches; in the British Museum Copy this has been cut up into three pieces, so that it is not *a blank* sheet as this author suggests, although curiously enough he mentions it in the reprint issued at Moguntia, 1682.

Craven (Revd Dr. J. B.) Count Michael Maier Doctor of Philosophy and of Medicine Alchemist, Rosicrucian, Mystic, A.D. 1568 = 1622 Life and Writings, 2 Plates. 8vo, Kirkwall 1910.

Collation (viii) 165 pp. & *1 page Errata.*

Another excellent Biography and an exhaustive Bibliography of the Author's Works.

Crucigerus (Eus, Chr.) Eine Kurtze Beschreibung der neuen Arabischen unnd Morischen Frat. laut ihren eigenen 1614 zu Cassel unnd 1615 zu Marpurg . . . durch E.C.C., von der Frat des Holtzen Creutzes Jesu Christi. 8vo. Liechtenberg (Rostock) 1618, *64 pp.*

Davenport Adams (W. H.) Dwellers on the Threshold or Magic and Magicians. 2 vols, 8vo. London, 1865.

— Witch, Warlock and Magicians 8vo. London, 1889.

Both of these works contain chapters on the order, they are written in a superficial style.

Dee (Dr. John) The Private Diary of, and the Catalogue of his Library of MSS. from the originals in the Ashmolean Museum. . . . 4to. London, Camden Society, 1842.

Contains a fine collection of Mystic Books.

De Quincy (Thomas) Works. 8vo. London, 1871.

"Historico-Critical Inquiry into the origin of the R.C.-Freemasons."

Dickenson (Dr. Edmund) De Quintessentia Philosophorum et de Vera Physiologia . . . 8vo. Oxoniæ e theatro Sheldoniano, 1686.

Collation (iv) 224 pp.

— De Quintessentia Philosophorum et vera physiologia; una cum quaestionibus aliquot de secreta materia Phisica Editio altera. 8vo. Rotterdami P. van Slaart, 1699.

Collation (ii) 224 pp.

This Author is reputed to have obtained his occult knowledge from a French adept who was a Rosicrucian and stated that the reason they kept themselves secret was to ensure their safety. Another Edition of this work appeared in 1705, and in Germany 1721.

Echo Fraternitatis Roseæ Crucis. 8vo. Dantisci 1616.

This work has been attributed to "*Michael Maier*" vide J. Ferguson's "*Bibl Chemica.*"

[**Eckhoffen the Elder,** (Hans Carl von Ecker und)] Der Rosenkreuzer in seiner Blösse zum Nutzen der Staaten hingestellt durch Zweifel wider die wahre Weisheit der so genannten ächten Freymäurer oder goldnen Rosenkreutzer des alten Systems von *Magister Pianco,* vieler Kreisen Bundsverwandten. 8v. *[Nurnberg, Bauer].* Amsterdam, 1781 (?), *223 pp.*

Another Edition was published at Amsterdam (?) 1782, 223 pp. Both of these are dedicated to *Bruder Phœbron, i. e.* himself, but in the first one, there is a curious misprint, the last page being numbered 232, it should be 223; the second edition has this mistake corrected, the text being exactly similar. (See also in connection with this Author article "Theoretischen Bruder" and "Schleiss (H.).")

This is a very important work inasmuch as at page 84 we find a large folding table in German of the order "*Fratrum Rosæ et Aureæ Crucis.*" This was reproduced in Kenneth R. H. Mackenzie's "*Royal Masonic Cyclopædia*" without any acknowledgment of its true source, which it has been left to me to discover. I am informed by my worthy colleague Dr. Wynn Westcott who was personally acquainted with Frater Mackenzie, that he would never divulge the source from whence he obtained this information, which I am bound to assume was taken from this Book, inasmuch as it tallies almost word for word with the later work, it contains the "Degree Membership, Number, Sign, Colour, Symbol, Name of the Brotherhood, Places of Centre, Places of Assembly," etc., and as far as I am able to judge this must have been written by a renegade Frater, as the rest of the work is too consistent to be a total fabrication.

Epistola ad illustrem ac rev Frat. R.C. metro ligata ad eosdem missa a L.G.R. (datum Holthusii in agro Mindensi, 1616. I Martii L.G.R. pædotriba ibidem).

Epistola ad Reverendissimam Fraternitatem Rosæ Crucis. 8vo. Francofurti, 1613.

This appears to be the earliest publication connected publicly with the F.R.C., I am unable, however, to find a copy in any Public Library, this title is taken from Lenglet du Fresnoy's Catalogue.

Favrat (Ludovico) Aurea Catena Homeri id est concatenata naturæ historia Physico-Chymica Latina Civitate donata notisque illustrata. 8vo. Franco, 1762, (fine folding plate at page xx.)

Collation (xx.) 630, (xlv.) pp.

A translation of this was made by a *Dr. Sigismund Bacstrom* in 1797, and from this MSS. an attempt to publish it in the Journal "Lucifer" was made in 1891, but it was discontinued. It is a very important Book, and considered by many to hold the key to Alchemy.

Ferguson (John) Bibliotheca Chemica, a Catalogue of the Alchemical, Chemical and Pharmaceutical Books in the collections of the late James Young of Kelly, and Durris Esq. L.L.D. &c. 2 vols. 4to. Glasgow, 1906.

Collation Vol. I (xxi) 487 pp. & Portrait.
Vol. II (ii) 598 pp. & Portrait.

This stupendous collection of Alchemical Books (the best that has yet appeared) was printed for private distribution by his family in accordance with the terms of the deceased's will; an act of benificence to genuine Students that is unequalled in History: long may his Name be handed down to posterity for such Princely Generosity: the Work is printed on hand made paper, the type I should judge was cast specially for the purpose, and the labour of compilation must have been immense, whilst the Notes of Mr. Ferguson comprising the Lives of the various Authors and copious matter of most detailed facts form a History of the Subject that is unequalled. The Cost of all this could only be defrayed by a Wealthy Gentleman whose purse was equalled by his desire to benefit genuine Students of the Hermetic Art whom fortune had not placed in such a favourable position.

Findel (J. G.) Geschichte der Freimaurerei. 8vo. Leipzig, 1866.

— The History of Free Masonry from its origin, down to the present day. 8vo. London, 1869, (Second Edition, 1871).

In this work Findel deals very impartially with the R.C. chiefly reviewing the order from the events that have happened in Germany, also subsequently with other orders, using this same symbol, notably J. G. Schrepfer's in A.D. 1768.

WORKS by ROBERT FLUDD,
alias DE FLUCTIBUS.

Apologia Compendiaria Fraternitatem de Rosea Cruce suspicionis et infamiae maculis asspersam veritatis quasi Fluctibus abluens et abstergens: auctore R. de Fluctibus, M.D. London. 8vo. Leydae, G. Basson, 1616, *23 pp.*

This work is an exposition of the Rosicrucian Faith, and was considered of so much importance that P. Gassendus (see Article) and Kepler endeavoured to refute it.

Tractatus Apologeticus Integritatem Societatis De Rosea Cruce defendens. In qua probatur contra D. Libavii et aliorum ejusdem farinæ calumnias quod admirabilia nobis a Fraternitate R.C. oblata, sine improba Majiæ impostura, aut Diaboli, praestigiis et illusionibus praestari possint. Authore R. de Fluctibus . . . 8vo. Lugduni Batavorum, G. Basson, 1617, *196 pp.*

This is a new and revised edition of the last work, the headings to the chapters being extracts from the "Confessio."

MSS. (Brit. Mus. 12 C. II.) Declaratio brevis Serenissimo et Potentissimo Principi ac Domino, Domino, Jacobo, Magnæ, Britanniæ, Franciæ, et Hyberniæ, Regi Fidei gr Defensoris dedicata, In qua sincera operis cujus dam publicati intentio Majestati ipsius. Regiæ luculenter per ipsum autorem Robertum Flud Armigerum et in Medicina Doctorem Regiæ Majestati subditissimum explicatur.

This MSS. is unsigned by Fludd, and has no letter of his accompanying it, but it evidently is a genuine copy of a letter he sent to King James, proving undoubtedly that he was the Author of the Two preceding works, unfortunately MSS. 12 B. VIII. Brit. Mus. was burnt in a Fire they had at their Binders, this was presumably the original and more valuable document, whereas the above is only a copy.

Tractatus Theologo-Philosophicus in Libros tres distributus: quorum (i), De Vita (ii), Morte (iii) Resurrectione . . . collecta, Fratribusque à Cruce Rosea dictis dedicata, a Rudolfo Otreb (i. e. Robert Fludd) Brittano Oppenheimii, J. Theo de Bry, 1617, *126 pp.*

Contains one of De Bry's magnificent Title Pages and deals with the first origin of the world from a metaphysical standpoint.

Utriusque Cosmi Majoris scilicet et Minoris Metaphysica, Physica, atque Technica Historia In duo Volumina secundum Cosmi differentiam divisa De Macrocosmi Historia in duos tractatus divisa, folio. A magnificently engraved Title Page by J. T. de Bry in his best style. Oppenhemii, 1617.

Collation (ii) 206 (ix) pp.

This is a Handsome Work in Two vols, the second being again divided into two parts each with separate titles and pagination. It deals with Metaphysics, Physics, Arithmetic, Music, Geometry, Military Arts, Astrology, Geomancy, and Chiromancy, &c., the plates being executed in De Bry's best style.

Tractatus Secundus. De Naturæ Simia seu Technica Macrocosmi historia in partes undecim divisa. Folio, fine Vignette Title. Oppenhemio, J. T. de Bry, 1618.

Collations 788 (x) pp.

A Second Edition was published at Frankfurt in 1624.

Microcosmi Historia. Tomus Secundus De Supernaturali, Naturali, Præternaturali et Contranaturali Microcosmi historia in tractatus tres distributa, Folio, fine Vignette Title. Oppenhemii, J. T. de Bry, 1619, *277 pp.*

An interesting Work dealing partly with Metaphysics and partly with Physics, also Actual Influences on the Human Body, with some fine cuts.

Tomi Secundi Tractatus Primi, De Technica Microcosmi Historia in Portiones VII. divisa. Folio. Fine Vignette Title. [Oppenheim, 1620 (?)]

Collation 192 (x) pp.

Tomi Secundi Tractatus Secundus De Prœternaturali utriusque Mundi Historia in Sectiones tres divisa. Folio. J. T. de Bry, 1621.

Collation (xii) 199 pp.

Veritatis Proscenium in quo Aulæum erroris tragicum dimovetur . . . seu Demonstratio quædam analytica . . . Folio. Francofurti, John de Bry, 1621, *54 pp.*

Contains a fine criticism of Kepler's attack on him in 1619, (vide Article Kepler)

Monochordum Mundi symphoniacum seu Replicatio Roberti Flud alias de Fluctibus . . . ad Apologiam . . . Joannis Kepleri, adversus Demonstrationem suam Analyticam, nuperrime editans. 4to. Francofurti, J. Theo. de Bry, 1622. *83 pp.*

Contains a fine folding plate and numerous cuts. This is a reply to Keppler's work "Prodromus Dissert Cosmog," &c., published 1621—1622. (see Art. *Keppler.*)

Anatomiæ Amphitheatrum effigie triplici more et conditione varia designatum. Fine Vignette title page. Francofurti, John de Bry, 1623.

Collation (ii) 331 pp.

A medical work full of plates of the human body in detail.

Monochordum Mundi symphoniacum seu Replicatio Roberti Flud, alias de Fluctibus . . . ad Apologiam viri . . . Joh Kepleri adversus Demonstrationem suam Analyticam nuperrime editam in qua Robertus Validioribus Joannis Objectionibus, Harmoniæ suæ legi repugnantibus, comiter respondere aggreditur, 1623.

This work is contained in pp. 287-331 of the Anatomiæ Amphit., and is a reprint of the 1st Edition published by De Bry in 1622.

Philosophia Sacra et vere Christiana seu Meteorologia Cosmica. Finely engraved title page. Folio. Francofurti, Officina Bryana, 1626.

Collation (viii) 303 pp.

This contains a fine portrait of our author.

Medicina Catholica seu Mysticum artis medicandi sacrarium. In Tomos divisum duos . . . authore Roberto Fludd alias de Fluctibus. 5 parts, Folio. Francofurti. Fine vignette title. W. Fitzerus, 1629.

Collation (xx) 241 (vii) pp.

Part II.

Integrum Morborum Mysterium sive Medicinæ Catholicæ . . . Folio, fine vignette title. Francofurti, G. Fitzerus, 1631.

Collation (xii) 503 pp.

A most voluminous work, with some excellent mystical plates. Contains a fine portrait of Fludd, although he appears older than his previous ones. Included with the medical matter we find a long article on Astrology.

Part III.

ΚΑΘΟΛΙΚΟΝ Medicorum Katoptron in quo quasi speculo politissimo Morbi præsentes more demonstratio clarissime indicantur et futuri ratione prognostica aperte cernuntur atque prospicuntur. Folio. (Francofurti) 1631.

Collation (iv) 413 pp.

A most curious work on Divination, whether by Geomancy, Urine, Chiromancy, or Physiognomy, it is all detailed at great length with many cuts.

Part IV.

Pulsus seu Nova et Arcana Pulsuum Historia, e sacro fonte radicaliter extracta . . . Folio, large folding plate at end, and a fine vignette title, [Franco., 1631 (?)], *94 pp.*

Part V.

Medicamentosum Apollinis Oraculum in quo ipse Catholicum Medicandi Mysterium seu Arcanum Medicinæ tam cælestis quam terrestris sacrarium . . . videtur.

This 5th Part is one large sheet, measuring 39 by 17 inches, and is connected by the catch-word "Medi" to Part 4.

Each part (except Part V) of this important medical work has a distinct title page and separate pagination, and, throughout, the plates and cuts are well executed, some of which are of a mystical order.

Sophiæ cum Moria certamen in quo lapis lydius a structore, Fr. *Marino Mersenno* Monacho reprobatus celeberrima Voluminis sui Babylonici figmenta accurate examinat. 2 parts, Folio. (Frankfurt) 1629.

Collation 118 (ii) pp.

This work contains Fludd's reply to Mersenne, who had attacked him in 1622 (see article "Mersenne").

Summum Bonum quod est verum Magiæ Cabalæ Alchymiæ *Fratrum Rosæ Crucis* verorum. . . . in dictarum Scientiarum laudem et insigniis calumniatoris *Fratris Marini Mersenni* dedecus publicatum, per Joachimum Frizium. Folio, *Fine Vignette Title,* with the inscription, "Dat Rosa Mel Apibus." (Frankfurt) 1629, *54 pp.*

The authorship of this work has been denied by Fludd, but it is very evident that he was largely responsible for its production and certainly approved of it. It is written in defence of the Rosicrucian Fraternity's claims, and contains therein the views of Fludd and those of his friends. It has recently become exceedingly scarce.

Doctor Fludd's Answer unto M. Foster, or the Squesing of Parson Foster's Sponge, ordained by him for the wiping away of the Weapon Salve . . . 4to. London, Nat Butler, 1631.

Collation (viii) 68 pp.

A counterblast of Fludd to a pamphlet issued by the Rev. Wm. Foster, called "Hoplocrisma Spongus, or a Sponge to wipe away the Weapon Salve: a treatise wherein it is proved that the cure late taken up amongst us by applying the Salve to the Weapon is magical and unlawfull." 4to. London, 1631. 56 pp.

Clavis Philosophiæ et Alchymiæ Fluddanæ sive R. Fluddi Armigeri et Medicinæ Doctoris ad Epistolicam P. Gassendi Theologi exercitationem Responsum, &c. Folio, fine vignette title (same as the "Summum Bonum"). Francofurti, G. Fitzerum, 1633, *87 pp.*

This contains Fludd's final answer to *Gassendus, Mersenne,* and another opponent called *Lanovius,* and is rather important, since, being, twitted by Gassendus as to the absence of any place of residence being assigned to the R.C. Fraternity, he (Fludd) evades this point by relinquishing the name Rosicrucians, as he knew he was unable to meet it.

Responsum ad Hoplocrisma - Spongum M. Fosteri Presbiteri ab ipso ad unguenti armarii validitatem delendam ordinatum ... Folio. Goudæ, P. Rammazenius, 1638. Collation 30 folios, and 1 p. errors.

Philosophia Moysaica in qua Sapientia et Scientia creationis et creaturarum Sacra vereque Christiana ad amussim et enucleaté explicatur ... Folio, fine vignette title. Goudæ, P. Rammazenius, 1638.

Collation (x) 152 folios.

This was the author's last work and, as such, fitly represents his matured opinions on Metaphysics, Philosophy, &c. It is not such a voluminous one as the "Microcosmi Historica," but is was the only one of any importance that he translated into English, and thus evidently intended it to be more popular than his others. The English translation which he himself accomplished was not published until A.D. 1659.

Mosaicall Philosophy, grounded upon the Essential Truth, or Eternal Sapience, written first in Latin and afterwards thus rendered into English by Robert Fludd, Esquire, and Doctor of Physick. Folio. London, H. Moseley, at the Prince's Arms, St. Paul's Churchyard, 1659.

Collation (vi) 300 pp.

A work on Philosophy and Science, illustrated with many cuts throughout and the only one translated into English.

Discursus de Unguento Armario, pp. 507 to 513 in "Theatrum Sympatheticum Auctum," by Sylvestrus Rattray. 4to. Norimbergæ, 1662.

Meteorum insalubrium mysterium: duabus sectionibus divisum ... His accessit Oyromantia sive Divinatio per Urinam nec non nova et arcana Pulsuum scientia. Folio. Moguntiæ, L. Bourgeal, 1682.

Collation—Part I (xvi), 503 pp.; Part II, 413 pp.; Part III, 93 pp. and large table at end.

This is a re-issue of three works, viz.: "Integrum Morborum," 1631; Καθολικον Medicorum, 1631; Pulsus Historia [1631]; wanting, however, the Dedications and Hieroglyphical Engraving, etc., of the first work.

Religio Exculpata—Autore **Alitophilo** (i. e. *Robert Fludd*) Religionis fluctibus dudum immerso, tandem per Dei gratiam et indefessam enatandi Operam emerso. 4to. (Ratisbon) 1684.

Collation (viii) 459 pp.

Fasciculus Geomanticus in quo Varia Variorum opera Geomantica continentur . . . 8vo. Veronæ, 1687, *647 pp.*
Another Edition 1704.

This appears to be a reprint of a portion of the "Utriusque Cosmi" relating to Geomancy.

Schutzschrift für die Aechtheit der Rosen Kreutzergesellschaft von dem Engländer Robert de Fluctibus, der Arzneygelahrtheit Doktor zu London Wegen seiner überaus groszen Seltenheit und Wichtigkeit auf Begehren aus dem Lateinischen ins Deutsch zugleich mit einigen Anmerkungen übersetzt von AdaMah Booz. 8vo. A. F. Böhme, Leipzig, 1782, *320 pp.*

A German translation of "Tractatus Apologeticus," 1617.

Wood (Anthony à) Athenæ Oxoniensis. 2 vols, folio. 2nd Edition, 1721.

In Vol I, pp. 590, 610, and f. 169, there is an account of R. Fludd's life and works; also W. Foster, his opponent, and a statement that Fludd used some of Simon Forman's Astrological MSS. for his own books (p. 372). This is an invaluable work of reference.

Fresnoy (Lenglet du) Histoire de la Philosophie Hermetique; accompagnée d'un Catalogue raisonné des Ecrivains de cette Science . . . . 3 vols, 8vo. Paris, chez Coustelier, 1742.

Collation—Vol. I (xxiii) 486 (xx), Vol II (xxii) 360, Vol III (xxii) 432 pp..

This is the best bibliographical work on Hermetic books up to the present that we have ever seen. It must have taken the author an immense amount of time and trouble to compile, and his notes evince an amount of knowledge that is most admirable. He mentions the F.R.C. as fanatics, but I am afraid that most people are dubbed thus who run counter to the orthodox public opinion. Look back in history at the Inquisition, Tycho Brahe, Mesmer and Mesmerism. What is called fanaticism in one age becomes the creed of the next. Who could have foretold in Mesmer's time, and even later with Dr. Elliotson, here in England, that the much-ridiculed Mesmerism would be the adopted pet of the medical faculty, who in a former age could use no epithet hard enough to abuse it? *Autre temps Autres mœurs.*

Gabella (P. A.) Secretioris Philosophiæ consideratio brevis a P. A G. Philosophiæ St. conscripta et nunc primum unà cum *Confessione* Fraternitatis R.C. in lucem edita. 4to. Cassellis, G. Wesselius, 1615, *68 pp.* (*another edition*, Frankfurt 1617).
A reprint of the *Confessio*, etc.

Gassendus (Petrus) Epistolica Exercitatio in qua Principia Philosophiæ Roberti Fluddi Medici reteguntur . . . . 8vo. Paris, 1630.
Collation (xliv) 360 (ii) pp..

Contains a free criticism on Fludd's works and the "Fratres Rosæ Crucis." This was really done to relieve the burden on Mersenne's shoulders, who was getting the worst of his conflict with Fludd. So Gassendus came to the rescue, although he did not entirely exonerate his friend from blame, as his language was not very choice in his description of his opponent. Fludd replied to all this in his work," Clavis Philosophiæ," Frankfurt, 1633, including Mersenne in his diatribe. A good deal of this controversy is to be found in the "Foster" work by Fludd, vide Nos. 184, 186.

Geheime Figuren der Rosenkreuzer aus dem 16 und 17 Jahrhundert. Erstes Heft Altona J. C. Eckhardt in Commission in der Heroldschen Buchhandlung in Hamburg, 1785. Zweites Heft Altona, 1788. Drittes und letztes Heft. Altona. Folio. N.D. (1788).

Collation—1st Part, 32 pp. (title and 4 pp. letterpress); 2nd part, 34 pp.; 3rd part, 32 pp.

This valuable work was published anonymously, and the contents of the MSS. are described in No. 372. It consists chiefly of very finely coloured plates symbolical of the Rosicrucian teachings and doctrines, besides which there are a couple of tracts. One is called, "Aureum Sæculum Redivivum, or the Golden Age Revived," by H. Madathanus, A.D. 1621; the other, "Ein Güldener Tractat vom Philosophischen Steine," A.D. 1625, or "A Golden Treatise on the Philosopher's Stone." This is the work that F. Hartmann reproduced as a wonderful find in an old monastery, but which was already well known to be in existence. (vide Article).

Geheimniss aller Geheimnisse, (Das,) ex Macrocosmo et Microcosmo oder der güldene Begriff der Geheimsten Geheimnisse der Rosen und Gülden Kreutzer, mit ihren drei Steinen der Wunder. 8vo. Leipzig, Böhme, 1788, *104 pp.* Contains a number of alchemical processes.

Godwin (William) St. Leon: A Tale of the Sixteenth Century. 4 vols, 8vo. London, 1799. (Several other editions have since appeared).

This Rosicrucian romance is founded on a passage that appeared in Dr. John Campbell's translation of the work "*Hermippus Redivivus*," which also contains other curious occult matter.

Gould (Robt. F.) The History of Freemasonry: Its Antiquities, Symbols, &c. 3 vols, 4to. London, 1886.

In Vol II, Chapter 13, this erudite writer discusses at great length the relationship of Freemasonry and Rosicrucianism, especially with regard to certain Brethren who belonged to both fraternities, notably Elias Ashmole and Robert Fludd, and also to refute the idea that Freemasonry had even a part of its origin in Rosicrucianism; some Brethren however entertain strong views on this matter, and urge that there is a great similarity between the two ceremonies, the older of which is claimed to belong to the R.C. Order.

[Grasshof (Joh.)] Aperta Acta Arcani Artificiosissimi das ist eröffneter und offen stehenden Kasten der allergrösten . . . . der Natur, des Grossen und Kleinen Bauers (von Chortalasseus auch Condesyanus genannt J.G. zu Stralsund). 8vo. Frankfurt, 1617, *229 pp.* (Other editions in 1523 and 1687).

— Responsum ad Fratres R.C. illustres, Heus Leo Cruce Fidis, Lux Sat Hodie, Nam quando Fide Curris onus Propulsans Ecclesiæ. 8vo. Vigebit, 1618, *14 pp.*

[Grasshof (Joh.)] Prodromus Rhodo-Stauroticus Parergi Philos das ist Vortrab und Entdeckung derer Brüder-schaft vom R.C. . . . mit Figuren gezieret durch F. C. R. U. G. J. A. (24 Marz). 8vo. *1620.* (VII) &. *78 pp.*

Grüneisen (C.) Die Christenburg, allegorisch-epische Dichtung von *J. V. Andrea* nach einer gleichzeitigen Handschr herausg. von c.g. 8vo. Leipzig, 1836.

Guaita (Stanislas De) Essais de Sciences Maudites (I) Au Seuil du Mystère. 8vo. Paris, G. Carré, 1890.

Contains an article on the Order of the *Rose Croix,* with an alleged extract from its secret constitutions. He further states that it now numbers at present upwards of 1,000 adherents.
As it further states that its affairs are administered by a Supreme Council, I presume it is still in existence at the present time, since its founder's decease.

Güttmann (Aegidius) Offenbarung Gottlicher Mayestät darinnen angezeigt wird Wie Gott der Herr sich an-fänglich allen seinen Geschöpffen mit Worten und Wercken geoffenbaret . . . 2 vols, 4to. (Frankfurt) J. W. Däsch, 1619 (Another Edition, Amsterdam 1675).

Collation Part I (xxviii) 530 (xiii) pp.
Part II, 514 (xv) pp.

Hartmann (F.) An Adventure among the Rosicrucians by a Student of Occultism. 8vo. Boston, Occult Publishing Co., 1887, *188 pp.*

A modern work of fiction.

Heckethorn (C. W.) The Secret Societies of all Ages and Countries. 2 vols, 8vo. London, 1875.

— A comprehensive account of upwards of one hundred and sixty Secret Organisations . . . New edition, greatly enlarged. 2 vols, royal 8vo. London, 1897.

A long chapter is devoted by this author to the subject and contains a deal of interesting matter, although he treats it from a sceptical stand-point and devotes no space to their spiritual doctrines and teachings. The work contains a fine Bibliography of works upon—The Ancient Mysteries, The Cabbalah, Illuminati, Freemasonry, Inquisition, Knights Templars, and Mystics.

WORKS by JOHN HEYDON.

A New Method of Rosie Crucian Physick, where-in is shewed the cause and therewith their experienced medicines for the cure of all diseases . . . 4to. London, 1658.

Collation (vi) 62 pp.

In this early work the author states in his preface that he is not a Rosie Crucian, but throughout the work appears to have hitched himself on to the title of R.C. without appreciating the true signification thereof. He is very verbose, and loses himself in pages of windy eloquence, for the book is little better than a lot of scribbling without much point. He evidently obtained further and deeper knowledge later on, as his later works evince; but this early one makes one think of the first plunge in a new bath. He refers, however, on page 41, to Sir Christopher Heydon as the "Seraphically Illuminated Rosie Crucian and learned Astrologer," so it is just possible that this was the source where he derived his R.C. teachings from, and which blossomed out to greater advantage in his later writings.

The Rosie Crucian Infallible Axiomata, or Generall Rules to know all things, past, present, and to come, usefull, pleasant, and profitable to all, and fitted to the understanding of mean capacities. 12mo. London, 1660.

Collation (xlii) 126 pp.

The author again states in the preface to this work that he is no Rosicrucian, but he first mentions that there are a Society of men known as Rosicrucians. He then goes on deliberately to copy out of the Fama and Confessio pretty well the whole history of C.R., his life and travels, without acknowledging what I presume he must have been aware of— their having already appeared 45 years previously in German. He further refers to the Book M, and states that he himself as having "put it into English wearing the title of The Wise Man's Crown," and then describes a vault where the sun never shone; nevertheless, it was enlightened with another sun and an altar in the centre covered over with a plate of brass, &c.; and further goes on to say (p. xviii) that "there is another vault or habitation of the Brethren in the West of England," and winds up by saying that, "Thus much at this time and no more am I allowed by my Mistress Euterpe to publish." I notice that one of the laudatory epistles is signed by Fredk. Talbot, a gentleman who wrote the author's life in the work, "The Rosie Crucian Crown." The book as a whole contains some real knowledge and is one of the most valuable he has written. The bulk of it deals with the subject of numbers and shows indubitably that he passed through the lower grades of the Society.

Harmony (The) of the World being a discourse of God, Heaven, Angles, &c with the nature and harmony of man's Body; the Art of preparing Rosie Crucian Medicines, &c., *portrait*. 12vo. London, 1662.

The Holy Guide, leading the Way to the Wonder of the World (a Compleat Phisitian), teaching the knowledge of all things, past, present, and to come, viz., of pleasure, long life, health, youth, blessedness, wisdom, and virtue . . . with Rosie Crucian medicines, which. are verified by a practical examination of principles in the great world, &c. A fine portrait of the author. 8vo. London, sold by Thos. Whittlesey at the Globe in Cannon Street, near London Stone, 1662. A work published in VI. parts.

Collation—(cxxviii) 37 pp., Liber I; (xvi) 169 pp., Liber II; (viii) 226 pp., Liber III; (vi) 83 pp., Liber IV; (vi) 145 pp., Liber V; (viii) 55 pp., Liber VI; Index at end, xxix pp.

This is an excellent work, and by many considered his best. It starts with a Chemical Dictionary; then Book I deals with philosophy; Book II Numbers a reprint of his work, the R.C. "Axiomata," with a fine plate (p. 161); Book III, Long Life; Book IV, Virtue of Minerals; Book V, Gold and Rosicrucian Medicines; Book VI, The Rosie Cross Uncovered, with a most charming piece at the end, called

"The Rosie Crucian's Prayer to God." The whole of this book is virtually a reprint of the preface to his work, "The R.C. Axiomata," published in 1660, and which I have already noticed.

The Wise Man's Crown: or, the Glory of the *Rosie Cross,* showing the wonderful power of Nature, with the full discovery of the true Coelum Terroe or first matter of metals, etc.; with the *Regio Lucis* and Holy Household of Rosie-Crucian Philosophers. Communicated to the world by John Heydon, 1664.

Hammegulleh, Hampaaneah, or, The Rosie Crucian Crown, to which is set down the Angels of the Seven Planets, and their Occult Power upon the Seven Metals, and Miraculous Vertues in the Coelum Terrae, or First matter of all Things, whereunto is added a Perfect Full Discovery of the Plantarva and Elixirs of metals, by Eugenius Theodidactus *(pseud.).* post. 8vo. London, 1664.

Theomagia, or the Temple of Wisdome in three parts—Spiritual, Celestial, and Elemental; containing the Occult Powers of the Angels of Astromancy in the Telesmatical Sculpture of the Persians and Œgyptians. The Mystical Virtues of the Characters of the Stars with the Genii, Ideas, and Figures of Geomancy, &c. The Knowledge of the Rosie Crucian Physick and the Miraculous Secrets in Nature, which have performed incredible, extraordinary things . . . 8vo. Fine portrait of Author. Pub. by H. Brome at the Gun in Ivie Lane and Tho. Rooks at the Lambe at the East End of St. Paul's Church, 1664.

Collation—(cxii) 272 pp., Book I, 1664; (xii) 228 pp., Book II, 1662; (viii) 249 pp., Book III, 1663; and Index VII.

This work is a very ably written and is entirely devoted to Geomancy, with Astrology and the Angels, corresponding to the Geomantic figures, their Sigils and influences for good and evil. Most of the modern Geomantic works are taken from this and earlier books. Altogether, our author presents the subject in a very exhaustive and lucid manner, and judging by the number of works he quotes, it must have taken him a considerable time to compile. A proof of this is the various dates to the parts, one being published each year.

Psonthonphanchia: Being a Word in Season to the Enemies of Christians and an Appeal to the Natural Faculties of the Mind of Man whether there be not a God . . . in five books. 8vo. London, printed by Tho. Mabb for Wm. Gilbertson at the sign of the Bible in Giltspur Street, 1664.

Collation (x) 166 pp.

Dedicated to Aubrey de Vere, Earl of Oxford, Kt. of the Garter, etc., offering him this work on "Rosie Crucian Philosophy." The second dedication is to F. Hollis, Esq., and in it he appears to have incurred the enmity of the Church by his doctrines, as this work is really a reply to charges brought against him by the Clergy, and, although he does not mention names, yet he quotes a sermon preached at St. Paul's Cathedral on 8th May, 1664, accusing him of Atheism. The work shows a more finished style and maturer judgment.

Hammeguleh Hampaaneah, or the Rosie Crucian Crown, set with Seven Angels, 7 Planets, 7 Genii, 12 Signes, 12 Ideas, 16 Figures, and their Occult Powers upon the 7 Mettalls and Miraculous Virtues in Medicines; with the perfect full discovery of the Pantarva and Elixirs of Mettalls prepared to cure the Diseased; whereunto is added *Elhavareuna* Presoria, Regio Lucis, and Psonthon books . . . 8vo. London, printed for Samuel Speed at the Rain-bow in Fleet Street, 1665.

Collation—(xlviii) 54 pp., Books I and II; (iv) 44 pp., Book III. I am unable to be certain of this Collation as the copy to which I had access was very imperfect.

This work deals chiefly with alchemy. The author has not forgotten to insert his life by F. Talbot, which has already appeared in some of his former works.

A Quintuple Rosie-Crucian Scourge for the Due Correction of that Pseudo-Chymist and Scurrilous Emperick, Geo. Thomson, being in part a vindication of the Learned Society of Physitians. 4to. London, 1665.

A pamphlet of 6 pp., in which the author inveighes in strong language against his opponent's cribbing from his books and misrepresenting him.

El. Havareuna, or the English Physitian's Tutor in the Astrobolismes of Mettals Rosie Crucian, Miraculous Saphiric Medicines of the Sun and Moon, the Astrolasmes of Saturn, Jupiter . . . all harmoniously united and opperated by Astromancy and Geomancy, &c. Fine plates of author. 8vo. London, printed for Wm. Gilbertson at the Bible in Giltspur Street, 1665.

Collation (lxx) 208 pp.

This work contains some very choice alchemical mystical plates, and shews to my mind that he evidently got hold of valuable knowledge, which he gives out in a covert manner. A Mr. Fredk. Talbot also gives an account of John Heydon's life, mentioning that he was related to Sir Christopher Heydon, whom I strongly suspect was the channel through whom he obtained his R.C. knowledge, as he speaks so eulogistically of him in another of his books, although it is very possible he may have picked it up in his travels, as Talbot states that he went to Spain, Italy, Arabia, Egyt and Persia. He was descended from Julius Heydon, the King of Hungary and Westphalia, and Cæsar Heydon in Rome, and was articled to a Mr. Mic Petley, an attorney of Clifford's Inne, afterwards fighting for the king; and, after travelling, wrote most of his books,—recounting a list of the wonderful predictions he made concerning his Majesty, etc. He also appears to have had a good deal of influence at Court, as when he got into trouble on one occasion we find that the Duke of Buckingham espoused his cause with great success. He was also not without vulgar copyists, and others who emulated his success. He appears to have been consulted by many high ladies about various divinations, but he did not marry, although of a handsome appearance. On the whole, from the internal evidence of his writings, he appears to have gone through the lower grade of the R.C. Order and to have given out much of this to the world. Whether he was chosen as a fitting instrument to do this at that time I am unable to say, but judging that it came so shortly after the publication of the important Fama, etc., in Germany, I should not consider it unlikely that those who ruled such matters should deem it advisable to start a movement in England and selected this man as their fitting instrument; contemporaneous with him was the famous Astrologer, John Gadbury.

Higgins (Godfrey) Anacalypsis: An Attempt to draw aside the Veil of the Saitic Isis, or an Inquiry into the Origin of Languages, Nations, and Religions. 2 vols, 4to. London, 1836.

This monument of learning and research could hardly be complete without a reference to the Rosicrucians. He makes mention of the Society in several places, and states his opinion that this and other Secret Orders existed long before Christianity. He further states that "The Papist Convocations and Councils had always endeavoured to suppress these Orders because they were Christians *before* the rise of *Romish* Christianity. Verb. Sap.

Hossbach (Peter W. H.) J. Valentin Andreä und sein Zeitalter dargestellt von w.h. 8vo. Berlin, Reimer, 1819.

Collation (xvi) 296 pp.

A fine work on Andrea's life and times.

Jennings (Hargrave) The Rosicrucian, or Curious Things of the Outside World, by h.j., with contributions by two other writers. 2nd Edition. 2 vols, 8vo. London, 1863.

— The Rosicrucians: Their Rites and Mysteries, &c. 8vo. London, J. C. Hotten, 1870.

— Second Edition, revised, corrected, and considerably enlarged. 8vo. London, Chatto, 1879.

— Third Edition, newly revised and corrected, and greatly enlarged. 2 vols. Royal 8vo. London, 1887.

We have here a work of a most discursive character. It contains a mass of ill-digested information upon Rosicrucians, Antiquities, Legends, etc. His remarks hardly crystallize; they are more suggestive than positive, and deal too much with the physical aspect of our subject. In the second and third editions he has deliberately cribbed the occult plates from *Welling's Opus*, published at Franckfurt, 1760, without any acknowledgment whatever. The same remark applies to the Gnostic gems in the 3rd edition, which are taken from an old work issued by the famous Plantin Press at Antwerp, 1657. It was written by *J. Macarus*, viz., "Abraxas seu Apistopistus . . . de Gemmis Basilidianis, etc.," and published in quarto, the plates being exceptionally fine ones of "The Gnostics," etc.

— Fifth Editions, revised. 8vo. London, N.D. [George Rutledge Sons Limited].

Collation (xvi) 464 pp. and 12 Plates.

Although the title page bears the imprint 5th Edition yet it only contains the prefaces to the first 3 Editions. I am unable to trace any Fourth Edition.

Keppler (Johannis) Harmonices Mundi Libri V . . . appendix habet comparationem hujus operis cum Harmonices Cl Ptolemæi Lib III cum que *Roberti de Fluctibus,* dicti Flud Medici Oxoniensis speculationibus Har-

monicis operi de Macro et Microcosmi insertes. Folio.
Lincii, Austriæ, J. Plancus, 1619.

Collation (viii) 255 pp.

This work was written attacking Fludd's work, "Utriusque Cosmi," on
Natural Philosophy, which was replied to by the latter in his work,
"Veritatis Proscenium, etc." 1621, which Kepler replied to in his turn
by his "Prodromus Dissert, etc., 1622" (see next work), to which Fludd
again responded by issuing his "Monochordum Mundi, etc.," in the
same year, 4to, and which was reprinted in the following year as a
folio at the end of his "Anatomiæ Amphitheatrum."

— Prodromus dissertationum cosmog. continens My-
sterium Cosmog ... Apologia adversus Demonstrationem
Analyticam c.l.v.d. Roberti de Fluctibus Med Oxon ...
In qua ille se dicit respondere ad appendicem dicti operis.
Folio. Francofurti, G. Tampachii, 1621-1622.

The 3rd part contains Keppler's Apologia.

King (C. W.) The Gnostics and their Remains, Ancient
and Mediæval. 2nd edition, royal 8vo. London, 1887.

The 1st edition appeared in 1864, but this one has been considerably
enlarged. The author devotes a number of pages to our subject, and
has raised a storm of abuse from the Masonic Fraterny by venturing
to assert that that Order had its rise from the R.C., who, after the
fuss in Germany in the 17th century, came to England and started
Freemasonry, Phœnix-like, out of its ashes.

Kloss (Dr. Georg) Bibliographie der Freimaurerei und
der mit ihr in Verbindung gesetzten geheimen Gesell-
schaften, systematisch zusammengestellt. 8vo. Frankfurt am Main, J. D. Sauerländer, 1844.

A monument of labour and research. It contains entries of upwards of
5,393 works, and I am indebted to this authority for many German
works on the Rosicrucians, which I should have been obliged to omit
otherwise. It is a marvellous compilation, and of late years has become
quite unobtainable, as it has long been out of print.

Kochheim (J. H.) von Hellrieden, Tractatus errantium
in rectam et planam viam reductio das ist Beständiger
unwider sprechlicher und ganz gründtlicher Bericht von
der wahren Universalmaterie, &c. (1 Dec.). 8vo. Strasburg, E. Zetzner, 1626.

Kurtzer Discurs von der Fratrum R.C. Confession oder
Glauben. 8vo. 1617.

Levi (Eliphas) (i. e., L'Abbe Alphonse Louis Constant)
Dogme et Rituel de la Haute Magie, deuxieme Edition
tres augmentée, avec 24 figures. 2 tomes, 8vo. Paris,
1861 (and several others).

— Histoire de la Magie, avec une exposition claire et
précise de ses procédés de ses Rites et de ses Mystères,
avec 18 planches (90 figures). 8vo. Paris, 1860.

Libavius (Andreas) D.O.M.A. Wolmeinendes Bedencken
von der *Fama* vnd Confession der Brüderschafft dess R.C.
eine Universal Reformation vnd Umbkehrung der gantzen

Welt von dem jungsten Tage zu einem irrdischen Paradehys etc. betreffend . . . 8vo. Franckfurt, bei E. Emmel, Peter Kopff, 1616. (Another edition appeared at Erfurt, 1617).

Collation 294 (vii) pp.

Liber Mutus in quo tamen tota Philosophia Hermetica figuris hieroglyphicis depingitur, ter optimo maximo Deo misericordi consecratus, folisque filius artic dedicatus authore cujus nomen est *Altus* (*i. e., Saulat Jacob*). Folio. [Rupellæ, 1677.] 15 Large emblematical plates, with 2 pages of dedication to King Louis XIV of France.

It is said that the whole of the physical Rosicrucian art of Alchemy is shewn in these 15 plates. They are certainly an exceedingly curious production, and those who have hitherto been ignorant of the existence of such a work should make a point of inspecting them whenever an opportunity offers. My copy is bound up with Manget's large work on Hermetic Chemistry (vide Article, Manget, J. J.)

Madathanus (Hinricus) *pseud.* i. e. *[Count Adrianus a Mynsicht]* Aureum Seculum Redivivum das ist die vhralte entwichene Guldene Zeit, so nummehr wieder aussgangen, lieblich, geblüher vnd wollrichenden güldenen Samen gesetzet, &c., by н м. Theosophus Medicus et tandem Dei gratia auræ crucis Frater. 8vo. N.P. 1621. (Several other Editions were issued.)

Collation 23 unpaged leaves.

The Author states at the end of the Preface that he executed his Essay "in Monte Abiegnus"—a palpaple crib from the Fama and Confessio.

WORKS by MICHAEL MAIER.

Maier (Michael) Arcana Arcanissima hoc est Hieroglyphica Ægyptio-Græca . . . ad demonstrandam falsorum apud antiquos deorum . . . originem . . . 4to. [Oppenheim, 1614?]

Collation (xii) 285 (xiv) pp.

Apologeticus, quo causæ clamorum, seu Revalationum Fratrum Roseæ Crucis et silentio, sive non redditæ responsionis, una cum malevolorum refutatione, traduntur. 8vo. Francofurti, 1617.

Examen Fucorum Pseudo-Chymicorum detectorum et in gratiam veritatis amantium succincte refutatorum. Vignette Title. 4to. Francofurti, Theodor de Brij, 1617, *47 pp.*

Dedicated to a Dr. J. Hirschberger.

Jocus Severus, hoc est Tribunale æquum, quo Noctua Regina Avium, Phœnice arbitro agnoscitur. Fine Vignette Title of the Birds. 4to. Francofurti, Theo. de Bry, 1617, *76 pp.*

Symbola Aureæ Mensæ duodecim nationum Hoc est Hermœa seu Mercurii Festa ab Heroibus duodenis selectis artis Chymicæ usu, sapentia et authoritate Paribus celebrata . . . 4to. Francofurti, L. Jennis, 1617. (Fine Portrait of Author at page viii.)

Collation (xx) 621 (xliii) pp.

Silentium Post Clamores, hoc est Tractatus Apologeticus revelationum Fraternitatis Germanicæ de Rosæ Crucis et Silentii eorum. 8vo. Francofurti, L. Jennis, 1617, *142 pp.*

In this work the Author professes to explain why the Rosicrucian Order treats its applicants with silence. This was translated into German vide next Article. Another Edition in Latin appeared in Frankfurt, 1624. (Collation 100 pp.)

Silentium Post Clamores Das ist Apologi und Verantwortung wieder etlicher ungestümer Clamanten (so sich in die Fraternitat r.c. auffzunehmen begehret aber ihres Gefallens keine Antwort erlanget) Verlästerungen und Schmachreden welche sie wider dieselbige aussgegossen . . . dahren weingers dieselbe zu ihren gesellschaft auffzunehmen Bedenckens getragen. Durch r.m.f. 8vo. Franckfurt apud Lucæ Jennis, 1617. *190 pp.*

Atalanta Fugiens hoc est Emblemata Nova de secretis naturæ chymica . . . figuris cupro incisis, adjectisque sententiis . . . plus minus 50 fugis Musicalibus trium Vocum, &c. 4to. Oppenheimii, Joh. Theodori de Bry, 1618.

Collation (iii) 211 pp.

These fifty plates and the epigrammatic descriptions of them supply to the *Adept* who holds the *Clavicula* a complete view of the system of the Universe, the essential unity of all things, the possible transmutation of matter and the highest form of Theosophy able to be conceived by earthly mortals (Quod Scis Nescis, 1866).

Tripus Aureus hoc est Tres Tractatus Chymici, Selectissimi nempe,

    (i) Basilii Valentini Practica . . . ex Germanico;
    (ii) Thomæ Nortoni, Crede mihi seu ordinale in Latinum translatum;
    (iii) Cremeri Testamentum . . .

4to. Francofurti, L. Jennis, 1618. *196 pp.* (Fine portrait of Author at p. 6.)

Thomas Norton, of Bristol, wrote his Ordinal of Alchymie about 1477, it was first published in English by Ashmole in his "Theatrum Chimicum," A.D. 1652; an English work with a Latin title. However, Maier seems to have anticipated Ashmole, as it first appeared in print in the above work. The Tripus Aureus is also published in Latin in the 1678 Edition of the Museum Hermeticum.

Themis Aurea.—The Laws of the Fraternity of the Rosie Crosse, written in Latin by Count Michael Maierus, and now in English for the information of those who seek after the Knowledge of that Honourable and Mysterious Society of wise and renowned philosophers. 12mo. London, printed for N. Brooke at the Angel in Cornhill, 1656.

Collation (xxx) 136 pp.

The Dedicatory Epistle is addressed to Elias Ashmole and signed by two persons under the initials

N. L.
T. S. } H. S.

Themis Aurea, hoc est de Legibus, Fraternitatis Rosæ Crucis. Tractatus quo earum cum rei veritate convenientia utilitatis publica et. privata nec non causa necessaria evolvuntur et demonstrantur. 8vo. Francofurti, L. Jennis, 1618, *192 pp*. italics.

This important work contains the Laws of the R.C. Order. It was republished at Frankfurt, 8vo, 1624, as a continuation of "Silentium, &c." Collation pp. 101 to 236. It was translated into German by R. M. F. 8vo, Frankfurt, 1618 (244 pp.).

Viatorium hoc est De Montibus Planetarum Septem seu Metallorum: Tractatus tam utilis quam perspicuvus . . . 4to. Oppenheimii, H. Galleri. Sumptibus Joh. T. de Bry, 1618, *136 pp*.

Cantilenæ Intellectuales, in triadas novem distinctæ, de Phœnice redivivo, id est Medicinarum pretiosissima, quæ mundi Epitome et speculum est, et Clavis ternarum irreserabilium Chimiæ Arcanorum. 16mo. Romæ, 1622. (Another Edition appeared at Rostock, 1623.)

Both of these Editions are exceedingly rare and are said to be the scarcest of this Author's work.

Viridarium Chymicum, das ist Chymisches Lust Gartlein in sich begreiffend, etlich und fünffzig Philosophische Suinenbilder deren Beschreibung in teutsche Reimen gefasset durch einen Liebhaber deren Wissenschaft. Oblong 8vo. Franckfurt am Mahn, 1688, *112 pp*.

A collection of 51 plates taken by an enterprising German from Maier's various works, reduced in size and edited by Daniel Stolz von Stolzenberg with a Commentary.

Marci (Fried) Rosenkreutzer Astronomia inferior, oder septem planetarum terrestrium spagyrica recensio, &c. 8vo. Nürnberg, Endters, 1674.

Mersenne (F. Marin) Questiones Celeberrimæ in Genesim cum accurata textus explicatione in hoc volumine Athei et Deistæ impugnantur et expugnantur, &c. Folio. Paris, 1623.

The author in this work accuses Fludd of dealing with Magic, and was answered by the latter in his work, "Sophiæ cum Moria Certamen," published in 1629. (See also Article "Gassendus" in connection with this controversy.)

Michelspacherus (Stephanus) Cabala, Speculum Artis et Naturæ in Alchymia . . . *Roseæ Crucis* Fraternitati dicata edita, quo hac in materia amplius nil desideratur. 4to. 1654. Collation 14 pp. and 4 plates.

A translation of a German work published anonymously, 1615. Vide Article "Sendtschreiben mit Kurtzer Philosophischen Discurz."

Murr (Christoph Gottlieb von) Uber den wahren Ursprung der Rosenkreuzer und des F.M. Ordens: nebst einem Anhange zur Geschichte der Tempelherren. 8vo. Sulzbach, J. E. Seidel, 1803, *160 pp.*

Musæum Hermeticum omnes Sopho-Spagyricæ Artis Discipulos Fidelissime erudiens quo pacto summa illa veraque Medicina . . . inveniri, ac haberi queat, &c. 4to. Francofurti, L. Jennis, 1625.

Collation (xvi) 483 pp.

This work contains one of De Bry's Engraved Title Pages, executed in his usual excellent style. It contains Nine Alchemical Treatises—less than the succeeding editions. It is a much rarer volume, however.

— reformatum et Amplificatum . . . continens tractatus Chemicos XXI. 4to. Francofurti, Hermannum à Sande, 1678.

Collation (xii) 864 pp.

This edition is enlarged to 21 Treatises, and contains Four fine folding Mystical plates at end, symbolical of The Rosicrucian Philosophy.

— The Hermetic Museum Restored and enlarged most faithfully; instructing all the Disciples of the Sopho-Spagyric Art how that Greatest and Truest Medicine of the Philosopher's Stone may be found and held . . . containing XXII most celebrated Chemical Tracts. 2 vols, 4to. London, 1893.

We have here the only English translation of this important Hermetic work. It is edited by the well-known Author, A. E. Waite, who, however, states in the Preface that the translator prefers to preserve his anonymity. The work has been well done and is a highly creditable production, whoever is responsible for it. I notice that there is one more Treatise in this Edition than in the former. This is because there is a Key to the four Emblematical Plates alluded to in my last notice of the 1678 Edition. This Treatise now appears under the title of "The All-Wise Doorkeeper," and is a most desirable addition.

Mylius (Joannis D.) Autidotarium Medico-Chymicum Reformatum. Libr. IV., *finely engraved Portrait and*

Mylius (Joannis D.) Anatomia Auri sive Tyrocinium Medico-Chymicum continens in se partes quinque. 4to. Francofurti, L. Jennis, 1628. Finely engraved Title.

Part V contains such excellent plates (5) of the process that I thought fit to include this with the others.

Petersen (J. W.) Leben Joh. Valentin Andrea's vom Bibliothecar J.W.P. zu Stuttgardt im Würtemberg, Repertorium der Literatur. 8vo. Stuttgardt, 1782.

[**Prock** (Baron)] Der Compass der Weisen von einem Mitverwandten der innern Verfassung der ächten und rechten Freymäurerey beschrieben: herausgegeben mit Anmerkungen einer Zueignungsschrift und Vorrede, in welcher die Geschichte dieses erlauchten Ordens vom Anfang seiner Stiftung an deutlich und treulich vorgetragen, und die Irrthümer einiger ausgearteter französicher F. M. Logen entdeck werden von Ketmia Vera, 8vo. Berlin und Leipzig, C. U. Ringmacher 1779.

Collation (v) 19—386.

Another Edition appeared 1782. Collation (viii) 429 (1) pp.

Renatus (Sincerus), *pseud* i. e. *Sigmund* Richter, Die Wahrhaffte und vollkommene Bereitung des Philos. Steins der Brüderschafft aus dem Orden des Gulden und Rosen Kreutzes, darinne die Materie zu diesem Geheimniss mit seinem Nahmen genennet, etc. 8vo. Breslau, 1710 and 1714.

Collation xvi and 126 pp.

A work on Alchemy, containing numerous processes. This Author has published several others, but this is the only one that mentions the R.C.: it contains the "Rules of R.C. Fraternity for the Initiation of new members."

Schmieder (K. C.) Geschichte der Alchemie. 8vo. Halle, 1832.

This is a fine work on the R C. Order and Alchemy. It was written by a Professor at Cassel to establish by Historic Proofs the truth of the transmutation of metals. It contains many valuable Bibliographical notes.

Schweighart (Theo.) Sub umbra alarum tuarum Jehova! Pandora sextæ Aetatis sive Speculum Gratiæ, das ist Die ganze Kunst und Wissenschaft der von Gott hocherl Frat. R.C. . . . 8vo. 1617, *74 pp.*

See also Art. "Sendschreiben," and "F. de Valentia."

— Speculum sophicum Rhodo-Stauroticun das ist Weitläuffige Entdeckung dess Collegii und axiomatum von der sondern erleuchten Frat Christ R.C. Allen der wahren Weisheit begirigen...durch T.S. Constantiensem. 4to.1618.

— Menapius (F. G.) Rosæ Crucis das ist Bedencken der Gesambten Societet von dem verdeckten und angenandten scribtore (sic) F. G. Menapio ob er pro Fratre zuhalten. 8vo. April, 1619, *54 pp.*

Alberti, who was a friend of Andreas, wrote under the assumed name of *Menapius*, and the name of *Schweighardt* is affixed to the third part in fun. According to *Kloss* he also assumed the following pseudonyms, viz.: *Gometz, Joh. Procopius. Georg Odaxus*, and it is conjectured that *Agnostus* himself might also belong to this collection.

Semler (Dr. J. S.) Zusatze zu der Teutschen Uebersetzung von *Fludds* Schutzschrift für die Rosenkreuzer. 8vo. Halle (J. J. Gebauer), 1785.

Collation (xxxii) 212 pp.

— Unparteiische Sammlungen zur Historie der Rosen-kreuzer. 4 vols. 8vo. Leipzig, Beer, 1786—1788.

Collation:—Vol. 1 [xxiv], 182 (1786); Vol. 2 [xxviii], 179 (1787); Vol. 3 [xii], 2C4 (1788); Vol. 4 [viii], 196 (1788). Chronological Register [xviii]. An Impartial Collection from the History of the Rosicrucians, with some fine plates, by a most erudite writer. He adopts the view that the order existed long before the 17th. Century, and proves the existence in the 14th Century of "An association of physicians and alchemists, who united their knowledge and their labours to attain the discovery of the Philosophic Stone."

— Briefe an einen Freund in der Schweiz über den Hirtenbrief der unbekannten obern des F.M.O. alten Systems. 8vo. Leipzig, (Grasse), 1786.

Collation (xxxvi) 156 pp.

This was answered by an Anon. writer. Vide Art. "*Etwas.*"

— Von ächter hermetischer Arzenei an Herrn Leopold Baron Hirschen in Dresden. Wider falsche Maurer und Rosenkreuzer. 3 vols. 8vo. Leipzig, G. E. Beer, 1786.

Sendivogius (Mich.) Cosmopolite ou Nouvelle Lumiere de la Physique naturelle, traictant de la constitution generale des Elements simples et des composez tradiut du Latin en François par *De Bosnay.* 8vo. Paris, A Pacard, 1618. (Another Edition, with a Second Title, Paris, 1691, also in Latin, vide Manget's *Bib. Chym.,* 1702).

Collation (xiv) 152 pp.

Sendbrief an alle, welche von der Brüderschaft des ordens vom R.C. geschrieben. 8vo. Leipzig, 1615.

Sendschreiben an die Brüderschaft des hochl Ordens der R.C. mit einem Kupferstücklein auf der allerseeligsten Frat Famam und Confession, *205 pp.*

The reputed author of this, and probably the 3 preceding works, is *Th. Schweighard,* alias *Florentinus de Valentia.* Both of these authors works may be considered herewith.

Sendschreiben an die glorwürdije Brüderschaft des Hoch Ordens vom R.C. von einem derselben besondern Liebhaber gestellet (geben zu *Camposala* den 29 Januar, 1615). 8vo. 1615.

Sendschreiben an die R.C., in centro Germaniæ. 8vo. Kazauer, 1617, *40 pp.*

Sendtschreiben mit Kurtzen Philosophischen Discurz an die Gottweisse Fraternitet des löblichen Ordens des Rosen Creutzes; auff derselben *Famam* unnd *Confession* einfältig gesehen, durch einen der Göttlichen von Natur Weisheit trewlich zugethanen (10 July, 1615). 4to. N.A. or P., 1615.

Collation (viii) pp. and 4 Folding Plates.

The Plates to this Work are charmingly executed, and exhibit some very fine Rosicrucian Symbolism on its Alchemical side, they remind one of the *Mutus Liber* of which I have made mention elsewhere. It has also been translated into Latin (vide *Article* "Michelspacherus")

Sendtschreiben oder einfeltige Antwort an die hocher Brüderschaft dess hocl ordens dess R.C. Auff Die von ihnen ausgefertige Famam uund Conf. Durch einen Liebhaber der volkommenen Weissheit gestellet uund aussgesandt (12 Januar, 1615). 8vo. Frankfurt, Bringer, 1615, *16 pp.*

Shelley (Percy Bysse) St. Irvyne, or The Rosicrucian: a romance by a Gentleman of the University of Oxford. 8vo. London, J. J. Stockdale, 41 Pall Mall, 1811.

Collation (iv) 256 pp.

A fine work of fiction founded on facts obtained from the Order.

Soane (George) New Curiosities of Literature and Book of the Months. 2 vols. 8vo. London, 1847. (Second Edition, with plates, 2 vols, 1849.)

In Vol II., p. 35, a chapter is devoted to Rosicrucianism and Free-masonry and the positions very fully reyiewed, the author coming to the conclusion, however, that the "Fama" was not intended to describe a Society really existing, although he adduces some excellent evidence to shew that it was put forward by Andreas, there being nothing to show on the face of it by whom it was written. This author has got the date of the 1st Edition of the "*Universal Reformation*" correct as being A.D. 1614, but he is hopelessly out in his subsequent dates: he evidently had a meagre library at his disposal.

Trismosin (Salomon) La Toyson d'or ou la fleur des thresors en laquelle est traicté de la Pierre des Philosophes, de son excellence, effects et vertu admirable . . . enrichies de figures et des propres Couleurs . . . 8vo. Paris, 1612, chez C. Sevestre.

Collation (16) 219 pp.

I have inserted this volume on account of its beautiful plates, which are very similar to many others contained in other works on the Rosicrucians; it is translated from the German, and this Adept was the one who furnished Paracelsus with the "Philosopher's Stone."

Valentia (F. de) Jhesus Nobis Omnia! Rosa Florescens, contra F. G. Menapii (J. V. Alberti) calumnias Das ist Kurtzer Bericht vnd Widerantwort auff die sub dato 3 Junii, 1617, ex agro Norico in Latein und dann folgends den 17 Julii obgedachten Jahres Teutsch publicirte unbedachte calumnias F. G. Menapii, wider die R.C. Societet &c. 8vo. *[Francofurti]*. N.P. 1617, *44 pp.*

Another Edition appeared in 1618, 46 pp. See also Articles "Sendschreiben," and "Th. Schweighard." *Arnold* suggests that J. V. Andreas was the author, under the nom de plume (F. de V.), and if so he also possibly wrote under the two other pseudonyms. Murr contends that J. V. Alberti used this also as his pseudonym.

WORKS by THOMAS VAUGHAN,
alias EUGENIUS PHILALETHES.

Anthroposophia Theomagica: or, A Discourse of the Nature of Man and his state after death; grounded on his Creator's Proto-Chimistry, and verified by a practical examination of principles in the Great World, by *Eugenius Philalethes*. 32mo. London, printed by T. W. for H. Blunden, at the Castle in Corn-hill, 1650. (Fine Portrait of Cornelius Agrippa, at page 52).

Collation (xvi) 70 pp.

Anima Magica Abscondita: or, a Discourse of the universall Spirit of Nature, with his strange, obstruse, miraculous ascent and descent, by *Eugenius Philalethes*. 32mo. London, printed by T. W. for H. B., 1650.

Collation (xiv) 56 pp. :— 1 leaf by H. B.

This Work has been reprinted in Dr. Westcott's Hermetic Series, *vide Article.*

Magia Adamica: or the Antiquitie of Magic; and the descent thereof from Adam downwards, proved: whereunto is added a perfect and full discoverie of the *Cœlum Terræ*, or the Magicians Heavenly Chaos, and first matter of all things, by *Eugenius Philalethes*. 32mo. London, Printed by T. W., for H. Blunden, at the Castle in Corn-hill, 1650.

Collation (xxxii) 140 pp.

Observations upon Anthroposophia Theomagica and Anima Magica Abscondita, by Alazonamastix Philalethes. Printed at Parrhesia, but are to be sold by O. Pullen, at the Rose in Paul's Churchyard. 8vo. 1650.

Collation (x) 94 pp.

Henry More (The Platonist) wrote under the name of *Alazonomastix Philalethes*; Vaughan could hardly expect his publications to pass unnoticed, and he aroused the ire of this Cambridge Scholar. Later on however he retaliated in the work called, "The Man Mouse, etc.," which in its turn called forth More's reply, "The Second Lash, etc."; but our worthy Adept was not to be outwitted, and wishing to have the last word, issued another counterblast in his work, "The Second Wash, or the *Moore* scoured once *more,* etc.," which ended the matter.

The Man Mouse taken in a trap and tortur'd to death for gnawing the margins of *Eugenius Philalethes*. 32mo. Printed in London and sold at the Castle in Corn-hill, 1650.

Collation (ii) 116 pp.

The Second Lash of Alazonomastix, containing a Solid and Serious Reply to a very uncivill Answer to certain Observations upon *Anthroposophia Theomagica* and *Anima Magica Abscondita*. 32mo. Printed by the Printers to the University of Cambridge, 1651.

Collation 208 (v) pp. and Index.

The Second Wash: or, the *Moore,* (i.e., Henry Moore), scour'd once *more,* being a Charitable Cure for the Distractions of Alazonomastix, by *Eugenius Philalethes.* 32mo. London, printed by T. W., and are to be sold at the Castle in Cornhill, 1651.

Collation (xviii) 188, and Page of Errors.

Lumen de Lumine: or, A New Magical Light discovered and communicated to the World, by *Eugenius Philalethes.* 32mo. London, printed for H. Blunden at the Castle in Corne Hil, 1651, another Edition London 8vo. 1910.

Collation (xviii) 101 pp.

Aula Lucis, or the House of Light, a Discourse written in the year 1651 by s.n., a modern Speculator. 12mo. London, sold by Wm. Leake at the signe of the Crowne in Fleet Street, between the Two Temple Gates, 1652.

Collation (x) 39 (xii) pp.
This is a work treating of Alchemy.

The Fame and Confession of the Fraternity of R.C. commonly, of the Rosie Cross: with a Preface annexed thereto, and a short Declaration of their Physicall Work, by *Eugenius Philalethes.* 32mo. London, Printed by J. M., for Giles Calvert, at the Black Spread Eagle, at the West end of Paul's, 1652.

Collation (lxviii) 64 pp.

Euphrates, or the Waters of the East; being a Short Discourse of that Secret Fountain, whose Water flows from Fire; and carries in it the Beams of the Sun and Moon, by *Eugenius Philalethes.* 32mo. London, printed for Humphrey Moseley at the Prince's Arms in St. Paul's Church-yard, 1655. (Fine Mystical figure from R. Lullie, page 31).

Collation (xvi) 124 pp.

A Brief Natural History, intermixed with a variety of philosophical discourses; and observations of the burnings of Mount Ætna, with refutations of such vulgar errours as our modern authors have omitted, by Eugenius Philalethes. 32mo. London, printed for Matthew Smelt, next door to the Castle, near Moor Gate, 1669.

Collation (xiv) 120 (1) pp.
As Vaughan died in 1665 I presume that this is a spurious publication.

Aula Lucis oder das Hauss dess Liechts durch s.n. einen der Kunst zu dieser Zeit Beflissenen in Englischer Sprache beschrieben . . . durch J.L.M.C. 8vo. Franckfurt, 1690, *38 pp.*

A German edition of the English work published A.D. 1652.

The Works of Thomas Vaughan: Eugenius Philalethes, edited, annotated, and introduced, by A. E. Waite, *plate*. 8vo. London, 1919.

Collation (vi) 498 pp.

An excellent reprint of the Authors works that are of Alchemical interest ; those dealing with his dispute with Henry More the Platonist are omitted.

[**Villars** (Abbe N. de)] Le Comte de Gabalis, ou entretiens sur les Sciences Secretes. 8vo. Paris, Claude Barbin, au Palais sur le Perron de la Ste., Chapelle, 1670.

Collation (iv) 327 pp.

The First Edition of this work, which treats of the Rosicrucian ideas of Elemental Spirits, "Gnomes," "Undines," &c. The chief figure in it is said to be taken from *G. F. Borri,* who is the imaginary Count de Gabalis ; although written in a satirical vein yet it contains profound truths ; possibly the author found it necessary in those days to disseminate knownledge in this fashion. It is also stated that Pope in his work, " *The Rape of the Lock,*" obtained his ideas of the Elementaries and the general outline from this work.

— The Count de Gabalis, or the Extravagant Mysteries of the Cabalists exposed, in five pleasant discourses on the Secret Sciences. Done into English by P A. Gent, with short Animadversions. 12mo. London, Printed for R. M., Printer to the *Cabalistical Society,* of the *Sages,* at the Sign of the *Rosy-Crucian,* 1680.

Collation (viii) 183 (12) pp.

[**Villars** (Abbe N. de)] The Count de Gabalis, a diverting history of Rosicrucian Doctrine of Spirits, viz.: Sylphs, Salamanders, Gnomes and Dæmons, shewing their various influence upon human bodies. 8v. London, 1714.

— Le Comte de Gabalis, ou entretiens sur les Sciences Secretes, renouvellé et augumenté d'une Lettre sur ce sujet. 12mo. Cologne, chez Pierre Marteau, N.D. (circa, 1690.

Collation (ii) 161 pp.

Wadzeck (F.) Leben und Schicksale des beruchtigten Franz Rudolph von Grossing, eigentlich Franz M. Grossinger genannt, nebst der Geschichte und Bekanntmachung der Geheimnisse des *Rosen-Ordens* ... 8vo. Frankfurt und Leipzig, 1789.

Collation (xvi) 271 pp.

Wohlgemeyntes Ausschreiben, an die Hochw Frat. des R.C. zweyer ungennanten Biederleuth. 4to. Oppenheim, H. Balthenius, 1617, *115 pp.* (Another Edition Regensburg, 1781.)

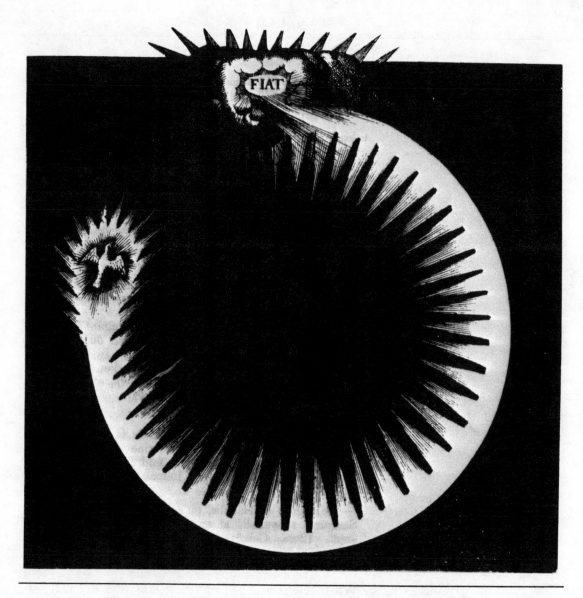

The Creation of the World. A plate by de Bry from Robert Fludd's *Utriusque cosmi ... Historia, De Macrocosmi Fabrica*, Oppenheim, 1617. From a cloud concealing the ever-secret Essence of the Father God springs the cosmic Word of the Son, expressing the creative Will, manifest in the Dove of the Holy Spirit which girdles the cosmos, at the same time setting bounds to the dark world of chaos in its luminous flight. Within the orbit of light a portion of darkness is ensphered and surrounded, thus being included in the world of Creation. In this graphic and highly unique way Robert Fludd, Rosicrucian apologist, solved the "presence of evil" in face of God's omnipresence — a problem which has plagued Church Fathers and Rabbis alike. Jacob Boehme's concept of "the darkness in God" — a teaching which made a great stir in his lifetime — drawn as it was from Rosicrucian teachings, becomes reasonable and clear in the light of this extraordinary engraving.

EDITORIAL AND REFERENCE NOTES

NOTE -   The following notes are not intended as "commentary" or "explanation" of the materials in this book. Still less do they make claim to "authority," and least of all are they put forward with dogmatic intention. — They have been compiled mainly as aids to the study of the text itself, and at the same time as a means of indicating other sources which can help to amplify and enrich the reader's appreciation of the subject as a whole.

p. 7, 1. 3-4:   *. . . our present-day comprehension of the significance of Christian Rosenkreutz . . .* The attention of the reader is drawn, first of all, to the Chronological List of *References to Christian Rosenkreutz in Lectures and Writings by Rudolf Steiner 1903-1924,* included in this volume. Extensive though these references may appear at first glance, *they are by no means complete,* since Rudolf Steiner repeatedly referred to the significance of Christian Rosenkreutz during the nearly 25 years of his continuous lecture activity. Therefore, to trace *all* such references, one would of necessity have to read the transcripts of a great share of his nearly 6,000 lectures — a formidable task indeed! — However, one point should be made clear: It is not possible to fully grasp the fundamentals of Rudolf Steiner's discussion of the significance of Christian Rosenkreutz without a working knowledge of the Science of Spirit (Anthroposophy) contained in his fundamental books. References to these written works of Rudolf Steiner are included in the Notes which follow.—

By the same token, one should not believe that the selections from lectures by Rudolf Steiner included in the main body of this book, or in the Reference Notes are presented with any dogmatic intention, for this would be an offense to the whole spirit of Rudolf Steiner's work. They are given solely with the wish to illustrate points made in the text on the one hand, and with the desire to acquaint the reader who perhaps may meet Rudolf Steiner's work for the first time through the pages of this book, with something of a first-hand impression of the general tenor of his indications regarding the significance of Christian Rosenkreutz.—

In addition to all that is indicated in the Bibliography and the following Notes, however, *one* communication of Rudolf Steiner concerning Christian Rosenkreutz is indispensable if one is to understand precisely *why* the latter is of such profound significance *in our time,* in addition to his importance in the spiritual history of humanity. This statement by Rudolf Steiner took the form of a letter written to Edouard Schure, author of *The Great Initiates,* in reply to certain questions which Schure had put to him. The document in question is dated, "Barr, Alsace, September, 1907," and the relevant section reads: "Christian Rosenkreutz went to the Orient in the first half of the 15th century in order to find the equilibrium between the initiation of the East and of the West. A consequence of this was the definite founding of the Rosicrucian orientation in the West after his return. In this form Rosicrucianism was to be the strictly secret school of preparation for what would become the public task of esotericism at the turn of the 19th and 20th centuries, after external natural science had achieved the preliminary solution of certain problems. Christian Rosenkreutz designated these problems as follows:

1. The discovery of spectral analysis, whereby the material constitution of the cosmos saw the light of day.
2. The introduction of material evolution into the science of the organic.
3. The knowledge of the fact of a condition of consciousness differing from the usual one, through the recognition of hypnotism and suggestion."

(Translated from the German original contained in Paul Regenstreif's *Beitraege zum Studium der von Rudolf Steiner gehaltenen Vortraege ueber Christian Rosenkreutz,* privately printed, Wiedenbrueck, n.d. (c. 1962), p. 4.) See also the article by Paul Regenstreif, *Ueber Christian Rosenkreutz* in *Mitteilungen aus der Anthrop. Arbeit in Deutschland,* Vol. 16, No. 3, Stuttgart, *Michaeli,* 1962, pp. 145-161, *especially* p. 156. Further details, *including Edouard Schure's presentation of this same material,* will be found in the same issue of the *Mitteilungen* in the article by Hans Reipert, *Ueber die Stellar-Spektralanalyse, op. cit, supra,* pp. 161, *seq.*

For a discussion of more recent literature on the subject of Christian Rosenkreutz and his teachings, see the article by Walter Weber, *Neuere Literatur zum Rosenkreutzertum* in *Blaetter fuer Anthroposophie,* Basel, January, 1960, 12 Jahrg., Nr. 1, p. 23, *seq.*

p. 11, l. 27: *The Thirty Years War* (1618-1648). 15 years before the outbreak of this devastating war, Andreae wrote *The Chymical Wedding* (1603) ; 7 years later (1610) the *Fama* was circulated in ms. form in the Tyrol; 4 years later (1614), the *Fama* was published; 1 year later (1615) the *Confessio* appeared in print; in 1616 *The Chymical Wedding* was published, and 2 years later The Thirty Years War broke out.—A similar time-pattern can be observed in the work of Rudolf Steiner as follows: 15 years prior to the outbreak of World War I, Steiner wrote his famous essay on the *Fairy Tale of the Green Snake and the Beautiful Lily* (Goethe's story based on *The Chymical Wedding*) in honor of the 150th anniversary of Goethe's birth (August, 1899) ; 7 years later (1906) at the conclusion of a cycle of 14 lectures, he spoke on *Rosicrucian Training,* and shortly after, on *The Path of Knowledge in the Sense of the Rosicrucians.* 4 years later, in August 1910, his Rosicrucian drama, *The Portal of Initiation,* appeared, and the next year (1911) he gave the two great Christian Rosenkreutz lectures at Neuchatel. The following year (1912) he spoke repeatedly about Christian Rosenkreutz, in Cassel, Vienna, Neuchatel, St. Gallen, Berlin, etc., and 2 years later World War I began.

The holocaust of the Thirty Years War. This war (1618-48) which began within three decades after the defeat of the Spanish Armada, was the result of political ambition and greed, religious intolerance and fanaticism. — In the 17th century more than 200 states of various sizes existed in the area of central Europe between the Elbe and the Rhone, the Baltic and the Mediterranean. In some, Roman Catholic doctrines prevailed, in others Lutheran or Calvinistic teachings. Jealousy, political intrigue, suspicion, endless bickerings and tensions were the order of the day. — At last an obscure incident — so obscure, in fact, that today it is not known exactly what it was — provided the lighted match, and the whole area exploded into one of the most terrible wars in history. — However, despite the violence with which the war began, it was only a very few years before the goals for which it was instigated were forgotten, and the armies degenerated into vast hordes of heartless mercenaries who sold their services to anyone who could offer the best prospect of plunder. One by one, outstanding military leaders were murdered, and plot and counterplot destroyed the last vestiges of command. — Everywhere bands of robbers roamed the countryside. Fields were left untilled. In city and country alike, famine and pestilence took a dreadful toll. — A reliable account gives ghastly details: "Miserable survivors in some places were reduced to eating the flesh of those slain in battle or left upon the gallows. Travelers were often murdered in order to eke out the almost non-existent food supply. Even graves were frequently opened for the same purpose." — The most infamous crimes, resulting from fanatical hatreds, often without any real or apparent objective, were committed by noble and commoner alike. Men seemed to have lost all vestige of manhood, and the beast of anarchy reigned in what had been one of the most populated and culturally advanced areas of Europe. — The ravages of the Thirty Years War were so terrible that the population of Germany alone was reduced by somewhere between one-half and two-thirds. Of all movable property, fully two-thirds had been plundered, most of it destroyed in one way or another. The value of human life was reduced to practically nill. For example, at the end of the war, in the duchy of Wurtemberg only about fifty thousand inhabitants remained alive out of a former population of over a half million. In Augsburg the population was reduced from eighty thousand to about eighteen thousand. Less than one-fourth of the population of Bohemia survived. — Human progress was at a total standstill, arts and crafts that formerly had flourished in central Europe disappeared, some of them never to reappear. Trade and communication were practically non-existent. — It is significant that in the ravages of the Thirty Years War and other characteristics of the 17th century, observers have discovered rather close parallels with certain events and trends in our present time.

p. 13, 1. 6:   ... *as early as 1603 The Chymical Wedding had been read* ... For an insight into the "historical moment" in world affairs at a variety of levels, cultural, political, scientific, etc., in the year 1600, see Walter Weber's article, *Ueber Sinn und Bedeutung der Chymische Hochzeit Christiani Rosenkreuz*, in *Blaetter fuer Anthroposophie*, Basel, December 1956, 8 Jahrg. Nr. 12, p. 454, *seq.* — (Two additional articles by the same author under the same title follow in the January and March 1957 issues of the same periodical, and are highly recommended for study.)

p. 14, 1. 2-3:   ... *surrounded as they soon were by charlatanry and fraud* ... An example of this is described by Rudolf Steiner in a lecture on June 29, 1907: "By the designation, *Preparation of the Stone of the Wise* was involved certain Rosicrucian secrets about which it has become possible to speak only in the present time. By that name were known certain rules for the entrance into the higher worlds, and these rules have existed ever since the founder of Rosicrucianism inaugurated this movement in 1459. You must bear in mind that this spiritual movement has always been handled with the greatest precaution and has always been kept secret. — Toward the end of the 18th and the beginning of the 19th century certain secrets of Rosicrucianism were revealed to the public in an unjustified manner, owing to a kind of treason. At that time several things connected with these secrets were printed, but from those publications one could realize that the people concerned had an inkling of these secrets, but did not understand them. Nevertheless they at least heard the right words, or picked them up, so to speak, — and in regard to the Stone of the Wise as well . . ."

Again in a lecture given on May 22, 1907, Rudolf Steiner mentioned the same subject: "At the time (of Goethe) when Rosicrucian wisdom was intended to flow gradually into the general life of culture, it happened, in a manner of which I need not speak further now, that a kind of betrayal took place. Certain Rosicrucian conceptions found their way into the world at large. This betrayal on the one hand, and on the other the fact that it was necessary for Western culture during the 19th century to remain for a time on the physical plane uninfluenced by esotericism — these two facts made it imperative that the sources of Rosicrucian wisdom, and above all its great Founder, *who since its inception had been constantly on the physical plane,* should, to all appearances, withdraw. Thus during the first half and also during a large part of the second half of the 19th century, little of the true Rosicrucian wisdom could be discovered. Only now, in our own time, has it become possible again to make the Rosicrucian wisdom accessible and allow it to flow into general culture." (Italics by Ed.) Publ. in *Theosophy of the Rosicrucians,* London, 1953, p. 10., new ed. 1966.

Further, in a lecture given on May 6, 1909 Rudolf Steiner said: "Many things have trickled through into outer life in regard to the Rosicrucian Mysteries, but much that is told is a caricature of the truth. Profound achievements of spiritual life were influenced by the mysterious threads of Rosicrucianism which found their way into civilization . . . But associated with the outer Brotherhood of the Rosicrucians is all the charlatanism, quackery and caricature that is unavoidable in our age since the discovery of the art of printing. Since printing was discovered it has been no longer possible, as it was in olden times, to let secrets remain secret. Everything — mature and immature alike — comes out caricatured and distorted . . ." (Publ. in *Anthroposophy, a Quarterly,* London, 1929, Vol. 4, p. 275, *seq.*)

p. 19, 1. 1-2: . . . *what the human soul experiences when it has opened the gates into the spiritual world* . . . Rudolf Steiner described true Rosicrucian Initiation as consisting of seven stages or steps ("though not necessarily consecutive") as follows: 1. *Studium,* Study; 2. Imaginative Knowledge; 3. Inspired knowledge, or Reading the Occult Script; 4. Preparation of the Philosopher's stone; 5. Correspondence between Macrocosm and Microcosm; 6. Living into the

Macrocosm; 7. Divine Bliss. — In terms suited to modern consciousness and capacities, the essentials of this path of spiritual development are described in Rudolf Steiner's *Knowledge of Higher
Worlds,* New York and London, 1963. The seven stages outlined
above are discussed in his *Theosophy of the Rosicrucians,* London,
1953, esp. pp. 159-168. Also see his *Theosophy and Rosicrucianism,*
14 lectures given in Casel, 1907, publ. in *News Sheet,* in English
transl., Vol. 10, p. 161, *seq.,* Dornach, 1942.

Careful study of the details Rudolf Steiner gives in lecture 14
(June 6, 1907) of his *Theosophy of the Rosicrucians* concerning
the two paths of Initiation: the Christian path and the Rosicrucian
path (each consisting of seven stages) and a comparison of these
with the events of the seven days of *The Chymical Wedding* will
prove very rewarding for a deepened understanding of the entire
significance of the latter work.

p. 27, 1. 16:   *. . . I have called this the Ahrimanic world . . .* See especially Rudolf
Steiner's lecture, *The Deed of Christ and the Opposing Spiritual
Powers — Lucifer, Ahriman, Mephistopheles and Asuras,* London,
1954. In the lecture on *Mephistopheles and the Earthquakes* (January 1, 1909), included in the above brochure, p. 25 *seq.,* Rudolf
Steiner used the name *Ahriman* for the first time; previously he
had spoken of "Mammon" and other designations for the evil principle opposite to Lucifer in tendency. It was *after* this that he
spoke about the Reappearance of the Christ in the Etheric World,
mainly in his lectures of 1910 and in the 1st Mystery Drama, also
written in 1910. On Ahriman, see also Rudolf Steiner's lectures,
Three Streams in the Evolution of Mankind, Oct. 1918, publ. London, 1965, also his lectures on *The Influences of Lucifer and Ahriman, Man's Responsibility for the Earth,* Nov. 1919, publ. London,
1954, etc.

p. 28, 1. 27:   *. . . Astrology . . .* See Rudolf Steiner's lecture cycle, *Man in the
Light of Occultism, Thesophy and Philosophy,* London, 1964, es-
pecially lecture 9. Also Hermann Poppelbaum's essay, *Truth and
Error in Astrology,* England, n.d. (c. 1950).

p. 29, 1. 24:   *he had to wait . . .* See *Knowledge of Higher Worlds* by Rudolf
Steiner, especially Chapters I and II.

p. 30, 1. 12-
    13:    *. . . the life-forces that engender growth . . .* Rudolf Steiner refers
to these as the *etheric formative forces.* See Guenther Wachsmuth's
book: *The Etheric Formative Forces in Cosmos, Earth and Man,*
London, 1932.

p. 30, 1. 16:   *... forces which destroy life ...* Rudolf Steiner indicated the important relationship between forces of consciousness and forces of death as observed by the Jena Professor of Philosophy, A. R. Karl Fortlage (1806-1881) and described in the latter's book, *Beitraege zur Psychologie als Wissenschaft, Leipzig,* 1875. Steiner dealt with this subject in his lecture cycle, *Das Karma des Materialismus,* lecture 5.

p. 31, 1. 10-
11:    *The spiritual impulses which ... form the human social life ...* See Rudolf Steiner, *The Threefold Commonwealth, The Inner Aspect of the Social Question, The Social Future, The Science of Spirit and the Social Question,* etc.

p. 32, 1. 16:   *Choosing the path.* This is a leading theme of Rudolf Steiner's Rosicrucian Mystery Drama, *The Portal of Initiation,* transl. by Adam Bittleston, publ. by Rudolf Steiner Publications, Blauvelt, N.Y., 1961.

p. 33, 1. 18:   *the spurious spirit-seeker.* See especially lectures 8 and 9 of Rudolf Steiner's Torquay (England) lecture cycle, *True and False Paths in Spiritual Investigation,* London, 1927, new edition 1967.

p. 34, 1. 5:   *a genuine relation with the spiritual world.* See especially, *The Science of Spirit,* by Rudolf Steiner, Blauvelt, N.Y., 1964, pp. 7-39.

p. 34, 1. 13:   *the threshold of the spiritual world.* See Rudolf Steiner, *The Threshold of the Spiritual World,* London, 1956, also the final chapters of his *Knowledge of Higher Worlds,* London, 1963.

p. 35, 1. 39:   *man and the animal form.* See *The Psychological Foundations of Anthroposophy* by Rudolf Steiner, N.Y. and London, n.d. also *Man and Animal* by Hermann Poppelbaum, London, 1960.

p. 37, 1. 11:   *the seven liberal arts ...* See the essay by Karl Heyer titled *Martianus Capella and the Seven Liberal Arts,* in *Anthroposophy Quarterly,* London, Vol. 5, No. 3, Michaelmas, 1930, p. 364, *seq.* This article appeared originally in German *Die Drei, Stuttgart,* Vol. 4, No. 12, March, 1925, p. 841 *seq.* — See also the important study by E. Schickler, M.D., *Medicine and the Seven Liberal Arts,* in *Anthroposophical Quarterly,* London, Michaelmas, 1929, Vol. 4 No. 3, p. 342, *seq.*

p. 37, 1. 35:   *the weighing of the souls ...* See Rudolf Steiner's book, *Theosophy,* London, 1965, Sec. III, p. 78, *seq., The Soul in the Soul World after Death.* A careful study of the entire book is indispensable to a clear understanding of the underlying significance of many of the leading motifs of *The Chymical Wedding*, and is warmly recommended.

p. 38, l. 10:   *Love*. See Rudolf Steiner's lecture, *Love and its Meaning in the World*, London, 1964.

p. 38, l. 29:   *community aims of mankind*. See Rudolf Steiner's lectures titled *Community Building*, New York, 1942, also references given to note on p. 3, 1.10, above. For the negative aspects of this subject, see Rudolf Steiner's *Secret Brotherhoods*, London, n.d. (c. 1935), new transl. *The Wrong and Right Use of Esoteric Knowledge*, 3 lects., 18-25 Nov. 1917, London, 1966.

p. 39, l. 30:   *can observe in a new way events of the sense world* . . . See Rudolf Steiner's, *Behind the Scenes of External Happenings*, London, 1947.

p. 40, l. 4:   . . . *the glorious Phoenix* . . . Reference to the famous bird, symbol of resurrection, known to the ancient Egyptians, Greeks and Romans. Heroditus, Pliny and Tacitus have discussed the Phoenix from many points of view, regarding it as the figurative depiction of the liberated soul. — In connection with the events concerning the Phoenix in *The Chymical Wedding*, see the *Verses Belonging to an Emblematical Scrowle*, by George Ripley, and *The Hermes Bird* by Raymond Lully, transl. by Abbot Cremer of Westminster, both included in Ashmole's famous *Theatrum Chemicum Britannicum*, London, 1652. — In Nicolas Caussin's *De symbolica Aegyptiorum sapientia*, Paris, 1618, the phoenix is shown as a symbol of the Christ, the Bringer of the powers of Resurrection to Nature and Man. — As liberated soul, the Phoenix has also been identified with the picture of the Higher Self, the Ideal Man, the true *Anthropos*. See Martin Ruland's *Lexicon alchemiae, sive Dictionarium alchemisticum*, Frankfort, 1612. — In Chinese Alchemy, the Phoenix and Dragon represent two forms of Mercury — the first, the higher form, the second, the lower. — For further details consult any standard encyclopedia.

An important indication regarding the relationship between the Bible character, Job, and the Phoenix is contained in the Section titled *Job, the Phoenix-initiate*, in Sigismund von Gleich's *Marksteine der Kulturgeschichte*, 2nd ed., Stuttgart, 1963.

p. 40, l. 5:   *secret of death and of birth* ∴ See Rudolf Steiner's *Occult Science, an Outline*, London, 1963, esp. chapter 3, *Sleep and Death*. Also his lecture cycles, *Earthly Death and Cosmic Life*, London, 1964,

The Innter Nature of Man, London, 1959, and the single lecture, *The Dead Are With Us,* London, 1964.

p. 41, l. 11-
12: *the fifteenth century as a turning-point.* See Rudolf Steiner's *Mysticism at the Dawn of the Modern Age,* Blauvelt, N.Y., 1960, also lecture 7 in his cycle on *World History in the Light of Anthroposophy,* London, 1950, and many other references in his lectures and written works.

p. 41, l. 18-
19: *. . . you will develop a feeling for a new path . . .* See especially Rudolf Steiner's lecture, *The Change in The Path to Supersensible Knowledge,* London, 1959, *also his supersensible knowledge (Anthroposophy) as a Demand of the Age,* New York, 1943, etc.

p. 41, l. 20-
21: *Christian Rosenkreutz' spiritual path as the legacy of the spiritual investigation of the fifteenth century . . .* As an example of the Rosicrucian impulse working into history, leading into modern times, see Rudolf Steiner's lecture, *Historical Characters and their Place in Evolution,* Dornach, Feb. 1, 1920, publ. as Supplement to *The Anthroposophical Movement,* London, 1933, Vol. X, No. 18, especially the following passage: "Out of this very same source whence arises inspiration for Bacon and Shakespeare, and even *proceeding from the same initiate,* flow forth for Central Europe the spiritual streams of Jacob Boehme and Jakob Balde . . . — Now mark what depth lies in the things I have been saying! From the self-same source of inspiration comes the work and influence of Bacon, Shakespeare, Boehme and Balde . . ."

p. 41, l. 33-
34: *Rosenkreutz makes his way to a great globe . . .* Rudolf Steiner is reported to have said in a conversation that such "globes" or models of the earth and heavens were connected with the Demeter Mysteries and that they were actually used in the Mystery Centers devoted to the Demeter cult. He also remarked that in the Mysteries in Tibet long ago there existed a model of earth and moon, so constructed that it was moved by celestial, etheric forces, even to the extent that the moon passed round the model earth and produced tides in the oceans represented upon it. — For further details concerning these Globes, see the Note to p. 105, l. 19, below.

p. 42, l. 19-
20: *a spritual knowledge of the heavens.* See Rudolf Steiner's *Man and the World of Stars,* New York, 1963, also *The Spiritual Hierarchies,* London, 1931, esp. lect. 9, also the single lecture on *Sun,*

Moon and Stars, Dornach, 1945. The writings of W. O. Sucher, particularly his *Isis Sophia, Outline of a New Star Wisdom,* England, 1952, and his *Man and the Stars,* England, 1955, based as they are on indications by Rudolf Steiner, are also particularly helpful.

p. 43, 1. 22: *true alchemy.* See Rudolf Steiner, *Cosmic and Human Metamorphosis,* London, 1926, particularly lectures 4 and 6, also his lecture cycle, *Earthly Death and Cosmic Life,* London, 1927, lecture 1. For bibliography of general works on alchemy, see Ferguson, John: *Bibliotheca Chemica,* included in the annotated bibliography in this book.

p. 56, 1. 12-
13: *. . . the special kind of spiritual knowledge demanded since the 15th century . . .* Basing his exposition on the indications given by Rudolf Steiner, especially those in the lecture of March 2, 1915 in the latter's *Zeitbetrachtungen,* Walter Weber shows that the human soul in initiation follows the same path it follows between death and rebirth. This path includes four stages and passes through four "Portals" as follows: 1. *The Portal of Death* leading out of the physical into the Astral (soul) world. This involves the "meeting" with *the Angel* (forces of the *head*) In *The Chymical Wedding* this is shown by the meeting of the brother R. C. with the angelic messenger on the first day.—2. *The Portal of the Elements* in the Astral world, involving the meeting with the *Lion* (forces of the *heart*). In *The Chymical Wedding* this is shown in the elements, particularly in the wind, confusion of the 4 ways under the cedars, the Lion guarding the gateway, etc. — 3. *The Portal of the Sun* leading from the Astral world to *Lower Devachan.* This involves the meeting with the *Dragon* (forces of the *will*). In *The Chymical Wedding* this Region of the Sun is shown by the Sun Temple at end of the 3rd day to the beginning of the 5th day. The *Moor* who beheads the Kings is the figure of the *Dragon* of the Door of the Sun. — 4. *The Portal of Saturn,* leading from the Lower to *Upper Devachan,* ultimately to the *Cosmic Midnight.* This involves the meeting with the *Upper and Lower Gods* as this experience was described in Greek and Egyptian mythology. The representation of the *Kings* in the Castle in *The Chymical Wedding* leads to the Cosmic Midnight. The Journey to the *Tower of Olympia* and the *Work* itself is a kind of "mirror picture" of the meeting with the Upper and Lower divine Beings. — Following this comes the return to the Sun Region, and the descent to physical earth existence once more. However, in highly artistic fashion, this descent into the physical is not related in all de-

tails in *The Chymical Wedding,* but with artistic reticence the "two leaves in quarto" which supposedly contain this account "are wanting", i.e., are missing, and "the Author . . . returned home" . . . (See Walter Weber's article for further details: *Ueber Sinn und Bedeutung der Chymischen Hochzeit Christiani Rosenkreuz* in *Blaetter Fuer Anthroposophie,* Basel, January, 1957, 9 Jahrg., Nr. 1, p. 20, *seq.*)

p. 62, 1. 9:   *Ezechiel Foxcroft (1633-1674)* — Foxcroft's boyhood home was Finsbury Court, Moore Fields, London, and his father, George Foxcroft, was a merchant of importance. On one occasion the latter was sent by the India Company to Fort St. George on a mission requiring considerable tact. He left England on Sept. 9, 1664, and returned in July, 1672 — an absence of eight years. During this period, while her husband was in India, his wife, Elizabeth, lived at Ragley as the intimate companion of Lady Conway. On July 11, 1672, Henry More, the Cambridge Platonist, a close friend of the Foxcrofts as well as of Lady Conway, wrote in a letter to the latter: "I hear Mr. Foxcroft is returned safe from the Indies, which I am glad of both for Mrs. Foxcroft's sake and his own. But I suppose this may be no occasion of any sudden removal of Mrs. Foxcroft from Ragley. Her husband that has traveled so many hundred miles if not thousands rather, to far strange countries will easily be persuaded to take so short a journey to Ragley to see his wife, before the time of her removal thence." (For data on George Foxcroft's experiences in India, see *The Burley Papers,* I, 441-2.)

Ezechiel Foxcroft occupied the position of Lecturer in Mathematics at King's College, Cambridge University, where his relative by marriage, John Worthington (1618-71), prominent Cambridge Platonist, was Chancellor. In the latter's accounts under date of September 29, 1958 appears the item: "Mathematic lecturer, Mr. Foxcroft, his year's stipend, 04/00/00." — At Worthington's death he left a rare folio edition of *Piers Plowman,* among other books, to Ezechiel Foxcroft, and a set of translations of the *Works of Jacob Boehme* to Elizabeth Foxcroft.

Another relative of Ezechiel Foxcroft was the famous theologian and philosopher (regarded as the "founder" of the school of Cambridge Platonists), Benjamin Whichcote (1609-83), provost of Kings College, Cambridge (1644), and Vice-Chancellor of the University (1650). (For a study of Whichcote's life and work see John Tulloch, *Rational Theology in the 17th Century,* 2 vols., London, 1874, reprint, 1965.)

A close friendship existed between Ezechiel Foxcroft and Henry More, as noted above. Among the latter's papers preserved in the British Museum Library (Additional Mss. 23,216) are frequent references to the young mathematics professor. For example, in a letter addressed to Lady Conway dated Oct. 13, 1670, More gives an account of a dinner he gave in honor of Franciscus Mercurius Van Helmont in his rooms at Christ's College, Cambridge. On that occasion Ezechiel Foxcroft was not only present but served as interpreter as well: "Van Helmont can speak French and Italian but Latin very brokenly, so that Mr. Foxcroft, understanding his Dutch, could with utmost ease conceive his meaning . . ."

A result of this occasion was the long visit of Van Helmont to Ragley—of utmost importance from a Rosicrucian point of view. In addition, this may have been the time when Van Helmont, identified as a Rosicrucian by Rudolf Steiner, perhaps called the attention of Ezechiel Foxcroft to *The Chymical Wedding of Christian Rosenkreutz,* and it well may have been he who advised Foxcroft to translate this work into English.

Van Helmont seems, indeed, to have had a gift for interesting scholars in each other's work. For example, on this visit to Cambridge, he interested More in Knorr von Rosenroth's work on *The Zohar,* an introduction which stimulated a long correspondence between More and Von Rosenroth, and an important contribution from More's pen to the great *Kabballa Denudata.* In similar fashion, Van Helmont had introduced Von Rosenroth to the Count Palatine of Sulzbach in 1668, who not only gave the scholar an important position in his council, but took an active interest in his work.

At Ragley, Van Helmont acted as physician to Lady Conway, and became her close friend and advisor in many things. Rosicrucian ideas were warmly discussed at Ragley, along with Alchemy, Mysticism and related subjects. There Van Helmont expounded the books of Jacob Boehme, which had been studied since 1667 when they had been purchased in London at the request of Lady Conway. Henry More himself had — temporarily at least — espoused the cause of Jacob Boehme when he wrote a poetic preface to Judge Durand Hotham's *Introduction to the Teutonic Philosophy,* London, 1650, one of the very first works on Boehme to appear in English.

p. 62, 1. 22:   . . . *Ralph Cudworth* . . . Valentine Greatrakes is reported to have treated the small son of Ralph Cudworth, and by his ministrations is credited with having saved the boy's life. (See M. H. Nicholson, *The Conway Letters,* New Haven, 1930.)

p. 63, 1. 6: *... Ragley in Warwickshire* ... Located about ½ mile south of the town of Alcester, Ragley dates back to medieval times. From the mid-eighteenth century it was the home of the Marquis of Hertford, and the main buildings were extensively remodeled about 1750. During the seventeenth century the Conway family occupied Ragley, and the estate became famous as a gathering place of several of the Cambridge Platonists, particularly because of the friendship between Henry More and Lady Anne Conway (1642-1684).

See *The Antiquities of Warwickshire* by Sir William Dugdale, London, 1656 on the early history of Ragley. For a very fascinating account of early family traditions of the Conways, see the article in the *Argosy,* 1880, vol. 30, pp. 378-387, titled *Lady Conway and Valentine Greatrakes, the Stroker,* by C. J. Langston, Rector of Beoley in Worcestershire. — For letters by Greatrakes to Lady Conway, see *The Rawdon Papers,* 1819, p. 210, *seq.* For further details on the history of Ragley, see William Smith's *A New and Compendious History of Warwickshire,* 1830, also J. T. Burgess' *Historic Warwickshire,* 1876. See also the modern study by M. H. Nicholson, *The Conway Letters, being the Correspondence of Anne, Viscountess Conway, Henry More, and their Friends.* New Haven, 1930.

p. 63, 1. 11: *... the many famous men* ... Among the names mentioned should be included one not so famous, perhaps, but of great importance for his Rosicrucian connections. This was a certain Albertus Otto Faber, a Helmontian physician, who came to London from Germany at the express invitation of the King in 1660. His tract, *Some Kindling Sparks in Matters of Physick,* dealing with medical subjects, was published in London in 1668. He was among the signers of a petition in favor of Valentine Greatrakes in 1666.

p. 63, 1. 12: *Franz Mercurius Van Helmont* ... A striking impression of this famous son of Johan Baptiste Van Helmont is given in the notes by James Crossley in the *Diary and Correspondence* of the well-known Cambridge Platonist, John Worthington (publ. by the Chetham Society, England, 1855, Vol. 2, part 1, p. 100) : "In the early part of his life Franz Mercurius Van Helmont traversed the greater part of Europe with a caravan of Bohemian gypsies to learn thoroughly their habits and language, and was so intimately conversant with every variety of man that his conversation ... is represented as in the highest degree striking and instructive. He preserved to his death the reputation of having acquired the great arcanum, and his carelessness with regard to money was such as almost to indicate that he had a perennial means of supply. During his residence in this country . . . several portraits were taken of him, now remaining in the various collections and perpetuating one of those countenances which, once seen, live in the memory and are never effaced from it." — The most famous of these portraits — that by Sir Peter Lely — is reproduced in this volume by courtesy of the Trustees of the Tate Gallery, London.

This portrait has had an interesting history. Probably given to Lady Conway by Van Helmont himself, it hung in the library at Ragley for many years. During the 18th century it was relegated to the cellars of the house, but was rescued from destruction by damp and improper storage by Horace Walpole (see the latter's *Correspondence*) and once again found a place of honor on the walls upstairs until it was sold by the Marquis of Hertford and eventually found its way to the Tate Gallery where it hangs today.

Henry More mentioned this portrait in a letter to Lady Conway (British Museum Add. Mss. 23,216, f. 107): "Mr. Lily (sic) told me he had drawn Mr. V. Helmonts picture which yett I had not the happiness to see . . . Mr. Lily did very kindly remember Mr. V. Helmont."

(For further data on Sir Peter Lely, see H. Collins Baker, *Lely and the Stuart Portrait Painters*, London, 1912.)

Incidentally, Van Helmont — who knew Henry More well, — made a number of drawings, tables and engravings for the latter's work on the *Apocalypse of John*, titled *Visionum Apocalypticarum*, included in More's *Opera Omnia*.

When Lady Conway died at Ragley, Van Helmont was with her, and in order that her husband — who was absent on business in Ireland — should be able to see her once again, made a double coffin, the inner part of glass, the outer of wood. In this he placed the body, preserved in spirits of wine according to a formula he had from his Rosicrucian-scientist father. Upon the husband's return the coffin was finally closed, placed in a leaden container, and conveyed to the little church at Arrow, accompanied by Conway, Van Helmont and Henry More, where it remains to this day.

Apparently Van Helmont left England soon after Lady Conway's death, taking with him her only written work, which was published in Latin in Amsterdam soon afterward. It was translated into

English and appeared in London in 1692 under the title, *The Principles of the Most Ancient and Modern Philosophy.*

Van Helmont had found an affinity to the teachings and customs of the Society of Friends (for example, he refused to remove his hat in the presence of Prince Rupert and Lord Craven in 1677, to their amazement), and when he died he was buried in an unmarked grave, dressed in the garb of a Quaker.

Franz Mercurius Van Helmont, son of a Rosicrucian of great importance, publisher and editor of his father's written works, traveler, linguist, philosopher, mystic, instructor of the deaf and dumb (he wrote his *Alphabet of Nature* for them) doubtless a Rosicrucian himself, physician, alchemist, was a wanderer like the gypsies whom he had loved from his youth. He is indirectly the original of the famous poem of Matthew Arnold, *The Scholar Gypsy,* and well fills the description of the youth in Joseph Glanvill's *Vanity of Dogmatising* (1661): "The lad ... who was by his poverty forced to leave his studies ... and at last to join himself to a company of vagabond gypsies, among which extravagant people, by the insinuating subtlety of his carriage, he quickly got so much in their love and esteem that they discovered to him their mystery . . . of their traditional kind of learning . . ." (According to his own note, Arnold read this passage and from it drew inspiration for his *Scholar Gypsy.* For further details see the article by M. H. Nicholson, "The Real Scholar Gypsy" in *Yale Quarterly Review,* XVIII (1929), pp. 347-63.)

See also Ernst Benz, *Die Christliche Kabbala,* Rhein-Verlag, Zurich, 1958, and Kurt Salecker, *Chr. Knorr Von Rosenroth,* in *Palaestra, No.* 178, Leipzig, 1931.

p. 64, l. 24:   ... *the great Silesian mystic, Jacob Boehme* ... The Boehme literature has become large through the years. As introductory study the Introduction to Rudolf Steiner's book, *Mysticism at the Dawn of the Modern Age,* Blauvelt, N.Y., 1960, esp. pp. 70-79, and from the text, pp. 212-19 will be found helpful. For studies on Boehme, see John Jos. Stoudt, *Sunrise to Eternity,* Phila. 1957, also Hans L. Martinsen, *Jacob Boehme,* Rev. ed., London, 1949. The best Boehme biography to date in German is by Will-Erich Peuckert, *Das Leben Jakob Boehmes,* Jena, 1924, which is included in a revised edition in the new reprint of the *Saemtliche Schriften* (Leiden 1730), ed. by Peuckert, Frommann Verlag, Stuttgart,

1960, 11 vols. — Among the wealth of essays on Boehme, the study by Albert Steffen in his *Der Kuenstler zwischen Westen and Osten,* Zuerich, 1925, pp. 159-190, also his *Jacob Boehme's Heart* in his book, *Remolding of Destinies,* New York, 1948, pp. 33-40, are recommended. In addition, among the rare works on Boehme which the editor of this present book has found helpful are Christopher Walton's *Notes and Materials,* London, 1855 (only 500 copies printed), Hermann Vetterling's *Jacob Boehme, The Illuminate of Goerlitz,* Leipzig, 1926 (only 50 copies printed). — For study of *Boehme texts* he prefers the 1715 edition (2 vols. bound as one), and for data on the various editions, translations, etc. of Boehme, the book by Werner Buddecke, *Die Jacob Boehme-Ausgaben* is of great importance. Rudolf Steiner's lecture on Jacob Boehme, given January 9, 1913, English transl. N.Y. 1942, is also recommended highly.

It is of interest that when Alexander Labzin's Russian translation of Boehme's *The Way to Christ* was submitted to the St. Petersburg censor in 1815, it was given only partial approval, the official in question stating that he feared "this work may spread the dark fundamentals of Rosicrucianism."

On the importance of the Moscow Rosicrucian Brotherhood for the development of mystical literature and the spread of these works in Russia, see especially Vernadsky, G.: *Beitraege zur Geschichte der Freimaureri und des Mystizismus in Russland.* This appeared in *Zeitschrift fuer slavische Philologie,* Bd. 4, Leipzig, 1927, pp. 162-178, esp. p. 168 *seq.*

For general information on the development and spread of Rosicrucian ideas in Russia, particularly in the 18th and early 19th centuries, see the following works and references cited in them: Zenkovsky, V.V.: *A History of Russian Philosophy,* 2 Vols., transl. by G. L. Kline, London, 1953. This is one of the most complete studies of the whole field, and the late Prof. Zenkovsky, though not in sympathy with Rosicrucianism, was a scholar of extraordinary insight and veracity. A shorter work, but also of importance for this area of study is Prof. N. O. Lossky's *History of Russian Philosophy,* New York and London, 1952. In this work, note especially reference to I. G. Schwarz (1751-1784), professor of philosophy at Moscow University (1779-82), an avowed Rosicrucian who made copious references to Rosicrucian teachings in his explanations of Boehme's *Mysterium Magnum.*

p. 67:   *The Chymical Wedding* ... The word Chymical is derived from the old Egyptian hieroglyph *K-H-M* which in ancient times meant not only *"black earth"* as opposed to the barren sand of the desert, but, in this sense, land suitable for human habitation, *hence Egypt itself*. In this root is also a relationship with a later Greek word, *chom-ia,* meaning *pouring, infusion,* connected with the study of plants in particular and growing things in general. Plutarch uses the word *chemeia,* deriving it from Egyptian *khame* (based on Hieroglyphic *K-H-M*), and calls it "the Egyptian art." The first use of the term in English is in *Piers Plowman* (1362) where it appears as *experimentis of alconomye* (the prefix *al-*is the Arabic article), and the variants in the *Piers Plowman* tests are: *al-kenemye* and *al-kamye.* — The prefix *al-* was dropped by middle of 16th century.

Traditions exist to the effect that what Plutarch called *chemeia,* "the Egyptian art," was founded by the Egyptian god Hermes (Thoth), and that this art was brought to Egypt by "Master Hermes" from Babylonia after the "confusion of tongues," at Babel. Tertullian speaks of Hermes as Hermes Trismegistus, the master of those adepts in the art. The latter — who occupied themselves extensively with the study of Nature,—therefore referred to their work as "hermetic art," taking the seal of Hermes as their emblem, which they affixed to the sides of their vessels (hence our modern expression, "hermetically sealed.")

Fundamentally, therefore, *Chymical* refers to a knowledge of nature, which in turn leads to a study of how matter is infused with life, involving principles of metamorphosis, birth, growth, death, etc. This naturally brings one to the problem of the relationship between spirit and matter, how the spirit incarnates itself, as it were, in matter, unites itself with matter. And the knowledge of the uniting of spirit and matter in this fashion is *The Chymical Wedding,* seen from one aspect.

But, since the human being himself participates in the phenomena of matter and spirit, he too shares in this "wedding" as a part of his growth and spiritual development, at progressively higher levels. The ultimate for him — described in the pictures of *The Chymical Wedding* — will be the *transformation* of matter through the working of his higher nature (described by Rudolf Steiner as "the higher ego") upon the lower principles of his being. In a sense, therefore, this book, *The Chymical Wedding* can be said to be a direct forerunner of Rudolf Steiner's *Knowledge of Higher Worlds.* Also see his lectures titled *How the Spiritual World Interpenetrates the Physical* (1914).

p. 68, 1. 1,

seq.: *... the Evening before Easter Day ...* According to the Perpetual Calendar and the first Spring Full Moon, Holy Saturday in 1459 fell on March 24th. In that year Easter apparently coincided with the date of Easter calculated according to the non- or semi-astronomical Easter Rule of the Roman Church — March 25th.

Rudolf Steiner once indicated that in a spiritual sense each day "begins" at 6 o'clock on the evening before. Thus the opening events of the spiritual initiation of Christian Rosenkreutz are pervaded by the Easter mood of Resurrection, and this accompanies the entire course of action spread over a whole week. —

Compare this with the mystical "journey" of Dante which also covers a full week, rather carefully articulated in *The Divine Comedy:* The action begins on April 7, 1300; at nightfall of the next day, Good Friday, Dante enters the *Inferno,* leaves it on the morning of Easter Sunday at 5 o'clock — and enters the *Purgatorio.* The events there continue to midday on the Wednesday after Easter; he enters the *Paradiso* at noon on that day, and the whole "action" is completed 24 hours later, on Thursday noon. (See Lord Vernon's *Readings in Dante,* based on the great commentary by Scartazzini, 6 vols., London, 1906.) Rudolf Steiner's lecture, *Dante's Divine Comedy,* Feb. 11, 1906, publ. in *English News Sheet,* Dornach, 1936, Vol. 4, p. 73 *seq.,* contains helpful indications on the spiritual aspects of Dante's work. Also see the two articles by Roberto Passaglia, *Die Erkenntnis des Uebersinnlichen in Dantes Goettlicher Komoedie,* in *Blaetter fuer Anthroposophie,* Basel, 1957, 9 Jahrg., Nr. 1, January, p. 14, *seq.,* also *ibid,* Nr. 2, February, p. 64 *seq.* —

It is of interest to compare the spiritual qualities of each day of the week with the particular events which occur in the week-long initiation of Christian Rosenkreutz. — In a spiritual sense, the week of seven days is a totality, an organism with definite inner relationships, dynamics, etc. For example, in the series of 7, 4 is the center-point, the "moment" of greatest tension, the "middle" toward which the action or development "rises," and away from which it flows. The principle of "beginning, middle and end" is basic to every work of art which involves *time* (as in *The Chymical Wedding*), or *dynamics,* as for example, in the arrangement of the columns of the first Goetheanun Building designed by Rudolf Steiner.

The *Geocentric* configuration of the planets for Easter Eve, March 24, 1459, shown in the drawing prepared for this book by Mr. Willi Sucher, clearly indicates the conjunction of Uranus and Pluto through the Node of the Moon.

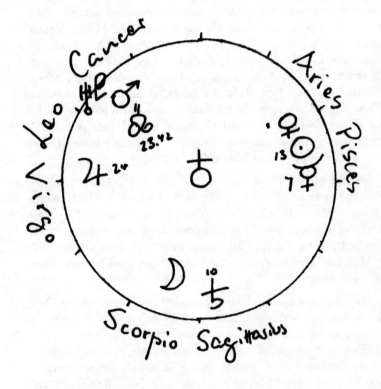

Geocentric
March 24, 1459, c. 6 pm
"Eve before Easter"

p. 69: *The Sign in the margin.* — This is the celebrated *Hieroglyphic Monad* about which Dr. John Dee (1527-1607) wrote his famous treatise which he dedicated to the Emperor Maximilian II (1527-76) at the time of the latter's coronation as King of Bohemia, 1564. A facsimile of the title page of Dee's book is included among the illustrations in this present volume. —

As can be readily observed, the Sign breaks down into 6 parts which, together with the whole, make a sevenfold totality. The components include the planetary signs for Sun, Moon, Venus, Mercury, Earth and the Zodiacal sign for Aries. United in one sign, as here in *The Chymical Wedding,* they indicate a harmonious constellation in Aries between Mercury, Venus, Sun, Moon and Earth. This is a sign *of total balance,* of harmonious relationship between the outer and inner, macrocosm and microcosm. *This is the Easter Constellation,* and Christian Rosenkreutz specifically states that his spiritual adventure began "the Evening before Easter Day," i.e., late in the day of March 24, 1459. —

This element of balance is carried into the very title of the work itself in the German original (modified by Foxcroft), which reads: *Chymische Hochzeit Christiani Rosenkreuz, Anno 1459.* (See facsimile of original title page reproduced in this book.) Rudolf Steiner states in his essay, p. 28, *supra,* that "with good reason" the year 1459 has been added to the title of the book. Rosenkreutz himself also speaks of 1459 as "a year of balance."

According to information kindly provided for this book by Mr. Willi Sucher, Easter 1459 was remarkable as the time of a configuration in Leo, Virgo and Libra (Balance). Virgo shows especially the "alchymical" aspect, with Jupiter, Venus, Neptune and Earth included in it. Jupiter stands at a right-angle aspect to Saturn in Saggitarius. Mercury stands in Libra (Balance). Mr. Sucher concludes, "The year 1459 was a 'Mercury year' and therefore the position of Mercury in the Balance is particularly important. Rudolf Steiner might have had this in mind when he spoke of 'the year of balance.' "

Another possibility of viewing this question of the "year of balance" is offered by the well-known historian, the late Dr. Karl Heyer, in his *Geschichtsimpulse des Rosenkreutzertums,* Historical Impulse of Rosicrucianism, 2nd ed., Stuttgart, 1959: "The year 1459 in the title points to the year when, in a decisive and actual manner the new Rosicrucian movement was established in the Western World . . . "

p. 70, 1. 8-9:   *... the searching out and understanding of the secrets of Nature ...* In the preface to his *Opus Mago-Cabbalisticum,* Georgius von Welling wrote, "Our intention is not directed toward teaching anyone how to make gold, but toward something much higher, namely how Nature may be seen and recognized as coming from God, and God in Nature." See also the remarkable dialogue reported by Rudolf Steiner between the Rosicrucian teacher and his pupil in the lecture given on Jan. 5, 1924, Dornach, publ. in *Rosicrucianism and Modern Initiation,* London, 2nd ed. 1965, p. 20, *seq.*

p. 71, 1. 27, *seq.*:   In the margin opposite this verse, both in the original German edition of *The Chymical Wedding,* 1616, and in Foxcroft's English translation, the following appears: *Vide St. Bernard, Serm. 3, de 7 Fragmentis.* This refers to a section in the collected edition of the works of St. Bernard of Clairvaux (1090-1153), edited by Andre Bocard, publ. Paris, 1508, titled *Seraphica melliflui doctoris S. Bernardi scripta.*

p. 72, 1. 7:   *For now a Cord shall be let down* — *...* In this dream about the cord, one is reminded of the motif of the "Mercurial chain" cited by Eunapius in his praise of Porphyry, when he said that the latter was "like a Mercurial chain let down for the benefit of mortals." This in turn recalls the famous *Aurea Catena Homeri,* The Golden Chain of Homer, based on the well-known passage at the opening of the Eighth Book of Homer's *Illiad*: Zeus asserts his supremacy in the words, "Let ye down the Golden chain/From Heaven, and pull at its inferior links/Both Goddesses and Gods. But *Me* your King,/Supreme in wisdom, ye shall never draw/To Earth from Heaven, strive with Me as ye may./But I, if willing to exert My power,/The Earth itself, the sea, and you,/Will lift with ease together, and will wind/The Chain around the spiry summit sharp/Of the Olympian, that all things upheaved/Shall hang in the mid Heav'n." — In Thomas Taylor's great translation of Proclus' *On the Theology of Plato,* Book vii, ch. 41-42, and also in his *Commentary on the Timaeus of Plato,* Book iii, are two noble passages related to the Golden Chain of Homer, q.v. — This theme of the Golden Chain extends down the centuries almost without interruption, and it is not without significance that it also appears — though in slightly altered guise — in *The Chymical Wedding.* — In the 18th century Goethe studied a book on hermetic lore titled *Aurea Catena Homeri,* Leipzig, 1738 — one of six works he mentions in his Autobiography as having formed the basis for his alchemical studies. Incidentally, the motto on the title-page of this latter work reads in translation: "He who does not understand the earthly, how will he understand the heavenly?"

A similar motif appears in one of the beautiful Hasidic tales — a product of the rich Jewish mystical current which flourished mainly in western Russia and Poland in the 18th and early 19th centuries. — "The souls of men descended from heaven to earth by means of a long ladder. Then the ladder was removed. And now, up there, they are calling the souls to return home whence they came. Some do not move, for how can one climb up to heaven again without a ladder? Others leap and fall and leap again, and at last give up. But there are those who, knowing full well that of themselves they cannot achieve it, nevertheless try over and over again until finally God catches hold of them and pulls them up." (See Martin Buber's works, especially his *Tales of the Hasidim*, his *Tales of Rabbi Nachman,* and his *Ten Rungs, Hasidic Sayings.*)

p. 74, 1. 22: *D.L.S.* Either *Deus Lux Solis* ("God, the Light of the Sun") or *Deo Laus Semper* ("To God Eternal Praise").

p. 75, 1. 9-
10: *... a Ribbon bound cross-ways over my shoulder ... four red roses . . .* This reference to the Roses and the Cross, along with similar passages in *The Chymical Wedding* and the *Fame and Confession R.C.,* has caused considerable discussion in the past, some writers identifying these symbols with the family coat of arms of Johan Valentine Andreae, others pointing to something similar in the crest of Martin Luther. Goethe, on the other hand, in his poem, *The Mysteries,* depicts the arrival of the pilgrim, Brother Mark, at a mountain sanctuary, where . . .

"Upon the arch above the closed portal
A symbol full of mystery beholding . . .
He ponders long: What does this sign convey? . . .
He sees the Cross and bows his head in seeing,
He feels anew the faith of all on earth,
The power of salvation steaming thence;
But as he looks, he feels his very soul
Pervaded by a new and unknown sense:
Who added to the Cross the wreath of Roses?
It is entwined by blooming clusters dense,
Profusely spreading just as though they could
Endow with softness e'en the rigid wood . . . "

Rudolf Steiner, in line with these thoughts of Goethe has pointed to the profound reality concealed by these symbols, and refers to them in many places in his books and lectures. The following passage will serve as an example, taken from a lecture he gave on June 24, 1909:

"Those who called themselves Johannine Christians, whose symbol was the Rose Cross, considered that just what was reborn for humanity as the secret of man's higher self, was preserved by that intimate community which grew out of Rosicrucianism. This community is symbolically indicated by that holy cup from which Christ drank with his disciples . . . that is, the Holy Grail . . . A temple was erected to house this vessel, and the Rosicrucians became guardians of what it contained . . . *The one who knows the secret of the Holy Grail knows that from the wood of the Cross springs ever new life, the immortal self, symbolized by the Roses on the black wood of the Cross.*"

p. 75, 1. 12:   *. . . I took Bread, Salt and Water . . .* In ancient times these three substances were regarded as symbols for fire, knowledge and life, respectively. In the individual man the bread corresponds to the fire of his life of activity, of will, the salt to his life of thinking, and the water to his life of feeling.

For further indications see: Lectures by Rudolf Steiner, January 13 and 14, 1923, Dornach, on *Salt, Mercury, Sulphur,* publ. in *Anthroposophy, Quarterly,* London, 1931, Vol. 6, No. 1, p. 1, *seq.,* and the lecture of Jan. 14th in *Dornach News Sheet,* 1934, Vol. 2, p. 21, *seq.*

On the relationship between salt and bread, see the article by Rudolf Hauschka, M.D., *Der Salz prozess und das Brot,* in *Natura,* Jan./Feb. 1930, 4 Jahrg. No. 4/5, p. 109 *seq.*

See also the article by Dr. Grete Bockholt, *Eine Gralsberg im Gehirn,* in *Natura,* Arlesheim, Sept. 1926, No. 3, p. 75 *seq.,* and another by Drs. Suchantke and Diefenbach, *Ein geheimer Bauplan in den Naturreichen und seine Offenbarung in den Salzen,* in *Natura,* Arlesheim, Jan./Feb. 1930, 4 Jahrg. No. 4/5, p. 89 *seq.*

In his *Opus Mago-Cabbalisticum, Homberg,* 1735, Georgius von Welling wrote, "Fallen Man, having come through sin and ruin into a state of putrefaction, must be regenerated, and maintained in a fixed and permanent condition, through *the sweet, fixed Salt* of eternal and gentle peace, Christ Jesus." This comparison between the Salt and the Christ is not infrequently met with in early Rosicrucian and alchemistic writings.

p. 75, 1. 22-23: " ... *I departed out of my cell with joy*. In his important lecture, *Salt, Mercury and Sulphur*, Dornach, January 14, 1923, Rudolf Steiner points out that the "releasing" or "dissolving" "mercurial process" can be observed in external Nature at Easter time, when the plants build up their new leaves and buds after the more "solidified" and "rigid" condition of winter. This vernal turning-point is a time of great joy in Nature, brought about by the redeeming power of *love*. The opening scene in *The Chymical Wedding* reflects this joyful mood of the Easter Festival of Resurrection.

For a description of the working of the salt, sulphur, mercury processes in their relation to the turning-points of the year and the Festivals, in a Rosicrucian sense, see the article by Christian Lahusen, *Von der Fortenwickelung des Christentums aus dem Geiste des Rosenkreutzertums in Blaetter fuer Anthroposophie*, Basel, Oct. 1956, 8 Jahrg., No. 19, p. 374, *seq.*

p. 76, 1. 1: ... *into a Forrest* ... Compare with the opening of Dante's spiritual journey in *The Divine Comedy*:

> *Nel mezzo del cammin di nostra vita*
> *Mi ritrovai per una selva oscura* ...

In Longfellow's translation:
> "Midway upon the journey of our life
> I found myself within a forest dark ..."

In similar fashion, Spenser's *Faerie Queene* IV, ii, 45 relates that they were

> "Seeking adventures in the savage wood ..."

The *Tesoretto* by Brunetto Latini, the "teacher" of Dante, which Rudolf Steiner referred to as "an initiation book," also opens with "a dark forest," "mountain" and "wild beasts."

p. 76, 1. 5-7: ... *the Birds chanted more pleasantly than before, the young Fawns skipped so merrily ... they rejoiced my old Heart, and moved me to sing* ... This mood of rejoicing in Nature and Man is the mood of Easter and Resurrection, for this "Second Day" is Easter Day itself. Rudolf Steiner indicated this mood of "rejoicing" in a lecture given April 10, 1909, titled *The Spiritual Bells of Easter* (publ. in *Easter*, London, 1956, p. 99, *seq.*): "It is precisely at the time of Easter that man's soul can become imbued with the unshakable conviction that in the innermost core of man's being lies a fount of eternal, divine existence, a fount of strength which enables us to break free from bondage to matter and, without losing our identity, to become one with the fountain-head of cosmic existence. To this inner fount we can penetrate at all times through higher knowledge. The Easter Festival is an outer sign of this deep experience within the reach of man, an outer sign of the deepest Christian Mystery ..."—In this light one can understand why it was precisely at Easter time that Christian Rosenkreutz and Dante experienced their "becoming one with the fountain-head of cosmic existence" in Initiation.

p. 77, l. 10-11:

... I espyed a Tablet fastened to one of them ... In the margin of the 1616 ed. of *The Chymical Wedding* at this point is written: *Tabella Mercurialis* (Tablet of Mercury) and the cedar to which the tablet is fixed is called *Arbor Mercurialis* (Tree of Mercury).

p. 79, l. 40:

Procul hinc, procul ite profani, "Far away remain, O you profane ones!" See Plate III of Heinrich Khunrath's *Amphitheater of Eternal Wisdom,* included in this book.

Of the many statements concerning this injunction which might be chosen, some of the best are quoted from classical sources by Rudolf Steiner in the chapter titled *Mysteries and Mystery Wisdom* in his *Christianity as Mystical Fact and the Mysteries of Antiquity,* Rudolf Steiner Publications, New York, 1961, p. 48, *seq.* and the Notes, pp. 207-209.

Among writers on Rosicrucian themes, Thomas Vaughan has given a remarkable exposition in his *Anima Magica Abscondita,* London, 1650, in these words: "But, Reader, let me advise thee: if by what is written here thou attainest to any knowledge in this point — which I hold impossible without a divine assistance — let me advise thee, I say, not to attempt anything rashly; for Agrippa tells me, 'Whosoever doth approach unpurified calls down judgment on himself and is given over to the devouring of the evil spirit.' — There is in the magical records a memorable story of a Jew who having rifled some spiritual treasures, was translated into the solitudes and is kept there for an example to others. I will give thee the best counsel that can be given, and that out of a poet: 'Demand a healthy mind in healthful frame.' — Thou must prepare thyself till thou art conformable to Him Whom thou would'st entertain, and that in every respect ... Fit thy roof to thy God in what thou canst, and in what thou canst not He will help thee. When thou hast thus set thy house in order, do not think thy Guest will come without invitation. Thou must tire Him out with pious importunities, Perpetual knockings at His door,/Tears sullying His transparent rooms,/Sighs upon sighs: weep more and more—/ He comes./—This is the way thou must walk in, which if thou dost thou shall perceive a sudden illustration, 'and there shall then abide in thee fire with light, wind with fire, power with wind, knowledge with power, and with knowledge an integrity of sober mind.' This is the chain that qualifies a magician. For saith Agrippa, 'To make search into things future and things at hand, or into other hidden things, and those which are foreshown to men divinely, and into true significations, as also to perform works exceeding the common course of the powers of Nature, is not possible apart from a profound and perfect doctrine, *an uncorrupted life and faith,* and is not to be performed by light-minded or uninstructed men.' "—

Out of just this kind of Rosicrucian approach, Rudolf Steiner once said prophetically to a group of scientists: "One day there will be Scientists who can show how matter is arranged according to the will of Christ, and to whom the laboratory table will mean what the altar does to the priest."

p. 80, l. 20:   *. . . these two Letters S.C. . . .* Either *Sanctitate Constantia* (Constancy in Piety), or *Spes Charitas* (Hope and Love).

p. 81, l. 2:   *Date et dabitur vobis!* ("Pray and it will be given to you!")

p. 81, l. 3:   *A terrible grim Lion.* Reminiscent of the lion confronted by *Christian* in John Bunyan's *Pilgrim's Progress,* written in 1675, 15 years before Foxcroft's translation of *The Chymical Wedding* was published. It has been suggested that the lion is an imaginative picture of Rosenkreutz' own inner, instinctual life which — as with everyone—is more or less held in restraint in everyday physical existence, but is "released" in the spiritual world. Hence the lion figures that aspect of Rosenkreutz which the latter must transform in the course of his experiences.

p. 81, l. 14:   *S.M.=Studio Merentis* (Merit in Study—*Studium* being the first step on the Rosicrucian path, as Rudolf Steiner has indicated), *Sal Mineralis,* (Mineral Salt), *Sal Menstrualis* (Salt of Purification).

p. 82, l. 5:   *S.P.N. = Salus per Naturam,* "Rescue through Nature," *Sponsus Praesentandi Nuptiis,* "Guest of the Bridegroom at the Wedding."

p. 83, l. 19:   *certain great Sr John's,* etc. The original 1616 text reads *Dessen doch etlich grosse Hansen.* This has been rendered by Weber, 1957, p. 24 as *Einige Grosshansen,* etc.

p. 84, 1. 4-6: *rustling of the heavens . . . Plato's ideas . . . Democritus' atoms* . . . The first probably refers to the Music of the Spheres, concerning which see Rudolf Steiner's lecture cycle, *The Effect of Occult Development*, London, 1945, lecture 3, p. 40, *seq.*, also Edouard Schure's *The Great Initiates*, New York, 1961. For an understanding of the reference to Plato's ideas, see Rudolf Steiner's *Christianity as Mystical Fact*, New York, 1961, p. 84, *seq.*, *Plato as a Mystic*. Democritus' atoms refers to the teaching of the greatest of the Greek physical philosophers, an older contemporary of Socrates, who taught that the atoms are eternal, invisible, so small that their size cannot be diminished, hence their name, *"atomos,"* meaning "indivisible." For Rudolf Steiner's comments on the atomic theory, see *Wonders of the World*, London, 1963, p. 184, *seq.*

p. 90, 1. 1-2: *. . . the bright Sun, having raised himself, etc. . . .* This reference to the Sun rising and standing at the highest point of the heavens is important, since it emphasizes the "new light" of the sun following Easter Sunday, for this is the dawn of Easter Monday, often referred to in Europe as "White Monday."—In his lecture given on March 27, 1921, titled *Spirit Triumphant* (in *Easter*, London, 1956, p. 52, *seq.*) Rudolf Steiner indicated that "The true Easter thought will never be within our reach if we cannot realize that whenever we speak of Christ we must look beyond the earthly into the *cosmic*. Modern thinking has made the cosmos into a corpse. Today we gaze at the stars and calculate their movements—in other words we make calculations about the corpse of the universe, never perceiving that in the stars there is *life,* and that the will of the cosmic Spirit prevails in their courses. Christ descended to humanity in order to unite the souls of men with this cosmic Spirit. And he alone proclaims the Gospel of Christ truly, who affirms that *what the sun reveals to the physical senses is the outer expression of the Spirit in our universe, of its resurrecting Spirit.* There must be a living realization of the connection of this Spirit of the universe *with the sun,* and of how the time of the Easter festival has been determined by the relationship prevailing between the sun and moon in spring . . ."

p. 92, 1. 31: *Lapiden Spitalanficum makers* . . . makers of so-called "universal remedies" or panaceas, i.e., makers of quack medicines.

p. 95, 1. 18-19: *. . . presented everyone with the Golden Fleece with a flying Lion.* The symbol of the Golden Fleece reflects the golden light of the supersensible, the purified etheric, life-forces, of which the ancients said, "He who hath this, hath all." In alchemical language, the Flying Lion, reminiscent of the winged lion of St. Mark, was called *Aurum Volatile,* Volatile Gold, and the symbol itself represents the purified heart forces. The image of the Golden Fleece upon which is pictured a Winged or Flying Lion, therefore, is a picture of the purified heart forces, shining like the golden light of the sun.— Among the illustrations in *The Secret Symbols of the Rosicrucians,* included in the present volume, this motif will be found in various forms.

p. 102, 1. 10: *A Draught of Forgetfulness* . . . At a certain stage of his spiritual initiation, Dante drank the "draught of forgetfulness" when he bathed in the river Lethe. This motif is a very ancient one, but plays a distinct role in modern spiritual training as well. See, for example, Rudolf Steiner's book, *Knowledge of Higher Worlds,* London, 1963, pages 64-5.

p. 102, 1.36: *a beautiful snow-white Unicorn* . . . An extensive literature exists concerning this famous creature, symbol of pure spiritual discernment. See particularly Shepherd, Odell: *The Lore of the Unicorn,* London, 1930; Lucas, F.A.: *The Unicorn and his Horn,* in *Natural History,* Vol. 20, pp. 533-35, New York, 1920; Jung, *Psychology and Alchemy,* London, 1953, esp. Chapter 6, part 2. Important bibliographical references will be found at end of article on the Unicorn, *Encl. Brit.,* 11th ed., Vol. 27, p. 581-2, also on the same subject by I. M. Casanowicz in Vol. 12, p. 344, of *The Jewish Encyclopedia,* New York, c. 1916. Since Christian Rosenkreutz—according to the *Fame and Confession*—was trained in the Middle East, points of interest will be found in the investigation of the Unicorn in the culture of that region. See Ettinghausen, Richard: *The Unicorn* in *Studies of Muslim Iconography* series, Freer Gallery, Washington, D.C., 1950. —It has been suggested that a connection exists between the horn of the Unicorn and organs of spiritual perception among human beings in earlier epochs. See Wachsmuth, Guenther, *The Evolution of Mankind,* Dornach, 1961, esp. Chap. 10, p. 127 *seq.,* on *Supersensible Perception and its Organs.* Compare Rudolf Steiner's *Knowledge of Higher Worlds,* London, 1963, p. 83, *seq.* For indications on the spiritual nature of the *horse,* see Rudolf Steiner's lectures on *The Apocalypse,* London, 1958, lecture 4, p. 78 *seq.* An extremely worthwhile and original study will also be found in the article by the late Karl Koenig, M.D., *Bruder Pferd,* publ. in *Die Drei,* Stuttgart, March/April and May/June 1966.

p. 102, 1. 38:   *the Unicorn bowed himself to the Lyon* . . . Included among the illustrations in this volume is a representation of this scene, taken from the magnificent Unicorn Tapestries series on display at the Cloisters of the Metropolitan Museum in New York. See Rorimer, James J. (Ed.): *The Unicorn Tapestries at the Cloisters, A Picture Book*, New York, 1946. It is of particular interest that these tapestries were created in 1499, just 30 years after the events of *The Chymical Wedding* took place. Useful information will also be found in Cyril G. E. Blunt's article, *The Lion and the Unicorn*, in *Antiquity*, Vol. 4, pp. 425-37, Gloucester, England, 1930.

p. 103, 1. 9:   *We were to wash our hands and heads* . . . A significant parallel is to be found in the words of Peter at the Washing of the Feet before the Last Supper: "Simon Peter saith unto him, Lord, not my feet only, but also my hands and my head" (John 13:9). Further insight into these words will be found in Rudolf Steiner's lecture cycles on the Gospels, also in Emil Bock's *The Three Years*, London, 1956, and his *Studies in the Gospels*, London, c. 1936.

p. 105, 1. 18:   *A terrestrial Globe* . . . One of the most famous globes of this type was made by Martin Behem or Behaim (c. 1436-1507), noted traveler, geographer and merchant. The globe was constructed at Nuremberg, and has interested visitors to that city ever since. For details, see: Ravenstein, E. G.: *Martin Behaim, his Life and his Globe*, London, 1909.

More famous, however, was the great *Globe of Gottorp*, created between 1652 and 1664 under the direction of the great traveler, Orientalist and archivist, Adam Oelschlaeger (Olearius) (1600-1671), with the help of the master-mechanic, Andreas Busch. Constructed of copper, 11 feet in diameter, the globe weighed about $3\frac{1}{2}$ tons, and 12 persons could be seated inside it at one time. There they could observe the course of the stars, and the planetarium moved by an ingenious arrangement of water-power. The sun was represented as a great crystal, the planets were shown in silver and gold, and the zodiac was represented in luminous precious stones. —The Globe, which soon became famous as "a wonder of the world," was set up in the garden of the castle of Duke Friedrich III of Holstein-Gottorp on an island in the Schlei. Finally, in 1725 the grandson of the Duke, Christian Augustus, gave it as a present to Peter the Great of Russia. After tremendous difficulties in transportation, the globe was finally erected in the grounds of the royal palace of the Tsar in 1754. Some years afterward it was damaged in a great fire, but was restored and removed to the grounds of the royal palace at Tsarskoie-Selo. When that town was captured by German troops in World War II, it was decided to return the Globe to its original home in the West. An account of its journey was published in a Bingen periodical, June, 1943. Finally, in June, 1946 the Globe was once again dismantled and was returned to Leningrad.

As a supplement to the story of the *Gottorp Globe,* it is of interest that another resident of the castle of the Dukes of Holstein-Gottorp, Prince Karl of Hesse (1744-1836), was a protector and patron of the Count St. Germain, and an enthusiastic student of mysticism.

From another point of view, however, the image of the Globe in *The Chymical Wedding* has to do, undoubtedly, with the spiritual relationship between man and universe, a subject of intense interest to the early Rosicrucians. Robert Fludd's writings were illustrated with many plates on this subject—several are included in this book —and other authors dealt with this same theme.

The theme of the Globe also found expression in a rare and little-known mystical work of the 17th century by Dr. John Pordage: *Theologia Mystica /or/ The Mystic Divinitie/ of the Aeternal Invisibles/viz.,/ The Archetypous Globe, or the Original Globe,/ or World of all Globes,/ Worlds, Essences, Centers, Elements, Principles/and Creations whatsoever ...,* London, 1683.

p. 111, 1. 3, seq.:

My name contains five and fifty, and yet hath only eight letters.—The well-known philosopher, Gottfried W. von Leibnitz (1646-1716), solved the riddle in this fashion:
My name contains five and fifty . . . letters:
In the alphabet, A is the 1st letter, L is 12th, C is 3rd, H is 8th, I is 9th, M is 13th. The total of these numbers is:

(A) 1 + (L) 12 + (C) 3 + (H) 8 + (I) 9 + (M) 13 + (A) 1 = 55. (Apparently the second I is *not* counted.)
... And yet hath only eight letters:
A L C H I M I A
1 2 3 4 5 6 7 8

—With this as a key, the solution of the riddle itself becomes an easy arithmetical exercise!

p. 113, 1. 13-14:

... I was all the night troubled with a Door which I could not get open ... This picture, reminiscent of many others of similar nature in fairy tales and myths, points to the spiritual fact, so well known

664

in earlier times, that it is the task of the human soul, upon falling asleep, to open the door into the supersensible world. Rudolf Steiner described in detail the experiences of the soul in relation to the spiritual world during the state of sleep in Chapter 3 of his *Occult Science, An Outline,* London, 1963, p. 60, *seq.* It is also noteworthy that Rudolf Steiner once indicated that the phenomenon of insomnia, so prevalent in our modern world, could be overcome if men would once again cultivate "a feeling for the holiness of sleep," involving a new appreciation for the beauty of the night as a time when spiritual powers are at work restoring the forces in man and nature which the activities of day have removed. (See Friedrich Rittlemeyer's *Meditation, Letters on the Guidance of the Inner Life,* Revised ed., London, 1948, esp. Chapter 2, p. 20, *seq.*)

p. 114, 1. 26: . . . *HERMES PRINCEIPS,* etc. . . . An approximate translation would be: "I, Hermes the Prince,/ Who after so many trials, / Which are put to human kind / By divine judgment, / And by the help of Art—/Am become a healing substance,/ Flowing here—/Drink from me who can,/Wash himself who may,/Make me impure who dares,/Drink, Brothers, and live!"/

The script which follows the Latin inscription has been translated by Kienast as 1378.

It is not without significance that this date is at the same time the date of the *birth* of Christian Rosenkreutz *and* of the *death* of the Bohemian and German King and Emperor, Charles IV, "last Initiate on the throne of the Emperors," as Rudolf Steiner indicated, and builder of Castle Karlstein, where *The Chymical Wedding* is depicted in frescoes. (See pages 14-15 and page 450 *seq.* in this book.)

p. 115, 1. 21: *three hundred sixty-five stairs (steps)*: It has been suggested that these indicate the patient, daily meditative work required if one is to enter the spiritual world in the right way. See Rudolf Steiner's book, *Knowledge of Higher Worlds,* London, 1963, p. 66, *seq., Some Practical Aspects.*

p. 117, 1. 23
     seq.: . . . *a small but unpressibly curious Altar* . . . This altar with its symbols is discussed in Rudolf Steiner's essay, p. 47, above. *The serpent with the skull* is shown as a motif in the title page of Robert Fludd's *Tractatus Theologo-Philosophicus,* 1617, dedicated to the Brotherhood of the Rosy Cross, reproduced among the illustrations in this present volume.

p. 121, l. 5,

seq.: *. . . many remarkable passages in this Comedy . . .* The word *Comedy* is used here in the old sense of the Italian *Commedia,* which means *a drama, a tale,* as opposed to modern usage. In the ancient theater, particularly in Greece, the true purpose of drama involved the principles of *Katharsis,* Purification, of which Aristotle speaks in his well-known essay. This "Comedy" in *The Chymical Wedding* follows this classic principle exactly. For a discussion of its main points, see Rudolf Steiner's essay, page 46, *supra.*

p. 122, l. 24: *the four Beasts of Daniel.* Reference to the account of the four great beasts which came up out of the sea in the Old Testament book of Daniel, Chapter 7, 3-8.

p. 123, l. 13: *Nebuchadnezzar's Image.* This is described in Daniel, Chapter 3, in the Old Testament.

p. 123, l. 26: *. . . who in a trice, made a great Globe of the World, and soon undid it again.* —Modern materialism has indeed built up a technical world "in a trice," like magic, but because it is based upon an exclusion of the spiritual, it does not last. It is soon undone again in the blind pursuit for something "new."

p. 124, l. 7-8: *Vivat Sponsus, Vivat Sponsa!* —"Hail the Bridegroom, Hail the Bride!"

p. 126, l. 34

seq.: *The beheading of the Kings and Queens.* See Rudolf Steiner's essay, p. 48, *supra.* This motif of the "beheading" has its counterpart in a fairy tale motif which has various forms. For example, in *The Gold Bird* in the collection of the Brothers Grimm, the fox loses his head and paws, and at once is transformed into a man. This motif is discussed by Rudolf Meyer in his *Die Weisheit der deutschen Volksmaerchen,* 8th ed., Stuttgart, 1950, p. 127. — The principle involved is that *through sacrifice alone* can higher stages of spiritual development come about. This Goethe has depicted wonderfully in the sacrifice of the Snake in his *Fairy Tale of the Green Snake and the Beautiful Lily,* based on themes from *The Chymical Wedding.*

It is of interest in this connection, that Rudolf Steiner once observed that much of the Rosicrucian wisdom was clothed in picture-form and made available to people at large through the medium of the fairy tale. Hence the importance of the genuine fairy tales — particularly those of the Brothers Grimm. — See also Rudolf Steiner, *Rosenkreuzerisches Weistum in der Maerchendichtung,* Lecture, June 10, 1911.

p. 127, 1. 26,
seq.: ... *the great lake ... seven Ships* ... The lake is a picture of the etheric world, and the motif of the souls (the descending flames) of the beheaded kings and queens entering into the ships is a reflection of the experience of the soul after death, as described in the ancient Egyptian *Book of the Dead*. See Rudolf Steiner's lecture cycle, *Egyptian Myths and Mysteries*, London, 1933 and his *Universe, Earth and Man*, London, 1955, etc. For the boats of the dead in Ancient Egypt, see: Murray, Margaret A.: *The Splendor that was Egypt*, New York, 1957; Budge, E. A. Wallace: *The Book of the Dead*, New York, 1960, reprint ed., etc.

p. 127, 1. 28: ... *About midnight, as soon as it had struck twelve, on a sudden I espied on the lake a great Fire* ... At the conclusion of this fourth or central day in the whole spiritual development of *The Chymical Wedding*, the *original* German text of 1616 contains a highly significant detail, generally overlooked in later reprintings. At this point in the 1st edition, the German word for "I" (*Ich*) which up to now has been printed with a small letter i, except when it has appeared at the opening of sentences, is printed with a capital "I." — But this capital letter disappears again at once!—With this graphic detail is perhaps suggested that Christian Rosenkreutz at this moment looks ·through the window into the spiritual (etheric) world with enhanced faculties of perception, his higher self, his higher "I" awakened by all that has taken place during the past hours at this vital turning-point in his experience.

p. 127, 1. 31: ... *I saw seven ships*. .. In his edition of the text of *The Chymical Wedding* in modern German (2nd edition, Stuttgart, 1957) Walter Weber has equated these ships with *the seven planets*. (*opus cit.*, p. 73.)

p. 129, 1. 11,
seq.: Kienast has translated this inscription as "Hye lygt begraben/ Venus, / dye schoen Fraw, so manchen / Hoen man / umb glueck, ehr segen, und wolfart / gebracht hatt." This can be rendered in English approximately as: "Here Venus lies buried, the beautiful woman who has robbed so many noble men of fortune, honor, blessing and well-being."

p. 130, 1. 13,
seq.: ... *here lies buried Lady Venus* ... Here Venus is to be identified with Demeter, the Goddess Natura. See Rudolf Steiner's essay, page 51, above, also his lecture cycle, *Wonders of the World*, London, 1963, esp. lectures 1 and 2. important indications are also to

be found in dramatic form in Edouard Schure's *Sacred Drama of Eleusus,* in his *Genesis of Tragedy,* London, 1936.

p. 131, top of page: Kienast has translated this inscription as "Wan dye Frucht meynes/baums wyrt vollends /verschmelzen, werde ych / aufwachen und eyn /muter seyn eynes / Konygs." — This may be rendered approximately as, "When the fruit of my tree fully melts, I will awaken and become the mother of a king." In other words, when the decaying fruit of the Tree of Life above the sleeping figure has entirely "melted," i.e., returned to its etheric state, and a "new beginning" can come about, then Venus, figure of the origins of life, Demeter-Natura, will stir to new activity and will be able to bring forth "a king", i.e., a man created in harmony with the highest ideals of humanity.

p. 134: *Drawing of the Pentagon.* The pentagon is the "picture" of Man. See Baravalle, Hermann v.: *Geometrie als Sprache der Formen,* 2nd ed. Stuttgart, 1963, and his *Darstellende Geometrie nach dynamischer Methode,* Stuttgart, 1959 for a fundamentl approach to the *experiencing* of geometric forms in relation to man and nature. Also helpful is Schuepbach, Werner: *Ueber das Geometrische im menschlichen Skelett,* Stuttgart 1947/48. For important indications see the article by Hermann v. Baravalle, *Die geometrische Figuren des Agrippa v. Nettesheim,* in *Anthroposophie,* Stuttgart, Oct./Dec. 1932, 14 Jahrg., Buch 1, p. 61. *seq.*

p. 142, l. 22, seq.: *... I saw the Globe hanging by a strong Chain in the middle of the Room ...* This action of the light as a force of resurrection in this passage in *The Chymical Wedding* is to be compared with a similar remark in Thomas Vaughan's *Anima Magica Abscondita,* 1650, "Trust not those impostors that tell you of ... I know not what fables, who pin also that new and narrow name *Chemia* on a science both ancient and infinite. It is the light only that can be truly multiplied, for this ascends to and descends from the first fountain of multiplication and generation. This light applied to any body whatsoever exalts and perfects it after its own kind: if to animals, it exalts animals; if to vegetables, vegetables; if to minerals, it refines minerals and translates them from the worst to the best condition ..."

On the fire from heaven and the reflecting mirrors, see *The Romance of the Rose* by deLorris and de Meun, Sec. 84, p. 386, *seq.* in the translation by H. W. Robbins, Dutton, New York, 1962, where Nature expounds the properties of the mirrors. — Though of course the *Romance of the Rose* in manuscript form is very much older, it was finally published in 1481 — just 22 years after the events described in *The Chymical Wedding,* 1459, took place.

p. 143, l. 24-5:   . . . *a lovely, great snow-white Egg* . . . This is the so-called "egg of the philosophers," known to the adepts of ancient Babylonia and Egypt as the symbol of the creation. To the Greeks, the egg was the symbol of the universe itself. In early Christian times the Easter Egg was associated with the Christ Event which transformed the creation and the creature. — The Easter mood of Springtime pervades the events of this "day" in the spiritual development of Christian Rosenkreutz. "Cutting the egg of the philosophers" is the subject of one of the illustrations in this present book.

Among the wonderful frescoes by Fra Angelico which adorn the walls of the cells in the Convent of San Marco in Florence is one of the Resurrection, in which the women are looking into the empty tomb below, while the Figure of the Risen One, surrounded by an egg-shaped nimbus of light appears above them. This painting illustrates in a most remarkable way the same motif of the "egg of the Philosophers."

p. 144:   *the Latin inscription:* In the notes to his German ed. of *The Chymical Wedding,* Weber indicates that the first two lines are fragmentary and — particularly the second — exceedingly difficult to translate. The words on the second side are: *Health - Snow - Lance.* The third side is inscribed: *It shall be.* The fourth side reads: *What | Fire: Air: Water: Earth | Of our Kings' and Queens' | Sacred Ashes | Were not able to annihilate, | The true community of Alchemists | in this Urn | Have Assembled | In the Year of Our Lord 1459.*

Kienast translated the script at the bottom of this page as *1459,* the Year of the events of *The Chymical Wedding.*

The motif of *Health - Snow - Lance* found beautiful expression in the famous Ninth Book of Wolfram von Eschenbach's *Parzival,* where Parzival, pondering his soul's health and salvation, leans upon his lance as he stands in the snow. See the first complete English translation of this work by Mustard and Passage, Vintage Books, New York, 1961, p. 245, *seq.* — This is one of the most central images of the whole story.

p. 145, l. 22:   . . . *his Feathers began to be curiously colored* . . . The role of feathered birds, feathered serpents, and similar creatures in fairy tales and mythologies of various peoples is well known. Mozart's opera, *The Magic Flute* with its "feathered man" is actually a drama of initiation. In that opera one can observe all the experiences of Christian Rosenkreutz in another form.

p. 150, 1. 36-7:

... *a bright Stream of Fire* ... Speaking of fire as "the universal fountain of life, order, distinction and beauty in the Universe," Oswaldus Crollius (1580-1609) wrote in the *Admonitory Preface* to his *D.O.M.A. Basilica Chymica Contiens,* Engl. transl., London, 1657: "Nature is that medium which by an harmonicall consent joyneth the lowest things to the highest, and some times is called Animall, sometimes Vegetable, sometimes Minerall, according to the diversity of the subject or receptacle. Those who diligently seek out the Hermetick Phylosophy and the marvelous works of God, know that that same Spirit and Minerall Nature which produceth *Gold* in the bowells of the earth, is also in Man. That Spirit in *Gold* is the same generating Fire, that Spirit in all creatures, and is the same and only generative Nature diffused through all things. This living, spiritual Gold, this meer Fire, hath now assumed a Naturall body; It is that which first moveth and ruleth Nature in all Naturall things, it preserveth all things, and all inferior things by a kind of harmonicall consent are governed by it ..."

p. 154, 1. 8-9:

... *Knights of the Golden Stone* ... In a remarkable passage in his *Letter on the Use of the Hebrew Language* (1767), the great scholar William Jones of Nayland (1726-1800) wrote: "The word *Aurum,* Gold, is Latin, which can be traced up to no Latin original; but in Hebrew the word *Aur* expresses a kindred idea; it signifies *Light,* to which Gold is more nearly allied than any other substance, from its color and its splendor; and in the symbolical language of the Chemists, Gold stands for the *Sun.* When we have once obtained a leading idea in Hebrew, it is pleasant to see how other words in abundance will fall in with it: for hence we have the word *Aurora,* for the Light of the Morning; *Horus* a name of the Sun with the Egyptians; *Orion,* the bright constellation, the brightest in the heavens; *ora* and *orios,* beautiful, because the Light is the most beautiful of all things; *ouranos,* the Heaven; and many others. So simple is the Hebrew, and so perfect in its construction, that even Light itself is not an *original* sense, for *Aur* is from *Ar,* a biliteral root, which signifies *to flow;* Light being in perpetual flux, and the most perfect of all fluids; perhaps the only *absolute* fluid in all Nature."—Consideration of this passage in the light of the concluding events of the 6th Day and this opening of the 7th will help one to understand something of the significance of the name given to Christian Rosenkreutz and his friends at this point.

p. 154, 1. 13-15: *AR. NAT. MI. and TEM. NA. F. — Ars naturae ministra,* "Art is the Priestess of Nature." *Temporis natura filia,* "Nature is the Daughter of Time." These two sayings not only reveal that the work which has been accomplished is "Art" in the highest sense, but that it involves the central principle of Rosicrucian initiation, the profound secret of "Dying and Becoming" in space as well as in time.

p. 154, 1. 20: *The Ships were twelve in number . . .* — Previously there were seven ships; now there are twelve. This points to the profound secret, described in Parsival's words, "Here time becomes space." In other words, Parsival comes to the Castle of the Holy Grail as he leaves behind him all that has been built up by Nature on the foundation of ever-evolving cycles of time, and enters into the precincts of a spiritual "space", a holy temple girdled by the eternal pictures of the Zodiac. See Rudolf Steiner's lecture cycle on *The Apocalypse,* London, 1958, especially lecture 2, also Emil Bock's *The Apocalypse of John,* London, 1957, p. 186-7.

p. 154, 1. 27: *Our Flags were the twelve Celestial Signs, and we sate in Libra.* — The sign of Libra, or the Balance points to a reaching out toward the external world and deeds in the physical sphere. It is a "critical" sign, for it indicates a question as to what man will do with the spiritual wisdom he has gained from the "Virgin Sophia:" whether he will put it at the service of the death-sting of the "Scorpion," of the intellect, or whether he will use it to transform the latter into the ascending "Eagle," rising upward to the light of the spiritual Sun. In the year's course, the path from the wisdom of the "Virgin" to the critical meeting with the "Scorpion" passes through the moment of Michaelmas, associated with the Archangelic Leader of the Hosts of Heaven. — And Rudolf Steiner has indicated the urgent necessity for modern men to find their relationship to Michael in our time. — Thus it is prophetic that Christian Rosenkreutz finds his place under the sign of "Libra," the sign of Michael, at the summit of his spiritual development. — See Rudolf Steiner's *The Mission of the Archangel Michael,* New York, 1961, his *Michaelmas, The Significance of the Impulse of Michael,* London, 1957, and his *The Michael Mystery,* London, 1956.

This relationship between the aspirations of the Rosicrucians and the Being of Michael was indicated by Rudolf Steiner in lectures given on January 4-13, 1924: "It is the peculiar characteristic of the Rosicurcians that in a time of transition these Rosicrucians had to remain in certain dream-like conditions. They could only, as it were, dream the higher truths, and had to watch what sober science found in Nature, next to them. And one can say that Rosicrucianism is characterized by the fact that their most enlightened spirits had a great longing to meet a spiritual being. They could only do it as in a dream. Only since the end of the last third of the 19th century is it possible for human beings to do in a conscious way what they attempted in a dream, namely to meet *the Spirit of Michael.*"

p. 156, 1. 16:   . . . *we came to the first gate where the Port r waited* . . . See Rudolf Steiner's essay, page 56, line 25, *seq.,* above.

p. 159, 1. 6:   . . . *to vow upon the following Articles* . . . These "Articles" or rules for their life are reflected in the concluding words of Thomas Vaughan's *Anima Magica Abscondita,* or *Discourse of the Universal Spirit of Nature,* London, 1650: "If thou dost intend to be a solid Christian philosopher, thou must, as Agrippa saith, 'live to God and the Angels,' reject all things which are 'contrary to Heaven'; otherwise thou canst have no communion with superiors (i.e. higher spiritual beings — Ed.). Lastly, 'be single, not solitary,' and avoid the multitude — as well of passions as persons."

p. 159, 1. 20:   . . . *that you shall not be willing to live longer than God will have you* . . . See the story of Signor Gualdi at Venice in *Hermippus Redivivus, or the Sage's Triumph over Old Age and the Grave,* etc. 2nd ed., London, 1749, p. 160, *seq.* Supposedly by a German physician, Dr. John Henry Colhausen, transl. by Dr. John Campbell, this curious work has been cited as having Rosicrucian implications, particularly in relation to the account of the mysterious Signor Gualdi.—

p. 160, top of
    page: *Summa Scientia nihil Scire,* etc . . . This may be translated as *The Highest Wisdom is to Know Nothing. Brother Christian Rosenkreutz, Knight of the Golden Stone, in the Year 1459.* For a discussion of the meaning of the expression, *The Golden Stone,* see Rudolf Steiner's essay, page 55, *seq.,* above.

In his *Anima Magica Abscondita,* London, 1650, Thomas Vaughan describes this Golden Stone in these words: "This, Reader, is the Christian Philosopher's Stone—a Stone so often inculcated in Scripture. This is the Rock in the Wilderness because it is in great obscurity, and few there are who know the right way to it. This is the Stone of Fire in Ezekiel; this is the Stone with Seven Eyes upon it in Zachary; and this is the White Stone with the New Name in the Revelation. But in the Gospel where Christ Himself speaks — Who was born to discover mysteries and communicate Heaven to earth — it is more clearly described. This is the Salt which you ought to have in yourselves, this is the Water and Spirit whereof you must be born again; and this is that Seed which falls to the ground and multiplies to an hundred fold."

p. 164, *seq.*: The first edition of the *Fama* was published in Cassel, "not later than August" 1614. It was titled: *Universal and General Reformation of the Whole Wide World; together with the Fama Fraterntatis of the Laudable Order of the Rosy Cross, written to all the learned and Rulers of Europe; also a short Reply sent by Herr Haselmeyer, for which he was seized by the Jesuits and put in irons on a Galley; Now put forth in print and communicated to all true Hearts. Printed at Cassel by Wilhelm Wessel,* 1614.

One of the earliest, if not the earliest ms. English versions of the *Fame and Confession* is the so-called "Crawford Manuscript" of 1633, preserved in the private library of the Earls of Crawford and Balcarres. On the flyleaf is written, "Balcarres, 1633," and the writer was Sir David Lindsay, created first Lord Balcarres, June, 1633, died 1641. He is known to have had a profound interest in alchemy, and "left in ms. several volumes of transcripts and translations from the works of the Rosicrucians."

This present translation, dated 1652 and ascribed to Thomas Vaughan, is based to some extent at least, upon the "Crawford Manuscript."

p. 164, 1. 12-
13: ...*Men endowed with great Wisdom* ... In writings on the subject of Rosicrucianism, the question of the antiquity of Rosicrucian wisdom has often been raised. With some authors, it is traced to Biblical times, while others see it as of later or earlier origin. Two passages from lectures by Rudolf Steiner bear upon this question. The first is from his lecture cycle, *Universe, Earth and Man,* August 16, 1908, publ. London, 1955, and reads: "The wonderful harmony between the Egyptian remembrance in wisdom and the Christian impulse of power is found in Rosicrucianism." — The second is from his lecture of June 10, 1911: "I have said that since the 11th, 12th, 13th and 14th centuries the spirit has worked as a

true Rosicrucian spirit, but it was always there, and has only assumed this last form since the dates mentioned. This spirit that is active at present as the Rosicrucian spirit goes back to very early ages of humanity. *Its mysteries existed in Atlantis.* The activity it has more recently developed, *becoming ever more and more conscious,* streamed not so very long ago in an unconscious way into the hearts and souls of men ..." (Italics ours.—Ed.)

p. 164, 1. 25:   *Porphiry.* At this point all German texts read, "the Pope," and the Crawford ms. reads *Popery,* hence "Porphiry" is perhaps a corruption.

p. 164, 1. 38-
39:   ... *although descended of Noble Parents* ... In his *New and Authentic History of the Rosicrucians,* Fr. Wittemans, Lawyer and member of the Belgian Senate, writes: "An important communication has been made by H. Roegsen (should be *Roesgen*) von Floss (sic) of the Hague, who writes: 'According to a tradition which exists in the family von Roegsen (*Roesgen*) Germelshausen, its members were included among the initiates in the German Mysteries. Although swept away by the current and become Christian, this family remained faithful to the neo-Gnostics who appeared in the Order of the Albigenses. The latter made adherents, especially in France, and they also had branches in Germany. The assassination, in 1208 of the Papal Legate, Pierre de Castelnau, furnished the Pope, Innocent III, with a pretext for accusing the Order of the Albigenses with it and having them exterminated. He confided this mission in Germany to the Dominican Order. The castle of Germelshausen was besieged, set on fire, and sacked. The whole family was exterminated in the most barbarous manner. But the youngest scion, Christian, escaped and fled, proceeding toward the East. Aided by co-religionists, he arrived finally in Turkey and Arabia where he was judged worthy of having revealed to him the secrets of the Order of the Rosy Cross, which had long been flourishing in those countries. Returning to Europe, Christian renounced his family name and took that of Christian Rosenkreutz.' " Wittemans, *History of the Rosicrucians,* London, 1938, p. 210.

p. 164, 1. 39-
40:   ... *in the fifth year of his age was placed in a Cloyster* ...
If the data contained in the note above is accepted as factual, then it well may have been that the boy was placed in the monastery as a means of protecting his life, to begin with. — In addition, the

well-known scholar, Dr. Johann Salomon Semler (1725-91), professor of Theology at Halle from 1752 until his death, and historian of Rosicrucianism, reports that this was the St. Agneten Monastery of the Augustinian Order near Zwolle, in the Netherlands. According to Semler's data, one of the fellow-brothers of Rosenkreutz was Thomas a Kempis (1380-1471), who wrote there a *Hortulus Rosarium,* and whose four books of the *Imitation of Christ* Theophilus Schweighardt called the *fons et origo,* fount and origin of the Rosicrucian "credo." See Semler, Joh. Salomo, *Unparteiische Samlungen zur Historie der Rosenkreutzer,* 4 Vols., Leipzig, 1786.

p. 165, 1. 2-
3:      ... *being yet in his growing years, he was associated to a Brother* ... etc. Dr. Solomon Semler (see note above) records that in the year 1393 the Bishop of Utrecht, Florentius Radewijns died. He had been engaged in alchemistic studies at the St. Ageneten Monastery with the Deacon, Gerhard Groote (1340-84). As their "adjunct and collaborant" a boy served them, whom in jest they called "Rosenkreutz," but whose real name was different. After the death of the Bishop, his patron and protector, the young *Famulus* Rosenkreutz went on a journey to the Orient. —

The life story of Gerhard Groote is related in connection with Ruysbroeck and the Brothers of the Common Life, in the introduction to Rudolf Steiner's book, *Mysticism at the Dawn of the Modern Age,* Blauvelt, N.Y., 1960, pp. 44-49. See also: Seeholtz, A.G.: *Friends of God, Practical Mystics of the 14th Century,* Columbia Univ. Press, N.Y., 1934. For a valuable study of the period of Eckhardt, Groote, Cusa, etc., see Jeanne Ancelet-Hustache, *Master Eckhart and the Rhineland Mystics,* Harper, N.Y., 1957.

p. 165, 1. 6:   ... *Damasco* ... i.e., Damascus. Famous as the scene of the great spiritual meeting of Paul with the Risen Christ, Damascus is a place of special etheric qualities, as has been noted by Emil Bock in his *Studies in the Gospels,* London, c. 1936 and in his *The Three Years,* London, 1956, p. 273, *seq.* Herman Beckh also pointed to this in his essay, *Die Rosen von Damaskus,* in *Die Christengemeinschaft,* Stuttgart, Vol. XI, No. 9, Dec. 1934, p. 264 *seq.*

It is noteworthy that while the Crusaders sought the Holy Sepulcher and those *physical* places associated with the life of Christ on earth, Christian Rosenkreutz sought out the *spiritual atmosphere* of Damascus where St. Paul had beheld the Risen, Etheric Christ. (See Rudolf Meyer's book, *Der Gral und Seine Hueter,* Stuttgart, 1957).

p. 165, 1. 10:   *. . . the Wise men of Damasco in Arabia . . .* i.e., *Damcar,* today *Dhamar* (Yemen) in southern Arabia, known in ancient times as "Arabia felix," located on the east side of the Red Sea, not distant from the northern part of Abyssinia (Ethiopia). Arabia felix has been identified as the country of the Queen of Sheba, and according to legend, it is the land from which the Wise Men came to Bethlehem, as related in the Gospel of Matthew. The country of the Queen of Sheba was known as the homeland of a rich star-wisdom, of a star cult. Here, it is said, was reverenced the appearance of the sun in the sickle of the moon, like a picture of the Holy Grail itself. — Incidentally, the name Dhamar is *Schobua* in Arabic, *Scheba* in Hebrew, which latter is rendered *Sheba* in the English Bible.—Many important details concerning the cultural life of Damcar, or Dhamar will be found in the book by Sigismund von Gleich, *Marksteine der Kulturgeschichte,* 2nd. Ed., Stuttgart, 1963, esp. pages 136-164. — In view of the above data and that which is given in the following notes, (esp. that for p. 165, 1. 26, below) and the works cited, it is startling to find A. E. Waite in his *Brotherhood of the Rosy Cross,* London, 1924, reprint, N.Y., p. 127 note 2, state that "Damcar is an invented name for a fabulous city and there is not the least reason to suppose that it has any derivation at all, while that which is offered is in no relation to the city or to anything that is said concerning it, etc." — Unfortunately this is not the only flat statement by Mr. Waite which can be queried in the light of more recent research.

p. 165, 1. 17
    seq.:   *. . . made a bargain with the Arabians that they should carry him . . . to Damasco . . .* In ancient times a caravan route which was extensively used, connected Damascus in Syria with Damasco (Damcar in Arabia, i.e., Dhamar in Yemen), passing through Transjordania, via Mecca, and on to the south.

p. 165, 1. 18:   *. . . he was but of the age of 16 years when he came there . . .* He was born in 1378, therefore he arrived in Dhamar in 1394 and remained there 3 years.

p. 165, 1. 24:   *. . . the Book M . . .* Sometimes identified as the *Liber Mundi,* "the Book of the World," also (by Kienast, *op. cit.*) as *Memoria* or *Memorabilia.* — Raymond of Sabunda and Thomas Aquinas both wrote about this book, calling it *The Book of Nature,* indicating that it related how the world, the universe, had been created. However, early traditions record that man has forgotten the art of reading this book, hence the famous religious works, including the

Bible and the sacred Scriptures of the Eastern peoples, have been given as an aid to rediscovery of this lost art. — In modern terms, as described by Rudolf Steiner in his *Cosmic Memory, Prehistory of Earth and Man* (New York, 1959), man has the task to develop spiritual perception which once again will enable him to "read" the Akashic Record, which in *The Chymical Wedding* and the *Fama* is called *The Book M,* The Book of Nature, of the World.

p. 165, 1. 26:   . . . *where he did learn his Physicks and Mathematicks* . . . When young Christian Rosenkreutz arrived in Dhamar in 1394, that place was a cultural center of some importance. At that time the ruler was the Turkish Sultan al-Malik al Asraf Isma'il (1377-1400). The study of the sciences in the precincts of the mosque of 'Udaina was based upon Syriac translations of Sanscrit works from India and Greek writings which also had come through Syria. — Undoubtedly the writings of the most famous of all Arabian philosophers and physicians, Avicenna (980-1037), were expounded by the scholars for their pupils in Dhamar, as they were in all the cultural centers of Arabia at that time. —(It should be noted that this was the great period of "break-through" of Arabian science and philosophy into Europe as a result of the work of scholars who had translated works in this field under the patronage of the Emperor Frederick' II (1212-1250), not always with the complete approval of the Church.)—For a history of Dhamar (Yemen) during this period, consult the two excellent works: Kay, H.C., *Omarah's History of Yemen,* London, 1892, and Lane-Poole, S., *The Mohommedan Dynasties,* London, 1893, esp. pp. 87-103. For a general view of the study of philosophy at this period, consult de-Boer, T. J.: *The History of Philosophy in Islam,* London, 1903. —See any standard encyclopedia for further details.

p. 165, 1. 30:   . . . *he shipped himself* . . . *into Egypt, where he remained not long* . . . At that time Egypt was ruled by Zahir, Saif al-din Barquq of the Burji Malemuke dynasty, which had only recently come to power. When Christian Rosenkreutz arrived in Egypt — probably in Cairo, seat of the government — in about 1397 — the whole country was in a state of great confusion and alarm. Barkuk had recently entered into relations with the Ottoman Sultan, Bayezid I, had slain the envoy of the Mongol conqueror, Timur, and had led an army into Syria (1394) in an effort to restore the Jelairid Ilkhan Ahmad to Bagdad and at the same time to stem the Mongol invasion. — With all Egypt stirred by these events, and the whole Middle East anticipating the arrival of the Mongol forces at any moment, it is no wonder that Christian Rosenkreutz "remained not long" in the land of the Nile. In fact, the above historical data substantiates this statement in the *Fama,* a point, to the best of our knowledge, overlooked by previous students of this Rosicrucian document.—For a reliable history of this period, see Muir, Sir W., *The Malemuke or Slave Dynasty of Egypt,* London, 1896. — For further details consult any standard encyclopedia.

p. 165, 1. 32:   *. . . came unto Fez, where the Arabians had directed him . . .* In early times Fez — especially during the years of Mahommedan rule in Morocco — was famous as a seat of learning, and was a cultural center of which the whole empire was proud. Its schools of religion, philosophy and astronomy were famous throughout the Middle East and Southern Europe. The geographer, Alhasan ibn Mohammed Al-wazzan (Lat., Leo Africanus) 1483-1550, in his book on Africa (Book III, Ch. 136) speaks of the scholars of Fez assembling each afternoon near sunset time in the precincts of the ancient mosque of Mulai Idris in order to dispute among themselves concerning their researches in alchemy, caballa and astronomy. — See especially, Gaillard, H.: *Une Ville de l'Islam, Fes,* Paris, 1905, also consult any standard encyclopedia for historical and cultural details.

In 1575 at Basel was published a book by an anonymous author, titled *Arbatel, de Magica Veterum.* This little work of 87 pages, bearing the sub-title, *Summum Sapientiae Studium,* The Highest Study of Wisdom, has been traced to teachings originating from the scholars of Fez.—For further details on editions of the *Arabtel* and its influence, see the article by Rudolf Rissman, *Anthroposophie des 16. Jahrhunderts,* in *Die Drei,* Stuttgart, 1964, 34 Jahrg., No. 1, Jan./Feb., pp. 29, *seq.*

p. 166, 1. 9:   *. . . commonly called the Elementary Inhabitants . . .* i.e., the Elemental Beings. It was through the indiscretions of the Abbe Nicolas Pierre Henri de Montfaucon de Villars of Toulouse (1635-73) in his book, *Le Comte de Gabalais* (Paris, 1670), that the relation of the Rosicrucians to elemental beings became known to the public. Incidentally, the Abbe himself was murdered at the end of December 1673 on the highway near Dijon, while traveling to Lyons.

The book, *Le Comte de Gabalais,* is prefaced by a motto by Tertullian: "When a thing is hidden away with so much pains, merely to reveal it is to destroy it."

On page 9 of the same work the Rosicrucians are spoken of: "They were agreed unanimously that these mighty secrets, and especially that of the Philosopher's Stone, are hard to find and that few people possess them, but all entertained a sufficiently good opinion of themselves to fancy that they were of the number of the Elect. Happily, the most advanced were at that time expecting with impatience the arrival of a German, a nobleman of high rank and a great Cabalist, *whose lands lie toward the frontiers of Poland.*"

(Rudolf Steiner has spoken of the elemental brings in many connections. See among others, his lecture cycle, *Man as Symphony of the Creative Word*, 12 lects., publ. London, 1945.)

Alexander Pope, when dedicating his *Rape of the Lock* to Mrs. Arabella Fermor, wrote: "The Rosicrucians are a people that I must bring you acquainted with. The best account of them I know is in a French book called Le Compte de Gabalis, which, both in its title and size, is so like a novel, that many of the fair sex have read it for one by mistake."

The book in question was published in English in 1680, *The Count of Gabalis; or the Extravagant Mysteries of the Cabalists, exposed in Five Pleasant Discourses on the Secret Sciences. Done into English by P. A.* (Peter Ayres), *Gent., London, Printed for B. M., printer to the Royal Society of the Sages at the Signe of the Rosy-Crucian,* 1680. — Another English ed. publ. London, 1714, and a modern edition appeared in London, 1913.

Influences of Rosicrucianism and the Rosy Cross have been traced in the literature of 17th century England, especially in the masques of James I and Charles I. Milton's *Comus* also seems to be derived from the same sources. *Undine,* Wieland's *Idris und Zenide,* Bulwer's *Zanoni,* and Mackay's *Salamandrine* are all based on Rosicrucian principles. Mention of the Rosicrucians also appears in Samuel Butler's *Hudibras,* Part I, Canto 1, etc.

p. 166, 1. 33:   ... *sailed with many costly things into Spain* ... At this time Spain was a very important center of Moorish cultural life, including studies in "black magic" and what was termed "practical metaphysics." The cities of Sevilla, Granada, Toledo and Cordova —along with the university center of Salamanca, once called the "devil's classroom"—were noted for these activities. Refer to cultural histories of Spain for details; consult any standard encyclopedia for bibliographical data. In his book, *The Zohar in Moslem and Christian Spain,* Ariel Bension gives an impressive picture of the cultural life of this period, (*op. cit.,* London, 1932, esp. Chapters 1-3) with special reference to Moorish mysticism.

p. 167, 1. 34: *Trygono igneo,* "fiery triangle." Kienast (in his book listed in the Annotated Bibliography in the present volume) suggests that this may have been composed of the united Zodiacal signs of the *Ram, Lion* and *Archer.*

p. 167, 1. 39: *Theophrastus Paracelsus,* 1493-1541. For details on his life and work see introduction to Rudolf Steiner's *Mysticism at the Dawn of the Modern Age,* 1960, pp. 59-67, and text, pp. 193-207. The best anthology of Paracelsus in English is *Paracelsus: Selected Writings,* ed. by Jolande Jacobi, transl. by Norbert Guterman, 2nd ed., New York, 1958. Also see: Hall, Manly P.: *The Mystical and Medical Philosophy of Paracelsus,* Los Angeles, 1964. A great wealth of literature on Paracelsus exists; consult any standard encyclopedia for details.

For a particularly useful and original study on Paracelsus, see Walter Pagel's book, *Das Medizinische Weltbild des Paracelsus, Seine Zusammenhaenge mit Neuplatonismus und Gnosis,* Franz Steiner Verlag, Wiesbaden, 1962.

p. 170, 1. 9: *upon the day C* . . . In the original text this reads *auff C. Tag,* i.e., *auf Christi,* or *Christiani Geburtstage,* hence Christmas Day.

p. 171, 1. 27: *the 100 years* . . . The Frankfort edition of 1617 says *of the 120 years.*

p. 171, 1. 35: *Protheus,* i.e., Proteus, the embodiment of the principle of metamorphosis. In Greek mythology he was a sea-god in the service of Poseidon. See Goethe's *Faust II,* Act II, lines 8152, *seq.* For a discussion of the principle of metamorphosis as it works in nature and man, see Rudolf Steiner's *Goethe the Scientist,* New York, 1950, esp. Chapters 2 through 6.

p. 172, 1. 13: . . . *in Gallia Narbonensi* . . . i.e., the province of Narbonne in Southern France. This reference is an important and suggestive link between the Rosicrucians and the earlier Albigenses and Cathars, for Narbonne itself was the scene of one of the most terrible massacres of Albigenses by royal forces operating under direction of the Inquisition in 1234. In the beginning of the 14th century a valiant insurrection of the Albigenses of Narbonne took place. See the important book by Deodat Roche, *Etudes Manicheennes et Cathares,* Paris 1952. Also see Ellen S. Davison, *Forerunners of St. Francis, and Other Studies,* Boston, 1927, esp. Chapter 6, *The Cathari and Allied Sects,* p. 201, *seq.* — Important footnotes in this work offer rich bibliographical data on the subject of the Cathars.

p. 172, l. 30
seq.: *. . . the tomb of Christian Rosenkreutz . . .* The proportions and design of this tomb have been found to have a correlation with the 53rd Figure among the plates illustrating the famous work by Georgius von Welling, *Opus Mago-Cabbalisticum et Theosophicum . . .* 1735. This book was carefully studied by Goethe during his University years, and is mentioned in his autobiography.

In connection with this 53rd Figure of Welling — reproduced in this present volume — the authors H. C. and K. M. B. in a work titled *The Rosicrucians,* London, n.d., suggest that to find the relationship with the Tomb of Christian Rosenkreutz one should "construct a circle surrounded by a seven-sided one (a heptagon) which in turn is to be surrounded by a dodecagon or twelve-sided one. The altar represents oneness of all creation. The four points the cardinal directions. The heptagon represents the 7-sided Tomb, and the dodecagon the digits of the number inscribed outside the door of the Tomb. Thus, the Elements are: *One,* the altar; *Four,* the quarters; *Seven,* the vault, *Twelve*; the number outside the doorway. If the seven-sided vault were represented by seven concentric circles, the diagram would serve for that of the solar system. A (the altar) would be the *Sun;* N.E.S.W., the quarters; B (the heptagon) the 7 planets, and C (the dodecagon), the Zodiac. In this case, the Tomb would indeed be 'A compendium of the Universe.' " — "In another sense, the altar can be considered as the Throne in the *Apocalypse of John,* the cardinal directions, the four Living Creatures, the heptagon, the 7 Spirits before the Throne, the dodecagon, the twice-twelve or 24 Elders."

In his work on the Rosicrucians, Hargrave Jennings reproduces the Welling figure. Again, the small circle represents the ceiling of the Tomb, the large circle, its floor. The seven sides represent the 7 planets, and the 12 outside the door correspond to the 12 signs of the Zodiac. "The connection between the earthly and heavenly suns is shown by the lines from the ceiling to the central circle on the floor of the Tomb." (Compare with the reproduction of the Welling figure in the present volume)

p. 173, l. 16
seq.: *. . . it was enlightened with the light of another sun . . .* Reference to the "ever-burning lamps" apparently well known in antiquity. The famous physician, Licetus of Rapallo in the Middle Ages was one of the first to write about these lamps. During the Papacy of Paul III (1534-49) a grave was opened in Rome (1534) and such

a lamp was discovered inside. It was assumed that this was the grave of the daughter of the famous Marcus Tullius Cicero, died in the year 45. The report states that as soon as daylight entered the tomb, the lamp flickered out.—The well-known modern writer, Will-Ernst Peuckert reported in his *Schlesische Sagen,* 1924: "In Trebnitz ever-burning lamps were found in heathen graves." (p. 305). Franz Spunda (1928) reported the existence of such ever-burning lamps in the Monastery of Vatopaedi on Mount Athos. The famous Abbot, Trithemius of Sponheim, "teacher of Paracelsus," provided such lamps at the direction of the Emperor Maximilian, and Agrippa of Nettesheim, Henry Cornelius, in his *Occult Philosophy* gives details about them. A tradition also exists that at the time of the dissolution of the monasteries in England under Henry VIII (about 1533-39), such lamps were found and were preserved in the Museum of Leyden. See Hargrave Jennings' *The Rosicrucians,* Chapter 3.)

In his famous treatise on *Natural Magic,* the well-known scientist, John Baptista Porta reports that in about the year 1550 on the island of Nesis in the Bay of Naples a marble tomb from ancient Roman times was discovered. When the tomb was opened, a brightly burning lamp was discovered, but quickly dimmed and flickered out upon the admission of air from outside. It was reported that the tomb dated from approximately the beginning of the Christian Era. (John Baptista Porta, *Natural Magick,* London, 1658.)

p. 174, 1. 33-
36:    ... *the dead body of our careful and wise Father* (Chr. Rosenkreutz) ... *a fair and worthy body, whole and unconsumed* ... This remarkable passage can be compared with Thomas Vaughan's words in his *Anima Magica Abscondita,* London, 1650: Speaking of a quotation from *The Occult Philosophy* of Agrippa of Nettisheim (Book 3, Ch. 43), to the effect that a wise man was surrounded on all sides by sparkling flames which issued from his body, Vaughan continues, "This, I believe was R. C., the founder of a most Christian and famous Society, whose body also—by virtue of that Medicine he took in his life—is preserved entire to this day, with the epitomes of two worlds about it. Such Elijahs also are the members of this Fraternity, who—as their own writings testify—walk in the supernatural light. 'To join our Society,' say they, 'it is needful that thou shouldst behold this light, for without this it is impossible to see, save only when we ourselves do will it.'—I know some illiterate school divines will cry out with the Jews of

old : 'Away with such a fellow from the earth!'—Truly these are the men to whom now I give advice that they read not our writings, nor seek to understand nor remember them, for they are harmful and as poison to such. . . . To them the gate to hell is in this book . . . Let them not mind it, buy it, nor touch it. 'Hence, hence ye Profane!' "

p. 176, 1. 13:   *Ex Deo Nascimur, in Jesu morimur, per Spiritum Sanctum Reviviscimus* . . . The initials of these words also appeared on the monument erected over the grave of Jacob Boehme at Goerlitz in 1624. Rudolf Steiner transformed them slightly, and they are included in the "seal" appearing on the cover of his first Mystery Drama, the Rosicrucian play, *The Portal of Initiation,* tr. by Bittleston, publ. New Jersey, 1961. In addition, he spoke on the spiritual importance of these words in the following lectures: *Pfingsten im Jahreslauf* (May 23, 1915), publ. Dornach, 1935; *The Mystery of the Trinity* (July 30, 1922) publ. London, 1947, p. 39; *Man's Life on Earch and in the Spiritual Worlds,* (Aug. 30, 1922), publ. London, 1952, p. 42, *seq; Star Wisdom, Moon Religion, Sun Religion* (May 8, 1924), publ. London, 1950, p. 37 *seq.;* in addition, the following lecture cycle is built up entirely on this theme: *The Inner Nature of Man,* publ. London, 1959.

NOTE: It is not without great significance that Robert Fludd, whose book, *Tractatus Theologo-Philosophicus,* 1617, deals with *Life, Death* and *Resurrection* (implicit in the Rosicrucian formula discussed above), dedicated the work to the Brotherhood of the Rosy Cross. A reproduction of the highly interesting title page of this work is included among the illustrations in this volume.

p. 177, 1. 2:   ... *the Book M* ... See the Note for p. 165, 1. 24 above, for details.

p. 177, 1. 11:   ... *Aurora or some clearness, or divine light in the sky* ... Through the original German text does not use the word "Aurora" at this point, the context is such that it is probable that the title of Jacob Boehme's famous book was suggested by this passage. The title page of the first English edition of Boehme's work reads in part: *AURORA | That is, the | DAY-SPRING | or | Dawning of the Day in the Orient | or | Morning-Rednesse | in the Rising of the | S U N* ... London, 1656.

p. 177, 1. 25:   ... *two Sacraments* ... The Frankfort text of 1617 reads, "We use the Sacraments as they are instituted, etc."—This is the most famous of all variants of this text, and upon it Nicolai built the argument that from 1617 on, the original tenets of the Rosicrucian Fraternity were modified to allow admission of Roman Catholics.

p. 178, 1. 1-3:   *. . . our Philosophy . . .* This refers to the Kabbalah, that Jewish mystical teaching which formed one of the three central pillars of Rosicrucian study. (See the notes to the illustrations for Khunrath's *Amphitheater*, p. 341 *seq.* in this book). The main work, often called "the Bible of the Kabbalists" is the classic *Zohar, The Book of Splendor.* According to the teachings of the latter, the philosophy of the Kabbalah was taught by the angels to Adam, was transmitted to the Patriarchs, and so on down through the ages. A vast literature on the Kabbalah exists, and can be traced in the bibliography at the close of Gershom Scholem's work, *Major Trends in Jewish Mysticism,* 3rd ed., revised, N.Y., 1954.

p. 178, 1. 23:   *fastigium.* According to Virgil, this word denotes the chief point, rank, quality or kind.

p. 178, 1. 30:   *parergon.* According to Vitruvius, a *parergon* is an ornamental addition to a principal or main work. Hence, in this case, "goldmaking" is but "an ornamental addition" to the real work of the Rosicrucian Brotherhood.

p. 178, 1. 32:   *Phy: aurum nisi quantum aurum!* i.e., "Phui! Gold, nothing but quantities of gold!"

p. 178, 1. 38-9:   *Contumeliam gloria Dei,* i.e., "An affront to the glory of God."

p. 179, 1. 11:   *Communicato consilio, singulatim.* The thought is that the learned of Europe, having studied the *Fama* and *Confessio,* are at liberty to express themselves in relation to the latter, either as a body or individually.

p. 180, 1. 13, *seq.*:   At the conclusion of a rare work titled *A Brief Consideration of Occult Philosophy, written by Philip a Gabella, student of Philosophy, and now published for the first time, together with the confessio of the Fraternitas R.C., Cassel, 1615,* printed so as to face the opening of the *Confessio,* is the following prayer:

"Eternal, unchangeable and infinite God, Who art existent in Thyself, from Whom all things spring and without Whom there is nothing; Who art good without bounds, great without limit, eternal without time, omnipresent without space; Sole Virtue, sole Perfection, embracing all perfections and all qualities far exceeding the perfection of our thoughts; when we have long tarried in contemplation of Thee we have realized that we are ignorant of Thee. Suffer us not then, O God, to be lost while seeking Thee through pathless ways. Grant in Thy fatherly and infinite goodness and compassion that by love, worship, adoration and supplication we may at length attain to Thy glory and majesty and meet Thee face to face and dwell in Thee, in the name of Thine only begotten Son, our Lord Jesus Christ; And that Thou wilt grant our request through the mediation of Thy Holy Spirit in Thy great love for us, Thou who art in very truth God greatest and best, we pray and beseech with ardent vows and lamentation. To Thee, one and triune God, true and living, be honor and glory, for all eternity, world without end, Amen.

—Philemon Philadelphiae R. C."

p. 186, l. 17-18:

. . . *some new Stars . . . in Serpentario and Cygno* . . . The new star in *Cygnus* appeared in 1602, that in *Serpentarius* in 1604. See Kepler's work, *De Stella Nova in pede Serpentarii*, with supplement, *De Stella Cygni*, publ. in Prague, 1606. In the present volume will be found an illustration showing the House of the Holy Spirit of the Rosicrucian Brotherhood, with the Swan and Serpent depicted in the heavens above. This is taken from the work of Theophilus Schweighardt. (Serpentarius is shown on modern maps of the heavens under its Greek name, *Ophiuchus*.)

Mr. Willi Sucher has kindly provided us with the following information: "In 1484 (the year of the death of Christian Rosenkreutz) the conjunction of Saturn and Jupiter, just entering Scorpion, is the most significant feature. In 1604 the same conjunction appears again—and yet again in 1901. —These conjunctions (called 'Great' conjunctions) recur in intervals of about 60 years. They move slowly forward in the Zodiac, i.e. each succeeding conjunction moves a few degrees ahead in the Zodiac from the former one. Thus the conjunctions in 1484, 1604, 1901, etc. have come in time all along the Zodiac from Libra to Sagittarius, to Capricorn, which it will enter in 2021. In 6 B.C. occurred in Pisces the famous 'Great Conjunction' which is associated with the beginnings of the great events in Palestine, leading to the earthly life of Christ. This conjunction of 6 B. C. is the *ancestor* of the conjunctions in 1484, 1604, 1901, etc.

"It is remarkable that 1484 should show the same configuration as in 1603/04, the time of the "opening of the tomb,' and then again in 1901, around the time of the 'birth of Anthroposophy.'"

On the 1603/04 conjunction and related matters, see the important work by Elisabeth Vreede, *Anthroposophie und Astronomie*, Freiburg i.Br., 1954, p. 332, seq.

p. 187, 1. 8-
10: *... the languages of our forefathers ...* On the origin of language, see Rudolf Steiner's lecture cycle, *Genesis, Secrets of the Biblical Story of Creation*, London, 1959, especially lects. 1 and 2. Also see Arnold Wadler, *One Language—Source of all Tongues*, New York, 1948, and his *Der Turm von Babel*, 1935. In this field the pioneer work of Hermann Beckh is of great value. See his *Neue Wege zur Ursprache*, Stuttgart, new ed. c. 1950.

p. 188, 1. 29-
30: *... the three double Horn ...* The Latin edition reads, "And his triple crown shall be brought to naught." The Cassel edition (1616) reads only "triple horn."

p. 189, 1. 22: *... lead a Christian life ...* The Latin edition reads "lead a life worthy of man." — Rudolf Steiner once spoke about the relationship between Christianity and Rosicrucianism (June 16, 1907, publ. in *Dornach News Sheet*, Vol. 10, 1942. p. 145, *seq.*) as follows: "... Around the 16th century men lost the vision of the spiritual world, and the materialistic conception took hold of humanity. Those who believe they themselves do not live in the very midst of such materialism are very much mistaken ... Before the dawn of our modern epoch, before the time of Copernicus and the 16th century, care was taken in Europe to establish the foundation of a new way of proclaiming spiritual truths. Around the 16th century lived certain people who were able to interpret the signs of the times. As early as 1459 a higher spiritual individuality, known in the external world as Christian Rosenkreutz, along with a very small number of men, founded an occult school for the cultivation of the ancient wisdom, but in a form suited to modern men.. This was the wisdom of the Rosicrucians, cultivated for the first time around the year 1459. This wisdom, however is nothing new; it is the ancient, primeval wisdom, but in a form suited to modern men. —What is the connection between this Rosicrucian wisdom and Christianity? *There is no difference between genuine Christian teachings and those of the Rosicrucians.* If we grasp Christianity in its essence, we grasp the wisdom of the Rosicrucians. It is not necessary to found a new religion, but Christianity should be grasped as the early Christians grasped it. Very few people today still know anything about the mysteries of early Christian development ... But a new era dawned (in the 16th century) and with it came the necessity of stating these truths in such a way that science cannot object to them. *This is the aim of true Rosicrucian wisdom.* Therefore Rosicrucian wisdom represents that form of religion which is suited to our time. . . If we were in a position to hear in all details what Rosicrucian wisdom has to say in connection with true Christianity, we would discover that scientific facts do not conflict with these descriptions. . . What does Rosicrucian wisdom wish to give us? — The knowledge of higher worlds, of those worlds to which man will belong when his physical body shall have decayed. It gives him knowledge of life, of the true nature of death and of human development. In this way it can give him strength in regard to religious truth and religious life."

p. 349, 1. 9:   *Marinus Mersennus,* a monk of the Order of the Minims, born at Osye, 1588, died Paris, 1648. He was a center of the learned correspondence of his time, at home in theology, philosophy, medicine, music, literature, history. He carried on a wide correspondence with famous men, including Descartes, Hobbes, Gassendi, etc. His great work, *Questiones in Genesim,* Paris, 1623, folio, contains about 1100 closely printed pages. It offers "a perpetual feast" to the curious, and includes a vast range of subjects, from Paracelsus' Homunculus to the mystic qualities of the number 77; from the correct mode of dancing to why a corpse bleeds at the touch of the murderer; from the questions of Trithemius to the exact shape and material of Adam's first breeches! —This work brought him into severe conflict with Robert Fludd.

p. 349, 1. 15:   *Agrippa of Nettesheim,* Henry Corenelius (1487-1535), see Rudolf Steiner's *Mysticism at the Dawn of the Modern Age,* pp. 54-59 and 189-194.

p. 349, 1. 26:   *Cardanus,* refers to Hieronymus Cardanus (150--1576), Italian mathematician, physician and astrologer. His highly interesting and active life is told in his autobiography, *De Vita Propria,* which was translated into English and supplemented by Henry Morley in the latter's 2 volume work, *Jerome Cardan,* London, 1854. Otherwise, consult any standard encyclopedia for details.

p. 356, 1. 31-
    2:   *. . . the true Architects built the House of the Word . . .* Compare this passage with that by Thomas Vaughan in his *Anima Magica Abscondita,* London, 1650: "Let them approach with confidence to the Almighty God who made the world, for none can give a better account of the work than the Architect. Let them not dispair to attain His familiarity, for He is a God Who desires to be known

and will reveal Himself, both for the manifestation of His own glory and the benefit of His creatures ... But it will be questioned, perhaps, how shall we approach the Lord, by what means may we discover Him? —Truly, *not with words, but with works;* not in studying ignorant, heathen authors, but in studying and trying His creatures. For *in them* lies His secret path, which though it be shut up with thorns and briars, with outward worldly corruptions, yet if we would take the pains to remove the luggage we might enter the Terrestrial Paradise, that Enclosed Garden (*Hortus conclusus*) of Solomon, where God descends to walk and drink of the Sealed Fountain ..."

p. 357, 1. 18-
19:     *... man himself was formed according to this image ...* See Rudolf Steiner's lecture, *The Temple is Man!,* publ. London, 1951. Also his *The Mysteries of Light, Space and of the Earth,* New York, 1945, esp. p. 18, *seq.* His lecture cycle, *Earthly Man and Cosmic Man,* esp. lecture 9, (London, 1948), and his *Universe, Earth and Man,* London, 1955, also shed additional light on this theme.

p. 358, 1. 3
seq.:   *... true seed of Abraham ...* See Rudolf Steiner's *Deeper Secrets of Human History,* London, 1957, p. 33 *seq.,* also Emil Bock's *Beitraege zur Geistesgeschichte der Menschheit, Das Alte Testament,* Vols. 1, 2, and 3. Stuttgart, 1950.

p. 359, 1. 21:   *... Hermes ...* See Edouard Schure's *The Great Initiates,* New York, 1961, esp. the section titled *Hermes, The Mysteries of Egypt,* p. 127 *seq.,* also Rudolf Steiner's lecture of February 16, 1911, titled *Hermes,* in *Turning Points in Spiritual History,* London, 1934, p. 84, *seq.*

p. 361, 18,
seq.:   *... children unto Abraham ...* See Rudolf Steiner's lecture cycle on *The Gospel of Matthew,* London, 1965, esp. lects. 4 and 9.

p. 362, 1: 35:   *... the godless nature of Barabbas, the son of dark confusion ...* See Albert Steffen's drama, *Christ or Barabbas,* transl. by A. D. Wadler and P. M. Allen, New York, 1950.

p. 368, 1. 20:   *The Cross of Christ consisted of two woods ...* This is clearly shown in the Crucifixion scene included in the famous Isenheim Altar by Gruenerwald, now displayed at Colmar.
For a most interesting study on the wood of the Cross, see Alfred Usteri's book, *Die Hoelzer des Kreuzes und ihre Beziehung zur Flora der Mittelmeerlaender,* Basel, 1942.

p. 370, 1. 1, seq.: *the blood* . . . For the significance of the Blood shed on Golgotha, see Rudolf Steiner's lectures publ. under the title, *Easter,* London, 1956, especially lects. 3, 6, 7, also his *Tne Occult Significance of Blood,* London, 1926, his *The Etherisation of the Blood,* London, 1955, and his *The Mystery of Golgotha,* a lecture given at Oxford, August 1924, publ. London 1940, etc.

p. 371, 1. 35-36: . . . *the parable of the Song of Solomon* . . . See the article and translation by Emil Bock titled *The Song of Songs, The Character of the Book,* including an analysis, in *The Christian Community Journal,* London, Vol. VII, Jan./Feb. 1954, pp. 2-24.

The rich imagery of the *Song of Solomon* has provided a source for many themes by mystical writers, among them the English Philadelphians, led by Jane Leade (1623-1704). The title of her principal work, *A Fountain of Gardens,* (1697-1701) was taken from the *Song of Solomon,* and this latter work inspired writings by a number of her co-workers and followers, including Dr. Samuel Pordage (1607-1681), Dr. Francis Lee (1661-1719), Thomas Bromley, Richard Roach, etc. See *The Behmenists and Philadelphians* by Nils Thune, Uppsala, Sweden, 1948.

p. 372, 1. 26: *the Lord Jesus Christ will appear to the chosen ones in this life.* . . . See especially Rudolf Steiner's *The Vision of Christ's Advent in the Etheric,* New York, 1942, etc.

p. 373, 1. 22: *within the grain of wheat* . . . This suggests the words of Christ, "Except a grain of wheat fall into the ground and die, it remains alone; but if it dies, it brings forth much fruit." (John 12:24) See also Rudolf Steiner's lecture cycle, *The Gospel of St. John in Relation to the other Gospels,* New York, 1948, especially lectures 12, 13 and 14.

p. 374, 1. 12: *the true and divine Alchemy,* see references given in note to p. 43, 1. 22, above.

p. 374, 1. 28: *diligent . . . patient* . . . See Rudolf Steiner's book, *Knowledge of Higher Worlds,* London, 1963, p. 78, *seq.*

p. 375, 1. 14, seq.: In this passage it should be noted that Fludd takes good care *not* to deny his Rosicrucian connections! Despite his statement about his "unworthiness," and that such gifts come through divine grace alone, he leaves the question entirely open.

p. 376, 1. 5: *"the first year of your nativity* . . ., i.e., of his entrance into the Rosicrucian Brotherhood.

p. 381:   *The Parabola.* Dr. Walter Weber, in his edition of *The Chymical Wedding* in modern German, 2nd Ed., Stuttgart, 1957, p. 183, indicates the importance of *The Parabola* as "a highly charming little work of art, directly related to *The Chymical Wedding* itself ... In it breathes the purest Rosicrucian spirit ..."

p. 388, 1. 1-
2:     *... these two lying before me dead ...* With this passage compare the words of Thomas Vaughan in his *Anthroposophia Theomagica,* dedicated *To the Brothers of the Rosy Cross,* London, 1650: "Death is a recession of life into the hiddenness—not the annihilation of any one particle but a retreat of hidden natures to the same state they were in before they were manifested. This is occasioned by the disproportion and inequality of matter; for when the harmony is broken by the excess of any one principle, the vital twist—without a timely reduction of the first unity—disbands and unravels. In this recess the several ingredients of man return to those several elements from whence they came at first in the access to compound. Thus the earthly parts—as we see by experience—return to the earth, the celestial to a superior heavenly limbus, and the spirit to God that gave it. Neither should any wonder that I affirm the Spirit of the living God to be in man, when God Himself doth acknowledge it for his own. (For to think that God creates anything *ex nihilo* in the work of generation is a pure metaphysical whimsey.) ... This Spirit was the Spirit of Life, the same with that Breath of Life which was breathed into the first man, and he became a living soul. But without doubt the Breath or Spirit of Life is the Spirit of God. Neither is this Spirit in man alone, but in all the great world, *though after another manner.* For God breathes continually and passeth through all things like an air that refresheth—wherefore He is also called by Pythagoras 'the quickening of all.'"

In the Preface to this same work, Thomas Vaughan makes the following statement: "I look on this life as the progress of an essence royal: the soul but quits her court to see the country. Heaven hath in it a scene of earth, and had she (the soul) been contented with Ideas, she (would) not have travelled beyond the map. But excellent patterns commend their mimes: Nature that was so fair in the type could not be slut in the anaglyph. This makes her ramble hither, to examine the medal by the flask; but whiles she scans their symmetry, she forms it. Thus her descent speaks her original. God in love with His own beauty frames a glass, to view it by reflection. But the frailty of the matter excluding eternity, the composure was subject to dissolution. *Ignorance gave this release the name of death, but properly it is the soul's birth* and a charter that makes for her liberty. She hath several ways to break up house, but her best is without a disease. *This is her mystical walk, an exit only to return."*

p. 439, 1. 5-7:

... *the legend of Flor and Blancheflor* ... A beautiful rendition of this legend, with the rich tradition surrounding it, is given in Eleanor Merry's book, *The Flaming Door,* rev. enlarged ed., England, 1962, Chapter 12, p. 286, *seq.* This material should be studied in connection with this excerpt from Rudolf Steiner's lecture given on p. 433, above.—The same theme has been discussed in connection with the Parsival story in Walter Johannes Stein's *Weltgeschichte im Lichte des Heiligen Gral. Das neunte Jahrhundert,* 2nd rev. ed., Stuttgart, 1966. — The connection between the Lily and Rose and the Rosicrucian wisdom is developed also in Gerbert Grohmann's study, *Die Pflanze als Lichtsinnesorgan der Erde,* Stuttgart, 1962, p. 26, *seq.*

A metamorphosis of the same motifs will be found in the famous fairy tale from the Brothers Grimm collection, *Snow White and Rose Red.* Among other themes developed in that story which are clearly Rosicrucian in nature, is the following: "Once when the children had spent the night in the forest and the dawn awakened them, they saw a lovely child in a shining white dress sitting beside their resting-place. It got up and looked at them in a most kindly fashion, said nothing, however, and walked off into the forest. And when they looked about, they found they had been sleeping right beside a precipice and would certainly have fallen over had they gone a few steps more in the dark. Their mother told them it must have been the angel that watches over good children." — Compare this with what Rudolf Steiner says in his lecture of January 29, 1912 at Cassel, published in *Christian Rosenkreutz,* London, 1950, p. 23, *seq.,* especially pp. 27-29.

p. 443, *seq.*:

The Temple Legend. This theme is also developed in Rudolf Steiner's lecture, *Ueber den verlorenen und wiedergefundenen Tempel,* On the Lost and Rediscovered Temple, given at Berlin, May 15, 1905. It is represented in dramatic form in Albert Steffen's play, *Hieram und Salomo,* Hyram and Solomon, Dornach, 1925. Important details about the Temple of Solomon will be found in the article by Rudolf Frieling, *Stifshuette als kultische Widerspiegelung der Schoepfung,* in *Die Christengemeinschaft,* 12 Jahrg.,

Heft 1, 1935/36, p. 7 *seq.* — Details concerning the same subject will also be found in Emil Bock's *Koenige und Propheten*, Stuttgart, 1953, pp. 119 *seq.*

p. 446, l. 1-2: ... *third and fourth sub-race of our fifth root race* ... See Rudolf Steiner's *Cosmic Memory, Prehistory of Earth and Man*, New York, 2nd ed., 1959, p. 48 and 222. Also see his Nuremberg cycle on the *Apocalypse*, lectures 3 and 5, his *Occult Science, an Outline*, and his *Spiritual Guidance of Man and Humanity*.

p. 447, l. 5: ... *the war of all against all* ... See Rudolf Steiner's lecture cycle on *The Apocalypse of John*, London, 1958, esp. lecture 8, p. 137 *seq.*

p. 447, l. 12: ... *a lady-in-waiting of Marie Antoinette* ... Comtesse d'Adhemar, *Souvenirs sur Marie-Antoinette*, Paris, Mame ed., 1836, 4 vols. The pertinent passages from this very rare work have been translated into English in *The Comte de St. Germain*, by Cooper Oakley, London, 1927, Chapter 3, p. 53 *seq.*, q.v.

See also the article by Gerlind Zaiser, *Ueber den Grafen von Saint-Germain und die Fortdauer der rosenkreutzerischen Einwirkungen auf die Entwicklung des Abenlandes* in *Blaetter fuer Anthroposophie* Basel, 1957, Jahrg. 9, Nr. 6, June, p. 216, *seq.*

p. 447, l. 15-16: ... *the Count of St. Germain* ... In addition to the book referred to in the note above, the following are recommended on this subject: Heyer, Karl: *Aus dem Jahrhundert der franzoesischen Revolution*, 2nd ed., Stuttgart, 1956, p. 51 *seq.;* references to the Count of St. Germain will also be found in Heyer's *Gestalten und Ereignisse vor der Franzoesischen Revolution*, Stuttgart, 1964, and his *Die Franzoesische Revolution und Napoleon*, Stuttgart, 1953. References also appear in his *Kaspar Hauser und das Schicksal Mitteleuropas*, 2nd ed., Stuttgart, 1964. Incidentally, in this latter book Heyer quotes a verbal statement by Rudolf Steiner to the effect that Professor Georg Friedrich Daumer (1800-75), the gifted and highly perceptive teacher of Kaspar Hauser, was, *"the last Rosicrucian ..."*

p. 447, l. 27: ... *the actual secret of Christianity* ... See Rudolf Steiner's book, *Christianity as Mystical Fact and the Mysteries of Antiquity*, Rudolf Steiner Publications, 1961. Also Rudolf Steiner's lectures titled *Christianity Began as Religion but is Greater than All Religions*, London, 1959, etc.

p. 451   *The Temple of Pansophia by Johann Amos Comenius.* This book was translated into English and published in London c. 1912 under Comenius' Polish name, Komensky, as author. An extensive literature on Comenius' life and work exists; consult any standard encyclopedia for details. Among recent publications, see the commemorative volume issued for the 300th anniversary of his major work, *The Great Didatic,* titled *John Amos Comenius, Selections,* ed. by Jean Piaget, publ. by UNESCO, 1957, including extensive selections from his works, bibliography, etc.

One of the most important works by Comenius of Rosicrucian interest is his book, *The Labrynth of the World and Paradise of the Heart* (c. 1640), in part a paraphrase of sections of works by Johann Valentine Andreae. Chapter 13, titled "The Pilgrim Beholds the Rosicrucians" is of particular interest, but as Manly P. Hall writes in his study on Comenius, it "does not add much to the general literature on the subject." (See *Collected Writings,* Manly P. Hall, Vol. 2, Los Angeles, 1959, p. 188 *seq.*)

See also the article by Eduard Lenz, *Die Pansophie des Johann Amos Comenius* in *Die Christengemeinschaft,* Stuttgart, 23rd Year, No. 3/4, March/April 1951, p. 103 *seq.*)

Important material will also be found in two articles by Rut Nillson, *Die Rosenkreutzerstroemung in Schweden,* and *Die Beziehungen des J. A. Comenius zu Schweden,* in *Blaetter fuer Anthroposophie,* Basel, 1958, 10 Jahrg., Nos. 5 and 6, p. 168 *seq.* and 106, *seq.* The first English translation (a bad one incidentally!), of Comenius' *Pansophiae Diatyposis,* from the Latin edition, Amsterdam, 1645, was made by Jeremy Collier and published in London, 1651, as *A Patterne of Universal Knowledge in his Pansophical Draught.*

ACKNOWLEDGMENT

The editor and publishers wish to thank Mr. Manley P. Hall and The Philosophical Research Society of Los Angeles, Calif. for their generous permission to include the following illustrations in this volume:

From Manly P. Hall's *Codex Rosae Crucis*, 1938, the plate depicting the *Temple of the Rosy Cross* from Schweighardt's book, 1618, and Michaelspacher's *Mountain of the Adepts*.

From Manly P. Hall's *Orders of Universal Reformation*, the early portrait of Johann Valentin Andreae, 1616, ard the title page of *Speculum Sophicum Rhodo-Stauroticum*.

We also wish to extend our warm thanks to Mr. Erwin H. Meyer-Steinbach of Stuttgart, Germany, and to Mr. Willi O. Sucher of Los Angeles, Calif., for their generous help in locating points of importance which have been included in the Notes above.

LIST OF ILLUSTRATIONS

— *Illustrations — Series B* —

— *Illustrations — Series C —*

THE SIGNATURE OF ALL THINGS. A drawing from the 1730 edition of the Works of Jacob Boehme showing definite Rosicrucian influences.

PRACTICAL APPLICATIONS

1707-X **Education** As An Art   Steiner/$1.95
1730-4 **ESPecially IRENE:** A Guide to Psychic Awareness
                                                                                Hughes/$1.65
1715-0 **Gardening** For Health: The Organic Way   Philbrick/$1.25
1701-0 Meditations on the Signs of the **Zodiac**   Jocelyn/$2.25
1739-8 Occult Powers of **Precious Stones**   Fernie/$3.45
1728-2 The Pictorial Key To The **Tarot**   Waite/$1.95
1713-4 **Methods** of Spiritual Research   Steiner/$1.65
1714-2 **Results** of Spiritual Investigation   Steiner/$1.65

REFERENCE

1767-3 Steinerbooks **Dictionary** of the Psychic, Mystic, Occult
                                                                        The Editors/$1.95

SPIRITUAL RESEARCHERS, BIOGRAPHIES

1722-3 **Caspar Hauser:** Enigma of a Century   Wasserman/$2.95
1702-9 Count of **Saint-Germain**   Cooper-Oakley/$1.95
1721-5 **Eleven** European Mystics   Steiner/$1.95
1732-0 Mother **India's Lighthouse:** India's Spiritual Leaders
                                                                        Sri Chinmoy/$1.95
1733-9 **Paracelsus:** Life & Prophecies   Hartmann/$2.45
1703-7 The **Unknown Philosopher:** Louis Claude de Saint-Martin
                                                                                Waite/$2.95

Spiritual Science Library

Beginning a series of clothbound library editions, 4-1/2" × 7-1/2"

6001-3 **Alchemists** Through The Ages   Waite/$7.50
6002-1 **Atlantis:** The Antediluvian World   Donnelly/$7.50
6003-X **Maya/Atlantis**   LePlongeon/$7.50
6004-8 **Cosmic Memory:** Atlantis & Lemuria   Steiner/$7.50
6005-6 Occult Powers of **Precious Stones**   Fernie/$7.50
6006-4 **A Romance** of Two Worlds   Corelli/$7.50

Additional titles in preparation. Send for complete catalog.
Multimedia Publishing Corp., Blauvelt, N.Y. 10913, U.S.A.

WHAT ARE THE SPIRITUAL SCIENCES

The Esoteric Tradition stretches back into prehistory and forward into tomorrow. It has left us names clouded in mystery, like Rosicrucianism, the Freemasons, Alchemy, Theosophy, the Guardian of the Threshold, the Akasha Chronicle, ordeals by fire and water, and countless others. Today a higher consciousness is in the process of birth, and what was mysterious is now being uncovered by increasing numbers of people. The Spiritual Sciences speak to the development of the new consciousness.

Steinerbooks

The Spiritual Sciences in popular paperback format, 4-3/16" × 7" rack-size; and quality paperback format, 6-1/8" × 9-1/4" giant-size.

ALCHEMY, OCCULT SCIENCE

1704-5 **Alchemists** Through The Ages	Waite/$2.45
3505-1 **A Christian Rosenkreutz Anthology** [7"×10"]	
[Steinerbooks Giant — 704 pps. Illus.]	Allen/$9.95
1735-5 The **Great Pyramid:** A Miracle in Stone	Seiss/$1.95
1720-7 **Lamps** of Western Mysticism	Waite/$2.45

ATLANTIS, SPIRITUAL HISTORY

1717-7 **Atlantis/Europe**	Merejkowski/$2.95
1724-X **Atlantis:** The Antediluvian World	Donnelly/$2.95
1729-0 **Maya/Atlantis**	LePlongeon/$2.95
1718-5 **Ragnarok:** The Destruction of Atlantis	Donnelly/$2.95
1716-9 **Cosmic Memory:** Atlantis & Lemuria	Steiner/$2.25
1705-3 **From Sphinx** to Christ: An Occult History	Schure/$2.25

COMPARATIVE RELIGION

1731-2 **Commentaries On The Bhagavad Gita**	Sri Chinmoy/$1.95
1719-3 **Occult** Mysteries of Antiquity	Steiner/$1.95
1706-1 **Reincarnation** & Immortality	Steiner/$1.95
1727-4 **Mysteries** of Egypt: Secret Rites of the Nile	Spence/$1.95
1711-8 Ancient Mysteries of **Delphi: Pythagoras**	Schure/$1.65
1708-8 Ancient Mysteries of the **East: Rama-Krishna**	Schure/$1.65
1712-6 **Light** of the Mysteries: **Jesus**	Schure/$1.65
1709-6 Mysteries of Ancient **Egypt: Hermes-Moses**	Schure/$1.65
1710-X Mysteries of Ancient **Greece: Orpheus-Plato**	Schure/$1.65

OCCULT FICTION

1726-6 The **Golem:** Mystical Tales of the Ghetto	Bloch/$1.95
1737-1 **A Romance** of Two Worlds	Corelli/$2.45
1725-8 **Vril:** The Power of the Coming Race	Bulwer-Lytton/$1.95
1723-1 **Zanoni:** A Rosicrucian Tale	Bulwer-Lytton/$2.95